ARTIST UNKNOWN

ARTIST UNKNOWN

An Alternative History
of the
Arts Council

Richard Witts

LITTLE, BROWN AND COMPANY

A *Little, Brown* Book
First published in Great Britain in 1998
by Little, Brown and Company

A CIP catalogue record for this book is
available from the British Library

ISBN 0 316 87820 0

Typeset in Baskerville by Solidus (Bristol) Ltd
Printed and bound in Great Britain by
Clays Ltd, St Ives plc

Little, Brown and Company (UK)
Brettenham House
Lancaster Place
London WC2E 7EN

In memory of two Arts Council staff:

Sir Hugh Willatt

Andrew Milne

Contents

Acknowledgements

Without Lawrence Mackintosh, head of secretariat at the Arts Council of England, this book could not have been written, a fact which the honourable Mr Mackintosh may not care to know, once he's read what follows. Through him all doors were opened and promptly locked behind afterwards.

Mary Wratten, the Council's director of personnel, worked, like Lawrence, beyond the call of duty to make sure the information I sought was as close to the truth as the Arts Council could ever get.

In pursuit of precise dates and long-forgotten facts I must have bored rigid the Council's librarian, Stephen Chappell, and his colleagues, though they were kind enough never to show it, while anyone who has ever contacted Sue Rose, the Council's indefatigable head of press and public affairs, will understand how welcome I found the no-nonsense service she and her staff provided. My debt to Lawrence, Mary, Stephen and Sue lies beyond all measure, which puts it in the realm of the South Bank Centre grant.

Sincere thanks to all of the following who gave generously of their time, and in several cases tea and cake, to help me in my research: Paul Allen, Ed Berman, Peter Booth, Val Bourne OBE, Melvyn Bragg, Yvonne Brewster OBE, Jean Bullwinkle OBE, Julia Carruthers, Peter Cheeseman, David Crombie, John Cruft,

Constance Cummings CBE, Sir Michael Davenport, John Denison CBE, Joanna Drew CBE, Mary Endacott MBE, John Faulkner, Anthony Field CBE FCA, Stephen Firth, Rod Fisher, Mik Flood, the late Alan Fluck, Edwin Glasgow QC, Sheila Gold, David Gothard, Sir Alec Guinness, Stella Hall, Mike Hill, Lou Hodges, Professor Richard Hoggart, Emyr Jenkins, Lois Keidan, Roger Lancaster, John Latham, N.V. (Dick) Linklater CBE, Charles Morgan, Clare Mulholland, Sandy Nairne, Jane Nicholas OBE, David Pease, Keith Pickard, Catherine Porteous, David Pratley, Hilary Pugh, Richard Pulford, Lord Rees-Mogg of Hinton Blewitt, Luke Rittner, the late Sir Kenneth Robinson PC, Paul Rogerson, Sara Selwood, Sir Roy Shaw, Ed Smith, Ian Stoutzker OBE, Basil Tschaikov, Leslie Upton, David Whelton, the late Sir Hugh Willatt, Faith Wilson, John Wilson.

I am sorry that Sir Hugh Willatt, Sir Kenneth Robinson, Dick Linklater and Alan Fluck passed away before they could read this book, and it was a disappointment that Lord Goodman was available for interview, but deeply unwell when the time(s) came. I interviewed three current members of staff, also six working artists who have served, or presently serve, on panels or committees, none of whom wished to have their names registered here at the present time. Of those whose names are listed above, some spoke off the record as well as on.

The late Linda Dorrell, to whom my previous book is dedicated, provided an interview she made with the retired Mary Glasgow a decade ago, which was a new source and an excellent addition to Glasgow's privately circulated autobiography. In 1994 I presented a radio documentary on the Royal Shakespeare Company, produced by Ed Butler. The tape, but not the transmitted programme, includes Adrian Noble's creditable response to my routine question about future hopes: one 'Gosh', twenty seconds of silence, another 'Gosh'.

Three foreign artistic directors of distinction offered me their views on the British scene, but as they considered they were giving opinions that represented their profession in general, they did not wish to be singled out. I know that by rights I should have interviewed Anthony Everitt and Mary Allen, but perhaps I would have found it impossible to keep a straight face.

Thanks are due instead to the staff of the following archives, libraries, press and information units: A.C.B. Ramsay, Head of Arts, Sports and Lottery Group of the Department of National Heritage; Jane Fenwick at the Glyndebourne Archive (an exceptional resource), also Sir George Christie for permission to reproduce material; Francesca Franci at the Archive of the Royal Opera House; Helen Anderson, press officer of the Royal Opera House; John Bos, secretary of the Covent Garden Community Association; Mira Bel-Hillel of the *Evening Standard.*

Nicola Scadding at the National Theatre Archive; Nick Lee at the Allen Lane Archive of Bristol University; Clare Hyde, head of press at the South Bank Centre; Madeline Nichols, head curator of the New York Public Library Dance Collection; Public Record Office, Kew; Edith Symonds of Mablethorpe Public Library, Lincolnshire County Council; Bobbie Mitchell of the BBC Photograph Library; Tracey Hurd of the House of Commons Information Office; Jane Pritchard of the Rambert Archive; Rachel Parflew and Stephen Walton of the Arts Theatre Cambridge; Lord Skidelsky of the Keynes Estate.

Nikki Smith of the New Scotland Yard Press Office; Ed Glinert of *Private Eye*; Sue Pratt at the Equal Opportunities Commission; Chris Rush, press officer of Salford City Council; Nick Salmon, chief executive of the Theatre Investment Fund; Elizabeth Earle of the Carnegie United Kingdom Trust; Sam McCauley at the Salisbury Playhouse; Ross McLauchlin, director of Jersey Arts Centre, the Channel Islands; Mike Barrow of the Department of Economics, University of Sussex; Maire McQueeny; Tanya Hudson of the BBC Radio Arts Unit; Ed Butler of the BBC World Service; Music Performance Research Centre, Barbican, London.

Isobel Johnstone and Emma O'Halloran of the Arts Council Art Collection, Hayward Gallery; Jane Ellis of Bristol Theatre Royal; Donald Neame, information officer of Chichester District Council; Jerry Bingham of the Sports Council Policy Unit; Don Carleton of the Bristol University Information Office; Clare Colvin at the English National Opera Archive; Tony Lucas at the Musicians' Union; Martin Brown of Equity.

Dorothy Ritchie of the Nottingham City Library Local Studies Archive; Judy Owen of the Nottingham Playhouse; Mark Curtis, chief executive of the Nuffield Theatre, Southampton; Phil Slorick at the Hallé Concerts Society, Manchester; Lisa Drysdale of the Royal Exchange Theatre Company, Manchester; Ann Meyer of the Royal Court Theatre, London; Sarah Gee at the Association of British Orchestras; Janis Susskind at Boosey & Hawkes Ltd; Neil Hoyle, Chief Executive of the Incorporated Society of Musicians.

Damian Smyth, public affairs officer, Arts Council of Northern Ireland; Duncan Cameron, senior communications officer, the

Scottish Arts Council; the Arts Council of Wales; Sarah Borley of Eastern Arts Board; Pamela Hoon of East Midlands Arts; Graham Wiffen of the London Arts Board; Northern Arts; Rachel Wallace of North West Arts; Paul Clough of Southern Arts; Polly Marshall and Judith Clark of South East Arts; Martyn Cox of South West Arts; Ann Smith Hajdamach of West Midlands Arts; Ian Aspinall of Yorkshire and Humberside Arts (with special thanks to the lady there who had to photocopy the entire 1995 annual report); Christopher Gordon, chief executive, English Regional Arts Boards.

Thanks to: Erica Wagner, who researched the newspaper files in the beginning; Sophie Walshaw, who transcribed many of the interview tapes; Martin Lovelock & Co.; Kim Shannon, as ever; James Hale, my literary agent. My editor at Little Brown, Alan Samson, deserves thanks three times over, the last for the cute way he has of saying I'm a slowpoke.

The spending of that which is another's
takes not away thy reputation,
but rather adds to it.
Niccoló Machiavelli, *The Prince*

Cocklebury-Smythe MP:
Yes . . . yes, the P.M. offered me a life
peerage, for services which he said he
would let me know more about in due
course if I were interested. 'I hear you're
a keen gardener, Cockie,' he said, 'we can
call it services to conservation.' 'Not me,
Rollo,' I said, 'all I use it for is a little
topiary in the summer.' 'Services to
sport,' he said, ignorant fool. 'No, no,
Rollo,' I said, 'I really have no interests of
any kind.' 'That will be services to the
arts,' he said.

Tom Stoppard, *Dirty Linen*

Introduction

The Arts Council has piddled about in the cultural life of Great Britain for half a century. Since the pioneering quango was set up in December 1939, it has spent, at current values, £3.6 billion supporting anything from Notting Hill Carnival's sequins to the Royal Ballet's shoe resin. It was conceived as an emergency wartime measure to help jobless artists outside London, but has grown to become the chief means by which arts organisations, producers and artists themselves receive the money of tax-payers, in turn to create work for the public's benefit, amusement, education, unease and annoyance.

As it expanded, the Council became the butt of ridicule and malice. Its existence has been threatened many times in Parliament, most recently in 1993 when the Council gave the impression it was cheerily butchering orchestras and theatres. Despite the Government's subsequent naming of the Council as one of the 'five good causes', the birth of the National Lottery in 1994 did little to improve its image. Around £300 million a year of lottery income is distributed by the Arts Council in addition to its £190 million government grant. Misjudgment over the use of money in its charge renewed the calls for the Council to be scrapped.

This book charts the extraordinary changes in the Council's fortune, reveals the good and bad side of its work, and exposes why it continually gets itself into a fix, like a Loonytoons cartoon character forever blowing out its brains, yet living to die another day. In the end, however, the book pleads for the Council's life and reminds the institution that what it first stood for is still worth pursuing.

The book also attempts to answer a question that vexes plenty of those who come into contact with the Council: why do committees packed with smart people often make stupid decisions? Many of those interviewed in the following pages have spent countless hours on the working groups, sub-committees, committees and panels of the Arts Council – even the Council itself – and endured the same puzzling experience. They have sat round the table and watched thousands of pounds 'float in the air and land in the wrong places', as Philip Hedley of the Theatre Royal, Stratford East once put it.

They might offer as a defence the lack of time the committee had, a muggy boardroom, misleading information bandied about, weak applications from otherwise fine artists, a permanent discrepancy between the small amount of money available to 'float in the air' against the sum total of the grants sought – that sort of thing. Yet afterwards, tramping to the tube station, there comes a queasy feeling that, though the right facts were fed in, the most irritating officer was off sick, insightful debate flowed from start to finish, the tea was hot and the biscuits crisp, and even the final decisions seemed virtuous – the result was a sodding dog's breakfast.

The doubts often begin, 'Who said we only had *that* amount of money to spend?', followed by the realisation that the panel has somehow been hypnotised into considering not how much to give an applicant but how little. As Sir Hugh Willatt, perhaps the most respected of the nine secretary-generals so far, revealed for this book, 'The basic, if unwritten, question we tackle is: What is the minimum amount each particular set-up can operate on for another year and remain solvent?' That is the one question, of course, that the applicants are rarely asked to answer for themselves.

Three petty experiences colour the writing of this text. First of all, I was commissioned by the Arts Council in 1987 to report on its Contemporary Music Network. There was an attempt at the time to hive off anything that the Arts Council ran, though the Contemporary Music Network was not likely to find any takers, given the plinky-plonk nature of the work it promoted. At one key meeting in the Council's Goodman Room, a jumble of experts offered their opinions as to the Network's future. One of these was Dr John Paynter, the celebrated music educationalist, who'd travelled down on a 6am train from York, only to twiddle his thumbs while the Council officers arrived from their hideaway two floors up, 'delayed'.

He kept talking about *his* report. The staff around the table furrowed their brows whenever he did so, as though he was a little bit loopy. In fact he'd been commissioned a few years earlier to write a structural paper rather similar to mine, except his was about strengthening the Network's educational role, not dismantling it. The staff simply had no knowledge of the work he'd done, and at that point I saw the sad, shelved future of my study, *Mail Order Music*, loom up before me.

Second, I was asked in 1984 by BBC North to attend a press conference at the Royal Opera House. Presenting its annual report, Covent Garden's chairman, Sir Claus Moser, asked for questions from the floor. The whole affair was very homely; Moser knew everybody there, except one. 'Yes, Rodney, I see your hand is up', 'Hugh, I'm all yours', 'Mr Sutcliffe!' and finally, 'Er, yes – you there'. I asked why the Royal Opera was stalling on a decision to return to the Manchester Palace for a short season. The city council believed it was something to do with working out the percentage of subsidy it required from them. 'What is the bottom line below which you will not go?' This was met with a nervous silence and a flurry of neck-craning.

'That's not a very helpful question,' Moser replied. I answered that it was helpful to me, BBC North, Manchester City Council and possibly a handful of its theatre-loving citizens. 'Well, I don't think I can go into it here.'

'Twenty-five per cent?' I recklessly persisted.

Moser answered instead a much more helpful query from Rodney Milnes of *Opera* magazine about how one could join the Friends of Covent Garden. By my intervention I felt I had joined the Enemies, though if it meant missing out on the benefits of this apparent complicity between the House and this country's *reptiles* (as these critics are called backstage), fine. Leaving the premium wine and peanuts to them, I withdrew wondering why the Council's largest client was also its most impenetrable.

Thirdly, I attended a kind of supporters' group wake at the ICA in 1995 for one of my favourite British theatre companies, Forced Entertainment from Sheffield. The funeral was premature and

the group still breathes, but it had slowly slid off the drama department's list of clients. Though it was self-evidently a touring
company that did shows with actors and actresses and props
and panstick and stage fright and everything that the Royal
Shakespeare Company would recognise as thespian, the Arts
Council drama officers found it too advanced and suggested it
should get its money from combined arts instead, otherwise
known as the 'dustbin department'.

Many people attended the ICA rally to show support, yet it soon
became clear that hardly anyone there understood how the
Council worked. It came across to them as an aesthetic MI5. This
experience led me to write this book in the hope that the general
public may understand more how the Arts Council conducts itself
and why it functions in its gloriously barmy way. Equally, though,
the book aims to address why it is that the Council is seen by
many in a murky light and what it should do to better itself. This
book goes to press before the Council's eleventh Chairman, Gerry
Robinson, takes charge. I hope it proves of use to him as an aide-
mémoire.

I was already aware that the Arts Council had commissioned its
own history to mark first what it considered its fiftieth birthday in
1995, and second the geographic shrivelling of its remit from the
Arts Council of Great Britain to that of England the previous year.
Andrew Sinclair's book *Arts & Cultures* came out as I was writing
this, but his view – that the history of arts subsidy begins at the
bottom rung of civilisation when Gilgamesh builds the Sumerian
city of Urak and ascends solemnly unto the utmost step where we
find The Lord Palumbo, accompanied by his Super-Orchestra – is
not quite mine. But then I didn't enjoy the £50,000 advance that
the Council gave Mr Sinclair to research back to 3000 BC.

Nor could I equal Sinclair's propensity to see the history of the
Arts Council in terms of its literature department. This tiny unit
didn't truly exist until the sixties and remains its least crucial
artform component. There is an understandable tendency for
authors to account for the Arts Council in terms of their own
trade, but the organisation was set up to serve the performing arts
principally and that's what I focus on. Sadly, therefore, my book
lacks the abundant quotes of Eliot, Leavis, Larkin and C.P. Snow
that fill so many histories of post-war culture (but I've got a rare
piece of Priestley!). I can offer merely the Arts Council's minutes,
extracts of 'confidential' papers and the thoughts of its staff and
advisers over half a century – in other words, what the Council

actually did, meant to do, failed to do, wished it had done, or thanked heaven it hadn't.

Sinclair saw the organisation's life driven as though by Shakespearean sovereigns, its Council a sort of Star Chamber, its directors unruly barons and the rest of the staff mere spear-carriers and serfs. Less like Shakespeare and more like his accountant, I've started from a structural approach, which explains the fetish for comparative tables and statistics, each of them compiled for the book and sent on to the Arts Council or the Department of Culture, Media and Sport for verification (by the way, I don't use the cultural survey figures of the Target Group Index – they're concoctions). Nonetheless, Sinclair has a point. Tom Jones set the thing up in 1939 so he could control it, and then Maynard Keynes took it over in 1942 so he could control it, then Bill Williams made sure he could control it ('You are the admiral. I am the captain. Get off my bridge') and on it went.

In the end, my book attempts to uncover the point at which the individual encounters the structure and from that what ensues. This may explain the all-out account of the Council's origins and why the book is organised into three sections: the pre-history (1918–1946), then the chief structural challenges arranged into key issues (1946–1998), and finally the Council's internal network and its future. The central section aims to show how problems, already planted like viruses, survived and re-emerged through the years, provoking farce and tragedy by turns to each of the principal artforms.

Above all, it is intended to establish the effect of these dilemmas on the creative work of artists and producers. Creative artists are here defined, quite crudely, as those who 'make something out of nothing': visual and performance artists, sculptors, authors, poets, playwrights, film-makers, choreographers, composers and improvising musicians, songwriters and so forth. They are the first division, often supported in partnership by a second, which comprises those who help them to realise the work and bring it to a public: producers and performers of all kinds, publishers, curators, conductors, directors, designers, actors and actresses. So when the book complains about the absence of creative artists on the Council, no disrespect is intended to the re-creative and entrepreneurs, but it is this first division that is normally meant.

The Council's impact on those who serve it is also defined, especially on members whose involvement with the institution has benefited their status through harvesting Her Majesty's medals, or ermine, or both. They prefer to be known as 'the great and the good', just as they wish the arts to be seen as all sweetness and light, and its management the very model of efficiency. More believable in my view is the claim that 'the arts show us what we are and what we might be'. This somewhat unsettling thought was written by a speechwriter for President Reagan to voice (it echoes Ophelia's mad line from *Hamlet*, 'Lord! we know what we are, but know not what we may be').

As for models of efficiency, a more convincing image of arts administration was presented by Peter Stevens, the outstanding theatre manager who worked at Nottingham Playhouse, the National Theatre and Chichester Festival Theatre during their key years. When I met him in his Sussex office, a framed photo of Sergeant Bilko stood on a shelf behind his desk. I asked him why it was there. 'When everything seems hopeless, I turn round and think, "What would Ernie have done?" ' That's more like it.

Part I

Before the beginning
1918–1946

The Arts Council has always been hazy about its maverick origins. It has relied too readily on vague memoirs, especially a warped account by Bill Williams, the iron-handed Secretary-General of the fifties who was involved from the start. He made sure that his perspective was the exclusive one. Here is an attempt to provide one which is inclusive.

Chapter 1

Hitler respects us

Keynes and Christie • Glyndebourne 1934
Cambridge 1936

John Christie enjoyed the company of Nazis, while Maynard Keyncs preferred the fellowship of boys. That is precisely why we have an Arts Council and not a Council for Music and the Arts, the Royal Opera instead of the People's Opera and an ingenious system of funding for the arts run by MPs rather than the royal family.

The arts structure that has helped or hindered Britain these past fifty years was shaped by the mutual hostility of these two Etonians. From and through Captain John Christie came Glyndebourne and its operas, the Edinburgh International Festival, the saving of Hammersmith's Lyric Theatre and everything that nearly was the Arts Council. In John Maynard Keynes' name stands the Royal Opera House and the companies it keeps, the Bristol Old Vic, the Cambridge Arts Theatre and the Arts Council itself. It was not solely their contrasting habits that fuelled this aversion for each other. Perhaps it was their time at Eton School at the turn of the century, where Christie was six months the elder, or later at Cambridge University, Christie still six months senior though Keynes ten inches taller and twenty times brighter. Whatever had happened – Christie, no Adonis, often called Keynes 'a bugger' – it drove them to compete in the arts where both remained rigorously amateur, and dramatic.

John Maynard Keynes (1883–1946) was a conscientious Liberal, borne out by the showy Rolls-Royce he bought off the tycoon Sam Courtauld and his regret that he 'did not drink enough champagne'. By training he was a fuddy old free-trade economist who lectured at Cambridge University and worked for the Treasury during the First World War. He provoked public outrage at the end of that war by walking out of the negotiations leading to the Treaty of Versailles. As a Treasury adviser there, Keynes was appalled at the vengeful scale of the compensations levied by the Allies out of a defeated Germany that was clearly unable to meet them. His subsequent pamphlet *The Economic Consequences of the Peace* predicted the disasters that would pass in Germany and generate the Second World War.

Keynes gained fame as a kind of Cassandra, a theoretical forecaster whose remedial ideas assuaged the Slump of the thirties. He advised the Government on how to deal with long-term unemployment by investing in programmes of public works ('The patient does not need rest. He needs exercise'). Questioning a self-regulating economy, his plan of government interventions to boost or bridle what the public spent became known as 'the Keynesian revolution', and he is nowadays the monetarists' demon. They blame his theories for the post-war money crises that eventually swamped the seventies.

Tall but podgy, his stout moustache crowning thick lips, this rather prissy Cambridge don sought insanity among artists, doting at a distance on show-offs and queeny sorts. Privately gay, his love for the louche portraitist Duncan Grant swept him into the company of a clique of dilettante artisans and writers. They liked to be known as the Bloomsbury Group, after the patch of London they haunted during late Edwardian days. The group included two sisters, Vanessa and Virginia Stephen. The former was a flimsy painter who wed the critic Clive Bell, while Virginia married the publisher Leonard Woolf and drew less fame then than she deserved as a novelist before drowning herself in a Sussex river during the Second World War. They assembled about them a queer little crowd of dependants, whom Keynes shadowed. 'Maynard Keynes came to dinner. He is like quicksilver on a sloping board – a little inhuman, but very kindly, as inhuman people are,' Virginia Woolf noted in 1915.

One morning the phone rang in the Bloomsbury flat that Grant shared with Keynes. Grant answered. It was the Prime Minister's wife. 'This is Margot Asquith. I want to speak with Mr Keynes.' Grant replied that he was still in bed. 'Well, tell Mr Keynes from me that if he does not get up earlier than this, he will never get on in the world.' Though he never ever got up sooner he certainly got on, professionally in economics and unprofessionally in the arts.

'Champagne' Keynes had no time for the ultra-right, tweedy squire Christie (1882–1962), whose cellars of heavy German wine supplied the King. Just before Keynes suffered his fatal heart attack on Easter Sunday 1946, he told a friend that the start of the Arts Council was 'a message to Christie'. But he had devised the thing to 'wither away' within ten years. Keynes would have been horrified to see, half a century on, its staff of 190 doling out no less than £450 million in a year to its ungrateful 'clients', while his Cambridge theatre would end up shuttered, as forlorn and crisis-ridden as the Arts Council he fashioned in order to fund it. The theatre would be opened again in delicate health in 1997 thanks only to the National Lottery, a means of funding art that would have dismayed him. Meanwhile Christie's colossal Edinburgh Festival thrives on a blend of subsidy and commerce, and the Christie family's smashing new theatre in the Sussex Downs remains privately endowed. Glyndebourne continues to set an internationally sublime standard for opera that eludes Keynes' tarnished Covent Garden year in, year out.

Back in the thirties Christie and Keynes were near neighbours. They sometimes caught the same train up from Sussex to London, one of the new electric kind. It was said they never acknowledged each other, but it would have been difficult anyway as Captain Christie travelled third class while Keynes sat in the first. The Captain relished games of inverted snobbery and Keynes was snooty enough to be miffed. Here was the agreeable side of John Christie, 'a boy and a schoolmaster impishly mixed together' as his *Times* obituary put it, who would wilfully wear 'garments generally associated with foreigners who have failed to master the English rules'. But he didn't know quite when to stop. He'd yank the rail-way company's lightbulbs out of their sockets if they annoyed him or unfurl his umbrella as a shield against the artificial light. Back on his inherited Glyndebourne estate he was volatile and ruthless with farmhands he thought lax. At a nearby pub Christie was known as Captain Grizzly.

He was the son of the MP for Lewes, the county seat of Sussex. John Christie took over the local Glyndebourne estate at the end of the First World War. He'd been a captain in the King's Royal Rifles and served gamely in the trenches: 'In spite of all, the thing that satisfies me more than anything is German music,' he wrote to his mother. Wagner was a passion. At the Glyndebourne house, 'Victorian . . . ugly and uncomfortable', he held amateur concerts in the Organ Room, entertaining – so he assumed – his servants and weekend chums from London.

In June 1928, he ran a concert version of the final act of Wagner's *Mastersingers*. Christie sang the comical role of Beckmesser, the town clerk who thinks he is God's gift to music and women. His operatic rival, the shining young knight Walter, was played by Steuart Wilson, a polished concert tenor brought in for the occasion. This amateur operatic showdown was prescient. Twenty years later Wilson became the Arts Council's first music director and Christie's worst enemy: 'You now call me a liar – I call you a fool. Shall we leave it there?' Wilson wrote from the Council, diva to diva.

Every summer Christie would trawl around the music festivals of Munich, Salzburg and his beloved Bayreuth, home and temple to the ultra-conservative Wagner clan. He evolved the notion of an English Bayreuth where he could produce Wagner's mystical opera *Parsifal* every Easter. But for a Bayreuth to be Bayreuth-ish it needed a family and bachelor Christie was nearing fifty. In 1930 he booked a jobbing soprano named Audrey Mildmay to sing Blonde in an Organ Room version of Mozart's *Die Entführung*. Lustful and in pursuit, he sent her Charbonnel chocolates, pheasants from Fortnum's, then a fox fur. Finally he announced, 'I am engaged to a moderate soprano.' He took her on a honeymoon of German theatres: 'We had an orgy . . . of opera.'

Christie didn't quite get his English Bayreuth. In 1933 he built instead a snug 300-seater opera theatre next to the house so his wife could cultivate her career in Mozart. It looked like a village hall, and he was able to build it thanks partly to the 'bugger' Keynes. In 1930 Keynes had sat on the Labour Government's Economic Advisory Council, trying to make sense of the mess left by the Wall Street Crash. Groping for solutions the Liberal switched his beliefs dramatically from free trade towards protection, from *laissez faire* to state investment, from the gold standard to its abandonment and a supply of 'cheap money'. He argued for schemes to get the economy moving and encourage business confidence, especially in the building trade. This suited Christie, who owned a building works. 'Too many buildings, alas: & gossip to the effect that Capt. Christie & the Ringmer building Co. are buying Botten's farm to build on,' Virginia Woolf sulked in her 1934 diary.

The state's enterprise schemes helped to finance the private opera house of Glyndebourne. Christie opened it in May 1934 with Mozart's *Marriage of Figaro*, with Mrs Christie as the servant Figaro would marry. Christie had calculated that he could afford to lose £800 a year on the venture (around £30,000 today). To make sure it got no higher he hired Germans to run the thing. Carl Ebert had been in charge of the Berlin State Opera. He was made Glyndebourne's artistic director. Fritz Busch had been music director of the Dresden State Opera. Neither of them were Jewish nor politically active but both were rather nervous of their career prospects in an increasingly Nazi Germany. Christie thought they were being 'damned silly' but he couldn't really say that to his manager, Rudolf Bing, an Austrian Jew and a socialist. Bing had been picked by Ebert and proved to be Christie's governing godsend; he eventually became the world's most famous opera manager when he took over the New York Met.

But if it was Keynes' cheap money that helped to build Glyndebourne, and it was the Germans who turned it into a world-class production house, it was Christie who made it the Ascot of opera. He favoured the terribly chic trend of wearing lederhosen and dirndls, just as he'd seen at the Salzburg Festival where millionaires pretended to be peasants. He also provided knitting to give the ladies something to do during the show. There is an assumption, even today, that guests must wear evening dress or face a firing squad among the picnic hampers of the Long Interval. This is strictly false, though the ruthlessly posh audiences of Glyndebourne remain the ugliest dressers in the business. Christie simply wanted a little bit of well-bred Germany in his back garden and his guests (guests, though they paid) were disposed to this, especially the clique of Appeasers who turned up every summer to discuss how the British might best get along with Hitler who, after all, was making the opera houses run on time.

Christie was a member of the Anglo-German Society. He and his wife travelled to Germany throughout the thirties and saw only a country pulling itself manfully out of the mire. In early 1939 he made a speech at a meeting of the Deutsche-Englische Gesellschaft in Hamburg. Mrs Christie sang in the Salzburg Festival of 1939, an event attended by the Minister for Propaganda, Joseph Goebbels, for by then Austria was occupied by the Nazis. Even Rudolf Bing had to speak out: 'Would she, not just metaphorically but literally, be shaking hands with murderers?' When the Second World War started Christie got a letter that asked, 'Where are your

German opera directors now? Behind barbed wire we hope.' But Christie reckoned he was safe from friend or foe, whichever was which: 'I don't think Hitler would bomb Glyndebourne. I'm sure he respects us.'

Sitting by the ha-ha at the lawn's edge, a Glyndebourne audience picnics and admires the Sussex Downs. Due south, a chain of shapely mounds and spurs is crowned by Firle Beacon, a 700-foot hump on which fires would be lit in earlier days to warn of danger. By the late thirties Captain Christie would have gladly set a fire going there, but one at the foot of the hill where the Bloomsbury Group lived in their cute farmhouses, Charleston and Tilton. He wished to 'cauterise the rubbish and littleness of their minds'. When we see the dilettante decorations and the Bloomsbury bric-à-brac that still litter Charleston farmhouse, shrine to the Bells and the Woolfs, Grant, Sackville-West, Lytton Strachey and Dora Carrington and Keynes, we get his drift. The walk of three miles between Glynde Rough and Tilton Bottom is aesthetically tiring.

John Maynard Keynes, who preferred his name pronounced Kaynz, leased the Tilton farmhouse under Firle Beacon supposedly because a Norman ancestor, William de Cahagnes, had owned it but really it was because the Bloomsbury set had leased the one next door. Leonard Woolf discovered Charleston back in 1916 and moved the clique over to their Sussex hideaway in dribs and drabs. It was from Tilton, where he took a layman's interest in pig-farming, that Keynes would write his notes of apology to the Christies whenever he was formally invited over as a 'figure of power', until Glyndebourne got the message.

As he was a dull economist by trade, it's intriguing how often Keynes was portrayed in the sparkling terms of the theatre. The stockbroker Oswald Falk wrote how at committee meetings 'he loved the footlights and was impatient if he were off the stage for a minute, almost more impatient if he were not the central figure on it'. The judge Lord Macmillan noted how 'I lost track of time when he spoke, like a fluent actor holding the stage'. Conversely Virginia Woolf emphasised how removed he was from the arts. 'His book [*The Economic Consequences of the Peace*] influences the world without being in the least a work of art: a work of morality, I suppose; . . . the perils of society . . . would submerge Maynard, if he were an artist.' He was removed from the arts no longer when in 1925 he married – as so many gays did in the ludicrous hope that it would disguise their disposition – a ballerina.

Lydia Lopokova was a Russian star of the Diaghilev Company in its fading days. Keynes first met her at a party for the touring troupe in 1918. When she returned in 1921 he persuaded her to stay with him in Bloomsbury. Their friendship ran mightily deep. To the dainty dancer he became 'her Lankiest'. When they married he asked his former lover to be best man: 'On Tuesday at 12.30 Maynard retires to St Pancras Registry Office with Lydia, & Duncan to witness (against his will),' recorded Virginia Woolf. The Bloomsbury set didn't like Lydia very much. In their eyes she was a cute but dim foreigner. Woolf summarised, 'Lydia ... I suppose a very nice nature, & direction at Maynard's hands.'

Undeniably he gave her direction – and a ballet group and a theatre. First of all Lydia wanted to pursue her profession, though she was on her last legs and not far off forty. But Britain was a balletic backwater; decent dancers changed their names and worked for exiled Russians in France. One such was Edris Stannus from Ireland, who had worked for Diaghilev with Lopokova under the name of Ninette de Valois. She and Lydia and a group of like minds set up in 1930 the Camargo Society of London, resourcefully supported by Keynes at the very time of the economic crisis he was sorting out for the Government. Under this wilfully recondite title (from a nineteenth-century Belgian dancer) they organised subscription performances in the West End, presenting the early work of the fledgling choreographers Frederick Ashton and Anthony Tudor. It fell apart in 1933 but sowed the seeds for a British ballet company – Keynes saw to that, as we shall see.

Keynes also decided his wife should act. She started with a try-out in his home town of Cambridge ('Maynard's pocket borough') while he promoted her talents among his contacts on the Old Vic board. Her London debut in 1933 was, in Woolf's words, 'a dismal farce'. The *Daily Telegraph* damned her portrayal of Olivia in Shakespeare's comedy *Twelfth Night* as 'humourless'. Her heavy accent was mercilessly mocked. Keynes wrote to his wife, 'Don't be too sad about the acting. I swear we will have another go.' Thus, at the very same time that Captain Christie was building an opera house for his wife, Keynes chose to build a theatre for his. Citizen Keynes.

We know many of his thoughts and plans because he spent a lot of time away from Lydia but wrote to her often. Mostly he stayed in Cambridge with his boyfriend and 'favourite pupil' Richard Kahn (ultimately Lord Kahn of Hampstead, Cambridge's post-war professor of economics). Kahn would also stay with the couple for long periods at Tilton, where Christie caught wind of this exotic arrangement.

At any rate, in November 1933 Keynes wrote to Lydia from Cambridge with the first news of an astonishing scheme:

> I am thinking out a plan to build a small, modern theatre for the College. Will you agree to appear in the first production if it comes off? The argument is this. The ADC [theatre] has been burnt down. Our Peas Hill site, upon which we intend to build soon, is of ideal size and position. Why should we not join with the ADC? – build a really good theatre to hold 400 to 500, give them Club rooms and certain rights over the theatre (say four weeks in the year) and have the theatre as we choose for the rest of the year?

While Christie spent his own money, Keynes sought partnership from the start. The project proved far more complicated than he'd assumed. In the end he had to accept financial responsibility for building and running the whole affair. To design the theatre he commissioned an architect pal, George Kennedy, who had previously run up some alterations to Tilton. He then invited a local cinema manager to govern the place. When Norman Higgins protested that he knew nothing about theatres, Keynes retorted, 'We shall learn by experience unencumbered by notions which may prove inappropriate to the present venture.'

He finally had to put up £20,000 of his own savings (around half a million today) and donate extra money to back a West End transfer of the plays featuring his wife. At this point Keynes showed, like so many business people do, that when it comes to the performing arts they leave their brains at the stage door. The scale of his investment propelled him to brood about every damn detail, from the tone of the table napkins in the restaurant (a service always on the verge of disintegration) to the tunics of juvenile ushers. He even sacked one of the actors to make room for a sixteen-year-old, 'a boy of great beauty and piquancy', and in Citizen Kane style featured his wife in four of his productions. Keynes' Arts Theatre in Cambridge opened on 3 February 1936 with a ballet gala starring Mrs Keynes, succeeded two weeks later by Mrs Keynes as Nora in Ibsen's *A Doll's House*, followed by Mrs Keynes in *The Master Builder*. From this glittering start the theatre survived increasingly as a cinema (a stroke of luck for the manager), until the advent of state subsidy, when Keynes did his best to jump the queue. While Christie stayed private, Keynes revealed just how 'unencumbered by notions which may prove inappropriate to the present venture' he could be.

Keynes the impresario was bewildered most of all by the theatre's audiences, which he hadn't considered until he saw them sat in their seats. 'Who are these people? Where do they come from? It is very queer; I do not know half a dozen people in the theatre.' Christie never made that mistake.

Chapter 2

Ding

The Thirties • Carnegie • Royalty
Hitler, Mussolini, Stalin and Beecham
Mary Glasgow's Survey

By the end of the First World War Britain was 'eager to compensate the wastage of war by some contribution to the arts of peace'. In this way the Liberal MP H.A.L. Fisher explained his Education Act of 1918. He added that 'the country was in a spending mood' to achieve it. It needed to be, for this remedial legislation required loads of extra cash from central and local government to make it work. At its core the act raised the school-leaving age, while at the fringes there were equally striking shifts. Teachers throughout the country were encouraged to run classes of massed singing, oratory and pageants.

This cult of collective performance induced a revival of competitive festivals, a zealously conformist movement that had last gained its peak in the years before the war. Now speech groups bid for alloyed cups with massed recitations of Tennyson. Youth choirs competed for carved shields by singing 'national' songs fussily arranged by Edwardian organists. It was the notion of 'community' that brought this on – that the performing arts and sports were equal means to shape this unifying concept, so vital to 'social discipline and the maintenance of a grand heritage' – and competition was the healthy way by which team spirit would be rewarded. Or, as one such contestant later put it, 'the arts as *drill*'.

All manner of team crazes were promoted in the twenties, from

cycling clubs to ukelele bands. While community singing proved
to be one of the strongest activities, it took the mass media of the
mid-decade to define the movement's zenith; Lord Beaverbrook's
Daily Express ran packed rallies in the Royal Albert Hall. No Cup
Final would start without the crowd hymning 'Abide With Me';
audiences in theatres and cinemas actually sang along to the
national anthem. This trend fed into 2,000 choral societies, each
comprising around 200 members, whose great moment came
each Christmas when they vied to perfect the longest, loudest and
least authentic execution of Handel's 'Hallelujah Chorus'.

These voluntary groups drove an active economy served by
instrument-makers, tailors, engraving jewellers, printers, the
music profession of conductors, soloists and orchestral players,
and, above all, publishers who provided the choral scores – an
optimum of 100,000 volumes per work, even when singers shared.
The economic weight of this movement and its crack-up in the
thirties created the Arts Council. It also explains why the Council's
music and drama budgets have always been the biggest and why
their persistent plights dominate its agenda.

The competitive festival scene grew impressively, so that by
1929 there were more than 14,000 events a year at which
youngsters ('costumed or uncostumed') recited Shakespearean
speeches to waged adjudicators, or tackled jaunty solo songs often
commissioned for the occasion. In that year it was estimated that
competitors paid at least 1,800,000 entry fees at two to sixpence a
time (around 60p to £2 at today's prices).

Though now we might question an event called both a
competition and a festival, the latter was tacked on to dodge a
selective entertainments tax. Yet there were many more of these
ventures to be found. Two hundred of the 6,000 brass bands in
existence competed in two rival national competitions, having
first won rounds in regional bouts. Their sight-reading skills were
tested by tricky pieces commissioned from established composers.
The revenue swishing around these enterprises fed servicing and
manufacturing industries as well as the artistic profession, but
local councils also felt the benefit out of hall hires or catering
profits, and whenever the Government's Treasury Department
looked hungrily at this market, it was fended off on the grounds
that the arts voluntary sector was a thriving but intricate ecology
that central intervention might damage. Then came the Slump.

Following the Wall Street Crash of October 1929, and the
worldwide collapse of trade and money value that followed,

Britain's average unemployment soared from 10 per cent to nearly a quarter of the entire insured workforce. By late 1932 three million workers were on the daily dole – figures of the time excluded farm labourers, married women and the self-employed. The impact on the voluntary arts economy was near catastrophic north or west of Watford, and at least 150 choral groups promptly folded when they could no longer afford scores or fees to professional musicians such as their conductors. In 1935 the composer Arthur Bliss paced round the country noting the effect of the Depression on everyday musical life for the BBC's journal the *Listener*. His findings appeared as a series of articles called 'A Musical Pilgrimage of Britain'. The title evoked a similar trek undertaken the year before by his friend, the author J.B. Priestley in *English Journey*.

Arthur Bliss (1891–1975) was an intriguing man to conduct this audit. A Londoner with American family money in the bank, he'd served as a Grenadier Guard in the First World War and yet he wrote a pacifist oratorio, *Morning Heroes*. The music he composed at the time veered insecurely between jazzy avant-gardism and Romantic stodge. Nevertheless, as the composer of the music in the trendy new film *Things to Come* he was a man of the moment, and it's fascinating to read how the unadorned reality of the Slump dug into his metropolitan conscience. In Wales he attended a choir rehearsal where he noted that the price of a choir's scores fixed their basic repertoire: 'A family of three, all unemployed, have to think twice before handing over 1s 6d each for the privilege of singing the Brahms *Requiem*.'

Bliss concluded that 'one sure test of a town's financial condition is whether their choral societies are rehearsing new works or not'. He ended the series with a plea that municipal authorities might adopt a more 'civilised and forward-looking attitude' to financial support of these groups and concluded in the BBC's house magazine with this: 'Is there any way in which the Broadcasting Corporation can lend its powerful aid?' If this seems an odd thing to ask in 1935, Bliss was being canny, as we shall see.

His request that these amateurs should be subsidised was one of many that grew through the thirties. The most senior advocate was Sir Hugh Allen (1869–1946), 'bald and bulky, like a country solicitor'. A veteran figure on the music education scene, he was one of a stuffy breed of organists who controlled the musical life of Britain, thanks in part to the emphasis on training in the 1918 Education Act. They had all run choirs and served the theocracy of public schools, developing practical skills in music with a proficiency in supervision; they were transitional characters in the early development of arts administration. Allen was Oxford's music professor, but at the same time he led the Royal College of Music until he retired in 1937. 'Back to Bach' might have been this organist's motto. He ran Bach festivals and set up the pioneer Bach Choir of London, crusading to cultivate an alternative to the nation's adoration of Handel – both Handel and Bach were Protestant composers, which had an awful lot to do with it.

Around the time of the Wall Street Crash, Allen had been president of a kind of guild of professionals named the Incorporated Society of Musicians (ISM), founded in the Victorian north to regulate independent music teachers but reconstituted in the late twenties to protect the 'honour and interest of the music profession' in general. Its teaching and playing members were caught out by the effects of the Slump in no fewer than six ways.

Firstly, the choirs and amateur orchestral societies usually employed professional musicians as *stiffening,* a kinky bit of jargon that means 'strengthening'. Choirs often paid professional singers to join the ranks, posing as anonymous bank clerks while they beefed up the corporate sound. Some came from cathedral choirs or music colleges, while instrumentalists were customarily booked through regional orchestras. A dozy journalist who noticed the same man singing in various Lancashire choirs sought him out and asked if he came from a large family. The custom of stiffening diminished dramatically after 1930 as the societies ran dry of subscriptions.

The second issue facing the ISM was that its music directors, conductors and pianists risked reduced fees and curtailed work; choirs either performed less or took on the job of leading rehearsals from within the ranks. Even the Huddersfield Choral Society, the most famous choir in the country and one with a record contract, couldn't afford to use its showy but brilliant choral conductor Malcolm Sargent as regularly as it ought, and there was much talk of sinking standards and falling sales as a result.

Thirdly, the choirs and the big festivals, whether competitive or not, commissioned less. Most of the country's major composers and their publishers had relied on lucrative choral commissions, such as that the young William Walton received in 1929 from the Leeds Triennial Festival for his rowdy *Belshazzar's Feast,* in which he 'threw in' a couple of brass bands in the belief that it wouldn't get played again. Fourthly, there was the fact Bliss had noted, that amateurs were cutting back on new music for motives of economy. They couldn't afford to hire or buy the scores, nor could they afford the royalties collected by composers from each performance. Fifthly, concert societies could no longer afford many of the costlier or mid-range recitalists and their travel expenses. Lastly, the market for private tuition dropped by a stunning two thirds within two years.

The ISM was not the only society to face these problems. Musicians' Union membership dived from 19,500 to 8,000, a plunge compounded by the demise of the silent cinema, where many instrumentalists earned a sole wage. For the ISM members the problems boiled down to one: they had lost work but they were self-employed and so couldn't join the dole. Allen believed that the solution lay with the amateurs, who were disorganised. The ISM therefore encouraged through its members the setting up of regional federations of music societies, offering mutual aid to each other. Scores could be exchanged and performance dates co-ordinated so that to lower costs professional artists toured within the region. By the end of 1933 there were eight such groupings, including the West of England, North-Western and Yorkshire. One year on, eleven federations represented 486 societies.

A federal system eased matters, but by 1934 the pressure on the ISM itself to take practical measures was acute. The latest of its annual presidents speculated on setting up some kind of crisis fund. He was William Gillies Whittaker (1876–1944), a kind of Scottish duplicate of Allen. Not only Glasgow's professor of music, Whittaker also ran the Royal Scottish Academy and he too was Bach mad. Whittaker saw the problem as dual: the amateur movement was disintegrating at a time when people had increased leisure and the professionals were unemployed when they were most needed. His solution was financial investment to bring together the professionals and amateurs in a new context that would protect the professionals' vocation, renew standards and resecure the amateur movement's financial base. If the investment could not be ferreted out in England, Whittaker knew exactly where he might find it in Scotland, home to one of the nuttiest charities in the world.

Andrew Carnegie (1835–1918) had made a packet out of American oil and steel in Pittsburgh. He honoured his Scottish origins by spending income from US $10 million of steel bonds on public libraries and church organs. In 1913 he set up four Scottish trusts, three of which were mandated to serve the United Kingdom – he was insistent on the whole of the UK to mark his Celtic regard for Ireland. The Carnegie United Kingdom Trust was the first of its kind and for twenty years had the field much to itself. It was the Arts Council in all but name, privately endowed. On £100,000 a year (£3.6 million today) the charity was devoted to 'the welfare of the masses', especially the 'rural masses'. Carnegie had also insisted that the four charities should be set up in his birthplace, Dunfermline, and that the trustees of the charities should be locals. Even the great and good of Dunfermline thought this barmy and in the end the Carnegie UK Trust had a board comprising half Dunfermline folk, half outsiders.

The Carnegie trustees believed they should spend some of the money on 'purely aesthetic objects', especially musical ones because of Carnegie's thing about organs, though they never really knew what they were doing. Granville Bantock's uncelebrated *Hebridean Symphony* was printed up thanks to them; the Carnegie also bought a second-rate site for the Sadler's Wells Theatre in the late twenties. At the same time, though, it subsidised tours by the Old Vic Theatre Company and the British National Opera Company, while at the other end it worked with the National Council for Social Service and the National Federation of Women's Institutes to develop drama and music animateurism in rural areas. Carnegie trustees would not have known such a term as 'animateurism' then. Britain adopted it much later from the French, to identify endeavours where professionals and amateurs undertook projects to mutually enhance creative skills.

So when Whittaker made his informal approach, the Carnegie was all ears; it was eager to help out over an issue where employment preserved a refined artistic harmony between professionals and amateurs. Whittaker deftly geared the argument entirely to amateur issues. He claimed there was need for subsidy to:

1. encourage people to perform for themselves instead of being content merely to listen (this was a dig at BBC Radio and a burgeoning gramophone industry);
2. reach a large number of people who, without aptitude of their own, would at least appreciate and support amateur performances;
3. raise the standards of performance among amateurs;

4. salvage the numerous small music societies that were in
   danger of extinction.

Whittaker got Hugh Allen up to talk the issue through with the
Dunfermline trustees in February 1934. Allen invited to this a
younger composer-organist, George Dyson (1883–1964), who was
to prove the most vigorous of this ISM trio. But the amateurs were
not corporately represented, they did not have their ISM, and to
the trustees of the Carnegie this proved a constitutional glitch.

Allen pointed out that some societies had built federal networks for regional co-operation. Dyson grabbed at the fact and
proposed the development of a National Federation of Music
Societies (NFMS). A second brain-storming session in June sorted
out a policy line for the Carnegie trustees, and on 23 February
1935 a meeting of regional federation reps in York resolved that
the NFMS should be established with Dyson as its founding
president.

A couple of weeks later the Carnegie trustees announced a fund
for music societies of £30,000 (£1.1 million today) for the period
1936–1940. The Carnegie carrot immediately lured 300 amateur
societies to join an NFMS constituted to 'advance education by
promoting the art and practice and public performance of music
throughout the UK'. It stressed 'UK' rather than 'Great Britain' to
indulge the Carnegie Trust and 'education' as its prime aim was
inserted in order to comply with charitable conditions – that is, to
neutralise the taxman. To settle which members would get what
the NFMS set up a joint committee in the summer of 1935 (it still
exists) to regulate a near-metaphysical formula tied to intricate
percentages of professional costs and overheads that gives to this
day the impression that this primly democratic body is run by
cryptographers.

In framing this national body of amateurs the ISM was simply
protecting its professionals. And the timing was perfect. Measures
promoted by Keynes and others at the head of the decade to get
the general economy moving were seen to be working. By 1936
music societies felt fitter, gave more concerts, employed more
professionals and commissioning grew again by 15 per cent. Then,
a year later, a dreaded relapse. While the Carnegie grants came
into their own and propped up the concert scene, average
unemployment veered once more from the controlled 10 per cent
of early 1936 to above 15 per cent. This time it impacted directly
on the brittle entertainments industry and the damage was visible

to all, whether the show was a symphony orchestra or a circus.

In December 1936, George Dyson called for 'some sort of help from His Majesty or his Government' to fund commissions for composers. He had a specific interest, of course. His *Canterbury Pilgrims* of 1931 was a genuinely popular work, the nation's most performed cantata by a living composer. Spurred by success Dyson shamelessly attempted to outshine Walton's *Belshazzar* with his own *Nebuchadnezzar* of 1935, a much more practical piece with nothing 'thrown in', but also a pitiable one, and while Walton got more royalties than he'd bargained for, Dyson got fewer.

'His Majesty or his Government,' he said, not merely 'the Government'. 1936 was a coronation year, the prosaic, stamp-collecting George V having died in January and his glib son Edward summoned to the throne. Dyson was down to do one of the marches for the coronation of Edward VIII, but the coronation didn't come. The Prime Minister of 'His Majesty's Government' objected to His Majesty's divorced American girlfriend; Edward abdicated in favour of his timid brother Albert, who became not Albert I but George VI – a symptom of the enduring dependence of monarchy on marketing. Thus the year passed with three kings on the throne. At the eventual coronation in 1937 Dyson's march was supplanted by one from Walton, commissioned not from the King's purse but as a present from the BBC, keen as ever to ingratiate itself with the Windsors.

Dyson, though, was not merely venting personal frustration as a professional composer when he invoked 'His Majesty'. He was also voicing a general haziness about patronage and subsidy, and the ambiguous role of the royal family in the cultural life of this country. There were, and there are still, royal schools, royal academies, institutes, societies, associations, warrants, commissions, leagues and even a royal body for drivers, the Royal Automobile Club. Those who have ever joined the RAC will treasure how much closer they feel to the royal family by subscribing to such a thing.

In music alone there was the Royal Concert Fund, the Royal Society of Musicians of Great Britain ('for the maintenance of aged and infirmed musicians, their widows and orphans'), the Royal Amateur Orchestral Society, the Royal Scottish Pipe Band Association and the Royal Military Schools of Music (the regimental bands ate enormous amounts of taxes, and continued to do so for decades, way in excess of the Government's arts grants). There was even a choir of amateurs sanctioned by Queen Victoria, following a dispute, to call itself the Royal Choral Society simply because it was otherwise the Royal Albert Hall Choral Society and already had 'Royal' in its title. At the time of his plea, George Dyson had been approached to run one of these outfits, succeeding Hugh Allen at the Royal College of Music.

Yet in regard to royal patronage music was a poor relation, and remains so; there has been a gap of a hundred years between Victoria convincing Sir Arthur Sullivan that he had it in him to write a great opera (he hadn't) to Prince Charles scratching about on a cello. In contrast the visual arts hardly ran a supporting institution that wasn't royal, even leaving aside the royal collection. There was the Royal Academy of Arts of course, not to be confused with the Royal Society of Arts, but also the Royal Hibernian and Royal Cambrian Academies of Art, the Royal Institute of Oil Painters, the Royal Institute of Painters in Water-colours (not to be mistaken for the Royal Watercolour Society), the Royal Society of Portrait Painters, the Royal Society of Painter-Etchers and Engravers, and others too picky to mention.

Many of them were stimulated or reclaimed by Victoria's German husband Albert in the middle of the nineteenth century as part of his remarkable plan for practical, parallel progress in the arts and sciences. Not just clubs for debate, they were constituted as exemplars, advocates, benefactors of mutual aid. They arranged salons for the display and sale of work (the Royal Academy's monstrous Summer Show is still with us) and, in all, these institutions were meant to drive the British arts forward to face the world.

The advanced spirit that vitalised them has faded through the years. A majority became engaged with exclusivity, engrossed with preserving an increasingly tenuous aesthetic and intolerant to fresh approaches. Above all, to none of these royally adorned affairs did the royal family pay a royal penny. They were sent minutes of the societies' meetings for their servants to scan, and they or their inbred cousins turned up now and again to open exhibitions, unveil portraits and shake the hands of the genuine, gullible patrons who really kept the things endowed. Yet to be a Royal Something opened many doors of privilege. It guaranteed not only an obsequious bank manager but also leverage to garner security utterly through prestige. The subsidy offered from Buckingham Palace was that of the royal name, not royal cash.

That is why George Dyson dragged His Majesty into it in 1936. Among the armchairs of the Athenaeum club, where Dyson and

Allen relaxed with powerful allies, there was talk of how to get a new source of cash to protect the ailing arts. The principal means of funding had been unstructured private patronage. The First World War and the economic crises that followed had eroded the surplus from property and investments that had otherwise empowered the great and the good to indulge creative artists.

Neither was there much cash left to invest in artworks and the presentation of the performing arts. The dominant player on the music scene at the time was the maverick conductor Sir Thomas Beecham, an impresario who spent his allowance from Beecham's Pills on operas and braved the bankruptcy courts more than once. He soon found out how tough it had become when he tried to set up a new symphony orchestra at the turn of the thirties (it finally emerged as the London Philharmonic). He complained bitterly that the English tax laws were so stringent that they veritably penalised his rich friends who wished to make the world a better place by patronising the arts. If only the tax laws were as generous as the USA, Beecham argued, where all manner of donations and investments are tax free. 'The Inland Revenue Commission sees only larcenists and Artful Dodgers where I see philanthropists and angels,' he griped.

His girlfriend, the odious bigot Lady Cunard, would frequently berate Cabinet ministers at dinner parties with pronouncements like this one, noted by Lady Astor in 1931: 'No wonder there is trouble in the land. The wealthy are not allowed the freedoms they have earned. The civil servants are choking enterprise. We could cultivate soup kitchens, but you rob us of the privilege.' With the country facing one of the most searing economic crises ever known, the argument that the rich should be made richer in order to relieve the poor was not an easy one to grasp, even at dinner, drunk. The fact was that the rich weren't as rich as they were, and for the last twenty years the landed gentry had been slowly losing their land. Private patronage craved alchemy.

Keynes came across then as a kind of alchemist. Once the great liberal free-trader, he'd transformed himself by a study of the Slump into a protectionist and won the arguments against unmanaged capitalism at the Government's Economic Advisory Council in the early thirties. He'd proposed tariff protection and government intervention with a programme of public works. The Treasury officials irritably countered that 'public spending could not add to investment and employment, only divert them from existing uses' while far from 'setting up a cycle of prosperity', such a plan would much more probably 'produce a great cry against bureaucracy and a suspicion of extravagance and waste'. Their misgivings now seem more valid than they might have at the time, but Keynes won the battle and provoked, almost as a fashion, politicians from right and left to consider 'a machinery of planning to replace failed market forces', as his biographer Lord Skidelsky has put it. The Arts Council was an exceptional product of that very process.

Back in the armchairs of the Athenaeum, thoughts on support for the arts started from an agreed position. Private patronage had seen its day and only an utter, improbable overhaul of the tax system could bring it back. The topic then drifted in two directions. The 'modernists' argued for central government funding in the manner so successful to contemporary Italy and Germany. The opposing, orthodox group contended that those countries were quite unlike Britain, being foreign. If cultivating the arts was a duty of anyone, it must be the monarch, not politicians who would use the subsidy to serve their trivial, impulsive, aggrandising agendas – look at those buffoons in socialist France. As though royalty could never be guilty of such a thing, the modernists countered. It's the money for the art that comes out of the Government, not the art itself, they added. And that money is the public's, produced from taxes. Local government already supports libraries, art galleries and concerts at municipal venues, and that largesse is also public, out of the rates. What's wrong with transposing an existing system from local to central government? Nothing much, aside from plebeian standards, the elitists mumbled.

It was true that other governments were showing off their subsidised arts. British visitors were impressed to see how central subsidy promoted artistic popularity and backed work of higher quality than they found at home. There were at least three shining paradigms in Europe: Germany under Hitler, Italy under Mussolini and the USSR under Stalin.

In fact the Soviet Union provided models of good practice, bad practice and most components in between. From Lenin's Revolution of 1917 to Stalin's state fascism prevailing two decades later, the complex chops and changes reflected a power struggle between radical practitioners, conservative artists and a growing class of administrators (apparatchiks). It's ironic to think how far Queen Victoria's husband might have recognised and endorsed the early arts structures of the Soviet Union, given the way his relatives were killed off in the process of cultural renewal. For a start, the great Hermitage and other state museums were protected, while 1,100 private art collections were nationalised. 'We must preserve the beautiful, take it as a model, use it as a starting point, even if it is old,' said Lenin, though his successor Stalin must have thought he said 'even if it is sold', for he peddled Rembrandts and Van Goghs to raise foreign capital for the cycle of five-year plans he launched in 1928. Old art paid for new art.

Soon after the 1917 Revolution, artists formed co-operative guilds of professionals rather like the Royal Societies of Britain. The acronyms sound quite eerie: OMKh (the Society of Moscow Artists), AKhRR (the Association of Artists of Revolutionary Russia), and OSt (the Society of Easel Painters).

In the government structure itself, the arts came under the Education Ministry (Commission), just as it was to do in Britain. The impressive Commissioner for Public Education, Anatoly Lunacharsky, retained the institutes of arts training, such as the Moscow Conservatoire and the Kirov Ballet School. Yet he also supported at first a radical movement known as the Proletkult (Proletarian culturo-educational organisation), which might be classed as a national federation of 400,000 amateurs with whom professionals engaged directly, creating mass events or looping round the country in steam-driven arts centres called agit-trains.

Commissioning was funded through a structure we would recognise. For example, the art department of the Public Education Commission (IzoNarKompros) set up an arts panel of expert practitioners (Kollegiya) such as Tatlin, Malevich and Kandinsky. They had funds to back the commissioning of work and acted as a junction between commissioning bodies and artists. A separate art fund provided cash for materials and studios.

In April 1932 Stalin ordered the disbandment of the guilds as part of the Second Five-Year Plan (1932–1936), and this was doubtless a good thing as OMKh, AKhRR and the rest had been at each other's throats for years. The Proletkult was dissolved, amateurism ostracised and large professional unions of party members formed. Administrators increased their control over commissioning budgets. At the same time Stalin's Central Committee (Cabinet) endorsed his novel aesthetic of socialist realism. To be precise, it was said to be his idea, as far as most policies supposedly sprang from Stalin's prodigious brain. Unfortunately for the unionised artists, socialist realism was never defined more plainly than vague homilies like, 'Socialist realism is Rubens, Rembrandt and Repin put to the service of the working class', a definition not very helpful to the abstract painter Malevich and totally useless to Composers' Union members like Shostakovich and Prokofiev. Administrators indicated that activities must be fully quantified and to lead the way they offered incentives such as bonuses to theatre staff for exceeding the planned target of seats sold. Artists were commissioned to provide a number of works within a given period of time; their output was monitored by apparatchiks.

The Public Education Commission was replaced in January 1936 by the KDPI, the Committee for Arts Affairs, a committee because it reported directly to the Central Committee, of which Stalin was formally the Secretary. Its control was entire, and formed a dual but integrated system with the unions. It was through the membership unions that aesthetics were controlled. In general the union secretaries were practising artists of undeniable experience and it was their task to guide professional colleagues towards the stylistic needs of the commissioners, who might be the Red Army's own theatre troupe or choir.

Although the mandates of the unions were vested in charters that could be revised at congress meetings, it's interesting to note that the Composers' Union, for example, didn't hold its first congress until 1948. In other words, structural flexibility was practical on paper only and in daily life artists confronted a management system run by bureaucrats from the top down. Nevertheless, here was a workable, dual structure of practical administration on one side and artistic counsel on the other. What flawed it in the eyes of most Westerners was the way that artistic matters were depersonalised. Aesthetic sensibility was governed from the state through the party by a team of grovelling lackeys – so very different from our own Arts Council.

In 1936 a national decree banned abortion. One of the Art Union members complained at a meeting, 'In two or three months hastily executed pictures on the theme of birth were strewn everywhere.' George Dyson wrote, 'Here are some fine artists spending their talents on frivolous poems, paintings and cantatas to the glory of the Five Year Plan. In England at least we still have God.'

As did Germany, at least until March 1933, when Adolf Hitler's National Socialist (Nazi) Party took full control of a country mired in economic chaos. The Nazi regime promptly established a

Ministry of Public Enlightenment and Propaganda. Its Minister was Joseph Goebbels, a shrewd populist who preferred the term 'Culture' to 'Propaganda' but could never persuade Hitler otherwise. Blatant as the title was, the Nazis were clear at least about their intent, while the British might have chosen something softer, like Ministry of Information – which is exactly what they called their version of it at the outbreak of war.

The Propaganda Minister set up in September 1933 the Reich Chamber of Culture comprising seven departments divided by métier: broadcasting, film, theatre, music, fine art, literature and journalism. As he'd ordained himself President of the Chamber, it must have been difficult for functionaries to determine when Goebbels was making policy as a minister and when he was doing so as president.

Professionals, 'intellectual workers' in Nazi jargon, were invited to join the Reichskulturkammer, though membership was formally limited to Nazi Party subscribers. No end of confusion was caused at the end of the Second World War when certain artists, like the senior composer Richard Strauss (a former president of the music division), claimed to Allied investigators he had merely joined a professional guild rather than a political party and there was no simple way of sorting this out. Clear cut though the Nazi power structure was – engrossed in form-filling and measurements – it knew that in cultural matters, in a system required to embrace the Horst Wessel cult along with the legend of Parsifal, a little ambiguity was convenient to the cause.

Goebbels aspired to 'mobilise the spirit' and he had a fairly forward-looking approach, with a particular concern to motivate German youth. He wanted to commission works to help define the image of a new Reich. The racist ideologue Alfred Rosenberg lectured him in the 'purity of the idea', how culture equalled race and its pursuit engaged the heritage of Goethe, Schopenhauer, Nietzsche and Wagner. Goebbels sneered that if Rosenberg had his way, 'there would be no more active German theatre, only cult, only concept (*ding*) and that sort of tripe'. Production of good new work proved difficult as many of the most inventive artists had left and radical work was formally derided as 'degenerate' (*entartete Kunst*). In 1936 the Education Ministry promoted a deluxe Schiller Prize for play-writing, but the award wasn't made as no fresh work of merit served 'the spirit of National Socialism'. On the other hand the films of Leni Riefenstahl and Carl Orff's cantata *Carmina Burana* are often revived today.

Germany already ran a traditional structure of state and municipal subsidy for the performing and visual arts – mainly opera houses, theatres, museums and art galleries. These Goebbels retained and by 1941, for example, Germany still operated 355 state or municipal theatres and opera houses and 175 independent theatres, not to mention 142 open-air venues for the presentation of pageants. The Ministry's budget came from a fixed percentage of a mélange of taxes, party subscriptions and nationalised company yields (including record companies and music publishers) that the state absorbed. Films were assumed to be profitable and were financed through the Film Credit Bank.

The Ministry first limited its intervention to dismissing Jews and 'undesirables' from employment or commissions. Goebbels especially enjoyed wrecking the careers of liberal academics, though he claimed that 'sniffing out ideologies' had no place in his scheme. Nazi leaders simply desired 'to be the good patron of German art and culture'. A notorious book-burning ritual in May 1933 was promoted by a student union, not his Ministry. Nevertheless he was heading an operation that could intervene at all levels of production, whatever the artform or mass medium, for he made sure that the seven divisions of the Reichskulturkammer had parallel structures.

Goebbels spent much of his energy on developing mass cultural services such as a national cinema industry and a directly controlled version of the BBC, RRG, for which he insisted that 'eighteen hours out of twenty-four' must be devoted to popular entertainment. He enjoyed flaunting his power and was personally aroused by two particulars: getting youths to strip off and strut and seducing film stars. To cultivate youngsters his Ministry worked with a creepy-sounding outfit, Strength Through Joy, which was merely the state's travel and leisure service. They partnered community song festivals for which they commissioned new pieces in praise of discipline as well as ballads about past martyrs (the Horst Wessel Lied served as a standard). They set up travelling theatre groups and bands of young professionals who performed in summer camps and, in all, developed a hierarchy of animateurs.

When foreign dignitaries came to inspect Nazi Germany, the public building programmes and cultural developments featured in their agendas. Reports reveal how consistently the foreigners were impressed. Praise came from several of the British establishment who were to become involved in the setting up of state subsidy at home, among them the Foreign Secretary and future Prime Minister Neville Chamberlain and the Cabinet Secretary Tom Jones. Jones visited Hitler privately in 1935 and returned with a gift of Hitler's signed speeches on the arts. Nevertheless, some – not Jones, though possibly Chamberlain – felt that the Nazis lacked a certain sophistication, and Goebbels' fetish for mass entertainment was a sign of vulgarity, even kitsch. Elitists like Captain Christie would have favoured Rosenberg's *ding*.

Much more acceptable to all were Mussolini's fascists. For a start, Italy was a kingdom like Britain and the leader of the PNF (Partito Nazionale Fascista), Benito Mussolini, sustained a career as its Prime Minister from 1922 to 1943. The British appreciated the constitutional structure and they believed they understood Mussolini, 'a wonderful man working for the greatness of his country', claimed Chamberlain. (He also played the violin – about as well as Hitler could paint or Churchill draw; amateur artists at the top often gear their cultural policies to cheer up those at the bottom.) Secondly, the print and cinema industries remained in private hands and the radio, EIAR, was run as a semi-public agency like the BBC. Thirdly, while the Italians began to ape the anti-Semitic and 'anti-degenerate' structures of the Nazis as they developed in Germany from 1933, there were some barefaced differences. Contemporary work was actually promoted, especially in architecture, and diversity was encouraged in all artforms. The respected Bergamo Prize for painting of 1939 attracted avant-garde entries, one of which won; the 1941 season of the Rome Opera House consisted entirely of works by living Italian composers.

The Ministry of Popular Culture (Minculpop) was responsible to the Government for this approach. Minculpop had grown bit by bit out of Mussolini's press office. It became a full-blown ministry in June 1935, when it covered the press and radio, cinema, tourism, music, theatre, the visual arts and literature. The Ministry directed these varied elements towards administrative norms and common goals – endorsing the state, chiefly. Artists were invited to join new guilds like the Royal Academy of Italy, active from 1929, as well as a confederation of professional artists, membership of which was frankly a credential for employment. At the same time, the fascists set up a chain of 'para-governmental agencies' (opera) and it was these that most fascinated the British.

The Opera Nazionale Dopolavoro was one such, a cultural education outfit funded by the Ministry of National Economy. Its president was appointed by royal decree (the first was the King's cousin) and its policies were determined by a council comprising delegates from member organisations and independent experts, joined by observers from the relevant ministries. OND existed to support and develop *cultura dopolavoristica*, mass culture, and to do this it received an annual grant of 1.07 per cent of the mandatory dues paid to the trade unions and employer associations, amounting to four million lire a year. By 1939 its membership comprised 23,000 local groups. The range of initiatives was remarkable, even eccentric. Mulberry Day and Grape Day celebrated harvests, cultural holiday jaunts were arranged (a kind of cross between Strength Through Joy and Club Med), while selected train discounts (third class only) aided workers and families wishing to attend special events, including operas where the upper tier or matinees were further subsidised per seat by the OND.

The Fascist Party itself lay behind a middle-class version of OND. The National Institute of Fascist Culture (Istituto Nazionale di Cultura Fascista) operated as a federation of regional branches under PNF control, grossing a national membership of 200,000. Its structure ran parallel to that of the OND, controlled by a council of advisers and funded from a mixture of central grants and subscriptions.

The NFIC organised several thousand public events – concerts, art exhibitions, film shows and talks. It was set up to 'reconcile traditional academic culture with the activism of the new generation of fascist intellectuals' and its ventures were directed at the bourgeoisie, 'that is, to the class that is capable of assimilating doctrine'. While Goebbels humiliated the intellectuals, Mussolini seduced them.

It was a report that featured the OND and the NFIC which interested Britain's Board of Education when, in early 1939, it had been requested to look into comparative frameworks for arts subsidy. The writer of the briefing notes was an assistant schools inspector who was chosen in part because she spoke fluent French, German and Italian. Her name was Mary Glasgow and she would become the Arts Council's first executive.

Glasgow added a comment about a system she had not been asked to report on. 'They wanted to know about Europe, so no one had considered the United States. President Roosevelt had been running all kinds of arts projects with government money.' Franklin Roosevelt, sired from millionaires and thus in politics 'a traitor to his class', was the Democrats' Governor of New York at the time of the Wall Street Crash. His record on progressive social policies got him elected President in 1933.

He fought the Slump with a 'new deal' mechanism of fifteen major bills promoting nationalisation (federalisation) of key commodities, including the banks. A Public Works Administration (PWA) was set up to create and directly fund a series of major construction projects, very much in the manner of the USSR and Germany, devised to reduce a 20 per cent unemployment. Within the PWA was a unit called Federal Project One (FP1) which between 1935 and 1939 spent US $46 million of federal taxes on commissioning work from unemployed artists, such as the 70 per cent of all theatre workers and the 65 per cent of all musicians on the relief roll.

The PWA director, Edward Bruce, instructed that FP1 should 'make him feel comfortable about America'. The theatre, music and visual arts departments, directed by experienced progressives from those artforms, promoted projects aimed to meet his demand. FP1 was centrally serviced by administrators, rather keen, like the Soviet apparatchiks, the Nazis and the British civil service, to numerate everything. Their figures testify to the formidable scale of the project: 2,566 public murals made, 17,544 sculptures, 108,899 paintings. Eleven thousand theatre workers were employed in twenty-two production centres, their work seen by an audience of twelve million.

When academic Hallie Flanagan was appointed national director of the Federal Theatre Project in 1935, she insisted that the project was not just an alternative to the dole, but that it should find some way to reach new audiences. This mission was met by the New York branch director, Elmer Rice, who not only funded *The Swing Mikado* and Orson Welles' all-black *Macbeth*, but also invented the Living Newspaper, documentary road-shows dealing with upfront issues. The Living Newspaper's *Ethiopia*, a jibe at Mussolini's attack of that country, was halted by the White House before it hit the streets.

The music division was led by a former manager of the Cleveland Orchestra, Nikolai Sokoloff. He set up thirty new symphony orchestras around the country, six of which have survived, and a Composers' Forum Laboratory as a hothouse to develop new 'art' music from novices like Elliott Carter. Sokoloff's assistants took a broader view of FP1's aims and created teaching programmes where 'travelling tutors' worked among the mainly black neighbourhoods of Mississippi state, grooming raw pianists.

A folk archive of field recordings was established in Washington DC, a unique resource still used for those studying the origins of the blues and allied black music. Yet FP1 did not make many 'feel comfortable about America'. Much of the money seemed to be going to 'New York kikes and commies' and, thanks to conservative senators and congressmen, Germany was not the only country resisting *entartete Kunst* . At the time Mary Glasgow wrote her report, much of FP1's funding had been blocked by Congress and the entire project was steeped in political rancour. That is probably why the Board of Education was not so keen to learn from the other side of the Atlantic.

So what did the Board of Education unearth from this exercise?

1. Models for the central subsidy of the arts exist elsewhere.
2. The traditional arts are incorporated within policies dealing with culture, a term which encompasses language and its dissemination and therefore includes broadcasting and the press. The disciplines are not mutually inclusive, however, and at the lower levels of policy they are separated.
3. Schemes that tackle the unemployment of professional artists exist in both the performing and visual arts.
4. Most of the models deal with the relationship between professionals and amateurs, though it is difficult to separate the purely political and economic aspects of this.
5. A relation between arts and education is strongly apparent in the policies of the governments.
6. There is no evidence that central government subsidy adversely affects a *laissez-faire* arts economy.
7. There are no models devoted to reversing a decline of a *laissez-faire* arts economy, though there is evidence from Germany that central subsidy safeguards it in a time of economic crisis.
8. The scale of the funding can be determined through a percentage of a national budget, or by commission fees per project, or through partnerships (viz. Italy). Most of the second tier concerns are membership organisations.
9. The apportioning of central funds is generally controlled by a ministry, though its disbursement is placed through a second tier, often authorised or advised by experts (viz. USSR) or patrons (viz. Italy) and processed by administrators.
10. In each model the level of direct political involvement and censure is very high. Where it is not there is trouble (viz. USA). There is a need for governmental direction, but the

British level of involvement can afford to be lower given that matters of propriety, for instance, are already handled by the Royal Household (the Lord Chamberlain censored work until 1967).

Jolly good. Totalitarian regimes showed the Board of Education how the thing could work. To set up a system of government subsidy all the Government had to do was to work out what it wanted to fund, how it would control the flow, how much it would offer (and where that would come from), under what terms, and what mechanism for distribution and monitoring would be most effective. Then in best civil-service tradition the survey went in the bin and all was forgotten. Almost.

Working together to deliver N3

www.n3.nhs.uk

Chapter 3

It began on the telephone

Music and Drama Bill 1938 • The League
of Audiences • The Glyndebourne
Conference • Tom Jones • CEMA

The Arts Council was created in order to block something better. Remarkably, it did so twice: in 1939, when it was called CEMA, and again in 1945 when CEMA changed its name (though not its form) to the Arts Council. On the first occasion it terminated a period of lively attempts to launch a system for direct government subsidy (1937–1939). The Music and Drama Bill of 1938 lies long forgotten. Even the bill's designers are unremembered: the League of Audiences. 'League' was a very between-the-wars word, like 'federation', indicating an alliance rather than a hierarchy, as in the League of Nations. It helped to conjure an epic image for the Arts League of Service, for instance, in reality little more than a band of young actors bussing round to village halls with short plays and folk dances. Included in their number was the precocious Donald Wolfit, honing his ego.

Although the League of Audiences sounds like a union for consumers, it prevailed as a pressure group to boost audiences for live shows. Its curious mission was the 'preservation of personal as distinct from mechanised interpretations of music and drama'. The budding gramophone industry and the emergence in 1927 of the British Broadcasting Corporation were then considered threats to the live performing arts, classical music in particular. The League elite saw Promethean danger in the unemployed switching on radios. They approached it in this patronising way:

> Many influential people share with thoughtful legislators a growing concern about the problem of leisure. Enforced unemployment has made it serious, and with the shorter working day, which is certainly of the future, it will become more so. Cultural recreation needs stimulus and direction.

The League therefore drafted the Music and Drama Bill, the very title of which reveals a common tic in the British perception of the arts. Music, and something. Music and Drama, Music and the Arts – the Council for the Encouragement of Music and the Arts, the Aldeburgh Festival of Music and the Arts, even the Almeida International Festival of Contemporary Music and Performance, and so on. Although there are more subsidised theatres and drama companies than there are orchestras, music dominates yet is set apart because its power is pitched above patronage. Music is an immense business with significant commercial clout, its turnover today exceeding a billion pounds annually in Britain alone. And frankly it was the music trade that led the League of Audiences to propose a subsidy trough. Drama followed on, unsure of its lines.

The West End world of play-producers and investors – Binkie Beaumont, Harry Tennent, the Alberys, Howard and Wyndham – were then rashly opposed to the 'imbalancing spirit of government hand-outs', while the co-operative movement and the trades unions supported in various ways the work of politically 'engaged' theatre groups and would have countered state interference from Conservatives in the guise of subsidy. The Old Vic under Lilian Baylis needed the money most, and if it hadn't been shored up by the private Carnegie Trust, Baylis would have been banging her drum and annoying everyone, like a lesbian Christie. It was the British Drama League that was most interested in the introduction of subsidy and for exactly the same reasons as music's ISM and NFMS.

Set up straight after the First World War, the League (that word again) contained 1,600 play-acting associations rooted around the country. The Drama League was a rather self-satisfied outfit, as we might assume of something comprising 100,000 amateur actors. Yet it firmly supported the call for a National Theatre. This was a crusade that had been going on in various forms since 1904 without the slightest success (even when it cynically tied itself to Shakespeare anniversaries), but it still attracted the odd private donation and the irrepressible championship of the playwright George Bernard Shaw. By 1938 the Shakespeare Memorial National Theatre Committee had enough money in the bank to purchase a patch of wasteland opposite the Victoria and Albert Museum in South Kensington. No theatre, just land, and that was that until the seventies.

Back in October 1937 the League of Audiences promoted its parliamentary bill supported by a number of minor MPs 'to organize in every constituency a demand from the electors that the Government shall give to Music and Drama the practical recognition which it already gives to Libraries, Museums and Picture Galleries'. Under the bill eight 'commissioners' would be appointed to 'encourage music and dramatic art and to awaken in audiences a sense of their powers and responsibilities', which sounds a near-mystical remit. One of the commissioners should be an existing MP who would answer questions in the House, probably a Cabinet minister. A parliamentary committee was set up to study the bill in February 1938. It didn't meet – formally it was postponed – and the bill never entered the business of the House of Commons. One man had ensured its stillbirth: Glyndebourne's Captain Christie.

John Christie thought the bill was a nebulous mess and he was doubtless right. He knew that behind the League lay Sir Thomas Beecham and his selfish agendas, which were not the same selfish agendas as those of Christie. In fact the League of Audiences had been taken over by toffee-nosed friends of Beecham ('Many influential people share with thoughtful legislators . . .') who had tried in one of his many vain ventures get a partnership deal between Columbia Records and the BBC for his new symphony orchestra. When it failed he took every chance to attack the Corporation, most famously in April 1937 at the conference of the NFMS, when George Dyson invited Beecham to give a speech on vaguely 'musical matters'. His verbal blitz on the BBC's music policy was so well covered in the newspapers (though not by BBC Radio) that the exposure gave the NFMS sensational publicity.

One of the sponsors of the Music and Drama Bill was the oddball MP and author, A.P. Herbert. He was the Independent member for Oxford University from 1935 to 1950, but his droll pieces for *Punch* magazine and his contributions to West End musical comedies ensured that anything he said in the Commons would not be taken seriously. Nevertheless he succeeded well enough because the wry tone of his speeches invariably caught his colleagues out. In early November 1937 Christie met Herbert, then sent him a summarising letter:

> I was glad to have the opportunity of talking to you about Music & Drama. Your experience should be invaluable in trying to set things right. Speaking primarily for Music, the facts as I see them are:– What is wrong is the representation of music. Music is represented by musicians. Their chief preoccupation is intriguing against each other. Politicians pay little heed to them . . . because musicians are small minded and generally incapable of organising. Consequently the Government is bewildered with the problem and cannot see how to get a contact with it.

This, by the way, is how Christie wrote, whatever the occasion – less of an argument, more a chain of unguarded remarks that insulted almost everyone he addressed. His wife, his secretary, his manager and his butler, Childs, would discreetly censor his drafts, though they could not sub-edit the disordered nuggets of bigotry that passed for analysis. He proposed to Herbert a structure for an independent arts body that would handle government grants as well as accumulate subscriptions. At the heart lay a Council of Power. Consisting of people 'who are essentially wise and experienced', the executive Council of Power would be supported 'by a much larger and more or less ubiquitous Council, who would preserve contact between my Council of Power and other people – politicians, etc.', though the executive 'should not be appointed by the large Council'.

Christie would keep the Music and Drama Bill's commissioners 'who would hold the purse strings'. The Government would pay for the headquarters and provide special funds to bring in foreign advisers for six-month residencies. If this last bit sounds bizarre, it emerges that deep down Christie wanted a fund for the training of new British conductors to usurp the monopoly of Beecham and the foreigner he had in mind was Toscanini. Christie's ideas tottered from the rational to the ridiculous, as with his ensuing proposal. Rational: the Government would not fund the Council of Power's projects. That funding would be provided by the local authorities where the projects took place. Irrational: in order to make the borough's events instantly popular, 'I should use dodges, such as allocating certain Seats of Honour to certain local magnates, in order to get their interest and to obtain local glamour.'

Yet some ideas seemed illogical when they were smart: 'I should expect that the Government would wish to make their contribution through the cloak of the BBC. So far I have found an interest in the scheme from the BBC.' Arthur Bliss had made his similar point two years before in his *Listener* series ('Is there any way in which the Broadcasting Corporation can lend its powerful aid?'). They both knew that the Labour Government in 1930 had done a back-door deal with the BBC to subsidise Beecham's opera ventures at Covent Garden, then called the Covent Garden Opera Syndicate. This had been arranged by the socialising wife of Labour's Chancellor of the Exchequer, Philip Snowden, who provided a subsidy of £25,000 over five years (£800,000 today). The grants were passed unobtrusively through the BBC via the General Post Office, which handled the BBC's licences, and in return the BBC was allowed (with a nominal fee added) to relay some of Beecham's performances. In the end £20,000 was supplied between 1930–1933 before the succeeding Coalition Government dropped the deal; the seasons faced bankruptcy once again. But Christie also needed the BBC's support for a different reason; to outsmart the anti-radio caucus of the League.

Of all the things he dreamed up, it was the notion of an executive Council of Power 'who are essentially wise and experienced' that most prevailed when the Arts Council was finally set up. The assumption we make fifty years on is that it is connected to the 'arm's-length' principle, that the Government delegated responsibility to an independent body for reasons of democracy. But this is far from so. Christie's very title, Council of Power, warns us of a different bias. There was a fashion in the thirties, from right and left, to consider structures that improved on, or reacted to, those devised by totalitarian regimes.

Being invariably populist, the fascist autocrats belittled the emerging 'intelligentsia', the reformist, academic 'legislators of progress' and their fellow experts. Hitler announced in 1937, 'The artist does not create for the artist, but just like everyone else he creates for the people. And we shall see to it that from now on the people will again be the judge of its own art.' This unnerved the normally sympathetic sorts like Chamberlain and Christie, who considered this change cheapening. In response, a re-analysis of elites evolved in this country. The right's line was typified by Captain Ludovici of Ipswich (1882–1971), once secretary to the sculptor Rodin and by 1935 a Rosenberg-style Nazi zealot who wrote in the *Listener*:

> There are in all societies wise and healthy men, true aristocrats, examples of flourishing life in their own persons, and they usually have reliable knowledge or instincts as to what should be done in most circumstances of life. And, as a rule, by using them as a guide and following them, you would be able to flourish also.

On the left, it was mainly the followers of Trotsky (and thus the rivals of Stalin) who engaged in debate on the issue of aptitude, as in this anonymous leaflet on culture, also of 1935:

> Artists place their abilities at the service of the proletariat. But it is their expertise which they transform to the task in hand. Those abilities are honed from a balance of technique and creative prowess. In that sense, that is what under capitalism we have called an elite practice, and it cannot be condemned merely because it has been recognised, though not wholly controlled, by the forces of capitalism.

Even the Liberal Keynes believed that the best government would be 'an intellectual aristocracy using the method of persuasion' and that the most important decisions are better made by a small group of intelligent people. One of the most exalted radio inventions of the Second World War was a programme called *The Brains Trust*, a panel of 'four wise men' who pondered questions sent in by the public. One of the four was, incredibly, Malcolm Sargent, the rakish choral conductor and butt of Beecham's blunt quips. *The Brains Trust* conformed to this idea of an independent clite not handicapped by short-term political reasoning.

It was a type of Brains Trust that Christie was inventing with his Council of Power. He insisted on 'a self-elected group of men' supported by 'a representative body whose chief work shall be to find out and put forward the views of any section of our musical life to the self-elected group'. In this we recognise the Arts Council and its panel system of advisers. It was to Christie's immense frustration that the MPs and civil servants, when they took his idea and formed the Arts Council, considered that a pertinent elite was the House of Lords. It is for this banal reason that the chairmen of the Arts Council are routinely ennobled, if they're not already.

Nonetheless, in sum John Christie had worked out a primitive structure for the Arts Council. We can recognise the Council itself 'who should not be appointed by the large Council', the greater team of panellists who advise them and 'preserve contact . . . with other people', and the artform directors in the guise of the commissioners. He even predicts the name, 'Council', and in doing so he exhibits the confusion felt by so many since, unable to fathom the difference between the Arts Council as a committee (the council of the Council) and the Arts Council as an administrative entity. He concluded his letter in the usual tangled manner: 'I take it that the immediate problem is to revise the Music and Drama Bill, but perhaps discussions on this, or on other lines, should precede the redesign of the Music & Drama Bill.' Christie contacted the League proposing a dialogue and then wrote to Neville Chamberlain in January 1938 ('Dear Prime Minister, I want to have a discussion with you about the Music & Drama Bill, which is occupying the attention of a number of MPs') and that is why the bill drifted off into the fumes of the Second World War.

Out of the blue Christie discovered a fresh ally. A second-rate concert pianist called Robert Forbes ran the Royal Manchester College of Music, where 'loveableness was not his most apparent characteristic', though he was tolerated because he was the college's first home-grown principal. As the latest of the ISM's annual presidents, he addressed its annual Christmas conference in 1937:

> We are turning out annually hundreds of gifted and well-trained musicians who are just as unwanted as the tons of fish that are thrown back in the sea because there is no market for it. The creation of an intelligent and discriminating listening public is needed, and the most direct way of accomplishing that object is the subsidy of music by the state and the municipality.

His remarks about a partnership of central and local subsidy attracted not only the attention of the newspapers, but also a batty letter from Christie whose views he had echoed, ending with the accompaniment of 'Rule, Britannia': 'I feel so sure that the trouble lies at the top and that no conscious effort is being made to achieve what I am quite certain the British Empire can achieve – the lead in music in the world.' Forbes agreed that more talk was needed and Christie created the Glyndebourne Conference.

Intending to gather the great and the good for a spring weekend, Christie invited twenty or so souls down to Sussex, including Forbes, to work out what was needed for his Council of Power and give it some public shape. He did not invite Sir Hugh Allen, whom he feared would be appointed one of the eight commissioners under the League scheme. He said of Allen:

> He has achieved nothing in the way of a standard at the Royal College. He is a dominant character and a very good speaker. He is, in my opinion, exactly what I am afraid of. To me he represents more work for the British musician and a lower standard.

Neither was Christie a keen supporter of subsidy:

> Everyone is calling out for subsidies for everything because they have been introduced in one or two cases. Can't they see all wrong people pocketing the subsidy? [i.e. Beecham] ... People should expect good performances to be expensive, but they should also expect them to be worth it.

To his credit, when he later gleaned Arts Council subsidy for Glyndebourne projects, he used it specifically to support new work.

On Saturday 5 March 1938, Britain's senior composer, the sixty-five-year-old Ralph Vaughan Williams, sat in the Organ Room of Glyndebourne. A supremely well-connected and popular gent, his 'down with factories and up with folk music' nationalism charmed even Christie, and the two of them shared a disdain for show-offs and royal honours. The Captain was peeved, however, when the composer agreed close to the conference to accept an international prize, offered by the Nazis, on condition that the entire money was handed to Jewish refugees. Vaughan Williams sat in the grand Glyndebourne room with the vain conductor Malcolm Sargent ('Do I bring black or white tie?'), the popular opera singer Roy Henderson and a bevy of music organisation chiefs to discuss with Christie the setting up of the National Council for Music and the Arts, as they finally chose to call it, though it was plainly the music bit

that occupied their thoughts; 'and the Arts' kept drifting in and
out of print.

The weekend was minuted. Christie's snotty comments on
poverty ('the poor cannot have Van Dycks') spurred the William
Morris-style socialism of Vaughan Williams:

Mr Christie:	What I am alarmed at is that the mob should control music, because their taste is so bad. It is a question of whether the movement should be controlled by professionals.
Dr Vaughan Williams:	Could I ask Mr Christie what he means by 'the mob'?
Mr Christie:	The cinema crowd.

In that astonishing weekend the group defined all the basics of
the Arts Council. Chatting away they fathomed the fundamental
problems that the Council would confront for the next fifty years.
Malcolm Sargent developed the theme of state and local authority
partnership, touching on arcane elements such as matched funding. This very subject would prove to be the most vexed that the
future Arts Council faced:

> More good could be done by the local corporation than the state
> with regard to local music . . . The combination of the state with
> the corporation would be the easiest method . . . If it were known
> that if £500 were given from the corporation and then £500 were
> given from the state funds, it would be a grand thing.

Sargent, of course, was looking how the scheme would support his
concert profession. Vaughan Williams countered him by stressing
the creative duty of the Council: 'I think it is important that we
shall become, not a nation of music-listeners, but of music-
makers.' At the time Vaughan Williams was writing his 'Serenade
to Music', set to Shakespeare and including a special part scored
for Roy Henderson to sing:

> The man that hath no music in himself
> Nor is not moved by concord of sweet sounds,
> Is fit for treason, strategems and spoils.

The most colourful moments came when they debated the

relation of the Council to the state. Jo Hodgkinson, then organising secretary of the League of Audiences (and later a Council drama director) asked, 'Where does the Music & Drama Bill come into your scheme? How would the commissioners be appointed? – by Parliament, Cabinet or the King?' Christie replied, 'By the King ... We wanted it to be by the King and not the Crown because we did not want a Party appointment.' Luckily the King's aide-de-camp, the old Earl of Harewood, was there to clarify: 'The King could not appoint anybody without the advice of his Ministers.' It was Hodgkinson who reminded them how valuable independence might be:

> The National Council of Social Service, which has no money and which was only a paper organisation, was chosen by the Government as the body through which it should spend money on the depressed areas. The Government selected that body because it had the respect of all the social services.

What divided them mainly was the issue that would ultimately corrode Arts Council conduct – whether to go for the best, or the most: 'raise or spread', excellence or equity, London or the regions, the elite or the masses. As Vaughan Williams claimed for his side, 'We want to make opera popular and the thing that everyone wants to go to, from the richest to the poorest. We may have to leave out perfection to get popularity.' And, as Christie replied for his, 'I quite agree that we should let the mob hear Opera ... There should be some performances which are reserved for the poor (our dress rehearsals).'

It took all of Jo Hodgkinson's tact to move this round to his independent body:

> The question is standard against 'spread-over'. Whichever decision you make it will be necessary to have a body of persons if the spending of that money is worthwhile. This body would act as an advisory body who would receive applications and would decide whether the sum asked for would produce the result which it ought to produce ... The Government was rushed into finding millions for the Physical Training and Recreation Act, and such a distinguished body as yourselves could soon rush them into finding money for music.

Hodgkinson was spot on to say that the Government could be seduced into spending. The Government, Conservative under

'National' cover, had been persuaded by the likes of Keynes to discard balanced budgets and penny-pinching in favour of investment. As far as the arts were concerned, a much-hated tax had been eased in order to make it cheaper to put on live performances during the Slump. Entertainments duty was like value added tax (VAT) today, a selective surcharge paid by audiences. In 1931 it imposed itself like this:

Band	Admission	Duty
1	2–2$\frac{1}{2}$d	$\frac{1}{2}$d
2	2$\frac{1}{2}$–6d	1d
3	6–7$\frac{1}{2}$d	1$\frac{1}{2}$d
4	7$\frac{1}{2}$–10d	2d
5	10–1s 0$\frac{1}{2}$d	2$\frac{1}{2}$d
6	1s 0$\frac{1}{2}$d–1s 3d	3d
7	1s 3$\frac{1}{2}$d–1s 8d	4d
8	1s 8$\frac{1}{2}$d–2s 1d	5d
9	2s 1$\frac{1}{2}$d–2s 6d	6d

In cash terms it penalised the concert hall more than the music hall, the rich more than the poor, and that is sometimes the point of a selective tax. But given the fiasco of back-door subsidy for Beecham's Covent Garden season, and the growing crisis over attendances for concerts, with the Old Vic at the top of the scale and vagrant circuses at the bottom, pressure was placed to lighten the burden for live acts. In the Finance Act of 1935, duty ceased on payments 'not exceeding sixpence' and was then applied incrementally further up the scale. Christie's Glyndebourne, the Old Vic and Sadler's Wells were then quietly advised that there was a way of skipping duty at the top end, through the old charitable ruse of claiming you are there for educational purposes, not business. By this action the Government lost at least £100,000 annually on entertainments duty alone (£3.6 million), though Keynes would have argued that the £100,000 enlivened the economy through consumer spending.

A letter from Christie to Neville Chamberlain reveals all:

Dear Prime Minister,
I want to thank you for the letter which you sent to me, as Chancellor, about Glyndebourne Entertainments Duty. Your letter was

accepted by the Customs House in the end and I am grateful to you
for it.

It was practical elements like this that were starting to unsettle the
government machine. Was this not more back-door subsidy for
the rich, and were not selective taxes more fair than blanket ones?
Would it not be cleaner instead to take the arts through the front
door, regulate state support and then make the buggers pay it
back over the counter like everyone else?

The issue broke in the House of Commons on 7 July 1937
during a debate on the 1937 Finance Act. A corny old luvvie called
Freddie Denville ('First appearance on stage at four weeks old;
founder of modern repertory companies in the provinces under
the title *Denville's Premier Players*') had been the Conservative
member for Newcastle Central for the previous six years and
finally wished to make his mark in Parliament. Denville moved for
'the relief of the living stage from any form of taxation'. He called
for the abolition of entertainments duty beginning:

> I suggest that there is evidence to show that employment will be
> largely increased and much more money saved to the state in the
> way of employment than is being obtained by this tax ... It is
> possible for any theatre to escape Entertainments Duty by using
> methods which in some cases are not questionable, but which in
> other cases are questionable. There is the theatre which is stated
> not to run for profit, but as an educational force ... Then there is
> the touring company. If it makes a claim that it is not being run for
> profit it can be exempted from Entertainments Duty. I would press
> the Chancellor of the Exchequer to do something to prevent this
> form of exemption, which if it is allowed will lead to disastrous
> results, morally and financially.

The Tory chiefs opposed their own party member, pointing out
that the duty's abolition would lose the Treasury £1,250,000 a year
(£4,131 million). Labour's Chuter Ede, a future Home Secretary,
rumbled, 'I am not sure that we shall not have to follow the
example of some foreign countries and see that the best forms of
the drama and the ballet are supported from public funds by
direct contribution.'

In short, the Government had heard a crescendo of calls for
central subsidy, was threatened with an imminent bill to establish
it for the performing arts, and had its civil servants gnawing on the

issue. While the Music and Drama Bill promoted a neat but vague scheme of commissioners, the Glyndebourne Conference was turning up with a more mature proposal – an independent group who would work with the Government but relieve it of sensitive burdens. Chamberlain chose to wait for Christie. But he hadn't counted on an inscrutable old cove called Tom Jones.

Tom Jones made sure he caught the start and end of each chain of Chinese whispers connected with 10 Downing Street. He had the means to check details and the weight to wield changes and for this reason he never broke his back-room cover. Thomas Jones (1870–1955) had been Lloyd George's confidant, serving three Prime Ministers as Deputy Cabinet Secretary between 1916 and 1930. At that point he reached the retirement age of the civil service, though he stuck like a limpet to Downing Street in a number of 'advisory' roles. Jones discounted the honours system as stoutly as Vaughan Williams and Christie did, though given the way he watched Lloyd George exploit it for cash, this is hardly surprising.

Born in a border mining village in Monmouthshire, Jones attended the local county school and the Methodist chapel, where he acquired skills as a compelling preacher. Mary Glasgow described him as a 'formidable little pyramid of a figure, with a small head and long, pointed nose'. By sheer aptitude and tenacity he ended up as the Professor of Economics at Queen's University, Belfast.

Coincidentally to that job, Jones was passionate about improving the Poor Law and health insurance for the working class. He worked as secretary for the National Health Insurance Commissioners of Wales, a speciality that brought him to the notice of the Liberal Prime Minister Lloyd George who took him into Downing Street in the midst of the First World War. Jones became adroit in handling domestic issues that stemmed from international crises. From that time on he seduced a great many wheelers and dealers with his charm and quick thinking and cultivated a chain of unofficial contacts as the perfect civil servant, 'the man that everyone can trust and no one can trust'. He seemed to be a Jones who kept up with the Joneses, but really he was the Jones the others followed. In Government circles he was generally known as T.J.

The Slump threw Tom Jones back into issues of working-class poverty. Now in his sixties, he not only administered the

Economic Advisory Board that Keynes had recently seduced, but toiled on the Unemployment Assistance Board, the National Council for Social Service's Unemployment Council and chaired the South Wales Coalfield Distress Committee. He was also evangelical about adult education, founding Coleg Harlech as a Welsh residential academy for that purpose. Yet surprisingly he was the lynch pin of the lobby supporting Hitler in Downing Street.

Jones was a key member of the 'Cliveden Set', a group of plutocrats and politicians entertained over weekends at the Berkshire seat of Waldorf Astor, who ran the *Observer* while his brother John owned *The Times* (T.J. joined the *Observer* as a board member). Waldorf's wife Nancy was the first woman MP (Conservative, 1919–1945) to sit in the Commons. The Astors' weekend parties gathered together the 'Appeasers', those who – to be kind about them – opposed a second war and thus sought the nice side of the Nazis; oh, and they were chronically stuck up and didn't care for Jews.

It was Tom Jones who'd returned from a private meeting with Hitler in 1935 laden with the Führer's signed speeches on the arts. He reported that, 'Hitler does not seek war with us. He seeks our friendship. If we fail him he will turn to Italy and elsewhere and we shall be sorry to have refused him.' T.J. was adamant that Hitler was 'a factor for peace' and sought a meeting between the Prime Minister Stanley Baldwin and Hitler in a 'neutral' setting. Cliveden was suggested as a host venue, then Leeds Castle, then Glyndebourne during the season, where all those dirndls and lederhosen would have made the Führer feel *gemütlich*. Baldwin finally decided he'd prefer to meet Hitler on really neutral territory, like a ship in the Channel. The Nazis thought a ferry not quite proper and the plan was 'torpedoed' – T.J.'s unfortunate choice of word.

Jones had his fidgety fingers in the arts, as Hitler had fathomed. His musical crony was the composer Walford Davies, one of those fake Welshmen like Lloyd George who served the principality well. Walford Davies (1869–1941) was an Allen-style organist, who had taught choral singing to both Edward VIII and George VI at military college. He succeeded Elgar as Master of the King's Musick in 1934, yet he was sympathetic to the folk-song movement of Vaughan Williams, and he'd talk ardently with Jones about the value of the discipline and skill found in Welsh village choirs and bands. Like Allen and the others he saw musical development in terms of mass education, sharing with Jones an enthusiasm for adult study, and he practised what he preached by giving very popular talks about classical music on BBC Radio.

By chance Walford Davies had chatted in the early summer of 1938 with Vaughan Williams about the Glyndebourne Conference. Vaughan Williams gave a jaundiced picture of 'the old pros feathering their nests', caring more for international opera than the national development of music-making. (Forbes of Manchester had written to Christie after the weekend: 'Frankly I was quite horrified at the outlook of people like Vaughan Williams, to whom standards of performance mean nothing.') In the Chinese whispers style so valued by T.J., Walford Davies passed this gossip on to him and Jones went to work.

It so happened that Christie had sent Prime Minister Chamberlain a copy of the structure of his National Council. This was a mistake. Being transitional it had all manner of foolishness in it and T.J. simply had to pick out shards of manifest nonsense to puncture Christie's progress. The 'outer ring', by then called the General Council, comprised on paper no fewer than 101 representative members (the Inner, Grand or Executive Council had twenty-one, not unlike the eventual Arts Council). While the Board of Education was handed a single place on the General Council, the ISM had sixteen, the universities six and ten seats were offered to members 'who have given service' to music and the arts but had 'no vested interest whatsoever' in them, which sounded like a dubious combination of Captain Christie and the Man on the Clapham Omnibus.

Christie soldiered on with his scheme – he held a progress meeting in July 1938 – while Jones scanned the copies of material flowing from Glyndebourne to Number 10 and conceived his own version of the National Council for Music and the Arts. Christie had stopped the passage of the Music and Drama Bill on the pretence of improving it; in the same way Jones thwarted Christie by feigning adjustments to the National Council. Happily for Jones he didn't have to do much because Christie committed two indiscretions that confused the situation and alienated the Prime Minister. First, in late 1938 he contacted a youngish parliamentary private secretary whom he'd taught at Eton. Lord Dunglass has flitted in and out of British history under a number of stuffy names, most dismally as Alec Douglas Home, a Tory Prime Minister for a few forgotten months in the sixties. Back then this Bertie Wooster of a fellow was a pretty reliable way of getting through to Chamberlain, so Christie now chose to exploit him.

He asked Dunglass to find out whether he could get direct subsidy for Glyndebourne from the Treasury. In the eyes of Downing Street this single question exposed Christie's National Council crusade as camouflage for his selfish ends. Dunglass sent Christie a hand-written note: 'I am met at every turn by the contention that a subsidy could not be justified, however meritorious the production, to something which caters largely for the comparatively wealthy.' Ending his memo with a terrifically ironic twist, Dunglass suggested that Christie might apply to a newish philanthropic outfit packed, like the Carnegie, with American money. It was called the Pilgrim Trust. Its secretary was Tom Jones.

Unaware of his slip, Christie then thought of ensnaring Chamberlain into the National Council. He contacted Lord Dunglass once more with a proposition to create a chairman:

> My own view is that Chamberlain would be almost the most suitable of all because he is a man who, of all the leading politicians, is almost alone in actually showing some interest in music. Sam Hoare has been to Glyndebourne, but I don't know him personally.

He went on to ask if the Prime Minister could recommend 'the great and the good' for the Executive Council, ending with the information that, 'I am going to Germany early next week and return here on the 17th'. The letter was dated 1 February 1939, seven months before Chamberlain sent Britain to war with the Nazis. The Prime Minister, setting aside major issues like arts subsidy to deal with minor ones like arming the country, gave Christie's request to an adviser who knew about these things, a certain Tom Jones.

T.J. compiled an assortment of 'the great and the good' and sent it to Glyndebourne as 'the Prime Minister's List'. The line-up did not include John Christie. It did include Tom Jones. There were eighteen names apart from Jones, ten of them peers and five of them knights. None had been to the Glyndebourne Conference. The youngest mentioned was the writer J.B. Priestley, then forty-five years old; most were in their sixties and, by the way, the majority were Cliveden Appeasers. The eye-catching names included Sir John Reith, the prudish Director-General of the BBC, Lord Justice Porter, who tried Lord Haw-Haw for treason, and the

MP Hugh Dalton, a champagne socialist who would later favour the Arts Council as Labour's Chancellor of the Exchequer. A solitary female was listed, the Conservative MP Baroness Northchurch, though the roll did include the chairman of the Midland Bank, 'R. McKenna (or Mrs)'.

Lord Macmillan (1873–1952) was included too, and usefully so. A Scottish lawyer by training, he specialised in cases involving public bodies. He was excellent in 'the promulgation of fresh charters', and helped the very first Labour Government in 1924 as Lord Advocate, though he was no socialist (neither was he related to Harold Macmillan, the Tory Prime Minister of the fifties). Judge Macmillan had chaired some rum things in his time, such as the Royal Commission on Lunacy and Mental Disorder, the Royal Canadian Commission into Banking Laws, and the 1925 Enquiry into the Coalmining Industry, which did nothing to prevent the 1926 strike. He also happened to chair the Pilgrim Trust.

It's hard from this distance to tell how malicious Tom Jones was with this list. More likely it was tactical, based on the calculation that few of the names could be bothered with Christie, nor Christie with chasing them. Hardly any of the people mentioned ended up on the CEMA (the early Arts Council) even though Jones had a prominent hand in launching it. In any case Jones was considering his alternative to the National Council, and the synchronous enquiry to the Board of Education that led to Mary Glasgow's little survey of subsidy in other countries may have started with him.

Jones saw the arts issue as one of unemployment matched to education, just as the ISM, the NFMS and the Allen mafia had done, his friend Walford Davies included. T.J. examined it first as a labour matter, as we might expect of a campaigning member of countless dole committees. He could not find the right mechanism to link the notion of subsidy to an economic element, such as entertainments duty, where the aid could be connected to income from tax. Pundits occasionally pursue this futile exercise today by relating the Government's income from cultural VAT to the level of arts subsidy, unaware that this ring-fencing *quid pro quo* is not how the Treasury bothers to view it.

The education issues that Walford Davies and Vaughan Williams consistently identified, however, did suggest that the Board of Education might be the vehicle for the transmission of subsidy. Arts and education had been parliamentarily entwined since the Education Act of 1918. The work of the Board of Education was predicated on a practical liaison between the state and local government, mostly in the funding and monitoring of neighbourhood schools and adult education institutes – it even included a number of financial systems between central government, counties and municipalities. Of course, Jones was thinking of schemes to help the village choirs of Wales, not the village hall of Glyndebourne.

In the meantime Christie was pushing ahead all too slowly. 'My dear Dyson,' he wrote in September 1939, at the outbreak of war, 'I believe that our Council should be formed now and that we should not wait for Peace.' Christie had time to work on the Council knowing that he could not produce operas without subsidy while the war was on, though he had not expected the fresh and overwhelming challenges that combat brought, evacuation being one: 'Glyndebourne has 260 children and 60 helpers and may be the start of a new Social movement when Peace comes,' he told Dyson. John Christie, the Baron von Trapp of Sussex.

In sum, T.J. saw that while Christie was flustered and guileless, state arts subsidy was a notion in vogue and certainly on its way; that Jones had the means to use government funds to develop adult education in the arts, and that wartime – when the world gets moist-eyed about its culture – was when the Treasury was most disposed to oil its rusty locks. The time had come. One problem remained. He needed to control the subsidy machine to ensure that 'the elitists' didn't overwhelm it, and to supervise it to his satisfaction he needed a stake in its financing. The solution lay at his fingertips, though it took him a time to notice: the Pilgrim Trust.

The Trust was a recent adjunct to the Carnegie, established during 1930 to conserve American–British relations following the Wall Street Crash. The money came from Edward Harkness of Cleveland on the back of loans he gave to start up Standard Oil. With Lord Macmillan as chairman and Jones as secretary, it spent its invested £2 million endowment (nearly £70 million today) on social causes, 'giving to those with whom life has dealt harshly the opportunity of attaining by their own efforts those qualities of character which are a nation's most precious heritage'. As T.J. ran the thing, it comes as little surprise to learn that its money set up adult education centres in Wales and published a study titled 'Men Without Work'. T.J. arranged to use a surplus sum of £25,000 (£800,000) in the Pilgrim vaults to challenge the Treasury to match it and support a number of adult education initiatives in the arts.

In late October 1939 he phoned Buck de la Warr, who was president for a short time at the Board of Education during the 'Emergency Government' at the start of the war. T.J.'s scheme was presented to him as a civil development of adult education whereby ordinary people placed in the extraordinary conditions of war might encounter music and drama performed and taught by otherwise idle artists across the country. Jones asked for a formal meeting to sort it out then he, Macmillan and de la Warr held an informal pre-meeting on 14 December. Buck de la Warr thought it was worth a one-off grant of £5,000 if the Pilgrim could stump up the same amount, pound for pound. Jones did not disabuse him, but he was very careful to verify the offer of a pound for pound match.

On 18 December 1939, the president of the Board of Education and seven of his staff greeted five visitors: Tom Jones, Lord Macmillan, Sir Walford Davies, Sir Kenneth Clark of the National Gallery and Bill Williams, the secretary of the British Institute of Adult Education. Mary Glasgow, now promoted as a full education inspector (HMI), minuted the meeting:

> The purpose of the Conference was first to discuss in principle the problem of cultural activities in war-time; and then to decide how the needs of various organisations and individuals concerned might be met. The discussion was confined to what have been termed 'practical' activities: music, drama, the arts and handicrafts generally, as distinct from other activities which are on the fringe of academic adult education.

Lord Macmillan said that the Pilgrim Trust was prepared to put up £25,000 'if a suitable scheme were presented by the Board'. He understood that the Treasury 'might be prepared to put up £ for £ in such an arrangement'. The Pilgrim Trust, he diplomatically suggested, would be glad to leave the initiative to the board in the first place, 'but we would wish ultimately to take the full share in the administration of the scheme'. Buck de la Warr was visibly indignant to be put on the spot at a higher price, but with all this new money coming in for adult education, a charity willing to run the thing for them and a high-ranking group staring at him, he was chagrined into acceptance.

Tom Jones wrote the following account of the negotiations in his autobiography:

> It began on the telephone. Lord de la Warr, then President of the

Board of Education, rang up the Secretary of the Pilgrim Trust to sound him out about an 'idea' and a possible grant; nothing very much, £5,000 perhaps . . . Lord de la Warr was enthusiastic. He had Venetian visions of a post-war Lord Mayor's Show on the Thames in which the Board of Education led the Arts in triumph from Whitehall to Greenwich in magnificent barges and gorgeous gondolas . . . – in fact, Merrie England. Lord Macmillan's grave judicial calm collapsed suddenly and completely . . . Supply and Demand kissed. Would £25,000 be any use? The secretary blushed and fell off his stool.

And blush he should, for penning this pack of lies. He failed to add a Treasury warning that the matching money could not be offered until May, at the start of the 1940–1941 financial year, to which Jones replied, 'We'll start spending our half now. Winter needs art even more than spring.' T.J. also neglected to chronicle the follow-up. A committee was established then and there out of all of those present. It would be called the Committee for the Encouragement of Music and the Arts. CEMA held its first meeting the very next day under its founding Chairman – Tom Jones.

Chapter 4

Music while we work

Walford's Holy Women
The Carnegie Wrangle • CEMA v ENSA
Air Raids and MI5

In all but name the Arts Council gave its very first grant away on 9 January 1940. It went to the National Federation of Women's Institutes. The sum of £300 (around £10,000 today) was offered by CEMA to cover the salary and expenses of an 'adviser organiser' for music. It also agreed to give grants to the English Folk Dance and Song Society (a blanket £500 to cover the first nine months of 1940), £450 to the National Council for Music of Wales to appoint an area organiser for the north of Tom Jones' principality, and £1,000 to the Rural Music Schools Association to pay for five 'trained pioneer teachers' to work in new areas around the country. No wonder it was called the Committee for the Encouragement of Music . . . and whatever.

Tom Jones had got his way. He'd set up the first state subsidy machine for the arts, even though it had no state subsidy in it yet. Christie was left gazumped, while Keynes and his Bloomsbury dabblers were oblivious of the breakthrough. The show was on the road, all too literally; CEMA's cash availed regional experiments in adult education and not a penny was spent on London professionals, as the first four grants emphasised. The odd thing was that only the Women's Institute had actually applied. Nearly £2,000 (£65,000) was offered to organisations who had not asked for anything, while a request from the Vic-Wells Ballet Company received the first Arts Council rejection. As the Vic-Wells later turned into the Royal Ballet, this fact may please those jaundiced against its subsequent prosperity. Jones, though, must have been deeply happy with all of this, even though everything else around him was going terribly wrong.

On the day after the first full CEMA meeting he chaired on 9 January at its office inside the Board of Education's base at Kingsway's Alexandra House, he had been summoned to see his old mentor Lloyd George. A campaign was bubbling to drop the Prime Minister, a hapless Neville Chamberlain duped by Hitler and left to control a headless chicken of a War Cabinet. Lloyd George wanted to supplant him 'and negotiate a peace'; T.J. was expected to do his duty down the corridors of Cliveden and Downing Street to get Lloyd George back in. Although many considered the white-maned Liberal defeatist to be antique, he was, in fact, only six years older than Chamberlain, as Tom Jones had to keep reminding colleagues.

Jones checked if there were rivals and was embarrassed to discover that the Astors and many of the Tory Party were indeed thinking of dumping Chamberlain for the Foreign Secretary Lord Halifax, one hell of an Appeaser and a crony of Jones. T.J. decided to back Lloyd George as first choice with the profoundly conservative Halifax as a fall-back. He did his very best to see either of them in because he wanted at all costs to suppress a third contender, Winston Churchill, who scorned appeasement and had blocked Jones on unemployment issues as Chancellor back in the twenties. So, within twenty-four hours of personal success, Jones was embroiled in fresh intrigue. He could have handled it all if another issue had not broken that would disarm his power irrevocably.

At the start of the war T.J.'s Pilgrim Trust chairman, Lord Macmillan, was selected to run the Ministry for Information. The Minister was making a thorough hash of his job. Macmillan never understood why Chamberlain had press-ganged him into the position in the first place, but it was really because Sir John Reith of the BBC declined it, not having worked out what the Ministry was supposed to do, and mischievously suggested instead the chairman of his BBC Advisory Council, Lord M., who had headed so many weird things in his time. The Information Ministry, a defective replica of Goebbels' propaganda corps, was mandated to 'get the British war aims understood', an instruction so open to interpretation that Macmillan complained:

One was being told to do a job by a man [Chamberlain] who
agreed that one ought to do whatever one was asked to do, but who
could not or would not tell one what the job was, nor, what, if any,
support he would give.

Good training for an Arts Council chairman there.

Macmillan could not be absolved from the howlers made in his
name. When the British Expeditionary Forces arrived in France
on 11 September 1939, the news was first announced from a radio
station in Paris. The War Office agreed with Macmillan's Ministry
that the Germans would have heard the broadcast and so the story
was cleared for British newspapers. As the first midnight editions
were being distributed, the Secretary of State for War considered
that more information was being given than necessary and had a
ban imposed. The police were commanded to confiscate copies of
the early editions from trains, even from the hands of readers.
While frantic editors began again with mint editions, at 2.55am
Macmillan's ministry allowed the ban to be lifted and returned the
original copies to the stations. Macmillan was rebuked. It didn't
help that a parliamentary question as to the size of his Ministry
revealed that the total number of staff was 999. '999 at Sixes and
Sevens' was not the kind of headline the Minister of Information
needed at the start of his campaign. Chamberlain, a man close to
being thrown out himself, chose to discharge Macmillan and
replace him at all costs with the BBC's Reith.

To get rid of him Chamberlain used the excuse of CEMA.
Macmillan was told at the end of December 1939 that the Prime
Minister sought his skills 'at the service of the arts'. He must move
over to CEMA forthwith. Macmillan, partly relieved but also
indignant, pointed out that CEMA was already chaired by Jones.
In order to lubricate his departure civil servants planned to
promote CEMA from a 'Committee' to a 'Council' on the promise
that the detached CEMA 'may well lay the foundations for a
significant extension of cultural education' (which sounds very
Jonesish, but meant a longer life was predicted) and that more
Treasury cash might be made available if Macmillan could work
out a ruse like the Pilgrim one, though they really meant he'd
have to winkle more private money. Thus CEMA was impulsively
elevated simply in order to solve an immediate political problem
elsewhere.

T.J. was happy to move over at a convenient moment, bustling
about as he was to get Lloyd George or Lord Halifax into Downing

Street. He also knew he could continue to control Macmillan through the Pilgrim Trust. It was agreed between them that CEMA the 'Committee' should cease at the end of March 1940, when CEMA the 'Council' could start the new financial year with the Treasury grant. Macmillan would chair while T.J. continued serving as his deputy. In the meantime, should anyone ask, Macmillan was in charge. Jones, the power behind the throne – on the throne – ran six meetings, twice a month, and with his committee of thirteen spent most of the money.

He'd started out with the Pilgrim Trust's £25,000 (£800,000). Within three weeks the committee had given 40 per cent away solely for music to be promoted by a number of organisations on which the members sat. The vocabulary used to justify grant-giving was fascinating. It was a mixture of pinstripe jargon ('widespread provision of opportunities'), academic vernacular ('cultural education officer') and made-up stuff. This was hardly surprising given the expeditionary nature of the committee, storming its way through the linguistic wasteland that would finally emerge as artsperanto.

From the Board of Education came three snooping staff, including CEMA's proto-feminist Secretary Mary Glasgow, who wrote the well-modulated minutes. They were led by the Board's president's number two (the number one, by the way, had changed between meetings from de la Warr to Herwald Ramsbotham), a tiny and alert Tory MP who was the only other woman present.

Thelma Cazalet Keir (1899–1989) was very well known to Jones because she was Lloyd George's 'honorary daughter' and used to play the piano at his Downing Street parties. Thelma, born a moneyed Cazalet and married to a passive Keir, displayed her feminist empathy through more than her dual surname; she once embarrassed the Churchill Government by demanding equal wages for women teachers. Endearingly naive, 'I always closed my eyes when we drove through the poorer parts of London to our grand house in Grosvenor Square', she followed her Tory brother into the Commons as the MP for Islington (East), joining Lady Astor in the Conservative seats.

She was considered an expert in the visual arts for no greater reason than her family friendships with the artist Augustus John and a picture scout called Francis Taylor, whose uncle ran a posh gallery in New York – Taylor's little daughter Elizabeth was staying

at the Cazalets' country retreat when she was spotted riding a
horse and offered a role in a certain film called *National Velvet*.
Cazalet Keir loved art in a Cazalet kind of way: 'My pictures . . . pay
me regular daily dividends which my stocks and shares often
refuse to do.' Thus for the sake of CEMA 'Miss' Cazalet Keir – as
the minutes put it – personified the Board of Education, the
Houses of Parliament and the art-collecting community, at least of
Islington (East).

Walford Davies, now knighted, was another Jones intimate. An
uncreative but popular Master of the King's Musick, Davies turned
out to be the most radical thinker present. He was supported by
the pushy Reginald Jacques (1894–1969), yet another back-to-
Bach organist who was canvassing for his conducting career, having
set up his own chamber group, the Jacques Orchestra, which had
turned all-string when his wind players were conscripted for
wartime military bands. It was his ensemble's empty diary that
brought him to the CEMA table, seeking dates. Yet Sir Walford was
preoccupied by animateur projects, such as the American FP1
scheme of peripatetic music teachers which Mary Glasgow had
reported on, with its mixed-up image of mediaeval troubadours
and door-to-door Hoover reps. Using a knowledge of Welsh needs
informed by his chairmanship of the National Council for Music
of Wales (the very same that acquired one of the first CEMA
grants), he transposed the scheme from Mississippi to Merthyr
Tydfil and called his crew 'Music Travellers'. Behind his back the
others dubbed these artistic evangelists 'Walford's Holy Women'.

It was decidedly the members of the Federation of Women's
Institutes and the Rural Music Schools Association that assisted
the scheme throughout the land. The latter was a terribly priggish
network based in the Home Counties and set up by a group of
'spinster' music teachers who were inspired by the USA's Neighbourhood Music Schools movement. They called the operation
Rural so that it wouldn't get confused with city music colleges. It
ran mostly between 1929 and 1950, when the scheme was then
swallowed up within the state system and the classes evolved into
the music centres of the county education authorities. Like a
musical Sunday school, and funded mainly by the Carnegie Trust
in its social service mode, the RMSA had by the start of the war 800
registered students in thirty-three centres (mainly in Hertford-
shire, 'with an incursion into Bedfordshire') whose prospectus
established that the 'primary concern is to promote musical
endeavour in its social forms. Students are encouraged to become

useful members of choirs, orchestras, quartets and music clubs.' It added sternly that all a new member needed was 'a desire to learn and willingness to work'.

This sort of bootstrap stuff appealed no end to Lawrence du Garde Peach (1890–1974). Another pal of Jones (he was the Liberal candidate for Derby in 1929), 'Peachy' represented the theatre profession, though he was little more than a brazen hack who boasted about his 400 radio plays broadcast by the BBC. This was strictly true, yet many of them were puny and penned for schoolkids in the style of pageants: 'They can also be acted on simple school stages . . . a pillar or two, a few steps, a rostrum, and a throne will be found amply sufficient.' Author of the *Ladybird Book of Pirates* and, in view of what was to follow, the beguilingly titled *Plays of the Family Goodman*, Larry Peach had amateur dramatic dabbed all over him. Together with Harold Richmond of the Drama Enquiry Committee and Frederick Shoeten-Sack of the National Council for Social Service, Peach would emulate Sir Walford's scheme in the domain of drama, especially if they did his appalling plays.

Even in the visual arts Jones seemed to have it sewn up. The Welshman Bill Williams (1896–1977) was Secretary of the British Institute of Adult Education and the creator of a decent project providing travelling art exhibitions for 'galleryless' towns, started by the Institute in 1934 and socialistically titled 'Art and the People'. But the Brylcreemed, suit'n'tie Bill Williams – Billy to J.B. Priestley – was much more ambitious than that. His involvement with the Arts Council would gradually swell along with his name until he'd taken the venture over, almost strangled it, and retired in 1963, still Brylcreemed, as Sir William Emrys Williams CBE. He made his debut at CEMA along with a handsome gentleman, slightly younger, somewhat smoother and certainly snootier, the director of the National Gallery Sir Kenneth Clark (1903–1983). His great-great grandfather had invented the cotton spool and the profits from 'Clark's of Paisley' feather-bedded the aesthete for his entire life, which he spent looking at paintings and passing on his thoughts about them.

K., as they called him, was just thirty when he was given the National Gallery in Trafalgar Square to run. His off-the-cuff arrogance alienated the senior staff (they once locked him out of the library), and K. damaged his reputation as a scholar when he conned the trustees into buying four paintings he attributed to Giorgione that were accomplished by the inferior Previtali, as his staff knew all too well. When war came the National Gallery's paintings were carted off to a cave in Wales and replaced by Bill Williams' 'galleryless' shows. The otherwise empty museum was enlivened each lunchtime when the pianist Dame Myra Hess and colleagues musicians, bucked by a similar experiment of gallery recitals during the 1939 London Festival of Music, played Beethoven and Brahms ('an assertion of eternal values') to moist-eyed crowds. That K. Clark's National Gallery was celebrated for this kind of populist affair rather than its legitimate work annoyed many in the elite art world, and from that time Clark carried inside himself a perverse feeling of failure.

K. was at CEMA because he'd asked Tom Jones for Pilgrim Trust money to engage otherwise idle artists to record buildings likely to be blown to bits by the Germans. Jones told him to turn up at the formative meetings and help get the scheme moving under the auspices of the committee. So Kenneth Clark the gallery boss was there to get money for artists, while Bill Williams the adult educationalist wanted to use the cash for exhibitions. Between them they formed a nervous alliance, unbroken ten years later when K. became the Arts Council's cool Chairman and Bill his bullying Secretary-General.

CEMA's ragbag committee was hardly Christie's Council of Power. It was more like a cocktail crowd tossing from one to another lucky-dip gifts supplied by the host. They would have seen it in a more momentous and altruistic light, of course. The rules of behaviour were being written as they went along, and they were there in good faith to get the operation moving as quickly as possible, it being winter in wartime. Take the inclusion of a member of Parliament: the Arts Council today is supposed to be seen as an apolitical 'arm's-length' body, and Thelma Cazalet Keir is one of only two serving MPs ever to have sat on it. Yet the National Trust ('for Places of Historic Interest or Natural Beauty'), an organisation not unlike the Arts Council in its relation to Parliament, has had two MPs in tandem on its board whose contribution to the Trust's work has been considered constructive. And though it's true that Cazalet Keir was a Conservative, properly speaking she spoke for a coalition, emergency government, and chiefly she represented the Education Board's president.

She was never certain, she later admitted, whether she could vote or not. Jones would have ruled, though nobody bothered to check, that only he and three others could do so – Bill Williams, ment.

Sir Walford and Sir Kenneth, even though all three represented outfits that would benefit directly from the early grants and Bill Williams was strictly speaking an employee. Through all the years since these novice days, Council members are supposedly recruited for their individual expertise. They cannot sit as representatives, nor can they debate an issue in which they have an interest. It was over issues of representation that critics would first question Jones' integrity – as if Jones gave a toss.

Nevertheless, with this distinctive clique Jones set to work allocating his all-American funds. On the table sat a chequebook from the royal bankers Coutts & Co., who served the Pilgrim Trust and have remained the Arts Council's counting house ever since, though, after fifty years, there has been treasonable talk of change (the day can't be far off when the finance director carries the Council's cashcard to the nearest hole-in-the-wall while clients line up for their share doled out in crisp tenners). CEMA's chequebook was printed in the name of the Pilgrim Trust and would be so until June 1940, when CEMA launched its own account. Jones signed each cheque as a sum was agreed and the man from the Treasury appointed to the Board of Education, Sir Alan Barlow, kept a tally. This assembly line procedure was Jones' way of keeping anile control of the Pilgrim Trust's largesse. He even chose to put the cheque in the envelope himself, though Mary Glasgow did the address and the stamp.

At the second meeting on 18 January, George Dyson turned up with two massive schemes Jones had asked him to examine. First:

It is proposed to invite the London Philharmonic and London Symphony Orchestras each to give ten assisted concerts within a radius roughly between 10 and 50 miles from London, mainly in the newer industrial areas. We hope that Sir Thomas Beecham and Sir Henry Wood will feel that this is a worthy support of the appeals that they have been making on behalf of these two great national institutions [the LPO wasn't even 10 years old].

In other words it was a political device to keep Sir Thomas and his crabby professionals happy, playing lunchtime concerts of 'lollipops', as Beecham called them, to munitions workers in Home Counties factories. Beecham christened these jaunts, after the title of the upbeat radio show *Music While You Work*, 'Music While *We* Work'. Second:

Fifty concerts on lines akin to those that have met with such success
at the National Gallery. These will be given in the canteens and the
halls attached to large factories in engineering and munition areas,
at the midday or the midnight meal hour, or at such other time and
place as is locally found most convenient.

One singer was asked by a foreman, 'Could you call around about
dawn and wake us up with "'Ark, 'ark, The Lark"?'

These serenades were free (the performers were paid a
standard rate set by the ISM), while the orchestra concerts could
be heard for a shilling (£1.50 in today's terms), which was the
amount Clark was charging for his National Gallery recitals. Mary
Glasgow pointed out that the Entertainments Tax wouldn't apply
if they only set them at sixpence.

'How much is the tax?' asked Jones.

'Twopence halfpenny. We can avoid it if the concerts are
deemed educational but only if we fill out a rather complicated
Customs Board form for each and every concert.'

'What do you reckon the administration cost of that would be?'
Jones persisted. 'More than threepence a concert? No? Then we'll
make a halfpenny profit on every person there. Isn't that a terrible
thing!'

Glasgow enjoyed Jones and his whimsical banter. She liked less
his little ploys, like the way these major CEMA ventures were billed
as 'The Pilgrim Trust Concerts'. Nor did Sir Walford appreciate
the italicised tag beneath the title on the posters, 'Honorary
Director – Dr George Dyson'.

Walford Davies' travelling minstrels were doing wonders. Mary
Glasgow was able to claim, through an anonymous piece in a June
issue of *The Times*, that:

during the months from January to the end of May this year 235
new choirs have been started and 34 new orchestral teams; 184
concerts and festivals have been arranged and in the whole scheme
some 32,000 individuals have co-operated. This is the result of a
first, restricted experiment only, and is the work of five pioneers.

This civil servant had learned a lot about communication from
Roosevelt's FP1.

In April 1940 the Committee converted into a Council and
everything seemed to be swimming along as the former Minister

of Information took over. Maybe it was just not Macmillan's year, but the whole thing promptly nose-dived. There was the issue of money for a start. Jones had spent all but £3,000 of the £25,000 Pilgrim grant, though the Government's matching money now fell due. However, Macmillan had been under pressure to find more private cash since the Treasury had upped the stakes by offering a maximum of £50,000 of matching grant-in-aid; by turning the tables on Jones it had not forgiven his trick in December. The Treasury was actually banking on a CEMA semi-funded by American money, whether the Pilgrim or Carnegie or a mixture of both, and saw its £50,000 as an enlightened incentive. The notion of a state subsidy machine attracting 50 per cent of its funds from private sources seemed as commendable then as it does to some today.

As a member of the Carnegie Trust, the only other charity in the land dealing with the arts on a significant scale, the Scot Macmillan was sure he'd find the money there – Dyson was also a Carnegie member and the Trust's secretary, James Wilkie, was invited to attend CEMA meetings. But despite Macmillan's best endeavours the Carnegie prevaricated. There were two plain reasons. At the high level of policy the Carnegie was already doing better what CEMA wished to do less well; it continued to support orchestras to give 'performances at popular prices' (and in doing so nurtured them through the war's worst days more thoroughly than CEMA managed), it financed the NFMS's professional-amateur formula and gave regular money to the Rural Music Schools Association for its animateur schemes. At the low level of spite, without which the arts are as nothing, Dyson thought Walford Davies was a twit.

Carnegie's Wilkie and Dyson were horrified by the haphazard way CEMA threw money at things, 'scattering its grants around indiscriminately without any indication of the extent to which it was prepared to go in supporting various organisations in the future'. Dyson was irked firstly by Sir Walford's 'sentimental' interest in animateurism and secondly by his dismissive comments on the orthodox repertory Dyson had decided for the orchestral concerts, where Davies would painstakingly read out the list of composers and works, muttering 'Mmmm', 'Oh!' and 'Really?'

In a marvellous moment of irony Davies suggested that Dyson's programmes should be 'considered' by a sub-committee. Dyson protested and was supported by the embarrassed others sitting round the table. Afterwards Wilkie pointed out to Dyson that one of the key problems facing CEMA was precisely that it didn't have sub-committees. Dyson, tail between his legs but malice in mind, reported to the Carnegie Trust that:

> CEMA had refused to form subcommittees to give detailed consideration of the three arts it covered, and it was obviously impossible for a fairly large general committee, composed partly of ordinary members without technical knowledge, and partly of members particularly interested in drama and art to have an intricate knowledge of the difficult problems involved in, say, running the factory concerts scheme.

Wilkie added that the issue stemmed from the Pilgrim Trust; it was not accustomed, unlike Carnegie, to the 'long-term administration of continuing grants'. The Carnegie had sixteen executive members, the Pilgrim just five. Indeed Macmillan believed that 'committees and subcommittees have been the death of democracy in this country', and he ought to have known, having chaired so many. Democracy grew ever more deathly for Macmillan as other arts organisations grumbled ominously about CEMA's activities, which were duplicating theirs or neglecting them.

Macmillan had assumed for instance that the British Drama League supported Peach's theatre programme, of which he'd written:

> The amateur dramatic movement has grown to large dimensions in recent years. In one Midland county, for example, there are over 150 societies [it's not hard to guess the county, given Peach's parliamentary aspirations for Derby]. Their activities have been dislocated by the war and they need to be reassured of the value of their work. We have been fortunate in securing the honorary services of Mr. Lawrence du Garde Peach to undertake this task. He has unique experience of the work of amateur players in rural areas.

Of course he did, though that was of little interest to Lord Esher, the chairman of the British Drama League and a governor of the Old Vic, who wrote to *The Times* before he wrote to Macmillan:

> The policy of the trust [as CEMA was then perceived] appears to reflect the old prejudice that found the professional theatre less respectable and therefore less culturally important than profes-

sional music or painting. Only the innocent amateurs, it seems, are now to qualify for the largesse of the Pilgrim Trustees – and this at a time when the Old Vic is closed through the lack of a couple of thousand pounds [an outrageous understatement], and when no single classical touring company takes the road to remind the provinces of the glories of English drama. Surely there is something wrong here . . .

Macmillan was stunned by this unexpected and public rebuke. *The Times* made it worse by printing an editorial on 15 June 1940 which seemed to praise, while questioning, almost everything that CEMA was doing. Its thoughts were steered by Esher, a peer with much spare time on his hands. Having acclaimed the 'immediate success' of the Music Travellers, it exposed then challenged the true nature of Jones' mission:

> But it is asked, not unreasonably, what has such music propaganda to do with war? Is not that rather an intensification of the peace-time work of the Rural Music Schools, and in some cases a duplication of existing local bodies, choirs, and competitive festivals? However excellent it may be in itself it clearly will not help such major institutions as the leading orchestras, Sadler's Wells Opera, and the travelling opera companies to ride out the storm . . . Is Sadler's Wells to receive no encouragement while it alone is providing opera and ballet on a generous scale and of high artistic excellence to a not ungrateful public?

This bogus piece of metropolitan pleading could have been countered by CEMA, if only on the grounds that Sadler's Wells and the orchestras were already getting grants from the Carnegie. But Jones promptly made enquiries of the Old Vic to politically redeem the situation, and not long after the Old Vic company, under its director Tyrone Guthrie, together with Sadler's Wells as a Vic-Wells coupling, was living in Burnley on CEMA money, with a 'sweetener' direct from the Pilgrim Trust.

Then came ENSA. Commonly known as 'Every Night Something Awful', the Entertainments National Service Association was run on government funds by the despotic Basil Dean to 'entertain the armed forces and war workers' in the belief that 'popular entertainments act as a lubricant rather than a brake to the war machine'. Its 1940 budget of £2,200,000 (£72 million) paid for 3,000 performances a week to the armed forces both at home and abroad and 1,200 shows a week in factories. Unfortunately for CEMA, a few of those workplace performances were given by orchestras. It had never occurred to CEMA that they would be competing with a popular entertainments outfit for the provision of symphony orchestras to sweatshops, not until one of Sir Walford's music workers reported overhearing a conversation that ran, 'Do you know we've had Beethoven's Fifth twice in a week? It's like the bloomin' buses – you don't get it for years then two come at once.'

Enquiries produced a letter from Basil Dean confirming ENSA's intention of presenting major concerts in munitions factories and garrisons. Dean pointed out that he had the staff and advisers he needed to carry out a far larger operation than CEMA could handle. The composer William Walton was vice-chairman of ENSA's Advisory Music Council, while the liaison officer was, as Dean recalled elsewhere:

> a creature of uncertain temper with a supreme indifference to the
> feelings of those who sought to hinder its unerring flight towards
> that rarified upper air where only the finest music can be heard.
> This was Walter Legge, the recording manager of HMV.

Legge would go on in 1945 to put the RAF Symphony Orchestra into civvy street as the Philharmonia and in doing so give the Arts Council a prolonged headache.

It being wartime, CEMA decided to do battle with ENSA and develop an orchestral programme 'on the largest possible scale' and to 'arrange broadcasts to be given in the near future describing exactly what it is hoped to do'. Jones promptly sent 'loyalty' cheques of £2,000 each to the Lancashire and Yorkshire orchestras of the Hallé and the Northern Philharmonic, and £1,000 each to the London Symphony, the London Philharmonic and the Scottish Orchestra in Glasgow. These freelance orchestras did not object, though they continued to work for ENSA.

Neither did ENSA complain, at least not to CEMA. 'Concern has been expressed by ENSA to the Ministry of Labour,' ran a salty CEMA note, 'over the differential fees paid by ENSA and CEMA for artists performing in factories.' CEMA retorted that 'the types of artists employed by ENSA and by CEMA are in almost all cases entirely different'. In fact ENSA was paying a rate agreed with the humble Musicians' Union and Equity, while CEMA was paying a higher rate set by the lordly ISM. ENSA went on shelling CEMA –

petrol charges, subsistence, schedules – until Macmillan could take it no more and called on the Ministry of Labour with a deputation. In response the Ministry set up an Interdepartmental Committee on Entertainment which finally determined in February 1941 that Basil Dean's ENSA should be 'the sole official body for providing entertainment for the forces and munitions workers'. CEMA was left, crestfallen, to make independent concerts in factories not solely engaged in war work, which deflated much of the blather about 'emergency conditions' and 'nourishing the war effort'.

The behaviour of Bill Williams didn't help either. He'd done little more than transfer his 'Art and the People' to CEMA, claiming an initial £2,750 of its cash (£90,000), including his fees. At the same time he'd started negotiations with senior army personnel who were keen to create education programmes for the ranks while they were stationed in Britain, psychologically to introduce the notion of eventual peace and to turn to advantage the idea of fighting *for* something. He offered to mould the Army Bureau of Current Affairs (ABCA) which would inform the troops as to their greater mission, and to open up debate on peacetime objectives. Somehow he introduced within this scheme art displays, a Play Unit through which Williams reproduced FP1's 'Living Newspaper' formula (thrusting two fingers at Peach) and a Forces Book Club supplying reading matter exclusively from the publishers Penguin. Nobody in the army seemed to know or care that Bill Williams was a senior director at Penguin, where he was called Pelican Bill for his work on the Pelican current affairs list. Apart from the pecuniary implications, the arrangement greatly helped Penguin overcome wartime paper limits.

The exhibitions, already financed out of government funds, were assisted again when they were hung on army barracks walls. Sir Kenneth Clark, for one, smelled a rat, or at least a Pelican. Yet when the RAF welfare director was first offered 'Art and the People' shows by Bill Williams, he wrote back all too merrily, 'Join the queue!' The Central Institute of Art and Design was sending RAF bases independent work volunteered by artists, hanging in mess rooms to evoke 'a homely and restful atmosphere to those who are called upon to take part in air operations . . . a definite benefit to their morale'. Pelican Bill made enquiries and was livid to learn that the paintings were being sent out from a certain 'central depot' in Trafalgar Square, donated 'through the kindness of the Director of the National Gallery'.

Bill Williams was already mad with K. Clark for the way he kept ridiculing Bill's 'lecturer-guides' which CEMA had employed to tour along with its exhibitions. While Williams was proud that these teachers helped to provide information and context, Clark quipped that they just 'stood in the way of people hoping to see something of the pictures'. Clark had recently said that 'the average man' could never be 'the ultimate authority on artistic merit'. Clark and Williams were never average, but neither could they determine which of them was more ultimate.

Clouded policy, pointless duplication, precarious liquidity – these issues flitted in and out of CEMA's agenda. It was not entirely Jones' fault, though mostly his. He'd forced the birth of CEMA to block Christie's elitist plan, made a negative version of that without considering the consequences, not troubled to audit cultural provision covered by other agencies, allowed his 'old boy network' to dominate recruitment, lost the Carnegie grant and failed to determine an effective pilot structure. To these charges could be added his screw-up of the negotiations for the level of government income: for the first four months CEMA spent only Pilgrim funds and from then on it was able to distribute only half of the £50,000 offered by the Treasury; but his muddle would benefit CEMA eventually.

On 10 May 1940 Winston Churchill was appointed Prime Minister. He exiled Lord Halifax as Ambassador to the USA. Lloyd George had been vetted for premiership by the Cliveden Set at Jones' request but they dropped him, deciding he was only 'good for six hours a day'. Lloyd George died in 1945, having accepted an earldom. Churchill excluded Tom Jones from Downing Street. T.J. withered away to Wales.

Lord Macmillan strove to solve the money problem. The Treasury gamble of starting CEMA the Council with £100,000 (£25,000 each from the Pilgrim and the Carnegie, matched by the Government) had failed. Macmillan thought he could bestow more Pilgrim cash though he hit a second snag set by civil servants, which he revealed at the end of a report to the Council:

> Apart from a number of minor donations, of which the largest was £50 from the Goldsmiths' Company, the amounts received by CEMA from private sources qualifying for the £ for £ grant were £25,000 from the Pilgrim Trustees and a further £12,500 recently promised from the same source. The Carnegie Trustees, who were

originally expected to contribute, have found themselves unable to
do so, but have relieved you of the maintenance of big orchestras
... We agreed that the work which CEMA is doing must continue
and that we cannot maintain that £ for £ stipulation, particularly in
view of the difficulties in which the Pilgrim Trustees are placed
owing to the acquisition by the Government of their American
assets.

The Treasury dropped the matching incentive, offered the full
£50,000 for five quarters from 1 April 1940 until 30 June 1941 and
offered £45,000 for the three quarters from 1 July 1941 until 31
March 1942 – a solid start of £3 million for two years at today's
values, contrasting well with the sums dispensed by the private
Pilgrim and Carnegie Trusts. That settled, Macmillan tried to
establish policy. He'd solicited three new members in a ludicrous
attempt to stave off criticisms of a carve-up between vested interests.

The first was the Earl of Crawford and Balcarres (1900–1975).
For some reason Alex Lindsay preferred this title to his more
poetic alias, Baron Wigan. A thorough layabout and Tory MP for
Lancashire's Lonsdale until May 1940, when Churchill chucked
him, he'd been recommended by his close friend Kenneth Clark,
whom he'd recently defended against mutinous staff as a trustee
of the National Gallery, for the only thing that enthused him was
exactly the kind of art that absorbed Sir K. As one obituarist acidly
observed, 'A period as honorary attaché at the British Embassy in
Rome gave him opportunities for developing his knowledge of
Italian Renaissance painting.' It was super to see his time in
government service had not been wasted and a second dilettante
authority on Italian Renaissance painting was surely just what
CEMA needed at this moment.

The next of Macmillan's additions exceeded K. Clark in
superciliousness. Sir Kenneth Barnes had virtually invented
RADA, the Academy of Dramatic Art in Bloomsbury that he
royalised in the early twenties. Unbearably baronial, Barnes had
been enlisted to add gravitas to Peachy's world of am-dram, but
failed to do anything much other than snort and demur.

The third, Margery Fry, was anonymously recommended by
Mary Glasgow in the guise of a Board of Education memo. K. and
the other men there knew her as the sister of the artist and teacher
Roger Fry, who had recently died. She shared her brother's house
near Holloway women's prison, from where she supervised the
Howard League for Penal Reform and taught voluntarily at the

jail. As the principal of Somerville College, Oxford, she became a persuasive promoter of vocations for women. The presence at CEMA of Cazalet Keir, Glasgow and Fry may have healthily emasculated the otherwise Athenaeum intimacy of the earl, the viscount, the three sirs and three doctors. But otherwise, it's hard to judge from the minutes what she was doing there.

Macmillan considered that these additions made for a good political balance, but it served only to split the team in two. K. Clark, trying to make honest sense of CEMA's role, hearing the murmurings of discontent from the professionals outside of the CEMA circle and seizing the chance of support from the stuffier sorts around the table, defined the purposes of the Council in this way:

1. The encouragement of interest, and the maintenance of a high standard in all branches of art by whatever means are found the most appropriate.
2. Help and encouragement for the general public.
3. Help for unemployed professionals.

Had it activated affairs, his definitions might have served as a transition to the Arts Council we recognise today, for the tensions and irresolvable agendas that the modern organisation has faced and still faces are sealed inside these seemingly simple statements. But then there has always been a world of difference between what the Arts Council puts on paper and what it does in practice.

If the arts establishment didn't care much for CEMA, the public did. Its programme of concerts, art exhibitions and work with amateurs was warmly received by mainly 'aspirational' town- and village-dwellers in the odd bits of the country it served. Yet at first the Council hadn't a clue about how it was supposed to spread its work around the nation, let alone monitor progress. It needed a map.

As a carve-up of the country, the Board of Education's county and local structure was far too intricate, so Mary Glasgow shopped around other departments for something clear and foolproof that wouldn't involve employing a lot of people to cover the ground. She was advised that a civil defence chart would do the job: mainland Britain chopped into twelve Regional Defence Areas, ideal, Jones joked, because 'we are defending the good people of this island against John Christie'. Area Number 1, for some reason, was Northumberland, County Durham and Yorkshire (North Riding). Number 8 was Wales, 11 the whole of Scotland.

London (and Middlesex) was 5, and England in all had ten regions. It's curious to think that a civil defence map should have inspired the pattern for the ten Regional Arts Boards we endure today; as it happens, it's a coincidence.

This configuration helped to solve an annoying problem that CEMA had set itself. When Jones made it clear with his first grants that there'd be nothing for London, he provoked the kind of criticism logged by *The Times*. He didn't care tuppence for that, but two things changed his mind: the severe Nazi bombing of the capital, especially the working-class East End, and the sheer economic sense of the subsidised Old Vic and similar touring groups of professionals earning extra income in an eager West End, which the performers would view as a 'reward' for their hard work in the sticks. According to Mary Glasgow's map London was no longer the culture-choked megalopolis but region Number 5, as deserving of CEMA support as region Number 4 (Home Counties East) and region Number 6 (Home Counties West).

To publicise its nationwide programme, CEMA spent no more than £500 a year. Most of it was devoted to a little monthly bulletin that gave accounts of CEMA activities and listed the 'fixtures', at least as far as it could. While it was allowed to describe the Avon Rubber Company Sport and Social Club at Melksham it could only vaguely wave a finger in the direction of 'an ordnance works in Ruislip', due to restrictions imposed by the Ministry of Information which did not wish to give the enemy the chance to drop a bomb on Eve Maxwell-Lyte (soprano) and Doris Plumber (piano) performing there.

The names of certain artists on the CEMA circuit immediately evoke the era: Browning Mummery, Vera Spring and Mona Fawcett (sopranos), the Blech Quartet, Topliss Greene (baritone) and Ella Pounder (piano). Some of the venues, too, sound surreal: the Forces Quiet Club in Liverpool, the Dick Institute in Kilmarnock and the RAF Camp Theatre of Rhyl. Yet it cannot be denied that wartime audiences got solid value out of CEMA. One of Walford Davies' Music Travellers recommended an exceptional but inexperienced contralto he'd heard. Thus the young Kathleen Ferrier launched her international career on 'CEMA safaris', as the regulars called them, first in her native Lancashire then on tour in Scotland – Stranraer, Wigtown, Kirkcowan and so on.

Though some might have balked at the bland soubrette tone of Violet Carson in the Burnley Central Girls' Club, they can be comforted now in the knowledge that she found a stronger voice as Ena Sharples in TV's *Coronation Street*. And – once they'd heard them trying their best at 6 o'clock of an evening in a dimly lit, freezing church hall with a damp piano – who could begrudge two young conscientious objectors fresh from the States and eager to serve their country as CEMA orderlies, tenor Peter Pears with his boyfriend accompanist Benjamin Britten? The Ministry of Labour for one, and the chorus of Sadler's Wells, as we'll see.

It shouldn't be forgotten that between 1940 and 1942, especially during the Battle of Britain, these artists earnestly worked in places deprived of basic utilities. Even proper concerts were announced with the prominent warning: 'Owing to Black-out and Traffic Restrictions all performance times are subject to alteration'. In the autumn of 1940, during the first days of the air raids, CEMA employed people to race into shelters with wind-up gramophones and records, like primaeval DJs. As one CEMA bulletin account has it: 'During the bad air raids musicians were ready to go at an hour's notice, on receipt of a telephone call, wherever they were wanted. When something needs doing urgently, overlapping is no sin.' It's true that, due to a misunderstanding, a string quartet and a string trio turned up at the same air-raid shelter in Farringdon and, not having the printed music to play together, holding torches onto each other's scores, took turns to thaw the atmosphere. Between them they played a selection of light music – the sort of waltzes and fake Hungariana their audience would normally hear through foreground chatter in smart tea rooms – with a slow movement from a Schubert quartet slotted in the middle. They were generally advised to play cheerful music, impudent enough to cover the sound of planes, blasts and collapsing buildings, but not too loud to block the 'all-clear'. Nevertheless, on this occasion it was the meditative Schubert that got encored.

Mary Glasgow recorded that Macmillan was moved to tears by an account of an air-raid shelter 'sing-song' in the autumn of 1940:

> One old man, who had been struck totally dumb by nervous shock, at last recovered his voice when emboldened to sing at a concert. As one cockney, at first dubious about such goings on, remarked later, 'It does seem to keep the roof up some'ow.'

These concerts not only soothed the working class; CEMA supplied the Code and Cryptograph School at Bletchley Park with string quartets. In fact the regional defence structure (though Mary Glasgow did not know this at the time, she said) had been recommended by an MI5 officer seconded to the Board of Education, and those Music Travellers cleared by security were mandated to provide MI5 with information gleaned from small talk as they freewheeled around their 'patches'.

The rural Music Travellers, teachers more than players, expanded within a year from the pilot five to twelve, one in each region. Their work was recorded in a bureaucratic way – hours spent where at what meetings or gatherings and with how many – without a hint of the artistic contribution they made. One account comes from a typewritten record of a choir member in Mexborough, South Yorkshire:

> Miss Hotson was invited by [our temporary music director] to conduct a rehearsal. It was considered as much a help to him as it was to us. She was very knowledgeable, but she did not make a fuss of showing it . . . Miss Hotson helped us with problems like the ends of words, when we tended to splutter over the final letter of 'Lord'. She showed us different ways of dealing with the 'd', such as one of us in each row sounding it while the others kept silent. We hadn't thought of that before! It was hard work because she would repeat things until we improved but it was good for us because we knew it was helping us to sound better . . . Miss Hotson came about once a month and sometimes brought with her novel music we could try if we wanted to. The only thing we did not like was that she was assisting other choirs in the area, and we knew that they would be improving too!

It's a crying shame that much of the grass-roots work of the Music Travellers has been written out of Arts Council chronicles. It was patently clear from the few contemporary records that have survived the war that their work was highly valued, cut across the barriers of professional and amateur mistrust, raised technical awareness (as the Mexborough report shows), developed collaborative schemes to enhance resources and helped to stimulate repertoire. In addition, they spread a perception of CEMA as initiating but not invasive, democratic and not blinkered by elitism; the impression drawn is that the travellers even managed to purge the scheme itself of its patronising air.

The Music Traveller for the south-west was the loopy but loved Miss Imogen Holst. She met Britten and Pears on CEMA tours and took on the task, for the rest of her life, of working for the composer, a vocation for which she had been prepared all too well by her father Gustav Holst, creator of *The Planets*. She also

composed as a part of her war work: 'I am compiling a collection
of rounds and canons for use in village socials and festivals.' Some
of her letters have survived and they offer up a vivid picture of the
wartime atmosphere, from rationing – 'Very many thanks for the
petrol coupons. On the marshes of Sedgemoor there are NO
BUSES WHATSOEVER' – to native snags:

21 January 1941

Dear Miss Glasgow,

I am so sorry to bother you, but we have a local lunatic here who is
the composer of *The Little Grey Home in the West.* She is called Miss
Eardley-Wilmot and she has taken it into her head that Queen
Mary would like her to take community singing in the Somerset
villages (where she does not go down very well!).

She wanted to know the HQ of C.E.M.A. Well, I suppose you get
scores or hundreds of letters from such people, but I'm afraid
you'll get one from her.

Eventually, after the war, some of the travellers who worked
with the Rural Music Schools Association and the Townswomen's
Guilds were absorbed into the state education system as music
advisers alongside the Carnegie Trust's kindred county specialists,
while others became CEMA's own music advisers in the regional
structure. The post-war County Music Advisory Service, which
evolved a whole range of Saturday music activities – youth
orchestras, steel bands, jazz groups – was heralded by the Music
Travellers' movement. Some would say that this was the greatest
legacy the Arts Council never left.

The drama work of Lawrence du Garde Peach is well preserved.
That is, the work of Lawrence du Garde Peach: *Mrs Grundy Comes
to Tea* (1940), *Napoleon Couldn't Do It* (1941), *According to Plan*
(1942), *You Never Know!* (1943). Lord Macmillan assured the press
that 'about 400 amateur productions were given in six months
which might not, and probably would not, have occurred without
this stimulus'. He didn't say 400 amateur productions of what, but
readers need not look beyond this paragraph for clues. The
professional Old Vic Theatre Company split itself into three and
toured out of London; one of those was led by Dame Sybil
Thorndike touring mining towns in South Wales directed by Lewis
Casson (Mr Sybil Thorndike). Tom Jones, of course, encouraged
it and used the Welsh Welfare Commission he'd chaired to
organise her agenda.

Jones promptly made Casson the Council's honorary drama adviser, later drama director, in order to get the Old Vic venture properly managed and in doing so glimpsed a solution to CEMA's overall scheme: Casson for professional drama, Peach for amateur; Reginald Jacques for professional music, Sir Walford for amateur (though Davies died suddenly in March 1941); Bill Williams' exhibitions covered the visual arts as far as CEMA wished to go. Kenneth Clark, incidentally, didn't pursue his professional 'war artists' plan through CEMA. He had found money more swiftly through the Ministry of Information, where he'd been given a job, for a scheme named the National Buildings Record. Through this he found the cash to commission the famous paintings of twisted planes by Paul Nash and the haunting drawings of tube shelters by Henry Moore which later toured under 'Art and the People', lecturer-guides standing at the ready, in the way.

The travelling art exhibitions proved a splendid source of public relations, actively covered by the local press. Bill Williams could claim that in the first year 270,000 people in 'galleryless' towns had seen the shows of loaned paintings (some from Clark's private collection) and reproductions, with examples of industrial and domestic design added. Pelican Bill's exhibitions featured 'modern' pictures. One such, of British and French work, included pieces by Wilson Steer, Augustus John, Walter Sickert, Matisse, Rouault, Derain and Othon Friesz.

Yet there is less information to be found today on the more radical 'experiments', to use a vogue word of the time. A CEMA bulletin of 1942 describes one such venture: 'There's evidence that art has a positive therapeutic value to those who are enduring physical and mental suffering. A collection of modern pictures has been sent to a convalescent home for service women.' The super-intendent of the home wrote ambiguously:

No doubt they have been greatly appreciated ... One parlour member doing the rooms hears remarks by the girls as to how they get to like them better from looking at them for a long time ... I do not suppose many of the patients have had much opportunity to look at the pictures, but the consequence is that they start looking without a prejudice against a modern style of painting. They have great ideas as to how they should be hung.

The bulletins are marvels of art in themselves. The language is effusive, rich in metaphor and unremittingly ridiculous. Here is an announcement about setting up touring art exhibitions in canteens:

> It is familiar practice to say grace before meat: CEMA now seeks to add grace to another kind of meat. Eating being a necessary and sometimes enjoyable occupation, and being also in this case a social matter, it is especially desirable that it should be carried on in premises which are not limited to victuals merely. CEMA, by adding to the simple wartime fare, a sweet or savoury, if not a banquet for the eye, is doing its proper work of enhancing a hum-drum business and of reminding people, even as they ponder the less than romantic possibilities of a romantic menu, that even total war cannot cheat all the senses. The satisfaction of the eye may compensate for the austerity inflicted on the palate.

Here is a neighbouring declaration about concerts in parks:

> Sports and games, dances and bun fights (if the bun be deemed worthy of any such contention) are a natural part of the arrange-ments for parks and public gardens. CEMA, with its programme of a hundred concerts, will be adding beauty to the buns, as elsewhere grace to the meat.

No wonder CEMA lacked a literature programme. A rare example of concision came in the issue of December 1942: 'The CEMA lorry knocked down a dog. Saved by a vet, it was christened Cema and handed over to a group of airmen as a "mascot".'

Mary Glasgow would have hated to hear that, for she loathed the acronym. She insisted on pronouncing it 'C-E-M-A' and spelled it 'C.E.M.A.' in formal correspondence, though this encouraged the outside world to invent fresh meanings. It was said that a gentleman in Huddersfield sincerely thought it stood for 'Concerts Every Monday Afternoon', while an RAF liaison officer considered it indicated 'Caution! Effeminate Musicians Around'. Lower in the ranks it became 'Couldn't Entertain My Arse', 'Camp Evacuate! Mad Artists!' and the widespread 'Classical Earache, Mostly Awful'. Artists countered with 'Can Entertain Mostly Anyone'. But Mary Glasgow emphasised the full stops to stem its most common corruption, 'SEMEN'. She would soon meet someone who would sympathise with her dismay. He would have the name changed in such a way that nobody could do anything but primly spell out its letters, one by one, by one, by one.

Chapter 5

The changeling

Wolfit • Shakespeare • Glasgow

Have you ever
seen a play
by
WILLIAM SHAKESPEARE
OUR
NATIONAL POET?

Whether the answer was 'Yes! I have!' or 'Never!', it made little difference to Donald Wolfit's box-office takings. Not so many people ventured into Holborn's Kingsway Theatre through the black-out of early 1940 as to give his season of the Bard the profit he needed. Wolfit, a thunder-and-greasepaint actor-manager, believed that the sun shone out of Shakespeare's arras. At the Kingsway he furnished the brave few with his Hamlet, Othello and Shylock, also Malvolio and Benedick to show he had wit. Only thirty-eight years old, he was regarded even then as an Edwardian relic, a passionate actor hoofing round the country with his own company of stageboard subordinates who – juvenile, antique or flatfooted – escaped conscription to the wartime services.

Two of the few who sat in the stalls were Maynard and Lydia Keynes and they loved what they saw. At that time Keynes worked among a special team of Treasury advisers counselling the wartime

Government on economic co-ordination, but he was still bursar of King's College, Cambridge, and headed the Arts Theatre there. Impressed by Wolfit's hamming he did three things. He advised Wolfit to set up a not-for-profit business to evade the entertainments tax, he invited the company to present a season of four plays in Cambridge during May 1940, and he offered the service of his manager, Mr Higgins: 'I am asking Higgins [the theatre's manager] to let you have a float of £30 at once, as suggested by Mr Selby [Wolfit's booker].' In return the actor set up the Advance Players' Association, a name no doubt inspired more by the £30 than an expression of policy. He invited Keynes to join the board and he accepted.

Meanwhile one of Wolfit's many makeshift managers, Charles Landstone, wrote to CEMA requesting a small guarantee-against-loss for the Cambridge run. He was told CEMA couldn't help. Keynes was incensed, with that bitter mixture of mental frustration and a kick-in-the-stomach pang familiar to those even today who receive an Arts Council rejection. Because of this seeming snub he sought Kenneth Clark's informal opinion, learning to his horror this new outfit CEMA was 'frittering the public's money' on amateurs. As we've learned, this was not strictly true at the time – it didn't go solely to amateurs and public money wasn't involved ahead of May. The Wolfit residency proceeded without CEMA's aid and Keynes' revenge on the institution was then conceived, though not yet hatched.

Wolfit wanted to perform for Cambridge John Ford's tragedy 'Tis Pity She's a Whore, sending Keynes a script, as records suggested that the play had not been performed by professionals for 300 years. Keynes replied edgily: 'I had not realised that the theme was so exclusively incest without mitigation or remorse. Clearly it is strong meat for the general public. On the other hand, the title, fortunately perhaps, is calculated to warn away the squeamish.' Keynes or Mrs Keynes or the two together possessed an intriguing allergy to bawdy stuff, though possibly at root they disliked negative representation, for otherwise they enjoyed the flamboyant and rhetorical, as so many ballet people do. Having been approached by T.S. Eliot, for instance, to put on in Cambridge Louis MacNeice's play Out of the Picture, Keynes rejected the proposal by quoting Lydia's response: 'too much . . . a bad reaction to life'. Still, this raises the question of why Wolfit would wish to offer the public a diet of tragedy and blood and guts in a time of war. As it turns out, everyone else did.

The Old Vic company at the Old Vic Theatre in Waterloo was offering a glum *King Lear* (with John Gielgud) and *The Tempest* when it closed prematurely in May 1940. CEMA helped the company's director, Tyrone Guthrie, to evacuate the drama, ballet and opera companies to a safer 'Vic', the Victoria Theatre of Burnley. At the same time the Old Vic arranged with CEMA's cash the famous coach tour of Welsh mining villages led by the socialist Cassons, Lewis and his wife Dame Sybil Thorndike, who was not far off sixty. They chose *Macbeth* and, aware of two issues – that the locals may not have been to a play before and that *Macbeth* was not quite a laugh a minute – they commissioned Lionel Hale to write a prologue that would ease the audience towards theatricality and the meaning of the play itself. If this sounds patronising, the tactic was by all accounts successful, and the near-Brechtian device of the company walking on stage in day clothes with the props in cases, delivering lines such as the following, doesn't seem so condescending:

Second actor:	Macbeth was a chieftain. He murdered King Duncan and made himself King.
First actor:	He had to go on murdering to keep himself in power.
Second actor:	With a spy in every house in Scotland and so on.
Sybil:	And you still don't see what this has got to do with 1940?
First actor:	No.
Sybil:	Don't you? You've just given a perfect picture of a dictator.
First actor:	Yes, but . . .
Lewis:	You needn't always think of dictators in terms of concentration camps and tanks and aeroplanes. Men don't change in a thousand years. What Macbeth wanted, what all such people want, is power. This is a play about a tyrant, a dictator.
Sybil:	Yes, and his wife, too. Macbeth isn't the only part in this play remember.

This CEMA tour was so successful they did it three summers running, adding a new production each time – Thorndike's expressionistic *Medea* ('It kindles a fire,' said one miner), George Bernard Shaw's *Candida* (done under orders from RADA's Kenneth Barnes to brighten the package, and a thorough flop), plus a new play by Laurence Housman, *Jacob's Ladder*. Over half of the Old Vic's drama work around the country during the war, however, was Shakespeare. Aside from *Macbeth* the tragedies covered were *Othello* and *Hamlet*, as well as that categorical oddball *The Merchant of Venice*. *King John* and *Richard III* embodied the history genre while *Twelfth Night* and *The Merry Wives of Windsor* lightened the load, but the cathartic tragedies won at the box office. And while young stars like Laurence Olivier and Ralph Richardson drudged abroad in the forces, John Gielgud dominated the West End with his own *Macbeth*, then *Hamlet* and *A Midsummer Night's Dream* (quite a dud, by all accounts). It's interesting to note that nobody throughout the war seems to have produced that gung-ho horror *Henry V*, and Olivier's famous film version opened in November 1944, far too late to be the 'spur to victory' often claimed for it.

Only fifty years before all of this, Shakespeare was generally considered box-office poison. His restoration has been more peculiar than we might assume and it relied on four forces, the fourth of which was CEMA. The style of actor-manager that Wolfit emulated was one, of course: a company was built around an avaricious egotist who played Hamlet in *Hamlet*, Macbeth in *Macbeth* and blacked up for *Othello*. Gielgud recalls that 'the tendency with Shakespeare before my day had been to give the actor-manager the limelight and the centre of the stage, with all the small parts just standing about giving cues'. This made Shakespeare vivid, unadorned and – to the unacquainted paying public – unclouded in its form. Then came the emerging profession of 'scholars' who opened out the readings available, pored over the varying versions printed in the seventeenth century, upgraded the secondary roles to promote the multi-layered spirit of the works, and unveiled the essential ambiguities that have allowed directors to this day to justify the nth production of the thirty-seven plays. Harley Granville-Barker, who directed Gielgud in the 1940 Old Vic *Lear*, wrote a set of 'prefaces' that are still valued as vital meditations.

The third element is the oddest, fired by the reforms of the 1918 Education Act that drew together art and education in the classroom. This union was fuelled by the desire to present to children a grand, unified culture, and one that promoted the kind of preterite nationalism generated by Vaughan Williams and his kind. Shakespeare provided that distinctive focus within British history. That this was projected through the education system, in

Shakespeare's case with set texts, allows us to understand why the CEMA founders, sitting in the Kingsway offices of the Board of Education, gave their initial professional drama grant to a tour of *Macbeth* among the mining villages of Wales, and how the first grant to a commercial company went to support a big stage *Macbeth*, as we'll see. They also aided Robert Atkin's summer seasons of Shakespeare at the Open Air Theatre in Regent's Park and the first production they funded was another *Macbeth*.

That CEMA got involved with this self-conscious construction of a canonic heritage caused living artists like Vaughan Williams some discomfort at the Council table, for it seemed that 'history was being made' at the cost of new work. An imposed idolatry on this scale also explains how twenty years on, with the most audacious application ever presented to the Arts Council, the young Peter Hall managed to attract its backing to start an astonishingly expensive, enduring project devoted principally to one bygone playwright: the Royal Shakespeare Company – one of the neatest titles ever handed to a marketing manager.

CEMA's Secretary scared her Council by claiming that Shakespeare sounded 'much improved in French', especially in the translations of Messiaen. They were alarmed because they thought the Board of Education had given them some sort of docile minute-taker, not an expert in foreign literature. She added that Shakespeare's comedies would have worked much better if he'd had the brain of Molière. RADA's Kenneth Barnes, fed up with all of this, asked bitingly if Molière didn't sound better in German. 'Which translations do you prefer? Neppl or Hofmannsthal?' she replied. It quickly became clear to the Council that Mary Glasgow had been foisted on them less as a result of her paper on arts funding abroad but more because she'd been a bloody nuisance as a schools inspector at the Board of Education and it was glad to see the back of her. Trenchant though she was, CEMA could not have started with a better chief.

Mary Cecilia Glasgow (1905–1983) was only thirty-four when she was seconded as the Secretary to CEMA. She has been described by an inveterate staff member, Mary Endacott, as:

> slight with gradually greying fair hair. She dressed elegantly and liked old jewellery, not that there was much about in those days. And she was a generous person, keen to get women promoted. Her house was in Justice Walk, Chelsea, which was a good address even

then, and she held parties she would invite us to – not riotous affairs but fun and classy. Miss Glasgow had a strong personality with quite a carrying, resounding voice. That might give the impression of a schoolmarm sort, but she didn't dash about and fuss. She had flair and was terribly well presented, with a definite obsession about France and French ways.

Glasgow was an Essex girl, born in Walthamstow, where her father taught at a local public school. Her mother and father had both studied classics at university and they were considered by their curtain-twitching neighbours to be 'advanced', modish liberals. When Mary was four her father was appointed inspector of schools for Newcastle-upon-Tyne, and from 1909 to 1923 she lived in the north-east and remembers being taught choral singing by William Gillies Whittaker, who we encountered in connection with the Carnegie Trust. Glasgow studied French at Oxford's Lady Margaret Hall, where she became branch treasurer of the League of Nations Union (her boyfriend was secretary): 'We called ourselves pacificists, but ostriches is a better word.' She evolved into an atheist, and carried through her life a distaste for religious malarkey (she once tried to get rid of a secretary who was an avid Christian Scientist). Her first job, shortly before the Wall Street Crash, was assistant librarian to the Board of Education from where she was promoted as a junior inspector for Leeds during the Slump. Her reports and interventions on foreign-language teaching were often considered meddlesome, but in hindsight they were progressive.

Her individuality shone through everything she did, from sailing in her second-hand canoe round Semmerwater to sponsoring Richard and Paula Rubner. They were German Jews. Their children had escaped to England in 1938 while Richard was held in Dachau, then Buchenwald. Thanks to Glasgow's sponsorship (a kind of bail) the Rubners, whom she'd never met, were discharged from Germany to Leeds, where she put them up until they could settle. Commissioned while still working in Yorkshire to write the briefing paper on arts funding abroad, her skills and that report brought her to the notice of Lord Macmillan. He asked for her to be seconded from the Board of Education as a multi-lingual translator to his mockery of an Information Ministry when war broke out, and she moved down to London. The subsequent transfer to CEMA three months later, possibly requested by Macmillan, was a lucky break for the astute if obstinate Secretary. As the arts body was serviced chiefly by this Board of Education employee, it can be said that Miss M.C. Glasgow established within arts administration everything that reeked of the civil service, from salary grades to tea breaks (11.15am, 3.15pm). Even though she herself was a maverick officer, Glasgow accommodated the rituals of bureaucracy. She remained on a Board contract until (let us be precise and Whitehall about this) 31 March 1944.

It was she who had to face Keynes back in May 1940 after he'd wittered to K. Clark about the Wolfit incident. Clark had suggested to CEMA that someone should try and pacify the economist, as he could so easily make trouble. Glasgow wrote in her memoirs:

> He had sent for me to 46 Gordon Square [his Bloomsbury hangout], and attacked me mercilessly for the short-comings of CEMA policy as he saw them. He made mince-meat of me when I tried (as I had to) to justify my masters on the Council. I reeled out into the night, bloody but I hope unbowed, feeling that I had been in the presence of a very great man.

A typically mandarin account, for it tells us nothing about the substance of Keynes' blitz. Elsewhere she offered a verbatim quote of his, though one that sounds like it was exclaimed later than this particular Gordon Square riot: 'I think it's time your Council began thinking more seriously about the professional arts, you've given far too much time and money to the amateurs, come off it.'

Kenneth Clark wrote that 'He was not a man for wandering minstrels and amateur theatricals. He believed in excellence.' But this interest in 'excellence' is not borne out by the facts: Keynes was keen about all manner of second-rate work, especially the overblown. Mary Glasgow considered that Clark never really understood Keynes. Clark himself admitted in his biography that 'although I was on good terms with him, we never became friends. One reason may have been that by this time he was too tired and busy to make new friends.' Charles Landstone, Wolfit's oddjob manager and eventually an Arts Council officer, got closer when he wrote, '[Keynes] loved glamour, he loved success, and he was not impervious to flattery.' What Keynes shared with Clark was this: that everybody might enjoy the freedom to benefit – intellectually, morally, spiritually – from an artistic heritage confined so far to a favoured few, in order to renew and thus perpetuate that heritage's value. This inclusive vision was the mark of orthodox liberalism. It did not, however, concern notions of social 'rights' nor 'access', nor the advocation of coercive education schemes, nor anything communal like animateurism. It was an individual matter, to be pursued as a personal initiative, that pursuit being itself a sign of sophistication. What concerned Keynes was that the structure should be open to enterprise, that it should not deny revelation to the curious or the novice. And, as almost any economist can tell us, an inclusive system most benefits invariably one class of person, the one in the middle, the bourgeoisie – an English term much improved in French.

One other aspect of the encounter between Keynes and Glasgow deserves mention. No doubt a psychoanalyst would be stirred by Mary Glasgow's choice of language: 'he attacked me', 'he made mince-meat of me', 'I reeled out into the night, bloody'. It's interesting first of all that neither Macmillan, who'd worked with Keynes in the Slump, nor Jones, who had also sat on committees with Keynes as a former professor of economics, chose to undertake the task. They sent this thirty-four-year-old civil servant to face the onslaught. Keynes was incontestably a misogynist, as so many homosexuals are. He was deeply reluctant to work with women and his anxiety was noted by the CEMA staff when he eventually entered the doors as Lord Macmillan's successor in April 1942. The Gordon Square incident speaks more for the courage of Mary Glasgow than for the integrity of Maynard Keynes.

Consequently Keynes had a new request sent to CEMA to support a national tour of Wolfit's Cambridge repertoire which would end in London. Lewis Casson wrote that the appeal could not be considered as CEMA was about to aid a tour by (his own company) the Old Vic. Keynes, understandably outraged, wrote back that 'If that is to be the policy it would save everyone a lot of trouble if an announcement were made that no outsiders need apply.' Glasgow was embarrassed and, over Casson's head, arranged a guarantee. Keynes forgot none of this and nursed the wound.

It was two years before CEMA returned into Mr Keynes' life and he could exact his revenge. In that short time his prestige had grown prodigiously, aided by those with influence around the new Government of Churchill who admired his views on global economics – a vital issue because Britain was virtually bankrupt yet placing massive armaments orders to the USA which it bluffed it could pay, and the Government was counting on advisers like Keynes to come up with something clever. Quite simply Keynes was being courted.

In October 1941 he accepted an invitation to join the Bank of England as a director and in the same month he joined the National Gallery's Board of Trustees. Aside from his Treasury role he was a director of the Provincial Insurance Company (how he must have scorned that word, 'provincial'), a governor of Eton, bursar of King's and editor of the *Economic Journal*, as well as running the Cambridge theatre and tending the Tilton farm. On top of all this Keynes had turned sixty and his heart was shaky; he occasionally took periods of rest under doctor's orders at Tilton. Nevertheless he, with his consort Lydia in tow, would undertake no fewer than six hazardous trips to America during the war to sort out international borrowing schemes. The first exploratory excursion had taken place in the summer of 1941, and the other five would ruggedly interrupt his CEMA work – but also feed him with an astonishing idea.

Yet his energy was boundless in contrast to the Pilgrims. By 1942 Lord Macmillan was nearing seventy and felt he'd had quite enough of the Council, which seemed to lurch inarticulately from wrangle to wrangle as it faced competitors, embittered rejects and the sceptics of its schemes. Tom Jones was tired of it all, too; he hadn't anticipated the strength of conceptual opposition – from figures such as the National Gallery's K. Clark – to employment schemes in adult education and rural animateurism. Neither Macmillan nor Jones had related their development of CEMA to the existing subsidy structure of the national and municipal galleries, and they hadn't done so because they were dealing with the performing arts and the provision of art exhibitions for 'galleryless' towns. They believed they weren't at all in competition, but instead they were developing a distinct, 'root up', complementary scheme. Coming from the world of alms and donations, they were astonished that a manifestly 'good cause' could raise so much disfavour, in particular from the rich, especially as it was set up as an 'emergency' measure.

Clark saw it quite differently. In his eyes grants from a national government should serve national resources. He would have been delighted to see a national theatre or a national opera house or a national experimental workshop – at least we can assume he might have indulged the argument since he supported the Institute of Contemporary Arts. A diffuse and unbridled project like Jones'

CEMA, which did not generate product nor acquire possessions for public benefit, was no fit activity on which to spend central funds. He gave the impression that he saw the nation not as a complex of towns and villages but as a network of collections and estates. Clark and his kind were being protectionist in their discontent, of course. They didn't regard the Pilgrim's CEMA as a competitor for their annual government grant-in-aid, but they felt that this rogue project deflected from proven national needs – the demand for an integrated structure that determined and sustained a national perception of 'civilisation', for want of a better word. Clark once quipped that charities like the Pilgrim and the Carnegie Trusts 'did not erect great beacons of light of inspiration to us all, but gave everyone little torches fuelled by flat batteries'.

So, the dispensers of little torches spun a line that the Pilgrim Trust had now seen the venture launched and it was time to withdraw, though the Pilgrim convention lay in pump-priming an initiative for three years and only two had lapsed. With the promise of a final grant of £12,500 (bringing the full total of American aid to £50,000 and thus tidily meeting the Treasury's initial target), they tendered their resignations. Their analysis was misguided: the actual groundwork they'd set in motion was highly valued and had an emphatic impact among sections of the general public. What really flawed them was marketing; none of the worth of the local community work was being argued and promoted nationally as they spent no more than £500 a year on 'publicity', and the leader writers of *The Times* could not bring themselves to enthuse earnestly about Walford's Holy Women singing sweetly in Merthyr Tydfil, while they could not ignore the baying in the Athenaeum from governors of the Old Vic.

The Pilgrims also failed to safeguard their policies within the Council, partly through Macmillan's aversion to committees in general and a slackness in getting artists round the table. Macmillan came from a setting where committees agreed on things and he regarded his job as chairman one in which he identified the quickest consensual route; he called his Pilgrim group 'our little brotherhood'. After the Pilgrims departed, it was left entirely to Vaughan Williams, as the sole practising artist, to push for policies that acknowledged a relation between professionals and amateurs, artists and the public. Frankly, it's astounding how far he got.

The new president of the Board of Education was left with the task of finding Macmillan's successor. Richard Austen Butler (1902–1982), 'Rab' in monogram, was a proud amateur painter and one of those seemingly progressive types who would later be defined as a 'one-nation Tory'. His eventual training reforms in the Education Act of 1944 established the relatively enlightened schools system that the post-war Labour Government would cheekily claim as its own. Butler saw it as a vote-winning move to 'harness to the educational system the wartime urge for social reform and greater equality'. CEMA's Treasury grant for 1942–1943 amounted to £100,000 and, with the Pilgrim's farewell present, furnished nearly £4 million at today's value; Butler wished to see CEMA spend it in a manner that would bring kudos to the department. His boss Winston Churchill advised him to appoint Kenneth Clark as the new chairman; Clark was a secret-service informer and often discussed issues of the day informally with the Prime Minister – his was probably the first name that entered Churchill's head. Yet Clark was passed over and it's difficult to know quite why, aside from his diffident nature; possibly a 'new broom' was preferred. At any rate Keynes' name was brought up by Butler's father-in-law, the cotton tycoon Sam Courtauld, who had known Keynes for years and sold the economist his old Rolls-Royce.

Keynes said he didn't want the job. He told Butler that he had 'only limited sympathy' with the organisation. In response Butler played to Keynes' vanity. First of all Rab was willing to support a change of direction if it meant something 'lasting' would come out of it, something 'bricks and mortar', which was one of Keynes' fixations, though the German bombing raids had already stimulated broad issues of rebuilding. Second, he bribed Keynes with a peerage. Keynes was the first of nine Council chairmen to be elevated, four of whom were plain misters until they chaired the Council – Keynes, Goodman, Pearson and Palumbo.

Mary Glasgow considered that Keynes was entranced by honours and accolades because

his parents were still alive, you know, and perhaps he needed to show off and prove himself. He also had a brother who was very clever and got a deal of attention. It was moving when Maynard Keynes died because his mother and father attended the funeral. Some did say that his early death was the price he paid for his peerage. He was put under terrible pressure by the government as the war came to its close, but he didn't make it any easier on himself; he was a dreadful meddler. He seemed to have a relentless need to express his opinions and flaunt his abilities at all hours, whether he was genuinely able or not.

Once he began his wartime visits to America, which we'll come to, Glasgow said that she had hoped for some respite from his compulsive participation. She was soon disillusioned:

He wrote to me practically every day, sometimes several times a day, as dictated missives flew into our headquarters in Belgrave Square from the Treasury or across the Atlantic. And they *were* missives, long discourses, lists of questions, detailed comments on all that was happening in the theatre, concert halls and picture galleries . . . He said he gave about a twentieth part of his time to us at the Council, and once complained that in order to run things properly a chairman ought to be devoting at least a quarter – to us it seemed the equivalent of any normal person's full time.

She admitted that he didn't hesitate to 'tear strips off me when my efficiency failed' and that 'his blame was cutting'. She cited this as typical of his notes from the States:

I was, therefore, considerably shocked by the light-heartedly enthusiastic way in which the Council gave the Executive Committee authority without, so far as I can see, any of the necessary information before them . . . No doubt you will be able to assure me that it is not quite so irresponsible as it looks from the Minutes which have reached me. There is rather too much of an air of 'warm endorsement' of half-baked ideas in these Minutes to leave me quite happy.

Yet this confidential note has been published in three different books about Keynes or the Council, and it's now clear that Glasgow 'leaked' it to promote her view that Keynes was a difficult chief. From the papers that have survived the war, this particular memo is by far the most tetchy and the evidence suggests that Glasgow bothered Keynes as much as he did she. The Chairman would receive almost daily wires of the following kind, packed with staffing problems – her business – and snags he couldn't possibly resolve by mail:

11.12.44

1. Drama Panel: Lewis Casson has been given leave of absence for roughly the next three months. Whether he will come back at the end of that time is, I think, problematical. The Panel itself has more or less collapsed. Athene Syler is the only one left.
2. Music Director: Reginald Jacques has decided to resign. I think this has been inevitable for some time.
3. The future of CEMA: There is still no news. Sir Robert Wood has been prodding the Treasury but, so far, without result.

Keynes' replies seemed soothing in comparison. They consisted usually of the latest information he'd gleaned from government officials, such as this reply from the same period:

The Accountant General feels that the suggested increase for small town drama work is something which should appeal to the Treasury and, that, therefore, it may be fairly easy to justify provided we have some good evidence to support it.

Nevertheless, the proof that Keynes didn't think much of Glasgow and her operation can be found in a confidential letter he wrote to Sam Courtauld in April 1944: 'I always feel that there is a fearful lack of discipline and order and that they are always on the brink of making a grievous mistake.'

Keynes and those in awe of him have given the impression it was his genius for conceptual midwifery that reared the organisation from CEMA (Amateur) into CEMA (Professional). All he really did was blow the cobwebs off Christie's National Council papers, copy its outline and trim its form. It was Christie, *in absentia*, who turned CEMA into the Arts Council. Mary Glasgow spotted the link but pointed out that 'it took Keynes's kind of genius to see the possibilities in the first place'. She added that the speed at which he changed affairs was phenomenal, but that his habit of intruding slowed things down again. She joked that Keynes could never be certain which character to copy out of *A Midsummer Night's Dream*. Perhaps he was Puck: 'I'll put a girdle round about the earth, In forty minutes.' Or Bottom: 'Let me play Thisbe too.' In that case the Arts Council played the Changeling.

Chapter 6

Let me play Thisbe too

The Ballets Jooss • Binkie Beaumont
Vaughan Williams • Forgery and Treason

Owing little to Shakespeare, Maynard Keynes swept into
CEMA like Genghis Khan. When he chaired his first meeting
on 21 April 1942 (the Council's fourteenth gathering) he had
never been a member nor had he sat in at a previous assembly to
learn form. He just drove off at full speed as he meant to go on.
Mary Glasgow's minute records that Keynes

> put before the Council a suggestion for including in future CEMA
> activities both opera and ballet; and in particular bringing within
> the Council's scope of existence the entire Vic-Wells organisation,
> Theatre, Opera and Ballet. 'Very broadly it would entail greater
> responsibility for overhead costs combined with a definite control
> of artistic policy.'

Before anyone could take a breath he raced on through his own
agenda:

> The Chairman also asked the Council's sanction for possible future
> cooperation with the Ballets Jooss. In order to use the Ballets
> which, he submitted, would be extremely valuable to C.E.M.A., it
> would be necessary to bring them back to England from the United
> States where they were presently unemployed.

Glasgow's deft placing of 'he submitted' shows how quickly she was alienated by his peremptory style.

Even Kenneth Clark, who backed Keynes' move to professionalism, balked at the Ballets Jooss. Kurt Jooss (pronounced 'Yooce', 1901–1979) was a German, a typically liberal 'Weimar' artist. He created pieces of dance-theatre driven by social contemplations contained within the conventions of ballet. His work included a stylish anti-war parable called *The Green Table*, where every few minutes Death stalks the stage to smother dancers with his skeleton suit. Even this sort of stuff looked dated by 1933 when the Nazis advised Jooss to quit Essen because he'd refused to sack his music director, a Jew. Visiting England, Jooss found private funding to set up with one of his men the Jooss-Leeder Dance School at Dartington Hall in Devon, where the German company joined him. The Ballets Jooss toured with decreasing support around England (the Manchester Opera House box office called them Bally Jooss-less) and the start of war utterly screwed the company. Dartington closed down, while the dancers engaged on a US tour found that they couldn't get back to Britain, mainly because they had German passports. Jooss himself, lagging behind to honour teaching commitments now cancelled, booked himself a boat passage to the States to join them but found himself placed in a British internment camp as an 'enemy alien'. The company toured South America while Jooss gave dance classes to fellow inmates, and when his crew returned to New York there was no work to be had.

Keynes knew of all this because he had admired their hammy stuff when he presented them at Cambridge in the thirties, and his offer to help the company was turned to advantage by Jooss during the war. He appealed to Keynes to set in motion his release from the internment camp and then, through CEMA – the Council did grudgingly offer its 'sanction' – to arrange the passage, one by one, of his German company in military convoys across the mine-laden Atlantic. Twelve veterans returned to England in 1943; short of men, the forty-two-year-old Jooss danced among them, touring, with the aid of CEMA grants, a variety of garrisons where squaddies were often informed they were about to see 'The Jews' Ballet Company'. A few civilian theatres put them on with CEMA support, but because they were Germans a friendly face backstage was a rare treat. Twice Keynes mustered extra funds above their normal subvention to honour unsettled debts. The money was banked at their base – the Arts Theatre, Cambridge. After the war the company folded in financial disarray.

The Ballets Jooss story is typical of how Keynes carried on. He developed an idea buoyed by his personal aesthetic preferences, wove an eloquent argument in the finest debating tradition which accentuated the best of every angle, and allowed no one to intervene except to define the opposite view which appeared defensive after his dogmatic reasoning. As Kenneth Clark said, in a phrase sometimes misunderstood, 'He never dimmed his headlights.' Certainly at the start of his reign he swept the Council along and seemed to assert resolute order in place of the casual consensuality of the Pilgrims.

Take the staff: at the April meeting he asked that the three artforms of music, drama and the visual arts should be serviced by personnel who would sign full-time contracts. Up to that date a sort of wishy-washy dual structure had divided those responsible for professional and amateur arts, and the former were titled 'honorary' although they were paid fees. On the pretence of 'clarifying the structure' Keynes consigned the amateur workers like Lawrence Du Garde Peach into a fee-based limbo while he boosted the professionals. Reginald Jacques, his orchestra not far behind, became the first music director; Lewis Casson, his family and theatre company never far behind either, was confirmed as the drama director. They were paid £1,200 a year 'plus expenses on the civil-service scale'. Bill Williams was offered the post of art director by K. Clark with a crocodile smile, and knowing the double-fee game was up, resigned and from then limited his battleground to ABCA and Penguin Books, though he remained a voluntary art adviser in the revised system. In response, Glasgow promoted a donnish middle-aged deputy who had been seconded in the usual wartime wriggly worm fashion to CEMA from the Ministry of Home Security, and to that from the Victoria and Albert Museum where he'd been Keeper of the Library. A bookish man but not, in any sense, a Pelican Bill.

Philip James (1901–1974), a vicar's son who married a canon's daughter, had already authored *Early Keyboard Instruments* (1930), *Children's Books of Yesterday* (1933) and *A Butler's Recipe Book* (1935), none of them published by Penguin. It's amazing that a man with such a musty background so speedily developed the art department into the distinct form by which it continued until the mid-eighties. He established CEMA's exclusive touring network supposedly to complement the 'Art and the People' tours that it separately funded, though the content was more conservative than that provided by Bill Williams. He also developed CEMA's own collection of contemporary works, guided by K. Clark over purchases haggled directly with a ragbag of artists. It could be claimed that the works of many of those in the CEMA collection were contemporary only in a literal sense. They were frankly outmoded in contrast to the French, dissident German or emerging American avant-garde of the time. But the CEMA acquisitions were challenging enough for some people, as Philip James would soon find out, almost to the cost of his job.

Thus Keynes planted his staff tree, uprooted from Glyndebourne: three branches, each administered by a definite authority – a prominent conductor, a famous actor and an ace cataloguer. He also ordered a search for a bigger office to house them all, a hunt that would end in November 1942 at 9 Belgrave Square (telephone Sloane 0421). At the same time Keynes started on the Council. He had inherited the motley crew gathered by the Pilgrims: RADA's Sir Kenneth Barnes, the Conservative MP Mrs Cazalet Keir, Sir Kenneth Clark and Dr Vaughan Williams. The composer was going seriously deaf and in this sense he was the first disabled Council member – a matter considered of no importance then though much value is attached to disability now. Four more were formally included: to add a Scottish voice at the behest of the Scottish Board of Education, Glaswegian playwright James Bridie (1888–1951; he was really a physician called Dr Mavor), the dreary principal of the Royal Academy of Music, Dr Stanley Marchant (1883–1949) and the education director of the British Council, Ifor Evans (1899–1982) who everyone assumed was Welsh though he was born and raised in Soho. Finally, Ivor Brown (1891–1974) was elevated to the Council from the rank of drama worker and publicist. Brown had been the Council's first choice as drama director. He actually accepted the job but out of the blue he was offered the editorship of the *Observer*, for which he'd been theatre critic (T.J., as an *Observer* trustee, masterminded the appointment). Brown's alternative promotion to CEMA's drama chair became strategic, for Keynes, alerted by Glasgow to the old Carnegie canard that CEMA lacked specialist control, endorsed her desire to create committees for each artform, but he didn't want Barnes to run the drama committee because Barnes bored the pants off him.

In fact Keynes didn't want anyone to oversee anything if he couldn't harness them, nor did he wish the committees to have a shred of authority. He merely required them to absorb the small print that otherwise bogged down the Council, but at the same time he was incapable of delegating judgments or trusting colleagues. Reflecting on the situation Keynes determined two things: that the committees would be merely advisory and therefore be given the anodyne description of 'panels', and that he would chair all three as well as the Council. When the list of the panels was announced to the national press, it looked a mite peculiar:

Music	Lord Keynes (chairman), Professor Stanley Marchant (deputy chairman), Mr Arthur Bliss, Dame Myra Hess, Mr Constant Lambert, Dr Thomas Wood.
Drama	Lord Keynes (chairman), Mr Ivor Brown (deputy chairman, later Ifor Evans), Mr Ashley Dukes, Mr Herbert Farjeon, Mr J.B. Priestley, Miss Athene Syler, Mr Emlyn Williams.
Art	Lord Keynes (chairman), Sir Kenneth Clark (deputy chairman), Mr Samuel Courtauld, Mr Duncan Grant, Mr Philip Hendy, Mr Henry Moore, Dr John Rothenstein, Mr W.E. Williams.

Cast away was the Pilgrims' communitarian fervour. Only Vaughan Williams remained on the Council as the sole practising artist to speak up for the crusading origins of CEMA and, as we see, Keynes barred him from the music panel, where instead he'd enlisted the harmless old organist of St Paul's Cathedral, Stanley Marchant, to dilute the composer's influence. As it turned out, Vaughan Williams proved to be cleverer than Keynes and outsmarted him at almost every turn.

In sum there were nine places on the Council, six more on the music panel, seven on drama and eight on art, counting Keynes as four of the sum. The deputy chairmen of the panels sat on the executive council as representatives, a formality which has become a sensible convention carried through to this day, except when it hasn't suited a minister to approve someone. Of the total of thirty advisory places, however, just three were occupied by women – a Tory MP, a pianist-cum-promoter, an Old Vic actress – although the island's population at the time, out of kilter in a period of war, was overwhelmingly female. No women artists were invited, and in truth the art panel itself was a thorough stitch-up, comprising close friends of Clark or Keynes, including the latter's former boyfriend Duncan Grant. Threaded through the system were Keynesian pro-ballet people such as Sam Courtauld, the alcoholic pit conductor Constant Lambert and the henpecked husband of Marie Rambert, Ashley Dukes.

The overall tendency of the panels was traditionalist, even if the soft sentimental left outweighed the soft sentimental right. Yet it cannot be denied that CEMA applicants would have gained benefit from the sound practical advice of the six creative artists (Bliss, Lambert, Vaughan Williams, J.B. Priestley, Emlyn Williams, Henry Moore) and five producers (Hess, Dukes, K. Clark, the Tate's John Rothenstein and the ubiquitous Bill Williams). But Keynes wasn't remotely interested in 'applicants'. He had his own agenda, his own list of good causes to spend the public's money on, and he hadn't forgotten his retort of 1940: 'If that is to be the policy it would save everyone a lot of trouble if an announcement were made that no outsiders need apply.' Now it was his turn to choose who was in and who was out.

Binkie Beaumont was in. He was in his thirties, he was in the West End, he was in the hot seat of the classy producers H.M. Tennent, he was in with Gielgud and he was in with Keynes. He was out as a gay of the classiest kind, but moreover he was out with the Customs and Excise Board. According to Beaumont's biographer, Richard Huggett, an actor asked him in late 1941 what was the greatest single threat to the commercial theatre, thinking on the lines of the blitz or the shortage of good actors. Binkie replied, 'It's that *bloody* entertainments tax. Do you realise, Hannen dear, that I have to pay twenty-five per cent of the gross receipts, not just the net? They tax not only profits but *every* penny which comes in.' This was true and it was a means by which louche sorts like Beaumont who escaped service in the war could help pay for it. The net receipts from the tax were high, especially when the Americans came over, avid for entertainment. In fact they equalled the entire annual tax haul for wines and spirits, or half of the takings from purchase tax:

Entertainments tax net receipts	£
1941–1942	15,941,438*
1942–1943	31,272,602

| 1943–1944 | 43,379,820 |
| 1944–1945 | 45,935,819 |

= around £520 million today.

Binkie – it should be made clear that this illusory nickname was self-imposed (he was christened Hugh), and the alliterative conceit ran in the family, for his Welsh father's name was Morgan Morgan – learned how Keynes had advised Wolfit on tax exemption and so he cultivated a friendship with Maynard and Lydia, who came to see most of Beaumont's productions starring John Gielgud, hoping that this Treasury guru would help him work a West End tax dodge. Keynes said yes, as long as it was something worthy of exemption, 'like Gielgud in Shakespeare'. Beaumont executed the deal at exactly the right time, with the right ingredients, setting up the non-profit company Tennent Plays Ltd just before Keynes took over at CEMA. At his second Council meeting, Keynes broached the arrangement that he'd already made with Beaumont, and Mary Glasgow – mindful that CEMA was set up to exclude this kind of thing, especially in London – wrote it down straight so that everyone could see what the transaction was really all about:

> Meanwhile an application had come from Messrs. H.M. Tennent regarding the forthcoming London production of *Macbeth* with John Gielgud and Gwen Frangcon Davies. It was desired to know whether C.E.M.A. would be prepared to sponsor this production in some way which would make it possible for Entertainment Tax to be avoided. It was agreed that this would be a desirable thing to do.

Binkie was offered a £5,000 guarantee against loss and Macbeth, with sets by Michael Ayrton and music by William Walton, opened at the Piccadilly Theatre on 8 July 1942 'in association with CEMA'. It was by chance that a week later the Thane of Tilton took his seat in the Lords. Binkie's guarantee was never claimed, but then nobody suspected it would be. It's curious that Keynes, commissioned by the Government to advise on wartime finance, knowing that Britain was completely in hock to America, would encourage commercial traders like Beaumont to hold back vital cash such as this tax. As a theatre producer himself, though, Keynes knew that a non-profit-making company could only by law recycle the money to support further projects, providing more work for artists and sustaining an arts economy. He sanctioned this system so long as he endorsed the projects that drove it.

Though it was the private Pilgrims and the Carnegies who introduced the guarantee-against-loss routine into arts funding, the economist honed it into a lasting and useful tool of leverage. A guarantee rather than a grant, or a mixture of the two, was normally issued when it was agreed that there was a link between a project being an artistic and economic gamble, the outcome of which could not be predicted, though a bottom line of support could be agreed. A level of subsidy might be required, not if the expenditure went over budget, but if the projected income was not quite realised – if the audience attendances were as high in numbers as had been hoped but most people had been lured by coach-party discounts, or one night a typhoon hit Shaftesbury Avenue. Unlike a grant, no guarantee money was shelled out until the project had been completed and the subsidiser had seen the accounts and believed them. Of course, this is not really why the guarantee system evolved; it was a way by which the subsidising organisation could gain a stake in a project, negotiate, influence, while keeping the project's cash bubbling in its bank. In Binkie Beaumont's case he wasn't even interested in the guarantee. He wanted the 25 per cent of gross takings that would otherwise go in tax put into his account, not that of the Customs Board, and Keynes obliged.

Lewis Casson didn't. CEMA's drama director detested the whole affair. He felt it was a fiddle and told Keynes so directly. He reminded the Chairman that CEMA had a policy of decentralis-ation and had subsidised equitable, low rates for major performers working in terrible conditions (he was a founding father of the actors' union Equity), while here was a commercial outfit paying differential fees for spineless homosexuals living in the lap of luxury. Keynes, shaking, told Casson that in this office he was working for CEMA not the Old Vic. He had to accept whatever the Council had agreed. Casson shouted back that next time that Tennents sent in a request to evade tax it should be voted on. Keynes hadn't expected this kind of behaviour and didn't quite know what to do, because strictly speaking he wasn't Casson's manager, Mary Glasgow was. She came in (apparently the slanging match could be heard through the building) and defended Casson's right to discuss any further requests with the applicant. Keynes, seething, conceded.

According to Richard Huggett, Beaumont met Casson during the *Macbeth* run: 'To everything which Casson said, Binkie merely smiled and said, "Lord Keynes doesn't think so. We've discussed the matter and his ideas are different from yours, Lewis dear. After all, he *is* the Chairman." ' Charles Landstone, however, noted that he saw Beaumont's eyes turn green with anger when Casson spoke. Huggett adds that Keynes invited Beaumont to lunch at the Treasury and told him: 'Tennent Plays Ltd can do any play you like. But Lewis insists on being consulted. After all, he is the Drama Director for the Council.' To which Binkie is said to have replied: 'Of *course* he must be consulted and of *course* he will always be free to give his opinion. Of course, we don't have to take any notice of it, do we, Maynard dear?'

But they did. Gielgud and Beaumont chose to follow *Macbeth* with a light Restoration comedy, *Love for Love* 'in association with CEMA'. Casson refused to set aside a guarantee for it, which was a little inconsistent as his wife was soon to open in a CEMA-supported production of *She Stoops to Conquer*. He was narrowly overridden at Council, as it was agreed that there were certain political benefits of having, as Kenneth Barnes put it, 'CEMA's name up in lights', though there were no West End lights to light at the time. The farce played successfully for no fewer than sixteen months through 1943 and beyond, and needless to say, it never needed a guarantee. At the same time Beaumont planned a repertory season of five plays as a virtuoso vehicle for Gielgud at the Haymarket (1943–1944), and when the list came to the Council even Keynes gave way to Casson. As the minute read: 'The chairman, before going abroad, suggested dissociating C.E.M.A. from three plays being presented by H.M. Tennent.' The five plays Beaumont proposed were *Hamlet* in a production by Keynes' Cambridge chum 'Dadie' Rylands (and poor it proved), *A Midsummer Night's Dream* directed by Oxford's Neville Coghill (even worse), *The Duchess of Malfi*, Somerset Maugham's *The Circle* and a continuation of *Love for Love*. The Council minute did not declare which of the three Keynes disowned. We can guess that no one round the table would support creaky old tat like *The Circle* even though it was the sole modern play offered, and assisting a revival of a comedy that had already proved itself viable would make a mockery of the guarantee scheme. The third must have been the Renaissance shock-horror *Malfi*, productions of which have been subsidised so many hundred times since by the Arts Council that it could only be Keynes' personal aversion, glimpsed already over Wolfit's *Whore*, that singled it out. This proved the beginning of the end for the agreement between Binkie dear and Maynard dear, partly because Keynes was increasingly called to America and couldn't keep an iron grip on Casson. The guarantee scheme was dropped even though the 'association' tag was retained by Beaumont until 1951. Casson considered he had won the battle.

Even so, Casson was ashamed that he lost J.B. Priestley over it. As a fellow socialist, he already had cause for remorse, having opposed a production of Priestley's oracular play *They Came to a City* by Beaumont 'in association', on the sophisticated premise that to be seen to back socialist plays might compromise CEMA and his role in it. Priestley was a drama panellist who felt that decisions were being taken without consultation and that the Pall Mall mateyness of Beaumont and Keynes disdained the advice of practical artists; consequently he was the first panel member to resign over a principle. It wasn't Binkie's commercialism that rankled but the following, which Priestley declared in a 1943 CEMA bulletin:

> Some people do take the line that ordinary English folk are so undramatic that serious drama will never flourish among them. This seems to me all wrong. I believe the ordinary folk like drama. The undramatic element in our society is the well-to-do upper class, and it is the Theatre that depends on the patronage of this class that soon becomes trivial. Some of our CEMA friends who have been busy bringing new audiences to the Theatre tell us that these new audiences, mostly workers, like good, strong stuff . . . My objection to commercial men in the Theatre is that they do not remain commercial and cannot resist pleasing their own taste and that their own taste is usually so bad.

When Casson quit CEMA at the end of the war, he left it with a sting. CEMA had done a deal with the British Council to fund an exciting exchange between Tennent Plays and the leading classical company of Paris, the Comédie Française (thus the first visiting company to receive Arts Council aid). Mary Glasgow discovered only by chance that the deal had been switched. Instead of Gielgud going to France, the Old Vic went. Her complaint to the British Council revealed that the change had been made at the bidding of CEMA's drama department. For his services to CEMA, Lewis Casson was awarded a knighthood.

Nor did Keynes enjoy a smooth ride with music. First off and simplest to handle was Glyndebourne's John Christie, who kept pointing out to anyone who'd listen that the new improved CEMA looked suspiciously like the National Council for Music and the Arts he'd proposed four years ago. Nevertheless, even if CEMA had learned how to improve itself Christie hadn't, and the moan of dismay whenever his name came up meant that Keynes could dispose of his rival effortlessly. As a minute reads in July 1942:

> The Chairman, the President of the Board of Education and the
> Lord Privy Seal had received a number of letters from Mr. John
> Christie in connection with his National Council. It was not clear to
> any of them what exactly Mr. Christie was asking for and none of
> them felt they had any spare time to go into the matter.

Vaughan Williams proved a more cunning opponent. However deaf the composer was growing, he encountered Keynes at the Council during a fertile period of his fifth and sixth symphonies (he wrote nine). While the Carnegie Trust and ENSA were stamping their feet about CEMA's irregular and copycat employment of the country's symphony orchestras, the music director, Reginald Jacques, felt that CEMA must move firmly in one of two directions – leave the ensembles 'alone in the desert or provide an oasis'. In September 1942 he presented his report to the Council, which:

> agreed that the symphony orchestras should now, if possible, be
> brought within the scope of CEMA's activities ... It was pointed
> out that the orchestral players' fees had recently been raised by the
> Musicians' Union ... It might even be desirable to put the
> orchestras on a salaried basis.

The Council welcomed this far-sighted notion, especially as it offered a chance to put one over the pious Carnegies. At last, said Vaughan Williams, here was an opportunity to improve the 'fee-bitten' lives of 'dedicated and admirable musicians'. Then Keynes put his foot in it. 'The Chairman felt that greater care might now be taken to ensure reasonable receipts at orchestral concerts.' Jacques protested that, if the Chairman was referring to CEMA's own promotions, many of them were taking place under emergency conditions in isolated towns suffering air-raid damage;

that was the point of the exercise. Keynes would have none of it: 'The Chairman felt that this might be increasingly offset by the arrangement of concerts in places which might be expected to produce a profit.' Like the West End.

The Council wasn't at ease with these glib balance-sheet views. Seeing Keynes isolated at the table, Vaughan Williams decided his time had come to challenge the Chairman's fundamental creed. He did it carefully so that Keynes was forced by his own logic to give ground. The composer 'raised the question of amateur work in general, and made a special plea that the Council should not dissociate themselves from amateur music-making activity.' He asked why it was, for instance, that CEMA was not allowed to provide the fees of professionals taking part in amateur perform- ances. Mary Glasgow responded that the ruling was one which had been made with the Carnegie Trust in the early days at their request. Vaughan Williams then asked the Chairman if this wasn't a 'restrictive and economically inarticulate' precept to prevent CEMA supporting professionals and Keynes had to concede this was so. He then asked if Keynes had any objection to the subsidy of professionals earning their living where such need could be shown, and Keynes had to reply that in his view CEMA existed precisely for such a purpose. As a result, 'the Council agreed that the ruling was obviously an obstructive one in practice and should now be disregarded'. With this single move Vaughan Williams established an astute system for funding amateur performances with professional presence that only Thatcherism questioned forty years on.

At another meeting Keynes began by setting aside the typed agenda to pursue his case for the Vic-Wells monolith, a campaign that would lead to the creation of the Royal Opera and the Royal Ballet. Vaughan Williams stopped him and requested if he might 'crave the Chairman's indulgence to clarify something I must have missed'. Keynes gave way and the composer asked, 'Under what heading should opera and ballet be taken?' Mary Glasgow recalled that there was an 'appallingly long silence, broken first by the unwelcome sound of Lewis Casson trying to stifle a laugh, as it was evident that Lord Keynes had not considered this elementary point'. The Chairman testily replied that opera and ballet should be discussed under drama, 'in view of existing theatrical arrange- ments'. By now the eyes of certain Council members were starting to water because the answer sounded so makeshift. Vaughan Williams adopted an air of mock confusion: 'Drama? There is certainly a logic to your choice. But an opera is composed – at least, on occasion – and I believe that ballets are often put together by choreographers. And theatrical? Well, that depends.' Vaughan Williams' mischief underscored the fact that ten years before he had created the dance score *Job*, with a scenario based on William Blake's mystical images devised by Keynes' sparkling brother Geoffrey. Ninette de Valois made a crass choreography to it, despite the composer's warning that he'd named it not a ballet but a 'masque for dancing' to stress its ritual rather than its narrative, theatrical, nature.

Under duress Keynes agreed that major issues of opera and ballet should be discussed and determined by the Council. Keynes had fallen into a trap, as Vaughan Williams, not being a panellist, now had a front seat to guide policy and contribute to the evolution of British opera and dance, and his line was nationalist rather than internationalist. Thereafter Keynes kept the matter under wraps by inventing an executive committee of like minds that would mould the project and negotiate essentials to pre-empt the Council. Later, in 1947, when his successor tried to craft a special committee for opera and ballet, it floundered as it was comprised wholly of the selfish clients it was set up to handle. So when Keynes diverted the project for his own pre-disposed attention, he set a concealed and subjective course which the Arts Council has since been unwilling or unable to correct. It has failed for this reason to build a competent framework to deal with its biggest clients; it is still incapable of controlling the Covent Garden monster Keynes conceived. Vaughan Williams' question remains unanswered.

A third intervention by Vaughan Williams hit the mark far better. Having digested that Keynes was at least giving the arts funding scene a distinct shape, he decided that it might indeed improve the position to have a clear demarcation of coverage between the three funding bodies – CEMA, the 'exploratory' Pilgrims and the 'nurturing' Carnegies – even though none of them seemed to be willing to discuss the issue together. He saw for a start that Carnegie spent more money on music than CEMA did. Back in 1939, on George Dyson's advice in a policy paper called the Hichens Report, the Carnegie Trust had embarked on a five-year plan to spend £150,000 in support of three categories of music it considered vital to the life of the country: professional orchestras and opera companies ('to give performances at popular prices'), amateur music societies and music education schemes. Much of the aid went essentially to maintain the struggling professionals and the Carnegies could not lightly withdraw its support just because a five-year plan was completed. But if CEMA, which Keynes was piloting towards 'stabilisation', unburdened Carnegie of the obligation at the right time, then a bunch of money would be freed up for a new phase in the amateur field.

Although Vaughan Williams was not a music panel member, he examined with the music director the cost of 'taking on the bands', and in late October 1942, Reginald Jacques reported to the Council that it cost the Carnegie Trust £8,000 a year in guarantees to aid the orchestras for their tours. Keynes proposed adding £2,000 to cover the Musicians' Union increase already noted and suggested that £15,000 be set aside for 1943–1944 as an orchestral fund, aware as he was that the Carnegie had a 'moral obligation' to the orchestras at least until the end of 1942. Vaughan Williams then asked

> whether it would be possible to recommend to the Carnegie Trust
> that the money thus saved by them on their orchestral scheme
> might usefully be devoted to the development of amateur music
> and, in particular, the appointment of County Music Advisers.

By this means Vaughan Williams turned inherent discord between funders into concord and reclaimed resources that, thanks mostly to the Carnegie Trust, nurtured the impressive post-war improvements in state music education.

CEMA's relations with the orchestras began at the level at which they have remained throughout the Arts Council's life – dreadful. Jacques had attempted first to rescue CEMA's reputation from the kind of wartime touring tangle noted in the *Annual Register* review of 1942:

> Full-sized professional orchestras were to be met up and down the
> country competing for box-office favour, often clashing with each
> other's dates, imposing their own haphazard timetables on local
> musical life, and hurling symphonies and concertos at a vast new
> population that had no previous experience of that order of music.

Aside from the bands run by the BBC, there were then two main orchestras in the capital – the London Symphony and the London Philharmonic – and five in the regions: the Hallé in Manchester

which was considered the best in the country, the Liverpool
Philharmonic, the Scottish Orchestra in Glasgow, the Northern
Philharmonic and one that had evolved out of a municipal seaside
ensemble in Bournemouth. Only the Liverpool orchestra was
salaried and this set all manner of snags, not the least of which was
the damaging 'deputy' system which allowed key players to stick
substitutes in their seats if they got better-paid work on the night
of the concert. Nor were they organised in any way that made
sense to Keynes. He assumed he could use the new scheme to
impose his preferred order on their constitutions and their
balance sheets. This sort of thing had not worried the Carnegies,
whose scheme supported specific concerts: £50 grant plus a £50
guarantee, with a general reserve of £200 to cover 'catastrophic
losses due to air raids' – this was called on by the London
Symphony Orchestra when Sunderland's Victoria Hall was
bombed flat a few hours before the concert.

Keynes wanted an 'all-over' guarantee based on the 1943–1944
season's work. That was merely the start. The following year he
imposed sterner conditions, but already there was trouble. In
December 1943, Keynes's insistence on looking at the accounts in
greater detail than the artistic programmes forced the music panel
to break off 'relations with the Bournemouth Philharmonic
Orchestra [sic] because they were not satisfied with the Orchestra's
conduct of its financial affairs'. Tightening the screw, CEMA offered
the remaining orchestras for 1944–1945 an outright grant of £1,000
together with a guarantee of £4,000 'to offer proper working
conditions to your players by putting them on a salaried basis' with
the proviso that the orchestra should be 'a properly constituted
non-profit-making organisation' on the lines of Tennent Plays Ltd.

In the case of the self-governing London Symphony Orchestra
there were two problems: it was seen by them as a restrictive
imposition affecting the players' remunerations, and as 70 per
cent of the shareholding members were away in the forces a
change of the articles of association could not be voted on.
Locked in an impasse of its own devising, Mary Glasgow wrote
stiffly on behalf of the Council to the LSO:

> It was our prime intention to give interim help to the LSO in the
> hope that its constitution could eventually be reconsidered . . . But
> the time has now come for me to warn you that, until such a change
> is carried out, my Council will be unable to renew its association
> with the LSO.

Within a year CEMA had managed to lose two orchestras out of the nation's seven that the Carnegie Trust had handed over. Jacques had done his best to develop good relations, but he was confounded by Keynes' dogmatic approach. While the Carnegies and the Pilgrims had appeared to the orchestras as not merely benevolent but caring, CEMA came across as oppressive and sneaky. It took the unexpected death of Keynes and the appointment of an orchestral player to the post of music director in 1948 before a pragmatic rapport could emerge, but by then London had spawned two more orchestras and fresh problems brewed.

None of this compared to the farce of fake paintings and charges of treason that fettered the work of Philip James, director of art. He was responsible for establishing a formidable schedule of tours more to the taste of Keynes and Clark than the advanced 'Art and the People' exhibitions set up by Bill Williams (the guides still in place), and in his initial contract he was 'responsible to Sir Kenneth Clark in matters of policy'. Despite Clark's dubious reputation among scholars, the last thing James had anticipated was the kind of criticism that sprang up out of the blue in the letters page of *The Times* in November 1943:

Sir, – An exhibition entitled 'Paintings of the French School from a private collection' is at present touring provincial cities under the auspices of the Council for the Encouragement of Music and Art [sic] ... The present exhibition contains some lamentable paintings wrongly attributed to famous artists ... I would refer in particular to three paintings attributed, with highly laudable comment in the catalogue, to no less a genius than Edouard Manet. One of these is a copy of the 'Madame Manet dans la Serre' which belongs to the National Museum at Oslo ... Anyone who has seen it must be shocked by the crudity of the copy sponsored by CEMA. The other two paintings wrongly attributed to Manet are entitled 'Still Life' and 'L'Ile de St. Ouen'. They are commonplace pastiches of the master's inimitable style drawn from no known prototype. None of the three paintings is signed...

I am, Sir, your obedient servant
THOMAS BODKIN
Barber Institute of Fine Arts,
The University, Birmingham.

K. Clark sent a tetchy response:

> One of CEMA's chief difficulties in wartime is to find a sufficient
> number of good pictures for its circulating exhibitions . . . When,
> therefore, Mr H.J. Bomford, with great generosity, offered to allow
> CEMA to circulate his collection of French art, the council were
> delighted at the chance . . . A word of sympathy must be offered to
> Mr Bomford, whose extraordinary public-spirited action has led to
> this attack. In future owners of fine collections will be less likely to
> lend them to CEMA or to any other public institution.

Good, replied Professor Bodkin, if it spares an innocent public
misled by CEMA that crude, fake work is really good and genuine:
'Many of them will feel that public money has been wasted on the
organisation of a show that is not calculated to advance the cause
of the fine arts which CEMA was incorporated to promote.'

In the following weeks *The Times* received all manner of
correspondence on the issue, covering issues of attribution and
authorship, the right of the public to see fakes, the 'common fault
of looking at pictures with one's ears' (an attack on the guides) and
the concept of two publics – 'the uninstructed and the instructed' –
who are looking at different but equally valid things in the same
object. It ended with a *Times* leader that concluded, 'It would
certainly be wise for CEMA when compiling future catalogues of
loan exhibitions to state clearly the limits of its responsibility.' Clark
acknowledged to Keynes that the censure had caused CEMA
damage. It grated especially because the criticism was not aimed at
contemporary work and it implied that 'CEMA doesn't know its
stuff' even on the safer ground of traditional art.

Yet neither could it be trusted with living artists. In 1942
Council member Thelma Cazalet Keir had helped to set up an
exhibition of work by the popular Welsh painter Augustus John,
then in his sixties. She was a friend of his family and as such was
exploited by organisations such as the Contemporary Art Society
to buy pictures from John at favourable terms, such as the portrait
of Dylan Thomas that the Society acquired. For CEMA she had
selected an exhibition that proved extremely well liked, which the
painter caught at the Temple Newsam gallery in Leeds. He wrote
to Cazalet Keir that he'd 'only detected four forgeries'. Unsure at
first whether or not he was joking, she was horrified to learn that
he was telling the truth and indeed there could have been more

fakes 'had he had a better memory than he did'. When she reported this to James and Clark, the latter told them to keep quiet as it was one of the most successful contemporary exhibitions they'd supported, and anyway 'the artist has only mentioned it, not complained'. Mrs Cazalet Keir did the decent thing and exposed the affair twenty years on.

Clark was probably right to subdue that episode, for the critics of CEMA needed little more ammunition. First there were the progressives who felt that the organisation wasn't engaging fully with growing artists. An article in *The Times* of August 1942, penned anonymously by Ivor Brown, had summed up the work of CEMA to date, which was a tricky job with the record of the Pilgrims on one side and the contrary aspirations of Keynes on the other. The visual arts were depicted pallidly:

> Painting and sculpture presented a problem rather different from that of music and drama. Painting is not to the same extent a communal art and C.E.M.A. could not encourage local painters any more than it encourages local composers or local dramatists. Its enterprise was therefore confined to circulating collections of modern painting.

Nevertheless, the article concluded with a plug to expand the collection of commissions and recent work that Philip James was assembling under orders from K. Clark:

> Private patronage was never enough to keep the art of painting in a healthy state, and much of the appreciation of modern painting comes from people who cannot afford to become collectors. For both artists and public a generous scheme of State purchases and commissions is essential.

Charles Tennyson, chairman of the Central Institute of Art and Design, responded:

> The United States recognized this some years ago and has by the creation of the Federal Art Project done much to bring the arts back to their proper place in the life of the people.
> By this scheme a very large sum has been expended by the Federal Government every year in the decoration of public buildings, purchase and distribution of works of art and handicraft, holding of exhibitions and prize competitions and so on.

Francis Huxley wrote from London Zoo:

> While agreeing with Mr. Tennyson ... Equally important have
> been the activities of the Works Progress Administration Art
> Project, which was instituted during the depression to help unem-
> ployed artists. This helped a great many artists to remain at their
> painting; the Federal Art Project then provided large numbers of
> commissions ...
>
> The general conclusion I came to was that any government
> agency which might be set up here for encouraging the arts should
> in the first place concern itself with all the arts, including design,
> and, I am inclined to think, the cinema, and not merely with
> painting or the fine arts, and that it should have certain broad
> functions in the sphere of adult education. Secondly, in addition to
> providing specific commissions for painters, musicians, and so
> forth, it should provide support for longer or shorter periods to a
> number of artists and other creative workers, especially younger
> men and women of promise.

Correspondence flowed in this progressive and utopian vein,
annoying and dismaying Keynes by turns. It seemed that everyone
knew more than the Council did. He had considered the timid art-
collection scheme, as had Clark, to be a stimulant to current
practice, though in fact it duplicated other wartime programmes.
Keynes was vexed that the scheme had simply allowed his
detractors to draw attention to his slender vision and exclusionist
bias, especially that he was far less engaged with living creativity
than with conservation of the status quo. Theirs was an accurate
charge, for at his second Council meeting: 'The Chairman
stressed the fact that CEMA travelling exhibitions at present
concentrated far too much on contemporary work and that more
should be done to make available to the general public examples
of traditional painting.' Keynes was supported by Sir Kenneth
Clark in his further wish to reduce the influence of the Bill
Williams educational approach. It didn't take any time for Clark to
lay into 'the provision, at growing cost, of guide lecturers for
exhibitions', and he quickly proposed more 'tasteful' subjects for
the Council's own exhibitions such as 'Portraiture' or 'East and
West'. From then on the exhibitions became increasingly
historical in focus – 'Dutch Paintings of the Seventeenth Century',
'Old English Landscapes', 'Book Illustrations Since 1800', Mr

Bomford's assortment of French fakes – though demand for the contemporary 'Art and the People' tours resolutely persisted.

All the more galling for Keynes then, when a Colonel Blimp-style Conservative MP, Captain Alan Graham, stood up in the Commons on Ash Wednesday 1944 and requested of the Chancellor of the Exchequer that, 'in view of the poor quality and debasing effect of the pictorial art evinced at the exhibitions provided by CEMA, he will reduce the yearly grant to this institution from Her Majesty's Treasury'. The Captain had been put up to it by prehistoric members of the Royal Academy led by its crusty president, Alfred Munnings. They followed this up with a letter to (where else?) *The Times*:

> We the undersigned are of the opinion that Captain Graham has postulated a state of things true to the facts. For the most part the exhibitions comprise paintings devised to carry on the baleful influence of what is known as 'modernistic' art. This is a subversive movement which, with its several 'isms', has been for many years endeavouring to undermine the traditional glories of painting and sculpture, thus to lower the standards of artistic ideas and technical performance.
>
> The exhibitions alluded to in the question seek to promulgate these disastrous ideas by means of attendant lecturers engaged to persuade the public who visit the shows that the works they repudiate and protest against, orally and in the Press, are nevertheless admirable.
>
> In view of the amount of public money spent upon this promulgation of objectionable painting and sculpture, we declare ourselves in sympathy with Captain Graham's laudable attempt to amend the evil by the double means of reducing national expenditure and openly opposing the aforesaid organized activities for a lowering of art standards.
> Yours, &c.,
> D.Y. CAMERON, RICHARD GARBE, OLIVER HALL, EARNEST W. HASLEHURST, JOHN HASSALL, ROBERT LITTLE, J. THORBURN McGRAW, CHARLES PEARS, FRANK O. SALISBURY, FRANK SHORT, JOHN STIRLING-MAXWELL.

Keynes replied promptly:

> The letter suggests that our policy was calculated to deprave public taste. It is, I think, scandalous that so distinguished a body of

signatories should write that sort of letter with so little preliminary inquiry into the facts . . . Out of the 25 exhibitions which we have circulated up to date [he excludes here the 'Art and the People' tours, which he treats as the effort of a client] there have been six mixed shows of contemporary artists, two of which were selections from the summer exhibitions of the Royal Academy (two of the signatories of the letter of complaint were represented in these) . . . Our panel is as mixed a bunch of fogeys of repute as you could reasonably hope to collect. We have undoubtedly reached, on the average, the age of discretion.

It was a clever letter, which played on the fact that the malcontents were really knocking 'Art and the People', which was not strictly speaking run by CEMA but was a regular client of it. Yet a more broad-minded chairman would not have devalued the status of new work in CEMA's programme but instead attacked the regressive intolerance of the Royal Academicians, a stand for which there would have been much support, as further letters showed. The way this attack on CEMA was led from the House of Commons brought a certain discomfort to bear at 9 Belgrave Square, but the insurgents had so overloaded their language that the organisation gained more sympathy than abuse. Philip James received a near-incoherent letter from Charles Pears accusing him of being 'a traitor of the stamp of Lord Haw-Haw' for allowing the guides to tamper 'with the very soul of art which may be lurking in the minds of those children who are bidden to see CEMA shows'.

Despite the bowel-churning acrimony, arts bodies generally welcome these sorts of attacks, especially when ungraceful criticisms fly from both reactionary and progressive forces. It shows, they believe, that they are in the middle of things and are therefore balanced, ecumenical, objective. This is a public relations deception, of course, invariably allowing the substantive matter to evade scrutiny – in this case the disinvesting of CEMA's engagement with creative development at Keynes' bidding. Neither the affair itself nor Keynes' cute letter constrained Munnings. At annual dinners of the Royal Academy his spiteful comments on Arts Council sedition would crop up as loyally as the Queen's Toast.

If the economist couldn't keep the artform departments in check, we could at least count on him to keep his eye on the till. Up to the time of Keynes' appointment, the quaint chequebook system of Tom Jones had worked well and the accounts always ended in the black. For the first financial year for which the expansionist Keynes could be said to be thoroughly responsible, that of 1943–1944, the figures read as follows:

Expenditure	£
Music	71,211
Drama	21,713
Art	13,782
Administration	28,968
Total expenditure	135,674
Income	£
Government grant-in-aid	115,000
Concert income	5,016
Exhibition fees	1,437
Donations	57
Total income	121,510
Total expenditure	135,674
Total income	121,510
Loss	14,164

The deficit equals around half a million pounds at today's value. It took a great economist to create a great loss.

Chapter 7

Would that employ men?

Building Barmy • The Erogenous Regiment • The Mecca Temple

Keynes was deadly keen on buildings. He half solved the Slump with a massive works programme, the one from which Glyndebourne's Christie had profited. There was his Cambridge Arts Theatre and his farm, but he had also plotted to build a grand hotel on the Sussex road cutting Tilton from Glyndebourne, and in 1930 he dramatically proposed pulling down the whole of south London from Westminster in the west to Greenwich in the east, 'providing hundreds of acres of squares and avenues, parks and public spaces'. In other words, he wanted to turn Southwark and Lambeth into Bloomsbury: 'Would that employ men? Why, of course it would.' Yes, it eventually employed a number of Germans.

It therefore came as little surprise to CEMA when Keynes 'turned the Council into an architect's eyrie' – after all, that had been Rab Butler's brief, though he knew full well it was Keynes' too. In a notable article for a book of visionary essays called *Britain & The Beast* in 1937, Keynes had griped:

> It is not matter for wonder that the high authorities build no more hanging gardens of Babylon . . . not even opera houses, theatres, colonnades, boulevards, and public places. Our grandest exercises to-day in the arts of public construction are the arterial roads.

He started in 1942 with the oldest surviving theatre in the country, that of the Theatre Royal in Bristol (founded in 1766). The city had suffered severe bombing but the wooden-framed, 700-seater theatre had sensationally survived, only to be put on the market early that year in a district desperate for warehousing. The playwright Herbert Farjeon drew the Chairman's attention to a local rescue campaign and Keynes grabbed the chance to provide a wartime oasis for the Vic-Wells syndicate; he wanted them nearer to home than Lancashire, which he considered 'little short of Iceland'. It didn't seem to bother him that CEMA was unincorporated and the deal would ruin the organisation if anything went legally awry.

It peeved him no end to learn from Casson that Vic-Wells company members were happy with the present arrangements whereby they toured mainly around the north and came to London for limited seasons at the 900-seater New Theatre (nowadays called the Albery) in St Martin's Lane. Casson didn't let on that Bristol had been surreptitiously blacklisted ever since the BBC Symphony Orchestra was evacuated there but abandoned it for Bedford because of the unrelenting bombing raids. The BBC didn't like its microphones to pick up explosions when the orchestra played – it was less concerned about the safety of the musicians than the morale of its listeners.

Only in 1946 would Keynes' plan be met in part when the resident company at the Theatre Royal was christened the 'Bristol Old Vic'. Keynes suggested that an exploratory report should examine the chances of the theatre paying its way, and to make sure he got the answer he wanted to hear he appointed Norman Higgins, his manager at Cambridge. This was typical of his behaviour (his architect friend did well out of such consultancies), and when it came to appointing someone to oversee the Bristol project, he chose the Wolfit manager he'd brought into CEMA as an assistant, Charles Landstone, a seasoned soul who'd 'seen it all'.

The Council minute for September 1942 is worth quoting substantially to display how at ease Keynes was with bold deals of this kind:

The Chairman made a report on the Theatre Royal, Bristol, which had recently been sold to a private purchaser [Clarence Davy, an obliging metal merchant] from whom it was being bought back again by an appeal committee constituted as a Board of Trustees for the purpose. He suggested that, in order to save the building and to bring it into use as a theatre as soon as possible, it might be possible for CEMA to rent it from the trustees [£600 annual rent plus £400 rates] and arrange for plays to be produced there . . . With these facts before them, the Council agreed that a 21 year lease should be taken out with the Trustees on condition that they should acquire the Theatre immediately under mortgage from the present owner. The lease should be taken out in CEMA's name.

That is precisely what happened on 31 December 1942, at which point, as Charles Landstone explained in his book on the venue, it became 'the first state theatre in the country'. Three months later Lewis Casson reported to the Council that the place would re-open on 11 May with Oliver Goldsmith's comedy of 1773, *She Stoops to Conquer,* by the Stanford Holme Company, 'which had been working in factory hostels, taken over by the Old Vic, and strengthened with the addition of' . . . his wife Sybil. He pleaded 'that this information might remain confidential for the time being', a brave request when we meditate on the lavish lead-in time marketing teams convince us they need nowadays.

CEMA's pilot venture in theatre management was reckoned a success and it went to Keynes' head. He had met by chance the general manager of London's Crystal Palace. This led to a series of inconclusive meetings to discuss 'the possibility of replanning this area of national property as a centre for artistic activities of all kinds after the war'. Keynes proposed that 'the Council might offer prizes for a suitable design', suggesting 'a sum of £5,000 might be appropriate'. He then urged that the Council 'offer prizes for the design of an arts centre in a damaged city like Plymouth', directing Mary Glasgow to approach the relevant MP, who just happened to be Lord Astor. Glasgow subverted this, feeling that these seemingly impulsive concepts were coarsely concocted to enhance CEMA's standing in Parliament.

Glasgow even had to put off others in order to accommodate Keynes' more speculative whims. Donald Wolfit heard that the London County Council was thinking of disposing of the lease of the Lyceum Theatre. He wrote directly to his Advance Players' board member Keynes, but he was annoyed to get a letter back from Glasgow, and enraged by her jaunty 'sod off' tone:

Lord Keynes has asked me to answer your letter to him of August 10th on his behalf. He is leaving the country for a short time.

You ask about possible help to yourself to acquire a lease of the Lyceum Theatre. Much as the Arts Council would like to support your claim, they cannot very well do so in this case, because they contemplate taking a lease of the theatre themselves! I should be grateful if you would keep this information to yourself for the present. I do not know how the negotiations will go or whether, in fact, our project will be realised . . . They intend to use the Theatre as a Concert Hall in order to make up, in some degree, for the present extreme lack of accommodation in London for orchestral performances.

Wolfit wrote back to point out that 'as London has lost ten theatres and only one Concert Hall, it seems this was an opportune time for the Council to have dropped the word "Encouragement" from their title'. Glasgow was right to be cautious. Nothing emerged: the Lyceum was bought by Mecca as a dance hall for a while, then left to the rats and winos, and while in the early 1990s a group funded by the Arts Council dithered (thanks to feeble advice) about turning it into a national dance house, Andrew Lloyd Webber and Apollo Leisure reverted it to a theatre after fifty years of Arts Council disregard – a sign at least that thirties enterprise has not been stilled by state subsidy. Nevertheless, Wolfit was wrong to overlook the national picture. Keynes had not ignored drama theatres outside London; after all, he ran one himself, in Cambridge, which needed such partners to house the tours it produced.

Aside from saving the Liverpool Playhouse as an Old Vic off-shoot, he learned that there were two nineteenth-century theatres each with seating capacities around 900 'which might soon come in to the market' in Bedford and Luton. He told a nervous Council that he had 'already consulted with the Treasury on this matter and there would be no objection to acquire the theatres on the Bristol model'. At each meeting Keynes came up with a bouncy new building idea until his toughest critic could take it no longer: 'Dr Vaughan Williams protested strongly that it was not the function of the Council to provide a setting for the arts, but rather to foster the arts themselves.' What a thought to put before the present Council.

Learning that Keynes was 'building barmy' (as Charles Landstone put it), the British Drama League under its director Geoffrey Whitworth visited the Council in June 1943 with three trustees who also happened to be governors of the Old Vic: the

League's chairman Lord Esher, Sir Reginald Rowe and Sir Ernest Pooley – a decent old dullard who would try to command the Arts Council on Keynes' death. They put forward a fascinating plan to set up a nationwide chain of civic theatres on the following terms:

1. That for the creation and maintenance of civic theatres there should be a combination of state and local financial aid.
2. That each theatre should have its own resident company which might on occasion be exchanged with those of other theatres, but would spend the major part of its time at home.
3. That the resident company should be sufficiently large to undertake a full repertory programme; and also to supply a subsidiary company to tour the surrounding district.

The Council and staff were impressed by the scope of the scheme and the care that had gone into the group's preparation. All, that is, but Keynes. Lord Esher pushed for a definite statement of support from CEMA, while Keynes questioned whether the League wanted money for tours or for buildings, and if the chain would be 'restricted to five or six large towns' or was meant to 'cover the country'. Esher wanted them everywhere. Keynes explained that the Council 'could not at this stage give any general endorsement to the civic theatre scheme without further discussion amongst themselves', which was fair enough given its immense implications, but went on to remind them that 'the Council was a body created during the war to serve certain war-time needs. They had no funds available for building, and, at present, no authority to ask for any.' At this point, Glasgow recalls, the visitors visibly 'chilled'.

It seemed to them that Keynes was interested solely in the preservation of existing buildings, not the creation of new ones like his own theatre. They concluded that the Cambridge experience must have jaundiced him. Pushed further, Keynes considered that the provision of such theatres in towns like Luton and Bedford could be 'an essential part of policy' only where 'no competition with the commercial theatre could be suspected', though 'the first thing to do was to investigate the legal position of local authorities willing to give financial aid to local artistic enterprise'. The *legal* position – this was the cocky voice of a Treasury mandarin letting on he knew more than his audience did, aware that all manner of changes were being planned on local government control once the war had ended. In the field of culture, for instance, there was a civil-service move to consider the arts as a separate field from education. Although brought on by the non-profit tax dodge which irritated a number of Whitehall officers, it came from an argument about the presumed increase of local government support for the arts following the war's close. As CEMA's subsidy came under the control of the Education Board, it was surely consistent that local authorities should fund the arts not only directly out of the rates but through education, too. This, to the delight of certain civil servants, would allow central government control 'under section 86 of the Education Act of 1921', whereby 'a local education authority may, with the approval of the Board of Education, make arrangements to supply ... facilities for social training in the day or evening'.

Keynes was aware of the effects of this sort of thinking on CEMA. If the arts were not an accessory of education, then CEMA should stand alone too, receiving its aid direct from the Treasury and thus becoming more plainly exposed to parliamentary inspection. The civic theatre question, so simple and inoffensive, raised the kind of issues being debated in the Treasury hothouse, and Keynes had no desire to spread them any further while he was getting his feet under the desk. Esher, a little nonplussed, asked if CEMA would simply sponsor a travelling exhibition of theatre building designs, including those already in existence for the proposed National Theatre. Keynes agreed that such a tour could be considered and the matter was left. There was an unfortunate side effect, however. Mary Glasgow had taken Keynes' cautious response to mean that he was uncertain as to CEMA's practical position on capital development. Bristol's Theatre Royal had been acquired on a lease through private intermediaries, not the local council. She formally requested Treasury advice on the civic theatres scheme. The Treasury 'determined that C.E.M.A. could assist approved local bodies, perhaps a Civic Trust, to acquire theatres on the lines of the Bristol experiment'. Although this echoed with greater detail the advice Keynes said he'd already received, in the light of what he had in mind, it would not be good news.

Keynes wasn't bothered too much about civic theatres in Luton, Bedford or even Esher. He had become haunted by 'a national house' for opera and ballet; naturally Lydia, now Lady Keynes, played a part in this bewitchment. A national theatre devoted to drama was a crusade carried along by others like George Bernard

Shaw and Labour's London County Council, who were always getting somewhere but ending nowhere. In this matter Keynes was solely concerned to find for the Old Vic a decent, durable home at which to present plays in London. He was far more inspired by the sister notion of a permanent national opera house, because a traditional theatre of the continental type always sheltered two parallel companies – one for opera, one for ballet – and it was ballet above all that drove him on.

The economist shared this passion with a generation of Oxbridge aesthetes. Ballet meant Diaghilev. When the flamboyant Russian 'impresario' died suddenly in 1929 the loss created at one and the same time an immense crisis and a liberation, not only for those of his Ballets Russes company but also for the development of dance and its allied arts. His choreographers and dancers were left scrabbling around for work through the Slump, first in France then anywhere that would take them. Those who survived the best did so in the United States, especially the young Georges Balanchine, whose refused request for a permanent British work permit in 1931 was the one of the dimmest artistic decisions ever made by the Home Office (and we wonder which native artists helped them make it). In truth the Diaghilev dissolution exposed the fact that some of his choreographers, like Massine and Lifar, weren't up to much and that the impresario's mighty impact was based more on the class of ancillary talent he had garnered for his stage spectacles – the scores of Stravinsky, the sets of Picasso, the costumes of Chanel, and so on.

Above all, the occasional visits to England of the Ballets Russes between 1911 and 1926 offered an exotic, ticket-only focus for the dilettante gay scene. 'A friend of Diaghilev' prefigures 'a friend of Dorothy' as a code of inclination, and though myriad ballet companies existed at the time, none could compete with gay Diaghilev's gift for decorative opulence nor with his cardinal advantage, an array of athletic boys: 'Men galore, whirling like dervishes or hurling themselves about as warlike tartars,' Ninette de Valois observed, 'and all this crowned by one – Vaslav Nijinsky – who showed Western Europe the heights that a male classical dancer could reach.'

Back in the nineteenth century the ballet scene offered otherwise closeted homosexuals like the composer Tchaikovsky an unfeigned haven. Only in part, however, was it enjoyed for the opportunity to enter an erogenous environment which relied, like waiters need tips, on the economic patronage of sugar daddies and pederasts. It's certainly the case that, for the benefit of sexual beings of all kinds, the ballet industry has continually exploited the sensual turn-on of kinetic bodies exhibited in space, engaged in subjects of artifice, ambiguity and transformation. Ballet thrives on displays of erotic objects, whether of 'girls' or 'boys', to use the dancers' own revealing vernacular; at the same time it is always offended when this is pointed out, for deception is its very motor. This staged seduction, though, could be found readily throughout commercial showbusiness, on which ballet's popularity was often dependent; both de Valois and Lopokova worked in pantomimes and revues. It was more the gold-braid world of the old Court Ballet that appealed to elitists like Keynes. They revelled in the rarefied combination of order, exclusiveness, deference and luxury. Despite the more democratic advances that had developed in dance through the years, Keynes and his kind craved to retain the absolutist hierarchy that ranked dancers in a pyramid of functions – *corps de ballet, coryphées, maître de ballet, prima ballerina assoluta* – which Stravinsky called 'the erogenous regiment'.

It was the fading world of imperial Russian ballet that drew Diaghilev towards dance in the first place. Diaghilev was not a dancer or a creative artist of any kind, or even a financial patron (other people paid his debts) – he was best described as 'a charismatic figurehead'. But the tubby layman's involvement with 'lyric theatre' defined a mode of gay disposition and patronage which has retained its grip on the world of dance, as witnessed by the devotional tone of the recent homages to Diaghilev set up in exhibition and concert form by the homosexual dilettante Sir John Drummond.

Keynes' temperament for ballet was fired by Diaghilev's example, but he went further than his companions by buying into the Diaghilev heritage through his unconsummated but congenial marriage to Lydia. Lopokova danced with the company far less than she liked people to believe – for a single season in 1910, then in 1916 when it visited the USA, where she'd been living for six years, and casually from 1918. She was one of many fine dancers who flitted in and out of the Diaghilev scene to form elsewhere a business network. Her English Lopokova-Massine Group of 1921–1923 employed Vera Sokolova (real name Hilda Munnings), Vera Savina (Vera Clarke), Anton Dolin (Patrick Healey-Kay) and Ninette de Valois (Edris Stannus). The first two had danced for Diaghilev and the latter two were about to do so;

he said that he liked English dancers because they were 'well-trained and dutiful'. De Valois signed a contract for two seasons, which Diaghilev declined to renew. She was replaced by the teenage pixie Alicia Markova (Alice Marks) who would encounter back in Britain a degree of backstage anti-Semitism; Lady Keynes commented on her 'wobbling Jewish feet'. Markova in turn would help to create the English National Ballet as a rival to the de Valois monolith.

Here was a reservoir of British dancing talent assisted by stern immigrant teachers who forged their livings from the daughters, hardly ever sons, of the well-to-do. Born in 1898 and still active at the time of writing, Ninette de Valois was propelled into dance by her pushy mother, whose husband was a lieutenant-colonel. Throughout her career de Valois has used military images to describe her tactics: 'I visualised the possibility of a sudden weakening – a position akin to that of an army, its lines stretched to a point where a breakthrough could be effected almost anywhere'. Doggedly ambitious, she set up at the age of twenty-eight her own dance studio in London which she loftily called the Academy of Choreographic Art. Several of her girls became the nucleus of the Vic-Wells Ballet, while her studio advanced into the Vic-Wells Ballet School. These improvements occurred because she came to the attention of the Old Vic's matriarch Lilian Baylis, who wanted in 1931 not only decent dancing for her dramas at the Old Vic but an opera company and a ballet group at her new sister theatre, Sadler's Wells (hence Vic-Wells). For this she started de Valois on £1 a week. Fees did not bother de Valois personally because she soon married a GP and back home in Sunningdale, Berkshire, she was known simply as Mrs Connell, the doctor's wife.

De Valois was an exacting teacher and a long-term strategist but a banal choreographer. Her creative skills worked better in the boardroom than they did on stage, which raises the issue that though prominent women such as de Valois have pioneered the growth of dance in Britain, it is not necessarily the artform itself they have advanced but the structures that have strengthened its promotion. In any case she developed her own company at the Islington theatre in an interesting time for ballet. The legacy of Diaghilev was being re-assessed. He, like others, had consistently commissioned new works in a period when audiences in all artforms relished 'novelties', but the economics of such a policy was becoming unsustainable without regular subsidy, especially during the Slump. Even though the Carnegie Trust supported the

Vic-Wells evolution, de Valois merely paid lip service to choreographic development by creating a number of dramatically crude works of her own devising; it was a lucky thing for British ballet that de Valois' competitor, Marie Rambert, was at this time cultivating the choreographic talents of Frederick Ashton (Ashton's name, by the way, was genuine even though he was born in Ecuador, while Rambert's wasn't: she was Cyvia Rambam).

The notion of ballet 'classics' was actually a new one, inspired in part by the policy of 're-interpretation' then carried out by the major Soviet companies at the Bolshoi and the Kirov. And just as the ballet industry was constructing a canon of 'classics', it had equally to fabricate a heritage of production, for none of the nineteenth-century works were recorded aside from the scenario and music – and that often in different versions. So when de Valois added what we would now call the 'classics' – *Coppélia, Giselle, The Nutcracker* – she did so in a piecemeal fashion with the help of Russian exiles who trawled their memories for the steps and positions they'd been taught; in this manner in 1934 Lopokova staged *The Nutcracker* for the Vic-Wells. De Valois admitted that such a resurrection 'was thought very old and extraordinary by a lot of the modern people because they didn't know [better]. They do now, we have no trouble. We have a proper classical audience – but we had to educate it at the beginning.'

While ballet is paraded to the public as the most orthodox of arts, it has relied wretchedly on the defective reminiscences of grizzled veterans. The rest is made up on the spot, the holes plugged with kinetic Polyfilla. Thus the conventional claim 'choreography by – or after – Petipa', or whoever they invoke, is one of the most misleading used in cultural promotion. There's a comical account in the *Dancing Times* from April 1965 of de Valois herself trying to revive a short piece she made in the thirties:

> It was surprising to find some middle-aged women occupying the floor. They were running about in short bursts, with knit brows and hands clasped over their heads, and appeared lost to the world . . . Festival Ballet were mounting *The Haunted Ballroom* and Dame Ninette called in her old Sadler's Wells dancers to help her . . .

Audiences and critics play along with this deception so long as it reinforces their own fancied notions of pedigree and heritage. To serve this retentive market de Valois developed her jerry-built repertoire, adding *Le Lac de Cygnes* in the mid-thirties (not called *Swan Lake* until the sixties: using French labels for Russian works was an affectation of Diaghilev exiles) and then *The Sleeping Princess* in 1939. Now known more readily as *The Sleeping Beauty* after its origin in the French tale of Perrault, *La Belle au Bois Dormant*, directors like de Valois then followed Diaghilev's snide conviction that some of his dancing princesses 'were not beauties'.

When Keynes saw this production at Sadler's Wells it delighted and depressed him. He was thrilled to watch a British company attempt this full-length work 'by Petipa', a perilous undertaking as it was chosen for a gala in honour of the French President at Covent Garden, attended by the royal family which included then two unsleeping princesses, Elizabeth and Margaret. The production was decidedly frayed due to the flimsy designs by Nadia Benois that she was constrained to throw together on a budget of tuppence. As the dance critic R.W. Manchester noted, 'It was handicapped from the start by a desperate shoddiness and by a poverty of design in the costumes which was nothing short of astonishing ... Even the Blue Birds weren't blue.' Yet the ballet itself conveyed to one 'friend of Diaghilev' an aching resonance.

In November 1921 Diaghilev had taken a sensational gamble and introduced to the West *The Sleeping Princess*, developed from the basic Petipa production of 1890. He premiered this extravaganza at London's Alhambra Music Hall, now the site of the Odeon Cinema in Leicester Square. Petipa's original Princess played the monster Carabosse for Diaghilev, and at a special gala the first Carabosse returned to his evil role; in this way Diaghilev invoked an inheritance. The staging was supervised by Nicholas Sergeyev, who later advised de Valois on her version with the help of his dubious notebooks.

At the Alhambra Lopokova played the humane Lilac Fairy who turns the death spell placed on Princess Aurora by Carabosse into a sleep of a hundred years. To some in the audience the evening felt as though they'd drowsed that long too, and despite passable houses the show folded in January 1922, losing a mass of money. Diaghilev fled London to evade bankruptcy, leaving behind the opulent sets and costumes of Leon Bakst. The gamble Diaghilev took, and lost on, lay in his nostalgia for the Russian Imperial style of his youth and his desire to reclaim the genre. Much of London found it lavish but passé, though to the aesthetes *The Sleeping*

Princess was nothing less than the summit of Diaghilev's achievement as 'a charismatic figurehead'.

Keynes visited the original Diaghilev production more than once and for him it expressed what he valued most in performance – a display of consummate technique, skilful artifice and graphic extravagance. It also delivered what he adored in art itself, by the dramatic depiction of the holistic culture of the royal court surviving the invasion of sexual evil. It heals itself through probity and optimism, all reflected through the filtering device of a romantic fable. When he saw de Valois' 'revival' of 1939 he realised how possible it could be to cultivate a classical ballet company in this country, one that would take up the challenge that Diaghilev had left in London in 1921.

He readily acknowledged to Lydia that the Sadler's Wells Theatre was no place to house such a venture, with its cramped stage, lousy acoustics and awkward location. The project deserved better and the conventional choice would have been the Royal Opera House in Covent Garden which had always been run privately or by syndicates. However, there were two problems. First, the Vic-Wells gala there in 1939 had been a farrago, exposing the inability of de Valois' ballet company to handle a real theatre with a proper stage; the issue of scale was about training and difficult to solve, though one that would need to be faced wherever the dancers went (and it was not only the stage: Sadler's Wells sat 1,500 while the Covent Garden's capacity was 2,200). Second, Beecham's insolvent operatic adventures there in the thirties had killed enthusiasm for further 'grand opera seasons'. The owners of the property were driven to lease the theatre to Mecca Cafés, who turned it into a deeply popular wartime dance hall. On enquiring about the details Keynes had been told that the lease ran for ten years from December 1939. There were other venues – the Lyceum nearly next door, Drury Lane's Theatre Royal – but none with the 'artistic echoes' of Covent Garden. He couldn't quite put his finger on the solution.

New York City furnished the answer. Lord and Lady Keynes visited the States no fewer than six times during and immediately after the war, five of those while he chaired the Council, and each trip lasted three months or so, as he crossed the Atlantic by liner each time:

1. *May–August 1941:* Washington DC, an exploratory visit

regarding Lend Lease funds from the USA to Britain. Keynes discussed Britain's needs with President Roosevelt.

2. *September–November 1943:* A conference 'hammering out the principles of post-war economy' which included talks about creating an International Monetary Fund and a World Bank.

3. *June–August 1944:* The Bretton Woods Conference, New Hampshire, where twenty-eight nations participated to agree to establish the IMF. Keynes suffered a heart attack; his contributions were applauded.

4. *September–December 1944:* Lend Lease Phase II, where the Americans desired Britain to aid them in their war with Japan.

5. *September–December 1945:* The new President, Hoover, called for the return of loans. Keynes went to 'beg' but he was 'over-confident and this led to grievous trouble', according to his biographer Harrod. The revised loan terms he achieved were quite inadequate.

6. *February–March 1946:* Savannah, Georgia. First meeting of the IMF and the World Bank.

This is the wartime schedule of a semi-invalid in his early sixties, under doctor's orders for his dicky heart, who was engaged fully at the Treasury, the Bank of England, and not least of all CEMA, where he chaired the Council and formally three panels. He kept in touch through the famous memos and wires Mary Glasgow complained about, with their exotic addresses – the United Kingdom Treasury Delegation, Box 680, Washington DC; via Treasury Chambers, Great George Street, SW1; Office of the High Commissioner for the UK, Earnsville, Ottawa.

It was the second trip in the autumn of 1943 that provided him with the remedy to the opera house problem. Time was allowed for the conference guests holed up in Washington DC to enjoy monstrous hospitality and sightseeing, including two visits to that vast theatre named New York City. Lydia introduced her husband to an entire *kolkhoz* of expatriate Russian and Diaghilev dancers there. One was Boris Romanoff (1891–1957) who ran the New Metropolitan Opera Ballet. It was new only because the old one had been disbanded in 1935 by an enterprising but overly optimistic manager to make way for the American Ballet under Balanchine. This outfit provided dances for the operas over three seasons until the Met's famous 'horseshoe brigade', elderly hostesses of the kind parodied all too easily in Marx Brothers films, complained about Balanchine's 'modernistic tendencies'.

Romanoff had danced for Diaghilev in the early days but knew exactly what the Margaret Dumonts of Manhattan wanted and gave it to them with cream on top. He told Keynes that a ballet company would never succeed on its own as long as its schedule was decided by an opera company, and that the only solution was to have two ballet companies tied to an opera house – a 'real' company that 'the opera management must leave alone' and an 'opera ballet' group for them to boss around. Further, Keynes would find it was the dancers that 'will make money for the opera house, while the opera singers will lose it, always'.

At this time New York City was run by as near a socialist administration as you could muster in America, headed by Mayor La Guardia (mayor from 1933 to 1945) who was actually a Republican. He invited the conference delegates to look around his latest cultural success, the City Center of Music and Drama. This old freemason facility on 55th Street, between 6th and 7th Avenues, contained a 2,800-seat auditorium. Home of the Masonic Shriners, it had been taken over by the city authorities for two reasons: the freemasons owed a stack of back taxes and, conveniently for City Hall, they were not, according to the statutes, using the place for which they secured possession, that is, public gatherings of a cultural or religious nature. The building had been known up to that point as the Mecca Temple. It was this simple little name that gave Keynes a clue to the solution he needed. In the end he tried to transpose the city's method of acquisition from Manhattan's Mecca Temple to Covent Garden's Mecca Ballroom.

Mayor La Guardia wanted the Mecca Temple turned into a theatre to provide 'cultural entertainment at popular prices'. Opening with a special concert by the New York Philharmonic Orchestra, the Center continued with Gertrude Lawrence in a play, a new musical by Kurt Weill, then the premiere of *Carmen Jones*. Most popular of all was an ensuing revue called *The Seven Lively Arts*, an assemblage featuring new music from Cole Porter, Stravinsky (*Scènes de Ballets*) and Benny Goodman, including dance for the Stravinsky from Alicia Markova partnered by Anton Dolin. The Lord and Lady saw this show on their fourth trip, their noses turned up against its 'vulgarity'. Though Keynes had little interest in the populist aesthetic that governed the City Center's policy, he was completely taken with the mechanics of acquisition and subsidy. It helped that the chief administrator was a money man.

Morton Baum was as tall as Keynes, more tactful and better dressed. As a successful tax lawyer of a certain age he was able to maintain his business as it suited him while giving his time to the City Center voluntarily. Keynes was impressed, not only by Baum's personal approach but also the city authority's 'admirable sense' in recruiting a business man to run a major theatre. In Baum's plan the initial city subsidy beyond the capital restoration costs covered the theatre's overheads, while a percentage of the box office was divided between publicity and a 'commitments fund' placed on deposit account to cover future administration calls; a share of performance profits would build a reserve.

Keynes liked this sort of stuff very much indeed. The need to meet the long-term demands of the theatre was built into its opening phase, with a goal of self-sufficiency. This practical model endorsed his view that subsidy could be treated as investment. He went back to a war-ravaged Britain convinced that he could turf Mecca Cafés out on a technicality and that the future manager of the Opera House must be a business man. Unpleasant though it is, by the way, to spoil a story, Morton Baum had spun Keynes a line and the City Center soon lurched into a string of crises.

Chapter 8

The twilight of the sods

Boosey & Hawkes • E.J. Dent
The Floorwalker • Death to Hollywood
The Sleeping Beauty

At a 'tiresome' Manhattan party late in 1943 Sir Thomas
Beecham met the Keyneses. The maverick conductor was
over there making money and enemies at the Met. Among the
neutral line of chatter adopted by people who can't get on but
have to, the knight probed the Lord and Lady about progress in
London and, according to Beecham, Maynard Keynes 'wittered
on non-committally' about his hopes for a national opera house
and what a shame it was that Covent Garden was a dance hall for
the next decade, and so on. Beecham became suspicious. The
next decade? Keynes also predicted that the war with Germany
would end within the year, though he wasn't sure about the one
with Japan.

He also didn't know as much as Beecham did about the Royal
Opera House. Its lease had been handed to Mecca Cafés by the
Second Covent Garden Property Company Ltd, whose chairman
was a Beecham vassal called Philip Hill. A director of Beecham's
Pills, Eno's Fruit Salts, Maclean's Toothpaste and Timothy White's
the chemists, Hill had sat on Beecham's Covent Garden board in
the thirties. He was basically a property analyst with aesthetic
rather than medicinal leanings. Following the encounter with
Keynes, Beecham wired Hill to check on the details of the lease.
He learned to his delight that it was not precisely what Keynes had

assumed. The lease stood for five years, 19 December 1939 to 19 December 1944, renewable for another five 'unless the theatre was required for its original use'. Beecham, whose bankruptcy prevented him trading, persuaded Hill he'd learned that there was a strong chance of the Government subsidising the place as a national opera centre and Hill should get the 'vested interests' in place to take over the lease by next December and turn the dance hall back into the kind of international opera house that would meet the needs of a world-class chap like . . . well, like Beecham.

Philip Hill didn't know where best to turn, for Beecham hadn't a clue how the war had changed Britain. The aristocracy no longer had the means to sustain through exorbitant subscriptions the kind of sparkling international seasons Beecham had presented in the thirties – in fact, that had become increasingly clear even then – and Christie had already commandeered what was left over.

There were other types of 'vested interests', though, such as the music industry. Hill started with Harold Holt (1885–1953). Holt was a successful South African concert agent based in London who had taken his 20 per cent cut out of soloists such as Menuhin and singers like Melba and Gigli, supplying stars for Beecham's Covent Garden seasons. He protested to Hill that though he was keen he hadn't the means, as selling international artists in wartime was more restricting than rewarding, but he wondered about two of his fellow board directors, Leslie Boosey and Ralph Hawkes.

They were certainly vested interests. Their publishing firm of Boosey & Hawkes had acquired the worldwide rights in 1943 to the music of a German composer regarded by many as the finest living writer of operas, Richard Strauss, whom Beecham had first championed at Covent Garden. Closer still, Holt pointed out, the couple had an American subsidiary, the Boosey & Hawkes Artists Bureau, that just happened to manage Beecham and his latest girl-friend, a well-oiled pianist. Even better, the Hawkes wind instruments factory in Edgware had been converted to a wartime munition works which would have done well enough by now to allow a few bob to be injected into something a little more peaceful, if such a thing was possible with Beecham involved.

Though Leslie Boosey carried extra clout as chairman of the powerful Performing Right Society, which was mandated to issue licences and collect royalties from performances of music, Hawkes was the driving force of the firm. He signed up the young pup Benjamin Britten on an exclusive deal in 1935, five years after his business had amalgamated with the ballad-mongers Boosey & Co., and he developed a roster of living composers such as Aaron Copland, Prokofiev and later Stravinsky – all of whom wrote ballet music. Hawkes also gave jobs to four executives thrown out of Austria when the Nazis took over the Vienna publisher Kalmus, and through them acquired the exiled composer Bartók. Aside from sheer altruism, then, there was a solid business reason for helping to establish an active lyric theatre in London. But helping was not the same as supervising, and that they declined to do.

By now Keynes was back in Britain and he contacted Philip Hill, who he did not otherwise know, to find out if there was anything in the Mecca lease on the issue of use that he might manipulate in the manner of Mayor La Guardia. Hill volunteered the whole story and Keynes, galvanised, invited Boosey and Hawkes to lunch. Keynes wanted a lease, not Boosey and Hawkes, and strictly speaking there was no reason why CEMA shouldn't pick it up. However, the Treasury guideline on acquisition, which Glasgow stumbled on, had discouraged that. Though Keynes could have challenged it he knew that the Covent Garden issue could be a controversial one as long as Beecham was implicated and he preferred the easy option 'on the lines of the Bristol model'. Thus he needed Boosey and Hawkes to be his metal merchants and acquire the lease so that he could set up a trust to sublet the theatre. Explaining this over lunch, he added his City Center ruse that Mecca couldn't invoke its renewal clause because B & H, unlike Mecca, were 'using the theatre for its original purpose'. Hawkes was no dunce and spotted the flaw: they were not using it for its original purpose, they were not using it for any purpose at all, they were merely middlemen. Keynes reckoned that Mecca would not spot this. Then Keynes pulled out his handgun.

He did not want Sir Thomas Beecham involved. Keynes swore that no government subsidy would come the way of Covent Garden if that 'crook' barged in. Amazed by his audacity, the publishers asked who he had in mind to run the place and what he proposed to put on. Keynes replied he wanted a businessman to manage it and the rest would be determined through committee. It was clear to them that Keynes wasn't sure what he wanted, only what he didn't want. Up to this point the publishers had assumed that Keynes was really looking for a home for the Vic-Wells twins of opera and ballet. Though he talked with enthusiasm about de Valois' company, he floundered on the subject of opera, evoking the international seasons of Beecham but seemingly unaware that the Vic-Wells sang solely in English. Hawkes recommended Glyndebourne as an alternative; it had brilliant management, impressive casts, international standards. According to Glasgow, Keynes added, 'And an imbecile of a proprietor. What goes for Beecham goes for Christie.' The lunch ended on this liberal, Keynesian note. Boosey and Hawkes left wondering who would be worse to work with – the knight, the captain or the lord.

Before they had time to decide, the captain called them to his table. Christie had heard of the affair through Harold Holt and so invited Boosey, Hawkes and Holt to dinner with his manager, Rudolf Bing, at the Café Royal. Despite the war, it's said they sipped their way through a magnum of champagne while Christie outlined his plan, which the publishers considered perceptive and far more vivid than Keynes' feeble bluster. Christie would buy the freehold, keep his Glyndebourne season through the summer while Covent Garden carried dance and run three brief seasons of opera in the autumn, winter and spring with a Christmas ballet. He was also willing to tackle the unmentionable – the standards of English singing and conducting and the need to build a proper company – by a strategy of developing the repertoire.

Covent Garden would be known as the People's Opera House, starting its artistic ascent with operetta. If Keynes would not provide subsidy Christie didn't care because he would go directly to the Government with a scheme to raise one million subscriptions each of £10, beginning with members of the Cabinet. Boosey and Hawkes couldn't fault the policy, only the balance sheet. However impressed they were with Christie, and probably more with Bing who they guessed lay behind the measured repertory plan, his financial scheme only served to remind them of the enormous scale of the enterprise and their belief that the Government would have to support it, forever and ever.

Philip Hill advised them to do what was best for their business and go where the money was. The lease they would acquire ran for five years, which is more than Beecham would last if he headed the House. Christie had a terrific team and perhaps they could be poached, but the man himself was a maniac and though he had resources and a mailing list of millionaires, charity began at home and he'd never subordinate Glyndebourne; no one could run two opera houses fifty miles apart on private wealth. Keynes was the chap with the big, blank cheque book and the only one with power to keep the thing running longer than the lease. So they wrote directly to the Treasury and received a written assurance that, should they assist CEMA, financial support would be forthcoming as Keynes had promised (and few doubted that Keynes himself drafted that reply). Thus at CEMA's twenty-ninth meeting in late July 1944:

> The Chairman reported progress in the negotiations for the acquisition of the Opera House by Messrs. Boosey and Hawkes. The lease had now been signed and the firm would take possession in January 1945. The arrangements had been discussed informally at a meeting of himself, Sir Stanley Marchant, the Music and Drama Directors, Mr. Boosey, Mr. Hawkes and Mr. Harold Holt. As a result a small policy-framing committee of himself, Sir Stanley, Mr. Boosey, Mr. Hawkes, and Mr. Holt had been set up. It was unfortunate that a statement had been issued to the press by the Boosey & Hawkes firm giving the names as members of a new 'Committee of Management'.

Unfortunate it was. Several columnists pointed out there was not a single artist on the committee. Kenneth Clark had been cosily added to the trust and he quickly suggested William Walton should be brought in as their token composer. This was an aesthetic and political mistake. Walton had become an increasingly reactionary loner, on the creative wane. His dislike of competitors, especially 'the nancy boys' Benjamin Britten and the young turk Michael Tippett, would prove unhelpful to the genesis of the opera house, especially when we consider the tally of sizeable operas written by them respectively: Britten seven, Tippett five, Walton one. But Clark was close to Walton, who was knobbing Clark's wife, the alcoholic Jane, with his encouragement. A second problem with the published list lay in its omission of two names almost everyone had expected to see there: Christie and Beecham.

Christie, naturally, took the opportunity to publicise in *The Times* his ideas for a people's opera house. Given Christie's lack of enthusiasm for 'the mob', this sudden support for 'the people' sounds as though war and those munchkin evacuees at Glyndebourne had socialised the squire. However, People's Opera is a very literal translation of the German term 'Volksoper', meaning at root a company that performs popular opera, operetta and now even musicals. For an opera house that has to build standards, repertoire and an audience, this is a perfectly sensible starting point. Yet neither CEMA nor the committee would listen to Christie. He wrote to the Chancellor of the Exchequer (in fact, he wrote to almost everyone of influence) complaining that 'Keynes refuses to see me, and I believe that he is in there, with the satisfaction of the Treasury, in order to keep me out.'

Esher, the Old Vic chairman who had now joined the Council, raised the matter of Christie's omission: 'The Chairman said that Mr Christie's name had duly been considered but that the Committee had decided against inviting him. Lord Esher said he was glad to know it was not the C.E.M.A. representatives who had opposed Mr. Christie's election.' Those CEMA representatives had not needed to say a word. The next Council meeting in September was chaired by K. Clark while Keynes counted beans at Bretton Woods. Though the group was inquorate, with only three other members present (Ivor Brown, Esher, James Bridie), they approved the following: the addition to the Covent Garden Committee of Sam Courtauld and Professor Edward Dent, the confirmation of Keynes as chairman of it, and his written request for CEMA to create a ring-fenced allocation of £25,000 for Covent Garden as part of the Treasury grant for the year 1945–1946.

The inclusion of the outrageous Professor Dent was entirely political, demanded by the Old Vic's Esher, and though it proved a worrying appointment for Keynes, out of Dent's bolshiness sprang English National Opera. E.J. Dent (1876–1957) is admired today for his books about operas, especially on Mozart. Back then he was considered a 'poofter' and bitch of the first order. Like Christie he was the wealthy son of an MP, like Keynes he was sired at Eton and King's, and like Vaughan Williams he was in imminent need of an ear trumpet. His contentious tenure as music professor in Keynes' 'pocket borough' of Cambridge from 1926 to 1941 concluded only when he had reached the age of retirement and returned to London to earn a living translating foreign operas. An obituary records that Dent, as a left-leaning atheist, 'delighted in uttering outrageous opinions about music that he felt had been accepted with unthinking reverence. His delight would increase if he knew he thereby shocked the respectable – especially if they were clergymen or women.' He was a forerunner of those academics whose knowledge seems to stretch effortlessly from mediaeval music to the avant-garde until you realise they've simply locked the nineteenth century out of their minds, and thus he could cope with the presidency of the old Royal Musical Association and the new International Society for Contemporary Music at one and the same time. As he made his money out of translations, it's hardly surprising that he preferred opera companies in England to sing in English.

On the Covent Garden Committee he represented that part of the Vic-Wells group recently renamed the Sadler's Wells Opera Company on the pretext that the Vic was closed and anyway the opera and ballet companies had their home at the Sadler's Wells Theatre, even though thanks to the war this was no longer the case; the public muddle over titles would carry on like this for years. It was Dent's defence of Sadler's Wells and what it stood for that explains one of the most puzzling developments in British opera. A future chairman of the Royal Opera House, Lord Drogheda, summed it up when he wrote:

> The Sadler's Wells Ballet Company was moved into Covent Garden as its permanent home ... It has never been clear to me whether the question of the Sadler's Wells Opera Company also being transferred to Covent Garden was raised, or, if it was, why it was not pursued ... they had a degree of professionalism lacking elsewhere. Much time could have been saved, and many subsequent difficulties avoided, had Sadler's Wells Opera also been included in the plan.

Keynes, as we've seen, was quite out of his depth with opera but he refused to bring into Covent Garden those with swimming certificates. While Dent had a clear grasp of operatic issues, he was mainly concerned to defend the position of Sadler's Wells. It was more than a question of operas in the local language against operas in their original languages, or the training of British singers to project properly, act and gain the proficiency to compete in the international market. Dent believed that the operatic form, even the comedies of Rossini, presented 'case studies in man's deepest desires and profound obligations' and it was essential that everyone in the nation should have the opportunity 'to experience its power and intelligence'. He feared that Keynes' Covent Garden would merely revive with the advantage of subsidy the 'vapid international seasons of yesteryear', based on the fame of the singers rather than the merit of the operas themselves, together with the imposition of artificially high ticket prices as a means of controlling the character of the audience. More practically he considered the transfer of the de Valois dancers as nothing less than asset-stripping. Between July and December 1945 the ballet company at the re-opened Sadler's Wells Theatre made a £9,000 surplus above estimates at the box office, while the value of the company in grant terms was an annual £15,000. The sets were being passed on to Covent Garden at cost price, such as £416 for de Valois' ballet *The Rake's Progress*. Keynes had learned from the Met's ballet director how far opera houses relied on ballet to balance the books.

That apart, Dent detested Keynes' snobbish obsession with tactics to attract the rich into Covent Garden while refusing to give time to discounted ticket schemes. Keynes was keen to use a seven-year covenant formula to encourage the wealthy to take up seats and boxes in return for charitable donations, not unlike Christie's £10 plan. It was really a fiddle for them to dodge surtax as Lord Drogheda remembers:

> Since tax on the top slice of a rich person's income was levied at a rate of 97.5%, the true cost to those on the highest income tax bracket of an annual donation of for instance £1,000 was no more than £25.

But Labour came to power in August 1945 and in his subsequent April 1946 budget, Hugh Dalton, alerted as Chancellor and thus arts minister to Keynes' intentions, withdrew the surtax concession. 'The true cost to the taxpayer of giving £1,000 instead of a mere £25 would be more than £500.' Keynes' scheme was shattered. Someone asked him why Dalton had done it. He replied, 'Hatred'. He must have recognised that hatred in Dent, too, who put it on record that he resented the time wasted on these kinds of 'clever but improbable' ploys to seduce tycoons. He reminded the committee that they would be using the Sadler's Wells name to sell shows and that Lilian Baylis had built up the Vic-Wells group as part of her crusade to educate 'ordinary people in their own language'. To avoid confusion he wished to rename the Sadler's Wells company the National English Opera, a title chosen to maintain Baylis's objectives. He wrote about it in 1945:

> If we had a National Opera in English on a level with what the Vienna Imperial and National Opera used to be in its own language, the position of a *Volksoper* at Sadler's Wells might be humble, but it would not be humiliating, as it is bound to be if the old doctrine is revived that Society can only be seen as opera in a foreign language.
>
> If on the other hand the doors of Covent Garden were to reopen once more to an 'international season', we know what would

happen. No doubt all the most marvellous stars in the firmament would be engaged to appear there; how much rehearsing they would do is a different matter. And there would always be a certain number of our own singers thankful to be allowed to sing the smallest parts for the sake of 'prestige' conferred by that historic house, just as all sorts of ridiculous people would be ready to waste money on boxes and stalls because they think they would be getting 'into Society' ... [You] may say that I am talking nonsense, but I know the history of opera in this country, however ignorant I may be of economics.

Dent's closing dig was aimed not only at Keynes but also the businessman who'd been found to run the place, David Webster (1903–1971). Generally described as short, plump and soft-featured, Lord Drogheda commented that 'one felt that he had never seemed young'. Drogheda added:

> He had a maddening habit of drumming his fingers on the table if he was put out about something, and he tended to whistle a tune *sotto voce* if there was a lull in the conversation and he felt ill at ease.

As a student of economics at Liverpool University, Webster had joined amateur dramatic and operatic societies, involving himself eventually with dance when he and his boyfriend helped others to set up the Liverpool Ballet Club in 1935, where Ninette de Valois met him; she was invited there once a year to stage bits of 'classics'. He also fancied himself as a critic and reviewed the odd concert for a local paper. Beecham's activities were loyally followed in Merseyside, coming as he did from St Helens, so when he conducted a rare production of Delius's *Koanga* at Covent Garden, Webster went and wrote a notice which berated Sir Thomas. Beecham, who knew his Liverpool, wrote to the paper: 'And who is this David Webster? I insist that all copies of the offending newspaper be burned on St George's Steps, and Mr Webster with them.'

In his day job Webster managed the Bon Marché department store. At the outbreak of the war he advanced to the position of general manager of the Liverpool Lewis's and coincidentally chairman of the Liverpool Philharmonic Society, where he contracted the orchestra into CEMA's factory concerts scheme under his conductor-in-chief Malcolm Sargent, thereby giving it permanence. K. Clark paid a courtesy call on him to discuss this daring development following a visit to his North Wales cave full of National Gallery paintings, and in this way Webster went on meeting by chance and one by one the characters who would determine his operatic future.

In 1942 Lord Woolton, who owned Lewis's, had him seconded to the Ministry of Supply where he was given the task of introducing sordid time-management schemes and ploys to root out slackers in ordnance factories. On a snooping visit to a factory in Edgware he met its owner, Mr Hawkes. So when Keynes asked for names of businessmen with a working knowledge of the arts, David Webster's name cropped up and, said Glasgow, everyone went, 'Ah, yes, Webster'. A cousin of Hawkes happened to be one of Webster's friends, and it was he who approached him, which is how these things were done in those days – and continue to be done. That is simply how, when a wise board would have snapped up Bing, the general manager of Lewis's in Lime Street became the general administrator of Covent Garden. Though they deliberately ignored Webster's want of familiarity with opera and ballet, they failed to discern a major flaw in his behaviour: he was a bone-idle prevaricator.

Vaughan Williams, locked out of the negotiations, felt on principle that a businessman running an arts institution meant that 'artistic common sense' would be sacrificed 'on the altar of economics', and quipped that if Webster made a mess of the opera house he was trained well enough to slip around the corner to Covent Garden market 'and land a job on a fruit stall'. Beecham later went one, or two, better in a widely reported crack which struck not only at the businessman's lack of operatic nous and the House's policy then of doing operas in English, but also Webster's bent: 'You know, I was walking past Covent Garden the other day and saw, to my great surprise, that they were actually announcing *The Twilight of the Sods*. It's about time.'

Keynes was confident that David Webster would work wonders and open the Royal Opera House in time for the end of the war, which he had predicted would finish well by Christmas 1944. Sad as it is to report, the war didn't live up to Keynes' expectations. Webster had to kill time by setting up a new budget system for CEMA after the first finance director was sacked (what an agreeable induction to offer to your closest client). Meanwhile Mecca didn't quit Covent Garden. As Ralph Hawkes had suspected Mecca Cafés contested the lease by arguing that Boosey and Hawkes would not be presenting opera. Keynes, frustrated, fell back on the La Guardia method and was forced to use a ridiculous manoeuvre based on the site's original 'convent garden'. The area was owned by the Dukes of Bedford and in a deal with one of them in the 1850s, a box in the theatre's auditorium, the Bedford Box no less, was given to the family in perpetuity including, it was put to Mecca, the land beneath it. Boosey and Hawkes signed the five-year lease but allowed Mecca to carry on with its dance hall until September 1945, from where Mecca moved down the street to the Lyceum.

Meanwhile the committee reformed itself as the Covent Garden Trust. Keynes stayed in charge. That Covent Garden's first chairman concurrently headed the Arts Council was then considered clever rather than venal. Though Keynes possessed total power he felt increasingly insecure as he realised the depth of detail the decisions on opera demanded, the number of quacks all too willing to offer advice and the quantity of critics ready to spot a slip-up. The time spent in America made it no easier, and he tended to give and then take back control to and from the most spirited specialists on the Trust, Dent and Hawkes.

Hawkes simply wanted to see the project work and was dismayed by the suffocating limits Keynes had imposed on fundamental factors like the selection of staff, while at the same time his chairman was inarticulate on artistic policy. Dent had entered swinging his longsword, converting the rest to his cause that the Royal Opera House had a national role – not only to boost opera in English but develop English opera itself. He cultivated a rapport with Webster to promote his aims, telling a friend, 'I am encouraging his self-confidence and love of power because I want to be one of the experts whose advice he takes.'

When the trustees came to discuss the opening production it was ironic that, though they desired to open the House with an English opera, they couldn't at first think of one. Boosey and Hawkes felt unable to press the fact that their composer Benjamin Britten had been commissioned in America to write *Peter Grimes*, which would become the most successful English opera of this century; it had been made available by them to Sadler's Wells. Dent won the Trust over instead with Purcell's *King Arthur*. Keynes didn't consider that good box office but Dent lured him with the varied dances that would show off the ballet company. In any case nothing came of it.

Keynes sought to be useful instead by advancing the association between dance in Britain and Russia to fill the House's agenda. He wanted a major Soviet ballet company to take a residency at Covent Garden. Nothing came of this either. He introduced himself to the USSR Deputy Commissar for Culture in this colourful way:

> Dear Mr. Stepanov,
> In London I am the Chairman of the Council for the Encouragement of Music and the Arts. This is a State authority financed by the Treasury which has been created during the war for the purpose of assisting drama, ballet, opera, music and the arts. It is the kind of State cultural establishment which you have known in Russia . . . So I can almost boast that I am Commissioner for Fine Arts in my country!

The Trust had already agreed that there'd be separate executives for opera and ballet under Webster's control, but it was left to Dent to caution them that there were two main jobs in an opera house – artistic and administrative – and two more jobs in opera, one of which delivered the music and the other the production. Accepting this division, which was not common to every major opera house, they stressed the need for a music director, having got nowhere with the incontestable candidate to head productions, Glyndebourne's Carl Ebert. Ebert stipulated that Bing be appointed general administrator and that the Royal Opera House should make its peace with Glyndebourne. He mentioned that Christie had found a high-flying music director for Covent Garden as a substitute for Glyndebourne's Fritz Busch, who was now working in the States. The young man's name was Herbert von Karajan. The Allies had banned him from taking jobs because he'd been a notable Nazi. Whatever was the Keynesian way of saying 'piss off', the Chairman expressed it to Ebert.

Keynes had already insisted that the inebriated time-beater known to his musicians as Incontinent Lambert should continue in his position as music director of Sadler's Wells Ballet. For opera they decided to consider other British conductors. Keynes wouldn't have Beecham, Webster had seen enough of Sargent, Marchant didn't rate Barbirolli (though he was by far the best around), Walton pondered Boult, while Hawkes suggested Eugène Goossens (1893–1962). He'd written operas for Covent Garden, directed the Carl Rosa Opera Company and was developing a wartime reputation in the States. Webster wired him in

Cincinnati to which he cabled, 'EXTREMELY INTERESTED COVENT GARDEN'. From then on Webster's pathological sluggishness ground negotiations down, his behaviour to Goossens being typical of that to others they contacted through the years, including the hallowed Bruno Walter. It took three months for Webster to reply to Goossens, overlooking basic details like salary and length of contract. Goossens replied instead to Hawkes, with all manner of misgivings, starting with Webster's tactless claim that good English singers were 'not well schooled in opera':

> Either their place must be taken by the foreign artist (with imperfect English diction) – thus defeating the main idea of the project – or else that whole idea of opera in English must be abandoned . . . Blame for the shortcomings of a production as well as credit for its good points should fall on the shoulders of a single individual – the artistic director . . . Webster's letter has finally made me realise that I cannot safely undertake the responsibility for a project the artistic outcome of which I cannot foresee and consequently take full musical responsibility for.

This was the common reflex of those with practical experience in opera.

Keynes made an interesting response to Hawkes by parading Dent's impact on policy: 'This is very disappointing . . . [Goossens] does not grasp or sufficiently appreciate that our purpose, whilst including the traditional repertory, is something rather different, namely, to build up an English opera that has its own traditions and standards.' Nebulous stuff, though it's clear Keynes considered that de Valois' ballet provided a blueprint for the opera company in the construction of 'its own traditions and standards'. There were three problems: English opera's de Valois was Beecham, Sadler's Wells had rejected any further asset-stripping, and though the Austro-German exiles of Glyndebourne would offer a similar, if not superior, service to that de Valois had relied on from Russians, Keynes had himself vetoed any association with them.

None of these obstacles was overcome, and when a faux-native opera company was finally introduced to the Royal Opera House in 1947 it did so with fabulous irony under a hack Austrian chosen for reasons described by K. Clark: 'David Webster didn't really know the field and would not turn to anyone who could advise him in case he would be overshadowed. He chose as Musical Director a minor figure called Karl Rankl.' One by one the aims

Keynes avowed all too easily were junked, until the Royal Opera House accomplished exactly what Dent had dreaded by selling out to singers and society. Dent's status didn't suffer for he was still a director of Sadler's Wells Opera, which scored a sensational victory when it gave the world premiere of Britten's *Peter Grimes* at Sadler's Wells Theatre on 7 June 1945. The very next morning opera houses in Sweden and Switzerland asked for contracts to perform it. 'First blood!' roared Britten's publisher, Ralph Hawkes. Two years later Covent Garden would seek permission to do *Peter Grimes* too, with the Sadler's Wells originals.

Covent Garden's security depended on CEMA's endurance, yet Keynes saw it the other way round. He told Mary Glasgow that it was his assurances to Rab Butler on the nurturing of a national opera house that safeguarded CEMA and gave it permanence, and that it was the principal concern of CEMA to protect its 'sister', for if one went the other would too, 'like the ravens in the Tower of London, though I hope more tuneful'. Glasgow wondered which represented the ravens, which the Tower. It was in order to guard the Royal Opera House that Keynes was concerned to buttress CEMA's legality and fiscal strength; its authority by means of a royal charter, its brawn through a five-year rolling grant. To mark this stability he wanted to scrub the organisation of its bomb-shelter smell.

Mary Glasgow, as keen as Keynes to cast off the wartime tone of CEMA's image, toyed with alternative names. 'Council' persisted throughout her substitutes, as did 'Arts'; both were legally essential. In one of her rare flights of diplomacy she asked for contributions. 'Music and the Arts' was a description backed by the art panel for some reason, but not by the music advisers. Although it was an obvious and preferred first choice, all agreed that 'National' could not be used as it would only give Christie another chance to claim that they had stolen his ideas. 'United Kingdom' was workable for the remarkable reason that the Northern Ireland Government had set up a CEMA (Northern Ireland) from 1 April 1944 with a skimpy grant of £4,300. However, CEMA (everywhere else) argued that the sister organisation would need to have its aid routed through London, which rules precluded; in truth the London CEMA couldn't be bothered with the province. After full and separate committees were established at the end of the war for Wales and Scotland, this routing principle would rankle for decades. Meanwhile, CEMA (Northern

Ireland) survived until the mid-1960s, from when it gave itself the worst-sounding acronym in the world of culture, ACNI (the Arts Council of Northern Ireland).

'Britain', 'the British Isles', or 'England, Scotland and Wales' were offered by the Gallic James Bridie as the only alternatives to the traditional 'Great Britain' – in fact he sarcastically suggested 'Scotland, Wales and England (in that order, so that you can't SEW an acronym, or have you considered "Scotland Etcetera"?)'. Vaughan Williams had proposed 'Council for the Promotion of the Arts ... or Development', but both Glasgow and Keynes vetoed words which suggested the Council might actually do anything – 'it will only allow critics to say we're not'. The Secretary-General and her Chairman were equally at one to ensure that whatever acronym emerged from the title, it would be utterly unpronounceable.

Keynes, echoing Christie, desired the 'Royal Council for the Arts' and he would have forced this through despite 'muttering around the table' had he not been thwarted by regal red tape.

Buckingham Palace courtiers pointed out that these things involved issues of precision, interpretation, discrimination and therefore required a great deal of time. Keynes, on the other hand, wanted his RCA set up for the opening of the Opera House in 1945. Advised that it would take up to two years if he insisted on using 'Royal', he calculated that in the intervening time the war's Coalition Government would be dissolved and that he must establish CEMA's permanence while 'our friends are at the same addresses'. As a title, then, 'The Arts Council of Great Britain' was ranked second best, but no one could fault its monogrammed frightfulness.

It's commonly supposed that the Arts Council was a child of Labour. Some remain confused whether it was born in 1945 when its permanence was announced, or 1946 when it was finally incorporated through its royal charter; whichever, the period was that of Clement Attlee's Labour Government. Though we now know that the organisation was established in December 1939 and the change between Keynes' CEMA and Keynes' Arts Council amounted to an acronym, the Arts Council was in fact authorised and proclaimed by the Conservative Government's Chancellor, Sir John Anderson, in a parliamentary answer on 12 June 1945. On that date the Government was spotlessly Tory, as the coalition had been broken to provoke a general election, though Anderson himself was a Scottish Independent, whatever that meant in those days.

CEMA itself was created by an emergency government dominated by Conservatives and nurtured through the war by Rab Butler. The executive body had been chaired by two Liberal campaigners together with a Tory judge. Its small Council contained a working Conservative MP, and in the six and a half years up to its change of name, its support for the exhibitions of Bill Williams' British Institute of Adult Education was as advanced as it got.

Even the Pilgrim period was orthodox in its pursuit of animateurism. CEMA focused on traditionalist forms such as voluntary play groups, communal exhibitions, choirs and orchestras; the support for adult education emphasised 'courses and talks in appreciation and interpretation'. Despite the progressive models realised in other countries, especially the United States, its programme generally dealt with performance and performers rather than creativity itself, or equivalently the relation of professional and even 'non-professional' artists to the public. There is a consistency of approach, then, when Keynes took over: creativity – through commissions, production development, residencies, bursaries, workshops – was disregarded. He didn't stop the Old Vic performing in mining villages, though he did prefer them to play at traditional theatres in city centres. Nor did he block all of the music workers, though he introduced a more centralised regulation of their activities and continually questioned their economic value.

Among the inconsistencies, capricious acts and reactionary aspirations that mark the Keynes period, one of the most curious aspects was his call for 'Englishness'. After all, here was an economist devoted to the erection of international support systems, leading an arts organisation he had dedicated to the constructing and strengthening of classical paradigms, those models based on the dominant cultural practices of imperial Germany and Russia. This reflected if anything the thirties immigration of talent educated and employed in those systems, not 'Englishness'.

Such a paradox helps to explain why, when he was offered a practical option of the 'national' Sadler's Wells Opera Company or the 'international' Glyndebourne to provide services to his national opera house, Keynes could choose neither. He and his appointees let the opera schedule stay unfilled until a year and a half after his death when adverse criticism forced the issue, though to no one's advantage apart from the agents of singing

stars. Even David Webster used 'Englishness' as an excuse for
lethargy when he wrote in an Arts Council bulletin of 1946:

> Those who regret that Covent Garden is not opening with opera
> should reflect on two points. First, that it augurs well for the new
> regime at Covent Garden that its first company should be one
> whose dancers and choreographers are British [not entirely true]
> . . . Secondly, that to prepare an Opera company largely British in
> personnel, of a quality in any way worthy of the singing traditions of
> Covent Garden takes time . . . While foreigners will not be excluded
> from the company, British artists will be given first chance; that
> operas will be given in English; that every encouragement will be
> given to our composers.

He added, incidentally, that 'prices will be reasonable'.

When talking or writing about CEMA, Keynes increasingly used
commonplace images of Englishness. It's understandable during
a war that this should be so. Britain was isolated in 1941 and the
image of a united, uninvaded island was fostered by the Ministry of
Information. Yet the period during which Keynes governed CEMA
was one in which bonds with wartime allies and the Commonwealth were amplified, while Keynes' work in America (negotiating cash for Britain's needs) must have made him conscious of the
strengthening grip of the United States on Britain's cultural
scene. America's Lend Lease aid amounted to US$49 billion for
Britain and the Commonwealth, China and the USSR, and in
order to reduce the amount owed, Britain counted pennies in a
system of Reverse Lend Lease that operated fully once the
Americans were stationed in the country.

CEMA was brought prominently into Reverse Lend Lease, and
not only through a calculation of how many Americans visited its
subsidised promotions. 'MEMBERS OF THE AMERICAN FORCES ARE
WELCOME TO ATTEND CEMA EVENTS' was a slogan stamped onto
posters and programmes and printed in bulletins, while concerts
and plays were specially arranged mainly for off-duty Americans,
including an Old Vic West End run at the Embankment's
Playhouse in the summer of 1943 entirely subsidised by CEMA and
titled *Salute to the Allies* (the theatre's main poster was improved
one night to read *Salute to the Alkies*) in which the season featured
Drinkwater's *Abraham Lincoln* and, to represent British talent, a
new play by the young Peter Ustinov, *Blow Your Own Trumpet*,
directed by Michael Redgrave. At such events CEMA, like ENSA,

found itself arranging segregated shows in line with the US military's racist policies of the time; it was left to performers such as Gielgud and the Cassons to disapprove.

It's all the more strange then that Keynes should make a BBC broadcast about the Arts Council on 12 June 1945, barking: 'Let every part of merry England be merry in its own way. Death to Hollywood!' The next day Keynes acquired an acid response from a Mr Pole, director of publicity for United Artists Films, to which he promptly apologised for his anti-American *faux pas* publicly via *The Times*: 'I meant to say Hollywood for Hollywood.' Pole wrote back reasonably that 'the film industry might be helpful to the Arts Council', though no one went on to prove him right. On the same day Keynes received the following letter, the first surviving example of the insane writing that, according to a later Chairman, counts for 'roughly 20 per cent of the correspondence one receives at the Arts Council on a rotten day':

Three CHEERS for your slogan DEATH TO HOLLYWOOD! And I would go further & say DEATH TO ALL CINEMAS! and the vulgar notoriety of so-called Film STARS! of either sex! & the pseudo art of photography.

The majority of cinema 'entertainment' appeals with few exceptions to all that is lowest, sordid, & sensual in human nature: murder, lust, crime, infidelity, divorce & gangsterism being the chief items in the programmes!

(signed) A Social Worker tho' not a prude!

High Wycombe

Why the Chairman of an organisation founded by American money – who spent during the war the equivalent of a year in the States negotiating terms by which that country would come to exploit Britain's economy, who dragged methodology back across the Atlantic and even a dance company – why he should ape Olivier in *Henry V* and 'Cry "God for Harry! England and Saint George!" ' remains intriguing. The Arts Council was not involved with cinema at any level, even though the British Film Institute had applied three times for aid and been denied it. He may have used 'Hollywood' as Christie used 'mob', to belittle 'the cinema crowd'. More surely it represented the kind of cultural and technological imperialism that he and his colleagues allowed to inundate the United Kingdom in return for armaments and food, so that the country would end up after the war, in Gore Vidal's words, as 'America's little battleship off the coast of Europe'. Keynes admitted at the time in a cable: 'Americans not willing to discuss British needs without reference to *strings*.' They meant commerce not orchestras, and through his Hollywood death wish Keynes was projecting his own remorse.

His sentence preceding the Hollywood gibe makes little sense either – we know Keynes had no time for Merry England nor for the devolutionary notion of 'every part of it being merry in its own way'. The sentence that follows it sounds more like Keynes: 'But it is also our business to make London a great artistic metropolis, a place to visit and to wonder at.' However, put the three sentences back together and you get crude sophistry. Although the speech is regarded as a keynote account of Arts Council ambitions and elements are routinely quoted, the entire text is a mishmash of untruths, PR bluster, glib homilies and cloudy logic. Keynes' summary, for instance, of the Pilgrim years is deceptive: 'It was the task of C.E.M.A. to carry music, drama and pictures to places which would be cut off from all contact with the masterpieces of happier days and times.' Yet, as we've seen, the plays of Larry Peach were entirely new if rather Home Guard in their style, while the Old Vic played *Macbeth* with a preface to highlight its wartime pertinence, even a Schubert adagio matched a prevailing mood of sobriety, and Bill Williams' exhibitions were devoted to contemporary work, including items by official war artists. Only in the exhibitions organised by Philip James might it be claimed that 'masterpieces of happier days' were offered, and the notion itself is bogus.

According to Keynes the Arts Council was grounded in Englishness: 'State patronage of the arts has crept in. It has happened in a very English, informal, unostentatious way – half baked, if you like.' Yet it was a trademark civil-service enterprise in the way it was run, involving even at its inception a room of twelve advisers and officers, comments recorded and minutes drawn up. By 1945 it had a nationally distributed staff of seventy serving an advisory team of fifty-eight. When Keynes wrote of the 'informal, unostentatious' English way, he had considered not the system but the power that drove it on, an authority harnessed by close associates under his despotic control. In doing so he echoed Lord Macmillan's view that committees were the death of democracy and his meetings 'were small and intimate. We were all of us personal friends.' That may well define the Englishness of an Establishment in action, though it is nothing to be proud of given the specious quality of the decisions made and the ease by which the peculiar aesthetic predilections of non-artists were converted into enduring artistic directives. In any case, this mode of informal Englishness could be found genetically in mainland Europe, Asia, the Americas or anywhere a clique gathered to invoke and expend power for mutual benefit.

When the Council discussed membership of its own body together with that of the panels in January 1945, Vaughan Williams urged 'the recruitment of workaday artists rather than distinguished names'. Keynes countered that 'there was practical value in a list of responsible names to sanction the activities of the Council with the professionals and the public'. Keynes might well have considered artists irresponsible, having married one; he was reluctant even to trust their majority participation in the panel system, despite his insistence that 'the panels would, in future, be purely advisory bodies concerned with artistic matters only'. Vaughan Williams never succeeded in rectifying to his satisfaction the loose mixture of the landed gentry, boardroom dilettantes, executive academics and nominal artists that occupied Council seats and headed panels, mainly because he was nominal himself. This combination has persisted despite Vaughan Williams' belief that practising artists were the best people to consult over the practising arts.

The institution may also have been considered English in the lack of a written constitution or an approved statement of objectives. It's ironic, then, that at the very same time he made his speech Keynes was constrained to establish in writing a set of basic aims to be presented in the royal charter of incorporation. There are certain legal platitudes that comfortably fill such documents, and Keynes was happy to stick with those in the knowledge that their inclusion was designed to keep the tax officers at bay.

Vaughan Williams was less keen to tolerate solicitors' patois and argued that the routine opening line 'to encourage the knowledge, understanding and practice of the arts' should be followed by something more affirmative than the lawyers' spineless phrase 'to promote the arts throughout the country'. He urged the adoption of the following words: 'To increase the accessibility of the arts to the public throughout the country.' He added another aim: 'To improve and maintain the status of the artists', while Thelma Cazalet Keir, still representing the education department, wanted to preserve the Council's animateurism in the following expression: 'To encourage and aid proficiency in the arts.'

While it seems from the minute that the Council agreed with all three additions, the royal charter signed on 9 August 1946 omitted all but the first. Nevertheless its inclusion preserved and accredited the Pilgrimism that Vaughan Williams favoured, though it was all that remained of it. It took the one genuine 'workaday artist' left on the Council to keep in mind the general public. When Vaughan Williams was finally offered a Covent Garden premiere in the early fifties, he composed a 'morality' rather than an opera; its title, *The Pilgrim's Progress.*

The 1946 royal charter contained one change for which solicitors had not quite bargained. Everyone on the Council wanted the term 'the arts' used throughout without any limiting definition. Vaughan Williams among others hankered to expand the Arts Council's remit to cover films and K. Clark greasily replied that 'the arts' could already be said to cover cinema, 'or at least those films for which you write the music'. Yet the final document speaks of 'the fine arts' throughout. Glasgow supposed that Keynes didn't like the expansionist tone of the Council's thoughts and 'reined it in' with this phrase, which commonly means the visual arts. In fact Keynes was simply trying to avoid paying rates on the building. The Scientific Societies Act of 1843 allowed exemption under a number of categories including 'the fine arts . . . provided that such Society shall be supported wholly or in part by annual voluntary contributions'. But rather like the tale of Mecca and the Opera House, the gimmick failed; local council officers decided that the annual government grant-in-aid was not quite the same thing as 'voluntary contributions'. Nevertheless, for this bizarre reason 'fine arts' was the chosen term, and the final document opens:

GEORGE THE SIXTH, by the grace of God of Great Britain, Ireland and the British Dominions beyond the Seas King, Defender of the faith, Emperor of India:

To all to whom these Presents shall come, Greeting:

WHEREAS it has been represented to Us by Our Chancellor of the Exchequer that for the purpose of developing a greater knowledge, understanding and practice of the fine arts exclusively, and in particular to increase the accessibility of the fine arts to the public throughout Our Realm, to improve the standard of execution of the fine arts and to advise and co-operate with Our Government Departments, local authorities and other bodies on any matters concerned directly or indirectly with those objects . . .

The document closes ten pages later with a general declaration that it 'shall be recognised as valid and effectual by all Our Courts and Judges ... not withstanding any non-recital, mis-recital, uncertainty or imperfection in this Our Charter'. There would be plenty of non-recitals, mis-recitals, uncertainties and imperfections resounding from it.

It took just one sharp mind from the Treasury to spot two facts in November 1945: first that Keynes had garnered Covent Garden a grant of £25,000 for the financial year 1945–1946, second that the theatre was closed and therefore not exactly offering anything that required subsidy. Faced with its inaugural crisis, the Trust squeezed into the end of the financial year a production by Sadler's Wells Ballet of *The Sleeping Beauty*, which opened on 20 February 1946. De Valois was given six weeks to pull the thing together. Materially the same production as in 1939, with slight amendments by de Valois and Frederick Ashton, it looked better for two reasons. First, the company had undertaken wartime CEMA tours to grand theatres with spacious stages in Liverpool and Manchester and so learned to cope with sizes akin to Covent Garden, though the company has since neglected to pay back the debt it owed up north. Second, a resourceful designer called Oliver Messel made fulsome sets of receding towers with luscious vistas and swanky costumes that furnished this neo-romantic production for two decades. The monumental scenery used up the staff's spare clothing coupons for fabric as well as all the working hours, so that *Sleeping Beauty* had to be danced at every show for a month while sets for other works were prepared. The accounts for the time show that Messel failed to provide receipts for over £2,000 (£70,000) handed over to him in cash.

The chairman of Covent Garden had selected the ballet, ostensibly because of its theme of birth and renewal, but equally to dignify his affiliation with the legacy of Diaghilev. George VI and his family attended and watched from the box next to the Keyneses, thus launching the imperial tone of unctious veneration, tiered exclusiveness and smug indulgence that Keynes had sought for his national opera house. That the Australian Robert Helpmann was virtually the only male dancer on stage (he doubled as the gallant Prince and the evil Carabosse), that the pasteboard opulence of Messel's sets still stank of glue and cheap paint, and that rats ran across the audience's feet in the gallery – nothing was allowed to spoil the devised myth of a triumphant rebirth, not even Keynes' heart. Shortly before the royal family arrived he suffered a tremor and was made to rest in his box while Lydia greeted the guests. The strain on Keynes was hardly surprising. Not only had he gambled his credibility on an opera house without opera to put in it, he had been under acute pressure over the Lend Lease issue which he had not handled well. A week later, on his last visit to the USA, he gave a remarkable speech that ultimately coupled these two worlds into a singular, romantic union.

Addressing the first meeting of the World Bank and International Monetary Fund founders in Savannah, he drew on the images of *The Sleeping Beauty* to express his hopes at the birth of 'the lusty twins':

> I do not doubt that the usual fairies will be putting in an appearance at the christening, carrying appropriate gifts . . . The first fairy should bring, I suggest, a Joseph's coat, a many coloured raiment to be worn by these children as a perpetual reminder that they belong to the whole world . . . The second fairy, being up-to-date, will bring perhaps a box of mixed vitamins A,B,C,D and all the rest of the alphabet . . . I hope Mr. Kelchner has not made any mistake and that there is no malicious fairy, no Carabosse, whom he has overlooked and forgotten to ask to the party . . . If this should happen, then the best that could befall would be for the children to fall into an eternal slumber, never to waken or be heard of again in the courts and markets of mankind.

It was Keynes who first succumbed to eternal slumber, soon after his return from the States. On Easter Sunday 1946, at his Tilton farmhouse across the way from Glyndebourne, a heart attack stilled him. He had died two months after the opening of his own 'opera house, though I would much rather call it a ballet house. That would be an innovation, and, by the way, it would fox Christie'. Lord Drogheda notes that Keynes died two days after Hugh Dalton's budget which smashed his surtax plan. Baron Keynes of Tilton left behind an Arts Council rebuilt to Christie's design but with nothing to drive it once he'd left it, and a city centre Opera House that couldn't do opera (and when it could, rarely well), while Christie re-opened his absurd village hall to produce opera seasons the world would envy. Keynes was clever and got it wrong. Christie was a nutcase but got it right.

Part II

The Arts Council's main issues, 1946–1998

'The things that matter are the big things'Lord Goodman, 1968

To paraphrase Lord Rees-Mogg, the history of the Arts Council falls into three periods, measured by the response of the public and Parliament to its actions, or inactions:

1.	*1946–1964*	*Yes*
2.	*1965–1981*	*Yes, but*
3.	*1982 and counting*	*Well, really*

Part II examines the Arts Council's track record by the way it has had to deal with a number of recurrent problems. The fact that the Arts Council's solutions tend to create new dilemmas further down the line is probably the major means by which the Council keeps itself in business. Created as an emergency measure, it seems happiest handling emergencies, or making them.

Chapter 9

A body corporate

On BBC's Radio 3 on 2 August 1987, the Arts Council's former and formidable art director, Joanna Drew, was interviewed by Julian Spalding, who later became director of museums and art galleries in Glasgow. He asked her what her policy had been. There followed an immense pause. No, it was more like a menacing silence, of the kind that only Radio 3 or Harold Pinter can get away with. Finally she replied, 'I don't think ... we believed in ... policy.'

From the moment Tom Jones opened his chequebook in January 1940, policy existed. If policy can be generally defined as a 'guiding course of action', then CEMA's was unwritten but tacitly understood by those around the table. Its contours shifted as new ideas or old enemies sought CEMA's cash, and the nearest the early Council ever came to defining policy was written in the charter of 1946, where the Arts Council becomes 'a body corporate' with powers 'for the purpose of developing a greater knowledge, understanding and practice of the fine arts exclusively'. Today we would call that a mission statement, or as Roland Muldoon of the Hackney Empire would have it, 'a load of bollocks'.

The greatest single change that afflicted the Arts Council in the eighties came from the executives' desire to declare a written policy. It proved as elusive as defining the arts themselves and ended in 1992 with an immense stack of forty-five reports struggling to spell out 'a strategic framework for the arts and media'. These were collectively mashed into a National Arts and Media Strategy. They provided much enjoyment for one client's family 'when we used them to build a bonfire on Guy Fawkes' Night'. Luke Rittner called this collection 'the biggest suicide note in the history of the arts'.

Not having policies and strategies that were written down didn't stop the Council from spending money for fifty years, but they would help us to understand what the Council thought it was working towards if we could detect them beneath the Council's actions. An insightful reflection on the early, reactive style of the Council was raised in interview by Catherine Porteous, now a JP and a member of the National Lottery Heritage Board, but then a young secretary to Sir Kenneth Clark when he chaired the Council in the fifties. She said that:

> In those days, even from a worm's-eye view of affairs, the whole idea of formulating policy and having targets and budgets and all that sort of thing was not developed as it is now, and probably not considered to be pertinent. I suppose it's partly to do with work in the war, when there was only one target, which was beating Germany. Everything else was secondary to that. There was more a sort of feeling of responding to events as they came hopping along towards you. If you think of the kinds of ventures the Arts Council got involved with – Covent Garden, the National Theatre, orchestras, touring exhibitions – they weren't drawn up by policy. In those days it was easier for somebody to come along with an idea and you'd say 'Let's give it a go,' rather than 'Well that doesn't fit in with our policy.'

Those 'vague ideals' were stimulated by ways of thinking, ideologies, that were rooted in the remarkably integrated background of many of those who served as officers, advisers and clients in the Council's formative years. Swinging through the variegated family trees of the Council's leading members and staff, we see scions of the military profession (Lewis Casson, Ninette de Valois, Dick Linklater, Martin Browne, Joanna Drew, later Nigel Abercrombie), the medical profession (Ivor Brown, Tyrone Guthrie, Benjamin Britten, Sir Kenneth Robinson), the sons of MPs (John Christie, E.J. Dent, Adrian Boult) and brokers

(John – and Val – Gielgud, Benn Levy). Mary Glasgow's dad was a senior educationalist, as were the fathers of Maynard Keynes, Ernest Pooley, Barbara Ayrton Gould, John Burrell and Philip Hendy, the Council member who replaced Kenneth Clark at the National Gallery. The sparse offspring of the working class included Tom Jones, Ifor Evans, Sir Ernest Bullock and sculptor Henry Moore, alongside the deeply aspirant Bill Williams and Malcolm Sargent. Dominating all, the parents who supplied the most significant number of staff and advisers all served one distinctive but declining occupation – that of the Church. To appreciate its influence, we must start where Part One finished, at the end of the Second World War.

The Council's first full-time appointment after the war was Steuart Wilson (1889–1966), the music director. As a tenor we encountered him at Glyndebourne in the twenties, and as Webster's deputy at Covent Garden we will read about him later in the scandal pages of the *Sunday People*. He came to the Arts Council in 1945 from the BBC, where he'd served as music director of the Overseas Service. We might assume that this famous singer was following the predictable path of someone who had retired from performing to sustain his life in the arts as a back-seat administrator out to help the next generation. He was chosen, in fact, because of his fame. It would be like having the well-liked baritone Thomas Allen as music director today. Mary Glasgow said of Wilson that 'he hated, in his days as a public servant, hiding behind the anonymity of office', and that was why she accepted him, ego and all.

Steuart Wilson turned out to be a crass despot who readily humiliated those below him, or above. Glasgow allowed him to carry on with his sneering ways because she thought that the price was worth paying to have someone so celebrated working at the Arts Council. He didn't last long. Knighted in 1948, he left the Council to rejoin the BBC as its director of music, solely, it seems, to wreck the career of Sir Adrian Boult – a story worth telling to show what Wilson was like. He had recently left his wife, two sons and daughter. Boult in turn married Mrs Wilson, who became Lady Boult, and paid for the upkeep and education of Wilson's children. At the time Boult was conductor-in-chief of the BBC Symphony Orchestra, and so when Wilson joined that institution he got Boult thrown out under a retirement ruse. The conductor was devastated and the case gained notoriety as an example of crazy bureaucracy crushing artistic common sense, but it was revenge, not red tape. Once Sir Steuart had achieved this, he left the BBC within a year of joining it for Covent Garden, where he tried to get rid of Webster. In both cases he railed against these figures of power in his high moral tone because he believed them to be homosexual.

Wilson's appointment to the Arts Council set a standard for Glasgow's recruiting style in two ways. One she said she promoted, 'the other I couldn't help, despite myself'. For the first, Wilson had genuine artistic experience in the field for which he was serving the Council. He was already rich and a salary meant little to him, as little as it did to Lewis Casson or Reginald Jacques. Against this, Glasgow had to weigh up Wilson's 'artistic temperament', which she considered to be nothing to do with creativity and much to do with his posh background. She thought he looked down on people because 'conceit was in his blood', and this atheist of a secretary-general blamed his behaviour on that fact that his father was canon of Worcester Cathedral. She noted that many of the people working by her side came from the families of 'professional Christians'. She smelled sanctity all around her and she flinched.

Like the music director, the art director, Philip James, was the son of a distinguished vicar. The drama director, Michael MacOwen, was the grandson of one, as indeed were Lord Keynes and Mary Glasgow. Wilson's predecessor as CEMA's music director was the son of a reverend, as was his successor in 1948, John Denison; in turn, Denison's successor was a Westminster Abbey choral scholar. Vaughan Williams' father was a parson, Walford Davies' a Congregationalist preacher and organist, Sir John Maud's the rector of St Mary Redcliffe in Bristol, from which he later adopted the name, to make himself better known to the arts world, as Lord Redcliffe-Maud. Ashley Dukes was the son of a vicar, Lawrence du Garde Peach, Anthony Blunt, Reginald Jacques and Sir Kenneth Barnes too. Sybil Thorndike and Laurence Olivier were reared by their reverend fathers, and it was said that both of them acquired their brilliant vocal skills by mimicking sermons.

It remains a truism that the arts have succeeded the church in 'telling us what we are and what we might be'. The cultural temples of the nineteenth century invoked ancient places of worship for deeper reasons than a fashion for the gothic; concert halls were decked out like churches, often with grand organs in pride of place, while Garnier called his Paris Opéra 'a cathedral of the lyric arts'. Yet this career move of the theocracy, to protect its lofty status by constructing for itself an alternative livelihood, can't solely be explained away by the dwindling fortunes of 'professional Christians'.

Vaughan Williams spent much of his life attempting to reform the liturgy. He did so as part of a campaign against Victorian self-righteousness and he saw what he was doing as belonging to a progressive crusade to restore pre-industrial values. At the age of thirty-four he edited *The English Hymnal* (1906). It was written as a zealous two fingers to the stodgy *Hymns Ancient & Modern* (1904) and it proved popular, selling five million copies. In 1925 he helped to compile the 700 tunes of *Songs of Praise* as 'a national collection of hymns for gatherings of all sorts and ages'; he was absorbed by the public pageants and civic ceremonies of the time, noting that they acquired a spiritual dimension beyond the routines of the church. The hymnal and *Songs of Praise* were still selling at his death in 1958, and rightly so. His introduction of secular folk melodies and settings by composers like Holst gave congregations glorious tunes to sing.

The composer was equally concerned with the problem of the churches' fading place in the musical landscape of the country. When he was born there was a church band or an organist in almost every village. He saw organisations like the Rural Music Schools Association and the county music services as regenerators of music's local inspiration, and he wanted the Arts Council to drive this deeper.

So, there was a level at which the move from clericalism to artistry was a moral one. This sheds light on Vaughan Williams' missionary phrase in the Council's charter: 'to increase the accessibility of the arts to the public throughout the country'. It's as though he viewed the nation as a network of congregations. And, further, when we view the surprisingly persistent celebration of orthodox spiritual values in the works of British composers, many commissioned with subsidy from the Council, we can imagine this is another way in which Vaughan Williams inspired Council conduct. Britten's reconciling *War Requiem*, Tippett's hippy-drippy pantheism, the devotional works of John Tavener, Diana Burrell or Jonathan Harvey among so many others: this is a disposition to sanctity the Arts Council has consistently encouraged, but one which does not reflect the advancing atheism outside.

It helps to explain why the dissenting, experimental practices of those around Cornelius Cardew, or his more conservative teacher

Alan Bush, found it less easy to obtain the support from the Council they deserved at the time. Once we've learned that the music department was led by choral scholars up to 1979, we can appreciate why God continued to get grants despite the atheism upstairs, shared by Glasgow and Williams, and why music remained the most conservative unit at the Council. When the progressive Sandy Nairne became visual arts director in 1986, he was astonished to meet as his music director counterpart Richard Lawrence, who looked like 'a wimpish choirboy'. Lawrence went on to work for the Royal School of Church Music.

This gas-and-gaiters parentage of those gathered around the original Council probably explains why they saw themselves as radical while we might consider them artistically conservative. They were brought together by anti-Victorianism. This bias linked Keynes, Clark, Casson, Walton, Vaughan Williams, Glasgow and Pelican Bill. When Mary Glasgow said of Keynes that he had little time for 'the missionary zeal' surrounding Sadler's Wells, she was referring to the campaign of teetotalism that brought about the Old Vic and its brother building, led by the tyrannical Lilian Baylis and her unpleasant aunt Emma Cons. They wished, in a censorious Victorian manner, to 'save' the working class from the demon drink by having them watch Falstaff and Don Giovanni, to name but two stage inebriates.

Keynes was the sort of liberal who detested this evangelical bullying. He brushed it aside as hypocritical puritanism. Lounging in bed of a morning, we can't imagine Keynes thinking much of Victorian values: rigour in the home, self-advancement and the 'immorality of extravagance'. Approved Victorian arts touted rectitude; Prince Albert justified artistic practice by its industrial, economic and moral benefits. Victorianism was as German as he. Keynes preferred French – the sensuality of ballet, aesthetic opulence, champagne by the ice bucket, a *ménage à trois*. (Vaughan Williams, by the way, studied composing in Paris with Ravel, to get away from 'German thinking'.) To Prince Albert it was art's practical usefulness that gave it value. Keynes admired more its enchantment.

The boyfriend of Keynes' boyfriend, Lytton Strachey, wrote *Eminent Victorians*, a mocking account of figures like Florence Nightingale, made to look like 'those queer fishes that one sees behind glass at an aquarium, before whose grotesque proportions and sombre menacing agilities one hardly knows whether to laugh or shudder'. In this way it becomes clear why characters like

Christie and the Royal Academy's Alfred Munnings were never encouraged to pass through the Council's doors; they were fishy relics of the last century. Munning's barmy sermons against modernism and his censoring manner were the cause of much sniggering at Council. A light-hearted, 'common-sense' stand against censorship is in fact the most obvious sign of its anti-Victorianism (though it didn't stop some executives from suppressing work when it suited them politically). Their placing of Shakespeare at the hub of artistic endeavour is an added indicator: a most ambiguous and profuse writer who probes duplicity and complexities. The work that appealed least to the Council's pioneers were those that to their eyes peddled simplistic propaganda, such as Joan Littlewood's Theatre Workshop.

Though the Council was united against cold-blooded probity, however, it doesn't explain the conflict between Pilgrimism and Keynesianism. Vaughan Williams and the Pilgrims renovated what has been identified as a Victorian counterculture, a kind of William Morris-style Christian socialism which supported the application of the arts to everyday life. They favoured co-operative endeavour; they envisioned a society sanitised of unethical competition, and for such reasons they stood against Prince Albert's promotion of industrial development and self-improvement. Keynes, though, had no time for rustic nostalgia, cultural nationalism or the comradely values that Vaughan Williams' boots ground into the Council carpet. After all, Keynes was a pig farmer.

At least we know what values Vaughan Williams was fighting for; it's less easy to say that of Keynes or Kenneth Clark. Their motivations can be drawn, however, from two books with (nearly) the same, awesome title: *Civilization* and *Civilisation*. The former was penned during the First World War and revised in 1928 by Keynes' Bloomsbury cohort Clive Bell (1881–1964), an art critic who eventually joined the Council's art panel. It was conceived at a time when Keynes was sheltered by the Bloomsbury set, and Virginia Woolf considered it read like the transcript of 'a lunch party at 50 Gordon Square', which, if true, is scary. The latter flourished forty years on as the script of a TV series by the Council's former chairman, K. Clark himself.

Bell and Clark try to define their books' title and the similarities are strong. Both consider that a civilised society is a good one. It is validated by its art. Both believe they know when a society isn't civilised: 'No characteristic of a barbarous society can possibly be a peculiarity of civilized societies,' writes Bell. They agree that distinct values promote civilisation: in Bell's case it's self-consciousness ('which leads to an examination and comparison of states of mind') and a critical spirit; to Clark it is confidence and durability ('The Huns ... preferred to live in pre-fabs'). Both argue that civilisation is practised best by Europe and never better so than in the West end of it. Above all, both Bell and Clark claim that the art which expresses civilisation is made by individuals who are supported by a society to do so. As Clark puts it, 'I believe in the God-given genius of certain individuals, and I value a society that makes their existence possible.'

Lytton Strachey had apparently said in the First World War: 'I am the civilisation for which you are fighting.' A generation on, the writer Stephen Spender thought this phrase defined the duty of a classic intellectual: to act as 'a visible, tangible, material example of civilisation'. This smug, self-reflective image engaged the Arts Council for forty years, until equal opportunities begged questions. At root, a record of the personalities that have determined and driven the activities of the Arts Council is a history of the British intellectual, which is truly a scatterbrained and disenchanting saga.

The difference between Bell and Clark's books, aside from the spelling of sibilants, lies more in their style. Bell is whiny and provocative. He's aiming to stir things up. Clark is a bit of a roué, charming and . . . well, civilised. In the wake of the 1968 riots he's trying to calm things down; the handsome quality of his writing is both casual and lucid. But Bell's the one who swayed Keynes. He inspired the economist to declare at the founding of the Arts Council that, 'the artist walks where the breath of the spirit blows him', which mirrors Bell's comments on artists, or rather the Artist, for he ignores the collective noun. Bell's Artist, by the way, is eternally male, even though his wife was a painter and *Civilization* was actually dedicated to Virginia Woolf.

The Artist is a special being whose public must be disposed 'to allow him to know best what is best for himself . . . Civilization, that elaborate protest of individual intelligence and sensibility against the flock instinct, will never accept reach-me-down standards or bow to the authority of shopwalkers.' He argues that this is crucially the case in Britain:

> An Englishman of any superiority must stand on his own feet, because there is nothing about him on which he could deign to lean. He must make his own way, because all public roads lead

through intolerably dreary country to intellectual slums and garden suburbs.

How close this is to Keynes' reasons, made public three years later, for why the whole of south London should be knocked down.

Bell believes that civilisation is generated by a refinement in creation and receptiveness that can be cultivated only by a special caste. To reach this conclusion he defines what civilisation is not, and it ain't darkies. He denigrates Australia's Aborigines ('the most barbarous of barbarous creatures'), the Veddhas of Sri Lanka, the forest tribes of Brazil, the 'miserable people' of the Gold Coast, the Yoruba of west Africa, and all native Americans including Inuits. It turns out that he never actually met any of these folk.

He writes: 'I fancy the savage rarely smiles; he grins. He never raises a shoulder or an eyebrow; intellectual graces are as meaningless as subtle shades of sentiment to him.' In contrast, it is the leisured few of England (and we guess Bell can narrow this down to a couple of squares in London WC1) who know how and when to simper and glow and thus save the world from the inelegance of Johnny Wog. Civilisation, he asserts, is an artificial product of reflection and education – and a liberal education at that, not a technical one.

> Civilization requires the existence of a leisured class . . . Unluckily, material security, leisure and liberty all cost money; almost all kinds of money-making are detrimental to the subtler and more intense states of mind, because almost all tire the body and blunt the intellect.

The less refined folk of England must pay for this leisured class to carry out its sensitive duties, just as it pays for universities and municipal picture galleries. 'This implies inequality – inequality as a means to good.'

Clive Bell was born to a moneyed family 'which drew its wealth from Welsh mines and expended it upon the destruction of wild animals'. He was educated at Marlborough and Trinity, Cambridge, from where he drank his way to Paris. There he explored the 'pure aesthetic' world of Cézanne and Renoir, evoked by Clark in his book as: 'No awakened conscience, and no heroic materialism. No Nietzsche, no Marx, no Freud. Just a group of ordinary human beings enjoying themselves' – smiling, not grinning.

Leaning against bars, Bell conceived his influential notion of 'significant form' which he wrote up in his eminent essay 'Art' of 1914. But back in Britian he found no agreeable bars to lean on, and thus he penned his tirade against its intellectual slums and his right to be subsidised to point this out. In this sense the Arts Council, shaped by his ally Keynes, was the bursary he had wished to see in place to support and sustain the leisured class he championed. It did so by giving the creators grants, while their intellectual peers, their 'receivers', were given jobs and boards.

The unwritten policy of the Arts Council reflects the infatuations of the drifting, capricious intelligentsia of this country, which is what we tolerate to call what became of Bell's leisured class. The kindred assumptions of Bell and Clark reflected those around them who enjoyed privilege but were not privileged to produce worthwhile art. They stood on the sidelines trying to make themselves somehow indispensable to those who engaged in creative work. That's why they understood a little more about artistic practice than did Keynes, by insinuating themselves with artists rather than ballet 'artistes', even if they failed to notice that the best of such artists confront society more than they flatter it. Keynes, though, understood better how to turn ideas into realities, however rickety the outcome.

Once the Pilgrim War had been won by Keynes' cosmopolitans, the Council chose not to parade policy, which would have been a very Victorian thing to do – to lay down strictures, determine objectives, measure the arts in terms of indicators, and all that. With this in mind we can appreciate more clearly the upheaval the Council braved in the eighties, when Mrs Thatcher restored those hated 'Victorian values'.

Yet it was these very values, of missionary self-advancement, that finally gave blacks a voice at Council, welcomed the promotion of women's work and debated issues about disability and the arts. The task for today's Council, if it is to save its skin and make itself useful again, is to discover a bold new harmony between the permissive and valuable anti-Victorianism that it sprang from and the need to account for its behaviour to those on one side who feed it money and those on the other that for decades it disenfranchised for grinning, not smiling.

Chapter 10

The food of love

To the public at large, symphony orchestras are symbols of corporate discipline, transcendent virtuosity, universal harmony, virile energy and restorative solace; to the Arts Council they are 'an absolute nightmare; a living hell of bad manners and disagreeable people, thick people', in the words of one officer, and to a former orchestra manager, 'If music be the food of love, those bastards gave me stomach ulcers'. The philharmonic ensembles of London brought the Arts Council to its knees in 1993 – but not for the first time.

There are no fewer than fifteen full-time symphony orchestras presently spread about the United Kingdom. Nine are independent. The BBC owns a further four: two in London, one each in Manchester and Glasgow. The BBC National Symphony Orchestra of Wales is co-funded by the Welsh Arts Council, and correspondingly the Ulster Orchestra in Belfast receives around 20 per cent of its income from the BBC. There are also five full-time opera orchestras and three freelance ballet orchestras. With the strength of each orchestra around eighty to ninety-five players, they account for a total of roughly 2,000 musicians under contract throughout the country. The four Arts Councils spend over £12 million a year supporting them, which comes out at around £6,000 a player. The orchestras and their 1994–1995 grants are distributed as follows (opera and ballet orchestras in italics):

Belfast	Ulster Orchestra	£ 826,000
Birmingham	City of Birmingham Symphony Orchestra	£1,149,000
	Birmingham Royal Ballet Orchestra	
Bournemouth	Bournemouth Symphony Orchestra	£1,570,400
Cardiff	BBC National Symphony Orchestra of Wales	£ 534,650
	Welsh National Opera Orchestra	
Glasgow	Royal Scottish National Orchestra	£1,821,750
	BBC Scottish Symphony Orchestra	
	Scottish Opera Orchestra	
	Scottish Ballet Orchestra	
Leeds	*English Northern Philharmonia*	
	(Opera North)	
Liverpool	Royal Liverpool Philharmonic Orchestra	£1,482,800
London	The London Philharmonic	£ 700,000
	(LP's South Bank residency)	£ 400,000
	London Symphony Orchestra	£1,140,000
	Philharmonia Orchestra	£ 700,000
	Royal Philharmonic Orchestra	£ 250,000
	BBC Symphony Orchestra	
	BBC Concert Orchestra	
	Orchestra of the Royal Opera House,	
	Covent Garden	
	English National Opera Orchestra	
	English National Ballet Orchestra	
Manchester	Hallé Orchestra	£1,251,000
	BBC Philharmonic Orchestra	

Dull as it is, the previous paragraph is both correct and possibly counterfeit. Although the big four independent orchestras of London call themselves 'full-time' or 'permanent', their musicians are entirely Schedule D, freelance players paid on a per-concert, per-rehearsal basis, earning on average £25,000 a year under terms which one London Philharmonic violinist explained as follows: 'We have no pension, we can go for weeks without work, and then have to work for 35 days without a single day off.' The London four, it can be argued, are really clumsy commercial businesses using public cash to bail them out year after year, thanks to a ploy contrived by the Arts Council.

The five main regional orchestras are not independent but run by societies governed by the local great and good, councillors and unelected dabblers, who can hire and fire key players, conductors and administrators by a nod of heads. As for the notion of national provision, no planners – at least no sober ones – would have peppered the symphony orchestras around the country in such a patchy fashion: six in London (including the ninety-strong BBC Concert Orchestra), three in the north-west and two in Glasgow, while the east, the north-east and the south-west have apparently no provision whatsoever.

'Yes, it is a curious situation,' an Arts Council music director chuckled, 'but the British orchestra scene is a hostage to history, chiefly to Beecham.' The Arts Council has consistently mongered the notion that it inherited this madness and any calamities are due to ingrained historical factors far beyond the Council's control. Yet, with only two remarkable exceptions which we'll come to, the independent orchestras were founded within the lifetime of the Council, and mostly with its encouragement (current names in brackets):

Liverpool Philharmonic Orchestra	1942
(Royal LPO	1957)
Hallé Orchestra	1943
City of Birmingham Orchestra	1944
(City of Birmingham Symphony Orchestra	1948)
Philharmonia Orchestra	1945
Royal Philharmonic Orchestra	1946
Bournemouth Municipal Orchestra	1947
(Bournemouth Symphony Orchestra	1953)
Scottish National Orchestra	1950
(Royal SNO	1991)

While none of the orchestras can deny that these are their true founding dates of incorporation as full-time orchestras, they like to pretend that they've been around far longer in order to exploit, for the sake of marketing, presumptions of pedigree. Both the Hallé Concerts Society in Manchester and the Royal Liverpool Philharmonic Society thirty-five miles away claim the credit for being Britain's oldest operators. Liverpool ran a largely amateur orchestra from 1840, while in Manchester the German Carl Halle directed an orchestra of forty professionals seasonally from November 1849 onwards. These became the Hallé Concerts in

1858; when he anglicised his name he added the acute accent as he hated being called Hall.

Directing the orchestra for thirty-seven years from this time, Hallé insisted on schemes for cheap seats, and he constantly championed new music from abroad, though somehow the boldness of his choices doesn't quite come across today: Brahms, Berlioz, Liszt, Grieg. When the Wagnerite Hans Richter was selected to succeed Hallé, this reflected the financial and aesthetic influence in the north-west of German industrialists and academics. The Hallé Orchestra was soon the best drilled in the country and its musicians were continually filched by rivals. It survived as a hothouse through to the 1970s until the death of Sir John Barbirolli, who rebuilt the 'Hallé Band' over twenty-five years from the middle of the Second World War (when there were basically four incumbent members left) until whisky got the better of him.

Notionally the capital's oldest ensemble is the London Symphony Orchestra, but there is nothing in its origins to brag about. Its founders comprised a grumpy rump of the Queen's Hall Orchestra who walked out in 1904 when the conductor Henry Wood imposed conditions to improve standards, pledging the same players to attend both rehearsal and concert. The LSO's founders flaunted their autonomy through adopting the system used in Vienna and Berlin by orchestral enterprises; they set up their own limited company and gained a self-governing status as members and directors, a system occasionally misconstrued as a 'co-operative'. All of the regular orchestral members became shareholders and appointed a small number of playing colleagues to form the board of directors who then hired the conductors and managers. The other three London orchestras adopted this in time, and when the Arts Council proposed the ruse of a non-profit status in order to give them regular grants, they created for themselves parallel concert-promoting trusts for that purpose.

The London Symphony Orchestra survived not because it was good – it was put about that LSO stood for 'Low Standards Operate' – but because benign conductors and soloists who earned decent money abroad would offer back their fees to keep their colleagues solvent, especially in the thirties. At that time the orchestra's secretary was a double-bassist, George Wood, who carried two books, one in each pocket of his coat. The left hand listed the phone numbers of all the players, the right hand receipts of those who'd been paid cash on the nail.

Prior to state subsidy, this century's London scene was far more fickle than musicians care to be reminded. An audit of the main freelance orchestras at the head of each decade shows an unstable picture until the post-war Arts Council settled matters:

1901	Queen's Hall Orchestra
	Royal Philharmonic Society Orchestra
1911	Queen's Hall Orchestra
	Royal Albert Hall Orchestra
	Royal Philharmonic Society Orchestra
	Beecham Symphony Orchestra
	London Symphony Orchestra
1921	New Queen's Hall Orchestra
	Royal Philharmonic Society Orchestra
	London Symphony Orchestra
	British Women's Symphony Orchestra
1931	London Symphony Orchestra
	BBC Symphony Orchestra
1941	London Symphony Orchestra
	London Philharmonic Orchestra
	(BBC Symphony Orchestra evacuated to Bedford)
1951	London Symphony Orchestra
	London Philharmonic Orchestra
	BBC Symphony Orchestra
	Philharmonia Orchestra
	Royal Philharmonic Orchestra

The Arts Council has expressed the view at various times that there are too many orchestras in London – 'two many', one music director quipped. He cited major cities around the world where you often find no more than a couple who keep each other on their musical toes, and it's often the case that a city – not necessarily a capital – supports one major ensemble which is rival to another somewhere else, as the football-style feud between Chicago and Boston bears witness.

Sir Thomas Beecham is certainly to blame for London's variety of choice. He set up the LPO with money from Sam Courtauld and friends as 'a spoiler' in 1932, because the BBC didn't give him the symphony orchestra it had recently created to broadcast classical music. Following a successful tour of Nazi Germany where his orchestra played Mozart for Hitler, Beecham evacuated to the

USA in advance of the war and left the LPO to fend for itself. When he returned to find it no longer agreeable to his control but self-governing, he created, to cash in on the renewed recording trade, an alternative in the Royal Philharmonic (RPO), which itself became self-governing in 1963 after his death. As we've already seen, the Philharmonia was created by ENSA's Walter Legge in 1945 to provide an ensemble out of decommissioned RAF talent to play for his EMI recordings, though it too gave concerts – its acclaimed debut under Beecham!

Far from dealing with the issue at source or striking at suitably weak moments (and there are many), the Arts Council has actually contrived, sometimes against its music department's will, to promote and sustain this crowded market. It could have disposed of the LPO in 1952, when a scandal and a policy shift debilitated the ensemble, or in 1957, when the directors 'decided it was impossible to continue on a permanent basis', or as late as 1994, when its members were forced into a pay cut, borrowed money from the Musicians' Union then lost their manager and music director. The LSO could have gone in 1954 or again in 1967, when it faced a variety of internal crises, or in 1984, when it teetered on the edge of financial collapse; the Philharmonia was vulnerable in 1964, when Legge withdrew and it became the New Philharmonia, while between 1970 and 1973 it faced profound problems.

While the London Philharmonic has always been the Arts Council's pet (with the longest record of any single client in any artform, receiving subsidy since CEMA's inception), the one band Arts Council officers have routinely desired to cull is the Royal Philharmonic, but ironically the annual grants given to that body are now so slim that the Council lacks a strong enough stake in the enterprise to effect its death. It could certainly have damaged it in 1963 after Beecham's own demise, or as recently as December 1995, when the players sacked their executives and watched their board nearly fall to pieces.

The RPO has been discounted ever since it started up in 1946, partly because it promptly landed the job of playing in the pit each season at Glyndebourne, and the combination of Beecham and Christie holding its life together was bound to peeve members of the Council, but also because Beecham set it up imperiously, without consultation and through a commercial arm called Anglo-American Concerts Ltd. This pursuit of the 'light-music crowd' through a one-rehearsal, one-concert drill devalued its status in the eyes of the Arts Council, and consistently so, for this is the band that gave us *Hooked on Classics* in the eighties. Back then, though, the Council couldn't fault it on artistic quality; the RPO was considered an outstanding group of players, while the LSO at the time was labelled 'dilapidated, artistically ruinous' in an Arts Council memo. The confusion between the standard of a performance and the choice of works an orchestra offers its public is one that the Arts Council still finds hard to unravel.

The London problem is deemed an issue of *quantity*, of over-provision: there are too many orchestras competing for audiences, or put the other way, too few concert-goers around to satisfy the orchestras' box-office needs. Alternatively, it is put that the Arts Council simply does not have enough money to meet the claims of four orchestras. The solution, however, is posed as a *qualitative* one of artistic standards, or more recently one of 'artistic vision': the orchestras that have the lowest standards or the feeblest ambitions should perish to allow the better ones to get even better. It is this misalignment of problems and solutions that catches the Arts Council out.

Let's look at the problems and the solutions in turn. If the concert-going public is too small, that could be a greater fault of the halls and their social image. In 1993 the violinist Yehudi Menuhin complained:

> Our orchestras are situated in two of the most dismal areas of London: the South Bank and the Barbican. At night these areas are quite frightening, especially for the elderly or those with children. It is difficult to find parking. Restaurants to dine [at] after a concert are virtually non-existent. Going to the South Bank or the Barbican is a deterrent not an inducement to concert-goers. That, and the price of tickets, is what is responsible for the difficulties of the orchestras. The Arts Council should realise this and act upon it.

Sadly for his argument, the Arts Council devised the prevailing South Bank and fondly rewarded the LSO for moving to the City of London's Barbican Centre. Menuhin, by the way, is president of the Royal Philharmonic.

Until the Council was created, London possessed a single symphonic venue, the Queen's Hall. Sited north of Oxford Circus where the St George's Hotel now stands, it was built at the end of the last century (the Queen concerned was Victoria) and housed

2,500, thus creating a statistical yardstick for London concert halls which has since proved overambitious. It provided a home for the popular Promenade Concerts which were taken up by the BBC and transferred to Kensington when the Queen's Hall was blitzed in May 1941, an action the Nazis took to avenge the British bombing of the Berlin State Opera House.

After the war the Council was drawn into plans to build a new Queen's Hall a little further north at Regent's Park where land was owned not by a borough council but by the King. All manner of other alternatives were proposed (we saw earlier how the Lyceum was brought into this), yet the issue dragged on with little competence, for nobody matched Keynes' resolve on building projects. Meanwhile Labour's London County Council erected on the South Bank an elegant Royal Festival Hall for the Festival of Britain in 1951, and though its dry acoustics have been fiddled about with ever since, it has been respected as a decent, second-division venue seating 2,900. Yet for several years the fact that it was local government that built and ran the place drove the Council to dabble with projects to create a 'national' concert hall under its own control. At the back of the collective mind has always lain a vague notion of a concert centre both north and south of the Thames, just as Lilian Baylis revamped Sadler's Wells as an Old Vic for the 'north bank'.

There has never been any hard evidence that London needs two symphonic concert halls, though it remains a commonplace thought, and is possibly derived from the impression that an orchestra needs a regular home: ideally two ensembles, ideally two halls. To complicate matters, the elevated position of the London orchestras in the Council's artistic hierarchy is a contrived one, as they are metropolitan orchestras – half of them with the city in their title – yet they've been frequently defended as national resources, while the Hallé, which has literally an international name, is considered regional. Though the music department's officers are careful nowadays not to differentiate between the status of the nation's orchestras in their language, Council members are not so subtle and awkward phrases are occasionally aired, such as 'a London orchestra of international calibre' or 'world-class', and it follows that a 'world-class' London orchestra needs a 'world-class' hall.

It was not until 1986, when the Thatcher Government axed the Greater London Council and placed the South Bank Centre into Arts Council care, that the Council suddenly defended the Festival

Hall as a 'national' asset with 'an international reputation', which is an ambiguous claim, and worse 'the world's largest arts centre', which is a pointless one. By then the north bank had been favoured by another local authority called the Corporation of London, which serves the square mile of the City. It opened the rival Barbican Centre for Arts and Conferences – a revealing title – in 1982, goofily shaped like a grand piano and hidden in the bowels of a posh housing estate where it is rumoured lost audiences are arrested for 'loitering with intent to find a concert'. The Barbican Hall holds a capacity crowd of 2,026, some of whom find their seats on time.

It was back in 1954 that the City burghers first had the idea of building this monolith on blitzed land, thus spurring the Arts Council to revive the Queen's Hall in competition: 'The Music Panel considered that the Hall would be of great value to the musical life of London, and that it should be rebuilt without delay', the Council was told in October 1954, only three years after the opening of the Festival Hall. A month later, though, the matter was propelled over the Council's head into the lap of the Conservative Government when Chancellor Rab Butler set up a Treasury committee to advise on the proposed rebuilding, sparked resentfully by the success of the Germans and Austrians in restoring their war-wrecked venues. A naive civil servant slipped up by calling the Queen's a 'third hall for London', naming Kensington's Royal Albert Hall as the second. The music panel's chairman, Professor Anthony Lewis, quickly put him right: 'London, as the world's centre for concert-giving, could well support two large concert halls, and musical opinion was unanimous that the Albert Hall was unworthy of high-standard performances.'

The drum-shaped Albert Hall is a relic of Prince Albert's 1851 Great Exhibition, just as a hundred years later the Festival Hall was built to mark that show's centenary. To raise the Albert Hall's funds, 1,300 people paid £100 each for a scat from the 6,000 available to be leased to them for a century, no less. At the end of the Second World War the manager of the Albert Hall tried to get the Council to buy out the 1,300 seat-holders, but despite Keynes' predictable enthusiasm, the Council turned it down while he was out of the country.

Though the Albert Hall is burdened with muddy acoustics, the BBC nevertheless keeps the summer Proms there because it can iron out aural flaws with microphones when it broadcasts the result. Thus the recent decision of the Royal Philharmonic to treat the Albert Hall as its London home shows how desperate that orchestra has become to ground itself in the capital fifty years on. Its players can take comfort in a comment of conductor Leonard Bernstein: 'There's no such thing as bad acoustics. Ears adapt.'

The 1955 Treasury committee on the Queen's Hall was soon out of its depth and requested the Arts Council to 'undertake a survey into the whole question of the housing needs of the arts' predicated on four elements they had so far deduced, the vast scope of which shows how easy it is, when civil servants get involved, for the personal impulses of politicians and mandarins to cloud artistic priorities:

- Building a small concert hall on the South Bank;
- An art gallery;
- A metropolitan opera house on the South Bank;
- A permanent 'London' [*sic* the inverted commas] orchestra on the South Bank.

When the Queen's Hall was eventually rebuilt a decade later and opened in March 1967, nobody could possibly have recognised it as the South Bank's Queen Elizabeth Hall. Accepted only with gritted teeth as a venue for chamber orchestras, in 1986 the place was gutted by the Arts Council's own South Bank team and turned from a feeble concert hall into a feeble theatre. What little is left of the Queen's Hall scheme is now known as RFH2 and tinkers with the performing arts in general. The art gallery got built in 1968 and was named the Hayward after a county councillor, while the opera house was not formally cancelled but definitely dropped. The permanent orchestra proposal – a pet idea of London County Council at the time – resurfaced like the Creature From the Black Lagoon in the early nineties and provoked the biggest number of departures in the Arts Council's history, including that of the Secretary-General. Then came the Lottery; someone is bound to call for the resurrection of a credible Queen's Hall, while recently the Albert Hall tapped the lottery board for £40 million, plainly to turn it into something it isn't.

Audiences are prone to overlook the fact that orchestras spend most of their time in halls rehearsing. Many players believe that working in a consistent environment improves the unity of their sound and the sophistication of their individual contributions.

The idea of a single, resident orchestra in its own hall is drawn in part from this, though quite why an outfit like the Royal Liverpool Philharmonic – which has had its own art deco hall for more than fifty years free of charge – is not corporately better than it is remains a mystery.

Until the LSO occupied the Barbican and the LPO the Festival Hall the four orchestras used converted churches or municipal rooms to practise in. Yet they still gave distinctive concerts that were considered supreme. Notions of tenancy and permanence may have been too readily accepted, but in any case the South Bank residency has proved a sham; the LPO had to pay such a high rental for rehearsals it soon bolted back to the churches. The ensemble has enriched neither its sound nor its repertoire by moving into the South Bank; nor reduced its deficit.

The demand of a band for its own hall has more to do with a conceited ambition to assert its identity. An Arts Council report in 1993 published market research findings that:

> audiences choose concerts on the strength of the programme first, the conductors and soloists second, and the orchestra third and very much last. Indeed, a majority of the audience emerging from the Royal Festival Hall will not know which orchestra they have been listening to.

It would be interesting to ask the same question of the musicians as they pass the stage door, for though each of the London four claims that 90 per cent of their members turn up consistently for major concerts, there is a detectable degree of traffic between them, and the same 1993 report comments that 'the personnel of the London orchestras is far from immutable. Talent tends to follow money or perceived concentration of artistic excellence.' It follows, then, that if the Arts Council cut three of the four ensembles tomorrow morning, it wouldn't matter which one survived because it would be bound to attract the best players.

Elements of chance and caprice test the nerve and prowess of orchestras from day to day. It's not only the continually unstable circumstance of conductor, soloist, programme, personnel, management, board, acoustics, stage lighting, publicity, cashflow, transport, backstage conditions, the nearest pub, accidents with instruments, accidents without instruments, or simply the sense of occasion; it's the accumulating combination of all these discrete variations that conspires to drive an orchestra's reputation.

In the thirties and forties the Hallé and the London Philharmonic were *the* orchestras; in the fifties the Philharmonia under Klemperer and the Royal Phil. By the late sixties the fusion of André Previn with fabulous players in the London Symphony Orchestra made that the chicest band in town, then the Philharmonia recovered under Muti, and so it goes on. There is not one full-time symphony orchestra in the country which is consistently bad or unfailingly great. Nor one conductor. That's why the Arts Council's use of artistic criteria against the *status quo* in order to spark solutions never works out.

In his recent attack on the state of play, Yehudi Menuhin criticised ticket prices, and there is no doubt that the London orchestras are commercially caught between a crusading desire to get all kinds of folk to buy seats and the strategic craving to ingratiate themselves with the affluent by retaining a Hollywood image of grandeur and exclusiveness. On the one side an orchestra begs you in its leaflets and posters to 'explore the passionate world of classical music', yet once at the concert you are expected to participate in a frigid ceremonial with the most peculiar rules: you must applaud before you hear a note of music, but only after the orchestra has stopped if there is not more to follow under the same title.

Orchestras have further retained the bygone, bloodstock convention of the 'season' from which they derive subscription schemes, and a full system of segregated seating areas: the Barbican has used twelve price zones (A–M: 'Seats in Area D suffer a limited view') and the Festival Hall no fewer than seventeen. While the subscription discounts are increasingly user-friendly in their descriptions ('You pay £189.00: you save £81.00 on eight concerts', boasts the LSO, careful to account for the pence), they are not actually based on anything related to the consumer.

One marketing specialist observed:

> The basic problem with orchestral subscriptions is that the pricing is all too crudely based on the revenue needs of the orchestra. You feel someone has decided they need to raise a box-office yield of a certain amount and then plays around on the spreadsheet until the right-looking discounted numbers come up. No one seems to have defined well enough their target audiences and those groups' expectations and income. There are indicators to help, the most basic being the 'unwaged' price, which is currently at the South Bank £5 or so. Someone on income support has a total daily living

allowance of no more than £5, so the message we seem to be sending is that if you starve for a day you can watch a concert, so long as you walk there and back.

No wonder musicians are amazed to learn that audiences consider concerts offer a poorer return on money than other events.

If your chosen dress is that of a white-tied retainer or a puff-sleeved nanny, however, and your repertoire is driven by the Hapsburg Empire, your confusion as a jobbing musician in the 1990s as to what you're doing and for whom is quite understandable. It used to be the case that orchestras played nothing but modern music and that was why the audiences came. Even in the thirties, new scores were welcomed as 'novelties'. The post-war orchestras reinvented a tradition on which to trade, bending the word 'classical' in order to transcend the twentieth century and what it represented. This was welcomed by audiences who valued nostalgia over adventure, though they are now dead or dying, leaving orchestras with a dignified but stagnant presence to play to. Yet the Arts Council has encouraged this.

In a brilliant report to the Arts Council in 1970, the free-market economist Alan Peacock showed that its subsidy was being used to offset the rising internal costs of orchestras, not to improve public access to them. Whether or not the music officers truly believed that the money was going to help to reduce ticket prices, it was certainly the impression that was projected in annual reports. His disclosure was never properly followed up and the condition is now entrenched.

Despite, latterly, a range of chancy marketing schemes and cringing poster campaigns of players camping it up for cameras, orchestras have faced the same types of audience that their predecessors have done throughout the century, described by one London violinist as:

nice, elderly couples whose kids have graduated; cultivated Jewish families with fidgety sprogs; cloth-eared critics; vicars, confirmed bachelors and spinsters; record collectors sitting with scores in their laps and probably timing the movements with a wristwatch; and loners who look like they've been let out of the mental home for a treat. But at least they come out of interest. The people I don't often like playing to are sponsors and their guests who look bored to tears.

Orchestra managers pitch an upbeat tone as they report their annual box-office earnings to the Council, but they know that their core audience is not merely replicating itself but dwindling, while alternative forms of listening to their music render concert-going little more to many than a ritual to be endured like church.

Recent research has found that while 42 per cent of people claim to like classical music, only 12 per cent go to a concert at least once a year while the remaining 30 per cent presumably visit record stores or listen to the two classical radio stations. The London orchestras have contributed directly to this problem; a significant source of their income continues to come from recordings, not only the classical repertoire rehashed in fresh formats (78s in the forties, LPs in the fifties, stereo in the sixties, CDs in the eighties), but also film scores and commercial ads – a source of revenue not available to their regional allies, by the way. When a marketing survey uncovers this kind of comment – 'I've got it on record, what's the point of going to hear an orchestra play it again?' – musicians are lost for an answer.

At least, the symphony musicians are. Some of their freelance colleagues spawned a neat response in the seventies, the 'period instrument movement'. They claimed to play Mozart as Mozart might have heard it, on instruments based on those of the time and in keeping with the style of the epoch as it's been estimated by academics. By this means they created an orchestral subculture which proved brightly attractive to audiences and record-buyers alike. Suddenly the symphony orchestras, which had shunned modern scores in favour of the 'classical heritage' found their stately-home repertoire occupied by a new breed of ensemble with cute names: the Academy of Ancient Music, the Hanover Band, the Orchestra of the Age of Enlightenment. Several of these were run by inglorious conductors posing as scholars, and in another sense they revived the Beecham style of entrepreneurism.

Moreover the period orchestras held a terrific advantage. They were cheaper. Concert promoters found they could book a smaller orchestra on the grounds of 'authenticity', with soloists already in the ranks and music directors who came as part of the deal, while indulging in the classical and early romantic repertoire once monopolised by the big bands. The ability of these ensembles to reclaim the nineteenth century, creeping up through the symphony's golden years, leaves the traditional orchestras with little of their own before Mahler. Of course, this game of interpretation can be played both ways, and it won't be long before performing editions of Klemperer's Beethoven supplant those for Period Beethoven.

The Arts Council embraced the authenticity movement as a welcome diversion, pinching money from the 'new music' purse to pay for it, and even suggested that the orchestras' societies should make way in their concert series to promote showcases for these intruders. Wrong, though understandable, is the desire of the Council to hide the modern music problem with the period-instrument solution. But when it comes to the symphony orchestras themselves the Council's final defence remains 'There is only so much money in the pot,' or, applying its version of plainer language, 'It is a question of supporting clients within the constraints of existing resources.' Yet it was never clear with itself what it was funding orchestras for, nor on what terms it has set limits.

Most of the Council's attempts to define boundaries and determine rules have been added in retrospect and have failed. For instance, money to fund extra sessions to rehearse music by living composers, which was first marked out in determining a grant, gets 'forgotten' by the orchestras. This stimulates the Arts Council to turn its stick into a carrot and set up a special fund of additional cash to get them to do the very same thing. In that yee-haw vernacular Keynes called 'Cherokee', an American orchestra manager boasted of late:

> When we use the term grantsmanship to signify the discipline of exploiting and leveraging subventions and charitable funds, it is not only the ability to secure the allocations that counts, but also the knack of re-investing and amplifying those opportunities. If you can get the money twice over for the same thing, that is not duplicity, it is enterprise.

However much the orchestras can squeeze out of the Arts Council in order to survive, their deepest problem is less financial than structural. A subsidised orchestra system existed before the Council began. It was the BBC. In 1927 the broadcasting monopoly celebrated its elevation from Company to Corporation with a series of symphony concerts played by its Wireless Orchestra combined with a band from Covent Garden. This 'national orchestra' developed into the BBC's house ensemble, but not without Thomas Beecham bumbling about, straining to create a superior orchestra for the microphones of the BBC and Columbia Records with the support of the Royal Philharmonic Society to serve its public concerts. From his melodramatic wrangles emerged the 'studio' BBC Symphony Orchestra of 1930, drily directed by 'Dame' Adrian Boult, and in opposition to it the 'live' London Philharmonic Orchestra of 1932, driven by the volatile Beecham.

The BBC created three problems. First it depleted other orchestras as it pillaged for players, chiefly from the country's best, the Hallé in Manchester. Second it established a snug and invulnerable economic structure entirely at odds with the world of music outside its studios – BBC musicians were lured by subsidised salaries few could resist so soon after the Wall Street Crash – and spread this distorting framework into the freelance markets of Birmingham, the north-west and Glasgow, where it caused persistent friction between the local-authority orchestras and their musicians (in the case of Manchester and Glasgow this has never been fully resolved). Third, provoked by the League of Audiences to 'keep music live', it competed on the concert platform, using its subsidy and monopoly power to promote itself on the airwaves against its rivals.

The BBC wouldn't see it like that, of course, and on the bright side we could say the first problem gave us three smashing orchestras, the second saved the careers of many regional musicians in the thirties, while the third revived the Proms, cultivated commissions and introduced new repertoire. Even so, when CEMA took over the grant role of Carnegie during the artificial environment of the war, it could not have predicted the problems that would be faced by the existence of two mutually exclusive subsidy systems in the succeeding peace. The structures not only fuelled hostility between the strapped Hallé and the upholstered BBC Northern Orchestra, but also sustained acrimony between the BBC Scottish, the Scottish National and Scottish Opera – a squally discord the Scottish Arts Council lucklessly revived in 1995 when it tried to merge the BBC and opera orchestras.

Moreover, the unique role the BBC Symphony Orchestra set itself as a trailblazer for the novel and the arcane is changing. It is starting to 'explore' the routine repertoire of the London four, which worries the independents no end. Certain BBC executives feel that they could dismantle their orchestras tomorrow morning in the knowledge that far fewer listeners would challenge the passing of these relics of pre-war broadcasting than they would the Philharmonia or the Hallé. Such an act would certainly improve the lot of the others. But it wouldn't give the Arts Council an extra penny to play with.

The first CEMA grants in 1940 followed in the steps of the Carnegie Trust, which supported the travel and outlay of the orchestras to remote towns for single concerts, while ENSA paid guarantees against loss for events it scheduled directly – in other words, the funding did not cover the orchestras' work at home. By 1944, at Keynes' bidding, CEMA offered annual grants of £1,000 plus guarantees, the aim being to ensure an orchestra's survival while it developed its own workload and revenue through its relation to the local authorities in its home territory – the LCC for the London Phil, Liverpool City Council (supported by several Merseyside boroughs) for the Liverpool Phil. The Arts Council had to make sure that it didn't put tax-payers' money into relieving the rates, and the game plan has proceeded from this base.

In 1946 the music panel launched a review 'on the special needs of the four permanent symphony orchestras', they being the City of Birmingham, Manchester's Hallé, the Liverpool Phil and the London Phil (nothing then of the 'problem'), each of them with a local authority bedrock. The four outfits signed an agreement to become 'Orchestras in Association with the Arts Council: only properly constituted non-profit-making orchestras of national reputation are eligible'.

Whatever conditions music directors may have tried to impose in the meantime, there has been no fundamental revision to the recipe. Even the idea of pegging grants to local-authority contributions as an attempt to make the boroughs offer stronger support has been aberrant, simply because, in the words of one former director:

> The Arts Council often found it difficult to talk to local officers and councillors. It was not just a matter of vocabulary, where the Arts Council typically came across as a bit paternal, but also of the significant gap in financial expectations. We rather felt we were being taken for a ride when a city claimed to pride itself on its orchestra while doing little more than covering rental charges for concerts in the city hall it already owned [a reference to Manchester City Council].

In 1995 the cash-starved Liverpool City Council gave merely £25,000 to the Royal Liverpool Philharmonic Society while the

Arts Council granted £1.4 million, a sum in no sense relative. Nevertheless, it is here that the chief problem and solution lies: in the relation of an orchestra to local subsidy, not national. In turn it raises the most fundamental issue: why keep such orchestras at all?

They are a consequence of the ambition of cities to compete in cultural status. The Berlin Phil, the Vienna Phil, the St Petersburg Phil, the Orchestre de Paris, the Leipzig Gewandhaus, the Amsterdam Concertgebouw: mercantile cities, not countries. National orchestras tend to be the invention of broadcasting systems: the Danish Radio Symphony Orchestra, the Orchestre Nationale de Radio France, the BBC Symphony Orchestra and so on. Over here we have four full-time civic bands: in Birmingham, Bournemouth, Liverpool and Manchester. There is in addition the fickle endurance of mutated 'scratch' orchestras such as the Brighton or Guildford Philharmonics, which have survived as a sign of how strong civic patronage once was. Two of the three provincial orchestras came out of the BBC radio system, those in Northern Ireland and Wales – hence the substitute name National.

Local subsidy – or rather, locally located subsidy – in the eighties powered the stunning success of the City of Birmingham Symphony Orchestra (CBSO). That and Simon Rattle, Ed Smith and the players themselves. The subventions came out of money siphoned from the abolition of the West Midlands County Council in Thatcher's blitz of 1986 (the figures for which the Arts Council over-calculated, aware that ministers hadn't done their homework), then from the European Union in the form of development funds which created a new home for the CBSO, Symphony Hall, the foundation stone for which was laid by EC President Jacques Delors.

Simon Rattle came to Birmingham from Liverpool in 1980, young and fresh at twenty-five, with muppet hair and modish ideas, exploiting the post-war supply of college graduates to bring the orchestra closer to his testosterone level. He took with him Ed Smith, a junior manager at the Liverpool Phil, and together they devised a development plan whose content was common-sense stuff but whose timing was simply perfect.

Conducting skills aside, Rattle's puppy charm and political nous was bound to win over a metropolitan authority desperate to rid Birmingham of its Spaghetti Junction image. Yet it was well known that the Tories would soon hand back power to the old city councils and relations would need to be not only transferred but regenerated. At this time came the Arts Council's decentralised plans in William Rees-Mogg's report 'The Glory of the Garden'. The opportunity to apply that policy for local growth, with national subsidy, was grasped in the CBSO's development plan. It called for (1) a new concert hall, (2) enlarged string section, (3) improved pay and conditions for players, and (4) new means to explore contemporary music. It was submitted both to the Arts Council and the City Council in May 1986.

Ten years on it has achieved its goals, but, says the CBSO, with little thanks to the Arts Council. While 'Glory' withered away courtesy of civil-service cynicism and Council dithering, Birmingham was seen rather strangely as 'William's thing', and as long as Rattle stayed wedded to the CBSO – which he has until 1998 – the Council did little more than pay lip service to the deal. It gave an initial £100,000 for the £600,000 plan, then withdrew. The orchestra was helped instead by short-term sponsorship from Merrill Lynch. In an account of the CBSO by its archivist in 1995, a table showed the relation of local-authority and central subsidy, revealing that the local grants were consistently defined at 20 per cent of turnover but the Arts Council piddled about before it matched the city:

	1964		1974		1984		1994	
	£	%	£	%	£	%	£	%
Earned income	83,880	58	173,195	44	996,597	54	3,232,450	58
City Council	·35,000	21	83,380	21	369,235	20	1,125,500	20
Arts Council	42,000	26	135,000	35	457,594	25	1,164,646	21

While Ed Smith complains that 'its grant has not kept pace with the rising costs of continuing to deliver a first-class orchestra', Birmingham was lucky in its timing. It has not suffered the financial stop-start indignities of Manchester's Hallé. When Barbirolli died in 1970 he left a deeply defensive outfit still fastened to the fifties; it still played the national anthem before every concert. As there had been a spate of foreign appointments to command the country's other orchestras, the Hallé board got the retarded idea that they had to appoint 'someone from these shores', as the chairman put it to the press. The result was disastrous and allowed a peppery BBC manager, David Ellis, to rejuvenate the BBC's Northern Orchestra into the impressive BBC

Philharmonic, the relative success of which called into question the Hallé's right to rule the region.

The Hallé responded with jittery attempts to drive itself back on course and finally succeeded with the recent appointment of Kent Nagano, a Californian of Asian background and an opulent conductor to have around; his ideas are as radical as Rattle's, his hair decidedly dishier, but he is very much a man on the move. The Hallé's impediment has been its inability to align perfectly good artistic leadership and skilled management at one and the same time, which has resulted in fall-outs, misguided format changes and financial losses of the kind Rattle avoided by bringing his management with him. In 1996 the local council clinched European Union cash for a new Hallé home, Bridgewater Hall, but the CBSO's rental deal at Symphony Hall appears infinitely smoother. The Hallé is a stakeholder in league with Ogden Entertainments and has to make the place work as a generic leisure facility.

Meanwhile the Arts Council's position in Manchester is a most curious one. Through a recent appraisal it has actually suggested a hold to Nagano's progressive agenda by insisting on 'a more flexible approach artistically' and allowing the organisation to revert to a bums-on-seats drive back to stock repertoire, which is not why Nagano was employed. The Council's policy in the eighties of supporting progressive artistic policies has now been abandoned for limp popularism, and it appears that the Hallé has had to strain to equal Birmingham's good fortune.

At least they have a local authority to work with. In London the LSO is alone in its link with the unelected Corporation of London. The other three have no relationship because, of course, there's nobody to have one with, ever since Mrs Thatcher's Government dumped the socialist Greater London Council in 1986, handing over the GLC's South Bank to the Arts Council. This is why the Council's recent attempts to handle 'the London problem' by itself ended so terribly, with the organisation isolated and exposed to inordinate ridicule. The orchestras have instead generated phantom relationships, not only in the London Philharmonic's tarnished South Bank residency, but also in the Philharmonia's novel link with Bedford and the Royal Phil's residencies at Nottingham, though the RPO has muddled the issue by additionally appointing itself 'Britain's national orchestra'. These arrangements merely camouflage the principal problem that they belong nowhere any more, the Philharmonia, the Royal Phil and the BBC Symphony having been originally set up to serve the airwaves and the record deck.

In truth they work in a city which doesn't really care if it has two or twenty-two symphony orchestras, because it is a capital that trades on volume, on its eccentric diversity. Professor Lewis made it clear to the Council of 1954: 'London *as the world's centre for concert-giving,* could well support two large concert halls.' Prompted by an exceptional commercial network of music publishers, concert agents and record companies, the city has sold itself this century on the quantity of its musical life and the prosperity in consumer choice, a condition that the Arts Council has encouraged.

With the inclusion of the BBC Symphony as the fifth, the existence of five orchestras competing in the classical repertoire bucks the capital's reputation as a supreme cultural marketplace. After all, we've already learned that it's the choice of conductor and soloist more than the orchestra that determines an audience's patronage, and the significant traffic of international performers is a phenomenon on which the city's apologists pride themselves. It's surprising that no one has invested in a concert hall at Heathrow, just to save the taxi fares and lodging of jet-setting divas.

The London orchestras therefore have the general public's ignorance and indifference on their side. Any attempt to axe one or more of them is seen as red tape meddling in the right of companies to turn an honest penny. As each orchestra gives well over a hundred concerts a year and makes assorted discs, it isn't difficult for the ensembles' managers to find among the dud nights and indulgently edited recordings something that has been declared an achievement which can then be touted about to prove that the orchestra is an incontestable treasure whose success is jeopardised by crabby bureaucrats.

Yet it would be foolish of the orchestras to rely on a public which has never heard a note of theirs, and so each has cultivated friends in high places who will turn out once a year to have the national anthem played at them. Patron of the Philharmonia is HRH Prince Charles, of the LSO HRH the Queen, of the RPO Her Mother, and of the London Phil HRH the careerist Duke of Kent.

Hard though it is to imagine the royal family sat round the dinner table debating the relative virtues of 'their' orchestras, it's the thought of the royal thumbscrews at the top end and the black hole of public opinion at the bottom that makes officers quake whenever the Council decides to tackle the 'London problem'.

Chapter 11

Give me excess of it

No fewer than nineteen key reports have been commissioned so far on 'orchestra provision'. Eleven of those looked solely at London, which doesn't mean to say that the others haven't had a go at imposing solutions on the capital as well. A chronological list of the reports is too dreary to contemplate even for a book about the Council, but the main ones are as follows:

1949   Report on Orchestral Policy in England.
1958   Facing the Music: Memorandum by the Orchestral
          Employers' Association.
1965   Committee on the London Orchestras (the Goodman
          Report).
1970   Report on Orchestral Resources in Great Britain (the
          Peacock Report).
1978   The Four London Orchestras (the Figgures Report).
1984   The Arts Council and the Four Independent London
          Orchestras (the Duncan Report).
1987   Report for the Working Party on the four London
          Orchestras (the Ponsonby Report).
1993   The Advisory Committee on the London Orchestras
          (the Hoffman Report).

Half of these called for reductions in the number of the London orchestras, only one for the maintenance of the four (Ponsonby dealt with the *status quo*); the earliest didn't quite see the problem looming while the most recent famously sat on the fence. At the heart of the matter lay two opposed sentiments, rendered in Arnold Goodman's study of 1965 and Alan Peacock's five years later. The solicitor Goodman wanted four orchestras, Professor Peacock two; the Council backed the lawyer and denied the economist. Yet all is not what it seems.

For a start Goodman was writing a report he knew he could personally implement. The debut Labour Government of Harold Wilson had chosen Goodman to take over in May 1965 as the next Arts Council Chairman, and meanwhile opened the door to the job by giving him this report to chair in December 1964, a study urged by the Musicians' Union as an employment matter. Here was an odd affair: the Arts Council commissioned the report 'in association with the London County Council' but the Government requested it to do so and determined its chairmanship; Goodman detected a certain discomfort down at St James's Square.

In his autobiography Goodman claimed that 'it was necessary to produce the report in lightning time so as to enable the Arts Council to determine the orchestral fates', but there is no evidence that this was the case; the Council had already set aside £10,000 as interim aid. He knew perfectly well that he could not compose the study as Arts Council chairman, only endorse it, but he also knew that the post was coming his way. The 'lightning time' was that of his own agenda. He also claimed, with the sort of self-satisfied irony that saturates his memoirs, that he did in the end report to himself, 'since my appointment in May 1965 as Chairman of the Arts Council – to whom the report was addressed – came shortly before its publication, a notion that delighted Harold Wilson'. The report was actually received and its recommendations approved by the Council on 28 April under the retiring Chairman, Lord Cottesloe. That it was indeed printed up later and presented to the Government allows Goodman a play on words and, if his book is to be believed, nothing Goodman did ever dampened the Prime Minister's delight any.

Goodman and his team admitted that there was not enough work around for four orchestras, though there was probably enough for three and a half. To reach this bizarre conclusion they had to address three questions:

Whether the present and potential demand for the services of [the four] makes it desirable for their number to be maintained, increased or reduced; whether, and if so, in what way, it is desirable for those four orchestras to be regrouped; what measures can be taken to improve stability of employment and working conditions among orchestral players.

A couple of provisos curbed the enquiry. One of them was plain and first posed by the Musicians' Union, that 'employment will continue to be provided for the members of the existing four London orchestras' – a timely invitation to regroup the forces, which is what the Council staff urged. The other condition had been planted by the music department to spoil things for the Royal Phil, which was having a tough time after the death of Beecham: that 'programmes and performances are of the highest metropolitan standards'.

The Royal Philharmonic and the New Philharmonia were entering self-governing status at a time when recording revenue and audience attendances were dropping pitilessly. If it wasn't for the swinging-sixties growth of the London film industry and the inventive use of classical musicians by groups like the Beatles, the 'extras' that kept players otherwise buoyant would have sunk them. But Goodman reckoned that the report was less to do with general conditions. He considered it was framed by the Council to kill off the Royal Phil:

> The Arts Council, as I was soon to discover, contained some exceptionally snobbish elements. The other orchestras they regarded as socially superior and right to be retained ... Strong pressure had been brought to bear on our committee by the Arts Council representatives and others to report adversely on the orchestra, but utilising the skilful services of Ernest Bean – then the general manager of the Royal Festival Hall and a name to conjure with where the arts was concerned – we concluded that there was room, and a need, for this orchestra and that it should not be dissolved. The conclusion was bitterly resented by certain people at the Arts Council.

It annoyed almost everybody at the Arts Council, especially as they couldn't exactly nobble the new Chairman to get the report shelved. Had it been produced in front of any other body under cooler conditions the Goodman Report might well have been set aside. It was a shoddy piece of work. Goodman crowed about how it took only four months from the first meeting of his team to its adoption, and though it is stylish in its language and its conclusions are crystal clear, the arguments are vague and silly by turns, based as they are on a batty set of figures provided by the Festival Hall's Mr Bean. Goodman's team constructed a grid which mixed up quantity and quality even in its core terms:

Good (G)   Relates to concerts at which the unsold seats
                  numbered fewer than 590.
Indifferent (I)   Relates to concerts at which the unsold seats
                  numbered between 590 and 1,180.
Bad (B)   Relates to concerts at which the unsold seats
                  numbered more than 1,180.

In other words, though not the words used anywhere in the report which used this device to hide some grim figures, a 'good' concert was one where the attendance was higher than 80 per cent, an 'indifferent' one had a 'house' between 60 and 80 per cent, and a 'bad' show attracted less than 60 per cent. By this means we were assured we would learn whether the supply of concerts (629 over three years were tallied) – concerts, not *seats* – 'were in excess of public demand'.

Leaving aside all manner of bothersome questions about prices and discounts (the Festival Hall had revamped a rather drastic voucher scheme during the period in question), the categories appeared to put the public more on trial than the orchestras. Thanks to an editing error in the text we learn that there had also been a Category D, 'Disastrous'; for patent reasons the team thought better of using it. Undaunted, Goodman then had the concerts divided into ''Adventurous' or 'Popular', as though 'Bad Popular' was some kind of lucid category. The total looked like this:

Season	Number	G	I	B
Adventurous				
1961–1962	101	21	28	52
1962–1963	82	14	21	47
1963–1964	91	15	18	58
Popular				
1961–1962	125	72	36	17
1962–1963	134	71	42	21
1963–1964	96	52	26	18
Total	629	245	171	213

It then listed the orchestras by turn, concluding that the New Philharmonia had 'ten failures', the LSO twenty-six, the BBC twenty-eight and the LPO thirty-four. The figures showed, however, that the Royal Philharmonic enjoyed a mere eight failures, and it was soon apparent that this ludicrous clutter of qualitative and quantitative terms was constructed solely to deny the conspiring assassins of the Royal Phil a scrap of statistical ammunition. In fact the orchestra was doing next to no work at the Festival Hall but had set up instead a rival series of popular concerts in the Odeon Cinema at Swiss Cottage. At any rate it was on a metaphysical basis that Goodman and his team deduced that there was enough work in London for 3.5 orchestras, though whether that work would be Good, Bad or Indifferent they didn't quantify.

Goodman knew perfectly well that the music department would not be fobbed off with a report so, in order to take the implementation of it out of its stifling hands, he invented another quango. This turned out to be his solution to all kinds of problems. He implied that the London Orchestral Concerts Board (LOCB, 1965–1986) was something he had personally crafted from one of his ample ribs. In fact Ernest Bean had already set up with the companies concerned a joint orchestral committee to tackle the day-to-day plight of four independent orchestras touting for an indifferent public. The LOCB was developed from this group by bringing together the Arts Council, the Orchestra Employers' Association, the Musicians' Union and the LCC itself, which from 1 April 1965 was renamed the Greater London Council. It was therefore the LOCB that a year later passed on to each orchestra a basic annual grant of £40,000 plus a subsidy per concert, the money it acquired having come from the Arts Council and the GLC in partnership.

It took the LSO to point out that Goodman's quango would cost £10,000 a year to run while Bean's committee cost nothing. Still, if you were a member of an orchestra Goodman's solution was G for Good and it lost no one a day's work, though it dodged the key issues and prolonged corporate torment for the bands, whose roller-coaster careers still scuttle between success and disaster, which is why the Arts Council has to return to the problem every few years and make a fool of itself.

Goodman alleged that he was rattled by the unprincipled snobbery of Arts Council staff, and that was what made him wish to defend the Royal Philharmonic by way of the report. A former Council member thinks differently:

There were a couple of conspicuous hints in the brief as to how to deal with the problem. Goodman ignored them, and frankly the reason was nothing to do with orchestral politics and everything to do with Goodman's elevation into the Establishment. I say this being Jewish myself, so you can't pin any anti-Semitism on me, though I'm ashamed to say I've heard a few insensitive remarks in my time at the Arts Council. But it was plain Mister Arnold Goodman who chaired the report, and he used his solicitor's role to be around the right people, when Harold Wilson got into Number 10, to pursue his fantasies: escorting fancy ladies to the opera, wining and dining the elite at his flat in Portland Place, showing off, intimating rabbinical good sense, and all that palaver. He wanted a knighthood, but he went one better and Wilson got him ennobled, using the excuse of the Arts Council to do it. That's what it was all about. The orchestra he saved was the one with 'royal' in its title. I'm not being far-fetched. When did Arnold get his peerage? The Queen's birthday honours in 1965. When did the Queen confer the exalted prefix on the orchestra? A few months after. He was also wanting changes to the charter, which would have to go by Her Majesty.

Indeed, the elevation of Baron Goodman of the City of Westminster was announced on 12 June 1965. His report, which saved the Royal Philharmonic, was made public at a press conference twenty-four hours later, the kind of cute coincidence a smart solicitor could best choreograph.

The Royal Philharmonic Orchestra got its name by a trick. During the First World War Beecham had helped out an ailing concert-giving outfit of vintage distinction called the Royal Philharmonic Society. He acquired the rights to use its name, and in 1932, when he created the London Philharmonic, he almost called it the Royal Philharmonic Orchestra, that is, the Orchestra of the Royal Philharmonic Society, until he had a row with one of the backers. He arranged for his new orchestra of 1946 to play for the RPS's annual subscription concerts and this finally gave him the opportunity to exploit its title, though it was still the society, not the orchestra, that enjoyed royal patronage.

The power of the word 'Royal' to turn cynics into bumsuckers should never be underestimated. British composer Richard Rodney Bennett remembers an episode in the late sixties when a group of American producers booked him to write a film score, met up in town, and asked him which orchestra he'd prefer to play it. He requested the London Symphony Orchestra, which by then was generally favoured among the four, but the producers proposed the RPO, which he didn't much rate. One of the Americans looked down a list of London orchestras and asked Bennett if he'd consider the Orchestra of the Royal Opera House. He accepted the compromise, though he thought it an unconventional choice. It was only then he learned that the whole object of the producers' exercise had been to get the world 'Royal'' somewhere on the film's opening credits.

In order to secure some dignity in its orphaned state following the death of Beecham, the Royal Phil in 1964, while facing all manner of legal snags, appealed to the Queen to ratify its title with categorical patronage, a request that was favourably received. Goodman had been alerted to this manoeuvre by Number 10, and the royalist in him saw the sense of it. As his peerage was under consideration at the same time, the argument runs, he didn't wish to debilitate the chances of the orchestra, nor indeed his own.

To anyone who didn't know what lay behind it the report was considered a wise piece of work, and 'has become a basic document in any discussion of the problems of orchestras and the funding of music', in the words of Maurice Pearton, who made an impressive study of the London Symphony Orchestra. Without doubt its positive review of the RPO raised some lively fringe issues, not least the fact that the orchestra was holding its own in Swiss Cottage and doing no worse than the others down at the South Bank. Goodman's report urged the GLC to rethink its policy and, basically, turn the metropolitan orchestras into suburban ones.

The cue came from the London Symphony Orchestra itself, which, in its 1965 submission reported by Pearton, argued:

> Greater London is large enough to 'take' four good concert halls – the Festival Hall as its central venue, a hall to cater for North London, one in the West, and one for those living South of the Thames ... It is far easier to build up and maintain a 'local' audience, than the transient customers one has to attract from a huge area to the Festival Hall.

The north, the west, the south – it's a mite ironic that the LSO didn't consider the east, which is where it ended up. Nonetheless it is instructive now to move forward to Yehudi Menuhin's 1993 proposals on solving the London problem:

> The orchestras ought to be relocated to areas which are congenial and alive and outside the inner city area. There should be four well-equipped concert halls in different parts of London for the four orchestras. Ideally they would be placed around the compass. For the north, how about Hampstead or Camden? For the south, Richmond or Wimbledon. For the west Fulham, Hammersmith or Putney ... These areas would benefit culturally and financially, and borough residents would lay claim to their orchestra.

The Philharmonia of Fulham, the Royal Phil of Ruislip; there's a certain ring.

From Goodman in 1965 to Menuhin in 1993 comes the same idea with three decades of inertia in between. No doubt the Arts Council was unconcerned because the issue was no longer national but local, while a GLC saddled with the South Bank wasn't about to cultivate rivals. Whether the property resources were around in the sixties to furnish such a scheme is hard to judge, despite the existence of a 'Housing the Arts' budget, partly because Goodman's coverage of the issue was so loose.

Now, however, the Council has an entire fund fed by Lottery loot which could cover Menuhin's bold if bourgeois plan. At the same time the Government restricts the Council to respond to proposals not make them, and there's presently no GLC to fill in the forms. Yet even in order to help, the Arts Council would need to ditch its *à la mode*, government-infected enthusiasm for coupling the arts with tourism, which gives it the excuse to pamper the South Bank. This tourism theme loops back to Professor Lewis's comment to the Council in 1954 about 'London as the world's centre for concert-giving', and reminds us of the Council's ceaseless confusion about its role in the capital. As one regional officer said when the 1994 changes turned the AC of Great Britain into the AC of England, 'It makes no difference; to me it's always been the Arts Council of London.' London, but not Greater London. And to think it started out funding anywhere *but* London.

So the Peacock Report was the opposite. Meaty, it covered the national scene, contained meaningful statistics, useful tables, impeccable research, terrific ideas – but deadly dull to read. It must have annoyed York University's professor of economics no end to have his report compared unfavourably to Goodman's poncy tosh, but the Chairman of the Arts Council saw to it that it was, for it was the good lord himself who received Peacock's paper.

Nobody could deny that the report was needed so soon after Goodman's; there were two reasons why. First the Labour Government was in difficulties with 'the pound in your pocket' devaluation of currency. This was shaking the regional orchestras' hopes of balancing costs against subsidy from local and central sources; in fact Peacock was written under Wilson's Labour and published under Heath's Tories, voted in once the public had lost confidence in Labour's economic performance. Second, the BBC had been making creepy noises about changes to its orchestras and the fear of upheaval in the music market craved an independent overview of the national scene. But there was more to it than that: though a new music director had arrived he was cut from the same cloth as the old one and his department remained resolute in its determination to 'Kill the Royal Phil'. Opponents of the Council should never miscalculate the 'won-the-battle-but-not-the-war' tenacity of its smarter staff, who, in bountiful civil service fashion will sit and count raindrops until the sun shines on their cherished schemes.

Why Goodman would have agreed to let Professor Peacock lead the report is a beguiling matter. He was probably duped by the music department. The new music director in question, John Cruft, recalls Peacock's suitability in the most emollient terms:

> He was considered a caring and sensible man who had by then not become so politically involved [an allusion to his proto-Thatcherism]. He was very interested in music, so much so that he composed pieces himself, which was an attractive advantage. The work was unpaid and demanded quite a lot of time and energy, which luckily he was able to give.

Yes, Goodman gave Peacock the job because he was an amateur composer.

Goodman had too readily assumed that the report, entitled 'A Report on Orchestral Resources in Great Britain', would leave London alone, but Professor Peacock made good arguments why he could not, and they hinged in part on the Arts Council's bias to the capital but chiefly on the uneven traffic of players from the regions to the centre simply because they could earn more for the same work, with extra cash from studio sessions added on. The final report contained no fewer than twenty-six dynamic recommendations, but two of them were bombshells:

1. That the salaries of players in regional symphony orchestras be raised at least to the level of earnings for comparable work in London.
2. That the LOCB announces as soon as possible that from the beginning of the 1973–1974 concert season it will offer appropriate financial support for two orchestras accepting contractual obligations designed to provide permanence and stability, and we commend the proposal to the GLC, the Corporation of London and the Arts Council for their urgent consideration.

In reply Goodman sank his big bum on top of Peacock's report. He wrote a flatulent preface to the published document in order to demean it: 'Number 2 is a far-reaching Recommendation which, having regard to the current musical situation, the Council has not felt able to endorse at this moment in our musical history.' He said more or less the same about the salaries, really because Goodman thought people in London deserved more simply for being clever enough to live there. He once commented, 'It is idiotic that the regions, which are pretty barren of talent, should run the show. You can't find that in Wigan or Warrington. They need a hard centre.' Peacock's point was quite different. Looking at the London orchestras in a national context, his team noticed that in 1968 the London four earned almost double that of the five regional orchestras:

> Whereas the [regional five] earn their performance income almost exclusively from concert-giving, the London orchestras spend a relatively small part of their time on the concert platform, and obtain a high proportion of their income from gramophone recording, television performances and, possibly, film studios, on all of which income can be forced up more nearly to balance costs than is possible in giving concerts.

The implication that the Arts Council of Great Britain should therefore use its subsidy to balance this national imparity, which drained the regions of ambitious players, was not a notion to impress Baron Goodman of the City of Westminster.

Even he must have been over-awed by the tables and figures. For the first time in British music, statistics were gathered that showed the development of subsidy, such as this one breaking down the income of the five regional orchestras, for which here, to make it even simpler, only the percentages are shown:

Sources of income	1954–1955 %	1961–1962 %	1968–1969 %
Performance income	60.2	54.9	46.1
Grants and subsidies:			
Arts Council and British			
Council	12.8	19.9	30.6
Local authorities	21.8	17.9	21.0
Private sources	1.7	1.9	1.3
Met from reserves (deficit)	3.5	5.4	1.0
Total	100	100	100

The worrying conclusion drawn, if the gap between box office and need continued to grow at the same rate as it had over the last decade, was that, 'for the regional orchestras as a whole, performance income would fall to about 30% of total expenditure by the mid 70s', while their dependence on national subsidy would rise above it. Through tables like this the report showed the lack of principle behind orchestral grant aid and issued a number of warnings about the future which it tried its best through the twenty-six recommendations to address.

Some of those now seem mad. Number 11 suggested that orchestra managements should prepare a budget showing their estimated income and expenditure for the next ten years: 'I'm lucky if I can work one out for the next ten weeks,' groaned a manager recently. Yet number 21 proposed that orchestras each use a part of their grant to appoint a composer-in-residence (this only started to happen in the eighties), who would also build bridges between the orchestras and local schools and colleges 'to compose for their available musical resources'. Most far-reaching of all was number 16, which urged 'that a greater proportion of public money' should be used for 'consumer subsidies', and it was the method of this money's distribution that was most audacious: 'We recommend that in all areas some part, and in deprived areas a major part, of grants should be awarded to music societies through Regional Arts Associations and possibly through the National Federation of Music Societies.' The idea of dragging the Arts Council's worst enemies, the RAAs, into the marketing of orchestras may well have triggered hair loss among Council staff.

Above all, the proposal to kill off two of the orchestras was convincingly put, not as a local London issue, but as a national one. The Goodman solution, steered through the LOCB, had simply not worked. The four orchestras were not getting the level of subsidy they believed they required to operate without scraping their reserves, they had not improved working conditions despite Goodman's abstract nudging of subsidy towards holiday pay and pensions, and their standards of performance were as come-and-go as ever. It was achingly obvious to the orchestras by then that a reduction would work in general favour of London's musical life. Goodman, who was not an authority on music or musical life, would have none of it. Peacock, amateur tunesmith, would.

As our source at the Council put it:

> I would say first of all that the common-sense solution, even in 1965, with all four orchestras in trouble but two established and two immature, would be to take the option hinted at in the brief of Goodman's report. That is, to strengthen the London Symphony and the London Philharmonic from the 70 to 80 members each had at the time towards the size of the Boston Symphony or the Berlin Philharmonic, around 115 players each. You would absorb players from the other two orchestras; well, OK, you would be reducing the total of around 300 members to 230 and dropping 70 into the freelance pool – or getting them back into the regions where some of them came from in the first place. By doing that you'd certainly have raised standards – quadruple woodwind, fuller string sections, back-up brass, permanent percussion specialists, better hours and breaks for individual members, and so on, all the things the top Americans have – while at the same time easing the dilemma of competition. That could have been done on the money. All Peacock really did was to remind us of the solution that should have been taken five years earlier.

By the time the Peacock Report was published the Royal Philharmonic and the New Philharmonia were in a deep financial pickle. Goodman was forced into a meeting with the orchestras in May 1971. By now culture's Buddha, he beamingly repeated his mantra to maintain four different orchestras, while behind his broad back the New Philharmonia and the RPO discussed a merger. When Goodman heard this he used all his powers of honeyed blackmail on the NPO's benefactors to forbid a musical marriage. Two months later, though, Ernest Bean reported to the

LOCB that he could foresee 'the Official Receiver conducting the *Farewell* Symphony' to a couple of the four. There were just two alternatives, he advised: increase the grants for all four orchestras to drive off insolvency but little else, or put all the money into two orchestras, just as Peacock had proposed.

Bean said this knowing that Lord Goodman was on his way out. He'd led the Arts Council for seven years; now the Tories were bringing in Pat Gibson, a director of the *Economist* and chief of Pearson Longman, the publisher. At this time the New Philharmonia was staring bankruptcy in the face; reserves were exhausted and in addition the 1971–1972 loss totalled £24,000 (£170,000). Its record company suggested a merger with the London Philharmonic, and once this had been dressed up as a 112-strong super-orchestra (very seventies, very flares and Jumbo jets), it was put before an eager Gibson. This whole business was driven by EMI assembling a star vehicle for Daniel Barenboim, the pianist turned conductor who was locked into London life due to his wife's multiple sclerosis. The package included sixty-five concerts a year at the Festival Hall and 100 sessions for the record company. A Council member considered 'it was like creating a football dream team out of other teams, and you just knew it could only work as a one-off'.

A group of City businessmen, no doubt music-lovers all, came in to examine the state of the field, and called the match off: Ronald Grierson, chairman of the Philharmonia Trust but also vice-chairman of General Electric and a director of S.G. Warburg; Ian Stoutzker, joint managing director of Keyser Ullman and chairman of the London Interstate Bank, who eventually bought the orchestra out of trouble by gaining its chairmanship then its presidency, a little like he would for a football club; Peter Andry of EMI; Lord Salisbury of the London Philharmonic's Council; the Philharmonia's long-suffering 'Anonymous Benefactor' who, or which, is really the same exotic trust that endows Warwick University; the Council's print-trade chairman Pat Gibson.

Apparently the super-orchestra would need just over £400,000 a year in subsidy, of which Stoutzker promised to provide half if the LOCB would cover the rest. But in November 1972 the Philharmonia suddenly pulled out of talks because until then the musicians knew nothing of it and believed that Barenboim had not yet proved himself worthy of the monopoly. The project was quietly swept under the carpet of the Festival Hall.

It's remarkable that the Arts Council staff, who were now getting their way in the matter, seemed to allow the scheme to evaporate. It confirms how far Goodman had disarmed the officers' powers. In fact it was Goodman's dislike of the music department – the 'exceptionally snobbish elements' which (he perceived) considered certain orchestras to be 'socially superior' rather than musically so – that fostered some of the entrenched problems. His memoirs describe the two music directors in his time:

> On my arrival at the Arts Council I soon became hugely impatient of the antics of the bureaucrats and was relieved when John Denison departed for his well-earned promotion as general manager of the Royal Festival Hall in succession to Ernest Bean not long after. But his successor John Cruft . . . was no better where the RPO was concerned. He too had evolved the theory that London had too many orchestras.

In fact, both Denison and Cruft had been distinguished orchestral musicians, and the problem for Goodman was that they not only knew the London bands inside out and could name most of the individual players concerned, they also knew all about orchestral life in general and he couldn't fault their facts. Denison had been third horn – that is, second in command – in the London Philharmonic for five years in the thirties ('I normally had a wage but it didn't always come on Friday. No one had the slightest security'), then principal horn of Birmingham's orchestra; he'd even entered Glyndebourne's pit before the war. His successor, John Cruft, played oboe in the London Symphony Orchestra and became a salient figure in its rehabilitation with the Arts Council during the late forties and fifties. Between them Denison and Cruft ran the music department for thirty years, so it can't possibly be said that the Arts Council lacked awareness of the ways of orchestras.

The combative Goodman was quick to turn their experiences back against them: 'For some reason, those who defect from the orchestra pit to administration view their former colleagues with contempt and animosity . . . You cannot, they say, turn that shower into a body of respectable human beings.' There may be some truth in Goodman's argument, which becomes most evident when bad players leave their seats to become bad conductors. There is certainly a body of opinion nowadays which maintains that the self-governing system is no longer sustainable because some players are not their best bosses.

One former orchestra manager and music panellist commented:

> Some of them I would consider rather like right-wing versions of
> the old trades-union officials: dogged and not able to see the wood
> for the trees, regarding an issue in terms of their next wage, not the
> next decade. And frankly, musicians are a rather rum bunch –
> some are deeply intelligent but eccentric, but many of them are not
> very bright at all.

At the same time, while many of the musicians of the fifties and
sixties had served in the forces and saw a dress suit as another sort
of uniform, the new generation of recruits were more progressive
(Rattle took advantage of this liberal swing).

Whether orchestras are now able to turn *themselves* round to
face the future is an issue of the moment, but Goodman's
poacher-gamekeeper notion is not borne out by the fact that the
Arts Council never made a fool of itself when Denison or Cruft ran
the department. Some would say that whenever non-players were
in charge, from 1979 onwards under Basil Deane, Richard
Lawrence and Ken Baird, it was not so successful. The latest
incumbent, Kathryn McDowell, worked as an assistant administrator for the Ulster Orchestra and her line, in the wake of the
1993 disaster, has appeared to be to do little to stir up the
orchestras, which is surely not a policy but a precaution. She is
backed by her chairman Gavin Henderson, a flamboyant
character once seen never forgotten, who used to work for the
Philharmonia.

The Arts Council keeps facing the same problems as though
they are fresh ones, learns little from its faults or failures,
manipulates the time and energy of outsiders to no great purpose,
and nourishes long-term problems through short-term remedies.
The dilemmas of the early seventies were stoked by the solutions
of the middle sixties, and so it runs on: the super-orchestra whim
was ruinously revived by Lord Palumbo in the early nineties, not
for a young Barenboim but instead a venerable Solti; Ronald
Grierson reappeared at the centre of the 'first time as tragedy,
second time as farce' orchestral beauty contests of 1990 and 1993;
the Royal and London Phils failed to merge in 1994 after their
players found out what was going on. As one manager declared,
'The Arts Council sees it as the Orchestra Problem. The
orchestras, I can assure you, see it as the Arts Council Problem.'

*

The four London orchestras are still with us, despite the following.

Early in 1978, Sir Frank Figgures and his team urged that the LOCB should 'make no further assistance to managements in difficulty and make public this decision'. Had this become policy the LSO would have perished. By the end of that year the London four complained they'd been 'frozen out of discussions to give just one of the four a substantial increase to bring it up to the highest international standards'. The music director John Cruft would neither confirm nor deny the rumour. Yet in November 1979 *The Times* reported:

> After a year of arousing both ire and uncertainty among London's orchestras, the plan for a new 'million pound orchestra' has been quietly buried by the Arts Council. Government cuts ensured the death of the scheme but, said an insider, 'It was never really a question of a £1m orchestra: the likely cost of such a body was estimated by orchestral managing directors at between £2m and £3m a year.'

In 1981 relations with the Council soured again when the London four realised that, without their help, a major modern-music series titled *Music of Eight Decades* had used up all the supplementary funds they had banked on. The latest music director, Basil Deane, felt that 'the big orchestras have not demonstrated a strong commitment to new music. We did not know that it would turn out that there would be virtually nothing left for other concerts.' The Council promised to reconsider its policy the next year. In April 1982 the House of Lords helped it along by debating the incident, poking fun at the Council in an exchange led by Labour's Lord Strabolgi, who just happened to be a life member of the Royal Phil:

> There have been complaints from the orchestras that they are not always fully consulted by the Arts Council. Moreover, the Arts Council want to see an increase in contemporary music being played as well as commissioned. At the same time, though, the Council are anxious for the orchestras to attract more concert-goers. I am sorry to say, that, on the whole, those two aims are mutually exclusive.

He pointed out an ironic fact, that though the Council said it wanted to make contemporary music more accessible to the public, there was no such aim in the charter – music in *general*, yes, but not specifically new. The Liberals' Lord Tordoff, a Hallé fan, mocked the Council's tone of voice:

> The Arts Council believes that there are 'no new vibrant ideas' coming from symphony orchestras. I suppose they could perform Verdi's Requiem seated on coffins, or they could perform Beethoven's Ninth in the nude. That might make it vibrant, but it would not make it more musical.

In April 1984 a major Council tome entitled 'The Glory of the Garden' proposed a 'great eastern symphony orchestra' to be based in Nottingham, which many recognised as a hint to the Royal Phil to move to the Midlands if it wanted to improve its subsidy, offered at an extra £280,000 a year. Yet it seems that hardly anyone in the area had been consulted. 'There is dismay in the region at the idea of a single orchestra. They want variety. I've spoken to sixteen major authorities and sixteen smaller ones out of our sixty-three and not one feels anything but dismay,' said the manager of the East Anglian Orchestral Association, whose grant was to be withdrawn to help pay for the scheme. The London four scoffed at 'an orchestra wandering around the East Midlands'. By December it was admitted that 'shifting a London orchestra is now almost certainly impossible', while Secretary-General Luke Rittner stated, 'The Council feels it needs more time to crack this nut.'

In November 1984 Neil Duncan, an Arts Council veteran affectionately known as Drunken Duncan, reported on the London four's work in the capital as well as their regional touring, where he confessed that 'the programmes available from the London orchestras are often routine and under-rehearsed'. Aware that the Government's imminent axing of the Greater London Council would mean an end to the LOCB, he urged that:

> all four of the London orchestras be directly funded by the Arts Council as from April 1986 . . . That the Council should withdraw financial support from any of the four orchestras which was unsatisfactory in financial position, quality of management or artistic standards [interesting order of priorities] . . . That at least one-third of its main London season concerts be repeated or toured.

To assist this grand tour, he invented ROTA (a Regional Orchestra Touring Agency) funded entirely by the Council and mandated to offer 'equalisation grants' so that 'a London orchestra would cost the same to a local authority whether in Walthamstow or Newcastle', which was a very 'Glory of the Garden' idea and like much of 'Glory' went west.

More boldly he believed that, unless the Council secured the £280,000 for London orchestras, it should persuade the City to throw the London Symphony Orchestra out of the Barbican and replace it with the RPO, which was about to start a stretch under Ashkenazy and Previn. But if the City fathers wouldn't play along then the Arts Council should withdraw its money from the RPO forever. Soon after his report was delivered, Mr Duncan left for a job in Hong Kong.

In 1987, a former BBC music mandarin, Robert Ponsonby, and his working party looked at the financial demands the four orchestras were placing on the Council's music budget, only to learn that a joint plan initiated by the London Phil and the Philharmonia for 'a dual residency' at the Festival Hall had been 'put on ice' by the Arts Council people recently hired to run the South Bank. This partnership was considered by some press commentators as little less than a takeover bid for the soul of the Philharmonia by the London Phil. Against the dual-residency scheme stood three doubts: 'Competitiveness between the two orchestras in this situation might make the plan unworkable; the number of concerts inherent in the plan would be unmanageably high; and the acquiescence of the third orchestra [the RPO, frozen out] would not easily be obtained.'

In that case, the working party wrote:

> the South Bank Centre might well consider as an alternative a close
> association with whichever orchestra is best placed to fulfil the
> following criteria: very high standards of performance ... the
> ability to plan more adventurous, interesting programmes ...
> maintain the existing level of players' income whilst reducing their
> workload ... market concerts in a way to maximise box office
> income ... secure financial resources from the private sector.

Ponsonby went on to carve up the annual subsidy, not in a general way, but per concert: forty by the LSO at the Barbican, thirty each by the others. He also supported the need by the LSO and the

LPO for a 'call fee', a 25 per cent increase in concert fees 'in return for an increase in the players' commitment to concert work', which is a sign of how undisciplined these ensembles had become.

Ponsonby's invitation to the South Bank to seek 'a close association' with one orchestra got terribly tangled with a kindred idea when property tycoon Peter Palumbo, the new Arts Council Chairman, arrived in 1989. Palumbo put forward the highly original notion of a state subsidised super-orchestra, rumours having already circulated that the concept was born at a prattling dinner party. Behind his back it was sniggeringly called the London Palumbo Orchestra – the LPO – or the Palumbo Philharmonic. He decided it would make its debut in Hyde Park conducted by Sir Georg Solti, who would be eighty in 1992. At the same time the South Bank was developing the Ponsonby option into a 'resident orchestra'. Easy as it is to see how two such outfits could get a couple of similar but unrelated ideas muddled up, that is how one of the biggest farces in British musical history began.

Chapter 12

'Tis not so sweet now as it was before

How Nicholas Snowman got his job as artistic demigod to the South Bank in 1986 remains a mystery to many. He was certainly awarded the directorship by Arts Council executives who hadn't at first thought of him at all. They wanted Michael Vyner, a thoroughly flamboyant music administrator who had to admit to them he was dying of AIDS. Why they chose Vyner it's hard to say, though he was fun and camp to have around. All he seemed to have done was to have run a chamber orchestra called the London Sinfonietta that had a job to find bookings and existed on Arts Council favours. But the Council needed to act swiftly, having found the whole South Bank Centre operation dumped on its doorstep by Mrs Thatcher in 1984. She was due to close down the Greater London Council on 1 April 1986, which had run the place pretty successfully – certainly better, some would say, than the Arts Council was about to do.

The Council's Chairman, William Rees-Mogg, gave the job of sorting out the South Bank's 'can of worms' to the Deputy Secretary-General, Richard Pulford. This former civil servant chose to split the top job there between administration and artistic direction and took for himself the management post. Pulford was the first of many to 'walk the little bridge they built for themselves between Piccadilly and Waterloo', and when he did so, he warned the Council that 'I'm not going to be the Deputy Secretary-General of the South Bank'. Once he'd crossed his bridge he admits he 'lost interest in the Arts Council' and turned, in the words of a former colleague, into 'one of the most formidable and confrontational clients we faced'. As Pulford's artistic cohort they chose Vyner, who chose Snowman.

Vyner and Snowman were pals because the former had succeeded the latter as manager of the London Sinfonietta, which Snowman had started up in 1968 as a career move with an ambitious young conductor, David Atherton. The freelance orchestra specialised in complex modern scores, though not by women – Vyner was a rigid misogynist. The Arts Council backed the Sinfonietta to the hilt in that loyal, one-off way it adopts whenever it knows it must be seen to back something contemporary but not too novel; the music department did the same with an unsophisticated venture called the Opera Factory, which also found asylum in the South Bank. Though the Sinfonietta contained some magnificent musicians, its programmes were generally a decade behind the times it claimed to address, it got too little work beyond its own promotions, and was soon outclassed by foreign competitors. Thankfully, the Sinfonietta has since been relaunched to tackle a wider view of the modern musical world.

Vyner forced the Sinfonietta and its poker-faced programmes on the Council's Contemporary Music Network year after year, and when CMN's Annette Morreau tried to bring in some more enterprising ensembles from abroad, Vyner went over her head to block their visits. So when he was offered the South Bank Centre he saw a way to protect his ailing outfit by making it the centre's resident ensemble. Here, then, is perhaps the fundamental motive, pursued by Robert Ponsonby in his report, for the South Bank Centre's evolution of the notion of 'residencies', which led to the choosing of a resident symphony orchestra.

Snowman (born 1944) had just finished working abroad as a supervisor for Pierre Boulez, the self-possessed composer for whom the French Government built in the centre of Paris a high-tech electronic music centre, IRCAM. (A splendid study of IRCAM, *Rationalising Culture*, was written by Georgina Born in 1995.) When Snowman arrived at the South Bank it seemed as though his brain was still detained in Paris. Certainly his planning of programmes would have satisfied his former French boss; he spent much of one annual budget, for instance, putting on a concert version of a French religious opera written by Boulez's old teacher. The riverside terrace was dug up to provide boules courts and dug back weeks later when it was discovered that no one who passed by knew how to play boules, nor cared to. Snowman seemed to be surprised to learn that London didn't wish to be Londres.

The South Bank Centre slid into a series of budgetary, programming and marketing crises over which the Arts Council has indemnified it for a decade. Exhausted and demoralised, the centre has since set up a whole new department to programme areas which were hitherto neglected. In turn the Arts Council has chosen to stick by its founding choice. In the words of a former South Banker, the Council's defence is that:

> Nicholas wanted to work closely with certain preferred artists by planning series and projects with them. He didn't want the South Bank to be a receiving house for other people's ideas. That satisfied the Arts Council, because otherwise the South Bank is an unwieldy beast.

Snowman's executive chairman at the time of symphony orchestra selection in 1990 was the industrialist Ronald Grierson, who'd run the Philharmonia Trust for fifteen years. When they decided to appoint a resident orchestra for the South Bank it was clear that someone else would need to make the decision. They appointed a committee headed by Sir John Tooley, the retired boss of Covent Garden. The London Philharmonic and the Philharmonia competed for the job, which guaranteed a permanent home, at least for five years 'or any subsequent year on two years' notice', and all the attendant luxuries such as rehearsals in the same hall as the concert, and priorities over programming and dates. When Tooley's committee made its choice, the managers of the two ensembles were summoned to Snowman's office. Unfortunately for David Whelton of the Philharmonia, he and his orchestra were touring the States.

The colourless, bespectacled Whelton recalls:

> I got a call in Boston in the middle of the night. I was told to catch a Lear jet reserved for me at Boston which would take me to New York, where I'd been booked on the early Concorde for London at the South Bank's expense. The orchestra was playing in Washington DC the next night with a host of diplomats attending,

but I was told it was all worked out and I'd been booked back on Concorde to get me there in time. I thought, 'This is it; we've got the residency.'

He arrived at the South Bank to be told by Snowman he hadn't. It would go to the London Philharmonic. Whelton went on:

You can imagine my feelings, suicidal feelings, when I got on the tube to the airport. I mean, I had to go back to the Philharmonia on an extremely prestigious date and tell them this awful news, and I'd gone halfway round the world to learn it. I was working out survival tactics on the back of a cigarette packet on the Heathrow tube. Amazingly, though, as I stood in the Concorde queue I saw in front of me none other than Ronnie Grierson.

The South Bank's chairman said he had some business in the States. Yet when Whelton arrived at the Washington reception after a successful but depressing concert sponsored by Parker Pens, he was stunned to see Grierson sitting at a lively table. 'By the way, I'm a major shareholder of *Schaeffer* Pens,' Grierson grinned. Called to make a speech in front of the orchestra and guests, Whelton didn't let the opportunity pass to underline, no doubt with a Parker pen, the grim irony of Grierson's presence at this loser's wake. Some might conclude, however, that Grierson, a good friend to the Philharmonia, went along to help Whelton think the future through.

However, the winner may not have felt so victorious once it had received a list of the South Bank's instructions: the wind department was to be restructured and a more abrasive repertoire of modernist works developed with the rugged Harrison Birtwistle as 'composer in residence'; there was a deal on hall hires for the rehearsals that was anything but a bargain and, above all, a music director was to be introduced.

This last requirement was a most interesting one in general, for it rightly called into question the relation of an orchestra to its conductors. Orchestras give the more regular conductors they work with all kinds of silly designations, in part to fool the public that behind the agent's invoice and the flight ticket lies a peerless intimacy and exclusive rapport, but equally to flatter the conductors, who collect these honorary titles like others do fridge magnets. The London Symphony Orchestra, for instance, parades the following in this way:

Conductor laureate	André Previn
Principal conductor	Colin Davis
Principal guest conductor	Michael Tilson Thomas
Associate conductor	Richard Hickox
Associate principal guest conductor	Kent Nagano

Snowman wanted a straight-down-the-line music director, someone with power to hire and fire the players and with whom he could work to plan the brave new repertoire he had in mind. The London Phil's problem lay in providing one. Up to that time its principal conductor had been a riveting if neurotic senior German, Klaus Tennstedt, who swiftly resigned as his cancer and private insecurities grew. The LPO's manager, John Willan, gambled with Snowman on an unknown twenty-nine-year-old Austrian with a put-on name, Franz Welser-Möst. It was a bet they lost, and the consequences were dire.

Soon disparaged by critics as Frankly Worst Than Most, his unconvincing appearances with 'his' London Phil at the Festival Hall, which formally began in September 1992, did little to persuade the public and the music business that the residency had introduced higher standards or stronger repertoire. The Austrian's autocracy only fuelled gossip about alleged right-wing connections as well as his subsequent grooming by a strange baron who, formally adopting him as a son, became the conductor's agent.

Audiences dwindled, at one point down to 40 per cent (a definite D on Goodman's grid), sponsorship dropped by half a million. The orchestra sacked John Willan; his eventual replacement was a city financier. It started rehearsing away from the South Bank to save money as it was otherwise paying £70,000 from its own income to be there. In February 1994 the players took a 15 per cent cut in fees while the Musicians' Union provided a £250,000 interest-free loan. *Private Eye* looked at the South Bank's 1994–1995 schedule and noted that 'while the Philharmonia is promoting 39 concerts, the Abominable Snowman's resident band . . . is able to mount only 21 in its *International* series, boosted by a further 10, low-budget, low-brow *Classics for Pleasure* programmes.' The residency required the LPO to promote fifty top-quality concerts a season; it was originally sixty – the LSO was obliged to provide the Barbican with eighty-five concerts a year. Welser-Möst later retreated to a less glamorous post in Zürich in order to hone his skills.

Meanwhile the back of David Whelton's fag packet had worked

wonders. Under pressure to win more dates for the Philharmonia
to keep up cashflow and momentum, he found them in Paris.
Thanks to a boardroom connection the Philharmonia landed
work at the Châtelet Theatre. It was run by the conservative city
authority of Mayor Chirac, half as a concert hall, half as an opera
house to thrust two Gallic fingers at President Mitterrand's new
national opera house at the Bastille. In a city where there is really
no orchestra worth hearing, the Philharmonia's success was a
sensation and, of course, the impact of this vindication back home
was all the stronger for taking place in Snowman's paradigm city.
To add insult to injury the orchestra championed the craggy
scores of Birtwistle, whom the London Phil had to accept as their
composer-in-residence not having played a note of his work. The
Philharmonia even poached the LPO's leader, David Nolan, two
principal wind players and its marketing manager.

Beleaguered, the London Phil sought a new alliance.
Broadsheets including the *Independent* carried a story on 13 May
1995 that the LPO would marry the Royal Phil: 'The merger will
be in the first instance only at an administrative level ... but
sources in both orchestras confirmed it was a precursor to an
eventual merger on the playing side, perhaps within six months.'
The orchestra's manager wouldn't go along with it and was
sacked, as it appeared that the idea had come from the chairman
of the LPO's trust, former Cabinet minister Lord Young, chatting
to his counterpart at the RPO, Sir John Morgan, a veteran Foreign
Office bigwig. They thought the new body might be called the
Royal London Philharmonic. The marriage plans fell apart when
the Royal Phil's musicians learned what was going on, and by now
the reader may well feel a creeping sense of *déjà vu* ...

... which will not be dispelled by the news that in July 1995 the
London Phil invited the Philharmonia to share its South Bank
residency from 1 September 1997. Bob St John Wright, chairman
of the LPO orchestral board, chirped, 'Inviting the Philharmonia
to join us in residency provides a unique opportunity to build on
its achievements at the South Bank,' and David Whelton chirped
back, 'We are looking forward to a completely new chapter in
London's orchestral life.' The South Bank hailed it as 'an historic
new agreement', historic certainly in the sense that neither
orchestra had a music director, nor would choose to have, and
thus the most basic element of the residency principle was
dropped. Readers are now invited to turn back to the section
about the dual scheme in 1987 and remind themselves of why, in

the South Bank's view, it wasn't going to work.

If this litany of folly wasn't bad enough, Palumbo decided in the middle of it all to cultivate his super-orchestra. Why the Secretary-General, Anthony Everitt, or his latest music director, Kenneth Baird, were unable to stop their Chairman is unknown, but they left their jobs once he had his way.

Almost everyone at the Council was concerned by Palumbo's plan as it re-emerged in early 1993, for in his eyes the super-orchestra would be entirely new, composed of the best players, poached presumably from the nation's fifteen bands, and thus it would not solve the existing problem but decidedly add to it. What possibly induced Palumbo, by the way, to choose such a difficult period to push his plan through might be explained by the fact that his term of office would end in April 1994, and hence he would be able to bow out in an acoustic blaze of glory on a gracious night in Hyde Park.

Maybe it was the grey-hued Baird who turned the plan round to face the London problem. He'd already fought the bands and fallen short in 1989 when, echoing the *Music of Eight Decades* wrangle, he wanted to 'reward adventurous programming' by giving selected concerts £15,000 each and ending blanket support. 'We will be particularly interested in music written in the last ten years,' he challenged, though this brave stand came to nothing. Now he had an opportunity for a reinforced invasion, but no doubt because the London Symphony Orchestra was protected by the City in its Barbican bunker, it was the remaining trio that was targeted. This move may have reflected what Baird thought of Snowman's achievement down at the South Bank, for what went for the LSO should have gone for the LPO, too, but subsequently Palumbo was happy to talk of 'the *two* super-orchestras', the LSO and the eventual winner of his contest.

In early July 1993 the trinity of managers was summoned to the Arts Council, where they were told that from April 1994 the Council would fund only one of them. The money would be won by the outfit that presented the best artistic plan, to be assessed by an independent team headed by Lord Justice Sir Leonard Hoffman. They were assured that it was an issue of artistic standards and that they would be judged on their 'artistic vision', which means they would be assessed on their aspirations not their track record, their paperwork not their music. A decision would be made in October 1993. Then, so as not to let the protesting orchestras play on the public's aversion to red tape, the Arts Council made a fatal mistake. Emerging all butch and brawny, it gave the contest a walloping press profile – so potent that even the tabloids gave it space – emphasising in its press releases the brave artistic step it was taking and through that the colossal cultural profit for the nation.

It is perhaps strange, then, that the music panel chairman of the time, philosopher Brian Magee, considered the issue a financial one:

> It is today's Government, not today's Arts Council, that has cut £5 million off that latter's budget from next April. But this is spurring the Council to do something it ought to have done years ago and focus resources on fewer London orchestras. It has decided to give more money to each of two than it has ever before given to any one, with the express aim of helping them develop into world-class institutions.

To get it over with, here are the allocations as they stood when the enquiry was announced, and then as they finally turned out in the following financial year:

	1993–1994	1994–1995
	£	£
London Symphony Orchestra	1,128,500	1,140,000
London Philharmonic	1,128,500	700,000
South Bank Centre residency	—	400,000
Philharmonia	711,500	700,000
Royal Philharmonic	400,000	250,000
Total	3,368,500	3,190,000

The grant total for the trio as it stood when the contest began was £2.24 million, and that was the kind of super-orchestra figure it was thought they were fighting for. The sums don't add up, however. Magee's music panellists, who saw Hoffman's delayed draft in early December, were under the impression that the exercise would eventually save £900,000. Thanks to lobbying by panel member Priti Paintal, of whom it would be nice to say she was there simply as a noted composer but who some suspect may have been placed as a token black female, the saving was earmarked to go on 'music education, regional developments, recordings, touring, jazz, Asian, Caribbean and African music'. It didn't.

She resigned from the panel after the meeting on this precise issue, while composer Robert Saxton had done so back in May over the entire concept of judging the orchestras, as did percussionist Evelyn Glennie twenty-four hours after Paintal. In any case £900,000 from £2.24 million leaves £1.34 million, and if that was the true sum the three orchestras were fighting over, it was hardly more than the existing grant to the London Phil. The difference between a mere orchestra and a super-orchestra was apparently £211,500, which is less than the contest itself cost to administer. Saving money was indeed behind this exercise, but somebody fudged the numbers. The figure of £900,000 was possibly invented on the spot just to keep the feisty Paintal quiet. Some hope. She set up a lobbying group, Main Music Agenda, which continues to prick the Council over the issue.

When 'Lenny' Hoffman was invited to chair the committee critics immediately protested that the Arts Council paid its staff handsomely to handle these sorts of decisions and ran a panel of specialists to advise them, so there was little sense in engaging an amateur to reach the kind of verdict it was set up to deliver professionally. Maybe, though, no one inside the Council building wanted the blood of two famous orchestras on their own hands. Instead they thought the choice of Judge Hoffman to be a terribly witty one, for he was Goodman's young aide back in 1965. Goodman wrote of this South African barrister that, 'he made an admirable secretary: he was good-humoured and patient, and, what is more . . . Hoffman had an instinct for selection that was near genius.' And so it proved, but not in the way the Arts Council had hoped.

Had they understood their Goodman Report better they would never have appointed Hoffman. Just as Goodman smelled a rat from the first moment and declined to be intimidated by Council staff, so the reasonable Hoffman refused to be influenced by the South Bank. Nicholas Snowman complained loudly that he had already selected his favoured orchestra back in 1990. The London Phil was simply the one Hoffman would now have to endorse, for the super-orchestra would be resident at the Festival Hall. Coherent as Snowman's stand was, his argument should have been resolved with the Council before it set up this confusing committee, and his failure to manage that ought to have told him something about his position. Snowman left the Philharmonia alone maybe because he felt its manager David Whelton might run rings around him. Hoffman had much fun with the chief's neurosis when he came to write the report:

> A section of the South Bank submission was devoted to explaining in somewhat dramatic terms how the selection of any orchestra other than the London Philharmonic would 'destabilise the Centre's finances', 'undermine the national and international reputation of the Royal Festival Hall' and cause it to lose audiences 'for all time'. If the Arts Council should contemplate withdrawing the funding of the London Philharmonic it will no doubt bear the dark predictions of the South Bank Centre in mind.

Snowman, to some, had already provoked those misfortunes himself.

In fact the report was more of a critique of its own existence, finding fault with the beauty contest at every level, not least the Council's inartistic and nebulous terms of reference which undermined the exercise:

> 107.   The Secretary-General wanted an orchestra 'at the very height of international prowess, expertise and reputation'. Even this is by no means unambiguous.
>   International reputation can be enjoyed by very different orchestras. If this is what the Arts Council wanted, we cannot believe that it would have framed the criteria we have been given.

However, Hoffman made the odd screw-up himself. In order to get a professional opinion he invited the chief executive of the Chicago Symphony Orchestra to examine the three plans. Henry Fogel's reputation was supreme, but even this American might have spotted the commercial naivety of giving him sight of the plans of three of his international rivals, had Fogel got that far. In addition the orchestras pointed out that two of their managers had only just started their jobs, while the South Bank would have sight of the Philharmonia and RPO plans in order to comment on them. How these problems were handled are lost behind the sealed doors of the committee.

In his report, delivered to the Council on 15 December 1993, Hoffman, with elegant irony, apologised that he was 'unable to offer the Arts Council the clear advice for which it asked . . . if such a choice has to be made, it must be made by others'. The final outcome, 'little change', can be examined in the 1994–1995 grants listed above, where all three orchestras continue to be funded.

The press, already galvanised by a cocky Council, went to work. The *Evening Standard* urged that 'heads should roll for the moral and financial damage this bitter fiasco has caused', the *Daily Telegraph* recorded a range of comments such as 'an utter waste of time and money' and 'I have no confidence in the people running the council ... a charade', while a *Guardian* editorial on 16 December reflected that:

> The London orchestral saga has been a total debacle. Nobody – not the council, its music panel, nor the orchestras – has emerged undamaged from it; and yesterday the Arts Council ensured that things will get no better in future by promising to review its indecisions on a regular basis.

It called for the resignation of 'the man at the top', though it didn't suggest who he might be. Palumbo was leaving anyway; Baird finally resigned just before Christmas, followed only in the spring by Secretary-General Everitt, who seemed to prevaricate even on the matter of his leaving.

In the end there was one surprising winner – the South Bank. As the 1994–1995 figures show, the London Philharmonic lost £400,000 which was handed over to the Council's mollycoddled client to spend as it saw fit on the residency. Even so, it's hard to feel much sympathy for the three orchestras. If the contest was as preposterous and wasteful as they claimed from the start, they should have banded together and declined to participate. The Council is able to play on the divisions within an artistic profession to push changes. That the results are generally worse than the problems that generated them is the Council's own fault.

If this litany of folly wasn't bad enough, the Council decided at the same time to commission a major review of the nation's orchestras in partnership with the BBC, the country's biggest single employer of musicians aside from the armed forces. It was prompted in 1992 by the realisation that the newly formed civil-service unit for culture, the Department of National Heritage, handled both the arts and broadcasting; it monitored equally the Arts Council and the BBC. Before the pin-striped snoops had a chance to examine blatant overlaps like the orchestras, the Council probably thought that it was better to take the initiative, marshall its facts and propose 'strategies' to protect what it served. In this sense the immense review obliged political needs, but sceptics believe the self-regarding BBC may have exploited the general goodwill surrounding it to gauge the weakness of its independent rivals in order to trespass into their commercial territory. In time this will bring about a new chapter of complications.

During the late eighties the BBC underwent a Thatcherite conversion, claiming no longer to be a public service but a Billion Pound Company. The introduction of an 'internal market', the Producer's Choice scheme of renting resources already provided and an increase in 'contracting out' invoked a foggy kind of entrepreneurism which affected not only the BBC's four orchestras but its smaller outfits like the Big Band, which has now gone independent and is no doubt available for quality weddings and leaving dos. The BBC orchestras suddenly had to quantify their 'productivity', a difficult word for some orchestral players to pronounce, let alone define or display.

To date the BBC has subsidised its salaried musicians out of public money garnered through the annual licence fee, even though they are basically radio resources and monochrome in look while licences are issued for colour televisions. In 1995–1996 the BBC spent £17 million on its orchestras, roughly 1 per cent of its entire revenue and half of that in London: £6 million to the BBC Symphony Orchestra and £2.3 million to the Concert Orchestra. A year before, the BBC's governors called for greater productivity from its orchestras by earning extra income – commercial recordings, jingles, film work, concert bookings (rather than self-promotions), tours by ballet companies and singing stars, anything to bring the quids back in. Up to then the BBC orchestras had been stuck in studios and let out each summer for the Proms or otherwise the occasional and poorly attended public concert. They'd kept clear of the commercial practices and core repertoire of the independents through a 'gentleman's agreement'.

Now the Symphony Orchestra was no longer run by a gentleman but by a lady, Louise Badger, a former music officer of talent at the Arts Council. In the middle of 1994 the BBC Symphony Orchestra lured its first commercial sponsor with a three-year pledge from Land Rover, a deal negotiated by the agents IMG Artists. The London independents' knees trembled when the BBC players accepted, though after a third ballot, a new-style contract offering their bosses more freedom to tally sessions and exploit recordings. Noting that 'under strict rules laid down by the Arts Council, no [concert] fees are to be used to subsidise commercial recording', a member of one of the London four complained that, 'the inevitable consequence of the BBC's new contract will be that most commercial recording work will pass from the independent sector to the BBC, where no such restrictions on subsidy seem to apply'. Today they are even competing to play commonplace repertoire.

As that player might have suspected, the Arts Council/BBC review didn't deal with anything so close to home. Having been held up while the Hoffman committee prevailed, the Arts Council resumed it as a white-flag exercise, sifting through the debris of Hoffman in an attempt to recover some credibility for its music department. The whole affair was handled in three hefty stages – a consultation document (107 pages), a report of consultations on the consultation document (185 pages), and a cut-out-and-keep Council strategy statement based on the report of the consultations on the consultations (seventeen pages). Here is an honourable system in action, honing material in order to shape up practical goals and tasks. The first paper asked twenty-three agenda questions. Some, like number 9 – Can an improved network of venues be developed in the Welsh/English borders? – soon fell off the agenda because nobody gave a toss about the Welsh/English borders. Major issues, though, can be traced from start to end, such as the vexed issue of audiences:

Agenda question 15: How can a new audience be reached?
    The potential for audience growth is a key area for further debate.

And how. In the second paper the rapporteur had apparently read forty-one contributions on this subject, and from that we learn that the ensembles' managers believe audiences don't come because 'orchestras need to develop clearer identities'; that education work should be considered as a major marketing tool, and that 'the importance of building relationships with audiences is emphasised', which is doubtless reassuring to someone out there. Finally, the decisive strategic goal that the Arts Council will pursue in response to agenda question 15, though grammatically garbled, is as follows: '[We want to see] individual orchestras which are firmly rooted in their respective communities and are actively exploring ways of capturing the imagination and commitment of a broader audience.' Another problem solved through language: a 'new' audience becomes a 'broader' one, 'reach' turns into 'growth', then 'building relationships', and ends up as 'actively exploring'.

The vocabulary caves in completely when clients try to get key terms defined. The Arts Council lists four bullet-point objectives: quality, adventurous programming, relationship with community, access. Here's Olivia Lowson, the music officer with responsibility for orchestras at the time of writing, when asked to define adventurous programming:

> It's an interesting debate. I haven't got a definition. Our approach to it is loose, and it includes programming new work and really just enlightened approaches in general. Period instruments are included in that. We're trying to move away from the old-fashioned, traditional concert; such as how it's presented, maybe cross-artform things.

In these circumstances, Lord Tordoff's vision of the Verdi Requiem on coffins no longer seems improbable. The answer she might otherwise have given is, simply, 'playing music by living composers', for there is nothing more daring the players and their audience could face. Yet the Council has never succeeded in finding ways for the orchestras to reconcile the needs of the publishing trade with the pressures of the box office, however generous its definition of 'living' or even 'composers'.

The final report 'Strategy for the Support and Development of Orchestras and their Audiences' of July 1995 is more positive about regional co-operation, but that's because other people are doing all the work. It points out the good news that three new associations have set up forums (or *fora*, as it insists). Yet the Northern Orchestral Committee, the London Co-ordinating Committee and the Association of British Concert Promoters were created independently of the Council and came into being somewhat because of worries about the Arts Council's status after Hoffman, and certainly over fears on local-authority funding, about which the Council appears impotent. Nonetheless, the idea that the northern orchestras should co-operate better within their patch comes not before time.

The London Co-ordinating Committee 'would not seek to reinstate the London Orchestral Concerts Board', the Council insisted, but for a 'long-term strategy' the Council had failed to take into account the desire of all three major political parties to create a London authority on the lines of the GLC after the 1997 general election. It's possible that the co-ordinating committee, rather like Mr Bean's of thirty years back, will spark a new structure to harmonise the three residencies: the London Symphony Orchestra at the Barbican, the Royal Philharmonic at the Royal Albert Hall, and the Philharmonia with the London Phil at the South Bank – better call that three-and-a-half.

Above all the Arts Council wants to believe that the 1995 strategy will secure a philharmonic rapport with England's orchestras which will last through to the next century. No more them and us, no reductions in numbers nor increases in sizes, no impositions of new music – no nothing, really. 'A process of organic development which builds on what exists, takes account of local will and initiative and responds to the demands of a changing society is acknowledged by the Arts Council as the most appropriate way forward.' Orchestra managers like this woolly stuff so long as it doesn't threaten them. Meanwhile the Council's sceptics will simply wait for the orchestras to stumble into the next big hole – and they still hope that the big hole is the Albert Hall with the RPO in it – responding when they do with the stock response, recently rehearsed by Olivia Lowson for this book: 'The Arts Council of England is not in a position to bale the orchestras out.'

This brings us back to the Figgures Report of 1978, which through its 'no lame ducks' policy would have culled the London Symphony Orchestra, and reminds us that the Arts Council is always in a position to bale out whoever it wants in order to 'maintain the status quo'. It also goes to show that orchestras like the LSO shift in their fortunes from season to season. Even a single concert is unpredictable. By the same token no quantity of long-term strategies, however hazy, can ever cope with them. The orchestras, it seems, will always be in a fix, and the Arts Council will always fund them to be so.

Chapter 13

The knot garden: a curtain rises

Britain and her allies blew up fifty-eight subsidised opera houses between 1942 and 1945. Not only did they destroy the German elite of Berlin's State Opera and Munich's National-theater, but also Vienna's Staatsoper and Milan's La Scala. The Nazis, however, failed to blitz a single subsidised opera house in Britain, but then there *were* none. Glyndebourne's idle village hall escaped precisely as Christie had predicted – 'Hitler respects us'. Equally, too, its forebear in Bayreuth dodged British bombs, though fleeing Germans raided Wagner's sombre temple and stole its costumes; Allied soldiers caught sight of assorted Wagnerian characters padding through the woods.

Thanks to American money of the kind that Maynard Keynes had bartered, the defeated citizens of mainland Europe restored their opera houses. Within a decade Germany – West, East – and Italy had rebuilt thirty-two of them. In the 1955–1956 season alone, while Covent Garden was facing a fearsome crisis, Berlin, Hamburg, Vienna, Augsburg, Wuppertal and Münster re-opened – the latter and seven others erected in British-occupied territory. One of the earliest theatres to open did so thanks to Brigadier Bertram Upton Sinclair Cripps of the First Welch Regiment.

When the British and American forces liberated Naples in 1944, the San Carlo Opera House had suffered little damage backstage but its foyer was ruined. 'Bertie' Cripps and his crew rounded up what they could find of the opera company and the orchestra and got them to entertain the troops with stock repertoire. This was done not so much to keep the starving Italians busy as his Allied soldiers out of trouble. Norman Lewis, an intelligence officer much impressed by the discipline of the local mafia, reported that 'one British unit to enter Naples cut the paintings from the frames in the Prince's Palace, and made off with the collection of Capodimonte china'. He later noted that 'a week or two ago an orchestra playing at the San Carlo to an audience largely clothed in Allied hospital blankets returned from an interval to find all its instruments missing'. The thieves were not Italians.

When it comes to high culture, Britons do not emerge from the Second World War as a race less philistine than those they fought. Peacetime pressure was put on Britain's post-war governments to challenge, even eclipse, the artistic equity of the Krauts and the Wops. At the very heart they thought they ought to have a national opera house in order to impress and entertain foreign big shots who understood this full-blown form, one which might compete with the very companies whose homes the British military arts had wrecked. It never entered Brigadier Cripps' head that he was boosting the contest by putting on Verdi for squaddies. Nonetheless, while he was rebuilding a great Naples troupe with salutary success, Covent Garden's David Webster was failing to create a British one, and it was the Brigadier's own Central Mediterranean Forces' San Carlo Opera Company that was the first to sing at the Royal Opera House, on 4 November 1946. Maybe the Arts Council should have commissioned the British Army to run the place (after all, its famous doorman was a certain Sergeant Martin), but nobody could have made a worse job of it than Webster, who left a legacy of disorder to his hapless successors, Tooley and Isaacs.

To Italians and Germans opera is first of all a national affair, as most of the great repertory they present has been written in the native language. For the British it's an international matter, not only as all the grand, resonant works are in foreign languages but also because Germany, Austria and Italy have sustained an investment in production, presentation and training that this country cannot, and never will, equal. When Keynes pursued the opportunity offered him by Rab Butler to open an opera house for his ballet company, he hadn't a clue how to deal with opera itself. In appointing David Webster, Keynes ensured that his ignorance would not be exposed, merely matched. Yet the key issues had already been brought to the board by Edward Dent, who made his money out of translations: you either go national, create a 'house' style with a brilliant company trained to deliver in English what the Germans deliver in German, or you do a Beecham and wheel on the foreigners to sing like fabulous canaries in front of flapping canvas in the knowledge that most of your audience isn't there to gain anything from the work itself but from the social log-rolling that shapes the interval. Dent, as we've already seen, warned Webster and Keynes of this directly, and yet they did nothing. The Royal Opera House flopped as a national resource, then failed to command the international market. Now it is merely a cosmopolitan player entirely at the mercy of agents and publishers. Still, it remains the Arts Council's biggest client, to whom the Council can never say 'no'.

The Royal Opera regularly re-invents its own history. It does so perhaps to convince the tax-payers and the tourists that it's a national treasure as old as royalty itself. The former chairman, Sir Angus Stirling, claimed:

> The Royal Opera House is one of the nation's great national assets. There has been a theatre on this site for nearly four centuries. As custodians of this building, the Board of the Royal Opera House has a duty to preserve this part of the nation's heritage.

In 1958 the House authorised a congenial fan, Harold Rosenthal, to write *Two Centuries of Opera at Covent Garden* in honour – inconsistently – of its 'centenary'. Two decades on the *Royal Opera House Covent Garden: A History from 1732* told us 'how it grew from a Georgian playhouse to become one of the world's most famous opera houses'. One decade further, in 1988, brought *The Royal Opera House in the Twentieth Century* by 'Frankie' Donaldson, wife of a former arts minister and board member; a book of charm, innocence ('although music has no class boundaries, appreciation of it among ordinary, untalented folk is most often found among those who have the greatest opportunities to hear it') and hype ('Once more *The Times* critic was ecstatic'). The Opera House's emblem is the royal coat of arms, its stage staff dress as eighteenth-century courtiers, its box-office phone number is 1066.

The House is not Georgian at all but was built in 1858 on the site of two previous theatres and could have been built on the site of a satanic shrine for all anyone cares. It first opened its doors as a year-round lyric theatre in 1946, acquired ownership in 1949 and gained incorporation in 1950. The Royal Ballet has existed merely from 1956, the Royal Opera from 1968. The first season there of Sadler's Wells Ballet fell in 1946, with Covent Garden Opera Company's *Carmen* in 1947 ('a dire penance' its most Christian critic wrote). When you have a building, three companies and an identity each of different vintage, it's easy to play games with dates. The Royal Opera House pretends that it has as little to do with the twentieth century as possible, and while it appeals for public largesse by displaying the antiquated conditions imposed on its dedicated workers, it trades on that self-same image to sell its seats.

Not only has it retouched its history, but its function, too. When Webster got the Covent Garden Opera Company up and running, or stumbling, in 1947, he assured the Arts Council:

> You will soon hear a company to rival La Scala, but with the advantage that it will sing in English. That is my aim, to create a unique genre. In time our singers, our dancers, our conductors, our producers, our designers, will take over La Scala.

'What? Singing in English?' Vaughan Williams retorted.

'They will sing English operas in Italy,' Webster replied. Funnily enough, in 1951 the opera house of Venice premiered Stravinsky's *The Rake's Progress* to an English libretto, while in 1954 it gave the world Britten's *Turn of the Screw* – though no thanks to Webster's 'unique genre'. Sir William Walton, composer and Covent Garden trustee, soon moved to Italy, too, but that's another story.

Webster's task should have been to build a staff which could cultivate repertoire related to the evolving abilities of the company and the size of the House. He needed to raise an integrated creative environment – an ensemble tone – at Covent Garden, which is how it worked in superior centres: Munich and Hamburg then, say Houston and Amsterdam now. If he wanted to bring about a 'unique genre' he should have built a house team coached to sing opera in the original language; by that means he would have been offering the public a product which contrasted with the vernacular of Sadler's Wells, while helping British singers to graduate into the international market. Instead he allowed the quirks and predilections of the semi-trained and the downright dilettanti to skew any chance of a grand perspective. According to the Earl of Harewood, who used to work for him, Webster 'basked in the occasional warmth generated by guest appearances of Kirsten Flagstad and Hans Hotter, of Schwarzkopf and Seefried'; he measured the success of trips abroad by the number of fine meals he ate, and on a first night enjoyed most the after-show buffet he hosted at his flat off Harley Street, as Lady Walton recalled in her memoirs. He acted like a blasé, fat poof – which is what Sir Steuart Wilson once called him to his face.

Yet Webster's lack of direction was no less logical than the half-baked vision that Keynes had peddled: Covent Garden's national role in projecting a native tradition. It was also Keynes who interpreted Butler's brief to mean that the Government would support a year-round opera house. He had no understanding of the *stagione* system, by which an opera house plans a limited run of, say, ten performances by the same cast but not on consecutive nights, and for artistic reasons rightly so, to encourage high standards of singing. It took more than fifteen years to mould a steadfast roster for Covent Garden. Nevertheless, Christie's idea of operatic seasons was a better one than the 'we never close' pattern put in place, and one of Covent Garden's basic economic burdens comes from Keynes and his successors not thinking through the structural options.

For some reason never so far recorded, Keynes hadn't liked the way the Old Vic created an English opera company at Sadler's Wells. Mary Glasgow suggested that he had little time for 'the missionary zeal' surrounding it, while Charles Landstone felt 'it simply wasn't flash enough for him – Sadler's Wells Theatre wasn't quite the thing'. Covent Garden was somehow meant to outstrip the Sadler's Wells Company as England's national opera and Keynes insisted that the place should be known as 'the national home of the lyric arts'. At the same time its first music director, Karl Rankl (an unfortunate, fitting name), was an Austrian and the leading roles were increasingly taken by half-decent foreigners. Though a few of the visitors gamely attempted English translations of works already written in their own tongue, others could only sing the words the composer had actually set. A *Guardian* review in 1949 exposes just how stupid it got:

> Libero de Lucia, a Swiss, sang in Italian and the rest of the company
> in English – or such at least was the intention. Mme Grandi sang in
> either language as best suited: thus after trouncing the American

baritone villain in English, she resorted to Italian to explain things to the tenor lover, and incidentally sang even better in that language.

Indignant at being involved in such nonsense and weary of disfavour, Rankl resigned in 1951. To some extent he'd been a victim of anti-Semitism. Despite all that had been learned from the war, Jew-baiting pervaded the House, stoked by the creepy Reginald Goodall who served on the staff, a Wagner-mad hack of a rehearsal conductor who later grew old enough to be considered, for no good reason, a sage. Goodall resented the fact that during Rankl's tenure thirty-nine operas were produced but no fewer than twenty-four of them were conducted by the Austrian, who, naturally enough, hogged anything in German.

Quality only improved when guest conductors were brought in. Through hard work insightful maestros from foreign companies such as Erich Kleiber and Rudolf Kempe raised standards, but they declined to work there regularly. Kempe was staggered by the lack of discipline and knowledge, not only in the House but also in the press: 'It seems something of an extravagance to bring Mr Kempe all the way from Bavaria to conduct middle-Verdi,' yawned *The Times*. Kleiber's biographer felt:

> He didn't sense at Covent Garden what he sensed at the Berlin Staatsoper and the Teatro Colón – the determination to put art first, at whatever cost, and with no side bets on friendship or social position, or safety of one kind or another.

Webster found himself increasingly reliant on aspirant divas like Maria Callas and Victoria de los Angeles to keep the public buzzing, while the gradual emergence of Commonwealth stars like Australia's Joan Sutherland and Canada's Jon Vickers gave Webster the false impression he was developing a talent-spotting flair.

Once Rankl resigned the music director's job was left unfilled until 1955, when Rafael Kubelik accepted the post for three seasons, during which he became increasingly depressed by the amateurism of the board and its senior staff. He departed grumpily in 1958, vouching that 'a good opera house must be an ensemble house'. Again there was an awkward gap until the arrival in 1961 of Georg Solti, a Hungarian Jew who, having refused to be intimidated by the anti-Semites, turned the fortunes of the House, though sadly not into something that gave back to music more than it took. Recalling his first impression of Covent Garden, fifteen years after it had opened, he felt, 'There was no one there who knew anything at all about how to run an opera house.'

Over in Islington the rival Sadler's Wells Opera Company was doing rather well, despite a grant less than half that of Covent Garden. Although the operation expended extra energy and offered more shows to the public than did the Garden, it had always run on half the cash. Before state subsidy in 1938, for example, the weekly expenditure figures compared like this:

	Covent Garden Grand Season £	Sadler's Wells £
Principal singers	1,500	300
Chorus	240	120
Ballet	150	100
Conductors	300	200
Orchestra	1,000	240
Miscellaneous	1,000	1,000
Total	4,190	1,960

The Arts Council unwisely widened the gap by clipping the turnover on Islington's balanced budget while offering Covent Garden what was effectively three years of start-up costs. In 1948–1949, the first full year of Covent Garden's operation, the House received £145,000 while Sadler's Wells got £40,000; by the middle fifties they received £250,000 and £100,000 respectively. In 1946 Sadler's Wells was in credit to the tune of £75,000. By 1957 its trust had accumulated debts of £40,000. Mary Glasgow reflected, wrongly:

> I don't think we neglected Sadler's Wells in my day, but Bill Williams, who succeeded me as Secretary-General, probably did. During his time there was an almighty crisis that nearly shut Sadler's Wells down, while Covent Garden was receiving half of the money available for all the artforms. On the other hand there was this rather vague, ill-expressed feeling that Covent Garden was the thing that mattered and we had to make a go of it. When you consider the legacy of Lord Keynes, it's this more than anything, I would say. You must remember that when he died he was chairman

of both organisations, and I wonder sometimes if the Arts Council hasn't a better memory about this than Covent Garden has. I think therefore we concentrated on the Royal Opera House, protected it rather solidly. Maybe we were a little terrified of what would happen if it didn't work out. That might have meant the end of the Arts Council, because the politicians were expecting us to support it and make it succeed. Apart from anything else, it's one of the few places they all go to that we, the Arts Council, fund. You had to run all the way with it. You couldn't pick at it. Sadler's Wells, though – it was sort of picked at already, when the ballet company was moved over after the war.

The titanic crisis that struck Covent Garden and Sadler's Wells between 1955 and 1958 was fuelled less by their rivalry in London than their work outside it. Covent Garden, Sadler's Wells Ballet and Sadler's Wells Opera were mandated by the Arts Council to 'tour the provinces' as part of their annual settlement. It was an attempt to stave off criticism that the Council pandered to London, though the touring patterns themselves were a wartime legacy. The first commissioned report on opera and ballet in 1950 had already stressed the need to provide 'more opera for the provinces'. In 1954, for instance, Covent Garden spent a fortnight in each of four cities – Cardiff, Manchester, Birmingham and Croydon (yes Croydon) – giving forty-eight performances from a roster of ten works, including *Aida* and *Carmen* but also Britten's new *Gloriana*, quickly nicknamed *Boriana*. In comparison Covent Garden's yield in London was 162 performances of twelve productions

Although the touring shows were sold on the premise that they were just what you'd get if you went to the Royal Opera House, they used 'singers of the second division and conductors of the third', according to the *Guardian*, while the critic of the *Scotsman* griped that 'the scenery looked as if it had been dismantled and rolled up in a Gladstone bag every Saturday night'. Sadler's Wells Opera and Ballet performed more outside London than in it. At the same time there was a third company that toured towns without subsidy and decidedly without flair, the Carl Rosa Opera. Having survived under a string of guises since 1875, it no longer had anything to do with Carl or Rosa but was run by the bossy Mrs H.B. Phillips on IOUs and a glut of wishful thinking. She would pawn jewellery in order to pay her singers. In 1952, when it found itself broke and unable to tour, an unwilling Arts Council baled it

out with a grant of £20,000, but only because the Carl Rosa had a
valkyrie of an ally in the House of Commons: the Tory MP Irene
Ward. On 17 March 1953 she tackled Rab Butler:

> MISS WARD (Tynemouth, C) said that she had received an
> assurance from the Financial Secretary that assistance would be
> given [to Carl Rosa]. Could the Chancellor give a similar assurance
> so that the company would be on the road in the provinces this
> year?

> MR BUTLER (Saffron Walden, C): I certainly endorse any letter
> sent by the Financial Secretary, especially to the hon. lady.
> (Laughter). The position about this company is one which excites
> considerable sympathy among us, but I must leave the negotiations
> between the Arts Council and the company to conclude.

The emergency grant grew uncomfortably regular and in
1956 Carl Rosa received £61,000, Sadler's Wells twice as much
(£125,000) and Covent Garden four times that amount
(£270,000). Together they absorbed an unsustainable 66 per cent
of the entire money the Arts Council had to spend, and it was clear
that this political solution would soon earn greater political
trouble to the detriment of Covent Garden, exposed with the
biggest grant but the smallest touring slate. A merger of Sadler's
Wells and Covent Garden was seriously considered, but the
Council was divided, if not confused, about the role of Covent
Garden as a 'national home' and Sadler's Wells as a 'metropolitan
centre' when both of them ran regional tours. It was feasible to
rationalise the two, and probably wise to do so, but, as Mary
Glasgow stressed, there was a pecking order and Covent Garden
couldn't be pecked.

The Council obeyed the law of the barnyard and chose to cull
Carl Rosa, using Sadler's Wells as the hired hand. It leaned on
Sadler's Wells, which was running an accumulated debt of
£40,000, thanks to inveterate Council parsimony. It first offered to
relieve the Wells of its immediate headache, Sadler's Wells
Theatre Ballet, the 'number two' company Ninette de Valois left
behind in Islington. In his book on the Royal Ballet – which was
what the number one company began to be called in this year –
Alexander Bland put the story in a manner only ballet folk could
be soft enough to swallow:

Early in 1956 Sadler's Wells, which was going through a financial crisis, decided that it could no longer afford to maintain the Ballet Company, which was losing £6,000 a year. Covent Garden acted immediately. 'Come back to us and bring all your dancers with you,' Webster telephoned to [John] Field. 'I don't know how we'll raise the money; but let's try.'

Really.

It also passed over to Covent Garden de Valois' ballet academy, which then acquired as a boarding school the White Lodge in Richmond Park, home to the Queen Mother when she was Duchess of York. Sixty thousand pounds of capital was borrowed and refunded by the Arts Council in annual globs of £15,000. The Council's complicity with thoroughbred education is often forgotten; blacks were vetoed at the school until the eighties, just as women were denied entry into the Covent Garden Orchestra until Solti forced change in the sixties. Anyhow, this curious device effectively asset-stripped the Wells and created the Covent Garden empire for Ninette de Valois, by gaining a royal charter which would confer the title 'royal' on all three enterprises, using the 'Royal' Opera House as a lever. The operation was planned from the coronation year of 1953, and the 1956 victory secured her a damehood one year later. A young solicitor was engaged to frame the integrated constitution – Arnold Goodman, who ten years on, through an orchestra, attained a peerage in a similar manner.

The Council attempted to turn Sadler's Wells Opera into a touring cartel, one which would absorb first the schedule of Carl Rosa, then Covent Garden. It exploited the weaknesses of the boards, playing on the operatic ambitions of decent members like Isaiah Berlin while learning that the great stumbling block was the chairman, Jimmy Smith. The whole exercise proved as easy as cutting butter with a hot knife, though the butter congealed rather messily. The Council kept Sadler's Wells waiting while the opera company's chairman warned that he would soon have to go to Canada on business. Finally, in late February 1957, it tormentingly offered Sadler's Wells a standstill grant (that is, the same money as the previous year) for 1957–1958 of £125,000 while imposing touring constraints which would limit earnings. The chorus went on strike.

Colonel the Honourable James Smith, as the chairman styled himself, issued a press release that he had resigned alongside all but one of his board in protest against the inadequacy of the offer, stressing that 'it is a waste of public money to produce opera which must inevitably be of a second-rate nature'. Once the Honourable Mr Smith had left the country for Canada the Arts Council suddenly discovered it was able to offer £142,000. The body of the board unresigned itself and in response the Council implied there might be better news next year if the Wells Trust and Carl Rosa could get together to discuss the 'rationalisation of touring plans' leading, the Council suggested, to some kind of merger. The chairmen of the respective trusts wrote to the Council in November 1957:

> We, the joint signatories to this letter, are writing on behalf of the Sadler's Wells Trust and Foundation and the Carl Rosa Trust to inform the Arts Council that we are mutually and unanimously agreed that amalgamation of the Sadler's Wells Opera Company and the Carl Rosa Opera Company will bring advantages both artistic and practical to both organisations.

They'd been duped, and in the ensuing negotiations with the Arts Council, three options emerged: plan A would cost £235,000 (their previous combined totals were £204,000) and provide enhanced touring for two aligned companies; in plan B, Carl Rosa would be disbanded while Sadler's Wells, maintained at current strength, would provide twenty weeks of touring; plan C, a holding operation with no more cash for either, implied cuts for Sadler's Wells. For plan A the Council proposed only £215,000, of which only £205,000 was allowed for operational use; for plan B it would accept nothing less than thirty weeks' touring; it condoned plan C, which on the money offered was the same as plan A, while expecting the companies to stick to their letter and merge. Secretary-General William Williams (whom we met pre-war as Pelican Bill) emphasised that 'if the two trusts should be unable to combine on these lines, there is no reason to suppose that either would receive a grant individually'.

It then transpired that the Carl Rosa chairman had not shown the merger letter to his board before signing it, and, given his history with the Arts Council, you would have thought he should, for he was none other than Sir Donald Wolfit. He resigned. The trusts cottoned on all too late to Williams' intent. Sadler's Wells trustees then negotiated separately to overhaul Carl Rosa's workload in return for preferential grants – £200,000 in 1959, £365,000 in 1961 – and Carl Rosa folded.

This episode exposes how resolute and sneaky the Arts Council became under the despotic Bill Williams, Secretary-General throughout the fifties. He hadn't counted, though, on the immense public disquiet, which reached a level similar to the orchestra farrago of 1993. The Arts Council was accused in the *Daily Mail* of 'banana-republic politics'. Prior to the general election of 1959 the three main parties individually considered dismantling the Arts Council in favour of a ministry, and it was a Labour document of the time that first proposed an arts minister post to keep a check on this kind of cavalier behaviour; Labour would introduce this when it gained power in 1964.

Press reports and a TV debate incited hundreds of letters of protest directly or through MPs, and Dame Irene Ward announced in the Commons that 'the well-loved provincial opera company, the Carl Rosa, is being murdered'. She attacked Bill Williams for 'getting his claws into the administration'. She herself clawed him one last time in February 1960, when she demanded of the Chancellor of the Exchequer 'by what authority his department decided to arrange for the Secretary-General, who has a salary of £3,800 a year, a special pension although he is over the qualifying age?' Indeed, he was sixty-three.

All these shenanigans were essentially set up to relieve Covent Garden of its touring burden, and that's what happened next. Had it taken over Carl Rosa's job, Sadler's Wells would have been playing towns like Warrington or Hull. Instead it absorbed more dates in cities it already knew. Its director, Norman Tucker (1910–1978), pointed out that up to 1959 Sadler's Wells toured eight to twelve weeks a year, but following the agreement it toured thirty-six to forty weeks using two separate companies, grossing 275 shows in the regions, 200 in London. He commented at the time:

[The] main problem has been to find a sufficient number of suitable singers to maintain the standard at which we aim . . . We often put too great a burden on singers by requiring them to move backwards and forwards between London and touring dates too frequently.

In contrast, Covent Garden concluded its formal duties in 1962 with a spell in Manchester and Coventry, where the new cathedral had just opened. From then on it had to be prised out of the House. When in 1981 a Manchester businessman revamped his city's Palace Theatre as part of a manoeuvre to force the Royal

Opera to earn its national title, the crew traipsed up a couple of times and blamed the City Council for its inability to win over the locals. Soon afterwards, Opera North began and this Leeds-based offshoot of English National Opera relieved the London companies of their touring duties – but then the Arts Council knew from the start that the businessman's challenge would benefit Opera North just as well, even though the theatre is now too big for it.

Williams hadn't expected militant public support for Sadler's Wells, and he certainly didn't foresee two exceptional developments. First of all London County Council barged in, setting up in October 1958 an independent enquiry on the state of the company. It was chaired by the Schweppes boss Sir Frederic Hooper, who invited Sir Adrian Boult on the team fully aware that he had been snubbed as an opera conductor by Covent Garden. It concluded that Sadler's Wells Opera's work in London deserved subsidy from the local authority, which it then gave: 'Assistance by the London County Council should be regarded as a deliberate contribution towards an adequate provision of opera as cultural amenity for the benefit of the people of London.'

Second, Sadler's Wells had done a deal with a commercial outfit and put on a sugar-rich operetta, *The Merry Widow*, in London's largest West End theatre, the Coliseum. A splendid success, it planted in the mind of the company's manager and Tucker's successor, Stephen Arlen (1913–1972), the idea of moving there permanently. The courageous Arlen found an ally in the LCC, which was then grappling with the problem of building on the South Bank a national theatre and a metropolitan opera house, an idea we encountered elsewhere. The Met would have been paid for by knocking down Sadler's Wells Theatre and flogging the land, a notion nearly everyone supported, for the theatre was and remains useless. The Met plan perished for no clear reason, but it allowed the LCC to envision the move Arlen had in mind. After acquiring a lease for the Coliseum, the opera company moved out of Sadler's Wells and marked its full-time debut on London's largest stage in August 1968 with *Don Giovanni*, directed by Sir John Gielgud with stage designs by a newcomer called Derek Jarman, who went on to make better films than sets.

The Arts Council frowned on this West End invasion. Not only was the Coliseum close to Covent Garden, it was bigger and more prominent than the 'national home' – Lord Drogheda said it made the House 'seem intimate'. Despite manoeuvres, the

Council failed to convince the powerful local authority that the dangers exceeded the opportunities; in any case Arlen's gamble paid off and the company maintained its home in St Martin's Lane, though in the process it killed him. Covent Garden marked the intrusion by the cheesy tactic of changing its name to the Royal Opera, aware that Sadler's Wells now had no need for its old title and was searching for a vivid substitute, which it found in 1974 by adopting Edward Dent's name of thirty years back: English National Opera. ENO now does everything Covent Garden failed to do for opera in English.

Ultimately the Arts Council's anxiety proved correct, if only to itself. First, in 1991 the Tory Government bought the Coliseum freehold and gave it not to ENO but the Arts Council. The £12,091,000 this cost can be seen in the Council's accounts designated for the opera company; nevertheless, the Arts Council remains the landlord. Second, the introduction through the Council of Lottery cash for capital projects allowed ENO to consider building a brand-new opera house somewhere else. While this unwise move was being considered through feasibility plans costing £2.5 million, Culture Secretary Chris Smith proposed in November 1997 that ENO and the Royal Opera should timeshare the refurbished Covent Garden Opera House when it reopened. In doing so, he cleverly exploited ENO's willingness to relocate. Here is a solution this book would have explored had not the Minister got there first, but with three provisos: that the companies should reside in seasons there (which would allow the Royal Opera to go private and free itself from subsidy), that the venue be headed by an independent artistic director and that the Royal Ballet be moved to the Coliseum, which it can share with the English National Ballet and dancing visitors under the leadership of an independent artistic director, as at the House. Otherwise, should ENO move out, the Arts Council would be lumbered with the vast emptiness of London's biggest theatre. Of course, it could always hold its council meetings there in full public view – seats at reasonable prices.

Chapter 14

The knot garden: a curtain falls

Two classic images are flaunted ceaselessly by Covent Garden to remind us of its good old days. The first is a photo of Verdi's epic *Don Carlos* from 1958. Within an ornate production – set and costumes by the soppy Italian film director Visconti, with conductor Giulini hidden in the pit – we see the Italian singers Gobbi and Barbieri, the Russian Christoff, and the Canadian Vickers with the Dutch soprano Brouwenstijn. The theatre director Peter Hall attended the show and swore 'it was the greatest operatic experience of my life'. The second is a video record of the central act from Puccini's *Tosca* on 9 February 1964, stunningly sung and acted by Maria Callas and Tito Gobbi and conducted by Calliario, in an equally ornate production by the soppy Italian film director Zeffirelli. There is nothing to tell us this is London rather than La Scala or the Met save for one telling presence – the arthritic camerawork of ATV.

There were two main reasons why Covent Garden shifted ground between these years to benefit itself, leaving headaches for its successors that the current regime cannot relieve. The first came from a confluence of economic factors. A new member of the board joined in 1958. Jack Donaldson, a chicken farmer – yes, a chicken farmer – and a close friend of the chairman, wondered not whether 'prestige' or 'special' productions like *Don Carlos* cost more but whether they lost more. The result, calculated in an exercise eventually called the 'Donaldson figures', amazed the board. It showed that international productions soaked up the same or less subsidy because the wealthy shelled out for the expensive seats, which were otherwise the hardest in the House to sell. While in 1957 a 'national' *La Bohème* averaged only 54 per cent capacity in paid attendances, an 'international' *Norma* averaged 93 per cent.

The opera committee prescribed:

> If in the opinion of the administration better performances can economically be given in a foreign language there shall be no objections to this being done. In other words, where there is a conflict between quality of performance and performance in English, the latter may be sacrificed.

Covent Garden's linking of cosmopolitanism with the dedicated pursuit of the wealthy grew from this directive, even though they were not mutually conditional, nor any basis on which to cultivate anything but a crude, sectarian policy for repertoire or access. In accepting this as a guideline, nobody questioned, either, whether the mismatch of income to expenditure in the national productions might be rectified – by then they had stars in their eyes. Kubelik considered *Don Carlos* worked so well because 'we brought in the top singers and then put them on display'.

At the same time the Government had faced 'a little local difficulty', as Prime Minister Macmillan expressed it, and his Chancellor had resigned. He appointed in his place a 'hermit', Derick Heathcoat Amory, one of those closet gays who devote themselves to boy scouts and find the odd night at the opera most congenial. He threw money at the House, wiping out the overdraft with an award of £100,000, and for three years (he retired in 1960) the Arts Council grant to the Garden was based on '43 per cent of allowable costs', the term 'allowable' being used simply because the Arts Council couldn't subsidise foreign tours. The 1959 grant swiftly shot up by a third to £473,000, which accounted for 49.5 per cent of the Arts Council's entire grant-giving, an elevated state never quite equalled again once other clients had twigged. In other words, Covent Garden was able to set its own subsidy, despite a ceiling set by the Council.

Because this upper limit rankled with Covent Garden's board, it was allowed to go one better and get its grant pegged to 85 per cent of the box-office receipts from the preceding year. Naturally this formula rewarded the raising of ticket prices and the policy that emerged from the 'Donaldson figures'. The accounts for 1962–1963 showed a surplus of £70,117, though unsurprisingly the following year's grant from the Arts Council was not reduced in consequence. When the present regime complains that the inadequate level of Arts Council subsidy prevents the lowering of prices, it has forgotten its own history – that it increased the cost of seats to acquire greater subsidy. Between the 1956 and 1962 seasons the top and bottom of the ticket rates grew in this way:

	Gallery		Stalls circle		Grand tier	
	Price	Value	Price	Value	Price	Value
May 1956	4s	£2.50	£ 1 2s	£ 13.20	£ 1 14s	£ 14.40
Don Carlos 1958	10s	£5.75	£ 3 3s	£ 36.40	£ 3 13s	£ 42.00
Otello 1962	12s 6d	£5.65	£10 10s	£112.00	£26 5s	£281.50
September 1962	12s	£6.45	£ 3 11s 6d	£ 38.00	£ 4 2s	£ 44.00
May 1965	13s	£6.15	£ 6 6s	£ 61.35	£ 7 17s 6d	£ 76.65

In five years the bottom prices doubled in value, while the top trebled (this was nothing to do with inflation – in fact comparative rates dropped a little, as the gallery values between 1958 and 1962 show). The middle range of seats tended to follow the upward drift of the quality sections. Before 1956 the entire range of prices had actually dipped in value; at today's charges a top seat would set you back £15.70, the bottom £3.45 when the House opened for San Carlo in 1946, and the small decrease over ten years is shown in the 1956 figures.

The remaining influential factors were political and social. Macmillan's Britain would soon apply to the Common Market. General de Gaulle, who opposed Britain's entry, was given a House gala on 7 April 1960. The Prime Minister was 'very close' to Ava, Lady Waverley, the widow of the Covent Garden chairman who was successor to Keynes. It was said she ground opera and ballet tickets into the clenched fists of Cabinet ministers, and Macmillan casually remarked, 'If we are to be serious about Europe, you had better make sure Covent Garden is serious too.' This was interpreted as an endorsement of a move towards cosmopolitanism and exclusivity. At the same time the Government had mounted a wining-and-dining campaign to undo the diplomatic damage wrought by the

Suez fiasco of 1956, and there were sixty-three embassies, five legations and three consulates in London to entertain.

Meanwhile, the latest Garden chairman, Lord Drogheda, a chronic snob, hankered to attract the richest people into the House, and in addition:

> It also seemed to me desirable that leading companies should develop a measure of involvement with the Royal Opera House: the more their sympathies were engaged, the more they used Covent Garden to entertain foreigners, the better the case I could develop to the Government, whatever the party in power, for continuing public support.

He launched the Premier Stalls scheme, an early corporate-entertainments wheeze taking the best seats out of public sale.

Furthermore, in October 1959 the board agreed to establish the Society of the Royal Opera House, which would comprise 'an exclusive set of people who will have no other privilege on the face of it than the glory of giving money to the Opera House' – on the face of it. In 1973 this 'exclusive set of people' mutated into the Royal Opera House Trust, a private club with its bevy of corporate and individual supporters on tax dodges, who are nowadays classed into Premium, Gold Star, Full, Individual and Country members (the last a puzzling name, possibly aimed at chicken farmers). The list has made entertaining reading in recent years as businesses crash and some of their executives, cultivated by Covent Garden, end up in jail, or Cyprus.

Richard Hoggart, the Council's socialist Vice-Chairman of the early eighties, became irate at the way the House sucked up to corporate sponsors. He had it out with the House's chairman then, economist Sir Claus Moser.

> I was bloody mad, because there was a banner across Bow Street saying 'Martini's *Traviata*'. Poor old Verdi. And when we got inside we found that Martini had taken over the Crush Bar. Fancy hiring that out during a show. The Arts Council's subvention for that production was ten times what Martini had given. So I said to Moser, 'This is outrageous. You're prepared to give them anything they ask for. You've got nothing but a little line to credit the Arts Council.' Moser replied with total confidence, 'But, you see, the Arts Council has to give us the money. Martini doesn't. That's why they have to be wooed.'

Hoggart retorted that the use of tax-payers' money had to be justified, and that anyway Martini wasn't doing it out of grace: 'They want the social groups A1 and B1, and if they don't get them from you they'll go elsewhere. And what's more, they get back their money in tax.'

In 1994 the House set up the Royal Opera Appeal, a provocative title in the circumstances, which aimed to acquire from rich folk £100 million of the £135 million it needed to partner the Arts Council's grant for redevelopment. This golden cache was sought with grand autonomy by Lord Sainsbury, a former Garden chairman whom some staff claimed acted 'as if we were the under-manager of his superstore at Penge', and also by the splashy Mrs Vivien Duffield, the so-called 'Queen of Arts' and leisured heiress to the Charles Clore property empire. 'The possessor of one of the largest fortunes and sharpest tempers in the country,' the *Evening Standard* told us, 'she spends most of her time giving away huge swathes of her money to charity. In between, she throws dazzling parties.' As her partner was Sir Jocelyn Stevens, chairman of English Heritage, Mrs Duffield was well placed to help the Garden in its controversial redevelopment. Yet when the appeal got off the ground two years later, suddenly, rather than the original £100 million, 'the intention [was] to match the Arts Council's £78 million with private money', a House spokesman declared. 'I never believed the British Establishment existed,' admitted the former Heritage Secretary David Mellor, 'until I became a minister and started going to dinner parties where I'd be lobbied about the Royal Opera House.'

These snooty developments were pioneered by the 11th Earl of Drogheda, Garrett Moore (1910–1989), one of the dimmest men ever to dither with the arts. His antithesis turned up in the form of the Seventh Earl of Harewood, George Lascelles (born 1923), who had a vague sort of job at the House after joining the board in 1950. Both were dilettanti, but Harewood was (and remains) brainy about opera while Drogheda 'knew less than nothing when he started and rose to nothing when he finished' at the end of fourteen years chairing Covent Garden. He survived by bolting himself onto other people's winning ideas – the 1958 *Don Carlos* was George Harewood's pet. Harewood left Covent Garden in 1960 in a demure huff (Drogheda cattily presented him with a mechanical canary) and ran the rival English National Opera between 1972 and 1985, after failing to succeed Webster when the floorwalker retired in 1971. In reaction Harewood turned ENO into what Covent Garden could have been in the fifties, and remains president not only of ENO but also of the National Board of Film Censors, on whose certificate his signature is screened twice daily throughout the land.

Harewood displayed an integrity at odds with his fellow bluebloods, who drift into the arts because they've nothing better to do. In 1950 he started up a little monthly mag written by excitable amateurs. It prospered as a *Reader's Digest* for opera addicts, dazzlingly titled *Opera*. But it was less this that attracted David Webster to invite Harewood onto the board than the fact that he was a member of the royal family. George Harewood was the present Queen's cousin and also, at the time, son-in-law to Benjamin Britten's publisher. He arranged for the coronation commission of Britten's opera *Gloriana*, which was premiered at the House during one of the most sour and sticky nights it has ever endured, diplomats clapping limply in kid gloves.

Once Harewood had graced the board, Webster offered to put him on the payroll, and his response to Harewood's 'What as?' shows how Webster organised his House: 'I think you had better come in a general kind of capacity and find your own level.' Between 1953 and 1959 Harewood had no designation whatsoever, until Drogheda imposed 'controller of opera planning' on him, soon after which he resigned.

How Webster got away with such wishy-washy direction has never been made clear, for his first operative Chairman, following Keynes' unexpected death in 1946, was a man considered 'the greatest administrator of his time'. Sir John Anderson (1882–1958), of Anderson Shelter fame, became Viscount Waverley during his time at Covent Garden. Not only Churchill's Chancellor at the close of the war, he also seems to have had a job in every nook of Whitehall at one time or another, including the chairmanship of a secret committee to create Britain's atom bomb. He got the Covent Garden post because he knew his way around the Treasury as well as Keynes did. Anderson smartly secured from his successor as Chancellor, Labour's Hugh Dalton, a letter which pledged the Government's enduring support for the House:

I recognise, however, that the magnitude of the Covent Garden undertaking and the difficulty in present circumstances of estimating its future needs places it in a special position, and that the State will be assuming a definite obligation to see to it that, subject to others playing their part, Opera is not let down.

Anderson carried this 1946 letter about him like a fetish, and though socialists may feel miffed that it was a Labour chancellor who vouched public funds to maintain the House for eternity, Dalton specified 'Opera', not 'Covent Garden'. It has been the House that has let opera down, and Anderson's style as a supreme mandarin allowed Webster to make a mess of it. Anderson brought a smooth and formal structural approach at board level which ignored the chaos beneath it. Drogheda noted that he had 'a somewhat inhibiting effect on discussion' and that criticism would be brushed aside with the comment, 'I feel we can safely leave Mr Webster to deal with that,' which everyone round the board table knew was rubbish, though nobody felt they could say so.

Drogheda therefore believed he must do the opposite. Whether or not he was by temperament a meddler, it became his style. It was felt he did so because he had no grand strategy and to hide this he'd poke about at lots of little things. He even wrote crabby notes to journalists not in his employ and handed them to their proprietors when he met them on newspaper business. Garrett Drogheda lived a successful life for one reason – he was very good looking. Solti believed that David Webster got on with the chairman because he wanted to lift his shirt. It's hard to say whether Brendan Bracken fancied him too, but Drogheda owed his power entirely to the owner of the *Financial Times*. Drogheda half joked that he had reached his intellectual peak at prep school (he left Cambridge degree-less) and when in 1932 a social encounter with Bracken landed him a job selling newspaper space for ads, he admitted, 'My knowledge of finance and advertising was nil, and I do not know what Brendan saw in me. He never interviewed me at all, which is just as well.'

At Covent Garden Drogheda stuck to this Establishment style. Frankie Donaldson, wife of the farmer friend Drogheda brought to the board, disclosed that 'small notes were made on the pad he carried about – reminders to help get a job for someone's son'. Or daughter, perhaps. When it was suggested that the House ought to have a reference library of set and costume drawings, he personally asked Colette Clark if she'd like to do it. She just happened to be the daughter of the Arts Council's Chairman, Kenneth Clark. Drogheda later commented, 'As things turned out, the compilation of the reference library never got very far. It was found to be too arduous a task.' However, 'the best outcome in fact was that some years later Colette Clark was asked by me to join the board of directors'. Lucky Ms Clark.

*

Though to some a library of set designs was hardly big opera business, most would agree that an artistic executive was a good thing to have, given the circumstances. The board of 1948 decided the House needed an artistic director to guide the production side – exactly as Edward Dent had emphasised in 1944. General administrator Webster made a sensationally brave appointment in a smart young drama director called Peter Brook, twenty-four, who'd just made an impact with *Romeo and Juliet* at Stratford. Basically hired as a house producer, his debut with *Boris Godunov* was hailed a disaster and two seasons later he bowed out with *Salome*, a public flop. His experience at the House may explain why this great craftsman today enjoys gelding operas at his theatre workshop in Paris.

Webster turned the artistic director post into an assistant general administrator 'with special duties on the operatic side'. He invited the veteran Sir Steuart Wilson, the Arts Council's first music director, who was the nastiest man ever to work at either building, to take it up. Full of himself, this tenor's right-wing arrogance and lack of tact boosted his charisma. He quickly made it clear he wanted Webster's job, but was so blatant and malicious about it that Webster didn't need to worry. Wilson declined to use his given title and called himself deputy instead; when his retirement age came up in 1955 he swept out using the Sunday press to incite a scandal, which we'll come to presently.

David Webster then decided that neither an artistic director nor an assistant general administrator was as desirable as an assistant *to* the general administrator, and board member Eric Cundell, who ran the Guildhall School of Music, recommended his thirty-year-old secretary, John Tooley. Tooley fitted well in this supporting role, but he was performing nothing like the job originally planned. Finally, and at a stage when there was no regular conductor, Benjamin Britten was offered a further mutation of the artistic director post, titled music director. Although this full-time composer accepted, he had little interest in the House by then and the work turned into a woolly consultancy before it fizzled out. How ironic, when we remember what Webster wrote for the Arts Council in 1946: 'Every encouragement will be given to our composers.'

If one consistent policy can be found in the life of Covent Garden Opera it is this: that no encouragement is given to our composers. In fifty years it has commissioned exactly six House operas – none by Benjamin Britten. The House wrongly claims that it commissioned two from this most celebrated of modern opera composers, *Billy Budd* (1951) and *Gloriana* (1953). The former was commissioned by the Arts Council for the Festival of Britain, and it was given to Sadler's Wells to premiere at the 1951 Edinburgh Festival. *Budd* proved too big for the Wells' resources and it was passed on at short notice to Covent Garden, which had been scolded about its lack of initiative for that special year.

Britten's coronation epic *Gloriana* was the Earl of Harewood's concept. His friend Britten agreed to do it only if it 'was made in some way official, not quite commanded but at least accepted as part of the celebrations'. Harewood arranged this through his brother Tommy, who was the Queen's private secretary. The money came from the Treasury via a special coronation fund. In fact Covent Garden didn't commission anything from anyone until 1970, when Webster was leaving. It certainly hosted the premieres of Bliss's *The Olympians* (1949) and Vaughan Williams' *The Pilgrim's Progress* (1951), but orphans are not quite the same as progeny. The best opera houses of the world have donated regularly to the present and future of music by commissioning and advancing the birth of new work, but Covent Garden hasn't had the spunk to contribute. Even when it has done so it has generally used extra cash from the Arts Council or the Gulbenkian Foundation to pay for the commissions. The failure of the House to engage with creative composers is as shameful as its obsessive pandering to snobs and its indulgence in shallow standards.

Covent Garden commissioned Sir Michael Tippett's *The Knot Garden* (1970) and *The Ice Break* (1977), Richard Rodney Bennett's *Victory* (1970), John Tavener's *Thérèse* (1979), Sir Harrison Birtwistle's *Gawain* (1991) and *We Come to the River* (1976) by the German composer Hans Werner Henze to a text by the English playwright Edward Bond. Some of these have sunk without trace. Notwithstanding the lack of any Britten, followers of modern music might have expected to see Peter Maxwell Davies listed; the House did his pungent *Taverner* – once, and grudgingly.

The sudden burst of premieres in the seventies came about because of the appointment of the remarkable Colin Davis as chief conductor. His tolerance of the kind of lyrical expressionism of Tippett and Henze didn't discourage Royal Opera to lure him away from Sadler's Wells. When Webster retired, his long-serving assistant, John Tooley, replaced him, and as general administrator he was under pressure to catch some of that trendy swinging London spirit before it evaporated. *The Knot Garden*, with its black and white gay couple and freedom-fighting student, and the Maoist 'actions' of *We Come to the River* are the radical chic legacy of the House; significantly, the Earl of Harewood omitted the Henze from the Kobbé opera guide he edited.

Birtwistle's 1991 mediaeval epic, *Gawain*, was really the result of a more recent regime atoning for the ghastly behaviour of its forebears. His masterpiece *The Mask of Orpheus* had been proposed to Covent Garden in 1970, when the 'dream team' of Colin Davis and director Peter Hall were meant to establish a new era for the House. Birtwistle was hot property thanks to Britten, who walked out of the young composer's manic *Punch and Judy* the previous year, giving that premiere a dose of 'young-firebrand-versus-old-fogey' publicity. Hall soon scarpered too, to both the National Theatre and Glyndebourne, dragging Birtwistle with him when it became clear that Covent Garden was not truly keen to support *Orpheus*. Glyndebourne coolly endorsed the commission until the score grew too complicated for the village hall, giving Glyndebourne the pretext to drop it, and finally, in this game of pass the parcel, English National Opera gave *Orpheus* the triumphant premiere in 1986 that Covent Garden had evaded.

The Mask of Orpheus was not the first piece aborted by Covent Garden. Back in March 1949 the Arts Council announced a half-baked competition, declaring it wished 'to commission a limited number of full-length operas in connection with the Festival of Britain'. A committee which included Edward Dent, Constant Lambert and Sir Steuart Wilson chose four scores from the submissions (there's no record of how many they saw) 'for performances which, the Council hopes, will be given by the Covent Garden Opera Company during the 1951 Festival of Britain. However, the Arts Council cannot enter into any assurances concerning production.' Although he was not paying for the commissions, Webster hadn't the slightest intention of putting them on even before he knew what they were.

A condition of submission was that composers had to use pseudonyms, and the committee was as horrified as Webster when they discovered the true names of the four winners: one of them was Karl Rankl, the House conductor they hoped to sack. The other three were equally embarrassing to the Establishment (could the mischievous Dent have guessed their identities?). Only one of the four, Alan Bush, was English, and he was a communist.

His opera concerned the peasants' revolt led by Wat Tyler. Arthur Benjamin was Australian and Berthold Goldschmidt not only German but a communist, too.

Although the Arts Council stumped up, none of the four works was produced. Goldschmidt pointed out the irony that his previous opera had also been commissioned but not placed before the public – but that was in Germany in 1933, thanks to the Nazis. When his Arts Council commission, *Beatrice Cenci*, finally came to be heard in London, in a 1988 concert performance under Odaline de la Martinez, it was generally considered a sensation. *Wat Tyler*, by the way, got its premiere in 1953 in Leipzig, where the East Germans were careful to thank the Arts Council of Great Britain for its generous gift.

Even when composers have made it to Covent Garden, they have left embittered. Webster was not the sole offender, for here's Sir Michael Tippett on the Tooley seventies, commenting that when he saw the House moving

> towards what I call 'gala performance' opera . . . I began to think I didn't belong. Each year there would be promises of revivals or new productions, especially *The Midsummer Marriage*, which were postponed – mainly because singers like Jon Vickers or Kiri Te Kanawa could not be persuaded . . . ENO were regularly blocked from presenting a Tippett opera because Covent Garden insisted they were planning for one.

John Tavener's experience over *Thérèse* 'still rankles with him fourteen years later', his biographer revealed. 'As he saw it, they felt stuck with an obligation they had incurred during the days of Peter Hall, and were hoping to discharge it with the minimum fuss and expense.' It wasn't even performed by the Royal Opera, which was touring Japan at the time, but by minor soloists with the London Sinfonietta Chorus and a scratch band in the pit. Tavener exclaimed, 'I am sure some accountant somewhere was saying, "My God, this is a modern opera! Do you realise we're going to lose on this? And there's no interval, so we're not going to have any bar takings!" '

By the middle eighties growing criticism of both the House and ENO for their lack of engagement with living composers forced them to take fatal actions. In a reckless response ENO threw Arts Council commission money at anyone who'd take it, producing a series of operatic premieres at the Coliseum whose creative emptiness underscored the apparently blasé tone of ENO's management at the time – the laddish trio of Poutney, Elder and Jonas. This criticism grew from the success of an independent music festival run by the young Pierre Audi at his pygmy Almeida Theatre in Islington. As it drew some of its funding from the Arts Council's drama department, this gave the Council the chance to close the sparkling festival down. The depressed Audi left for Amsterdam to run Netherlands Opera, which now sets the pace for new work on the international scene, and he handed his theatre to a couple of arch thespians who now put on proper plays for full-blown luvvies.

The bulk of the musical cash saved was handed over by the Arts Council to ENO's Contemporary Opera Studio, a meagre and timid operation seemingly invented to keep the Council's music panel happy. Each summer it would put on a display of skimpy things in the Almeida Theatre. The COS, ditched in the early nineties, was resurrected with much fuss by ENO's successor to Jonas, a former television director called Dennis Marks, who professed a desire to champion new work. However, instead of appointing an artistic director to run the COS – a post ENO advertised – Marks invited a composer he knew, Mark-Anthony Turnage, to associate himself with it. Turnage's publisher is Mrs Marks. But Turnage settled instead in December 1994 for a more prominent rank, one created for the occasion and titled composer-in-association of ENO in its entirety. To the COS he became simply a 'consultant' – but as in the end it has done next to nothing anyway, it doesn't seem to matter. Marks resigned (some say he was dismissed) in September 1997.

The Royal Opera House went one better, or poorer. The Council's music director at the time, Ken Baird, pushed the House to do something about its shabby creative reputation in the wake of the Almeida's success. Seizing their chance to advance the cause of contemporary music in the House, two subordinates proposed the Garden Venture, a workshop to introduce young composers to the world of modern opera. The trouble was that the duo seemed to know little about modern opera themselves. A music festival director recalls:

> They came and asked me for names of young composers who might be interested in opera workshops and I trawled my address book. I was surprised later when I saw the first few of those names commissioned to create operas for the House! I got the impression

that political pressure had turned a nice little unit of research into a public monster.

To make matters worse, the Garden Venture adopted a neat financial ploy invented for new dance by Julia Rowntree and John Ashford at the Place Theatre and called the Place Portfolio, but the House screwed it up. In the dance version members of the public were invited to put up £25 each to help fund a new production which was then matched by an investment company as sponsorship. Under a promotional scheme of the time, that total of £50 was matched by the Association for Business Sponsorship, delivering £100 from the initial investment of £25. The House completely missed the trick and merely invited readers of the *Independent* to cough up £100 each. After twenty-one assorted pieces and acres of acrid press reviews, the House swung the axe. In sum, that is how the House has treated this country's composers. As Spike Hughes wrily noted about the neighbouring fruit market, 'It grows nothing; it sells everything.'

Singers were a different matter. As Covent Garden became increasingly dependent on jet-set divas to sell its seats, their fattening fees dislodged the priorities of expenditure, while the agents' leverage over ever-lengthening schedules limited the Opera House's own repertory plans. When the House put on the premiere of *Billy Budd* in December 1951, the American baritone singing Billy was booked at three months' notice – not advisable, but do-able. Now the agents prefer three years, so they get it.

The House goes out of its way to ingratiate itself with the 'stars'. It's said that Placido Domingo enjoyed the exclusive use of an apartment discreetly run by Covent Garden in Neal Street where he could entertain whom he chose. On the other hand they lost Elizabeth Schwarzkopf forever and Luciano Pavarotti for ages because it was rumoured the celebrities overheard disparaging remarks from the directorate. Producers, too – with whom the House has an unimaginative record – are treated with skittish deference, despite the way the Garden pretends to frown on the recent growth of 'producer's opera'. It knows that this development is essential to marketing, for producers provide the vital elements by which old operas can regain their sense of novelty.

Vulgar as it may be, one perception of the House is that artistic relationships and jobs have sometimes been advanced not through professional skill or creative vision, but through sexuality.

This has never been defined more clearly than in the *People* on Sunday 24 July 1955:

MUSIC CHIEF LEADS BIG
CAMPAIGN AGAINST VICE

A campaign against homosexuality in British music is to be launched by Sir Steuart Wilson, until last month Deputy General Administrator of the Royal Opera House, Covent Garden. Sir Steuart, 66, told the *People* last night:

'The influence of perverts in the world of music has grown beyond all measure. If it is not curbed soon, Covent Garden and other precious musical heritages could suffer irreparable harm.

'Many people in the profession are worried. There is a kind of agreement among homosexuals which results in their keeping jobs for the boys.'

And Mr Walford Haydn, the famous composer and conductor, said: 'Homosexuals are damaging music and all the other arts. I am sorry for those born that way, but many acquire it – and for them I have nothing but contempt. Singers who are perverted often get work simply because of this. And new works by composers are given preference by some people if the writer is perverted.'

BUT Mr David Webster, General Administrator of the Royal Opera House disagrees. 'Music is flourishing,' he said. 'It is nonsense to say that there are jobs for the boys, as Sir Steuart alleges.'

But Mr David Webster was gay. He was so at a time when it was illegal and a prison sentence beckoned. What brought this on is hinted in Walford Haydn's phrase – and we are indebted to the *People* for telling us that this nonentity is famous (great name, though) – about new works by 'perverts'. *The Midsummer Marriage* was premiered just six months earlier. The composer, conductor, choreographer, producer and no doubt the tea boy were probably 'perverts' in Mr Haydn's eyes. But then, most of Covent Garden's living composers have been gay: Britten, Tippett, Richard Rodney Bennett, Peter Maxwell Davies, Hans Werner Henze. The objections aired by Steuart Wilson were induced by his envy of Webster's ill-earned status, yet this kind of sexual polarity is endemic in the arts: Christie against Keynes, Wolfit against Gielgud, Walton against Britten, and so on. There was certainly a feeling around the war that homosexuals evaded service and exploited the absence of 'patriots' to command positions they would otherwise fail to achieve. Webster was considered as such, Britten too. When Sadler's Wells premiered *Peter Grimes* in 1945, members of the chorus and staff, and in particular a group of bellicose women, were blatantly hostile to Britten and his boyfriend, Peter Pears, who played the leading role. His next three operas contained no chorus and when Britten next composed an epic, *Billy Budd*, he wrote for men's voices only.

To some the House has been a debonair cruising base since it opened. We've already observed the reason why this should be so in ballet, while gay disposition towards the extravagance, exaggerations and subterfuge of opera has been covered in Wayne Koestenbaum's book *The Queen's Throat* of 1994. Prevalence of homosexuality at key levels of the diplomatic service, the court and the Church is by now well documented, and therefore the main ingredients by which a national opera house can trade as a discreet, gay enclave both backstage and front of house are in place.

A refined social cosiness developed long ago between some of Covent Garden's staff and the prevailingly gay opera critics of the press. It took the antics of Sir Joseph Lockwood to draw general press attention to the social use gays made of the House. For instance, Lockwood ran EMI from 1954 to 1974 and hosted visits to his box by the company's gay pop stars, such as Freddie Mercury of Queen. Further, it was even rumoured that an outfit providing discounted seats for young people was being exploited to bring 'trade' into the auditorium of which Lockwood and his friends took advantage.

In any case, the golden-shower days of the Garden may be over. As metropolitan sexuality has become less covert, thanks to the liberation movements of the sixties, the House finds it increasingly difficult to maintain its hold on this vintage aspect of its social function, or more to the point the 'pink pound' that emerges from it. Put simply, the gay scene has outgrown the sanctuary of the House. Covent Garden's appointment of Keith Cooper, its latest marketing manager (or director of corporate affairs, as he was known), followed from the need to update the House's image in line with this shift in public affluence and openness. Cooper successfully attempted the same job for Opera North and ENO by using sexy photos on posters – bums on ads to get bums on seats. However, his success at the ENO had some interesting results which seem now to put Covent Garden at a disadvantage. In the spring of 1996 a little, *Opera*-like mag from gay New York, *Parterre Box*, covered London:

After the tweedy stuffiness of Covent Garden, the English National Opera and its environs were a breath of air. ENO is *crawling* with queer people! Onstage, backstage, inside, outside, gay men and lesbians *rule* . . .

There's actually an in-house men's bathroom you can retire to for sexual assignations and still hear the music (several couples took advantage of this convenience during *Turandot*). And what better way to begin your night at the opera than with a cruisy welcome from buff boy takers and ushers?

Gay entrepreneurs have even opened a cruising bar right next to the Coliseum. Its name is Brief Encounter.

Chapter 15

The knot garden: a curtain fails

Pink pounds are not the only kind Covent Garden has had to hustle. It's needed Council pounds too, and in order to ensure that it was never caught short of those, the Arts Council connived with the House back in the fifties to create the most audacious joint post in the history of arts subsidy. At the Garden it was the one we might expect to be the most boring, the company secretary and accountant, taken up by Mr D.P. Lund (died 1974) who began his work there in 1951. Before his arrival the accounts were run through Boosey & Hawkes; in fact, up to 1949 the accounts belonged to 'Boosey & Hawkes, Covent Garden Branch'. Douglas Peter Lund only worked afternoons. In the mornings he was employed by the Arts Council as its accounting officer. It was at this very time that Covent Garden received 40 to 50 per cent of the Council's total funds.

Lund wrote letters to himself, both from Covent Garden to the Arts Council and the other way round. He joked that he saved both outfits postage by carrying the envelopes and cheques in his briefcase as he walked between offices to hand the letter from himself to himself, and cashed the cheques he'd signed on behalf of the Arts Council to his alternate employer. Lund was said to be a very good accountant, which is why the Arts Council was sad to lose him in 1965, when he left, 'in order to devote himself wholly to the affairs of the Royal Opera House'. If we consider Keynes' joint chairmanship of the funding body and its main client to be ever so slightly dodgy, Peter Lund's dual duties take the breath away. The Council's music director of the time, John Denison, emphasised how close-run and casual the financial traffic became:

> Of a night Webster might ask me to call round to his home in Weymouth Street and we might walk round the block while he would say something in the nature of, 'There's not enough money in the safe to pay the company on Friday,' and we'd discuss arrangements. Covent Garden always had £50 to £100,000 too little. People don't appreciate how close to the ground it was.

Still, Mr Lund got a CBE for his efforts to hoist it up.

If the public cares to keep an eye on the tryst between Covent Garden and the Arts Council, it's confined to do so through the Council's annual accounts, which are passed on to public libraries. The House's presence in the budgets has always posed a mighty challenge to the Arts Council, which wishes it could slip the Garden's vast fiscal girth into the accounts without calling attention to it, though it's as hard as hiding Pavarotti. In the forties they tried to keep whatever bits of it they could out of the accounts altogether, by getting a supplementary grant going solely to the Opera House voted through Parliament. This could not continue as the money had to enter the Arts Council books in accordance with parliamentary accountability – actually, ministers wanted the opportunity to pass the blame onto the Council when they saw the House going out of kilter, once Rankl's operas started up. This explains the giant leap in the Covent Garden grant from £30,000 in 1947 to £145,000 in 1948 (£1 million to £2.5 million at today's values). The actual 1947 grant to Covent Garden had been £98,000; the bulk of this was nodded through the House of Commons as a supplementary sum.

Such a device, though, had the unfortunate effect of alerting MPs to the scale of the Opera House's cost. Any reference to Covent Garden in the order papers would ensure the behatted presence of Carl Rosa's valkyrie, Irene Ward, and her barbed questions to the Chancellor about Covent Garden's 'commitment to the provinces'. It was Dame Irene, by the way, who first spotted that chancellors never seemed to be sure whether Covent Garden was 'national' or 'international' in its remit. On the other hand, chancellors certainly knew that her Carl Rosa was neither.

The Royal Opera House soon found a new home in the accounts. It was essentially elevated, not to say isolated, and placed in a compartment at the head of the grants list so that the eye couldn't compare it directly to smaller acquirers of subsidy. This siting had the added advantage of rarely telling readers the full story, because the Arts Council would routinely give the company extra bits of money recorded in other columns on other pages. However, the Arts Council of the fifties and sixties could not hide the fact that it was handing over a sum never less than 35 per cent of its entire subsidy to one client. It was able to reduce the percentage proportion (while at the same time increasing the core grant) only when the Labour Government started tossing more money into the Arts Council coffers from 1965.

The Council had one persistent and firm response whenever it was quizzed about the Garden's grant. It would point out that the grant was really a compound, covering the costs of three separate companies: Covent Garden Opera, the Royal Ballet and the 'second' ballet company – which had worked its subordinate way through a number of condescending names – as well as the theatre itself and the school. At the same time the Council would use this corporate concept of Covent Garden to block panels and committees from interfering with it. Although the music panel formally dealt with both music and ballet until the late seventies, it was never allowed to pore over Covent Garden because of its 'complex and corporate nature'. That had to be dealt with 'upstairs'.

When the dance boom of the late seventies prompted the creation of a dance department and a dance panel, its members (several of them graduates of the sixties revolution) got bolshy about all the money going to the Royal Ballet without any comment invited from them as the Council's dance advisers on the issues of artistic standards, repertoire development, access or even education – after all, the Royal Ballet ran its own boarding school. Furthermore, the finance staff were unable to tell them at panel meetings how much the ballet side of Covent Garden actually got. The issue was 'too intricate to give a helpful indication' or 'problematic, as the overheads cannot be apportioned in manner constructive to the Panel's needs'. So when Clive Priestley's independent report on the running of the Royal Opera House came out in October 1983, senior management was peeved to learn that this seasoned civil servant had worked out a formula to express the grant's various elements. The finance director, Anthony Field, called it 'cutting Tooley into pieces'.

Rancour turned to relief when it was pointed out that the monolithic grant to Covent Garden could now be carved up among the artform columns of the accounts, ensuring that the full picture could only be seen by someone with a keen eye, a calculator and plenty of time to waste. Charles Morgan of the National Campaign for the Arts points out that the figures shown in the published Arts Council accounts and Covent Garden's annual reports are rarely consistent in their internal detail; you'd think they'd at least attempt to tell the same story. But that is how it stands today.

Covent Garden never has enough subsidy to do what it should, but it gets too much for what it does. Exerting their brains to comprehend this mystery are the fourteen members of the board. Under them sit three subsidiary boards: for ballet, opera and development. Since it started to meet in 1946 until the 1997 closure the main board has comprised seventy-five of the great and good, five of them women, and despite assumptions not all of the men went to Eton. No, only one quarter (eighteen) of the total are Etonians. A further third went to lesser public schools (three to Rugby, three to Winchester), though the economist Lord Robbins started out at Southall County School – well done! One third were peers when they arrived, during, or at the close of their tenure; 40 per cent of them knights. While only three have been working artists – the composers Walton, Goehr and Michael Berkeley – thirty-one (that is, just under half) have also sat on the Arts Council or its panels, including one director of music, a deputy secretary-general and four chairmen: Keynes, Clark, Goodman and Gibson. So anyone wild enough to suggest that this group of prestigious charity workers is in any sense an unelected, even unrepresentative, self-perpetuating, inartistic, lionising club out for honours and baubles, perhaps, need only check the figures.

The Garden argues that it is awfully hard to find the right people. They must be deeply distinguished because the pre-eminent are invariably people of probity, and anyway the public expects to see notable names. In any case the celebrated have casual access to the most desirable phone numbers. Board members must be able to sort of read budgets and know a little something about opera or ballet. They must have daytimes free for meetings and evenings free to entertain at shows. Put that all together and maybe that's why you end up with Bamber Gascoigne.

The problem of filling posts becomes most acute in the case of the chairman and the general director, which is what Webster's job was retitled in 1988 when Jeremy Isaacs took it on. Isaacs set up and ran Channel 4 TV; his cultural industry background, linking commerce with creativity, loosely fell in line with Keynes' notion that a businessman should run the place. He came at a time when those outside the world of TV voguishly believed that those inside it must be wonderfully gifted. It seems it didn't take long for Isaacs, Dennis Marks (BBC TV to ENO) and Liz Forgan (Channel 4 to BBC Radio) to disabuse them of that theory. Like the old white dot on the TV screen, Isaacs faded from Covent Garden in late 1996, earlier than contracted because, it was said, he had a TV show to work on. He left on his desk a renovation and closure plan that the Arts Council Chairman condemned in public as 'quite frankly, a shambles', and over which the staff were balloted for strike action. Still, as his predictable knighthood was secured in the 1996 New Year honours, Isaacs had little private need to hold on. Yet remarkably he rejoined the main board.

The general feeling is that Isaacs might have done something to revitalise the place but he soon flunked and consumed progressivist hopes. An executive of one of the leading foreign opera houses says of him:

> I am sure Jeremy understood the need to modernise the organisation from top to bottom. But he went in there and lost himself. It seems to be an organisation which allows this to happen. Is it so difficult in England to find the right combination of people at the top to push the reforms that are absolutely necessary?

Similar problems faced the music director Bernard Haitink. This decent, dependable Dutchman tackled opera first at Glyndebourne, where he did some of his finest work. He arrived at the House in 1987, after ending not only his rock-steady partnership with the Amsterdam Concertgebouw Orchestra but also a sustained marriage. Haitink came with a 'new start' reformist programme to purge the place of greedy stars and create an ensemble company with 'a family of singers and producers who enjoy working here and are willing to rehearse'. He wanted to drop seat prices and introduce surtitles so that the audience could follow the text. Surtitles aside, his aspirations sadly came to little. Seat prices continued to rise each year (top tickets £263, then the highest in Europe), while the ageing Pavarotti sang for sponsors' guests. Dent's wartime warning had turned into not only a reality, but a policy.

Haitink's frustration is doubtless shared by Nicholas Payne, the latest recruit to the muddled deputy job which started with Peter Brook, now titled 'director of opera'. Payne had strengthened Opera North, but whereas his self-evident though decent ideas for repertoire development worked in Leeds – promoting the neglected French repertoire of the nineteenth century, for example – they faltered in London. One such was Massenet's hollow *Chérubin*, premiered on Valentine's Day 1994, on which the sober skills of producer Tim Albery were frittered while the Russian conductor Rozhdestvensky walked out of rehearsals – all for a stick of candy floss. For its fiftieth birthday the House chose to put on, of all things, Pfitzner's *Palestrina*, a ponderous homily by a stale German composer from the turn of the century. It could at least have produced Goldschmidt's *Beatrice Cenci*.

Despite assurances that the House has professionalised its administration and improved its services, we still recognise the ramshackle features of the Webster fifties. In May 1995 a Royal Ballet show had to be cancelled and ticket money returned because the stage was still covered in opera scenery. A PR disaster broke soon after when it was announced that the schools matinees scheme was to be junked, twenty-four hours after the press had blitzed the £78 million Lottery award as elitist, after which followed the embarrassing erosion of Payne's hyped Verdi Festival. Crashing into all this came the backstage bungling revealed in Double Exposure's 1996 TV documentary *The House* on which a London *Standard* columnist wrote:

> We're left with the impression that behind the crimson and gold magnificence of the Royal Opera House there is humdrum inefficiency, staff truculence, internecine guerilla warfare between rival factions and a wing-and-a-prayer organisation.

On the very night in February 1996 that an episode of *The House* was shown to three million BBC2 viewers, a conventional production of *Aida* proved the accuracy of the TV show, as reported by the *Standard*'s Alexander Waugh:

> *Aida* was nearly half an hour late starting because rehearsals had over-run and the sets weren't up in time. Director Nicholas Payne apologised from the stage and announced that the evening's star

performer Julia Varady had withdrawn (yet again) – this time due
to an attack of bronchitis. One brave heckler accused him of lying.
When a hieroglyphic screen failed to rise above knee-height on the
first scene it really looked as if the whole operation had fallen to
pieces.

It appears that the administration would like the British public
to think it *has* fallen to pieces, for that is the only way it will obtain
tenable support for its bricks-and-mortar redevelopment. The
affair has been going on since 1969, when the old fruit market
next to the House was due to move out to Nine Elms. The Department of Education and Science set up a committee to consider
possibilities, and when the Labour Government returned in 1974,
it spent £3.1 million to purchase 2.1 acres of land next to the
House to allow for improvements and extensions. The Garden
had pointed out how crammed and dilapidated the place had
become, especially backstage. Nobody questioned then what the
House had been doing with previous government supplements
into the capital account for repairs and renovations.

Still, something had to be achieved if Covent Garden was to
compete with the new English National Opera at the Coliseum.
Phase 1, containing four rehearsal studios, modern dressing rooms
and offices, was finally opened by Prince Charles in July 1982. It
cost £9.5 million, of which £3 million was additional subsidy.
Phase 2 remains to be built at the time of writing. Five separate
phase 2 masterplans had gone before the City of Westminster's
planning committee for consent, and up to then the House had
spent a staggering £23 million on the project (£7.5 million in
professional fees, £1.9 million in legal fees, and so on) without a
single concrete improvement. In 1983 the projected cost of phase
2 was £98.4 million with a deficit of £23 million; by 1991 it became
£175 million with a deficit of £90million; by 1996, £213 million.
Glyndebourne's new opera theatre was built at a sixth of the
Garden's cost, and without a pound of public cash.

The whole wretched business of prevarication and confusion at
the House is complicated in its specifics and far too stodgy to
relate, but the chronological detail can be found in a clever spoof
of a Covent Garden programme, published by the Covent Garden
Community Association in June 1995 under the title 'Il Rigmarole
della Casa d'Opera Regale' (or 'Cock Up in Covent Garden'). The
issues centre around the feeling of the Community Association,
led by a canny architect called Jim Monahan, that the Garden had

been cavalier and smug in the way it expected to knock down old buildings and replace them with 'an extraordinary melange of stone and metal cladding', including shops and offices, to serve its needs. It was the commercial element in particular which roused the discord.

The Arts Council has supported the redevelopment from the first. It should be borne in mind that the Ministry of Works acquired the land for the existing building in 1949; at the time, there being a Labour Government, many regarded the ministry's compulsory purchase order as 'nationalisation'. The extra two acres were handed over in 1981 to the Royal Opera House Development Land Trust, which was really the House and the Council working in partnership; the Council is a trustee. Accounts for 1980–1981 include the following note:

> The Covent Garden property is held jointly by the Arts Council and the Royal Opera House, Covent Garden Ltd, subject to and on the terms of a charitable trust known as the ROH Development Land Trust, and the rights and interest of the Arts Council in such property, as set out in a trust deed dated 27 February 1981, include a charge in excess of £3.15m over any proceeds of sale from such land.

Controller of the ROH Development Land Trust was David Money-Coutts, a director and former chairman of the Arts Council's bank. The snag arose with the advent in 1995 of the Lottery. Covent Garden submitted an application to the Arts Council's lottery unit for a whacking £78.5 million to subsidise its £213 million redevelopment. According to objectors, the application was flawed because the Arts Council as a trustee would benefit, while rules under the Lottery Act forbade it to fund a company of which it was a 'member'. Council countered on the technicality that a trustee-ship was not the same as membership, which is an intriguing judicial point better left to lawyers, but an awkward moral one.

The figure of £78.5 million is curious. Under Lottery rules Covent Garden need only find 25 to 30 per cent from other sources. In that case it could have applied to the Council for £135 million, leaving it with £78 million to find by other means – in other words, transposing the figures. As £50 million was supposed to be raised through the retail value of the site, the remaining £28 million might have been donated largely by Lord Sainsbury and Mrs Duffield from their own funds, as it appears they'd already agreed to supply £10 million apiece. But we can imagine the Arts Council and the ministry calculating the political damage to the Lottery of a bid exceeding £100 million from a publicly unpopular body.

This raises the interesting question of what kind of arrangements might have taken place before the project was submitted, because the rules direct that the Council 'cannot solicit applications', which presumably means they cannot limit them either. There is no top line. The Council's lottery director observed in October 1994 that 'If we give a small grant to every village that asks for one ... we won't have enough left to fund the ROH extension.' At that time, a month before the Lottery opened, he supposed he'd have £80 million from takings for the first year. If the Garden elected to bid below the £100 million because it misjudged the money available, it would have been a surprising decision, because its trustee James Butler is deputy chairman of Camelot. If it chose to do so for the sake of public relations, then it was futile, because the outrage couldn't have been fiercer.

On 20 July 1995, the Arts Council announced that its principal client had won the £78.5 million it sought, in two stages of £55 million and £23.5 million. The nation's media went to town, most stylishly in the number one tabloid, the *Sun*:

FURY AS MORE LOTTERY CASH GOES DOWN THE DRAIN
IT'S THE GREEDY BEGGAR'S OPERA
Exclusive by Lenny Lottery

A storm erupted last night over the extra £100 million Lottery handout for opera lovers – instead of ordinary Lottery punters. Furious Labour MP Tony Banks blasted the Arts Council for dishing out cash to 'people who never bought a Lottery ticket in their lives'. He stormed, 'Most of the millions raised by the Lottery come from working class punters. But they are getting nothing back.'

Arts Council chairman Lord Gowrie defended the payouts insisting opera was not 'just for toffs' despite £120 ticket prices. He said, 'Opera audiences I have seen around the country are very often struggling professionals. '*They are middle class people – not very rich toffs.*' He added he would like to have given the Royal Opera House an EXTRA £10 million to help lower ticket prices.

The *Sun* set up a phone vote hotline called You The Jury: 'What do you think? Should opera get £100 million of opera cash? YES 0891 400 698: NO 0891 400 699'. A day later no fewer than 15,000 people had phoned 699. Jane Kerrati, a wine-shop manager from Bristol, protested, 'Charities are closing through lack of funds and the money keeps pouring into the opera. It doesn't make sense.'

Musician Jane Larnie of Islington said, 'It stinks. They should use the money to help ordinary and disadvantaged people, not fat cats.' Though it might be expected that the *Sun* would try this gimmick, the *Guardian* did, too: 'Subsidising arts and sports is a cheap way out for the Tories,' reckoned Manny Penner, seventy-one, of Bow. 'The Lottery is a levy on the poor to pay for the rich.' In response Covent Garden's chairman, Sir Angus Stirling (sixty-two, Eton and Trinity, Cambridge) said: 'It's not about elitism. It's about conveying to the people dance and opera to the highest level these arts have attained.'

By March 1996 it was rumoured that the Arts Council had passed on to Covent Garden £2.3 million of the Lottery award with the promise that 'it could draw up to £20 million more without any hassle'. Yet the Council had awarded the first tranche of £55 million on condition that 'the project must achieve full planning consent from Westminster Council *and satisfy all conditions* [author's italics]'. Five months earlier Westminster Council had given planning permission but with thirty conditions attached. The House tried to satisfy these with little success. Following a committee meeting on 29 February 1996, Westminster insisted that a fresh planning application be submitted, effectively outdating the earlier permission. The Council apparently handed out the money anyway, the condition now reading: 'and *assurances to the Arts Council's satisfaction* [author's italics again] that any conditions will be met'. As Mary Glasgow said, 'We concentrated on the Royal Opera House, protected it rather solidly. Maybe we were a little terrified of what would happen if it didn't work out. That might have meant the end of the Arts Council.'

Around the same time it was announced that Sir Angus Stirling would step down as Covent Garden's chairman. From the autumn of 1996 his successor was Peter Gummer, brother of Tory Environment Secretary John Gummer and a key figure in the promotion of the Conservative Party. He remains chairman of Shandwick, one of the world's largest public-relations groups. Peter Gummer was elevated to the upper chamber as Lord Chadlington on accepting his Covent Garden appointment. Gummer had previously chaired the Arts Council lottery board, which awarded the £78 million to the House. It's rumoured that he coveted the Council's Chairman job when it went instead to Gowrie and that the Garden post came as consolation.

Back in September 1994, Gummer had written a robust article attacking Anthony Everitt, the former Secretary-General who'd claimed in a column that the House had become 'Britain's most unpopular arts organisation', a charge made well before any Lottery outrage or TV documentary. Gummer lunged:

> As chairman of the Arts Council Lottery Board, and, until recently, chairman of the working party established to monitor the implementation at the Royal Opera House of the proposals made by Lady Warnock and Price Waterhouse, I am angry that your article will perpetuate myths . . . The underlying argument is that of access: that the ROH is a place of privilege for an elite few . . . The Opera House management has pledged that savings brought about by increased efficiency flowing from the development will be ploughed back to push some prices down.

He singled out for special mention the very school matinees that were scrapped ten months later. Baroness Warnock's report, by the way, recommended that the redevelopment plan should be shelved until a more suitable period, as it was consuming too much management time. Price Waterhouse likewise recommended that the general director should not oversee the development process. What Gummer therefore achieved in his role as monitor is unclear.

The phase 2 redevelopment began in earnest on Sunday 10 March 1996, when the eighty-strong staff of the Brahms & Liszt wine bar and Caffe Piazza were escorted out of their premises by security guards the House had hired. These restaurant sites were due to be incorporated into phase 2, though the evicted waiters weren't. More likely they'd join a dole queue of 110 singers, musicians and technicians from the House axed in order to offset an overspend of £3 million during the 1995–1996 financial year which, the Arts Council urged, had to be balanced in the next. Blame for the deficit centred on the cut-price Richard Jones production of Wagner's *Ring*, which reportedly failed to reach even half of the box-office targets set for it, despite sublime musical direction under Haitink. While estimating the ominous options available (including the laying off, during rebuilding, of 300 of the 820 staff remaining), the finance director chose to depart right in the middle of an audit. His deputy took over, but he had already been made redundant in the cuts and was only there working out his notice. By March 1997 the deficit had not been eliminated but in fact had risen by 50 per cent to £4.5 million. Soon afterwards, Mrs Duffield and Lord Sainsbury saved the House from going bust by contributing £2 million between them in a one-off rescue deal, which shows the impressive degree to which this duo went to retain their stake in Covent Garden's survival. Bring back Mr Lund?

Isaacs was not replaced in the traditional manner. Instead the board chose to downgrade his job and retitle it 'chief executive'. This purely administrative post was advertised and won by Genista McIntosh, who used to work in a similar position at the National Theatre. Although McIntosh had never worked in opera, she was the first chief in the fifty-year history of the House to have had solid experience of the performing arts. Known to all as Jenny, she was deeply admired in the drama world, where she had proved she could handle a top job well. It was assumed that she'd sort out the many immediate management problems, leaving Nicholas Payne a freer hand to devise the opera programme, while presumably Lord Chadlington would preside over the pressing PR woes. Chief among those was a malevolent press reaction to the delayed closure plans when he finally announced them in April 1997 – the ones that the Earl of Gowrie too considered 'a shambles'. Though executives were supposed to have secured another habitat for the Royal Opera and the Royal Ballet between July 1997 and the end of 1999, the companies were left homeless, 'wandering around London like the Flying Dutchman', according to the opera-loving Labour MP Gerald Kaufman. The extra revenue costs involved were meant to be covered by £20 million from the Lottery.

'Shambles' was in public service again soon afterwards, on 13 May 1997, when Lord Chadlington had to announce that McIntosh had walked out of her job after just four months. He claimed that she departed 'due to ill health', but few were convinced. When Jenny McIntosh wrote to *The Times* two days later to confirm that 'the decision to leave was mine alone', her letter was dissected in civil-service style to reveal what it didn't say. She hadn't said she was ill. More interestingly, she'd done nothing to scotch the rumours that there was discord in the House between the demands of public subsidy and private wealth, between the aspirations of the accountable Ms McIntosh and the ambitions of the free-floating Mrs Duffield.

'Scandal' supplanted 'shambles' when Chadlington announced he had already found a successor to take over as chief executive. It was none other than Mary Allen, the Arts Council's Secretary-General; she would start in September. Allen, who had said, 'I've never done a job for more than three years.' Allen, whose 'hands-on' experience of arts management comprised a couple of seasons at a little arts centre in Brentford. Allen, who sat in on Jenny McIntosh's interview, though she was not interviewed herself. Allen partnered Chadlington on the Lottery scheme that gave the House its £78.5 million. They gained the respective positions of chairman and chief executive of the client they had rewarded, the National Lottery's biggest single winner. It looked to all the world like an unhealthy Arts Council coup. Some claimed that Allen's move ran counter to the Council's own procedural and ethical code of practice, though this was denied. Detractors also pointed out that Lottery assessors were forbidden for at least twelve months from taking paid work from clients they had assessed, and the House had not yet been judged for its second tranche of Lottery cash.

Suddenly, it seemed, the House had an executive chairman and the old number one job became number two. Parliament convened a select committee in July 1997 under Gerald Kaufman to examine these startling developments. In a hasty response the Arts Council tried to pre-empt criticism of its lax role by hiring a solicitor, Edward Walker-Arnott, to report on its monitoring of the House's Lottery grant. When the Council received the Walker-Arnott Report in October 1997 it refused to publish the thing. Seeing as Mr Walker-Arnott was dealing with transparency of operations, this was a surprisingly untransparent gesture from a Council that needed all the friends it could find. A summary of the report implied that the most contentious aspect Mr Walker-Arnott addressed concerned the Development Land Trust, and it may have been this issue that prompted the Council to withhold his findings from public view.

Back to shambles. Gerald Kaufman's committee proceedings seemed to attract as much media coverage as a grim murder trial. 'It's a shambles, isn't it? It really is a shambles . . . You come along here and say you need more state money. It doesn't seem to me that you're running the thing efficiently and competently,' Kaufman told Mary Allen. She in turn announced that the box office was down on expectation and the operating deficit could rise to £7.7 million by April 1998. This encounter sparked two pieces of political theatre. First Culture Secretary Chris Smith attempted to recapture the thunder Kaufman had stolen from him. Smith dramatically declared that he had asked the former National Theatre head, Sir Richard Eyre, to report by May 1998 on the idea that the Royal Opera House should become an independent receiving house for the Royal Opera and Royal Ballet together with the English National Opera. Then, on 4 November 1997, Lord Chadlington announced to the select committee that the entire House operation was ten days away from bankruptcy. Two days later he stated that he'd found £15 million from certain 'anonymous donors' to ensure that the House could continue its homeless programme up to the reopening. Here was a sharp PR manoeuvre in action.

Yet his gambit failed to save him. When Kaufman's histrionic report was published on 3 December, it branded the entire board 'incompetent' and called for Chadlington and the others to resign or face withdrawal of the Arts Council's grant. As the report also criticised the Council for its feeble conduct over the House, Kaufman urged Chris Smith to personally supervise a substitute board. Chadlington stepped down smartly and the board agreed to follow once others were found to take their places. Sir Colin Southgate of EMI Records, a patron of New Labour, took over the chair in January 1998. Mary Allen, however, defied the report's call for her to quit.

However, we shouldn't allow these melodramatic turns to mask the deeper issues which face the House when it reopens in 1999. Covent Garden needs a total overhaul of its artistic identity, its public function and its creative duty. English National Opera flourished where the House was unsuccessful in serving opera in English, while Glyndebourne (at home and on tour) prevailed in original-language productions. When quizzed about this failure for the *Kaleidoscope* radio show, embattled board member Michael Berkeley retorted that while Glyndebourne 'uses young singers', the House was pre-eminent in exuding experience and promoting maturity. What stopped it from prospering was cash to buy in the best: 'The basic problem,' he declared, 'is money.'

Isaacs, too, blamed the unceasing crisis of practical headaches on the Council's revenue subsidy: 'The ROH gets by on less than a quarter of the subsidy given in Paris, Munich or Berlin without their governments batting an eyelid.' This is a much-loved aria chronically sung by Covent Garden chiefs. Here's a 78rpm version from 1956:

> The £250,000 annual grant which Covent Garden receives through the Arts Council looks small beside the subsidies granted to establishment opera houses in other countries. The Paris Opéra and Opéra Comique between them receive £1,347,575; the Vienna Opera roughly £750,000.

Claptrap. We can understand why administrators tout it; they know the government funds the Garden to compete with mainland Europe. The houses abroad, however, work on differing principles, with varying priorities, commitments and resources. Flanders Opera gets exactly twice as much as Covent Garden, but then it serves two cities with a dual programme of opera and dance.

Although many of the names keep changing in this litany of 'it's not fair, they have more cash', two establishments are most often cited as the House's peers – Vienna and New York's Met. Yet both of these are city operas rather than national ones, and unlike the House they seek and obtain municipal maintenance. More to the point they are deeply reactionary in spirit and capacity. They top the premier league as defined solely by the agents who live off them, but not by creative artists, producers and those who see opera contributing to the domain of living art. Covent Garden has not played in the top league ever – it simply hasn't sold its shows on to others, which is the strongest mark of international merit.

And there is no house quite like the House, which runs one opera company, two ballet companies and a boarding school. It beggars belief that a dance company now living and working in the Midlands still handles its accounts through Covent Garden's books, yet that's what has happened to the old Sadler's Wells second company which, after many bizarre changes of name, is now called Birmingham Royal Ballet. The motive behind this strange affair was exposed by Boris Romanoff to Keynes back in 1943: 'Dancers will make money for the opera house, while the opera singers will lose it, always.' Here is how Covent Garden started out in 1948–1949, when the opera and ballet were running fully together for the first time:

1948–1949 schedule	Expenditure £	Income £	Balance £
SW ballet season no.1	64,854	65,356	+502
CG opera season no.1	42,613	24,542	–18,070
Opera tours	23,393	24,001	+608
SW ballet provinces	18,350	26,338	+7,988
SW ballet foreign	6,053	7,964	+1,911
CG opera season no.2	134,563	82,865	–51,698
SW ballet season no.2	71,399	71,876	+477
Opera provinces	18,566	11,296	–7,270

Sadler's Wells Ballet (what we would now call the Royal Ballet) made £10,878 while Covent Garden Opera lost £76,430. The House's problem these days is that both Royal Ballet and Royal Opera have become burdens. The Royal Ballet lost its star quality and foreign pulling power years ago, after the glittering start of a commercial season at New York's Met in 1949 arranged by Sol Hurok. The following year's tour of the States brought in a profit to Covent Garden of £50,000 (£770,000) and the House began to get dependent. As the dancers became over-used and fatigued, the foreign press turned tepid. At the same time ballet companies abroad gained post-war strength, and the USA moved the creative focus towards itself when Balanchine advanced ballet, Martha Graham dance theatre and Merce Cunningham new dance. Britain became a ballet backwater, brightly lit by the sporadic defections of Russians such as Rudolf Nureyev and Natalia Makarova (not to say defecations like the Panovs). After the one-off brilliance of Frederick Ashton, choreography in British ballet took a dive from which it surfaced glitteringly in 1984 in the form of Michael Clark (suspended from White Lodge for sniffing glue) before he seemingly glug-glugged out of sight in a sea of drugs. The Royal Ballet is left without a purpose in the world of dance, without a truly living repertoire, but with a great deal of backstage eye-scratching which its fair-minded director, Anthony Dowell, can do little to quell.

When Kaufman's report of December 1997 was issued, the sentence most quoted by the media was this one: 'We would prefer to see the Royal Opera House run by a philistine with the requisite financial acumen than by a succession of opera- and ballet-lovers'. By this single phrase the new Government showed it was as lost as the old ones in pinpointing Covent Garden's true needs. The place has been stuffed with moneyed philistines since it opened. Though Kaufman saw off the dippy board, he failed to fathom the past fallibilities of the House or to reflect on a regenerated role for its future. The House now needs the advice of working artists and producers – perhaps the composer Peter Maxwell Davies should chair a task force. This is where the vital reforms must begin if Covent Garden is to start giving more to the arenas of creative art and the breadth of British society than it has taken from them.

Chapter 16

Some foul play

Regional drama policy: 1945–1960
London: 1945–1960

On 19 June 1996, the IRA bombed the centre of Manchester. The city's Royal Exchange Theatre caught a shockwave and thereafter its company had to work from a tent pegged near Salford. Prime Minister John Major visited the scene and announced that arts Lottery cash would be offered to repair the damage, which affected not the 'space pod' arena itself but the huge room in which it is suspended. How ironic. The Royal Exchange Theatre was built to last for twenty-five years, no more. It was already twenty-one years old when the bomb exploded. IRA hawks have done the theatre-goers of Manchester a favour, in a Brendan Behan kind of way.

Around the United Kingdom there are fifty-five subsidised companies like the Royal Exchange, housed in buildings of assorted dilapidation and bad design. With or without the Prime Minister's say-so the Lottery will sort them out, so that their press officers will no longer enjoy annual photos in local papers of buckets collecting raindrops from their stages' ceilings. Yet it won't answer the bigger issues that all these companies face: why are we here, what are we, who really needs us?

Most of them are called 'reps' – repertory theatres – or civic theatres, though they are neither. Whatever they are, they keep themselves abundantly busy: 'Subsidised regional theatre operating own productions for around 40 weeks a year, together with Sunday concerts' (Derby Playhouse); 'A mixed programme theatre, built around a professional company – opera, concerts, dance, youth & schools drama and music, films' (Theatr Clwyd); 'Mainly in-house productions of large-scale musicals and plays with commercial managements which either transfer to London or make national tours' (Theatre Royal, Plymouth). The Arts Council, brisk as ever, calls them 'publicly-funded, building-based, self-producing drama companies'. They are structural relics of a pre-war age, which is why they stick with bygone words like 'repertory', even though many of them were formed way after 1945.

The mad maze which is our theatre system was supposed to be centrally planned. It was the one thing the new Arts Council was expected to construct. The muddle we've ended up with exists for three reasons. Firstly, the 1945 Government decided to back the civic-theatre movement which we encountered in earlier pages. It became the Arts Council's duty to make sure the scheme thrived, through deals with the town and city councils. In January 1945 the Council publicly expressed a desire for 'a repertory theatre in every town in Britain'. This took place in that optimistic time before television and cheap heroin, when 'a good night out' meant live entertainment at a theatre, not a nightclub. However, not 'every town in Britain' shared the Council's zest.

Secondly, the post-war theatre scene renewed pre-war systems. In particular an intricate liaison was sustained between West End runs, provincial try-outs and the needs of the 'Woods', as Laurence Olivier called them: Holly— and Pine—. The film and growing television industries fed off those plays and players which succeeded in theatre's 'live network'. Olivier was obsessed with conquering the one-dimensional and three-dimensional worlds equally, which Charles Laughton had sought to do before him, Peter O'Toole and Kenneth Branagh after. The perpetual traffic of talent – and want of talent – between film, television and the stage has remained a paradoxical but stable economic factor in the survival of live theatre. The commercial theatre's stake in this arrangement counted on sustained runs and touring which increasingly involved the Council. The Council became entangled with this commercial formula, both in the regions and in the West End, at the same time as it was trying to build a contrasting system of civic theatres, and the tension between residential work and touring has fogged its dealings at every level since.

Thirdly, theatre grew young again. It even graduated: Bristol University offered the first drama course in 1947; the National Student Drama Festival opened in 1955. Just as poetry had been the fashionable art of the pre-war graduate, drama became so post-war. There was even a period of creative transition, when a trend for verse-plays gave us lofty work from Christopher Fry, Ronald Duncan and the like; writers such as Tony Harrison continue to combine the two. The fertile expansion from the mid-fifties to the mid-seventies drew its vigour from a belief that theatres were the new, vital centres for social debate, inspired by advanced work from America, France and Eastern Europe. The Council struggled to cope with these new approaches as well as the old ones.

Whatever benchmarks were set by writers and performers, they were achieved despite the to-and-fro bumbling between political parties, the local authorities and the Council itself. There were three 'waves' of theatre building, for instance. During the first, when the Council had most control, the least happened, and when the most happened the Council had the least control. The occasional 'Save Our Theatre' photos of bannered thespians posing tragically outside Number 10 Downing Street display the public face of a structural problem which started when Keynes bought the Bristol Theatre Royal 'for the good of the nation' in 1942.

We've already seen how snootily Keynes handled the British Drama League when it came to the Council in June 1943 with its alternative approach to buying up old theatres. The league proposed a robust network of purpose-built playhouses, with permanent companies inside them. Mary Glasgow considered the behaviour of Keynes shameful, because the project was brilliantly prepared, with all manner of local variation entertained. But Keynes had foreseen that the scheme wouldn't work without a massive reform of local government. The League itself represented amateurs mainly, and its proposal came out of that fascinating alliance of professionals and hobbyists that buoyed many wartime endeavours. The amateurs wanted local councils to maintain civic theatres, not for themselves, but to share with salaried professionals who would form a genuine repertory company; not what they had then, or we have now:

> The programme-policy of a Civic Theatre should be based on a true repertory system as opposed to the 'short run system' which most of

the so-called Repertory Theatres with resident companies were practising before the war ... That is to say: a repertoire of several productions must be built up, any one of which can be performed as desired ... Adequate time can be given to each new play introduced into the repertoire. Two or three different plays should be presented every week ... The repertoire to consist of (a) classical plays, (b) new and original plays, (c) contemporary plays and translations.

Those miserable but widespread 'weekly reps' persisted, however. Sir Peter Hall encountered one as a novice director at Worthing in 1954. He found that the company not only performed that week's play every night but rehearsed next week's in the daytime. Next week's play was read through on Tuesday morning and act I was staged in the afternoon; acts II and III were staged on Wednesday. On Saturday morning the whole play had a run-through, on Monday afternoon there was a dress rehearsal and that night it opened to the public: 'The whole process then began again.' In the same period the playwright John Osborne worked as an actor and remembers Folkestone, where the stage was so tiny that, as an unexpected dinner guest halfway through a scene, he had to drag his chair behind him when he came onstage.

The civic-theatre scheme was designed to wipe out this nonsense. When Keynes died in 1946, Glasgow carefully tried to get to grips with the proposal, to soften an amount of political pressure. It wasn't hard for the regional officers to build liaisons with local authorities, because there were already touring companies around their 'patches', presenting shows with the assistance of council officers. Glasgow soon learned that:

However well you could place the *moral* point before them, there was no financial motivation. The British Drama League, I think, wanted a parity scheme [50 per cent state cash, 50 per cent local], and it was our deputy drama director, Charles Landstone, who calculated what this 50 per cent meant. It was something like the old threepence in the pound, and I imagine that somebody along the way simply doubled it, which is probably the only artistic reason why we had that Act suggesting sixpence!

In 1948 Labour passed a Local Government Act. Section 132 gave town and parish councils the legal power to spend money on the live arts. Out of each pound raised from the local rates, a sum not exceeding sixpence ($2\frac{1}{2}$p today) in England, or in Scotland four and four-fifths pence (2p, give or take one fifth of 240th of a pound) could be used for the following:

1. the provision of an entertainment of any nature or of facilities for dancing;
2. the provision of a theatre, concert hall, dance hall or other premises suitable for the giving of entertainments or the holding of dances;
3. the maintenance of a band or orchestra;
4. any purpose incidental to the matters aforesaid.

A number of Corporation Acts had allowed cities like Manchester, Liverpool and Sheffield to do this sort of thing much earlier, but not at such a scale as sixpence in the pound. Dancing, by the way, meant the social knees-ups of Mecca Cafés Limited, and this explains that curious void on the first floor of the Royal Festival Hall, now a dismal setting for exhibitions. It used to be the ballroom, in line with Section 132 (a) of the 1948 Local Government Act. The target of this legislation, however, was the building of theatres and the creation of drama companies to put in them. Although this statute is now seen as the benevolent and far-sighted step of a socialist regime, it was really a nervous, unstudied gesture brought about by the likes of Labour's friend J.B. Priestley backing the British Drama League on one side and a frustrated Arts Council on the other, fed up with seducing dim mayors and stingy town clerks.

Charles Landstone, who we encountered at various times with Wolfit and the Bristol Old Vic, wrote a lucid report on the civic-theatre system in 1947, which was revised as a pamphlet in 1950. He was, incidentally, upset to be denied a promotion to drama director at this time. Dick Linklater worked as a regional drama officer and remembers that:

> Landstone used to pace up and down, up and down – in a real state – and he said that he felt he'd been insulted, after all the work he'd done in the war. To placate him they gave him the title of associate drama director, which meant that he could attend Council meetings with John Moody, the new director, who was more of an opera man. But once there, John would say so-and-so and Charles would immediately interrupt him – 'No, not at all'. Bill Williams [took over as Secretary-General and] said, 'I want you to understand that the drama department speaks with one voice.'

That was the end of Landstone, who became president of the Council of Repertory (later Regional) Theatres.

His work on the civic scheme was clear-minded. He calculated the relationship between a town's population, the rate it garnered, the size of auditorium the town could sustain and from that the size of company and type of repertoire that could run in it. He based his calculations on a commercial statistic that the size of an audience 'who could be relied on to form a regular audience for a good class repertory' would be 3 per cent of a town with a population over 70,000. From this he derived the following:

Size of town	Desirable size of theatre	Comments
Under 70,000	capacity 350	Should not be encouraged.
Over 70,000	capacity 350–450	A hard struggle (without a margin) on weekly repertory.
80,000	capacity 350–450	Might leave a margin.
100,000	capacity 350–450	Could support a 500-seater on weekly rep, but with a hard struggle might scrape through on a fortnightly rep at 350–450 capacity.

And so it went on up to cities of 300,000 ('capacity 700, three-weekly repertory'). Sound stuff, but completely untied to the political scene. Almost no local authority sustained $2\frac{1}{2}$p in the pound on the arts, or anywhere near half of that amount. Only Coventry and Sunderland came close, and only for a buoyant while. The former opened Britain's first true civic theatre in March 1958, named the Belgrade in homage to its twin city, which supplied some timber to build it. The Scunthorpe and Rotherham Civic Theatres opened in 1960, with capacities of 340 but no companies of their own. Ten years on from Landstone's paper, the brave new civic creations totalled one and two halves. The Belgrade, the Royal Festival Hall (1951) and Bernard Miles' Mermaid Theatre in the City of London (1959) were the sole artistic erections of the fifties.

Still, there were forty-four resident companies running repertory seasons in England, twenty-three of them in real theatres built anywhere between 1766 (Bristol Old Vic at the Theatre

Royal) and 1937 (Oxford Playhouse, home to the Meadow Players). A further twenty stock companies of different sizes and calibre were housed in buildings converted from other uses. Eight of those could be considered part of the post-war civic movement and, with Coventry, that brought the total within a decade to nine – plus Rotherham and Scunthorpe:

Building/company	Formerly	Date
Chesterfield, Civic	Cinema	1949
Derby, Playhouse	Church schoolroom	1953
Guildford Theatre	Court house	1946
Hornchurch, Queen's	Cinema	1952
Ipswich Theatre	Lecture hall	1947
Leatherhead, Theatre Club	Village hall	1948
Manchester Library Theatre	Library basement	1947
Salisbury, Playhouse	Chapel	1945

Conversion was a practical answer to the shortage of building materials (157,000 pre-fab homes were put up between 1945 and 1950), and the 1949 Housing Act emphasised subsidies for renovations rather than construction.

By 1960 the Arts Council was giving annual grants to just nineteen of the total of forty-four English building-based companies, 60 per cent of them in the southern counties and 40 per cent of them in the Midlands – nothing north of Chesterfield. The Council's failure to forge a coherent and widespread system did not solely lie at town-hall doors. Keynes had set problems for his successors when he purchased the Bristol Theatre Royal and followed that deal with one in Salisbury – the Arts Theatre, later known as the Playhouse. Both were managed directly by the Arts Council; Bristol's audited accounts were printed in the Council's annual report for seven years, progressively in the red.

The Council got shut of them both not long after the Salisbury company's attempt to run a county touring system as a 'neighbourhood service' foundered; the actors once turned up at the wrong town and simply carried on earning their wages while an audience elsewhere faced an empty stage. A similar plan in Yorkshire – a 'repertory circuit' by the West Riding Theatre Company – soon fell apart, as did a scheme in Swansea, though another touring around the Midlands survived: eventually the umbilical cord was cut and the Arts Council

Midland Theatre Company formed the home team for Coventry's Belgrade.

The visionary plans of wartime waned, along with the spirit of the public. Crudely put, theatre companies found full houses during the war and half-empty ones afterwards. Faulty memories accuse television for this, but the BBC made headway only when it relayed the coronation in 1953 and ITV didn't exist until September 1955. Theatre-owners blamed a resurgence of home-grown films for bad box office, but 'the pictures' did no harm to the profession and much good to the playhouse publicity machine. Ealing comedies and dramas by Rank still offer a glimpse of the delightful but mannered quality of acting around at the time, and a number of those actors to be seen there served on the Council's drama panel between 1945 and 1955, including Alastair Sim, Edith Evans, Miles Malleson, Ralph Richardson, Irene Worth, Laurence Olivier, Alec Guinness, Flora Robson, Leslie Banks, Michael Redgrave and even Noel Coward (1947–1950).

What seems to have happened is that those who enjoyed the theatre now did it for themselves, and the amateur drama movement thrived once more. The national decline in box-office fortunes affected the old commercial theatre managements and the new subsidised ventures equally. In reaction to the plunge the Arts Council blustered along as best it could – it had handled nothing like this before. Just after the war, for instance, the drama department had been dealing with: two companies under direct management (Bristol, Salisbury); two companies 'in association' with the Arts Council (Cambridge Arts Theatre, Glasgow Citizens' Theatre); twenty-six companies 'associated' with the Arts Council; four tours under direct management; and three seasons under direct management.

By 1951 the Council had dropped the direct management of all but the little tours run by the regional offices. In other words, instead of addressing the problem, the Council disembarrassed itself. Direct drama touring reduced once Bill Williams took over from Glasgow, and he dismantled the system completely when he shut the provincial branches. By 1953 Bill Williams was writing in the *Adelphi* magazine of the 'chronic ill health of the repertory companies'. As part of his obsessive plan to reduce everything in the arts so that the Council could control it all, he promoted a Charles Landstone idea as one of his own – a theatre grid – aimed at just ten cities (one of them London) which, he admitted, were all 'university cities'. It's here that a notion with two separate components is first expressed: theatres connected to universities and the idea of 'centres of excellence', of powerhouses and regional magnets which would raise the quality of performance and reception, infusing the region somehow with 'quality'.

In exploring these ideas, the Arts Council officers figured out that it was cheaper to move audiences to actors than the other way round. The touring system rapidly lost any appeal it had left. Instead, audiences could be bussed in. 'Travel subsidies' were born. His table of ten cities, however, was a mere wish list. It even contained confusing and unresolved variants: 'Newcastle or York'. Not only did it not align with regional reality (except in Bristol, Liverpool and Cambridge), but its airing offended the Council-aided reps elsewhere.

Williams unintentionally made it worse by retaining the antique tag 'associated company' for no more than eight of them. This suggested to the public that the eighteen companies which effectively lost this label were third division – which, frankly, may well have been true. It also insulted a number of local authorities who complained about it and so blunted the Council's future ability to bargain with them. But Williams was a determined sort, and he knew his Chairman, Kenneth Clark, was easily bored by town-hall politics. None of this speculative planning meant much anyway, as next to nothing was happening in the real world. By July 1961 *The Times* could claim in a leader that: 'The intelligent foreigner visiting Britain to see how one of the most civilized countries in the world houses its arts is likely to find little of significance and interest outside London.'

But by the time Williams retired in 1963, the nation's theatre landscape had changed so sharply that the Council would never quite catch up with regional, or national, developments, as we'll see.

London ran its own agenda. Keynes had ensured that the Council's liability to the capital was greater than its liability to the kingdom outside it. We might say this was due to the scale of commitment to the Royal Opera House and the 'national' Old Vic, but thanks to the war London had lost a lot of its population, and the Arts Council was drawn into government policy to build the capital up again. When Bill Williams took over in 1951 he fortified the links, so that within five years 82 per cent of the

Council's entire grant was spent on companies housed in the capital. But ironically the Council came a West End cropper on something that cost it nothing. The word 'association'.

A 'foul stench of Yanky slime filled the Aldwych Theatre' when Binkie Beaumont presented a British premiere on 12 October 1949, 'in association with the Arts Council of Great Britain'. This 'putrid smut' starred Vivien Leigh, directed by her freshly knighted husband Sir Laurence Olivier, and the offending play was known to critic Kenneth Tynan as 'A Vehicle Named Vivien' but to everyone else as *A Streetcar Named Desire*. This fervent portrayal of a prostitute sliding into a breakdown was already a hit for Tennessee Williams on Broadway. Beaumont sensed immense success when Olivier first asked him to partner the enterprise.

What caused the Arts Council to slide into the mire like Blanche Dubois was not the lurid language of the popular press used to describe the production, nor the puritan tone of Lady Ravensdale, who told her Public Morality Council: 'It is no excuse to say that this abominable play is well acted and directed. Our senses are being dragged down to the lowest possible denominator.' It was more the fact that nineteen other commercial producers had sought the rights to present the money-spinning show in London.

Their failure sparked a resentful backlash against Beaumont and his ways with the Arts Council, for it was through the Council's special treatment that Binkie was saving on entertainments duty – he was not alone in this deal, but he was unshamed and paramount. The equivalent today would be if Sir Cameron Mackintosh were allowed to keep the entire 17.5 per cent VAT charge on ticket sales of *Les Misérables* because of the show's link with the Royal Shakespeare Company. As the Council Chairman of the time, Sir Ernest Pooley, remarked to Beaumont: 'Everything you touch seems to turn to gold.' The gold in Binkie's bank grew thanks to his Midas 'association' with the Arts Council.

Led by Jack Hylton, the nineteen ne'er-do-well producers conspired to damage Beaumont. Heartened by spicy press coverage, they lobbied MPs. In the Commons on 8 December, Wilson Harris (Cambridge University, Independent) asked the Chancellor of the Exchequer about:

the nature of the association between the Arts Council of Great Britain and Tennent Productions Limited, in the production of the

play *A Streetcar Named Desire*: in what proportions any profits earned
by this play were divided between the two bodies, and what restrict-
ion was placed on the uses to which such profits might be put.

Labour's Financial Secretary replied that the relationship was one
of long standing and not confined to this play, and that the Arts
Council had no right to 'partake in the company's profits . . . but it
provides that all profits can be expended only on objects or
activities approved by the Council'. His uneasy answer opened the
debate out to a brood of backbenchers, who were astonished to
hear that Binkie Beaumont was hoarding untaxed profits because
the plays he put on were commonly considered by the Arts
Council to be 'educational'.

The deal was certainly working to the company's advantage.
Royalty payments were increased for promotions by Tennent
Productions, as were expenses; certain meals at the Ivy were
known as 'non-profit dinners'. *Streetcar* was bringing £6,000 a
week to the box office (£100,000 today), tax free. It was
suggested that the Chancellor should look carefully at 'clause 8
of the Finance Act, 1948, to ensure that relief goes to deserving
plays which may need it, and not to possible undeserving plays
which manifestly do not need it'. The peppery dialogue ended
with this exchange:

Mr Boothby: What precise educational value has this play?
                 (Cheers.)

Mr Hall: I have not seen the play, and, although obviously
                 opinions may differ, I am told it has won in the
                 United States at least three literary prizes.

Mr Marlowe: Is the right hon. gentleman aware that this play is
                 only educational to those who are ignorant of the
                 facts of life? (Loud laughter.)

A parliamentary subcommittee was set up, before which Binkie
gave a polished performance and Pooley a poor one. Labour's
Chancellor, Stafford Cripps, was livid and told Pooley he must
sever the connection with Beaumont at once. Pooley complied,
but not before Mary Glasgow had asked for permission to 'say her
piece' to the Council and defend the liaison with Beaumont. She
didn't need to do so except for moral reasons; the attack on
Beaumont continued beyond the Arts Council climb-down, and
way after it withdrew its 'association'. In 1954 six MPs, led by

Labour's gay-hating Woodrow Wyatt, promoted the Theatre Companies Bill in order to redefine what 'non-profit' meant in the theatre. Details got so complicated over differences between, say, a company director and a stage director, that in the end the Government simply did away with the levy for live art when it revised the Entertainments Duty Act in 1958. The tariff on ticket sales was revived in 1973 as value added tax.

Through her avid speech, Glasgow was felt by Charles Landstone to be defending the honour of the late Keynes. She was effectively pointing out to the Council that it lacked his grit, and her statement proved 'the beginning of the end of Miss Glasgow'. She later recalled her main point:

> Hugh Beaumont was saving the West End from itself. He was the most adventurous producer in the country. Not only did he underwrite work with very high production values, better sometimes than the Old Vic which we were funding to the hilt – he had an exceptionally good eye for casting – but he brought in new plays the others wouldn't have looked at. He put on new work by J.B. Priestley, James Bridie, John Whiting, Norman [NC] Hunter, [Rodney] Ackland. He financed the British premieres of plays by Arthur Miller, Tennessee Williams, Thornton Wilder, and Jean Anouilh. He put on plays without french windows in them. Those who would have wished to present *A Streetcar Named Desire* never took the kinds of risks on new and foreign plays of quality that Hugh did. He was making some contribution to the development of the art form.

Though this sermon was considered a homage to Keynes, Glasgow was really protecting the integrity of the present Council. It emerged for a start that the mechanism Beaumont and Keynes had devised, that of Tennent Plays Limited, had been wound up in 1947 because of a technical difficulty involving the Hammersmith Lyric Theatre, and a new arrangement was made between Beaumont and the Council in that same year, which is why the MPs referred to Tennent *Productions* Limited. In other words, Glasgow was justifying a recent arrangement.

Secondly, there was more at stake than the unsubsidised West End. Beaumont sat at the centre of two 'mafias', as Olivier once called them, at a drama panel, for which he later apologised to his friend. One was the Company of Four, founded in 1945. Surprising as it sounds, Glyndebourne's John Christie had set this up, with his manager Rudolf Bing. He did so as part of a typically barmy, spider's-web scheme to take over the artistic world. He wrote in March 1944 that he would create a National Glyndebourne Trust:

> to control a corporation which shall run Covent Garden, the Hay-market, the National Theatre ... the New Queen's Hall, the National Gallery and the National Portrait Gallery and the other galleries and so become a Headquarters of England's Art ... We might get one of the Royal Houses in St James's Palace as our Headquarters.

Christie's corporation sounds suspiciously like our Department of Culture, Media and Sport.

In the event Christie created first of all the Children's Theatre Company, as a further kind of present to his wife, for which Alec Guinness successfully penned a stage version of *Great Expectations*, directed by the novice Anthony Quayle. As an outlet for this, and a chamber-opera project which was brewing with Benjamin Britten (it emerged as the English Opera Group), Christie considered buying Hammersmith's deserted Lyric Theatre. CEMA had recently rented it for the Old Vic and others, then bluntly abandoned the place. Rudi Bing nosed around and discovered that the Cambridge Arts Theatre was considering a second home in London, as was the Bristol Theatre Royal, which was semi-connected to the rootless Old Vic. Further, Binkie Beaumont and Tony Guthrie were separately nursing plans to sift through the talent to be found among actors recently demobilised.

Once Christie had stumped up the initial outlay for the busi-ness, the Company of Four – Rudi, Tony, Binkie and Mr Higgins, Keynes' old cinema manager – took over Hammersmith's Lyric and presented seasons of decent plays (Wilder, Saroyan, O'Casey, Cocteau) which were normally 'tried out' on southern tours, fol-lowed by sporadic West End transfers. But by 1949 Glyndebourne had reopened and Guthrie had meanwhile developed a taste for epic gala productions at another Christie enterprise, the Edinburgh Festival. Beaumont was left handling the whole Hammersmith operation through Tennent Productions. He passed the Lyric on to his boyfriend and his secretary to run. So when Mary Glasgow made her speech, she was thinking of the effect Beaumont's expulsion would have on the drama touring scene of the south and the survival of the Lyric, which the Council would be deserting for a second time in five years.

Beaumont's other mafia was known as the Group. Quite why it's hard to explain, because there wasn't much of a group aside from Prince and Emile Littler, two property-owning brothers who seemed to have little time for each other. In 1965 Prince successfully sued Emile over a libel concerning a booking matter. From then on – earlier, according to Peter Hall, who dealt with them separately in 1960 – they never communicated. The 'group' concerned was really the collection of theatres they owned which was spread around the country, 150 of them in 1950, including sixteen West End theatres which had been bought cheaply during the war. To these Prince Littler added the Theatre Royal, Drury Lane in 1944, and the massive Coliseum. By that time he had also acquired a majority shareholding in HM Tennent, the unsubsidised wing of Binkie Beaumont's production empire.

This informal group of showmen, then, controlled much of the hardware and the software. They fixed high rents to stop inter-loping producers from invading their cartel, and because they owned thirty-four of the fifty-three big theatres (that is, 65 per cent of the number ones) of the main cities, including Belfast, they controlled an entire national system of regional try-outs, West End runs and post-London tours. So when Mary Glasgow intervened at the 1949 Council meeting, she also had in mind the regional disorder that could ensue by ending a rapport with the Group. Ultimately the Arts Council chose to create an entire department in 1970 to address the problem it had set itself twenty years earlier.

Yet this touring-theatre scene declined in volume, repertoire and quality without help or hindrance from the Arts Council. The producers and owners of the West End achieved this themselves, with Beaumont and the duelling Littlers. Their best profits had come from long-run West End showcases for 'star' actors and actresses, and the regional agenda was arranged to serve Soho. Increasingly, though, the importance of the regions declined as they made their money from direct imports of American musicals. Prince Littler, for instance, presented *Guys and Dolls* and *The Pajama Game* at the Coliseum, and *Carousel* at Drury Lane. The economic focus fell on a gradually refined roster of theatres, and the 150 commercial playhouses outside the capital suddenly appealed as real estate.

By 1959 the total of these active venues had dropped to thirty, according to the author John Elsom in his valuable survey of 1971, *Theatre Outside London.* They were left open to shelter the dwindling number of musicals loaned from Broadway, which by now were competing with their own back catalogue transferred to film. Of the others, some had been turned into cinemas, but the film-exhibition industry was in trouble, too: in 1957 the BBC announced it was buying twenty Hollywood movies to show on TV. Further conversions aided the colonising of the British Isles by American entertainments of the kind that required of their public a little more involvement than placing their bums on seats, and the cult of bingo halls and bowling alleys grew.

The producers were no fools in all of this. They promptly developed interests in leisure holdings and commercial TV companies. Prince Littler was chairman of ATV from 1956, and the influence of the Delfont and Grade dynasties in British television continued long after Bernard Delfont promoted his London Palladium Theatre live every Sunday night on the TV sets of the nation.

They fought each other for reliable product, transferable formats and bankable artists, and by the end of the fifties the commercial scene of the regions had been gutted by this executive cannibalism. The West End, being a dinosaur slow to get the message from its tail to its brain, survived another seven years before it galumphed into the Arts Council with its pre-glacial begging bowl.

Chapter 17

A hawk from a handsaw

Regional drama policy: 1960–1965
London: 1960–1965

The borough council that built the Belgrade Theatre in 1958 was led by Labour, which had run Coventry for the past twenty years. It had used a bit of the sixpenny rate, suggested by Labour's 1948 Act, to pursue a wartime scheme supported by MPs of all parties, and it did so under a high Tory Government which did nothing to obstruct the operation. In fact, in this period the Conservatives increased the amount of central money flowing into local government: Whitehall's contribution rose from 28 per cent at the start of the war to 40 per cent by 1960. At the same time local authorities were encouraged to develop the bricks-and-mortar schemes that advanced high-rise blocks, bypasses, shopping precincts, civic centres . . . and theatres.

Instead of sending town halls state aid tied to specifics, the Local Government Act of 1958 offered a more relaxed general grant. At the same time the Recreational Charities Act, the New Towns Act, the Charities Act (1960) and others created by Macmillan's Tories widened terms for collaborations between councils, charities, educational institutions and the private sector on capital schemes. That they didn't extend to issues of revenue is significant. These were devices to assist the construction trade, of course, but also to produce new arrangements for the urban blending of retail and leisure on American models, a notion which would end woefully with Billingham's Forum in the north-east.

Yet between 1960 and 1965, from which time Harold Wilson's first Labour Government asserted itself, it could be claimed that the following seventeen theatres were built thanks to a climate of enterprise cultivated by the 'You've never had it so good' Conservatives:

Birmingham	Cannon Hill Studio	1965	capacity 300
Chichester	Festival Theatre	1962	capacity 1,360
Corby	Civic Theatre	1965	capacity 545
Croydon	Ashcroft Theatre	1963	capacity 750
Eastbourne	Congress Theatre	1963	capacity 1,678
Guildford	Yvonne Arnaud Theatre	1965	capacity 568
Leicester	Phoenix Theatre	1963	capacity 274
London	Hampstead Theatre Club	1963	capacity 157
	Jeanetta Cochrane Theatre	1965	capacity 351
	Royalty Theatre	1960	capacity 1,035
Manchester	University Theatre	1965	capacity 300
Nottingham	Playhouse	1963	capacity 756
Oxford	Playhouse	1964	capacity 700
Southampton	Nuffield Theatre	1964	capacity 500
Torquay	Princess Theatre	1962	capacity 1,514
Weymouth	Pavilion Theatre	1960	capacity 465
Worcester	Swan Theatre	1964	capacity 353

In 1959 Harold Macmillan's Tories had bribed their way to another term of office with a give-away budget, one over which Mrs Thatcher was later to lecture him: 'I think part of our post-1959 problems arose from an extremely over-generous budget.' It drove an expansionist agenda steered by the Chancellor, a reclusive gay called Derick Heathcoat Amory, who favoured the arts and directly turned around the economic fortunes of the Royal Opera House at this time by throwing blank cheques at it.

Heathcoat Amory was responsible for the budgets of 1959 and 1960, after which he calculatedly retired. His replacement, the more orthodox Selwyn Lloyd, delivered less generous budgets in 1961 and 1962, after which he was sacked. It's important to be clear that this little 'window of opportunity' was opened by one Chancellor for two years and sharply closed again by another, for it helps to explain why the most startling developments in British theatre life took place during this time in the bizarre manner that they did.

A few of the buildings in the list above are known today only for their crises and closures, but two stand out as standard-bearers of Britain's conservative theatre practice. Chichester's Festival Theatre (1962) and the Nottingham Playhouse (1963) are not commonly ranked together. The former is deemed a Glyndebourne-style private venture, while the latter is considered the finest flowering of the civic-theatre scheme. Not quite so in either case. Both involved local government in deals, but while Chichester proved a cinch, Nottingham was a scandal.

Sir Hugh Willatt (1909–1996), the Arts Council's Secretary-General from 1968 to 1976, came from Nottingham. In the thirties he worked for his father's legal firm by day and acted in a radical amateur-dramatic company at night. He was involved with the local Co-operative movement, members of which joined in the call for a professional troupe with its own civic theatre on British Drama League lines. By 1948 this had gained Nottingham a first-rate company involving players like Leo McKern and Alfred Burke, though no building. The actors worked instead from a scruffy old cinema on a noisy thoroughfare 'where the audience sat as far away as they could from the traffic lights'. It had been acquired with a £5,000 loan from the Conservative city council, which supported the venture as an example of 'voluntaryism' – local people getting together with their own time and money for the good of the town. Willatt Senior joined the theatre's board as solicitor, eventually handing over his role to Hugh, who rose through the trust to the post of vice-chairman.

Willatt Junior got on rather well with the Arts Council's drama man in Nottingham, Dick Linklater (1918–1997), who moved to the London headquarters when the branch was closed down. In 1955 Willatt was invited to join the Council's drama panel, eventually succeeding Benn Levy as drama chairman – and Council member – five years later. Back in Nottingham this hapless one-upmanship peeved the actual chairman of the Playhouse board, who was an ambitious vice-chancellor of the city's university. At any rate, one day in 1955 the local Labour Party secretary, Tommy Ives, came up to Hugh Willatt in a pub and said, 'I know you're on the Arts Council [panel], and I know they're flogging the idea of civic centres and such. Look, don't do it like that. Do one *big* thing, and it'll get the backing you need.'

Willatt considered *big* to mean a 750-seater theatre based on Charles Landstone's leaflet, and he invited Secretary-General Bill Williams to put the case at a business lunch of the city's great and good in January 1956. 'If the local authority would, for example, provide the land, the Government would provide the money for the building,' Williams lied. He later promised a core subsidy of £5,000 a year if the company was given a proper venue, and this gave Willatt ammunition to brave the snake pit of the city hall.

Nottingham Corporation at this time was blighted by Tory and Labour alike. The parties fought tooth and nail to destabilise each other. Labour ran the council on a minority between 1956 and 1960, when the Conservatives took over again until 1963, and the genesis of the Playhouse was stalled by squabbles between the parties themselves. Even within the groups there were divisions between members who supported 'voluntaryism' and those who favoured gung-ho municipal enterprise, an argument that split Labour as well as the Tories. Throughout the entire episode each party used seedy tactics to discredit the other, and the Playhouse scheme got entangled in an obstacle course of police files, race riots, gifts of fridges, surplus tarmac, refreshment kiosks, Jaguar cars and the sacking of Chief Constable Athelstan Popkess.

In 1958 Tommy Ives had joined two Labour councillors on a trip to East Germany. They'd gone to inspect a planetarium with a view to buying it for the city. It sat with the Playhouse as their '*big thing*', which they were to finance through a £600,000 fund acquired when gas, exotically, was nationalised ten years before. The planetarium was slated to cost £150,000, the theatre £300,000. Chief Constable Popkess had been tipped off that the trio had acquired gifts of communist cameras. Gifts of any kind being disallowed, he summoned Scotland Yard to investigate. This wasn't the police's first encounter with apparent town-hall graft. At the same time a Labour councillor was charged with taking money from two traders who wanted to build a refreshment kiosk on corporation land proposed for the Playhouse. Claiming *sub judice*, Popkess was unable to report to the watch committee about the camera business, so it suspended him, which prompted the Home Secretary to intervene. It was in these strange circumstances that the Playhouse became a pawn of political shenanigans.

On the eve of the 1958 council election, the Conservative Party bought up a whole page in local papers to print an ad: 'The Socialists intend to spend £250,000 (a quarter of a million pounds) on a *Playhouse*. This reckless and feckless spending can be stopped IF – and only IF – EVERY Conservative votes tomorrow.' Next day Labour increased its majority. The ad backfired further when a petition in support of the Playhouse was signed by 3,300 locals, including prominent businessmen and card-carrying Tories. At the same time, though, it strengthened the resolve of several Labour worthies that the Playhouse project was becoming a liability and therefore the £300,000 could no longer be offered as a grant. In 1960 a new Labour leader ruled that the Playhouse should pay a full economic rent and reimburse its Gas Fund loan, adding 7 per cent interest to the cost.

Details of the civic mischief are described in a diligent study by Nick Hayes, 'Municipal Subsidy and Tory Minimalism', in the 1994 edition of *Midland History*. His account takes in the batty behaviour of the Labour Lord Mayor who, pushed by pressure from the Arts Council, passed the building scheme in 1960 entirely on his casting vote, yet refused to put his name to the construction contract two weeks later. He was loudly told that if he didn't sign he'd be thrown out of the party. Work started on the site and continued until May 1961, when the Conservatives came back to power and cancelled the contract. It is at this point that the reader may care to recall the business about Macmillan's 1960 and 1961 budgets. Instead, Tory leader William Dyer proposed a bold alternative.

He would offer the site free of charge to Moss Empires (a part of the Group), which had closed down its commercial theatre in Nottingham two years previously. Dyer proposed that Moss should build a 1,500-seater theatre (double the Playhouse capacity), which he considered to be 'more the size of theatre the city deserves'. Curiously, the director-designate John Neville had pushed for a bigger size, too – he wanted a 1,000-seater or so – but his arguments were stifled by the Arts Council. Moss inspected the site. It also took heed of the city hall's snake pit. Prince Littler let it be known that Moss Empires 'wish not to become involved in local politics, nor to be portrayed as the people who wished to prevent the building of a civic theatre in Nottingham'.

The Tories, admitting that the scheme had gone too far to be killed off, rallied round the Playhouse. Though they shifted their view from commerce to subsidy, voluntaryism to municipal adventurism, Labour had already seen to it that there'd be no money lost in doing so. 'Liaison will be maintained with the Arts Council, whose views on these points are known to be sympathetic,' declared Dyer, knowing full well it was the drama panel chairman's dream to see the place up and running. The fine new theatre opened on 11 December 1963 with Shakespeare's

Coriolanus, directed by Tyrone Guthrie and starring the theatre's new chief, John Neville, in the title role. Even then, there were problems, as *The Times* reported:

ACTORS COMPANY CRITICIZED
NOTTINGHAM COUNCIL STATEMENT

'Deplorable and unprecedented' was how a 300-word statement issued in Nottingham tonight described the behaviour of unnamed members of the new Playhouse company at a Council House reception after the opening of the theatre by Lord Snowdon. Members of the company arrived at the reception an hour later than the other 550 guests and walked out after complaining that there was no food left for them.

   Mr. Frank Dunlop, a co-director of the new theatre, said: 'The council seem determined to class the company as hooligans, so I don't see how they are helping their own theatre.'

They weren't helping at all. Costing £370,000 to build, the Playhouse was loaned £310,000 from the gas fund. It was left to the board to scrape together the remaining £60,000, which it failed to find in full – one businessman gave £5,000 a week before the opening. In response to the Nottingham City Corporation, the Playhouse agreed to pay a rent of £26,000 a year against an annual council revenue grant of £13,000. Over twenty years the Playhouse was committed to replenish the gas fund, plus 7 per cent interest. Difficult as it is to keep in mind, this rotten deal was set up by Labour councillors and, to put it in perspective, the local sixpenny rate at this time yielded in excess of £120,000 a year, which means that Nottingham was spending less than three farthings per head on its civic theatre.

   As we've seen, the Arts Council was involved in this project from the beginning. Dick Linklater was by now its deputy drama director. The drama panel's chairman at the time of opening was none other than Hugh Willatt. He must have sweated blood to get the Playhouse built; its survival is a living tribute to his tenacity and vision. But not even Willatt, Linklater and the authority of the Arts Council under Pelican Bill could prevent this bum deal, a frayed remnant of the Drama League's valorous wartime plan.

   Neither could they prevent the embarrassing scenes that followed once John Neville asserted himself, an abrasive yet popular actor-director. He felt increasingly compromised by the funding position of the theatre. Despite successful seasons – 'Audiences have trebled from the old Playhouse days by a theatre which is only half as big again,' he bragged – Neville found that the Arts Council covered the overheads rather better than the artistic work he was contracted to develop, and the Playhouse board seemed too inhibited by its close rapport with London to back him up. When – with a Labour Government and Labour councillors in power – the 1967 grant yielded £7,000 less than he wished (£65,000 today), he resigned, accusing the drama department of interfering behind his back in local matters.

The Playhouse board and the Arts Council were frankly relieved that this dominating character had quit, but amazingly, Jennie Lee, the Arts Minister, stepped in and announced, 'You are staying in Nottingham, and we are supporting you.' Neville was further assisted by the 3,000-strong Playhouse Club, who organised a sit-in at a board meeting, where trustees were pelted with screwed-up programmes. *The Times*, too, voiced its endorsement of his criticisms, adding:

> One also suspects the influence of the Arts Council in the board's statement that it believes artistic directors should move on every five years. This opinion . . . echoes the Arts Council statement of a few months ago that it was time MR. PETER CHEESEMAN left the Stoke-on-Trent Victoria Theatre. As MR. CHEESEMAN managed to regain his position there may still be a chance for MR. NEVILLE. Nottingham can ill afford to lose him.

It did lose him, though Peter Cheeseman ran the Vic very well indeed for a further thirty years. John Neville later admitted that he didn't know how to handle the board of trustees: 'It was a mystery . . . why the local butcher, baker and motor mechanic should be held to know more about running the theatre than the professionals. I am no airy-fairy, arsie-tarsie artist with my head in the clouds.' The difficulties at Nottingham, then, were not limited to a confusion in local government over the value, dimension and bankrolling of prestige theatres, but extended to how they were to be governed internally. As artistic director, Neville faced an abrupt transition from the actor-manager model that had been common up to then towards a corporate approach which obliged him to seduce the butcher and the baker before he could convince a seated public. Knowing this, it becomes clearer now that the decline of artistic authority and vision in regional theatre life was a measured process already present like a virus in the non-profit structures imposed from the first by the Arts Council.

In comparison, Chichester was a breeze. One of its city councillors watched his TV on 4 January 1959 and saw Tyrone Guthrie promoting the Shakespeare Theatre built for him in Stratford, Canada. Guthrie stressed the value of a thrust stage, which pushed the actors out into an arena framed by the audience. This was a theme at the time when live theatre was finding ways to emphasise its three-dimensional quality in contrast to its flat competitor, television (it's rather ironic that a TV company was broadcasting this). On hearing that the Canadian town was around the same size as Chichester, Leslie Evershed-Martin (1903–1994) simply decided to provide his musty borough with a matching theatre.

Evershed-Martin was an optician by training who contributed to the evolution of contact lenses, though this gave him no great stock of private wealth. But having been an independent mayor for two of his eighteen years in the council chamber and having spent four years at the county council, he knew the strengths and weaknesses of those in local office. He also knew private sources of support because he'd led a fund-raising campaign to build a home for the elderly (which is how some now judge his theatre). Evershed-Martin was drama-mad, too; in 1934 he'd founded an amateur outfit called the Chichester Players.

He began his campaign with the town clerk, then the director of education of West Sussex, the Dean of Chichester, and so on through the characters that could individually make or break the project. Finding adequate goodwill, he discovered at the same time the kind of prejudice against small civic theatres that gave the Nottingham board so much grief. Guthrie's theatre scheme softened local anxiety: yes, the theatre's as large and distinctive as you wish, with a thrust stage and a capacity of 1,374; no, it finds full houses because it's open only for a festival period, just like Stratford-upon-Avon and nearby Glyndebourne.

Evershed-Martin never involved the Arts Council. The town clerk had told him that to do so would fuel local animosity, because the Council had discouraged a 350-capacity civic theatre in Chichester a few years earlier. He therefore enjoyed the irony of showing Bill Williams and his Council executive round the completed theatre just before it opened, and they in turn thanked him for crafting a theatre that cost them nothing. From his fellow councillors he secured an area of Oaklands Park on a ninety-nine-year peppercorn rent and, before that was announced, properly resigned from his ward. The peppercorn, by the way, remains just that, and each year Chichester District Council accepts precisely £0.00 in the way of rent. A significant amount of the private cash Evershed-Martin raised came from Lord Bessborough, a board member of ATV who wrote terrible plays and ran a private theatre to act them out on his Sussex estate.

The only hitch concerned the city's unrelated refusal to build a public swimming pool at this time, because a doctor on the council didn't think much of chlorine. The affair allowed the press to sniff around for comments like this from a young waitress: 'I'd have preferred a swimming pool. I mean, a theatre's more for old people, isn't it?' Nonetheless, the 'hexagon on stilts' opened in June 1962 at a cost of £126,000 – under half the cost of the Nottingham Playhouse, with close to double the capacity, a statistic consistent with theatre economics.

To shape up the artistic side, the optician visited Tyrone Guthrie, who was working in the summer of 1959 at the English Stratford, and it was Guthrie who deftly suggested that Laurence Olivier should be Chichester's artistic director. It's now well known that the fifty-three-year-old Olivier had reached a creative crossroads. First, he was frustrated by his commercial failures as an actor-manager throughout the fifties. Second, Olivier was driven by personal dilemmas which resulted in his third marriage, to the actress Joan Plowright in 1961. He now wanted to raise a family in the quiet of Sussex.

So when he received an approach by letter from Evershed-Martin in January 1961, he jumped at the chance to make something out of Chichester, as though it gave him a fresh, or last, opportunity to prove himself as a leader. Olivier was offered a salary of £5,000 but would accept only £3,000 (around £33,000 today) and donated a further £500 to the building fund. Selecting and directing all three plays of the debut season in the summer of 1962, he chose also to act in two of them.

He later offered this reason for accepting the Chichester job:

> I had recently had two theatres seemingly pulled down about my ears, the St James's, in the eight years running of which I had squandered my entire resources, and a little later the Stoll, which saw its last performance in *Titus Andronicus*, and I began to think that my presence in a London theatre would only be enviable to a member of the IRA.

Prescient words: it was he who declared the Royal Exchange open. Olivier was facing the same kind of commercial adversity that challenged the Group and its competitors. Here in Chichester was a business opportunity where from the first the risks he took were entirely artistic. Olivier wished to prove he was not only 'the world's greatest actor' but also its most versatile director and cleverest executive. He needed to do this because of something he tried desperately hard to keep hidden from Evershed-Martin, though he failed – a matter we'll come to shortly.

Despite the odd councillor who carped, 'Why don't they do things like Brian Rix? People would go to see *him*,' Chichester's debut proved a public, financial and artistic triumph, mainly due to a brilliant production of *Uncle Vanya* directed by Olivier, who cast himself as Astrov. Part of its attraction lay in the thrust staging; few thought it would serve 'naturalist' work like Chekhov. The company included Olivier's new wife, along with Michael Redgrave, Fay Compton, Sybil Thorndike and Lewis Casson, Keith Michell and John Neville (who would the next year take over at Nottingham).

Olivier's choice of actors backed his claim that, 'I am hoping to provide . . . an actor's theatre', a barb aimed at the young Peter Hall, who he believed was turning Stratford into a 'director's theatre'. Sixty per cent of Chichester's leading casts had been, were or were to be drama panellists at the Arts Council, and Casson, of course, was its first drama director. One year later, the Council was to find itself enmeshed forever with Olivier's entire company, though not at Chichester.

Both the Festival Theatre and the Nottingham Playhouse have survived a number of snags and shifts, but they still plod on. Chichester has actually expanded, with the building of a studio theatre – the Minerva – sponsored at first by Japan's Nissan and now subsidised in part, though only through the feeble regional board of South East Arts. Dick Linklater, who retired to a pretty Oxfordshire village, noticed that his neighbours travelled for their theatre to Chichester more often than to Stratford. However, while the Festival Theatre has been true to Olivier's vision of an 'actor's theatre' (and as he coined that phrase on TV, it's hard to know where the apostrophe lies), Neville gave Nottingham a broader mission, related to play-writing as much as performing.

Like several 'proudly regional' theatres that trade in such a paradox, the early Playhouse measured its success by the number of productions that transferred to London. Nottingham's included Brecht's *Arturo Ui* and a *King Lear* starring Michael Hordern. More important were its premieres, including Peter Barnes' *The Ruling Class* (1968), Howard Brenton's *The Churchill Play* (1974) and Trevor Griffiths' *Comedians* (1975). While it seems that its contribution to new work has atrophied since, the Playhouse has become a casualty of a more general trend. Alternative approaches to making work evolved through the seventies which bypassed such repertory company routines as the writing of playscripts. Theatres like the Playhouse were locked into structures and convictions already timeworn when they opened for business. Now, like the others, it relies on TV personalities and adaptations to grab the public's attention.

Through three and a half decades Chichester has presented 142 shows in its main house, including twelve musicals (only one of them by Sondheim – well done!) and twelve play premieres, of which the most distinguished appeared in the opening years. Gutsy John Arden wrote two of them, *The Workhouse Donkey* (1963) and *Armstrong's Last Goodnight* (1965), while the showy Peter Shaffer garnered sensational success with *The Royal Hunt of the Sun* (1963) and *Black Comedy* (1965), both of which transferred to London and New York, requiring a move from thrust stage to proscenium that Evershed-Martin hadn't thought about. Robert Bolt's *Vivat! Vivat Regina* of 1970 was the last premiere to stand up to Shaffer's achievement, and Chichester has since gone the way of most other theatres in the land by depending increasingly on adaptations of books – six in the past decade, including in 1996 (this is how sad it's got) a Jane Austen.

This would have surprised Olivier, who thought that adaptations were 'a matter for Hollywood'. He left a healthy Chichester in 1965, which is a generous departure date considering how he'd stitched up Evershed-Martin right from the start, for on 10 August 1962, near the end of the debut season, it was announced in the press that Olivier had been appointed director of the National Theatre. This was the news he'd tried to keep out of Chichester, though he intimated to Michael Redgrave one evening there 'that Chichester was to be a launching pad for the National Theatre, and that he and I would lead the company in the national's first season. I was overjoyed.' The National Theatre didn't actually exist. Neither did its company, yet it was now clear that the summer troupe Olivier had assembled in Sussex would supply what he needed. The building was another matter, and it might be argued that if Chichester was so good why didn't that become the National Theatre? The reason why a National Theatre had to be built in London had little to do with the nation but an awful lot to do with London County Council.

More a tale of delays than achievements, the bungling history of the National Theatre has been well covered, most efficiently in the eponymous book by John Elsom and Nicholas Tomalin. Back in 1848 a publisher had first proposed for London a Shakespeare National Theatre. Shakespeare's name dipped in and out of the title over the years, especially when supporters thought his birthday might help set a deadline. The director Harley Granville-Barker produced a vivid plan in 1907, 'A National Theatre: Schemes and Estimates'. He revised it in 1930, adding a list of his supporters, which included many who would become involved with the Arts Council – Hugh Allen, Kenneth Barnes, the Cassons, Ivor Brown, E.J. Dent, Ashley Dukes, Vaughan Williams – but no Keynes, no Clark and nobody from the Bloomsbury set.

The bones of what we'd recognise on the South Bank today were there in his practical blueprint – two theatres (today three), a year-round programme, three producers ('at £1,000 annually') and a repertoire of forty-nine plays a year performed by seventy-one actors and thirty actresses. He also added a pension fund and a training school, though that was pushing it a bit. Given that there seems to be so much Lottery cash swishing around nowadays that the Arts Council can afford to fund the hilarious resurrection of the Globe Theatre, it would be no less fanciful to build Granville-Barker's National Theatre *exactly* as he conceived it. Sir Peter Hall would have to run it, of course, seeing as he's run everything else.

In previous pages we left the National Theatre as a pre-war hole in the South Kensington sod. Following the war the hole, in *Great Escape* fashion, reappeared at the South Bank. London County Council had swapped plots because the leader of Labour's LCC, a former trades-unionist called Isaac Hayward, was determined to create a cultural enclave there, which he began with the Royal Festival Hall for the 1951 Festival of Britain. Meanwhile the arthritic Shakespeare Memorial National Theatre Committee and the Old Vic got together in January 1946 to form a joint council, chaired by the Tory MP for Aldershot, Oliver Lyttleton, who was only in on the game because his mother has fussed about with the scheme for donkey's years.

The Old Vic got involved because it was homeless, but also because of its ability to provide the leading players. At the time the Old Vic was run by the glittering trio of Laurence Olivier, Ralph

Richardson and the stage director John Burrell, a polio victim who paced around on crutches. When he joined the Council's drama panel Burrell was probably the first disabled panellist, a point worth noting only because the Council seems to think it invented disability in the eighties.

Just after the war Ralph Richardson had reportedly warned Olivier over the National Theatre developments:

> Of course, you know, don't you, that, all very splendid as it is, it'll be the end of us? It'll be of government interest now . . . They're not going to stand for a couple of actors bossing the place around any more . . . We shall be out, old cockie.

And out they were, in July 1948, when Olivier in Australia and Richardson in Hollywood received a memo from the Old Vic's chairman, Lord Esher, an hereditary peer of paltry brain. He told them that the company could no longer be led 'by men, however able, who have other calls upon their time and talent'. Imagine saying that to Hall and Nunn nowadays.

Olivier was heading an Old Vic tour down under, while Richardson was filming *The Heiress* in order to subsidise his return to the stage company (it was in this very year, by the way, that they'd both been knighted). The trio were horrified to find themselves replaced by a couple of Arts Council staff – Llewelyn Rees the drama director and Hugh Hunt, who ran the Bristol Old Vic. This crude takeover may be considered a further example of the Arts Council's attempts to fortify administrative rigour in its principal clients, but it was a rum business all the same. Olivier's subsequent isolation from subsidised theatre explains away his staunch attempts to set himself up as a commercial actor-manager in the fifties, like Gielgud before him. At the same time, his Old Vic successes gave him a taste for a resident, integrated company.

The Old Vic's standards rapidly slid. It had set up a progressive centre for experimental work led by Michel St Denis, but by 1952 it had closed in administrative disarray. The better players sauntered over to the summer seasons of the private Shakespeare Memorial Theatre at Stratford-upon-Avon, which was capitalised by Flower, the brewery family. Meanwhile the National Theatre had grown no further than a 1949 Act of Parliament. The Labour Government had pledged that 'the Treasury may undertake to make . . . such contributions to the funds of the Trustees as they think fit (not exceeding one million pounds) in respect of the cost of erecting and equipping the theatre in accordance with the scheme'. A million pounds then equals £16.5 million today, so it was a plentiful sum. But when the Tories came to power the National Theatre Act of 1949 was left sitting on the shelf, and they merely looked on while the South Bank foundation stone was laid, then moved, twice. Though in 1954 Lyttleton was ennobled as Lord Chandos, he was unable to persuade other Tory peers that the country needed a 'national' theatre, in part because the 'national' Opera House had proved an embarrassment. He and Esher did little more than get the National Theatre added to a list of cultural capital projects in London that a Treasury committee was covened to examine.

This 1956 enquiry was supposed to determine where the new Queen's Hall concert venue should go, but it delved further, because it was also brought about by the asset-stripping of Sadler's Wells by Covent Garden and the maddeningly swift refit of theatres, concert halls and galleries in all the occupied zones of the 'defeated, barbarous' Germany. The Treasury was rather taken with Isaac Hayward's scheme to develop the South Bank where, it seemed, all the bits and bobs London needed could be located – another concert hall, a gallery, a new opera house, a national cinema and – well, why not? – a national theatre. Newspaper debates aired a variety of opinions about 'a cultural ghetto', and it took the baronial tone of Sir Donald Wolfit to bring drama to the fore in May 1956:

> There is no theatre in this country at present where young people can see a repertory of the great classics of the language. It is only in these great plays that the great tradition of the theatre can be kept alive.

Rather a lot of 'greats' there, though possibly not enough to satisfy Wolfit. Buoyed by the Treasury's interest, LCC officers started to polish up the South Bank plan.

These seem to be the main reasons for Lyttleton and Esher to busy themselves once more with the National Theatre, and why in early 1957 Oliver Lyttleton went to see Laurence Olivier (the chance euphony of their names is delightful) to sound him out about heading the National Theatre, should it happen. The actor answered, 'I don't think I'm really the right man for the job, but I can't think of anyone better.' Olivier never thought he'd come across a likely competitor, certainly not someone younger and less experienced than he. Yet he did, the next year, in Hollywood.

Peter Hall was only twenty-eight in 1958, a Cambridge graduate from a Suffolk working-class family, but already renowned as the director of *Waiting for Godot*. Shakespeare was an obsession of his and when he left Cambridge he worked with friends in the Elizabethan Theatre Company ('formerly the Oxford & Cambridge Players') who toured the country in the early fifties with help from the Arts Council's regional offices. Dick Linklater remembered meeting the fledgling but immodest company, proposing to them that they tour *Hamlet* for him. He even suggested that Hall might direct it:

> I was amazed when he said that it was too early in his career to do *Hamlet*, he'd rather wait a few years, 'but let's get Peter Wood to do it instead'. I mean, it was such an impertinent remark. But I felt even then that his self-assurance would work to his advantage. He was someone who knew where he'd end up, and I saw he was a chap worth watching.

Landing at the age of twenty-four a job at the little Arts Club Theatre in Great Newport Street (where the Unicorn Children's Theatre now resides), Hall promoted new foreign plays – almost by chance, according to his autobiography – including Beckett's audacious *Godot* and Anhouilh's well-bred *Waltz of the Toreadors*. A winning *Love's Labour's Lost* at Stratford's Shakespeare Memorial Theatre in 1956 led to further work at its summer festivals and finally to its chairman, Sir Fordham Flower, offering him the job of managing director, starting in 1960. Hall convinced Flower and most of his board that an entire change of approach would benefit the Glyndebourne-style arrangement in the Warwickshire town. Quite simply, Hall invented the Royal Shakespeare Company.

To establish a permanent operation, he cleverly emptied Stratford's financial reserves of £175,000 (£2 million today) in order to milk funds from the Arts Council. Linklater recalled:

> He came in and said he wanted to bring the summer company to London, that was all, but we weren't fooled for a moment. We guessed what he was up to. He ran down the reserves at Stratford on a season at the Aldwych Theatre in 1960–1, in order to get subsidy from us, and, as you can see, he eventually did it.

Not all of the Stratford board had backed the deal. One resigned, warning Hall that his plan would bankrupt Stratford and ruin the West End. He added that he would do his best to dissuade any theatre-owner from leasing him a London home. It was Binkie Beaumont who voiced the fears of the generation that included Olivier, which believed, quite rightly, that subsidy would deform their market place.

Perhaps only Hall, entirely post-war in his theatre career, could have contemplated and carried out a brazen leap from the world of commerce to that of subsidy. The notion came from abroad, of course – the Berliner Ensemble and Jean Vilar's Théâtre National Populaire were two state-fed companies Hall knew – as did his idea that a permanent company structured around Shakespeare should also present new plays and contribute to the evolving world of drama. But the National Theatre idea had been revived, too, and Hall was aware – given that nobody seemed to know quite what a 'national' theatre was meant to be in terms of repertory – that his Royal Shakespeare Company might be the one able to seize the nation's dramatic crown, and purse. His timing was near-perfect. He knew it would take a little time from his debut in 1960 to effect any change, but there was a valuable emotional goal to help him: that of Shakespeare's 400th birthday on St George's Day, 1964.

For the Stratford season in the summer of 1959, Hall was asked to direct Olivier in *Coriolanus* and Charles Laughton in *A Midsummer Night's Dream*. At the start of that year the two stars were in Hollywood filming *Spartacus*. Hall's first wife, Leslie Caron, was working there too, in *The Man Who Understood Women*. Hall took the opportunity to visit California, sounding out Olivier and Laughton on their Stratford roles. It was thus in America that Olivier first got wind of Hall's audacious plan for Stratford and it floored him. The actor and the director then worked together in England on *Coriolanus*, which boasts these lines:

> I have lived
> To see inherited my very wishes
> And the buildings of my fancy.

So, in the same summer that a Chichester optician came to Stratford to meet Guthrie, Olivier took Hall to lunch, spoke of the National Theatre and asked him to be his number two. Hall replied that he would be his own number one, and the race began.

Olivier chivvied his lordships Esher and Chandos, who were in luck, twice over. First, Heathcoat Amory was Chancellor. A deputation of MPs from both parties had a private meeting with the Treasury's financial secretary to promote the South Bank scheme. Heathcoat Amory's parliamentary secretary, Sir Edward Boyle, confirmed to the Commons in November 1959, 'The Chancellor had invited the Arts Council to review the priority to be given to the National Theatre within the limited expenditure [that is, the £1 million written into the 1949 Act].' Second, the Arts Council had changed its chairman. In came Lord Cottesloe, an hereditary Tory peer who'd served on the LCC for ten years as a councillor for Hampstead. He cultivated his presence on arts committees to cover the fact that he was obsessed with rifle-shooting. Cottesloe needed a 'project' to assert his own style and so he gunned for a National Theatre. Olivier was now sure that he would win the contest.

Suddenly, Esher and Chandos were no longer lucky, twice over. First of all, their joint council submitted its report in October 1960. The Chancellor who received the brief, however, was no longer Heathcoat Amory but Selwyn Lloyd. He hadn't commissioned it and whether he read it or not he already knew about Stratford, which by now had applied for a royal charter. The report had tried to pre-empt competition between Olivier and Hall by employing the LCC's South Bank plan as an artistic melting pot, which would cost £2.3 million. The Old Vic and the imminent Stratford-in-London company, together with Sadler's Wells Opera, should be incorporated into the South Bank, it proposed. Lloyd asked if all of the parties were happy with this idea. Lyttleton (Chandos) was pushed to reply that 'negotiations with Stratford are still proceeding, though the Chancellor's recommendation of the report's findings will help to tie any loose ends'. This was coarse evasion and Lloyd knew it. Not even Sadler's Wells was keen on the terms.

We know about the negotiations between the joint council and Stratford, or lack of them, because Emile Littler had recommended an arts-friendly solicitor, Arnold Goodman, to draw up a constitution for the South Bank scheme. In his fulsome autobiography, Goodman related that he took his draft document up to Stratford, where he met Fordham Flower and Peter Hall:

> and various other faces . . . They looked at the document with lacklustre eyes and minimal interest. Who, they said, is to be head of the organisation? I coughed slightly, since no one had told me, but I opined that it was likely to be Sir Laurence Olivier. There was an exchange of glances.

Goodman left knowing that Stratford would not be led to the South Bank. Lyttleton booted him off the job.

The second reversal took place at the Arts Council, which was disconcerted by the birth of two bellicose siblings which would shortly be craving to be fed on lots of its money. Cottesloe was behind the scheme to get Hall's company tied up with the Old Vic, seeing Waterloo, Stratford and 'the provinces' being served by a united company of 150 players, split into three or four gyrating units. It was a genuine attempt to meet Selwyn Lloyd's perfectly reasonable gripe that he couldn't see why a new building must have a new company, especially with the Old Vic already at Waterloo and Stratford aiming to go permanent with its stake in London.

There were two factors which prevented Cottesloe from pursuing the blanket scheme. On one side lay the intransigence of Stratford, which, we must remember, had not yet received any Arts Council aid and was a respected private initiative with a dignified track record – not the sort of thing a Tory like Cottesloe would wish to damage. To add to its stature Hall's debut London season, Christmas 1961, was a terrific success, including in it a premiere, *The Devils* by John Whiting. On the other side stood the Chancellor, whose party was setting up a campaign in early 1961 to strengthen its local-government hold in the shires and recapture cities like – well, like Nottingham. The Shakespeare Memorial Theatre was very shires. In contrast, the South Bank scheme was promoted by the LCC as a Labour initiative, in advance of its local election in April 1961. Now that Labour had placed the National Theatre directly on the political agenda, the Tories were obliged to snub it.

Lloyd told Cottesloe that if he'd bide his time about the National the Government would drop more money into the drama pot to benefit regional schemes which could include Stratford. Either Cottesloe didn't mention a glaring point, or didn't think of it, but the Peter Hall plan was more about London than Stratford. These manoeuvres explain why finally, on 21 March 1961, Selwyn Lloyd announced in the Commons:

> Although some people believe that the right thing is to have a large new building, costing a large amount of money, on the South Bank, and then form a National Theatre Company to put inside it, there are other people who think that the better way is to build up the existing institutions like the Old Vic and the Royal Shakespeare Theatre of Stratford-upon-Avon, and, at the same time, help repertory in the provinces.

The Hansard report is clear that Lloyd didn't specify figures, though he seemed to give the impression to many that the £1 million set aside in the Act would be incorporated into a revenue grant of between £300,000 and £400,000 to the Arts Council, earmarked for drama. Labour MP George Jeger, election PR in mind, thundered:

> Is not the Minister aware that . . . owing to the deplorable manner in which the Government has handled the question of a National Theatre, there is a considerable doubt whether we shall ever see one; and that we shall have to rely on the LCC to provide it?

Looking again at the dates, we can appreciate more clearly why Laurence Olivier was so happy to take on Chichester when he replied to Evershed-Martin's letter on 3 March 1961. There was no National Theatre, no company to work in it and no money. Moreover Peter Hall was gambling corporate reserves on a company lacking a proper London home. Eclipsing both, Olivier was going to get a new theatre, privately endowed, and a company of his choice; with a new wife as well he could afford to be happy as Larry.

But Cottesloe at the Arts Council felt let down by his own side. The extra drama money amounted to £349,000 but was spread incrementally over three years:

1960–1961	1961–1962	1962–1963	1963–1964
£155,000	£223,000 (+£68,000)	£336,000 (+£113,000)	£504,000 (+£168,000)

Coerced as Cottesloe was to keep quiet until the LCC election on 13 April was over, the Labour Lord Silkin tried to embarrass him by calling for the issue to be raised in the Lords a week before the poll. The Tories forced the date back, allowing Cottesloe to speak in the upper chamber on 20 April, where he vented his frustration: 'Nobody in his senses looks a £300,000 to £400,000 gift horse in the mouth, but let no one think that it is a substitute for a National Theatre.' Lord Esher added, 'It is very natural that [the LCC] should wish to crown that centre with a National Theatre before the worldwide Shakespeare celebrations in 1964 come upon us.'

The LCC election had found in favour of Labour again. Isaac Hayward remained leader, but on 6 June he was joined in a visit to

the Chancellor by his Tory counterpart, Sir Percy Rugg. Hand in
hand, they offered to add £1.3 million from the rates to the Act's
£1 million to get the theatre built in time for Shakespeare's
birthday. Rugg had rallied round, once the election was over,
thanks to fresh inspiration.

First there was America. Just as Keynes had been stimulated to
create Covent Garden by Mayor La Guardia's City Center, the
LCC grandees were stirred into action, if not competition, by John
D. Rockefeller III and his deluxe allies, who were launching the
Lincoln Center for the Performing Arts in Manhattan. Then there
was France. In 1959 De Gaulle had set up a Ministry of Cultural
Affairs under the writer André Malraux. Up to this time the
French had pursued a policy of *décentralisation dramatique*, by
which seven dramatic centres were planted around the country
and funded as though they were national theatres with regional
bases, a system which has been mucked about with through the
years, but remains in place today. Malraux looked again at the
Comédie Française in Paris, and cut off a portion of its grant to
dole out to the more radical partnership of Madeleine Renault
and Jean Barrault. Though this shift of focus makes for a
fascinating story in itself, the international publicity gave the
impression that Paris was expanding its resources to create three
national theatres in its capital. All parties in the LCC were nettled
by this cultural jockeying, hence the *Henry V*-style meeting
between Hayward, Rugg and the Chancellor.

Selwyn Lloyd told the Commons on 3 July that the LCC offer
'creates a new situation'. It didn't really, as Hayward had indicated
back in the fifties that the LCC could match the government cash;
though the £300,000 was an addition, the new situation was really
the election result. A week later Lloyd confirmed through clever,
negative words that the £1 million was available, as was the
revenue money listed earlier. The capital sum was now worth £6
million less at today's value than when it was first announced in
1949. Nonetheless, his greenish light allowed Stratford to proceed
independently of any South Bank scheme (though the Arts Council
kept plugging for an amalgamation through until the autumn).
Equally, on the face of it, Lyttleton could go back to Olivier and say,
'It's on.' It was pointed out to Cottesloe, though, that now Olivier was
building a starry company for Chichester the Old Vic looked more
than a little vulnerable, not to say worthless. Even the extra drama
cash dripping in couldn't support three companies. In short, Cottesloe shopped Esher and his Old Vic to make way for the National.

It took a year to pull the strands together. On 3 July 1962 the Chancellor gave the Commons a written answer through his flunkey, Henry Brooke, father of the future Arts Minister:

> The first step must be the appointment of a National Theatre Board which will be responsible for creating and running the National Theatre company ... I also propose to appoint in consultation with the LCC a South Bank Theatre & Opera Board ... I am glad to say that Lord Cottesloe, Chairman of the Arts Council, has accepted to preside over this body.

And what a useless git he proved. At some point Cottesloe pushed the Metropolitan Opera House into the Thames, and it was another fourteen years before he got the doors of the National Theatre opened – except, that is, for the smallest of its three theatres, which remained for a time a bricked-up void due to cost cuts. Maybe that's why they called it the Cottesloe.

The other wing of this flightless bird flapped with vigour. The NT board first met a month after the Chancellor's reply, on 9 August 1962, and appointed Olivier director. Now we can see how it wasn't Olivier's fault that he had to keep the business a secret from Chichester during its opening season, but also why it can be said in the same breath that he stitched up Evershed-Martin. The Chancellor's timing might even have been influenced by the Festival Theatre, which opened two days after his Commons statement. But he also had in view the need to turn his scheme in the public's mind from a Labour initiative to a Tory one. This is probably why he split the project under two boards, putting the hopeless Cottesloe in charge of Labour's capital scheme.

By contrast, Olivier's company found itself paraded in the Queen's Speech on 25 October: 'My ministers have taken important steps to enrich the nation's cultural life by setting in train the establishment of a National Theatre.' Cottesloe arranged with the gullible Esher for Olivier's Chichester company to take refuge in the Old Vic theatre at Waterloo 'until the National Theatre was ready' – they took out a five-year lease – and the National Theatre Company opened at the Old Vic on 22 October 1963 with, predictably, a Shakespeare, *Hamlet*, starring Peter O'Toole. Here it could be said that Olivier extracted his revenge on Esher, who had sacked him from the Old Vic fifteen years before. The Old Vic Company was wound up, though the board stayed on as owners of the building. *Hamlet,* by the way, lasted four and a half hours, in a version less cut than it would have been on a Binkie Beaumont stage. This was the public's first indication of what full-blown subsidy would bring to British drama: sore bottoms.

By Shakespeare's 400th birthday the Arts Council was lumbered with two 'national' companies, both of them promoting London seasons but neither with a desirable metropolitan home. Things would remain that way until the National opened in 1976 and the RSC moved into the Barbican in 1982 – both theatres, we should remind ourselves, the product of local government. The constant, queeny duelling between the two of them continues to this day, especially over their annual grants.

Peter Hall maintained that his Royal Shakespeare Company always got less than the National because the vengeful Goodman saw to that when he was Chairman of the Arts Council. Maybe. The relative proportions have fluctuated back and forth through the decades, though in general there's a 10 per cent gap in favour of the National. Here are some samples, showing the percentage of the drama department's spend awarded to them, with an interesting twist at the end:

	NT £		*RSC £*	
Sixties				
1963–1964	45,000	9%	47,000	9.5%
1964–1965	142,000	26%	88,000	16%
Seventies				
1973–1974*	450,534	18%	420,000	17%
1974–1975	1,017,500	32%	694,250	21%
Eighties				
1983–1984	6,869,446	30%	4,660,312	20%
1984–1985	7,005,870	29%	5,286,000	21%
Nineties				
1993–1994	11,167,000	28%	8,470,000	21%
1994–1995**	11,167,000	42%	8,470,000	31%

* 1970s and 1980s: percentage achieved by adding NT and RSC grants to remaining drama total, as in this period their grants were listed separately.
** First year of the Arts Council of England, therefore percentage of total drama grant spend shifts.

In truth, they have both been underfunded. Take their wages bill alone; each employs 700 to 800 people. They run between them eight theatres on three sites, plus numerous rehearsal studios dotted about town. Their relationship with the Arts Council has been far more fractious than the funding body's association with the Royal Opera House or, more recently, the South Bank Centre, because the Council set those up and will (have to) die defending them. Covent Garden has been there from the first, while the National came on stream twice – the first time in 1963, in the middle of the first big period of regional expansion, then in 1976, when it took on its new building at the South Bank during a year of ruining inflation, which coincided with the end of a second wave of regional development. Every time either of the pair make a fuss for more money, the forty-odd regional theatres (each with their own MP) drown them out. Never mind what measures the Council's drama department tries to erect to safeguard the nationals, it will always be compromised by historical demands elsewhere.

What the pair really needed to sort out between them was what they were giving the public now that they were both in business. It was fine for Olivier to contrast his 'actor's theatre' with the 'director's theatre' of the RSC. To the Arts Council and the tax-payers, essential questions remained. What is a National Theatre without Shakespeare at its heart? And, as the RSC promised to find the new Shakespeares, did this leave the National counting on the Irish – the Wildes, the Shaws, the Becketts, the Behans – as this country had done up to now? The latter was a question posed by one Brendan Behan, by the way.

It became London's rep, simply that, not a National Theatre at all. Yet it was a rep with a 1994 grant equal to that shared by thirty-three other reps outside the capital. However, it has to be admitted that when Richard Eyre came along in the eighties he certainly gave it a staunch national identity. He turned it into the National Theatre of America.

Chapter 18

Outrageous fortune

Regional drama: 1965–1980

The problem with your drama is that you are xenophobic. You say you have the greatest playwright the world has ever seen – Shakespeare. How you know he is unrivalled, when you fail to perform anyone else of his prestige, Schiller for example, is a miracle only the English can achieve. You have the greatest actors, of course, though how you know this when you don't speak another language is again a miracle. But if I said Jean Barrault was as sparkling as Laurence Olivier, I would be falling into the trap you are in already.

This is the opinion of a leading French director who went on to match specific British actors to their confrères in France – failing only to find duplicates for Jean Marais and Vanessa Redgrave (yes, there's a French Donald Sinden) – but added more seriously:

You use your theatre to make yourselves exclusive, when for me theatre is a way to open yourself to the world. Let me say I come to England and Scotland maybe once a year for many years, so let me be as cavalier as the English: I think many of your actors are extremely skilful and display character with refinement, your directors are superficial (there are interesting ones nevertheless – Declan Donnellan, Deborah Warner, etc.). Your designers can be resourceful but lack

The shrewd composer Ralph Vaughan Williams (1872–1958) opposed Lord Keynes'
plans for buying up buildings such as the Royal Opera House, protesting that 'it was not
the function of the Council to provide a setting for the arts, but rather to foster the arts
themselves'.

Left: German-loving John Christie of Glyndebourne (1882–1962) wore lederhosen for the private opera festival he launched on his Sussex estate in 1934. His aristocratic guests (*below*), some of them Appeasers, maintained more deluxe standards as war loomed in 1939.

Right: The economist John Maynard Keynes (1883–1946), 'smiling not grinning', in his study at 46 Gordon Square, Bloomsbury in 1940. It was here in that year that he barked at the Council's first Secretary-General, 'You've given too much time and money to amateurs, come off it.'

Below: Dr Thomas Jones (1870–1955) broadcasts a talk on his Downing Street career in 1938. Tom Jones created the Council in 1939 to stop Christie producing one himself. This well-connected Welshman fed his organisation American money from the Pilgrim Trust, of which he was secretary.

CEMA's war effort.
Left: Diaghilev ballerina Tamara Karsavina talks to Council member Kenneth Clark at the National Gallery's opening of a CEMA travelling exhibition about ballet decor in October 1943. *Below:* As part of the 'Holidays at Home' scheme, CEMA ran concerts such as this one in a Chelsea bomb crater, August 1942. *Right:* The Pilgrim Players theatre troupe pretending to be lost in 1943. *Below right:* Workers at an unnamed factory watch scenery being unloaded for a CEMA show in November 1942, which confirms just how desperate they were for entertainment.

TOPHAM PICTURE LIBRARY

Left: William Emrys Williams (1896–1977) – otherwise known as Bill Williams, or Pelican Bill, on account of his publishing career – dominated the Council as a member from its inception in 1939 until he retired as Secretary-General in 1963. He hated his predecessor (*below*), Mary Glasgow (1905–1983), and had her pushed out. She went on to create trail-blazing foreign-language schools programmes for Associated Television in the fifties.

ASSOCIATED TELEVISION

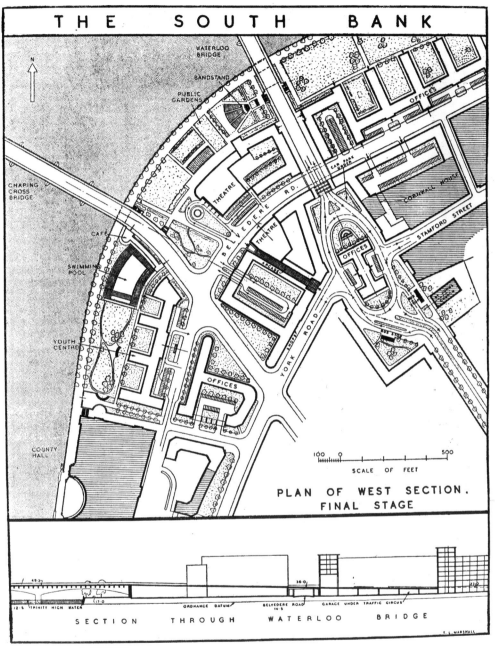

A London County Council plan for the South Bank in 1943, very much of its time. It would have given London two theatres (one eventually a concert hall and ballroom), a bandstand, a youth centre, a swimming pool, a shopping arcade – and flower gardens where there is now much concrete and a car park.

Sir David Webster (1903–1971), seen here pouring champagne for Margot Fonteyn after the New Year Gala of 1956, ran the Royal Opera House from its inception by the Arts Council in 1946 until he retired a quarter of a century on. An indolent chump with no experience of opera, he set the amateurish tone which to many has marked Covent Garden's direction ever since.

HULTON GETTY

Above: Laurence Olivier (1907–1989) dwarfing a model of the National Theatre just as the exalted actor dwarfed so much else. Leaning by him, and apparently blocking Waterloo Bridge, at the little Arts Council gallery at St James's Square in 1967, is the theatre's architect, Denys Lasdun. It would be ten more years before the troubled theatre got built.

Below: The royal opening of the South Bank's Hayward Gallery in 1968. The Tories had just recaptured Greater London Council and so the new GLC chairman, Sir Louis Gluckstein (left), accompanied the Queen and the Arts Council's Lord Goodman (right), which peeved Goodman no end. Far left is Labour's white-haired Arts Minister and Goodman's 'missus', Jennie Lee.

ARTS COUNCIL

Left: John Neville relaxing in the Nottingham Playhouse boardroom. Actually he's playing Richard II, one of many roles he brought to Nottingham when he was the artistic director there (1963–1967): 'It was a mystery to me . . . why the local butcher, baker and motor mechanic should be held to know more about running the theatre than professionals.'

Below: The growth of alternatives to the repertory theatre system caught the Arts Council out. Companies such as Forkbeard Fantasy, seen here in their 1976 *Cranium Show – a wildlife documentary,* have continued to produce touring shows of visual ingenuity despite the Council's capricious shifts of policy.

Above: The Arts Council's grand headquarters at 105 Piccadilly from 1969 to 1990 was chosen by Lord Goodman. It served only to emphasise the gap in tone between his establishment vision and radical developments such as the Cartoon Archetypal Slogan Theatre (*below*). CAST's Clare and Roland Muldoon now run the splendid Hackney Empire.

Right-handed Secretary-General Sir Roy Shaw (1975–1983) (*above left*) and his left-handed successor, Luke Rittner (1983–1990). As bureaucracy bloomed, Rittner's Council leased more offices behind 105 Piccadilly, building a bridge to connect both parts in the mid-eighties (*below*). Staff think it was possibly Richard Pulford (right), deputy to Rittner (left), who suggested that the bridge should be opened by the youngest member of staff – and perhaps we can see why. The Council eventually sold off the back offices at a loss of £1.65 million.

Above: Hapless conductor Franz Welser-Möst (left) celebrates with Nicholas Snowman the choice of the London Philharmonic as the South Bank Centre's resident orchestra in 1990. An SBC insider reported that an hour or so later the special cake had been dumped in a bin, uneaten. It had cost £700. The residency was one of several episodes that have coloured Snowman's tenure as the centre's chief. It seemed he wanted to create London-sur-Seine. Boules courts (*below*) were built beside his patch of the Thames, but only the SBC staff – on the opening day – cared to play much, and the commissioned sandpits were soon cemented over.

Above: Powers behind thrones in 1984. Front row, left to right: indefatigable minute secretary Mary Endacott; Roy Shaw's secretary, Vere Paterson; Sue Starbuck; Virginia Casey. Behind them are head of secretariat Lawrence Mackintosh on the left and the Chairman's chauffeur, Charlie Brannan, on the right.

Left: Come on punk, make my day. To many in the early eighties, the polished executive veneer of regional director David Pratley defined a new Council mood – 'the Suits arrive at 105'. Actually, he's a very nice bloke.

Above: Eighties Chairman Sir William Rees-Mogg addresses his many fans in the Council room at 105 Piccadilly, which seems to have been hosting a bring-and-buy sale at the time. *Below:* When the antiquarian Rees-Mogg was replaced by Peter Palumbo (centre), the arts world and an active press welcomed the change, though not for very long. Luke Rittner (right) soon found he couldn't get on with Palumbo and dramatically resigned.

ARTS COUNCIL

Above: Linda Ludwin (standing), chair of the East Midlands Dance Agency, accepts the award to present a Year of Dance during 1993 in Palumbo's 'Arts 2000' crusade. The Lord Palumbo (left), Princess Diana and Secretary-General Anthony Everitt (right) enjoy the joke, which is more than the people of the East Midlands were able to do as grand plans failed to materialise and the Year of Dance stumbled more than sparkled.

Below: Secretary-General Mary Allen and Chairman the Earl of Gowrie on the Chairman's terrace at the Council's Great Peter Street headquarters in 1994. Unlike their predecessors, who usually stood in front of works of art, it is significant that they chose as their backdrop the Houses of Parliament.

ARTS COUNCIL

imagination, your technicians are clever but are satisfied too quickly, and many of your playwrights lack formulation. Also, you steal from artists in other countries and you make believe you don't.

Formulation? Not explained any clearer than something to do with disclosing form: maybe accepting conventions too readily.

The director added that the British public apparently has a problem with the 'presence' of drama, due to the fact that the French still enjoy the theatre of the Church while we watch the telly. Almost endearing, it seems, is the fact that we 'have made efforts to improve the physicality of your theatres, with a more interesting individuality than some countries, such as Scandinavia. But not in the West End, which I call the West Hell.'

Her point about the standard of the theatres themselves came as a relief. When the Old Vic Company was sent abroad just after the war, Harcourt Williams and his fellow actors were not only amazed by the 'intelligence of the audiences watching work in a foreign language', they also felt 'spoiled rotten' by the facilities: 'What struck me most about the continental theatres was their spaciousness, not only behind the scenes but also in front of the house. In comparison ours seemed so cheese-paring, niggardly.' It was practical experiences like these that led to the way theatres such as the Nottingham Playhouse were conceived – actors' apartments were included in the draft design of 1958 – though the frugal habits of local government invariably shrank noble ambitions.

While Germany, France and the Low Countries led the way in reviving damaged buildings, America provided pristine models for theatres and museums: the South Bank board planned in the sixties to borrow from the Lincoln Center the chic architect Philip Johnson to design the National Theatre. Yet major changes in the material shape of spaces were due more to technical trans-formations, in lighting and sound diffusion, than they were to the comfort of audiences and casts. Wartime advances in the technology of illumination, amplified sound and recording had given to peacetime new concepts and equipment, the installation of which did much to divide the new theatres from the commercial veterans that still seemed to be run on coal gas, paraffin and barking at the gallery. In sum the physical refashioning of theatres following the war was a result of imported advances which we tend to acknowledge less than we should.

The summit of Britain's adventure in theatre design was achieved at the Royal Exchange Theatre of Manchester. In contrast to playhouses a hundred miles around it, the Royal Exchange seems to have dropped in from the Planet Zog. Placed in the bigger picture of international reforms, it looks very much a token of the seventies: a flamboyant flying saucer floating in a Victorian trading hall, enclosing an in-the-round auditorium. It is blessed with an acoustic ranging from the intimacy of a bedsit to the boom of a cathedral.

The Royal Exchange's opening, in September 1976, rounded off the third and final wave of theatre-building in the regions, motivated this time by the creation in 1966 of an Arts Council fund called 'Housing the Arts'. This title was taken from a two-part Council report written in the late fifties, which examined the need for arts buildings first in London then the regions. Little more than a sluggish response to the Treasury and LCC studies that plugged the South Bank, it nevertheless triggered all three political parties at the time to propose a vote-catching capital fund. As we've seen, the ruling Tories got in first with their £350,000 supplement of 1961–1964. When Harold Wilson's party grabbed power in October 1964, Labour allowed the uplift to stay in the drama budget for the following year, but at the same time cordoned off a further supplementary sum of £150,000 (around £1.5 million – not much) projected by the Treasury for the Tories and gave it this natty name, which politically was much more streetwise than the Tories' handling of the same resource.

Housing the Arts existed until 1988 (after a six-year gap the Lottery essentially took over its function). It paid over a portion of costs for many kinds of building. Too many, as it turned out. Of the theatres it helped to build, there were two kinds: what we must now call civic-style, because they were no longer a sole product of town-hall pride, and those designed within university developments in the late sixties. Of the first kind there were, unlucky for some, thirteen:

Billingham Forum Theatre	1968	capacity 643
Birmingham Repertory Theatre	1971	capacity 898
Bolton Octagon	1967	capacity 422
Chester Gateway	1968	capacity 500
Leatherhead, Thorndike	1969	capacity 530
Leicester Haymarket	1973	capacity 752
Liverpool Playhouse (renovation)	1968	capacity 762
London, Greenwich Theatre	1969	capacity 426
London, Shaw Theatre (Euston)	1970	capacity 458

Manchester, Royal Exchange	1976	capacity 740
Mold, Theatr Clwyd	1976	capacity 600
Sheffield, Crucible	1971	capacity 546
Weston-super-Mare Playhouse	1969	capacity 670

Six new theatres ought to be added to the list, though they didn't follow this pattern. In 1963 the offbeat American Jim Haynes opened Edinburgh's trailblazing Traverse Theatre Club in a former brothel. Dealing doggedly with new work (it still does), it moved to a purpose-built though pygmy space with a capacity no greater than 120 in 1969. Its founder tried to establish a Traverse of the South in the short-lived Arts Lab down London's Drury Lane. At the same time his fellow countryman Charles Marowitz launched a related micro-venture called the Open Space Theatre in a Tottenham Court Road basement, and a third American, Ed Berman, established the Almost Free Theatre nearby.

The spirited intervention of these bohemian expatriates in the capital's theatre life promoted what a commentator called 'the backside of the dollar bill'. It seems that America's progressive domination of Britain had dug so deep that we even scooped up its venturesome counterculture. The Arts Council didn't know quite how to handle gumptious efforts like these, which sprang up without notice, and we'll return to the whacky tale of its dealings with Charles Marowitz in a later chapter.

Waterloo's Young Vic, on the other hand, stemmed from pressure by the Arts Council on the National Theatre to get involved with young people. It opened in 1970, but broke off from the National four years later. A similar venture, the Cockpit, opened in north London at the same time, dedicated mainly to education projects. Theatre for young people appealed strongly, almost sentimentally, to the Labour regime. The Arts Council exploited this concern by setting up a special panel, chaired by the seasoned actress Constance Cummings, which was rather shamefully killed off once Labour left office.

Three of the eleven university and college theatres, listed next, were part-funded by the Gulbenkian Foundation, which means that their publicists have been lumbered with this off-putting name ever since. Back in 1959 Lord Bridges had chaired an enquiry set up by the Foundation which emphasised that 'adventurous programmes of plays do not pay. It is doubtful whether any system of regional networks of local authorities can do much to

remedy this state of affairs . . . The main hope lies in universities.'
The Gulbenkian clearly thought it had better put its money where
its chairman's pen suggested, but looking back, its cash was frittered:

Brighton, Gardner Centre (Sussex University)	1969	capacity 482
Canterbury, Gulbenkian Theatre	1969	capacity 342
Cardiff, Sherman	1973	capacity 472
East Grinstead, Adeline Genée (College)	1967	capacity 330
Exeter, Northcott	1968	capacity 433
Hull, Gulbenkian Centre	1969	capacity 200
Lancaster, Nuffield Theatre Studio	1969	capacity 220
Leeds Playhouse	1970	capacity 721
London, Collegiate Theatre (Bloomsbury)	1968	capacity 560
Newcastle, University Theatre	1970	capacity 450
Newcastle, Gulbenkian Studio	1970	capacity 200

In sum, then, at least thirty new theatres of various sorts
appeared in the decade between 1966 and 1976, and to crown, or
drown, it all, the delayed National Theatre opened on the South
Bank at the same time as the Royal Exchange.

This entire period is a most vexing one to sketch. The Arts
Council helped wonderful projects to flourish, but it also induced
others for which the consequences were pitiful. Both of the
Labour regimes in the sixties and seventies (1964–1970, 1974–
1979) and the intervening Conservative rule of Edward Heath
(1970–1974) persuaded the Arts Council to expand its activities,
its apparatus, its budgets and its client list – even its offices – without considering the artistic intent. The Council indulged itself like
there was no tomorrow. Tomorrow dawned in 1979.

As long as its policy was 'responsive', it's hard to blame the
Council for the booby traps it placed in its own approaching path.
Everyone in the sixties seemed to be 'planning for growth'. It was
assumed, for instance, that there'd be a 30 per cent rise in the
country's population by 1999, and car ownership would increase
'at a very much faster rate than the population'. That explains why
Theatr Clwyd was planned by local government officers with a vast
carpark in the middle of a North Wales nowhere. We now know
that the birth rate dropped and auto production along with it –
and that's mainly why Theatr Clwyd is often in a financial fix.

While Labour's encouragement embraced all the customary
artforms, it was drama that reaped the greatest benefit. To do as it

was told, the Council reversed the direction of the Williams years but without, we now see, any steering agenda beyond 'a policy of reaction'. The new Chairman, Lord Goodman, used this void to press his own metropolitan interests, but so did the others in executive positions. Hugh Willatt, the Nottingham solicitor who had served as chairman of the drama panel since 1960, became Goodman's Secretary-General in 1968. His predilection for drama was partnered by the increasing influence of his finance director, Anthony Field, a canny, perm-haired theatre queen who had started out in the West End counting chits for the Wingates, a family dynasty that owned the Comedy Theatre and the Curzon Cinema.

Willatt's arrival rucked the pecking order of his departments. It had been the music department, out of the three artform units, that traditionally handled the biggest budget, due to the weight of opera and ballet. The following table shows the position each decade of the spends and relative percentages of the three main units, with the period 1968–1971 featured to pinpoint the change when drama took over from music, which occurred in 1969:

	1945–1946		1955–1956		1965–1966	
Drama	£ 29,556	20%	£ 64,601	11%	£ 766,066	25%
Music	£ 99,535	68%	£ 514,819	85%	£ 2,189,514	71%
Art	£ 17,080	12%	£ 23,434	4%	£ 121,641	4%

	1968–1969		1969–1970*		1970–1971	
Drama	£1,833,712	33%	£ 1,403,079	47%	£ 1,419,538	45%
Music	£3,342,742	60%	£ 1,227,507	41%	£ 1,302,057	43%
Art	£ 324,215	7%	£ 322,344	12%	£ 398,233	12%

	1980–1981		1990–1991		1994–1995**	
Drama	£9,593,817	57%	£31,757,364	51%	£26,765,537	40%
Music	£4,130,994	25%	£27,570,163	44%	£36,130,435	54%
Art	£2,989,495	18%	£ 2,852,661	5%	£ 4,239,539	6%

The first year the 'big four' (NT, RSC, ROH, ENO) are removed from departmental budgets (but National Theatre is not yet open at the South Bank).
**First year Arts Council of England.*

The increase was spent chiefly on the National at the Old Vic, the RSC and the reps. In 1965 the drama panel had divided the English theatre scene it supported into 'seven major reps, fourteen smaller reps, and thirteen small theatres', a total of thirty-four. By

1970 it was funding 'forty-five regional reps and six London companies', a 50 per cent increase in five years, in addition to which the ranking was abandoned and, as we've seen from the list, there were more new theatres to come. The massive growth of the grants to the regional reps was a breathless response to the fact that, in every single case, their needs had been underestimated from the first.

The Council had lured local authorities into getting involved with theatre-building knowing full well that both the capital and running estimates presented to them had overestimated income and played down speculative components including inflation. It was as though a political calculation had been made that if councillors had been strung along far enough to scan draft budgets, they'd be disposed to favour confident predictions over cautious ones. Not only that, but as John Faulkner, drama director (1976–1983) pointed out:

> It wasn't just that the basic running costs of the theatres hadn't been contemplated, but also what you could do in them. Once a company was operating, it realised it could do more and more – education activities, lunchtime shows – whatever it was to exploit the space it was in, and these had unforeseen consequences on the figures.

Sir Hugh Willatt confirmed that:

> What they didn't understand is that there are set factors on taking on a building which will inexorably rise. The income predictions may calculate a capacity level which can't realistically be exceeded. There comes a point therefore where the charge of the building can only be offset by increased subsidy. In the end it's a simple economic issue, which artistic arguments can't address.

The expansions induced by the Arts Council started with increased government grants to it, as can be seen elsewhere. Housing the Arts grew from its initial £150,000 to £770,000 (around £5.5 million today) within five years. But it was a fund independent of the artform departments, and this is how things started going wrong.

The Council was watching its back over its regional spread because Labour regimes are prone to favour decentralisation in anything that comes their way – though, as it turned out, Edward Heath was too. The rudimentary Regional Arts Associations were seizing their chance to gain ground and so Willatt's predecessor was given the title of chief regional adviser to keep tabs on affairs. It was for political reasons, therefore, that a regional department developed. Neil Duncan, its first director, had a thing about arts centres which were meant to deal with little bits of everything, and eventually the Arts Council found itself developing with local authorities three separate systems for the delivery of live performance: reps, arts centres and number ones. On top of that, inflation swept in from behind like a pantomime villain. One of its chief causes was the rising price of oil, a component that affected the running costs of theatres and arts centres directly and obliquely.

A list of the grants to the reps through these years gives the impression of lavish generosity, but it hides the pinch-fist effect of inflation, which peaked at 29 per cent in 1975. Let's take three examples of model reps that together form a geographic triangle only ten miles by forty, give or take Spaghetti Junction. This trio were active before the Goodman-Willatt regime began; the vintage Birmingham Rep was revamped in 1971, which explains its exuberant increase a year later. The figures show their respective Arts Council grants every other financial year, throughout two Conservative and two Labour governments:

	1964–1965	Value today	1966–1967	Value today
Birmingham Rep	£17,550	£179,000	£40,588	£380,000
Coventry Belgrade	£17,500	£178,000	£41,413	£388,000
Nottingham Playhouse	£18,310	£186,000	£44,481	£417,000
	1968–1969	Value	1970–1971	Value
Birmingham	£49,027	£427,000	£51,875	£403,000
Coventry	£47,952	£418,000	£54,200	£421,000
Nottingham	£55,391	£483,000	£68,151	£530,000
	1972–1973	Value	1974–1975	Value
Birmingham	£119,530	£727,000	£149,000	£781,000
Coventry	£74,171	£451,000	£91,000	£477,000
Nottingham	£87,934	£535,000	£145,000	£760,000
	1976–1977	Value	1978–1979	Value
Birmingham	£238,000	£743,000	£240,900	£613,000
Coventry	£98,000	£306,000	£122,000	£310,000
Nottingham	£214,250	£669,000	£269,835	£686,000

We see that Nottingham enjoys an 800 per cent increase over ten years, from £18,000 (1964) to £145,000 (1974). Yet in value that equals merely 400 per cent. Readers may think that even a 400 per cent growth is rather dandy and suspect that Willatt and Linklater may have indulged their teething child. The figures speak for themselves: Birmingham Rep received identical treatment with a value increase of 440 per cent. In all cases, we notice that during the seventies the values slid as the cash increased – not quite Brecht's Germany, but it helps to explain why the reps started their public whines over money while the Council pointed to ever-greater grants. The Council was chronically unable to overcome two problems: first, underestimating the likely cost of an uneven complex of companies working in their own theatres and second, the impact of exceptional inflation.

Even though inflation is barely an issue now, the Council's failure to catch up with need got locked into the system. Nowadays the regional reps are supported by the Arts Council at one remove. It passes the money through the irrelevant network of Regional Arts Boards. That's merely a political device which doesn't absolve the Council's drama department from dealing with the problem. The sad fact is that the Council can't truly solve the issue without dumping some of the regional theatres it encouraged to have built when the Government fed it amphetamine three decades back.

The reps were not the only snag. Goodman was dazzled by the West End, and with thoughts of endless free tickets (and Ivy lunches) in mind, in 1967 he set up a theatre enquiry, chaired by the former Secretary-General Bill Williams, no less. Its report – 'Theatre Today in England & Wales' – took three years to emerge. Never had an Arts Council paper had a more misleading title. It was less concerned with theatre in 1970 than with the survival of what theatre had been in 1950, and the provinces were treated mostly as touring dates for West End leftovers. Pelican Bill even used its pages to praise his own leadership: 'In its early years [the Council] was charged with a task as fantastic as the Feeding of the Five Thousand, and what it managed to do on its meagre budget for its first 18 years borders on the miraculous', Williams wrote to his disciples.

The report asked:

What are the causes of the dry-rot which afflicts the commercial theatre? ... Can the theatre continue as a mixed economy of

private enterprise and public ownership? . . . Is there a case for
Government investment (rather than subsidy) in the theatre?

It then answered its own loaded questions with three key
proposals: a touring grid of twelve to eighteen big theatres around
the country, a theatre investment fund of £100,000 (£800,000 at
today's values), and a new company to be based in London
specialising in . . . Shakespeare.

The last notion eventually induced all manner of competing
nonsense, involving the homeless Prospect Theatre at the vacant
Old Vic, a resurrection of the Old Vic group itself and the English
Shakespeare Company – all of which ended in tears. It also
heartened Sam Wanamaker's mad plan to recreate the open-
topped Globe Theatre on the South Bank, though any project that
induces American tourists to stand for three hours in drizzle is
somehow welcome.

The Theatre Investment Fund (TIF) appeared finally in 1976
once Labour regained power. Heath's Tories would have started it
themselves had it not had Goodman's sticky fingers all over it.
Whether the TIF has really done the business since is debatable. It
still exists, without Arts Council money nowadays, and its list of
recent investments is pathetic: *Tommy*, *Buddy*, *Jolson*, *The Adventures
of Noddy* and Cliff Richard's *Wuthering Heights*. It prevails
principally 'with the aim of supporting and encouraging new
producers in the commercial theatre', though three of its
contemporary signal investments are shows produced by TIF
council member Cameron Mackintosh: *Oliver!*, *Martin Guerre* and
the gay ballet by Matthew Bourne, a very shallow *Swan Lake*.

The theatre grid, meanwhile, opened up new relations with
local authorities throughout the seventies and eighties. Touring
was only an issue, we should remind ourselves, because Williams
had neglected it in the fifties in favour of reps. It was typical of his
cheek that he should point to it as a problem his successors ought
to solve. The grid dealt chiefly with the old commercial theatres,
those number ones in regional cities still vertical and open for
business other than bingo, and the whole scheme found support
from an unexpected source: the former Arts Council member
Lord Redcliffe-Maud.

Redcliffe-Maud had been appointed by the Wilson Government
back in 1966 to chair a 'royal commission on local government in
England'. A previous commission had proposed turning the
London County Council into the stronger Greater London

Council of 1966. He examined the rest of England and proposed a small number of GLC-style metropolitan authorities for large conurbations in the north and Midlands. By the time his report got to Parliament in 1970 the Tories had come to power and they faffed about with it. Yet on 1 April 1974, six metropolitan counties came into being: Greater Manchester, Merseyside, South Yorkshire, Tyne and Wear, West Midlands and West Yorkshire. They would exist along with the GLC until Mrs Thatcher had all seven 'handbagged' in 1986. A former Regional Arts Associations director said of them:

> They basically had a lot of money and nothing to do, so naturally they got involved with the arts. Just as the GLC had developed its South Bank Centre, so the others had to have showcases that could take the National Theatre or an opera company – something which could offer cultural kudos. The Arts Council used this artistic pride business to tart up old theatres. It made Tony Field a happy man.

The Arts Council developed the DALTA scheme (Dramatic and Lyric Theatre Association) to harmonise a touring grid of dates and venues and to co-ordinate the marketing of them. Commercial theatres in the scheme were mainly part of the Group, which persisted beyond the deaths of both Binkie Beaumont and Prince Littler in 1973. The deal benefited the Group by extending the life of diverse West End productions, and by revitalising their regional real estate in advance of their sale to the local authorities. The breadth of companies involved in the DALTA scheme – whether the RSC, the National, Prospect Theatre or commercial enterprises – all had people perfectly capable of doing this sort of daily co-ordination for themselves. But in the happy-go-lucky mood of the times the venture added empire-building resources to the Council and gave it central control of the network it had proposed.

Nonetheless, when DALTA was converted into the touring unit in 1975 (shortened jauntily for a time to ACT), this move proved to be the most ill-advised shift the Council had inflicted on its structure since Williams abolished the regional departments in the fifties. Quite simply, it took a whole domain out of artform control. Divisions and conflicts of responsibility between the drama and touring departments swiftly emerged and remain unresolved to this day. The Council also allowed touring's starting officer, Jack Phipps, to augment and optimise his position there;

in his business-suit style he ran it as Phipps & Co.

The unit had been set up to address an issue about number ones and their 'product' that had been burning hot in the fifties. In stirring the embers it merely sparked a wan glimmer of provision. The National Theatre, the Royal Opera and English National Opera resented touring, and even when they did so, regional audiences soon cottoned on that they were seeing second-division casts rather more than first. The RSC did it differently by concentrating on a congenial relationship with Newcastle-upon-Tyne, and it continues to take a different road, being itself regional. Yet this whole touring department business was based on false expectations, inessential duplication of tasks and above all a misguided populism, which sought to placate a provincial bourgeoisie who wanted, as Christopher Logue put it in a poem of the period, to see 'Rudolf Nureyev and Margot Fonteyn dancing in the Swansea Civic Centre'.

In sum, the Arts Council was involved at one and the same time with two contrasting structures for the receipt of drama around the country – the number ones and the arts centres – as well as cultivating in opposition a production system of repertory theatres. Through Housing the Arts it was also dealing with three disparate kinds of buildings. All of them required revenue subsidy. On top of this barely controlled development, inflation flowered, value added tax was imposed by the Heath Government on theatre tickets from 1973 onwards, and decimalisation had been introduced. 'Call me old-fashioned, but decimal coinage was the worst of them all,' argues former dance director Jane Nicholas, 'because it doubled the going rate. Instead of them using the unit of a ten-shilling note, they used the pound instead – we forget this now – and from that time there was never any chance for certain companies who depended on their box office to break even.' If all that weren't enough, a meddlesome group turned up that the Council hadn't counted on. Artists.

Chapter 19

Out of joint

Alternative drama: 1955–1980

In 1968 the Arts Council of swinging London was clear about its dramatic aims. It was there to sustain the sort of theatre it had known since Hitler invaded Poland: Shakespeare, the West End, reps. So when thespian hippies and street-theatre Trotskyites started to piddle against the Council's doors that year, the department hadn't a clue how to handle them.

For the following decade it would try to come to terms with a jumble of artists who made it clear that they were more interested in fresh audiences than grand buildings. Indeed, officers couldn't at first differentiate between the plural styles these performers followed, and it was Goodman who first spoke at a Council meeting of 'the unwashed Alternative'.

This wasn't the first time in the life of the drama department that it had encountered 'alternatives'. In the fifties and early sixties, the Council struggled with four unconventional artists: Joan Littlewood, George Devine, Sam Wanamaker and Arnold Wesker. These trailblazers were involved with buildings, respectively the Theatre Royal at Stratford East (the compass point was trenchantly added to distinguish it from Shakespeare's home town), London's Royal Court, Liverpool's New Shakespeare Theatre and Centre 42, which we now call the Roundhouse. How the Arts Council dealt with each one relied entirely on the applicant's relation to the old-boy network.

The most remarkable of this artistically deviant quartet was Joan Littlewood (born 1914), who now lives in self-imposed exile in France, like Peter Brook. She was a working-class RADA student who bolted to Manchester before the war to co-found the socialist Theatre Workshop with her husband Ewan MacColl, the folk singer and composer. They tried to get a CEMA subsidy, then the same from the Council, and her highly coloured reports of their rejections by the snooty MacOwen and his drama department give readers of her punchy memoirs, *Joan's Book* of 1994, a feeling that the Arts Council was then 'an outfit with its head up its arse', which is, of course, a wildly different view from the one promoted by this book.

She outlined that:

> We had been playing one-night stands in villages, including mining villages [a dig at the Old Vic], from 1945 to 1953 and in all that time we had received nothing but opposition from the Arts Council, though we had been invited to Norway, Sweden, Germany, France and Czechoslovakia . . . 'The finest company to come out of Great Britain,' they said. But not in the opinion of the Arts Council. If we were to survive we would have to sell ourselves in a shoddy market – the West End.

It seems that MacOwen didn't like the Theatre Workshop, not strictly because it came from the left (the Council then answered to a Labour Government) but because of his anti-Victorian opinion that it was blatantly evangelical and 'crude' in its style. Yet Littlewood went on to succeed brilliantly for a while in the West End with plays and musicals, especially *A Taste of Honey, Oh, What a Lovely War* and *Fings Ain't Wot They Used T'Be*. All of these had started out in a discarded East End playhouse which she and her manager, Gerry Raffles, rented and brought alive for £20 a week in 1953: Stratford's Theatre Royal. It wasn't only the work that gained favour but also the talent she nurtured around her. The eminent designers John Bury and Sean Kenny started out at Stratford East, for instance. Many actors who are television names graduated there, including Roy Kinnear, *Steptoe*'s Harry H. Corbett, Barbara Windsor and TV's *George and Mildred* – Yootha Joyce and Brian Murphy.

Never was there more hand-wringing by Council members than over Stratford East, once it had won over the West End. Dick

Linklater remembers Sir Kenneth Clark regretting, 'We really ought to have done more for Joan,' when he retired as Chairman. Sir Hugh Willatt excused the Council's behaviour to her on two counts, starting his defence with a reminder that:

> she used to get on the stage after a performance and say, 'Those buggers at the Arts Council don't know they're born!' I never remember a note for the drama panel or the Council objecting to her on political grounds. The main point was whether she was serving the audiences she claimed to serve.

Willatt believed it was panel member Peter Ustinov who first pointed out that most of the audience at Stratford East had travelled from places 'somewhat west of it. Her clientele appears to be more Hampstead Central than Stratford East.'

The second point concerned the West End profits of shows guaranteed in the East End by the Council. Littlewood summarised:

> From August 1945 to March 1960, Theatre Workshop received a total of £4,150 from the Arts Council of Great Britain and a lot of criticism, but when we transferred a play to Wyndhams, Sir W.E. Williams, their Secretary-General, laid claim to ten per cent of the profits. 'We want that *Taste of Honey* money,' wrote Jo Hodgkinson.

Littlewood's style of operation simply didn't fit into the pigeon-holes the drama department had assembled for itself. Nor did she help to build a factional alliance for her cause. Her view of another of the alternative quartet was typical:

> One day I thought we should start a war of theatres, so halfway through [Brendan Behan's *The Hostage*], when the social worker and her fancy man have irritated everybody beyond endurance, I told Howard Goorney (the caretaker) to have them stowed in two dustbins to be labelled 'return to the Royal Court', where they were currently performing Sam Beckett's *Endgame*. The Royal Court didn't respond. They were too soft-centred – very middle class and proper, like their leader, the anti-Semitic George Devine. As for their John Osborne, 'Angry?' said Behan. 'He's about as angry as Mrs Dale.'

Mrs Dale, the posh doctor's wife who ran her daily radio diary of the time, was not the sort of middle-class and proper person to venture into Sloane Square's Royal Court Theatre. It was the inveterately modish bourgeoisie who queued to see John Osborne's *Look Back in Anger* when it opened in May 1956, racking up profits of £45,000 (half a million today) through a London run of two years. Nearly everything else the Royal Court did, though, made a loss, yet it had Arts Council backing from the first to help it through. It did so because of a most peculiar set of circumstances involving three pairs of ill-matched couples getting together as the English Stage Company, the name by which Royal Court grants are still listed in the Council's accounts. Half of them were people the Arts Council could trust whatever they did, and they carried the dodgier half.

This Victorian theatre in Chelsea had closed in the thirties. Its owner chose to open it again in 1952 as a club theatre, and a 'non-Jewish Jew', Oscar Lewenstein, was recruited as general manager with the brief that he could put on anything he wanted so long as 'it did not lose money'. Lewenstein was an active communist who'd worked in the Unity Theatre movement, but he teamed up in 1954 with the reactionary playwright Ronald Duncan, who earned a living as – and again here comes the spooky motif that appears mysteriously throughout this book – a farmer. Their slim point of contact lay in their agreement that there was a whole realm of work, especially Duncan's, that was meant for special occasions, not repertory. Their focus fell on plays and the intentions of their authors.

They wanted to create a playwrights' theatre, 'in which the play came first and everything else, director, designer and actors served the play'. Duncan wrote the overcooked libretto to Britten's opera *The Rape of Lucretia,* so he was in with the composer's circle which included the Queen's broad-minded cousin the Earl of Harewood, who was then working in his vague job at the Royal Opera House. George Harewood declined the chairman's role at this new theatre company, but joined the board anyway and agreed instead to chair the artistic committee, which was handy when it came to dealing with the censoring powers of his cousin's Lord Chamberlain.

Through friends of friends they found a board chairman in Neville Blond, a semi-retired businessman connected through marriage to Marks & Spencer. Blond really joined because he wanted to share privileged boardroom backchat with royalty. Harewood suggested George Devine (1910–1966) as artistic director. He was then working with Harewood at Covent Garden on Walton's opera *Troilus and Cressida*. Lewenstein remembered that Devine had come to see him a couple of years previously because he and the fledgling director Tony Richardson wanted to take a lease on the Royal Court and set up something that now seemed not unlike the playwrights' theatre, though they lacked backers.

It really is astonishing how these things start – a communist producer, a member of the royal family, a curmudgeonly play-wright, a businessman with no knowledge of the theatre and the now-legendary Devine who, by all accounts, was an unpleasant fellow. He certainly didn't get on with the down-to-earth Blond who, inspired by the good fortune of *Look Back in Anger*, would say to Devine, 'Which of these pieces you're offering me is going to transfer and make us some brass?' Meanwhile Ronald Duncan was hostile to Osborne's play. He didn't like the 'kitchen-sink' style of it for a start, and in addition he felt it depressed the audience into a sense that there was 'no hope in the world'. In fact, he liked hardly anything the Court put on and whined at board meetings like an elderly colonel ranting about beatniks. But he refused to resign.

Thanks to Harewood's careful handling of the artistic com-mittee, the Court stayed faithful to Lewenstein and Duncan's brief, and that play-writing feature has prevailed. Whether the Court has truly earned its esteem is another matter. It's now forgotten which of the Council's chairmen said to which secretary-general, 'The Royal Court is our alternative theatre. At least, it's as far as I'm prepared to go.' The Council placed the Royal Court in a relatively privileged position while it denied Littlewood's Theatre Workshop. It did so because of Harewood's clout and the fact that the Court 'did more this-and-that than Littlewood did' – Littlewood tended to run a tight house style. It has consistently received 3 to 5 per cent of the drama department's budget. And though it retains the size and scale of activity of a provincial rep, all of which are now devolved to the Regional Arts Boards, the Royal Court remains protected by the Council.

There's a sneaking feeling around that the Royal Court (and what a fortunate name) trades on the detective work of others. It retains its dominant status thanks to boundless bourgeois loyalty, especially that of the more languid drama critics. The Court's 'a bit naughty', a Council member once said, referring to its much-flaunted stand against the narrow-minded. But naughtiness cuts both ways: 'Of all theatres, the Royal Court is the last one you would expect to apply censorship,' wrote the director Ken Loach and his (Jewish) journalist sidekick Andrew Hornung in the *New Statesman* of February 1987. They were reacting to the sensational cancellation thirty-six hours before the first night of *Perdition*, a play by Jim Allen about Zionists who traded with Nazis in wartime Hungary. The duo suspected it was Lord Goodman and other high-ranking Zionists who pressured the Royal Court to withdraw, while a board member considered it just 'an internal cock-up of the highest order'. Whichever, some perceived the pull-back as a chronic act of folly by the artistic director of the time, Max Stafford-Clark, and it is noted here as a reminder that the Royal Court's record is rather more smudged than it lets on.

At any rate it exudes a self-regarding confidence, which always counts for much in the metropolitan arts scene. Joan Littlewood didn't like the place because behind her back it tried to poach *A Taste of Honey*'s author Shelagh Delaney. A consistency at least, because it seemed to do little for women writers until they'd emerged elsewhere, or more visibly once women's writing found a market niche in the eighties. Moreover, John McGrath, the writer and founder of the 7:84 Company, had worked at the Court but complained about its 'pernicious' system of 'turning authentic working-class experience into satisfying thrills for the bourgeoisie'. This is a charge that occasionally sticks, though the Court had a chance to redeem a progressive dynamism through its recent artistic director, the admirable Stephen Daldry, who chose to move on in 1998. But it certainly explains why Pelican Bill favoured Chelsea over the East End.

One of the plays that George Devine declined to put on was Brecht and Weill's *Threepenny Opera*. His colleague Oscar Lewenstein acquired the rights and 'hired' his own Court for a run in 1956. He chose as his director an abrasive American actor who'd settled in England to avoid the anti-communist witch hunt of Senator McCarthy, Sam Wanamaker (1919–1993). Born in a Russian-Jewish ghetto of Chicago, Wanamaker was apparently mesmerised by a mock-up of Shakespeare's Globe Theatre at the World Fair there, and later worked as a student on a similar replica in Cleveland, Ohio. This would lead in 1971 to the start of his campaign to create a copy near the original site in Southwark. But back in the fifties he was known to the Council as the bothersome artistic director of Liverpool's New Shakespeare Theatre Company.

Without doubt Liverpool holds the record as the city that most reliably exasperates the Arts Council. Its Playhouse declined

Council aid for years, spoiling Bill Williams' notions of theatre grids and suchlike. Then all three theatres there wanted money at the same time – the Playhouse, the Everyman and Merseyside's Royal Court. Wanamaker was the first to ask for aid in 1957. His programme was very Unity Theatre and when his name came up at a Council meeting, someone muttered that he was 'a Liverpool Littlewood'. Luckily for Wanamaker, he was protected by the drama panel's chairman of the time, the splendid Benn Levy (1900–1973). Levy was a West End playwright and socialist MP who'd worked as a Hollywood scriptwriter. He married the American film actress Constance Cummings, who came to live in London and contributed nobly to the Council's cause. He won everyone over at the Council for three reasons at least: Levy was chums with stars such as Charlie Chaplin and Laurence Olivier (who directed one of his plays in New York in 1958), he called everyone 'ducky', and he'd periodically set fire to himself by lighting his pipe and then putting it in his pocket.

Levy's tactic was to call the bluff of naysayers in a laid-back tone. He'd say things like, 'Sam? Oh come on, we all know Sam,' as though they all did, or if they didn't they should before they spoke about him. Hugh Willatt remembers Levy remarking to an obstreperous Council member, 'Well, that's Sam for you, isn't it? He does things his own way. He'd rather send a telegram than a letter.' To which the member mumbled, 'Oh, yes, I suppose so,' as if he didn't want to be caught out by this inscrutable remark. Though Levy used these ruses to protect radical artists, he wouldn't be able to get away with such gimmicks nowadays, more's the pity.

Another Jewish radical, who applied too late to get the Levy treatment, first made his name through one of the Council's associated theatres, the Coventry Belgrade. The work of Arnold Wesker (born 1932) was picked up by the Royal Court. Yet he was less interested in such bourgeois outlets, despite the success of his traditional and well-crafted trilogy *Chicken Soup With Barley, Roots, I'm Talking About Jerusalem* (1958–1960). Wesker tirelessly sought to build an alternative structure through the trades-union movement. In 1960 he set up the Centre 42 project to engage workers artistically. He started with a number of chaotic arts festivals around the country, and in 1964 he bought a Victorian train shed at Chalk Farm as a mixed-product theatre. Since then the Roundhouse has endured the saddest history of any arts building in the country.

Guitarist Jimi Hendrix believed that the place was 'haunted by an audience of ghosts', which would at least explain the failure of Wesker, and the several who succeeded him in 1970, to sustain its creative use. Wesker had hoped for greater support from the Trades Union Congress, as unions were growing in membership, but there was little warmth or cash coming back to him. The Arts Council had as little as possible to do with Wesker's scheme at a time when it may have succeeded, because Wesker was a brash artist and there was no royalty on his board. Typically, the Council got fully involved twenty years later in an embarrassing scheme to turn the train shed into a black arts centre, which we'll come to. The incredible history of the Roundhouse is worthy of a play by, say, Arnold Wesker.

The Council's variable approach to these four independents was guided by the radicals' uneven ability to employ a wad of old buffers between Council officers and the spirited artists themselves. So it's not so surprising that, even though it had been warned of change, the Council hadn't a clue what to do when a new generation of artists challenged the dominance of Williams' 'limited number of permanent institutions'. By 1968 the People Show, the Brighton Combination and Wherehouse La Mama (for the name blame the spirit of the time, or at least the smoke) had joined characters like Berman, Haynes and Marowitz in exploring new patterns of work and uncommon venues. There was a general feeling around the Council that these things were genuinely significant, and the Council would look stupid if it didn't at least check what was going on. Goodman was determined to sideline these upstarts and safeguard the *status quo* by setting up a separate category to deal with 'new activities'.

He invited the gormless Michael Astor (1916–1980) to chair a new activities subcommittee in order to report on what 'the hippies were up to'. Willatt remembers:

> Goodman had his eye on the Astor wallet. As Astor fancied himself
> as a bit of a dilettante in the arts, Goodman thought he might pay
> for some of this new stuff, save us some money, and so he thought
> Astor was just the chap to chair this new venture. Well, he wasn't.
> The whole thing was chaotic.

In July 1969 it evolved into a full committee with an allocation of £15,000 (£125,000: puny). No one seemed to notice it had sown confusion for itself by lumping together new drama groups with visual artists who centred their work around performing – what became called 'performance art' and 'live art' – and others who were concerned with the different business of installations. Hugh Willatt complained, 'We'd go and see their activities and all they did was talk about it. We'd wait and wait for them to actually do something.' Tony Field recalls a committee meeting where a performance group offered to provide lunch.

> They sent in twenty little packs with a bread roll dyed purple, a blue banana and a black tomato and we all had to sit and eat these things. Oscar Lewenstein was on the committee and turned up late, so someone gave him his ration but forgot to warn him. He went back home on the Brighton train, opened his food pack in the buffet car, and I don't think he ever recovered from the looks he got on the train that day.

Lord Goodman claimed, 'We never expected a new Art to emerge, and it didn't.' Oh yes it did, and Goodman's failure to recognise performance art and what evolved from it caused a mess of trouble from that time on. It explains the belated introduction of a combined arts department, known to insiders as 'the Dustbin'. But crusading companies like the People Show trekked around the country on one-night stands (they're still active; they number their shows and are now on 103), and because they formally fitted into the drama department's new small-scale touring scheme, they opened up a whole structure for relatively radical work, much to Goodman's displeasure.

Suddenly drama's annual accounts between 1970 and 1979 listed company names of increasing un-Royal-Shakespeare-Company-ness: the Yorkshire Gnomes, Nice Pussy, the Cartoon Archetypal Slogan Theatre, Phantom Captain, the Wakefield Tricycle Company, Sal's Meat Market, Big Girl's Blouse, Forkbeard Fantasy (still going, splendidly) – and the John Bull Puncture Repair Kit, whose filmed account of their bid to convince residents in a Liverpool cul-de-sac to turn themselves into frolicking bandits for a supposed remake of *Viva Mexico!* remains a treasure ('The director needs your house to look more *adobe*').

By 1976 the Council and the Regional Arts Associations were spending around £1.5 million (£5.4 million today) on no fewer than 106 'non-building based' drama companies of various sorts around the country. To put that into perspective, the grant for the National Theatre alone, still at the Old Vic, stood at £2.5 million.

The Council's contribution for this adventurous development settled at around 5 per cent of the drama budget.

Included in the list were new companies devised to give voice to issues raised by the sixties liberation movements. There were women's groups like Pirate Jenny, 'queer' ones such as Gay Sweatshop, and black ones like Temba. In many cases they appropriated or parodied conventional theatrical forms to raise issues for social debate, and sympathetic Council officers could justify their grants to malcontents because they'd locked themselves into artistic and administrative conventions. Socialist groups like 7:84, Red Ladder, North West Spanner or Belts & Braces used a variety of techniques drawn from showbiz; Belts & Braces even ran a band. They were able to progress beyond the rough and ready tone of the street theatre and cartoony agit-prop of the early seventies, which soon got tiresome and not a little patronising.

Yet, to put it as crudely as they first did, many of these groups weren't able to work up new conceptual structures. Even before Thatcherism took a hold, they had forfeited their audiences by touring weakly presented copies of reactionary play forms that could be handled much better by the larger reps and the nationals. Left-wing worthies such as David Edgar (once of the General Will), David Hare and Howard Brenton (ex-Portable Theatre) had found a welcome in the big houses, and wrote capaciously. They replaced the relative veterans John Arden and Arnold Wesker, who'd endured calamities with RSC casts of the time over their working methods. In contrast, Edgar was also willing to script escapist tosh for the RSC like *Nicholas Nickleby*. At the same time, the small companies that pursued the most old-fashioned ways from the first survived, like the Actors' Touring Company, Foco Novo, Joint Stock and the overweening Bubble Theatre, with their work sometimes transferring to established playhouses. The gaudy and profitable musical *Return to the Forbidden Planet* was originally Bubble's pastiche of a Hollywood film based on *The Tempest*.

While all manner of diverting and profluent stuff was taking place elsewhere, the Council failed to fathom it. Officers tended to support new work in terms of its play-writing, for which the department had a 'new writing' fund. But some groups were using improvisation, collaborative actions and visual theatre; there was hardly a running script to be found in the rehearsal room. The most daring products were created by British artists who'd gone abroad to study radical foreign work such as that of Germany's Pina Bausch company, which related to dance, or the dream-like stage images of the USA's Robert Wilson.

But the Council saw it too late. By the time that Leeds' Impact Theatre Co-operative had got going in the early eighties, or Rational Theatre and the like, the Council was shedding clients. In that sense it stifled an entire vein of progressive work, which ended up cloistered in the ICA's dreaded black box down the Mall, where their successors still lurk. It was the 'oddball' dramatic bohos like Forkbeard Fantasy and the Ken Campbell Roadshow which transcended this exceptional period, and it is no coincidence that the endlessly inventive, hit-and-miss Campbell was invited to open the National's Cottesloe in order to baptise it with an off-centre image it hastily cast off once he'd finished his run.

The Cottesloe, by the way, was a sort of added extra to the South Bank's National. It appeared thanks to a further development that the Council found no easier to control than the others, that of the 'Fringe'. Rooms, or little more than rooms, accommodated a new wave of companies which sought intimate spaces for a confluence of artistic and economic reasons which started with the simple fact that they lacked any other kind of home. Titchy billets like the Almost Free Theatre had inspired a number of pub back rooms to be prised open. Present studios like the Bush and the Gate started out in this way, and their prosperity impacted on the nationals.

However, the latter exploited this development simply to reduce risk, artistic and economic. The Royal Court's attic had been used by Clement Freud as a private restaurant. They now turned it into the Theatre Upstairs, while the RSC opened its Other Theatre in Warwickshire, then the Warehouse – followed by the Pit – in London. There was hardly a major regional rep that didn't attempt to build a black box in a grubby nook backstage. These actions were simply a consequence of the need of the dominant houses to trade on this 'alternative' energy, though they used the structure for less novel ends and marginalised it. As John Faulkner has already pointed out, the costs were unforeseen and the Cottesloe, for instance, was periodically closed down, or 'left dark' as actors prefer to say, which shows what kind of priority untested and intimate work truly had on such places.

The Arts Council accommodated all of these trends while it had the spare cash early in the splashy seventies, and it felt hurt by the begrudging tone the artists often tendered in return. One of the problems was the sort that by now the Council should have learned to live with – the internal structure of companies. Some were co-operatives, which was a perfectly acceptable way to work under the law – the strait-laced Royal Exchange even ran itself as a collective of artistic directors. Yet in the eyes of the Council it proved an annoying practice: 'Simple decisions took forever to arrive at.' Others were just plain difficult to rumble.

Drama director John Faulkner recalled one such company:

Paine's Plough was very clearly the creation of playwright David Pownall. You got wonderful plays and incisive performances which didn't rely on sets and costumes for success. But as a structure, what was the relationship between this beautiful, clear work he created and the memorandum and articles, the board structure, the entity that was Paine's Plough as an endeavour? At one level Paine's Plough was more of a text than a business, or a collection of creative people rather than what we had turned them into in order to receive a grant. This may seem a rather philosophical point, but I think it was a fundamental and vital issue. The Arts Council had matured to a stage where it worked more comfortably with bricks and mortar, boards and balance sheets, than it did with creative concepts.

This ushered in a deeper problem. A whole range of dramatic activity was now spread about, based often on communal procedures and co-operative ways of working. These small-scale companies were a matey lot, yet they were impelled to compete with each other for a relatively thin amount of Council cash. They were active around the country, hyperactive even, and very visible. They garnered prominent coverage from the racy new genre of 'listings' magazines. Prestige came their way; Belts & Braces' version of *The Accidental Death of an Anarchist* played for two years at Wyndhams in the West End.

All of this conspired to raise the question of why great dollops of dough were reserved for the restricted National Theatre, or the bigger reps, which were neither building audiences nor engaged with advanced work. This busy swarm of 'non-building-based' companies stung the Council into pondering fundamental questions about itself in order to defend the way it spent its budget. Ironically, it was this thrust from the new left that pushed the Council into the arms of the free-market ideologues at the end of the seventies, and led the way to policy-making, interventionism, and the dreaded navel-gazing of weekend retreats, one of which nearly saw off the drama department.

Chapter 20

List, list, o, list!

Regional drama: 1980–2000

First came the cuts of December 1980, when the soft left regime of Roy Shaw and Kenneth Robinson was impelled by the new Thatcher Government to withdraw support from forty-one of its weaker clients. Dramatic targets were predictable. The Old Vic, bravely revived by Timothy West, deserved all it didn't get, if only for the toiliest-and-troubliest *Macbeth* ever staged, with Peter O'Toole soaked in tomato sauce. Neither had many at the Council been disposed towards the National Youth Theatre, due to dark rumours about its gay boss, Michael Croft, and his juvenile members. Ed Berman – who, please note, had by now become an inner city *farmer* – ran a satirical play about the cuts at Kilburn's Tricycle Theatre, titled *Show Trial*, in which Roy Shaw starred in effigy. 'It's at worst a kangaroo court, at best a charade,' the Secretary-General griped, suspecting it was really called 'Shaw Trial'.

Berman's caper may have been the sole creative result of these cuts, but his revue reinforced how effortlessly the Council could alienate both radicals and conservatives, for Shaw also received a very public and somewhat crocodile-tear plea from the Arts Minister, Norman St John-Stevas, to preserve 'the broad base of theatrical endeavour in this country'. The Council took this to mean the nationals and the reps; support for all scales of touring took a dive of 45 per cent between the touring and drama departments from 1979 to 1983. The Old Vic and its Prospect touring wing were wound up, leading the executives of the four main number one regional theatres to write bitterly to the Council of 'the desperate shortage of product of good quality and appeal to enable the major touring theatres to continue'. A leader in *The Times* sighed in disbelief that:

> over the past few years the Council has spent large sums, and encouraged local authorities to spend even more, on modernising some of the main provincial theatres. Having helped create this, it is now under pressure because there are not enough high quality productions.

As Merseyside's Peter Booth put it, 'The words *chickens* and *roost* sprang to mind.'

This void galvanised the veteran director Anthony Quayle, who had run Stratford very successfully in the fifties by inducing stars to shine there. He promptly set up the Compass Theatre Company to fill the touring holes, for the noble reason that, 'I am distressed by the divisions in society . . . and a company that is not based in London can create a sense that it belongs to everyone'. Or no one, as the Council suspected. Compass pushed plays covered in dust – Garrick, Pinero, William Douglas Home. Yet it provided what the host theatres and their most regular attenders wanted, crimplene and Quality Street as they were. From this point on the congenital failure of the Council to determine whether it was really in business to assist creativity and 'respond to the future' or to develop access and keep old things open was utterly exposed. After all this time it had simply ended up recreating with public funds the Binkie Beaumont provincial tour, but without the power to assert his artistic clout, the Council being a facilitator rather than a producer. And while Beaumont had been in business to make money, the Council was compelled to spend it.

Had the Council not made the mistake of devising a touring unit detached from the drama department, this wouldn't have happened, of course. A couple of touring reports were commissioned in 1985, but they were produced to refine the *status quo*, not to challenge it. Yet this was only one part of the acute dramatic dilemma now facing the Council. The local authorities were in deep trouble, too. A Labour-led city like Manchester had reaped a rich harvest from the seedlings of the seventies. It had two number ones, two civic theatres (the Library and the Wythenshawe Forum), a major rep (the Royal Exchange) and a youth theatre (Contact). Now fighting a tight Tory Government, it was desperately over-extended and it became clear, after Thatcher's second election win in June 1983, that she was going to abolish the Greater Manchester Council along with the six other metropolitan author-ities around the country, including Greater London's.

In October 1983, with Tories Rees-Mogg and Rittner now in place, the Council attempted to make some sense of this looming disaster by retreating to a hotel in the middle of the Yorkshire moors. Out came 'The Glory of the Garden – A Strategy for a Decade'. 'We are not people who believe that London always knows best,' wrote the former editor of *The* (London) *Times*. He did so from conviction, but also perhaps because a Commons select committee on Education, Science and the Arts had told him to spend more dosh in the regions.

The first part of 'The Glory of the Garden' identified 'thirteen strategic areas for a rolling programme of regional development'. They were in fact eleven principal cities – the seven 'metros' including London, plus Bristol, Leicester, Nottingham and Southampton – a radius of thirty miles drawn around them (fifty around London), with a finger wafted vaguely above Devon and another over East Anglia (or Siberia as it was known to the Council). Then, without naming names exactly, the drama section focused on the reps that existed in those cities, adding Plymouth's Theatre Royal and sort of Ipswich, sort of Norwich. They were expected high-falutinly to 'bear a much greater responsibility for ensuring the theatrical experience of the wider community in the whole of their regions'. They should be magnets, emanating artistic forces reaching thirty miles around them.

Not only would they put on their own shows and tour them around their patch, they'd take in others, too, and not only drama but dance as well. They'd expand their seasons of studio work for new writing and house independent small-scale companies to help them do that. Theatre-in-education and young people's theatre work would be enhanced to cover the region around them. Overall, the 'Garden' plan was ambitious but reasonable, resourceful, politic, and altogether Disneyland. 'They were treating theatres like fucking arts centres. A producing house and a receiving house are Chalk and Cheeseman,' cracked a former theatre head. 'And they were virtually telling the other twenty reps to fuck off and die.'

The trouble is that the Council's panels were filling up with a new generation of arts-centre types who saw the reps as tiresome throwbacks, working by habitual and uninspired practices. Rather like an old print union on a daily paper, they were hostile to self-evident improvement. Local audiences, which the reps were increasingly losing, expected more from their theatres than a duteous play every other month. In his notable 1984 tirade against the theatre scene, *All Together Now*, Steven Gooch cattily listed the identikit annual programmes the reps set up 'to guarantee the 60-per-cent-box-office capacity approved by the Arts Council': one Shakespeare, one Restoration comedy, one Chekhov or Ibsen 'or foreign at any rate', one slightly more obscure classical play recently done by the National or the RSC, one 'modern' play (maybe *Godot* or Ayckbourn), one old favourite, the Christmas panto and one other.

School exam boards usually set the 'one other' – if it wasn't already the annual Shakespeare. Reps were playing safe for two reasons. First, the move to four-weekly runs of plays had improved standards of performance and offered longer rehearsal periods. Yet the risk of running a new or unusual play for twenty nights, or whatever it was, multiplied by 60 per cent of a 700-capacity (that is, seeking 8,500 people to see it), meant that the reps simply had to 'play safe – safe play', as Hugh Willatt put it. Secondly, some of the reps' artistic directors were useless gits – sluggish, uninspired, certainly uninformed of advances abroad, and set against experiment almost as an ethical stand.

To lure these (twelve, thirteen, fourteen) reps to be more adventurous, the Council waved a wad of cash in each of their undeclared faces – £250,000 down and more of the same if their local authorities matched it; that first £750,000 would represent £1.2 million nowadays. This was called 'challenge funding': 'This principle lies at the heart, for example, of the Council's hopes for the future development of its major drama clients in the regions.' Several others who weren't in the 'strategic areas' were now mere distractions to the plan and they were devolved to their nearest Regional Arts Association.

However, in common with nearly everything else connected with 'The Glory of the Garden', Rees-Mogg's money tree failed to bear much fruit. Its bait to reconstruct the involvement of local government didn't work, particularly with the seven metros that were busy digging fiscal graves on Thatcher's orders in advance of her 1986 pogrom. The abolition, or 'gravestone', grant of £4

million from West Yorkshire laggardly paid for a new Leeds Playhouse, which opened in 1990 and was named the West Yorkshire
Playhouse in memory of its money, which would be a bit like
calling Nottingham's development the Gas Fund Theatre.

Though the Arts Council's 'parity drive' flopped, it became a
concern of the drama director between 1986 and 1994, Dr Ian
Brown, who – in the view of some of his panellists – allowed it to
dominate the agenda. Brown could argue that he was only obeying
orders. His instructions came from the 'Garden' and the subsequent Cork Report of 1986, for which he was the secretary. Over
several years drama director John Faulkner and his successor from
1983 to 1985, Dickon Reed, had pressed for a full drama review,
the last one having been Williams' of 1970. It was only when weeds
surfaced where Rees-Mogg had desired a 'Garden' of buds that
the Council agreed to a major study of theatre needs. It was
brought on by a number of unsettling cases, one such being in
Manchester, where the Royal Exchange had supposedly been
promised an extra £1.3 million through a parity agreement
between the Arts Council and the Greater Manchester Council.
The theatre began to make expansive plans, but abruptly received
a letter from Rittner calling off the deal, due, it was alleged, to
GMC dithering. The theatre's manager claimed, however, that
'Rittner told us to ignore the letter ... They wanted to put
pressure on GMC to come up with additional funding.' None
emerged as pledged.

Around the same time, a new generation of hard-left
councillors in Bristol (Bristol Old Vic), Islington (Almeida),
Camden (Shaw) and Liverpool (Playhouse) sharply questioned
their theatres' core programmes, asking instead for local plays and
multi-ethnic productions which 'celebrated the community',
which several of the directors who ran the places couldn't fully
comprehend. A director in Bristol tried hard to comply, but
resigned when he apparently found himself caught between
conflicting advice from the Arts Council and the local Labour
Party. Kilburn's Tricycle under Nicholas Kent and Stratford East
under Philip Hedley, however, succeeded exceptionally in
meeting the challenge, but then they had a 'community' of eight
million to play to.

Thus, by fiddling with the funding system and forcing cuts,
Thatcherism had exposed extreme divisions and hostilities in
local government. As for their arts provision, the debate had
moved on a stage from the fifties. It was no longer a question of

whether to build a civic theatre, but instead what such an amenity should be doing for the locals who paid for it. Both right and left now believed that theatre existed to 'celebrate' culture, rather than confront or probe the state of play. Politicians of the right favoured enduring native values and remembrances of national history; those of the left a healing community spirit, one which accented and reconciled what had once been marginal, for which issue-based plays had to be composed. We can now see that these were emanations of rejoicerism, that chauvinist trend which stemmed from the episode of the Falklands War in 1982, when Mrs Thatcher ordered the country to 'Rejoice!'.

In came Sir Kenneth Cork. The first accountant after Keynes to have his likeness hung in the National Portrait Gallery, Cork ran a family firm specialising in insolvency. He was the liquidator who mopped up when John Bloom's washing-machine empire rinsed its last in 1964, and the growing calls on his skills as British industries fell to pieces led to the lord mayoral chain of the City of London in 1978. A little like Keynes, Cork sought relief from the carefree amusements of accounting in the tedium of theatre life. He became an RSC governor and chairman (1975–1978) and found City sponsorship for its Barbican project.

His Arts Council study 'Theatre is for All – Report of the Enquiry into Professional Theatre in England 1986', is a fine piece of work, apart from its ugly cover. Cork was assisted by experts like actress Diana Rigg – Emma Peel to his John Steed – and the critic Michael Billington, who'd worked at Lincoln's Theatre Royal in the sixties. Yes, it was a fine piece of work. And a useless one.

It failed to deal with what this rickety stack of theatres and companies was now supposed to be about. Starting with Williams' 1970 report, it looked at the subsequent developments, reported on budget cutbacks and tut-tutted. Cork then came up with eight main recommendations, and here the reader is invited to consider whatever became of these moderately inspiring ideas:

- Six regional reps be designated as national companies.
- A system of national new writing theatres.
- The National Theatre and the RSC to take a larger responsibility for touring.
- Drama school students to get mandatory grants.
- A theatre development fund of £5 million.
- A new capital investment fund for buildings.
- Drama panel to be elevated to board status.

- A 1 per cent levy on BBC and ITV to support new drama projects.

As a former drama panellist commented:

Cork was an odd one. It was like watching a comet zipping out of the blue and over your head to some other part of space. But the Cork people did have a go at constructing a sort of system. It was just impossible to turn the gooey mess that the Arts Council had got itself caught up in in the eighties into this lovely structure in Cork's head.

John Faulkner agreed:

I set the terms for Cork with my last chairman, the actor Tony Church. We wanted a real debate, not a sort of Polyfilla thing. The drama issue had become so knotted and entangled, and the Cork report worked best as a response to 'The Glory of the Garden'. It showed it up. And it has to be said that Cork was a wonderful thorn in the Council's side, because people would tell him that this and that was really Government policy, and he would simply pop off to the people at the top and find out whether that was true.

In a marvellous passage, 'National and regional balance', Cork wrote:

We have analysed the effects of the first year of 'Glory of the Garden' allocations. These show that the proposed shift of funding from London to the regions has not yet led to the envisaged spread of benefit in the regions. On the contrary, non-'Glory of the Garden' companies are in fact marginally worse off in real terms than they were before . . . Overall, the effect of the policy is not yet either to improve the general lot of theatres in the regions nor to develop a great deal of new activity.

By 1988 resolve had evaporated, and the Policy Studies Institute issued a glum report that ' "Glory of the Garden" has failed to make the spread of resources more even or equitable.'

Now we might see how far it is true that the Cork Report secretary, Ian Brown, allegedly drove this cause into the dust when he took over as drama director in 1988. Whether lack of cash was truly the issue, rather than stale vision, artistic directors could now use subsidy as a convincing excuse. Cork reported a real decline of

5 per cent in the drama department's funding of theatre between the start and the middle of the decade, adding that the National and the RSC now took half of the money available. Hugh Willatt had warned back in the fifties about the point of no return ('where the charge of the building can only be offset by increased subsidy. In the end it's a simple economic issue, which artistic arguments can't address'). However, John Doyle of Liverpool's Everyman explained to the *Guardian* in 1990 what happens conversely: 'Your product erodes. The one flexible area of a budget is the artists themselves and the product you put on stage.' David Thacker, then director of the Young Vic, agreed that if you asked him to name the ten plays he'd most like to do, 'I bet you that nine I wouldn't be able to do because we couldn't afford that number of actors. And so that has to be the most serious effect on our policy.'

In Willatt's terms, Britain's theatres had been led by their boards behind a barrier where artistic policy no longer imposed itself. Around this time, for instance, Nottingham Playhouse unhealthily placed an administrator as 'executive director' above an artistic director. Adventurous stage directors bypassed the crisis completely by moving into opera houses, which offered big budgets and international opportunities. And although Ian Brown did his best to rectify the failed implementation of fair proposals in 'Garden' and Cork, the degree of sensitive negotiation and trade-offs the Council and the local authorities had to undertake (much of it fruitless) led to a measure of grapevine paranoia unparalleled in the Council's history.

Brown had been a lecturer at Crewe and Alsager College. One of his panel chairs said:

> He was a bit of a didact, and he would walk into a local authority dangling his scales. He expected a parity of grants between the town hall and the Arts Council, which, given the cuts and capping they faced year by year, was wholly impractical. He saw himself, though, as the architect of a dramatic landscape. He also wrote plays.

The crunch came in May 1993, when the Council retreated to Woodstock, but not for 'three days of peace and music'. It was the spruce Oxfordshire Woodstock where Lord Palumbo, like Country Joe and the Fish, sort of hollered 'Gimme an F, gimme a U, gimme a C, gimme a K,' at the drama panel's chairman, Brian

Rix, who dropped his trousers in response. This retreat was labelled, with rare irony, an 'artistic review'. The arguments were about cutting cash in advance of the disappointing government grant the following year, not about the state of creativity. Prior to this fateful weekend, a number of advisory meetings had been held and at the session for the drama panel, members were asked to speculate on the priority of the theatres it would like to develop. From the vague waffle that followed, drama officers considered the bottom ten – or twelve, it's never been clear – of the panel's conjectural catalogue to be the most 'vulnerable'.

It's vital to recall here that the Council had whittled down its roster of reps from fifty-four in 1983 (thirty-seven regional, seventeen London) to thirty by 1993 (nineteen regional, eleven London). In devolving to the Regional Arts Associations those reps not much rated, the drastic cuts it was toying with would be inflicted on clients the Council had once prized, while those mediocrities it had relegated would survive. Here was one of several incongruities and ironies spinning round this barmy episode.

This Woodstock meeting under Palumbo resembled a kind of jolly public-school debate. Department directors were asked to bid for funds. Sue Hoyle, the dance director, seemed to come off best and Brown worst. Instead of forfeiting a possible cut of £640,000, drama lost £1.4 million, and suddenly the cobbled-up tally of susceptible theatres became an active hit list, though there was never at any time a printed inventory. Only seven of the ten – or twelve – were ever known: four regional (Bristol Old Vic, Coventry Belgrade, Plymouth Theatre Royal, Oldham Coliseum); and three London (Hammersmith Lyric, Watford Palace, Greenwich).

Brian Rix resigned, complaining of the Council's 'fatuous so-called policies and strategies and visions'; probably the first farce he'd turned down. The rest of the panel let it be known that they were going to discuss the issue by meeting 'away from the Arts Council building', which, according to Paul Allen, Rix's replacement, 'put the wind up the executive', and is a device future panellists might care to use one rainy day. Allen's panel insisted that any cut should be spread evenly across all clients. Meanwhile, the press had got hold of the 'list' from an anonymous circulated account of the issue that came their way in July. At a meeting held in the National that month, a gathering of the country's major directors and managers passed 'an expression of no confidence' in the drama department. Stephen Daldry for the Royal Court thundered that theatres were now under attack on two fronts, by: 'an Arts Council that is collaborating in its own suicide, and a Government that is not committed to supporting the cultural life of this country.'

Daldry was sharp in seeing separate fronts, for the imprecise but common opinion at the time was that Palumbo's Council and the Tory Government were as one. But when, in the Commons on 12 July, MP and former RSC actress Glenda Jackson tackled the number two Minister for Heritage, Ian Sproat, about the Council's 'stated policy of closing ten regional theatres', Sproat told her to complain to the Secretary-General, not to him. As shadow Heritage Minister of the time, Ann Clwyd took it up more forcefully on 21 July with Sproat's suave boss Peter Brooke, but Brooke quite rightly ran a mile:

Mrs Ann Clwyd: Has the Secretary of State no sense of shame that this could mean the dismemberment of the system of regional theatres? Is he aware that regional theatres are the backbone of what has made British theatre among the best in the world?

Mr Brooke: The honorable lady makes a series of references to regional theatres . . . It is for the Arts Council to make those decisions. The Arts Council made its decision at Woodstock. It is right that it should stand up and defend and explain them. If I may say so, the honorable lady is threatening an immediate invasion of the arm's-length principle if she wishes me to substitute my judgment for that of the Arts Council.

Following a strong letter in August to *The Times* from the retired Willatt and Linklater, in which they questioned whether the Woodstock cut was not 'a breach of trust' in the Council's bond with local authorities, the Council met in September and abandoned the list that didn't exist. Paul Allen points out that 'they never actually reversed their decision over the cut, but they kept finding little ways of putting money back again'. The *Daily Mail* called the episode 'a grotesque, silly-season pantomime' for which, it hammed, 'the foulest torture devised in a ghoulish Renaissance shocker is not too good for these Arts Council miscreants'. Brown found himself de-Corked, eventually resigned, and moved back to counselling students rather than leisure officers. Three months later the orchestra fiasco added to the Council's public shame. It looked to all the world exposed in the very position that Joan Littlewood had described: with its head up its arse.

Both the theatre and the orchestra disasters of 1993 had sprung from the Council's genuine need to impose radical solutions on perennial problems. The drama department wanted to turn back to the days of Williams and pretend that all these annoying reps had never existed. It did so for itself in 1994, simply by handing the remaining reps on its books over to the Regional Arts Boards – except for the Royal Court, to which it added (for no good reason that springs to mind) that mortuary for musicals, the Donmar Warehouse in deluxe Covent Garden. Though it's hard to make a firm comparison, the reps now get less money under the regional boards than they did under the Arts Council (1983 was the last time that they all appeared in the accounts together, and we should remind ourselves that clients thought it a bad year):

		£	Value
1983–1984	Building-based companies	9,127,508	15,485,000
1994–1995	Building-based companies	14,666,649	–

This devolution complements what the Council did in 1951, when it decided to disembarrass itself of direct provision. A pertinent move, then, because nowadays the lists of plays put on by a variety of theatres rather resemble the old Beaumont repertory, but this time it's Shaw, Priestley, Coward and Rattigan wrapped by directors in inverted commas of irony. While these exhumations can be justified as 'rediscovering Britain's dramatic heritage' (thank you, the Arts Council's National Strategy of 1992), it is surely not how Shaw or Priestley would have wished this century to end.

Equally, some reps have now got together to co-produce, sometimes together, sometimes with commercial producers, and best of all with theatres on mainland Europe. However, certain directors will not be pleased to learn that one respected foreign producer says of them:

Unfortunately they can only afford to participate in what I call my B list of projects. The nearest my A list comes to Britain is probably Amsterdam, Rotterdam or Brussels. I am not proud to say this, and I think it's a pity that Britain has such money problems. But we all have problems, you know. It's a matter of how you deal with them. There seem to be too many *little* problems in the way for British theatres to see a way ahead.

Those little problems start with the drama department. It now runs a budget of twenty-two cat's hair divisions, plus one category of allocation cleverly called 'unallocated' (six clients were funded in that in 1996). On viewing this depressing, red-tape segmentation, one can quite appreciate why Brian Rix pulled his pants up and bounded out. The department could help the country's drama scene by stirring all its money in one big pot and starting again, advised this time by practising artists and producers (none of them from the West End, no more than a third from the reps or a third from Oxbridge). That wouldn't solve a leading problem, however, namely that – let's be frank – the development of reps has been a thorough mess. There's not enough money around to let them do what they ought, and some of them have lost the artistic nous to know what they should be doing anyway.

Funding channels are now split between fourteen organisations (ACE, ten RABs, the three provincial councils). This makes a solution to the basic problem nigh impossible, however 'integrated' their limbs, and that problem remains the same as it was five decades back – buildings or productions? Does the money go best through writers and performers, their shows, the venues or touring schemes? Ignoring for a moment the howling of herds of actors, to whom the nightly drop of a curtain is more terrible than the shutting of a hundred hospitals, a number of this country's reps are artistically barren and could hand over to bingo without much of a fuss from the rate-payers around them. It's a shame, but at least with bingo there's a chance of taking something valuable home.

Any hopes the theatre profession may have held that the Arts Council might at least sort out its own snarls to their benefit were dashed by the release of its drama policy in late October 1996. The date of its publication is significant – two weeks before the Cabinet met to discuss the following year's budget which would determine the Arts Council's grant. It is believed that the policy document was not really written for drama people, but for a number of key MPs in those marginal constituencies which housed a rep, including Heritage Secretary Virginia Bottomley herself. Mary Allen, Secretary-General from 1994 to 1997, suggested this when she said at the policy's launch, 'If we get a standstill grant there will be temporary closures for some theatres. We want £6 million extra for drama alone.' This is not a figure mentioned in the policy document itself, by the way, which is nothing more than twenty-six pages of waffle. There is not a firm decision to be found in it, except that 'this strategy cannot be achieved on current resources'. One wonders why it doesn't say what can be done, given that both the Government and the Opposition had already told the Council it wouldn't get more money.

When in January 1945 the Arts Council said it wanted to see 'a repertory theatre in every town in Britain' it was an absurdly ambitious proposal, but a clear one. Now it says, 'Every community – whether a conurbation or a rural setting – should have access to quality theatre created by artists of integrity and vision.' This is ambling about in a whimsical landscape. It goes on to list nine basic principles, roaming from fuzzy inclusiveness – 'Everyone who receives public funding has a responsibility to encourage diversity in artists and audiences' – to dodgy prescriptions of the kind hidden inside this opening phrase: 'Drama should be emotionally and intellectually inspiring and educational in the broadest sense.' Should there not have been a comma after 'inspiring'?

Most likely the Council is reduced to fumbling because it has completely lost control of the various elements that form the ragged patchwork of drama provision. The policy concentrates on issues of 'integration' between itself and the ten Regional Arts Boards on which it dumped all the reps – it's like a soft-worded memo to regional clerks from central office, trying hard to avoid offence. Thelma Holt, the chair of drama at the time of writing, admitted that when her panel called for a policy review, 'we were at the time welcoming integration ... but anxious about the sudden delegation of our theatres throughout the country, as we were not wholly confident that a mechanism was in place to serve them'.

She has little right to be confident now. Her document concedes:

In 1994–5 real spending on drama projects was three-quarters what it had been in 1986–7 ... The 18 regional theatres funded by the RABs suffered an overall reduction of 3.46% in real terms ... a fall of 13% in audiences . . . sponsorship and donations fell by 32% . . . 33 companies have accumulated deficits totalling £6.58 million in 1995.

None of this can it address, it admits. Nor does it seem to be looking any more to the local authorities to help with these appalling problems, even though that's where some solutions lie. Yet at the same time it contains a deeply creepy warning for the reps:

> Where there is an agreed loss of artistic creativity, *or a failure to develop work of relevance within the immediate locality* [author's italics], then the funding system and the theatre should together consider whether a change of artistic direction is required.

That seems to be all that's left of half a century of dealings with local government.

Fifty years ago the Council was given the opportunity to work with local authorities and create a healthy, coherent drama scene for the whole of the country. At the time, Council member Lady Keynes told Chairman Pooley, 'If I want to see some good theatre, I'm afraid I ferry over to France,' to which Pooley replied, 'Well, if I have my way, madam, not for long you won't!'

Fifty years later a former drama panellist admitted, 'If I want to see theatre that's insightful, I go to Belgium, France, Holland. I don't go to Liverpool, Nottingham, Hammersmith.' It seems that Pooley never had his way, while our neighbours had Pooleys who did. Yet the 1996 drama policy starts with this: 'Just as German culture has found its highest expression in its musical tradition — or the Italian Renaissance in its visual arts – so the English genius has been seen, above all, on the stage.' Poor old Büchner, Kleist, Wedekind, Brecht, Handke, Müller, Bernhard, Ibsen, Strindberg, Chekhov, Gorky, Beckett, Cocteau, Artaud, Genet, Duras, Arrabal, Lorca, Pirandello, De Filippo and scores of others, all wasting their time. And poor old Turner, Bacon, Moore, Freud, Britten, Cardew, Greenaway, Loach, George (and Gilbert), wasting theirs.

Chapter 21

Get thee to a nunnery

London: 1965–2000

Three Americans gathered in the offices of the National Theatre on London's South Bank in April last year. They were not visiting stars waiting for the curtain to be raised, for it was early afternoon on a Saturday and the place was virtually deserted.

Ooh-er. With this sinister start a 1986 *Sunday Times* report suggested that the National Theatre and the RSC had been driven into disrepute. What transpired inflicted damage on those companies, on the men who ran them and on the Arts Council over an issue that has never been resolved.

Halfway through Mrs Thatcher's second term of office, the Sunday paper's editor, Andrew Neil, had set his Insight team on Peter Hall and Trevor Nunn, by that time the respective directors of the National and the Royal Shakespeare Company. Neil's Dobermann hacks dealt more normally with gun-runners and drug barons, but Insight devoted a full page of the issue dated 29 June 1986 to suggesting 'how both men have managed to amass fortunes while their theatres remain dependent on heavy public subsidies'. Under a photo of Hall and Nunn chortling merrily in Glyndebourne's sunny garden ran the headline: 'Laughing All The Way To The Bank'. It was never made clear whether the bank in mind was South or Midland. Not surprisingly, writs flew.

The reporters castigated Hall for the money he collected on Peter Shaffer's *Amadeus* and for the millions he was likely to make on the next Shaffer, *Yonadab*. They also calculated that he gained more than the National Theatre did on these shows. Nunn was reproved over *Les Misérables* and accused of moonlighting to make fortunes out of *Starlight Express*, *Cats* and *Chess* when he was supposedly running the Royal Shakespeare Company. In both cases, the Insight team got a number of their facts wrong. They certainly seemed to sow confusion with their figures. To cap it all, *Yonadab* was a terrible flop and no one but the critics made any money on it.

As for Insight's estimations, they claimed that Peter Hall earned £2 million from *Amadeus* on Broadway while the National took only half a million. He crossly replied the following week that he made only £720,000, while the National's share was double that. It transpired that Insight had been looking at the complex web of percentages by which theatreland operates and bamboozles itself internally. There are some percentages that various people like directors get before the show has paid for itself, and different percentages after it has (if it does), plus a share of the net profits. In addition there are deals for transfers, tours, film rights and the change that fell out of punters' pockets in the stalls for all we know. Hall took his standard 4 per cent of gross box-office takings pre-profit and 5 per cent post; this compared to 0.9 per cent pre and 1.035 per cent post for the National's share on Broadway. He confirmed his own figures to the press, though the National kept its books tightly shut.

While it's easy to understand how the National earned more than Peter Hall out of the entire undertaking of *Amadeus*, from the South Bank to a cinema near you, the figures didn't seem to add up on Broadway, Insight's bedrock. Hall's right of reply the following week did little to pacify public unease; a bonus of £700,000 (£1 million today) sounds lush even to readers of the *Sunday Times*. When he claimed he only had 'a small house in Chelsea, about £75,000 in the bank and a salary of £50,000', he was reminded about the business company he ran, his grace-and-favour Glyndebourne home and his salary as artistic director there. Of the country estate he replied airily, 'It's not an asset, it's a *facility*.'

Hall subsequently issued a writ for libel but never carried it through because, he admitted with a touch of irony, he couldn't afford to. Nunn pursued an action for some years which was settled out of court in February 1991 after the *Sunday Times* agreed to clarify some points it had raised in the original article. However mistaken Insight's particulars were, the issue did damage at three levels: first, to the public's understanding of subsidy and the working of the theatres that received it; second, to the relation between the two nationals and the rest of the aided theatre world; and third, to the rapport between the Council and the country's leading directors. Commenting on the article, Hall declared: 'I'm not saying that the Minister and the Arts Council set it up, but they are certainly taking advantage of what is happening.'

There's no evidence that either the Arts Minister, the likeable Richard Luce, or the Council took advantage of any kind. No sudden removal of subsidy followed, no 'ten minutes to clear your desk, Sir Peter, if you can remember where it is' stuff. It seems that Hall may have been catching up with a battle a year old which he'd already lost. The minister he had in mind was the previous one, a certain Lord Gowrie, against whom there was no evidence, either. Hall's feeling of betrayal came from a dip in the annual grant that arrived a year before, in April 1985, followed by a subsequent standstill. This shift had been flagged eleven months earlier in 'The Glory of the Garden'. It was argued in that very public document that the National wasn't doing the level of countrywide touring that it ought and that the Council would 'challenge' it to find new money from local authorities in the regions, whose cash the Council would match. Incidentally, the National's forgoing of this mischievous offer assisted a cheeky and popular small-scale touring group called the Not the National Theatre Company.

Why hadn't Hall fought the critical mood of the Council as it was known prior to the Ilkley retreat in the summer of 1983? Possibly because he was busy in Bayreuth, directing Wagner's *Ring*. Why was he so riled by the 1985 budget? Maybe because the National was carrying an extra half-million deficit thanks chiefly to his troubled *Jean Seberg*. He'd tried to overcome matters by calling for an uplift of £1.5 million, but got only £136,000.

For the record, the National's grants increased in cash terms (1986 and 1987 were the standstill years), but fell gradually in relation to the total money the Government gave the Council to disburse, as the following figures show. Yet this internal downturn in the Council's priorities was kept in line with inflation, if that makes sense. In other words, the National was not the victim of careless calculations, it was simply failing to meet imposed policy criteria; the consistency of the percentages between the cash figure and the value nowadays demonstrates this. The figures here exclude the annual grants the National acquired from its own local authority, the GLC. As a control sum in this rather intricate exercise, the last grant of Callaghan's 1979 Labour Government is included at the top of the table. Its presence shows that the fall of the National Theatre in the Council's priorities was a slow but consistent one.

Year	Government grant	Value today	National Theatre	Value today	% value
1979–1980	£63.1m	£160.5m	£4,806,500	£12.2m	7.62%
1983–1984	£96m	£162.9m	£6,869,446	£11.65m	7.15%
1984–1985	£101.9m	£164.6m	£7,005,870	£11.3m	6.86%
1985–1986	£106.05m	£161.5m	£6,995,200	£10.65m	6.6%
1986–1987	£135.6m	£199.7m	£7,811,400	£11.5m	5.77%
1987–1988	£139.3m	£197.0m	£7,811,400	£11.05m	5.61%
1988–1989	£152.4m	£205.5m	£7,917,000	£10.7m	5.22%
1989–1990	£155.5m	£194.5m	£8,060,500	£10.08m	5.18%

There's little question that the Tories were gunning for Hall, and the *Sunday Times* exposé appeared to form part of whatever plot there was. Nunn was an added extra in all this, but no less affected, as we'll see. Hall was quite open in telling the public that he used to support Labour but that he had voted for Mrs Thatcher in 1979, and he was equally candid in saying that he regretted doing so afterwards. 'Have your cake and eat it' seemed to be his motto. Tories were particularly irritated by Hall's press conference in the National Theatre's foyer on 7 February 1985, in advance of the dissatisfying grant for the next financial year. As Hall had to stand on a coffee table to command attention, it's known as the 'Coffee Table Speech', and no doubt one day they'll put a plaque on the thing and nail it to the foyer wall.

From this table he claimed:

In the old days the Arts Council used to fight the government, and the Minister used to try to get more money for the arts. Now the Minister executes Treasury policy and the Arts Council meekly follows suit. If that continues we shall not have a subsidised theatre . . . I believe the Arts Council has betrayed the National Theatre.

This heartfelt speech even seeped through to the tabloids, though they treated it as one more arty-farty mope.

What brought this quarrel to a climax was a meeting with the Earl of Gowrie, who was the most Thatcherite of the four arts ministers some suggested she kept in her handbag like sweets. To Gowrie's credit it has to be said that he had little time for pathetic whingers snivelling about money. This makes his resignation just seven months after the encounter with Hall all the stranger. He sulked to the press that he couldn't continue to be Arts Minister as he wasn't getting paid enough. But Gowrie was more gung-ho and 'come off it' then than he became later as the Council's Chairman, and Hall was horrified to be told by this minister that if he needed more money then there was plenty about in the City, and if there were problems with his South Bank *facility* there were loads of empty theatres across the river he could put his plays in.

Probably Hall and his National Theatre chairman, Lord Rayne (who headed a property company), had hoped they could negotiate their grant directly with the Government, which was a fashionable thought of the big companies at the time. A report on the Royal Shakespeare Company by a senior civil servant, Clive Priestley, in October 1983 said (startlingly, given the atmosphere of the period) that it deserved a bigger grant, and possibly one direct from the Treasury. This irked the Arts Council and the National no end, the latter because nobody was saying the same on its behalf. The National's board swiftly commissioned a similar audit from Priestley's boss at the Efficiency Unit, Lord Rayner (Marks & Spencer's chairman and plainly no relation to Lord Rayne). So when Hall spat venom at the Arts Council from his coffee table, it may have been part of a campaign to protect the big companies from the implications of 'Garden' devolution.

When the Insight team made its claims a year later, Hall and Nunn had every reason to suspect they had been brought on by vindictiveness 'upstairs'. Yet the article wasn't about their hostility to the Council or the Government. It gnawed on a bone of contention that was still lying around from the days of Binkie Beaumont: that seedy-looking link between taxes and profit, subsidy and commerce. A key difference now was that the anti-gay brigade couldn't smear their sexual bigotry around the issue, for Hall and Nunn had wives and kids – lots of them. At the time Hall was on the third of four marriages with five children in tow (now six). Nunn's tally is three wives and four children.

Hall has always been a family man in the sense that he has

gathered around him and championed a loyal group. His talented children have found work for themselves through his freelance production company, but some of the luckiest students alive were those who crossed his path at Cambridge University when he studied there in the early fifties. In his brightly written and deftly evasive autobiography of 1993, *Making an Exhibition of Myself*, he listed the university chums who would later benefit from working with him – directors Peter Wood and Toby Robertson, designer Timothy O'Brien, hammy musician Raymond Leppard and the donnish Shakespearean scholar John Barton. All men, by the way. He did find time to write one sentence in his book about three women theatre directors whose names he could recall (page 316).

Peter's friends were welcome at his RSC; Barton is still a solid if not stable fixture there. No wonder actors in the early days said that once Hall took over at Stratford in 1960 it was like going back to university. That tone endured – partly because Barton stayed on as associate director – when Hall slowly started to release himself from the helm in 1968, as though transposing himself by degrees to take over his funding rival, the National Theatre, which he finally acquired from a grateful but guarded Laurence Olivier in 1973.

Hall certainly deserved the job, for his handling of the RSC was terrific, quite extraordinary. He took that almighty risk in 1960, for instance, spending the Stratford reserves to anchor the company in the West End and win over the Arts Council, for ever and ever. Hall and Barton tampered with Shakespeare's texts to offer the public a fresh coherence by means of cycles of plays, like *The Wars of the Roses* for the 400th birthday in 1964, or *The Hollow Crown*. He built a brilliant ensemble company, one avid to reform verse-speaking. He supported Peter Brook's last experiments in England, from his 'Theatre of Cruelty' *Marat-Sade* to the white box *A Midsummer Night's Dream*, both preserved on film. He's directed hits and flops by turns, but he's never offered the public anything so crass or superficial as some directors supply at the RSC today.

In the life of the Arts Council there's been no one in his own or any other artform the equal of Hall in the way he's blended creative output, political ambition, practical scholarship and unrelenting celebrity status (at twenty-six he was Leslie Caron's husband) to refashion this country's drama scene. Of course, a stage director is not truly at the artistic front line like a playwright (Ralph Richardson said a director's job was to 'point me to the centre of the stage and shine a big light on me'), but try to name a famous visual artist who's moulded a national gallery from scratch, or a leading film director in this country who's changed the production and distribution scene for the better, and the nearest you'll come to it is conductor Simon Rattle's transformations at Birmingham. So it's quite astonishing, ten years down the line, to find Nunn standing at Hall's right hand like the king's anointed cub in a Shakespearean chronicle.

Both came from Suffolk working-class families, both went to Cambridge, where they acted and directed. Both married actresses – both more than one – whom they directed. Both have staged fine work and tosh by turns (notably dismal musicals). Both have led the RSC and (once Nunn took up his job there in September 1997) both went on to run the National. Both groom Shakespearean beards of a morning. Come to that, both have forenames of two syllables followed by surnames of four letters, the last two of which repeat. In name they sound, in fact, like characters by Samuel Beckett. Quite uncanny.

	Hall (born 1930)		Nunn (born 1940)
1960–1968	RSC managing director	1964–1968	RSC assistant director
1968–1973	RSC associate director	1968–1978	RSC Artistic Director
1973–1980	NT director	1978–1986	RSC joint artistic
1980–1988	NT joint director		director
1988–1996	Freelance director	1987–1997	Freelance director
1996–	Old Vic director	1997–	NT director

What interested *The Sunday Times*, however, was less these parallels than the commercial ones. To make the point it did – that directors earn their living from directing plays, and make more money in the commercial arena than in the subsidised one, even when shows cross over from one to the other – is less than Insight-ful. Pasting this revelation onto the smiles of the two national company chiefs led the public's gaze away from the more curious issue of why their theatre companies were keen to take popular work out of their own houses and into venues owned by other people. And by concentrating on 'Broadway hits' it misrepresented the record of the duo.

Nunn has certainly made a fortune from *Cats* (1981), *Starlight Express* (1984), *Les Misérables* (1985, the only RSC-related show of these), *Chess* (1986), *Aspects of Love* (1989) and *Sunset Boulevard* (1993) – four of those when he was co-director of the RSC. But Hall's record with musicals is terrible: *Via Galactica* (1972), *Jean Seberg* (1983), *Born Again* (1990). He's done much better at opera, though he's not the international leader he's often assumed to be. Both Hall and Nunn possess breadth, which is a very welcome quality in a boss of a national body, but in terms of calibre they're frankly shadows of foreign talents like Chéreau, Mnouchkine or the late Antoine Vitez in France, Elizabeth LeCompte in the States, or Peymann and Stein in Germany. Insight was really identifying a trend and an aspiration which started not in the boardrooms of the National or the RSC, but with the Arts Council.

When Goodman and Tony Field finally activated the Theatre Investment Fund in 1976, they were supported by the new Secretary-General, Roy Shaw, and the Labour Government, swayed by Goodman. The TIF helped to address four concerns: first, the mushy mood of regret whenever one passes a theatre that's 'dark'; second, the desire to establish a new generation of producers in the Beaumont mould who would keep these big theatres open; third, the need for all that good work being done in the regions to be seen in London; fourth, the populist notion that musicals are the operas of the working class (which brings to mind Christie's *Volksoper*), and consequently the Council has every right to support good examples and productions of the genre.

Tony Field remembers:

> We were down to twelve big theatres in the regions but still forty in the West End, and there was a continual crisis about productions to put in all of them. Arnold and I would sit for hours discussing problems such as these, though he would use the phrase 'You are pushing an open door', because we could both see the solutions, but they were obstructed by legal difficulties. How can a government-subsidised charity help a commercial company? By law we can only give money to [non-profit companies and] trusts.

Field admitted that at root the problem was one of the national companies and their role outside their own buildings.

> Peter Hall would answer, 'OK, I'll tour Strindberg's *Dance of Death* for twelve weeks with Olivier in the lead but I'll have to shut down the Cottesloe for twelve weeks to pay for it. I can't do everything.' I

hate to say it, but the Arts Council never really honoured – well, it wasn't an agreement but let's say a general pledge, to give enough touring funds to the National and the others to execute their touring commitments.

On balance, the logic was there. The Council had compelled the national houses of drama, opera and ballet to tour, in order to counter popular and parliamentary criticism that four London companies ate up one third of the Council's grants (27 per cent nowadays). In order to tour properly, the companies needed big, well-equipped theatres. The Council had done deals with local authorities to restore number-one venues with Housing the Arts assistance and to set up trusts to run them.

Yet the cost of the companies subsidised to visit these revived number ones was too high for the theatre managers to keep up a viable operation, so the presence of the 'nationals' was nominal. Add the Christmas panto, one-night stands by popular artists and the odd commercial run and still there were 'dark' weeks. Hence the need to pad them with more product, but not the sort that would compete with that provided by the national houses. Overall, it might be said that the Council was handling a problem of its own making by nourishing a tapeworm of solutions, but that was the logic at any rate. As with all such reasoning, as it ground its way through the Arts Council's procedural mill it came out the other end all mangled up, and instead of obliging the regions, what transpired served more readily the West End.

As Goodman and Field digested these issues and their legal drift, they kept coming back to a novel event that took place in 1954, when the Council still owned the freehold of the Bristol Theatre Royal. The Bristol Old Vic there filled an emergency hole in its programme with a hastily concocted musical about a magic piano that made everyone dance – the piano device was used by its author Julian Slade to save on an orchestra. *Salad Days* proved an unexpected hit and transferred to the West End for 2,283 shows at the Vaudeville. It worked in both Bristol and the Strand because it was a twee little show that was magnified by West End lights to look like a big camp one. A box-office and royalty deal was struck between Bristol's trust which paid for the premiere production and the commercial company that brought it in to the West End. Rather like a barrister citing a classic judgment to bolster his case, Goodman considered it might serve as a legal model, one which benefited the West End, the regional producing house, the theatre public, and the Council's fair name. Creativity, on the other hand, had little to do with it.

One day early in 1978 a 'mad young chappie' came to see Jack Phipps and Tony Field at the Arts Council headquarters. As Field recalls:

> He made a living touring Agatha Christie plays for £250 each. He'd put on *Murder at the Vicarage* and then he'd change the set's doors and windows round and turn it into *Murder on the Nile*, or something like that. But when he came to see us he'd done his homework quite well, and he was interested in the fact that the Leicester Haymarket rep had decided to do the American musical *My Fair Lady* as its Christmas show.

Cameron Mackintosh is now a multi-millionaire thanks in part to this meeting. With reason he calls Field 'my godfather' and singles him out as such at public gatherings. As it turns out, Mackintosh, the son of a timber merchant, devoted his life to the lyric stage once his aunt had taken him as an eight-year-old to see *Salad Days* at the Vaudeville. Subsidised musicals were therefore nothing new to him when, at thirty-two years of age, he walked into the office of Phipps & Co. Mackintosh proposed that the Council should give his project some backing in return for which he'd enter into business with the Haymarket through Moss Empires, build an enhanced production and run a tour around the region's number ones after it closed in Leicester. Phipps and Field were intrigued, because here was a scheme ranging across their subsidised domain – a civic rep, new touring product, the number ones – melded by a potential Binkie Beaumont.

As Field recounts:

> We fudged together a deal with Cameron and I went to the Council and said that there was this wonderful play by George Bernard Shaw called *Pygmalion*. They all nodded. Well, I continued, it has been put to music and it will be played at the Leicester Haymarket, and we have this excellent young impresario who wants to give money to our company there, if we will help it to tour the regional theatres afterwards. That's how I sold it to the Council.

The Council put in a guarantee of £40,000 (£120,000) for the one show, which, though modest, equalled the entire annual grant to the theatre from Leicestershire County Council.

Mackintosh booked Liz Robertson, Tony Britton and Peter Bayliss as the leads, and it toured the regions as promised on 70 to 90 per cent capacities. The press was told that 'the production is the latest move in the campaign to keep alive the big provincial theatres'. But it also made a loss. Leicester-Mackintosh's *My Fair Lady* had aspired to Beaumont qualities and it cost an incurable £25,000 a week to tour. Its set was lavish in contrast to contemporary commercial product, and it was dubbed by stagehands 'the heaviest show in town' – in one theatre the existing nine and a half tons of balancing weights couldn't hold Professor Higgins' book-lined study. Of course, this opulence was exactly what the West End was angling for, and from this time on commercial producers saw the subsidised stage as a source from which the old-fashioned spectacle might be retrieved as an audience-winner.

The best way for the Haymarket to recoup its costs was to get *Lady* into the West End. The Arts Council was now drawn into the equation through its lost guarantee. A tricky set of negotiations stalled the deal. Alan Jay Lerner, the musical's author, complained about 'nine months of tough fighting', from which the Arts Council acquired first call on its guarantee and 4 per cent of the net profits. What had started out as a regional exercise had turned into a West End gamble. The Council finally got its money back and Mackintosh suggested they put it into another touring show, *Oklahoma!* Field succeeded again in his spiel on the Council – 'It's a sort of American folk opera based on a book called *Green Grow The Lilacs*.'

Yet when Mackintosh knocked a third time, now with a mint British musical in mind, Council staff reminded him that British shows didn't work any more and threw the project out, even though the lyricist was a certain T.S. Eliot and its composer the son of the principal of the London College of Music. Mackintosh hired a subsidised director instead; Nunn moonlighted. This British musical that the Arts Council knew would never work was called *Cats*.

Mackintosh has turned out as Goodman and Field had dared hope. He is perhaps their Binkie Beaumont II. Not only does he dominate the West End, and trawl the subsidised scene for casts, directors and product, not only is he gay, he's even resurrecting the Group. In 1991 he teamed up with veteran producer Bernard Delfont to run, under the name Delfont-Mackintosh Theatres Ltd, two West End venues – the Prince Edward and the Prince of Wales. By late 1996 it was estimated that Mackintosh would eventually buy out Mayfair Entertainment Group, which owned eight central theatres, including the Donmar and the Albery. Mayfair happened to be a subsidiary of Tony Field's old employer, Chesterfield Properties, and the rumours started as soon as its director, George Biggs, left Mayfair to work for Delfont-Mackintosh in September 1996. The biggest West End owner (ten theatres) remains Stoll Moss, now run by the Australian Janet Holmes à Court, but she is reliant on the success of four of Mackintosh's biggest shows: *Miss Saigon, Oliver!, Phantom of the Opera* and *Starlight Express.*

Just as Beaumont associated himself with the Royal Shakespeare Theatre, Mackintosh did so with the National. As a contribution to programming he gave £1 million in 1990 for the NT to stage American musicals, starting with Sondheim's limp *Sunday in the Park With George.* He also joined up in ownership of an arts centre in Oxford, the Old Fire Station, where he could try out material such as his *Moby Dick.* Around the same time he endowed with £1 million a chair of showbiz at Oxford University to advance the study of making musicals.

Courting the Establishment helped Beaumont immeasurably, especially when Keynes inducted a tax arrangement for his benefit. Mackintosh's contributions have certainly done no harm to him, either: he recently received a knighthood, an honour that it was felt was denied Beaumont because of his gay ways. They both evolved clever little tactics to *manufacture* success for themselves and their shows. Mackintosh reportedly bought up seats for his own Broadway run of *Miss Saigon* to make it appear a sell-out, it was revealed in 1992. Though that's perfectly legitimate over there, London runs on more benevolent routines. It is sometimes appropriate for his Mackintosh Foundation to obtain tickets for his West End shows, which it passes on to needy paupers so they can enjoy *Oliver!*

The difference now is that, while Beaumont was implacably opposed to subsidy 'poisoning' his elevated patch of the West End, Mackintosh introduced it with *My Fair Lady,* and now he is able to benefit from the talent sustained by its existence. In his recent and most troubled show, *Martin Guerre,* the production team he employed, led by Declan Donnellan of Cheek By Jowl, had been hitherto nurtured by grants, while his star actor Iain Glen was an RSC regular. Another difference may be that, while Beaumont aimed for high production values to match the quality of content, Mackintosh seems satisfied to fill the West End with drivel that looks good. He can produce vehicles for tourists, but none named Desire.

Back to the Arts Council. When *My Fair Lady* opened at the Adelphi in October 1979, the show found itself in competition for trade with another subsidised musical – *Chicago* from the Sheffield Crucible. Here was nothing new: from the late sixties subsidised companies had nested in the odd West End niche under the Group's standard terms. Goodman's annual essay in the Council's 1971 accounts noted, 'It was interesting to look at the list of 40 or so theatres open in London on a recent evening and to find out that 13 were either subsidised directly or occupied by productions which started in one or other of the subsidised theatres.'

He wrote London, not the West End, and productions not musicals, and a number of regional productions would continue to percolate into the capital from then on. It's hard to say they set any great example by doing so: Nottingham Playhouse brought a retitled version of Agatha Christie's *Ten Little Niggers* to the Duke of York's in 1987. The difference with *My Fair Lady* lay in the scale of the production, the Council's investment and the involvement from the first of a commercial producer measuring up the show with a West End yardstick. For Tony Field and Lord Goodman this was a defining moment, where their hours of pondering now turned empty theatres into full houses. By 1980 there were twenty-seven transfers from regional reps to the West End, including those mentioned.

Roy Shaw drew attention to this wonderful news in the 1981 annual report: 'In this way the subsidised sector helps the commercial by taking some of the risk out of a very risky business.' Unfortunately, the attendance figures of the Society of West End Theatres (SWET), defensively vague as they are, tell a less happy story. Only the average weekly attendance percentages of this period remain, but they reveal that these shows merely kept the commercial businesses ticking over rather than providing those fresh audiences the Council had presumed:

Theatre	Originator	Production	Capacity	Audience
Adelphi	Leicester	*My Fair Lady*	1,500	60%
Ambassadors	Birmingham	*Mother Dear*	460	30%
Apollo	Oxford	*Before the Party*	750	30%
Arts	Almost Free	*Dirty Linen*	340	33%
Cambridge	Sheffield	*Chicago*	600	44%
Piccadilly	RSC	*Piaf*	792	40%

Even worse, producer Larry Parnes pointed out that the financial discounts involved for concessions and party bookings for Sheffield's *Chicago*, for example, dunked the financial 'take' below 25 per cent of the full value of an average week's tickets. What the West End cravenly relied on was the summer tourist trade, especially Americans, but at the time IRA bombs kept these visitors at bay. West End producers pinned their hopes on flashy musicals to lure them back. By 1987 half of the shows in theatreland would be musicals.

There was one useful outcome of the Council's second-hand complicity in West End deals: secretary-generals could now speak to Mrs Thatcher of the arts' evident contribution to the tourism industry in keeping theatres open in the capital's heart and putting musicals in them, which was what foreigners flocked to most. It was Tony Field, by the way, who devised the well-known ticket booth for tourists in Leicester Square, which was at first an Arts Council caper:

> I'd seen the TKTS scheme for unsold theatre tickets in New York and I told Arnold that we really should have this here. I went to see SWET, who threw me out, but in the end I got the London Tourist Board to lend me a caravan. The West End theatres wouldn't play ball and we started out with spare tickets from a few subsidised companies. It soon fizzled out, but eighteen months later SWET finally picked the scheme up and it's still there today. I must say I'm delighted.

This is the background, then, to the nationals' foray into the world of big bucks and frozen turkeys. At the head of the eighties both Hall and Nunn were easing themselves away from governing roles. 'My heart is no longer in this shit-heap,' Hall had written in his diary. Sir Hugh Willatt sympathised that 'they must have felt more like factory bosses than artists', especially when the RSC entered the blemished Barbican in 1982. Both directors brought in associates to spread the executive load, Hall choosing a group of allies on the Royal Exchange model, though this never really worked, while Nunn delegated to Terry Hands.

The Arts Council, too, had to face up to the reality of funding these giants for the first time: the National had only moved into the South Bank in 1976, and the Barbican was the RSC's first proper London home. Money was now a problem, not a solution – 'It was like inflation had banged on the door of the Arts Council's

Swinging Sixties party and finally brought Superintendent Thatcher round to close it,' said a panellist. While Hall and Nunn worked increasingly elsewhere to earn real fees (well, think of their alimonies), the nationals were obliged to take notice of the profit-seeking West End invasion by regional reps.

Peter Shaffer's *Amadeus* was the National's first international winner. Now famous as a film, this play 'took the piss out of history' by turning Mozart into a giggling tyke poisoned by his rival Salieri. Under Hall's direction, it opened at the Olivier in November 1979. 'If I am to do *Amadeus* it may be one of my last chances of making money, real money,' we find in his published diary, and it was kind of *The Sunday Times* subsequently to point out how far he'd prospered. *Amadeus* was a one-off, but it drew the RSC to reciprocate. *Nicholas Nickleby*, directed by Trevor Nunn, opened at the Aldwych six months later in June 1980. Setting the pestilent fashion for staged adaptations of novels, this eight-and-a-half-hour epic of not-very-much-really was designed to show off the technical skills of the RSC. It was as though Nunn chose to tell theatreland, 'You thought *My Fair Lady* was flash? Look what we can do, and book us.'

And booked he was, a year later by Andrew Lloyd-Webber and Cameron Mackintosh to direct another adaptation, of poems about cats. Meanwhile the RSC thought it had found its *Amadeus* in *Poppy*, a pantomime treatment of the opium wars by Peter Nichols, which became the first new play in the Barbican. It was originally sought by Philip Hedley at Stratford East, and Nichols admitted, '*Poppy* was written for a proscenium stage, like Stratford East . . . I am by no means sure an open stage can do it justice.'

Nichols was correct to be nervous, and the expansion imposed by Terry Hands to make it fit the Barbican virtually sank the production. Nichols promptly announced his retirement from the theatre. On writing about this incident at the time, James Fenton remarked in *The Sunday Times* on two trends that he considered contingent – technical extravagance and dramatic hyperbole:

This week provided a curious example of the difference between commercial theatre and the grand subsidised houses. In the commercial theatre the tendency is necessarily towards economy of means . . . It is in the subsidised theatre that you are more likely to find the extravaganza. There, the word which opens all the locks is 'celebratory' as in the sentence: 'We want a show which will be massive, affirmative, celebratory.' *Nicholas Nickleby* was the pioneering celebratory show. [The National's] *Guys and Dolls* is another. What about *Poppy*?

Fenton felt that to Nichols the musical was less celebratory than Hands wished. That the audience could sense this tension may be the very reason why it failed. A new generation of musicals was emerging in the manner that Fenton had outlined, the 'British musical', in which music became an increasingly present though insignificant element in works that should really be called 'technicals'. Andrew Lloyd-Webber is no Puccini, though their respective music enjoys a can't-quite-place-it affinity, and the shows he's done with Nunn succeed entirely because they look good. Nobody but the cast can remember a tune from *Starlight Express*, and they can only because he pays them to do so, but everyone leaves humming the skates. This explains the RSC's sole success in the genre, *Les Misérables*, which was really *Nicholas Nickleby* degutted and restuffed for the tourist trade. Though the RSC lacked the nerve to invest in *Les Mis*, leaving it to co-producer Cameron Mackintosh, the musical still brings in £1 million or more a year from profits to the RSC accounts, which we trust they spend wisely.

A year after *Poppy*, the National lost whatever it made on a snickering Mozart in *Jean Seberg*. Even before this new musical had been seen, the press condemned its presence at the South Bank on moral grounds. Michael Coveney summed up in the *Financial Times* the arguments of those like him who were 'concerned about our most heavily subsidised theatre presenting the work of a Broadway team'. Hall admitted that he'd been asked a year before to direct it on Broadway by the composer – 'Get me the *Amadeus* guy,' Marvin Hamlisch was reported to have ordered.

This pre-emptive attack by the drama critics was curious. They had given the thumbs-up a year earlier to a National production of *Guys and Dolls*, the brilliant – American – musical. Its popularity led both the National and the RSC to browse through dog-eared songbooks and stage *Kiss Me Kate*, *The Wizard of Oz* and *Carousel*. Yet it seemed that while the National could put on old Broadway shows, it shouldn't be allowed to create new ones. This paradox was underlined by the National's inability to choose anything that stood a chance, and in the end the press were right for the wrong reason. There's little question that musicals today are inferior to the Broadway classics because the composers of them lack flair and rely instead on stage effects to excite the audience. But then, the quality of the music generally used in plays at the RSC nowadays sets some of the lowest standards in Europe, and that too seems to be an issue of executive choice.

As it turned out, *Jean Seberg* was as big a disaster as the harrowing life of the film star it was based on, and its existence was made worse by the fact that the National had signed a contract promising a run of seventy-five shows on the South Bank. How ironic that they could have pulled it off and revived *Guys and Dolls* otherwise. With this kind of folly going on, it's little wonder that the Arts Council's new team of Rittner and Rees-Mogg had no option but to look quizzically at the National's position.

Still, even *Seberg* wasn't as bad as the RSC's *Carrie.* This shocker opened at Stratford in February 1988. One week before, the *Financial Times* called it sight-unseen 'a money-making wheeze', and one week later, sight-seen, 'a bloody mess'. Terry Hands had directed an independent try-out on Broadway in 1985, but the investors backed away from what they saw. As one of them admitted, 'Somehow the idea of a musical based on a young girl experiencing menstruation didn't appeal.' The German producer of *Cats* eventually put money up. By this time Hands had taken over from Nunn at the RSC. The RSC's 1986–1987 season had not been good, leaving a deficit of £1.2 million, and Hands needed his own *Les Mis* gravy train. Here it wasn't. Following the statutory try-out at Stratford, *Carrie* transferred to Broadway, where it closed after five nights, losing £4 million. Hands left the RSC soon after, to be succeeded by the current director, a brainy, perennial schoolboy called Adrian Mole – sorry, Noble.

Although the *Carrie* calamity deterred the RSC from staging another dud called *The Garden of Eden*, it didn't prevent the Royal Court from supposing it could do better. Ian Dury's rotten *Apples* of October 1989 provoked Cork Report member Michael Billington to write in the *Guardian* that if they thought *Apples* had anything to say about the state of the nation they'd made an error of judgment, but if they'd staged it as a box-office bet, then they'd succumbed hopelessly to Thatcherite market forces: 'Either way, it is not very reassuring.' Meanwhile the RSC tried a new approach to sensation-giving in 1990 with *A Clockwork Orange*, which delivered them a clockwork turkey for Christmas. They keep trying, bless them, and as late as 1996 they made a broken spectacle of *Les Enfants du Paradis*.

Why these extravaganzas fail is self-evident. First, the nationals do them whenever they need to make money out of tourists, not out of the burning commitment to the genre that drives Cameron Mackintosh. A former chief administrator of the National Theatre in Hall's days, Michael Elliott, once talked about his depression when he sat with a group of National directors plotting new productions. You would think, he said, they'd act like children with train sets, all gleaming eyes and zeal, but not a bit of it. He recalled mentioning new work that had been offered for staging, proposing dates, and watching them jadedly ramble through their diaries in the hope, he felt, they had something less stressful to do at the time.

The infinite *ennui* that overwhelmed those who work at the South Bank or the Barbican was more than a matter of bad air-conditioning, he reckoned. It's commonly expressed that the RSC loves Stratford, where it focuses on fresh air and Shakespeare, and tourists make the trip to see it, while it loathes London, where it must invent things to compete against the West End for the same tourist trade. The National, meanwhile, still lacks a clue as to what it's there for, so it does a bit of this, a bit of that.

Secondly, musicals may flop even when the dramatic and cast-list ingredients are right. Andrew Lloyd-Webber and Cameron Mackintosh have both suffered recent failures. The self-styled composer's *Aspects of Love* and *Starlight Express* bombed on Broadway. Mackintosh lost a fortune on *Moby Dick* in 1993, and his 1996 *Martin Guerre* was so inept in its structure he had to take it off and rework it. That's part of the secret, of course: to rework it, to be brutal, to cut and force changes.

Mackintosh succeeds because 'I do what I like . . . To me they are shows which make me want to jump up and down, to dance and sing.' (Stephen Sondheim pointed out that Cameron is an anagram of Romance.) His skill, it's often agreed, is packaging. As a fellow producer asked:

> Can anyone remember an RSC production by its poster, or even just an RSC poster? But nearly everyone can conjure up the poster of *Les Misérables* in their mind's eye. It's the gimmicks on stage, certainly – the helicopter in *Miss Saigon* – but the whole package, from the show's timing to the merchandise, is what Cameron handles best.

As a producer Mackintosh apparently has fifty 'angels' behind him, investors who believe as strongly as him in the stuff on stage, but equally study the nightly box-office records. It seems that it's not quite the same in the boardroom of the Royal Shakespeare Company.

Whatever is going on there, it obsesses journalists. The RSC has enjoyed a poor, almost vindictive press in recent years. According to them, under Adrian Noble the company seems to be mooching along, no longer striding around in gorgeous, fur-lined leather boots – the Shakespearean signature of Nunn and Hands. Noble is often a good director and certainly no fourth-form fool. He has faced two major problems. First, the consequence of the Arts Council's failure to address the findings of the 1983 Priestley Report, which showed that the operation was under-funded. Second, London – or rather the Barbican. Noble inherited a condition that started when Hall invented the RSC to bring Stratford into London, where he prospered even though the company was housed in odd scraps of the West End.

Hall was invited to work on the plans for the Corporation of London's Barbican Centre, so that when the company moved in during 1982, his successors were given a space designed by him in order to develop an epic style which was in his mind's eye but which never materialised. Not only that, but the entire centre was woefully conceived, obscurely located and later run with difficulty by a Tory peer called Baroness Detta O'Cathain, who used to work for the Milk Marketing Board. Gossips cruelly suggested that she treated the RSC executives as though they were a clump of feeble-minded farmers in need of a good talking to about sterilisation.

By October 1990 these structural problems merged when Terry Hands decided to close the Barbican theatres until his successor Adrian Noble arrived in March 1991. Noble (born 1950) subsequently announced that the RSC would no longer work year-round at the place. From April 1997 the company would spend twenty-two weeks a year elsewhere, much of the time in Plymouth, building in the south-west the kind of relationship with local authorities, the education sector and native audiences that it has had in the north-east. It was a noble move in more than one sense, but it irritated the Critics' Circle, who had only just worked out how to get to the Barbican in time for a show.

Yet what will the RSC do in London for the remaining thirty weeks? Hall created the company to play Shakespeare and premieres. Shakespeare it does, over and again, but new work not enough. Writers griped that Noble had marginalised them. Yet his appointment in 1996 of three associate directors – Michael Boyle, Katie Mitchell and Stephen Pimlott – may be a sign that the RSC will once again engage 'with the future' better than it has in the recent past. Appointing others to share the load is certainly a sign of transition, as we saw with both Hall and Nunn.

Meanwhile, at the National, the competent and decent-minded Richard Eyre furled up his Stars and Stripes and handed his office over to Trevor Nunn in September 1997. Eyre's Americanisation of the National during his tenure from 1988 may have grown from a perfectly valid disapproval of translations – after all, that's the only way we can deal with the European heritage through which the bulk of British play-writing has been stimulated this century. Perhaps Eyre possessed an evangelical lust to introduce great work born across the Atlantic, but that wouldn't explain why he made such feeble choices as *Johnny on a Spot* or *Broken Glass*, while some feel he ignored truly significant work such as that done by the Wooster Group or Robert Wilson. If so, perhaps he did it to till up tourist dollars. After all, he had three theatres a night to fill.

Whatever the reason on this side of the ocean, the concord was contrived on the other side by those who saw Broadway crashing like the West End. The growth of trade between London and New York developed from this crisis: the Royal Court made a cash deal with Jo Papp at this time, for instance, to produce American work. Eyre's contribution was probably stoked by the agents of two ageing playwrights: Arthur Miller and Stephen Sondheim. They seemingly cultivated opportunities using the British subsidy system to sustain their clients' careers. Arthur Miller came over to the National and railed that the New York stage had hit the 'bottom line', warning British theatre staff in 1989 that 'any discussion in this country which does not fasten on the question of subsidy is useless . . . the ticket will not pay for it'. In the event Eyre paid for the tickets of Miller and Sondheim.

Nunn is surely too seasoned to be affected in this way – some say too old. The millionaire of musicals was fifty-seven when he started at the National, which was a cause for press criticism, though let's not forget that Nunn was about the same age as Olivier was when he took it on. Nunn has done next to nothing for new work, but one feels he recognises that and will set up a structure to deal with this issue, which otherwise the National has sidelined for years because it seems that no one has had the guts to tackle it full on.

In the early eighties a Canadian store-owner bought up the Old Vic. Finding himself with a tacked-on studio which came with it, Ed Mirvish gave the space *gratis* to the National so it could experiment. John Faulkner moved over from the Arts Council to run it for a while, but it's hard to say what went on in there, aside from the sort of exercises actors do for free in such places but earn a fortune doing on TV under the name of 'Improv'. Richard Eyre made an attempt to address the theatre world outside by building up relations with small-scale companies like the Asian group Tara and the ambitious mime company Théâtre de Complicité, neither to great purpose. He then invited the gifted Canadian artist Robert Lepage to work there, a careful move to make the National appear modish. Nunn simply has to do better than this.

First, though, he faces a situation that is quite new. His old company, the RSC, has moved out of town for half the year. Rather nice, Nunn might have thought, to have a capital city to yourself; all those actors and backstagers who wouldn't leave London to dock in Plymouth, all those tourists. The trouble is, Peter Hall thought so, too. In a nimble move he took over the Old Vic, basically to fill the gap left by Noble and to revive an authentic repertory system, one that the British Drama League recommended to Lord Keynes fifty years ago. Nunn found his old predecessor – twice over – breathing down his neck from Waterloo. What a clever man, that Peter Hall. It wasn't his fault that the Canadian store-owner suddenly decided to sell the Old Vic one year into the deal with the veteran director.

One now wonders whether Hall is ingenious enough to pull off his old RSC ploy a second time and get new money out of the Arts Council to fund his repertory company. He needn't waste any time looking in the 1996 drama policy for guidance. It spent just six short paragraphs on what it called 'the companies established by Royal Charter', which became its latest excuse for treating the NT and the RSC as special. The NT formally became the RNT in 1988, against the advice of everyone, with the possible exception of some marketing twit who convinced the board it would enhance chances of sponsorship. Well, it didn't.

The Council calls the pair 'flagship organisations' (just like that, cloaked in inverted commas, as though it's not sure what those words mean) and only warns them that their future funding needs will be measured 'in the context of how those needs and strategies affect and benefit the needs of theatre throughout England'. It doesn't say why. Or how. It doesn't know why, or how, any more.

Chapter 22

What Joanna Drew

Visual Arts: Arts Council Collection • Arts Council Touring • Hayward Gallery Hayward Annuals

When Dame Barbara Hepworth donated her sculpture *Crucifixion* to Salisbury Cathedral in 1970 she didn't expect to be crucified in return. Local resident Colonel Body was among the first to condemn the artist and her art: 'The work is obscene and profane ... To put these monstrosities on consecrated ground is wicked.' He lived close by the cathedral and had witnessed outside his house the erection of an open-air summer display of modern sculpture. Crowning well-bred work (of manifest holey-ness) by Henry Moore and other veterans stood Dame Barbara's dramatic object of 1966, cast of primary-coloured bronze and set four-square like a sunscreen by Mondrian.

'There are many people with art qualifications who prefer and cherish the old forms of architecture and who consider modern art hideous and nerve-wracking,' wrote a Mrs Nunn. 'Is the Arts Council justified in spending large sums of public money in order to obtain this kind of result?' a neighbour of the Colonel wrote to *The Times*, while another railed that, 'The Arts Council has ruined seven centuries of beauty by shedding its junk in our midst.' A bomb was planted under Hepworth's showpiece. Though the explosive was easily defused, Wiltshire County Council ordered the work to be removed forthwith. 'We hope the Arts Council will have the decency to apologise for the trouble it has caused,' wrote a Mrs Moody to her local paper. Thing was, the show had nothing to do with the Arts Council.

Some six years later *The Times* (then under the editorship of future Council chairman William Rees-Mogg) derived further scandal out of sculpture. It reported:

> The Tate Gallery, unrepentant about its purchase of a piece consisting of a pile of 120 bricks, put them on show yesterday. They are the work of Carl André, the American sculptor, who received an offer to buy them in 1972 when the Tate had seen a photograph of them. But by then he had returned them to the brickyard and got his money back because he could not find a buyer. So he bought some more, crated them and sent them to the Tate.

Columnists of every major paper wrote facetious articles attacking the Tate on the lines of Bernard Levin's *Times* review entitled, 'Art may come and art may go but a brick is a brick for ever'. Five of these diatribes lashed the Arts Council for wasting public money on common building materials.

Andre's *Equivalent VIII* was really a rather elegant example of work that fused two current and related trends, conceptualism and minimalism. The 120 firebricks were not literally 'a pile'; they were set almost in the shape of a grave, reminding those in the know of the great Brancusi's *Endless Column* laid along the floor, and their total number was chosen for meditative reasons (1 x 2 x 3 x 4 x 5). Nevertheless, two-thirds of the bricks had to be treated for stains after a visitor sprayed them with blue food dye. 'The press and the public kept throwing those bricks at me,' recalled the Secretary-General of the time, Sir Roy Shaw, 'and I kept throwing them back!' For the trouble was, the bricks had nothing to do with the Arts Council.

There are at least 1 x 2 x 3 x 4 x 5 examples of this kind threaded through the history of the Council, where that institution has been assumed to be guilty of foisting 'hideous and nerve-wracking' modern art on the public. In the case of the Hepworth this is because that was precisely what the Council had previously done. From the fifties, when the outfit began to take seriously its responsibility for touring pictures and sculptures, it promoted certain examples of modern work, mainly those of a conservative and spiritual tone that the Council's Chairman Kenneth Clark championed and privately patronised. Chief among them was work by Henry Moore and Moore's ally Barbara Hepworth. This we'll explore shortly.

The ballyhoo about the bricks sprang from another source, that of the tax-payers' confusion about this country's major art houses and the subsidies they enjoy. Mr Tate's Gallery is funded directly by the government, not through the Arts Council; there have been very few galleries that have received annual grants from the quango. Yet the Council has organised some of the Tate's most famous shows, though it's been the latter rather than the former which has lived off the success of them. Certainly the art department has been the only unit at the Council that has done most things itself rather than give money to others to do it. This is called 'direct provision', an expression against which the country's gallery-owners wield garlic and silver bullets. So, before we look at the peculiar things the Arts Council's visual arts department has actually done in the name of culture, it's necessary to paint a picture of the scene slightly out of its sight.

The remarkable idea of paintings belonging 'to the nation' came about in the eighteenth century. This notion was advanced just at the time when Britain itself was deciding quite what it was as an entity. Between the Act of Union with Scotland in 1707 and that with Ireland in 1801 – between Rob Roy and Wolfe Tone – it's hardly surprising that 'nationhood' and cultural identity should be studied with a blend of Enlightenment logic and the self-interest of the land-owning elite, at least those who sensed that they stood at the brink of the Industrial Revolution. The titles of three fashionable books of the era hint at general trends of thought: *A Philosophical Enquiry into the Sublime and Beautiful* by Edmund Burke (1757), *Anecdotes of Painting in England* by Horace Walpole (1762), which was the first published study of native artistry, and *An Inquiry into the Nature and Causes of the Wealth of Nations* by Adam Smith (1776).

One of the weirdest polemical writings from this period was an enormous poem by a lawyer and amateur artist named Martin Archer Shee. His *Elements of Art* argued the economic need for the nine muses of culture to adopt the English language and nurture a national style of painting:

Shall Britain then, without a sigh, resign
To Gaul's proud sons the glories of the Nine;
Content, ambition's better laurel yield,
And fly, defeated in the graphic field!

Enrich'd by commerce, and renown'd in arms,
Has taste no trophies, and has Art no charms?

He thought the solution he sought lived in the shape of Sir Joshua Reynolds, the bum-licking portraitist who helped to establish the Royal Academy in 1768 as a means of advancing his status, and that of thirty-nine of his fellows, from back-door artisan to palace celebrity. 'Sir Sploshua' proved not to be 'the star to set alight the heavn's beam', and though there was a painter emerging who would turn out to be the first British artist of international fame, it's doubtful that Mr Archer Shee would have recognised the hero he craved in the pastoral artist John Constable; certainly the Royal Academy hadn't. At any rate the twin peaks of Reynolds and Constable set standards in the contrasted forms that 'graphic' Britons would emulate to this day: creepy portraits, cloudy landscapes.

A leading attempt to set up some sort of 'national' collection came about in 1777, when it was suggested that the private purchases of Britain's first Prime Minister, Sir Robert Walpole, should be exhibited to the public in the manner that galleries were adopting abroad. This move followed a tendency of the time to rehouse pictures, sculptures and other valued objects away from the traditional treasuries and cabinets (such as the Tower of London, where the crown jewels are still shown) and instead in galleries designed to deal more effectively with issues of display, climate and security. St Petersburg's Hermitage opened in 1764, Vienna's Belvedere in 1776, Madrid's Prado in 1786, and the Louvre in Paris in 1793; each was a royal venture, by the by, though the French Revolution rather scuttled the lofty gesture from Versailles. It was in rivalry to such developments that a British gallery was pursued. While the Government dithered, Walpole's collection was flogged off to Catherine the Great for her Hermitage and that was that.

The National Gallery itself was brought about by a Russian Jewish emigré, J.J. Angerstein (1735–1823). He had worked in the City, where he reformed the insurance company Lloyd's of London. Angerstein 'amassed a princely art collection of outstanding quality', mostly foreign paintings by artists such as Titian, Rembrandt and Claude Lorrain, some of which he bought cheap off the back of the French Revolution. When he died his estate offered thirty-eight of his acquisitions 'to the nation'. The Government bought these for £60,000 along with his house at 100 Pall

Mall, which it opened to the public as the National Gallery in 1824. Yet 'national' at this time meant 'paintings belonging to the nation', for it reflected the cosmopolitan taste of a collector rather than British artistry: Angerstein had bought some Hogarths and Sploshuas, but little else of note that was native.

In fact it was the state rather than the nation to whom he bequeathed these works, and it is without doubt the fidgety role of the government in the acquisition and distribution of collections that has led to the baffling legacy of institutions that today deal with the display, preservation and commissioning of art in this country. That it was the Government and not royalty that handled such matters is characteristic. Kings George, George, George and George kept their collections to themselves. It was the present Queen who first agreed to provide a public gallery round the side of Buckingham Palace to show off part of the royal picture collection, in 1962.

Other collectors offered works to the National Gallery when a variety of tax reliefs to legacy duty (imposed as a sign of the times in 1796) encouraged the development of bequests and gifts 'of national, scientific, historic or artistic interest'. A new building was designed in nearby Trafalgar Square where the nation's treasure store stands today, and the National Gallery Act of 1856 strengthened its value as a tax haven – one run by civil servants, for those employed at the gallery were government officials. Yet throughout the reign of Queen Victoria, critics questioned the use of the word 'national', as the Gallery had little truly 'national' in it.

Finally, in March 1890, a sugar refiner called Henry Tate offered sixty paintings from his collection of recent British work to the Trafalgar Square showcase. Amazingly, there was much controversy over the inclusion of Tate's gift, mainly over issues of quality. He was offered instead a number of discouraging spaces around the capital, including, of all things, a tunnel. Eventually in 1897 – when an incoming Liberal Government extended better encouragement than its predecessor – the National Gallery of British Art was built with £80,000 of Tate's own cash on the sleazy site of Millbank Prison.

Structured as a detached annexe to the National but commonly called the Tate Gallery, it had begun by showing recent works by Victorian artists and developed its collection in two directions – British work of all periods and international modern art. The National Gallery ran the Tate as a sideline but continued to accept for itself collections of international work, which led it to house comparatively recent paintings by the French impressionists, while the Tate held works by Turner – who had influenced them – as well as by British artists drawn by French example to impressionism. Their collections grew in this clashing way.

Staff at the Tate had to wait until St Valentine's Day 1955 to gain some freedom when a separate board of trustees was set up for them, and only in 1996 did the respective directors of the National and the Tate (surely each the cleverest the galleries have ever had) eliminate the inconsistencies in their stock. Now the National holds foreign paintings up to 1900, while the Tate starts its modern collection more or less at 1900. Thanks further to Lottery largesse, the Tate has rightly chosen to split its address, devoting Millbank to historical British work while converting for the year 2000 the Bankside power station to house contemporary art from around the world. That it took a hundred years to sort this out speaks volumes for the dilatory way in which civil servants have dealt with artistic matters. How quick to do things the Arts Council appears in contrast.

Beyond London the municipal gallery movement was spurred by Prince Albert's view on vehicles for mass education. The 1845 Museums Act and the 1850 Free Libraries and Museums Act encouraged local authorities to build public galleries and develop art collections for them. The factory town of Salford launched the first of these in 1849, and by 1880 a hundred new museums and galleries had opened around the country. Nearly all of them persist today. Such places displayed at first a lot of contemporary work, especially Victorian 'improving' pictures which illustrated moral dilemmas, but none of them presented something that we would consider normal and expect to find today, if only as a device to continually attract visitors: the exhibition – special, newsworthy, transient. These galleries, the National and the Tate included, were built to project a sense of permanence. It would become the job of the Arts Council to usher into them, especially the Tate, the short and sweet.

The Council was able to make and tour shows for the nation's galleries from its earliest days because – thanks chiefly to Keynes, K. Clark, Thelma Cazalet Keir and Pelican Bill – it had contacts among the country's top private collectors from whom it could borrow pieces; in fact, they often lent their own works under the printed tag of 'Private Loan'. More pertinent still, the Council itself stockpiled pictures and sculptures. To understand why a grant-distributing quango was able to assemble its own national collection, we must once again delve back to the days before it existed.

Keynes was twenty-seven when the art critic Roger Fry ran his infamous 1910 exhibition of post-impressionism in London at the commercial Grafton Galleries, the one by which much of artistic Britain woke up to the twentieth century and began to worship Cézanne. By the time Fry had organised a second show in 1912, the Bloomsburyites were buzzing around it. Keynes' boyfriend Duncan Grant contributed, as did Vanessa Bell, while her husband Clive wrote a catalogue introduction: 'We all agree, now, that any form in which an artist can express himself is legitimate ... We expect a work of art to have more in common with a piece of music than a coloured photograph.' One more dig at Victorianism.

Keynes began to collect for himself French work of this kind, including four Cézannes, a study by Seurat for his *Promenade à la Grande Jatte* and later some Picasso, Derain, Braque and Matisse: not bad for a jobbing economist (but then Cézanne was the son of a banker). At the close of the First World War a sale of Degas's collection took place coincident with a Paris peace assembly. Keynes persuaded the Treasury to stump up FF550,000 (£20,000) so that the National Gallery might bid for some paintings there, and he travelled to the 'Vente Degas' with Charles Holmes, the National's director. 'I shall try very hard on the journey out to persuade him to buy a Cézanne as a personal reward to me for having got him the money,' Keynes wrote to Vanessa Bell. Holmes declined to purchase anything by the godfather of cubism; he even underspent the Treasury grant. It would take Keynes' friend Sam Courtauld, the rayon king, to place such work on London's gallery walls, and he did so in 1923 by giving Holmes £50,000 for the Tate and telling him what he could buy with it.

Courtauld and Keynes picked up British work, too, especially anything influenced by the French, which included the daubs of Mrs Bell and Mr Grant. In 1925 the two plutocrats created and financially guaranteed the London Artists Association (LAA), 'a small organisation formed on co-operative principles ... [for artist members] to get a better market ... [by] acting as an agent ... providing them with a small guaranteed income and taking upon itself the entire management of their affairs'. Group and individual exhibitions were promoted by the LAA in London and elsewhere. By 1930 it claimed to have sold 700 works of art at an average £30 apiece. A commission of 30 per cent was taken off the selling price to cover framing and administration, while the artists were assured £150 a year of basic income.

It will come as little surprise that its members included Bell, Fry and Grant. Other beneficiaries of the scheme whose work Keynes personally collected included William Roberts, William Coldstream and Victor Pasmore, who was then working as a clerk at London County Council, at least until another kind of Clark gave him enough cash to take up painting as a profession. The LAA did not survive the Slump; Keynes was rattled when Grant and Bell resigned, moving over to the dealer Agnew's. Nevertheless, by the time Keynes joined CEMA in 1942 he carried a working knowledge of the contemporary art market and possessed a personal stake in the promotion of distinct artists.

He was not alone: sitting with him at the Council table were two more collectors, Thelma Cazalet Keir and Kenneth Clark. All three advised the Contemporary Art Society, which had been founded in 1910 with private bounty and subscriptions to help museums build collections by buying work from living artists, as well as running an annual art market (which survives). Clark also advised the Government and the royal family on purchases and commissions, and he ran his war-artists scheme at the Ministry of Information. Between them they could determine which kind of 'national' art should be promoted and which shouldn't.

When CEMA was handed over from Tom Jones to Keynes in 1942, the Pilgrim Trust earmarked a part of its pay-off for the purchase of new paintings and watercolours by living artists which CEMA could tour as a mixed show. Keynes thought this another wasteful duplication of existing services and a further example of the Pilgrimist fixation with art as employment. Yet the only touring scheme the Council supported was that set up by Bill Williams for 'galleryless' towns. There was now a need to provide exhibitions for the actual galleries, including the National, where permanent collections had been hidden from the hazard of German bombs. As we've already witnessed, Clark and Keynes were keen to see a more conservative style of presentation than Williams provided. Thus their art director, Philip James, supplied many shows that didn't include living artists, often using reproductions of 'Old Masters' in plush frames. He even sold for profit full-colour prints of Gainsborough's *Mr & Mrs Andrews* – well, someone had to.

James complied with the Pilgrim's proviso to buy new paintings, but his gathering hands were tied by his panel chairman, K. Clark, who made sure that the Pilgrim's award didn't divert *his* artists from *his* war effort. The CEMA war collection comprised seventy-five pictures. Around forty painters received fees for one or two works each, including – of course! – Mr Grant and Mrs Bell. Names some might recognise nowadays included Edward Burra, Lawrence Gowing, Ivon Hitchens, Rodrigo Moynihan, Victor Pasmore, Ceri Richards, Ruskin Spear and L.S. Lowry, from whom the Council bought direct a brand-new oil painting called *July, the Seaside*. Otherwise the remaining artists are likely to be known only to those scholars at the Courtauld Institute researching Early Twentieth-Century British Crap.

Philip James later agreed that this CEMA spree on the art market was 'a rather lame affair', but he was 'constrained by the existence of similar schemes' – and by the fact that his Council had a hand in those cliques against which he competed. They were saving their enthusiasms for the existing schemes in which they already held a greater economic stake. It was as though Council subsidy was denied an active place in the art market. From its very first purchase the Council collection had a bargain-basement feel to it. No Henry Moore, no Nashes Paul or John, no Wyndham Lewis, no Bomberg or Spencer or Sutherland or Sickert (who died in 1942). Put these names together and you've more or less covered the range of British work as it appeared by the end of the Second World War – except in the Council's collection.

When K. Clark took up chairmanship of the Council once his war-artists scheme had closed down, he had the purchase grant increased and he encouraged the department to look at what was missing from the stockroom. It seemed he wanted to turn the clock back and start again. To represent the veterans he had championed elsewhere, the collection acquired five Sickerts, seven William Roberts, four Hepworths, five Sutherlands and nine each of Pasmores and Pipers, bought (mainly from the commercial Leicester Galleries) in order to give 'a more coherent chronological presentation of the development of British art since 1900', as a curator of the collection tactfully put it. Acquisition of more modern work was apparently led by Millbank: 'In this way the Arts Council serves to supplement the purchasing policy of the Tate.' This would not be the only way that the Council eased the Tate's deficiencies, as we'll see.

From 1942 to the present around 6,800 works have been acquired for the collection from roughly 1,700 painters, sculptors and photographers. Of these, Henry Moore is king, thanks to the adjustments by Clark and James: twenty-one bronzes and drawings, acquired between 1948 and 1968. David Hockney is queen: there are no fewer than sixteen works of his. 'When

Hockney was fresh out of college in the early sixties we bought something off him, and he'd turn up at the office now and again with bagfuls of pictures, and say, "Hello. Would you like to buy some more?" ' recalled the finance deputy of the time, Tony Field.

Whether you talk to critics or dealers, the Arts Council collection – once they've remembered it exists – appears to them a mixture of crud, curios and shiny gems. Most prized of the possessions, at least in terms of use and insurance, have turned out to be those acquired in the fifties from emergent artists such as Leon Kossoff, Frank Auerbach (ten each) and Lucien Freud (three portraits). There are two Francis Bacons 'now worth millions', including *Head VI*, one of his screaming popes. Bacon was plainly bought as an investment, for the Council otherwise shunned the Irish drunk and his discomfiting portraits, a fact that he and his friends enjoyed pointing out to foreigners.

The ICA 'independents' of the fifties are represented by Richard Hamilton (five), Eduardo Paolozzi (eight), Joe Tilson (six) . . . and so we stroll through the decades, a little bit of this and a little bit of that to represent the scene at the time: Anthony Caro (five), Euan Uglow (nine), Bridget Riley (seven), Gilbert and George (five), Michael Craig-Martin (five), Andy Goldsworthy (fifteen, a job lot) and Damien Hirst. Year by year, a committee or a guest curator would use an annual fund to add to this stockpile of British flair. Sometimes they'd collect for a show that was driven by a theme, which explains quirks like a formal Fox company photo of the royal family, a training print of an abdominal operation from St Bart's Hospital and a twee cartoon strip by Posy Simmonds from the *Guardian*.

While the collectors' motives moved back and forth between representing the range of a period, supplementing the Tate, serving the immediate needs of touring and investing in future talent, the haul grew in a skittish and compromised way. As one art director admitted:

> There is a lot there which is considered worthless, both financially and aesthetically. If there's no call for it from the outside world and it's just sitting in store it's not worth much anyway. Of course, interest in particular artists comes and goes. Look at someone like John Latham [born 1921]. It seemed as though you couldn't lend his work for love nor money ten years ago. Now it's all over the place.

Latham once sued the Council for acquiring his work under false pretences, though he admits this was a ruse to indict the Council as an entity. The only means he found to do so was to take the Council to court for a contractual breach over the work of his the collection acquired ('they should exhibit it, not store it'). From Westminster County Court the case went as far as the Court of Human Rights in Strasbourg, which eventually ruled that the Arts Council lay beyond its jurisdiction as it was independent and not strictly 'a department of government'.

None of the collection is sold back onto the market; it gets used or grows mould. Here the Treasury's argument against selling is the same as the one it gives to the Tate: what you have bought with tax-payers' money has become a government possession and it can't be hawked off. Besides, it would be politically awkward to see national possessions sold to foreign buyers, who are most likely to offer the best prices. As the present curator of the collection, Isobel Johnstone, admits:

> Exceptionally one or two (possibly two of three) Andy Warhol *Beuys by Warhol* screen prints, purchased for an Arts Council Andy Warhol Prints touring show, were sold to add to purchasing funds – the best example was kept for the collection itself. The prints had been bought as an overspend on normal purchasing funds. It was becoming very unusual for the collection to buy prints by foreign artists (now we do not do it at all) and this was why the sale was justified. Subsequently it raised problems for the finance department and it is unlikely to happen again.

As a penalty the Treasury can reduce the main Arts Council's grant by the amount the art department gains through a sale. This limitation seems ill advised, though, especially when a great deal of the collection consists of pieces by relatively young artists who mature. It remains a mystery why, for instance, certain early work couldn't be exchanged in part for something more characteristic, estimable or simply fresher from the same artist.

Solely for insurance purposes, as they say on *The Antiques Roadshow*, the Council's collection is today valued at £25 million. There is no proper way of settling a value on it because of the range (or value) of artists and genres covered. 'Oh, the bloody business of commodities. This valuation business is pretty silly,' agreed a former art department member.

> You can add up what you spent on it, of course, and get a valuation

of cost. But that means nothing to the market, which surely makes some use of the collection as a value indicator. Art-market conditions directly affect the estimate. When the market dropped in the early nineties (in the wake of the slump) so did the collection's value, down from £22 million or so in 1990 to £17 million in 1992 – £1 million of that alone fell off one of the Bacons.

In consequence the Council's art collection is the most bankable asset it owns, but one tied in its worth to a commercial market which the Council only to a degree is in a position to influence. Another member warned that its value to the Council can be an ambiguous one:

> If I remember rightly it was in the early nineties when it was rumoured Lord Palumbo wanted to flog the collection off for the money, and in preparation of that it was re-assessed in terms of market value. Ironically, this was done by Lord Gowrie's Sotheby's. At first it had been suggested – incredibly! – that Palumbo wanted to employ the collection as collateral on a loan for the Royal Opera House.

Isobel Johnstone added, 'However far this collateral affair may have gone it was probably scotched when it was made clear that such things cannot happen where charitable trusts are concerned, and the Treasury would never permit the sale of the collection.'

Above all, the oddest thing about the horde is that it's as homeless as a *Big Issue*-seller. Squirrelled away in the basement of the Hayward Gallery, single items are sent on short loan to public organisations who apply for them, though members of the government can also borrow pieces to grace their rooms. When Tony Blair arrived at Number 10 he decided that a painting which had been 'hidden away in the Prime Minister's private quarters' should be put on public display. Very kind of him, though it was our friend *July, the Seaside*, which the Council had bought for the nation from Lowry in the war.

'Every few years there'd be a suggestion from some town in the regions that it would build or adapt a gallery if we gave it our collection. The most recent was Halifax,' recalls a former art director.

> But many of these places wouldn't engage with contemporary work normally; they wouldn't go out and buy it themselves. They're also missing the point of the collection, which has derived more than one function. If our two Bacons fell to pieces tomorrow, at least they

were seen by more people in more places than anyone else's Bacons.

The collection becomes visible only when parts of it form a travelling exhibition, in the manner by which it was born back in 1942. Nowadays the shows are run from an Arts Council rump stuck in the South Bank Centre and suitably called National Touring Exhibitions, but back then the Council supervised the two separate schemes already mentioned: one principally of contemporary art for 'galleryless towns' started before the war by Bill Williams, and its own more traditional shows for city and town galleries. Williams himself later wrote that, 'In the CEMA period [this] created a comprehensive and economic machinery of art-circulation throughout the country.' This was true, but only because the Tate and the National were institutions limited by space and inclination to permanent display, but bereft of their collections to circulate under wartime conditions. So when Williams went on to say that, 'no other non-profit-making body has yet emerged capable of performing a task of such magnitude at such a modest cost', he was being cheeky.

The Council ran a monopoly on countrywide tours when the war ended (aside from the Victoria and Albert Museum, which tended to handle the decorative arts through its own circulation department). Alternative schemes were simply squashed, including a 1949 network proposal by five regional galleries to provide varied shows for municipal museums and 'galleryless' towns. They naively sought subsidy for this from the Council, and they wanted to set it up because the Council had 'absorbed' Pelican Bill's 'Art and the People' enterprise that year after Williams had lost interest in it. In reality the department soaked up this subsidy into its existing touring scheme.

While the Tate and the National Gallery had in the meantime redeveloped their national circulation or loan programmes (with the encouragement of the post-war Labour Government), after Bill Williams became Secretary-General in 1951 he invited them to pass over this marginal work to the Arts Council, and in the middle fifties they complied, making available 270 pictures and sculptures from the Tate and 300 pieces from the National.

Frankly, Williams made the deal for political gain. He'd seen how well the art department staff had honed their skills, and contacts through the embassies, to a level that could make exhibitions of crowd-attracting, international quality suitable for the capital. Given the fiasco of the national Opera House and the ditherings over the National Theatre, it was through the visual arts that the Council would attempt to protect its 'national' remit and seduce the Macmillan Government and high society. After all, its Secretary-General and its Chairman were former grandees of the galleries. Pelican Bill had recently closed down the Council's regional offices, making redundant some of the art specialists there. Now the regions would have the shavings from the 'national' shows, with whatever could be cobbled from the Council's own collection and the 570 pictures that were suddenly surplus to national requirements.

Thus Bill Williams wrote in 1959, 'The Greater London public alone, representing as it does nearly a third of the whole population of England, must inevitably command a higher proportion of what is available.' He then tried to make the regional public pay on the nail to support the privileges of Londoners by introducing admission to touring shows: 'Why should the public pay for admission to a municipal concert-hall or a municipal repertory theatre and yet pay nothing to visit a municipal art gallery?' His answer could be found in the 1850 Free Libraries and Museums Act. And this from the creator of Art and the People. Now it was Art or the People.

From this moment the Council would blatantly focus on London at the cost of the regions. Yet it was not the first time that the art department had provided prestige shows for the capital. The director of the Tate then, Sir John Rothenstein, actually believed that the Arts Council was created at the end of the war to provide shows for his gallery:

> The demand [to see works of art], which did not abate with the conclusion of the war, led to the formation of the Arts Council and to a modification of policy with regard to temporary exhibitions. In 1946 the Tate accommodated an Arts Council exhibition of the works of [the Belgian] James Ensor.

Nonetheless it was through such high-pitched displays of foreign work at the Tate that the Arts Council made its own reputation and that of the Tate itself – Van Gogh in 1947 (157,500 visitors over five weeks), Art Treasures from Vienna 1949, Matisse 1952, Mexican Art 1953 (121,526 visitors), Braque 1956, and so on. These often used specialists hired by the Council for the occasion as curators. Even the big 1950 exhibition of Henry Moore was organised by the art department, as was the 1952

Graham Sutherland show at the Venice Biennale, not to mention most of the official presentations for the Festival of Britain.

Surpassing all these, and Pelican Bill's calculations, half a million visitors ascended the steps of the Tate to see the Arts Council's Picasso show of 1960. Much comment was made about 'the crowds' that the Tate couldn't readily contain. Costing £58,000 to mount, the exhibition made £112,126 and threepence on the door (£1.3 million), causing conflict with the Treasury. By chance the Chancellor of the time was the arts-friendly Derick Heathcoat Amory, and the Council was able to hatch a special-projects fund of £30,000 (£350,000) out of the profit. Now, thanks to the swarming throngs, the Council could vocally promote the cause its art staff had craved since the end of the war. A vital Council report at this time, published in two volumes and called 'Housing the Arts' (1959–1961), included this comment:

> The Committee has come to the conclusion that London is definitely short of suitable art exhibition space, particularly when its present accommodation is compared with other great cities abroad, such as New York, Paris and Rome. It accordingly welcomes the London County Council's proposal to build an Exhibition Gallery on the South Bank ... and recognizes the importance of close collaboration between the Arts Council and the London County Council in the use of this gallery.

When the Council had moved to St James's back in 1947, K. Clark suggested to Mary Glasgow that a part of the ground floor might be used as a 'symbolic' gallery, meaning a makeshift one, 'so that we have a showcase in London under our direct management'. After all, the Cambridge, Cardiff and Edinburgh offices had made rooms available for art objects to be shown. 'Open until 8pm on Tuesdays and Thursdays', the Arts Council Gallery was visited by 37,000 in its first full year. Some of the touring exhibitions were placed in it, which at that time consisted mainly of 'works of historic value and importance which during the war had been preserved in places of safety' as well as hangings from the contemporary collection. Though the gallery provided a neat home-grown solution to supplying a London (thus press-reviewed) display of small touring shows, 'Philip James was a little depressed about working with the bomb-damaged Tate on such an *ad hoc* basis for the big exhibitions,' recalled Mary Glasgow, 'and the department had ambitions to run its own national gallery.'

In 1949 the Council took up a lease for an exalted set of rooms behind the Royal Academy, known as the New Burlington Galleries, where the Museum of Mankind was until recently. Key shows were put on there, but mainly those of a conservative style which, wrote Mary Glasgow in the year she was dumped:

> had been treated by some critics as an opportunity to complain of the lack of patronage of contemporary painters by the new organisations entrusted with State funds . . . There are many ways of answering such a challenge and perhaps the best is to admit that there is something in it.

New Burlington was anything but a success, being at the back of something else and hard to promote, so in 1955 a frustrated Council relinquished the lease on it. This explains Bill Williams' renewed interest first in the Tate's repaired Duveen suites and second in a commissioned exhibition space. He was sparked by the London County Council's bold plan, subsequent to the Festival of Britain, to build an arts complex next to the Royal Festival Hall on the South Bank. Both Chairman K. Clark and his successor Lord Cottesloe were keen to see a grand new 'national' gallery placed there for the sole use of the Arts Council – one forgoing a permanent collection but instead devoted to prestige exhibitions. It was a piece of luck for the Council's cause that Cottesloe was made chairman of the South Bank's capital project board, once the Tory Government had given the scheme the go-ahead in 1962.

To anticipate the result, here is a chronology of Arts Council galleries:

| London | | Cambridge |
Large	Small	
New Burlington 1949–1955	AC Gallery 1947–1968	Office Gallery 1942–1956
[Tate (Duveen)] 1955–1967		Arts Council Gallery 1956–1969
Hayward 1968–1985	Serpentine 1970–1985	Kettle's Yard (Trust) 1970–
Hayward (SBC) 1986–	Serpentine (Trust) 1986–	

Following the Picasso triumph, calls on the department's expertise grew acute. Though covering a major artform, it had the smallest share of the annual government grant-in-aid (around 3 per cent), mainly because it was bringing cash back in the form of loan fees and ticket money. Yet the office employed the most staff of any department. They were engaged in setting up, transporting and taking down exhibitions 'peg to peg' – twenty employees by 1959, and rising. 'The Royal Opera House only takes four cheques a year, and nothing comes back in from the place. But imagine the number of transactions, money in and out, extra manual costs – drivers, packers, warders – involved in all these art shows,' noted a former employee. In addition the unit produced scholarly exhibition catalogues of good quality, hundreds through the years, and in this way the tiniest department grew the biggest public face.

Both the department and its panel enjoyed an exceptional continuity in staffing and membership. Granted, it was a club, but a club that included a number of outstanding and tenacious individuals, and also a few 'graphic' Britons. William Coldstream, the 'social realist' portrait-painter, chaired the art panel from 1953 to 1962, when he progressed to the vice-chairmanship of the Council until 1970. His pupil Lawrence Gowing also sat on the panel from 1953 to 1965, and served two terms as deputy chairman up to 1981. On the staff side Philip James had been the art director from 1942 until he retired in 1957 – fifteen years in charge. Gabriel White, his successor, started out as James' deputy in 1945, and he went on to govern for another thirteen annual reports.

Three interviewees for this book used similar words to describe Mr White: 'delightful/lovely/heavenly', though when your name's Gabriel White you're surely halfway to heaven anyway. He'd been an etcher who worked through the war as an expert in camouflage (which could explain the ready compliments). Both James and White were conservatives whose interest in contemporary art mirrored that of K. Clark: James wrote a monograph on Henry Moore while White authored books on his brother-in-law Edward Ardizzone and Sickert. White would retire soon after he'd seen the Hayward Gallery opened in July 1968.

Yet even longer-lasting and mightier in impact than these two perennials reigned the skilful Joanna Drew. 'Adamantly single-minded' in her own estimation, Drew starred at the Council from 1952 for thirty-six years, entering as a junior but eventually running both the department and the Hayward. Born in 1929 at Naini Tal,

India – but only Indian like Cliff Richard is Indian – she was the daughter of a brigadier.

> My mother was a fair artist and so I was sent to Dartington School in Devon, which was unique then in its access to the arts. I worked for a painting diploma in Edinburgh, but my style was negligible and, no, I don't think I would have got an Arts Council award had I persisted.

Drew joined the department as an exhibition organiser, 'but people didn't have to have titles in those days. It was really like some of the early Regional Arts Associations used to be – full of enthusiastic, well-meaning amateurs running things themselves.'

Drew witnessed all the key moments in the life of the art department up to 1986, when the Rees-Mogg regime cast off its historic load and handed over the collection, the touring shows and the Hayward itself to the South Bank Centre administration it was setting up after the abolition of the Greater London Council. Then she went to run the Hayward until 1992, from where she turned freelance.

> Though that transfer was a watershed, you have to go back further to find the single biggest error of judgment ever made at the Arts Council. That was Williams's shutting down of the regional offices in the middle fifties. We never really recovered from that. It was a misbegotten attempt to get the local authorities to contribute more to the arts, and instead it created these monsters which are now the Regional Arts Boards. Through the years the regional galleries with which we had connections were devolved to them. Now I'm pretty sure they all live on less money than they would have had they stayed with us. Of course, it's ironic many of these galleries didn't at first think of us in terms of support so much as rivalry.

While the Council's dinky exhibitions were chugging their way around the regions in the sixties exactly as they had in the fifties (though no longer with the help of regional staff), post-war baby-boomers were not just creating rock albums and fab gear but also groovy new galleries. It was hello Robert Fraser, farewell Leicester Galleries. Swinging London's commercial scene faced a turn-about, first to handle pop and kinetic art, then conceptualism, time-based art, and all the subsequent trends derived from the tussle for artistic leverage between America and Europe, which happily left 'graphic' Britons splashing about in the centre.

Outside London these shifts inspired the creation of spaces that 'wanted to act like trendy London galleries on tax-payers' dosh', as an officer once roguishly put it. Bristol's Arnolfini emerged all hip in 1965, as did Oxford's Museum of Modern Art (MOMA), with Birmingham's Ikon following a year later. Together with the seasoned Midlands Art Group in Nottingham and evolutions of the arts-centre scene around the regions, a more maverick approach to the presentation of modern art conflicted with the Council's assembly-line method and preconceptions about suitable work. Many received small, grudging annual grants from the Council, with little assurance of continued support.

Joanna drew some of the sniping.

It was first of all for the major exhibitions which appeared in the provinces that an organisation like ours was needed which had international links in-house. This capacity was resented as some kind of stranglehold by the new generation of independent galleries like MOMA. Our touring programme was focused on the local-authority sector, so in that sense we weren't in competition at all. And people in the regions took our exhibitions because they wanted them. They weren't imposed.

She did hold a monopoly, of course, along with the chequebook and the bank. Not only did the art department run the Hayward Gallery, but from 1970 it took on a disused tea pavilion in Hyde Park as a venue dedicated to showing contemporary work. This looked to some like the Council copying MOMA in the middle of London, trying to catch up with trends. Its two galleries, the touring scheme and the Council collection became, for self-evident economic and administrative reasons, bolted together to form a powerful machine. From 1978 onwards Drew was simultaneously the Council's art director and boss of the Hayward.

Yet the new and regenerated exhibition galleries – and here we can complicate the picture with such developments as the photography galleries in York and Covent Garden (both 1971) and Glasgow's Third Eye (1974) – were led by new minds on the scene with fresh approaches to artworks, their display, their interpretation and the broadening of access to them; approaches that 'the Arts Council was always ten years behind', a curator claimed.

Drew's strongest argument was economic:

We were supervising a system where the percentage return on a centrally run touring programme was infinitely more cost-effective than the work of the independent galleries. By the way, the young firebrands who were sniping at us from MOMA and Whitechapel were people like Nick Serota and Sandy Nairne.

Serota is now boss of the Tate, while Nairne succeeded Drew as the Council's art director (though now you'll find him at the Tate as its number two).

Advances like the independent gallery movement were at first readily accommodated by the Council, thanks to the substantial grant increases enjoyed in the late Labour sixties during Jennie Lee's period as Arts Minister. However, by the mid-seventies galloping inflation produced a sequence of funding crises akin to the regional theatre problem – and the remedies of Thatcherism. It was in the insecure climate of the early eighties that the gallery malcontents finally won their battle against direct provision.

As Drew remembers:

The Council had set up a sequence of independent working groups to look at our activities, to pre-empt the civil service poking around. One was set up to look at direct provision and it was chaired by Gerald Forty, who'd just retired as head of fine arts at the British Council. It was such a Stalinist stitch-up. To me it was obvious what the outcome would be, that it would call for us to abandon direct provision.

By then Sandy Nairne was running the ICA's art gallery. In his words:

Nick Serota was in charge of the Whitechapel at the time and we decided to write a joint submission to the Forty committee, so that we couldn't get picked off individually as somebody pushing for their own ends. I believe at first Forty wasn't convinced that there was any need for change, but he listened to a lot of evidence and became convinced by the arguments, especially that the touring scheme was counter-effective in not encouraging local-authority galleries to develop their own expertise. In turn I think that Joanna worked on her panel members well and they wouldn't accept Forty's conclusion, to discontinue direct provision and to set up the Hayward and the Serpentine as independent trusts. It went to Council, who also backed Joanna. Now, what happened next is that

Forty succeeded for a completely different set of reasons, because of the impending collapse of the GLC and therefore the change of status to the South Bank. The Hayward and the exhibition machinery would become part of the South Bank Centre under Arts Council control, because Thatcher pushed this solution on the new chairman Rees-Mogg.

Drew recalled the change:

Funny old Rees-Mogg. You know, he wanted to revive the St James's-style exhibitions in our headquarters at 105 Piccadilly, because he enjoyed them years ago. So to humour him we held one exhibition in the Council Room. He chose the topic of Samuel Johnson, on which he rather famously has a fixation. To add insult to injury I had to pay for the damn thing. I told Finance, 'You can bloody well take it out of the Chairman's allowance,' and quietly they did. So he wanted to keep the collection and the touring for reasons like this, but he was happy to get shot of the Hayward. When he accepted the Thatcher deal over the GLC he was appalled to discover he'd flushed the baby out with the bathwater.

Drew left 105 to save the bathwater. She already knew every leak and rusted hook in the place, for she had been thoroughly involved with the Hayward since it opened in 1968.

Back then, when we moved out of the Tate and into the Hayward, the Tate was paranoid that we were going to eclipse it, and insisted that the Hayward could not show international blockbusters on twentieth-century masters or schools. Ha! They were absolutely furious when we opened the Hayward with Matisse. We carried on with shows of this calibre, and in general there were five large exhibitions a year, most using the two floors of the gallery, but shows that covered the world and all periods – Florentine frescos, Haiti, early Soviet art – and to start Norbert Lynton was our director of exhibitions.

Drew took on Lynton's job when he moved on in 1974. She stemmed the trend of falling attendances, partly by developing the education programme, getting the school parties in, and counting them.

Despite the giddy variety of shows (it became known as the Wayward Gallery), several exhibitions were an eye-opening success. The concrete shell they were placed inside was not.

> Squat, boorish and offensive to the eye, its grim hulk makes no
> attempt to entice the visitor ... The Hayward is marooned in a
> dreary expanse of unembellished concrete, which implies that art
> has no role to play in the public spaces of society today.

So wrote Richard Cork, now art critic of *The Times*, and his committee in a report commissioned by the GLC. They added that the place had failed to make itself familiar to the nation, unlike the Tate or the National.

This was not merely a matter of its hidden-away site, but also its policy: 'The Hayward's programme sometimes seems arbitrary and capricious, moving around the map of world culture without any sense of coherent purpose.' Part of its problem, they felt, lay in the lack of a permanent collection to stimulate context. But, as we know, it had one, stuffed in the basement. The dilemma was that the Council's collection didn't gel with the jet-set shows the staff put on with such flair. 'When will the Hayward show something by working British artists?' the Council was often asked. Joanna drew up a solution: the Hayward Annual.

Attempting 'to present a picture of British art as it develops', thirty-three artists were chosen by three selectors (Michael Compton of the Tate, artists Howard Hodgkin and William Turnbull) to show work in the first Hayward Annual held in the summer of 1977. Unhappily, reviewers already sensed a *déjà vu* tone to this avant-garde survey. Caroline Tisdall of the *Guardian* wondered why people like David Hockney were included: 'The Sixties were the prime time ... for the generation that now rules the roost through established reputations and Establishment positions.' She pointed out that of the thirty-three, thirty-two were men and the sole woman artist just happened to be Mrs Turnbull.

An exhibition lecturer was sent home when no visitors asked for him to take them round. When a sourpuss TV reporter called Fyfe Robertson surveyed the Hayward Annual for the BBC, he made fun of the 'childish pictures' and dubbed the show 'absolutely useless'. Quick to spot a publicity opportunity, Drew invited the curmudgeon to a public talk where David Hockney agreed with Robertson that 'ordinary people' had a right to an explanation of modern art. But Robertson left saying: 'It was just an example of verbal diarrhoea, which the art Establishment is so skilled at producing.'

The next year Drew answered some of the criticisms. The Hayward Annual II selection team comprised five women and no men. The *Times* review was headed 'Ladies' Night at the Hayward', though seven males as well as sixteen females were represented. Again most critics thought it had failed in its purpose. Tim Hilton wrote that 'its unspoken rationale [is] that second-rate art deserves as much showing as first-rate'. At the opening reception, artist Rasheed Araeen distributed leaflets asking, 'Why are black artists always excluded from official exhibitions/surveys like the Hayward Annual?' For the third exhibition, in 1979, some more (male, white) artists of certain vintage made the choices, and John McEwen of *Art Monthly* began to spot a trend: 'Artists are the worst people to select art . . . What happens is they grab one slot for themselves and then divide what remains between friends. At very best they nobly overlook their own work in favour of the next best thing.' Considered 'immature' as a display, the show was branded 'a poor ad for British art'.

For the fourth exhibition (summer 1980), Drew answered a few more of the carpers. Critic Tim Hilton was invited to select the work alongside painter John Hoyland. They tried a new tack and began with a 'Preface' to the show of eighteen artists aimed to define 'established standards'. This gave bits of the Council collection an airing upstairs – Pasmore, Ben Nicholson, Lanyon, Caro and one woman (not Hepworth but Gillian Ayres). However, the Preface reportedly gave visitors the impression that the first team had been hived off from the rest, or as one put it, 'It's an exhibition of teachers.' Thanks to the predominance of abstract painting in the show, a member of the public complained that 'it was like a journey around Allied Carpets'.

In 1981 there was no Hayward Annual. The selectors had argued with the art department about its intention to develop the Preface idea with a bigger exhibition of twentieth-century British drawings and sculptures. Having pointed out that most of the artists were decidedly dead and that their inclusion was therefore hardly in the spirit of a Hayward Annual, they resigned. In 1982, for the Hayward Annual V (or VI), Gillian Ayres joined artists Euan Uglow and Kenneth Armitage in selecting drawings from open submission. A £7.50 application fee was charged, and from the 2,200 drawings received a quarter were selected. Unfortunately a pipe burst in the office above the store where the entries were being held and many of the works were damaged (this is possibly the only recorded occasion when new British art was destroyed by accident). Nicknamed the Conté Crayon Contest, the show 'seems too much concerned with placating the various factions of the art world and not enough with attracting the public', wrote Marina Vaisey in *The Sunday Times*.

In 1983 there was no Hayward Annual. Instead the budget was put into the Sculpture Show, a joint venture with the Serpentine. It was outside the Hayward that a protester poured petrol over David Mach's Polaris submarine made of tyres and in the process burned himself to death. There was no Hayward Annual in 1984. Instead of artists or critics making choices, for the 1985 Annual (VI or IX) the commercial art-dealer Nigel Greenwood was controversially invited to be the sole selector. 'The 1985 Hayward Annual is not a journey through contemporary art; indeed, it is not about art at all. It is about Nigel Greenwood's personal taste,' argued *Art Monthly*. Although the show included many different pieces, from one of the Council's Bacons to Nicola Hicks' goat and Dhruva Mistry's bulls, it was labelled by the press 'a shoddy affair', a 'narcissistic and sentimental exhibition'. Oh dear.

In 1986, Hayward Annual VII (or X) was subtitled 'Falls the Shadow'. Whether this was a reference to the demise that year of the GLC or of the Hayward Annual itself, it served for both. Selectors Barry Barker and Jon Thompson decided to feature foreign artists such as Mario Merz (alive) and Yves Klein (dead). It was attacked as 'pointless' and 'arid' by some of the press, but deemed elsewhere 'better than the others, if that is saying anything'. *Art Monthly* asked whether 'the Hayward will ever get it halfway right'. The Annual was annulled.

By now the Arts Council had taken over the South Bank in its entirety and fixed up its own people to run the place, including Joanna Drew as the Hayward's director. If Drew thought she had the gallery to herself once again to put on the blockbusters she organised so brilliantly, she must have been surprised to learn that the whole centre would be integrated under the direction of an obscure music man, Nicholas Snowman. 'It was simply an administrative marriage of convenience, a most odd affair,' she recalled.

Suddenly she was asked:

> to run up shows to fit in with musical themes. It started when Peter Hall was leaving the National Theatre and wanted to direct some late Shakespeare. Snowman thought this would be a way of linking the bits of the Centre, having us all tackle Late Works. Could I put

on some late Titian or Rembrandt, I was asked. No I bloody well couldn't. We could have managed late Picasso, but the Tate bagged that. Everything became a marketing concept. I had to do pretty terrible shows like one for the French Bicentenary – imagine how many other countries had the same idea and were fighting for works to display – then a Vienna exhibition which cost £80,000. It was a pointless sort of activity. When we had a Corbusier we'd organised, five chamber concerts were arranged to coincide with it. The cost of those concerts equalled that of half the entire exhibition. And the finance was fixed at the South Bank so that visual arts were cross-subsidising the music budgets which went repeatedly out of kilter.

After she left, the Hayward sagged while the Tate bloomed.

If this account of Joanna Drew's career to date offers anything but a positive picture, it's a slip. She remains one of the seminal and highly respected figures in the art world. For her promotion of French work (how Keynes and Glasgow would approve) she gained that government's Chevalier l'Ordre National du Mérite, and also acquired the rank of Officier, l'Ordre des Arts et Lettres in 1988 ('Ten years before, they made me a chevalier in that order but I think a knight sounds much more fun than an officer, don't you?'). In terms of the Council and its history Drew embodied a practice, fading now, that was guided by discriminating devotion to an artistic inheritance defined earlier as 'anti-Victorianism', and a concern that British artists work best when they're inspired or at least informed through exposure to foreign creativity. Drew didn't need policy, she just *did* it. And one valued thing she did was to make the horrible Hayward not national but international and worth the drudge of visiting.

Her style did raise issues of radical practice, cultural diversity and equal opportunities which her routines couldn't bear to confront. Drew's successor at the Council faced them instead and gave the department a new vitality after its 1986 decimation. Sandy Nairne started with a diminished budget of £2 million but he advanced through 'policy, which I believe essential to fuel debate'. He was the first art director who could write 'innovation, access and advocacy were the key words this year' and believe it. He spotted the drift of certain artists toward video, live art and installations and established an officer post to overhaul policy on performance, which led to the improved reform of combined arts as a unit. Following the 'Glory of the Garden' promise finally to give money rather than exhibitions to local-authority galleries, he discovered that 'this was the only bit of "Glory" that actually seemed to work', though like most 'Glory' policies, it couldn't be pursued far enough.

Photography he took more seriously than before, as well as art in public places through the 'Percent for Art' scheme, which he freshened:

> I brought in Conrad Atkinson, who, as an artist devoted to cultural democracy, had been firmly hostile to the Arts Council but who had set up the first Percent for Art scheme, in Lewisham. We needed to learn from experienced artists like Conrad.

Above all Nairne tackled racism with specific funds – the Black Visual Artists Resources Project, the Black Visual Arts Exhibition Franchise Scheme – which culminated with INIVA, the Institute of New International Visual Arts. Set up in central London with a cash spill-out from the 'black arts centre' Roundhouse scam of the late eighties, INIVA will 'address cultural histories other than the European'. We await the results.

While the Council nearly demolished itself with the music and drama policies of 1993, the art department has remained resilient, despite losing a little vigour since Nairne's departure to the Tate. Maybe this is because it is the only unit that simply deals with living art and new work. If a glimmer of good practice can be found any-where inside the present Council, it might be here. The Salisbury Saviours could stick a bomb under the Hayward tomorrow, the Churchills could revive a family tradition and burn the Sutherlands in the Council collection together with the rest of it, but the Council's art policy is fortified by the sway of practising artists. As Bernard Levin could have written, 'Bricks may come and bricks may go but art is an art forever.'

Part III

The system and its future

This section aims to explain how the Arts Council works internally, through both its structures and personalities, and how it could improve its chances of serving the arts.

The Arts Council was empowered by royal charter, not by an act of Parliament. This gives it a stable form, as any parliamentary threat of change has to face the challenge of obtaining royal assent, and shifts have to be enshrined in a new charter. Thus it is not a government body, though its members are appointed or approved by Her Majesty's relevant minister. Members of Parliament usually call it a 'quango': a quasi-autonomous non-governmental organisation. Civil servants prefer to use other terms for the 1,500 miscellaneous institutions like the Council, expressions that tend to be both precise and cloudy at one and the same time, which is very Whitehall of them: non-departmental public bodies, semi-private bodies, fringe bodies, non-ministerial public bodies and so on.

Nevil Johnson of Nuffield College, Oxford has offered this definition: 'By quango is meant the appointed public agency, established by statute or ministerial decision, to perform executive tasks in place of central government.' The distance between the government and the Council is commonly called the 'arm's-length principle'. Nevertheless, the relation of the Council to the government's minister of the time is critical, as we'll discover.

Chapter 23

How to house an Arts Council

'We never seemed to have enough room,' thought Mary Endacott of the different buildings that have housed the crammed staff and the crowded advisory meetings of the Arts Council. There have been five headquarters. Although Luke Rittner in the eighties thought 'for about ten seconds' of moving the whole operation to Birmingham, the groan of disbelief from those around him was enough to bury the issue between the flagstones of London's West End, where the Council has forever trodden.

1940–1942: Alexandra House, 25–33 Kingsway, WC2

This functional block of offices was named after Queen Alexandra, the Danish wife of Edward VII, for whom Kingsway was christened. It stands at the south-west side of Kingsway, near Barclay's Bank, and was commandeered for wartime use by the Board of Education. For that reason, as Mary Glasgow puts it, 'I was given a desk in someone else's room and the Committee for the Encouragement of Music and the Arts opened for business on January 1st, 1940.'

The only information Glasgow has left us about the building related entirely to wartime conditions, because she had to work from there during the Blitz. She did her share of fire-watching on the roof and occasionally slept in the basement along with other members of staff. We also know that MI5 had an office, or at least an officer, there because she obtained from him the national civil-defence structure on which CEMA based its regional framework.

Alexandra House was retained by the Education Ministry. It still houses the Office of Her Majesty's Chief Inspector of Schools and, more recently, Ofsted, the watchdog for standards in education.

1942–1947: 9 Belgrave Square, SW1

The house lies on the northern side of this Belgravia square, part of the estate owned by Earl Grosvenor, south of Hyde Park Corner and north of Victoria station. It was occupied in the nineteenth century by the Earl of Essex, who was married to a singer, Catherine Stephens. She outlived him and stayed on. In that sense the place enjoyed an artistic provenance before CEMA went stumbling around it in the blackout.

Mary Endacott first worked there just after the war and has retained a clear memory of it. The detail that she remembers above all, with good reason, is that the most junior member of staff was detailed to light the fire in the morning.

> I think the property had been rented by a section of the Board of Education, but it wasn't a convenient building for them and I think that's why we got it instead. It was a pretty drab place – blackout was still up and no decorating had been done. Apart from the fire there was only a rudimentary central heating. The rooms weren't right, and you always had to go through someone else's room to get through to another office. The Council Room itself was very squashed, partly because there was a large table. I actually think that very one was used for many years as the Council table, and travelled along with us. For all I know it's still somewhere in the organisation.
>
> The music department was in the basement. Steuart Wilson was down there, and he had access to a garden. He was fairly flamboyant, and he gave a garden party with a dreadfully strong tipple to drink. But overall, I can't emphasise enough how inconvenient the building was, and how dilapidated our furniture – broken-down desks, wobbly trestle tables. And look at it now at 14 Great Peter Street.

1947–1969: 4 St James's Square, SW1

The building stands at the north-east corner of this elegant square, which was built up in the Restoration. Re-erected after a fire in 1725, number 4 was occupied by the Earl of Kent until 1908, when this town house became the home of Waldorf Astor until 1942. It was here that Tom Jones held his crisis meeting in 1940 with the Cliveden Set to boot out Chamberlain and replace him with Lloyd George. The Astors handed the property over to the Free French Army, and once they'd freed France, the Astors sold it to the government on condition it was used by the new Arts Council. The Council restored it, including the installation of central heating – except for Mary Glasgow's room.

Catherine Porteous, Sir Kenneth Clark's young secretary, described the headquarters:

> You came from the street into the hall and there was an aristocratic-looking, elderly lady called Mrs Martin, who held court at the reception desk. She had a rather plummy voice and acted more like a concierge than a clerk. On the left was an office which may have been Lady Astor's morning room. It was huge; a big, round table in the middle, and a great bookcase. It looked out onto the square. On the other side of Mrs Martin, behind her desk, there were two or three ground-floor rooms which were used as small galleries for public exhibitions. Further beyond you went into the kitchen, which acted as a canteen; it was where you got a cup of coffee, nothing grander.

From then on it was a rabbit warren of officers' and secretaries' quarters:

> There were a whole lot of little rooms, which had probably been butlers' pantries and storerooms. These housed the secretaries. When I worked there, I remember a lady called Phyllis who had been Mary Glasgow's secretary, and when Miss Glasgow left she should have left too but she didn't, and so they put her in what I can only call a cupboard. Sitting in her cupboard she cut out things about the arts from the newspapers. They were killing her with kindness. Then there was the telephonist called Irene, a nice and cosy lady who was very plump. She always wore a palm of purple violets between her very ample bosom. Whether they were real or false I was never sure – I mean the violets.

A grand staircase led to the Secretary-General's room, which, when Mrs Porteous worked there, housed Bill Williams. Next to that came his secretary's office. And at the back of his room, looking out the other way, was Eric Walter White's lair.

> Then I remember a sort of landing and then Mr McRobert's room. From then on you went into the highways and byways of the departments: music – John Denison and Mona Tatham; art – Gabriel White (an absolutely heavenly man); and the drama department – Jo Hodgkinson – which seemed to me to be the slightly poor relation for some reason [it was housed in the one-time nursery]. I also have a memory of a stationery store, which was run by a lady who used to go mountain-climbing in Yugoslavia. K. said once that she'd come to a sticky end, and, astonishingly, she was murdered on one of her treks.

Of her own work there, she revealed:

> I had a little office, and next to that . . . Well, one day when K. was travelling away, which he did often, I got restless and peeked round. Next to me was the wardrobe lady of Opera for All, which was a little touring unit the Arts Council ran [it became Opera 80, later still English Touring Opera]. She was making costumes, and she let me help her. I learned an awful lot about dressmaking during my time at the Arts Council.

1969–1990: 105 Piccadilly, W1

Lord Goodman chose this because he wanted something grand he could waddle out of into the public gaze. What better address from which to hail a cab than this swanky mansion, built so that the original residents could say they lived near the Duke of Wellington, down by Hyde Park? Goodman was surprised to hear that the staff thought it was too big, too costly in its lease, and not exactly near anything they would need to visit, aside from the prostitutes of Shepherd's Market, who could be viewed from the higher back windows. The nearest shop was Fortnum & Mason.

It remains the most famous Council address. For many years people spoke of 'One-o-five' (a touch of Orwell's Room 101) in a way they wouldn't talk of 'Fourteen' today. Staff worked there for two decades at a time when the Council served the most clients and had the largest committees, but also when it was most vulnerable to the criticism of being elitist. Many visitors agreed that it produced a posh impression, but one that diminished the further they moved up and away from the ground floor.

Behind the majestic reception hall, at which 'you could sit for hours meeting friends and enemies as they waited for the nean-derthal lift to arrive', stood a wide, red-carpeted staircase of the kind stars saunter down to reluctant applause on West End stages. Theatre director Peter Cheeseman swore he would travel from Stoke-on-Trent once a year, stand at the bottom of the staircase and shout, 'Can I have some money?' After an infinite pause he would hear drifting down the ghostly answer, 'Noooooo.'

Council meetings were held in a huge room at the front overlooking Green Park, where, according to director Jonathan Miller, 'we sat at an enormous table with people silhouetted against the light of Piccadilly windows . . . [like] a singing version of the Beefsteak'. There were a couple of other committee rooms, equally imposing, and the top floor – the seventh – contained the staff restaurant where, on summer days, officers and visitors could enjoy the view south of Green Park and the Thames from a terrace. The six floors sandwiched between the restaurant and reception contained all the departmental offices, the highest of which sheltered executives. The chairman had a bathroom by his study: 'Someone kept stealing in and using it after hours. I don't think we ever found out who, but it was someone whose nights were more sanitary than their days.'

By the late seventies the staff had run out of space. When the Council unwisely chose to open its own bookshop for a time at 8–9 Long Acre in Covent Garden, the music and literature departments moved out there ('bang between the opera houses') and smartly asked to move back when it dawned on them that they were cut off from the rest of the operation. A modern building behind 105 Piccadilly, 1–5 Yarmouth Place, became available, and so the Council leased it and constructed an extraordinary glass bridge between the two units. The trouble was, when the Council vacated to Westminster in 1990, it did so during the recession and it just couldn't shake off its extension. After paying charges on the empty property for three years, it finally disposed of it at a net loss to the tax-payer, in that cost alone, of £1,653,000.

1990 onwards: 14 Great Peter Street, Westminster, SW1

How Peter Palumbo must have enjoyed his little joke of moving to a street which – by chance, of course – had a certain ring to its name. Others saw the shift down to Westminster as a sign of the Council's desire to trade more actively with politicians. They could equally have seen it as a wish by the ardently Anglican Chairman to invoke a more spiritual mood, for the chosen building was formerly the address of the Society for the Propagation of the Gospel in Foreign Parts, and it enjoys a breathtaking view of Westminster Abbey's outline from east to west (it's the abbey of St Peter, hence the name of the street). Unfortunately, this panorama can be seen only from the Chairman's office.

First-time visitors are often unsure if they've arrived at the right place. 'Palumbo wanted something to identify the building from the outside that was discreet and elegant to his way of thinking,' a staff member recalls. 'So he commissioned an enigmatic scroll in slate with "Arts Council of Great Britain" chiselled into it.' Not long afterwards, the Arts Council changed its name to that of England, and the exquisite, expensive sign became obsolete.

What happened next highlights a subdued problem that the Council tries to pretend doesn't exist: the vast aesthetic gap between the artform staff and the service workers.

> Sam Turner [the services manager] put up these signs that might have said 'Now Wash Your Hands' for all the decorum they exhibited. One of the directors fumed rather unfairly, 'How could this have happened? This looks so unattractive.' Few of the artform staff had thought it out as Sam had done, [reasoning] that perhaps something clear and elementary was what your ordinary folk need to find out they're standing outside the Arts Council's headquarters. That the servicing staff had no aesthetic connection with the rest of their colleagues is a condition which speaks volumes about the Council's infrastructure.

Great Peter Street provided the first opportunity for the Council to flaunt all it had learned in recent years about disabled access. A senior staffer admits that the access plan turned into a shambles, and what was supposed to have been built in had often to be added on. As another staff member amusingly recounts:

> Though someone was put in charge of finessing the design of the new building, we were driven nuts with alterations and revisions – to what end and what cost I can't begin to say. Look at something

simple like the toilet signs, for instance: those silly Swiss milkmaids in pigtails and skirts on the ladies' loos. They were apparently insisted on by the Council because blind women can feel them. How do you know where the door is in the first place? You know, if you think about it, isn't the milkmaid a bit beside the point?

A former officer voiced a common complaint that the building was:

Unathletic. There are four lifts, and you're forced to take them everywhere. Ever jogged in one? Memos were once sent round begging staff to propose money-raising ideas. Someone in the dance department came up with the best suggestion, given the nature of the building: coin-operated lifts.

Panellists complained bitterly about the meeting rooms:

The one at the top is the size of a rabbit hutch, and smells like one. The one in the basement had little windows at street level, and you could see passersby bending down, peering in and gaping at us. So now you have blinds cutting out the light. When you've travelled 200 miles to the big city and you can't see it, you feel a bit swindled.

This was the first headquarters for which the Council was able to plan its needs. Unfortunately, it miscalculated. The lottery unit soon needed more staff. In order to accommodate them, the twelve-strong finance department was moved to a rented building. Now the Council is searching for another home.

For the record, the Council has owned or owns the following properties: the South Bank estate (including the National Theatre, National Film Theatre, Hayward Gallery and South Bank Centre), 28 Sackville Street, 5 Record Street, the Coliseum, the Wigmore Hall, the Serpentine Gallery, and a portion of the Royal Opera House land currently under development.

A former regional arts director recalls an argument about the best kind of building for an arts organisation. 'In the end we agreed that there are two alternative models to choose from: a phone box or a barge.'

BT NHS

Working together to deliver N3

www.n3.nhs.uk

Arts Council

Royal charters

Although the Council refers to 'the charter' that empowers its purpose and operation, there have been four to date, six if you include the new ones for the Arts Councils of Scotland and Wales:

1. 9 August 1946
2. 7 February 1967
3. 31 July 1985 (a supplement)
4. 1 April 1994

In each case revisions of an administrative nature have been made with good reason. The only changes to the artistic objectives of the Council took place to widen the perspective of the term 'arts', which is never actually defined at any time – probably a good thing. In 1946 Keynes specified the 'fine arts', which had been an acceptable phrase already used by royal flunkeys to exempt certain societies from paying rates on their properties (an account of this can be found in Part I).

The original charter stipulated 'the fine arts exclusively', while Goodman's charter of 1967 states:

The objects for which the Council are established and incorporated are as follows:

(a) to develop and improve the knowledge, understanding and practice of the arts;

(b) to increase the accessibility of the arts to the public throughout Great Britain; and

(c) to advise and co-operate with Departments of Our Government, local authorities and other bodies on any matters concerned whether directly or indirectly with the foregoing objects.

The 1994 charter for the Arts Council of England maintained these, but just said 'the public' and dropped 'throughout Great Britain', which means that the ACE now deals with many more people, or fewer – the big wide world or little England. In any case, some Council members and critics believe that (a) and (b) are mutually exclusive. Two of the original appointees of both CEMA and the ACGB coined contrasting maxims to define the job the two objectives invoked. Ivor Brown conceived 'the best for the most'. Bill Williams countered with 'raise or spread?' In his case it was definitely raise, not spread.

The 1985 supplemental charter was necessary solely to allow Mrs Thatcher to hand the South Bank estate over to the Arts Council when she dissolved the Greater London Council on 1 April 1986. The Council

> shall hold the South Bank Estate . . . for its general purposes and in particular to maintain and develop the same as a centre for the arts for the benefit of the people of Great Britain in general and of London in particular.

This estate:

> means and includes the several hereditaments situated on the south bank of the River Thames in the London Borough of Lambeth and respectively known as the Royal Festival Hall, the Queen Elizabeth Hall, the Purcell Room, the Hayward Gallery, the National Theatre, the National Film Theatre and Jubilee Gardens and the grounds appurtenant thereto respectively together with all such lands adjacent thereto or in the vicinity thereof.

As far as this handover went, the Council never rose or spread, and the South Bank Centre (which comprises the first four facilities in the list) has arguably shuffled into a shambles.

Council minutes

Of the reams of printed paper the Council disgorges, the most splendid to read are the minutes of the Council meetings, as drafted first by Mary Glasgow, and then for thirty years by Mary Endacott. They remain confidential, though Lawrence Mackintosh maintains an archive where they may be consulted, so long as the Secretary-General gives permission; papers over thirty years old should normally be available to the public anyway.

Lord Armstrong, Cabinet secretary in Mrs Thatcher's time, believed that the purpose of minutes, as a testament to debate and decision-making, was less to report what people said than to record what they wish they had said. Arts Council minutes have benignly offered the impression that members were more on the ball than they probably were. Mary Endacott remarked:

> I wrote the minutes for six different chairmen (Pooley, Clark, Cottesloe, Goodman, Gibson, Robinson, Rees-Mogg), so they are distinct in style for that reason. Secretary-generals each have a view on the subject, too. Bill Williams was a great one for brevity, for instance, and so I had to write very concise minutes. But his Chairman, Clark, was 'got at' by some members of the Council, who liked to have the low-down when they themselves were not at a meeting. They wanted to read what *really* went on. So when policy matters came up, Sir Kenneth asked me to do something fuller, and I worked somehow between these two demands.

The trouble was that the detail took over. 'One really lost one's sense of direction. They got so full that members got to the point of saying, "I'm sure I made an interjection at that point." So, once they were full they could never be full enough.' When Richard Pulford joined as deputy Secretary-General in 1979, he was used to civil-service practice.

> He encouraged me to put the gist of the argument down in the form of a circular paragraph: Whereas on the one hand members of the Council thought so-and-so, on the other hand some members thought the opposite, but the general feeling was . . .

This made some of the members feel they didn't exist. I remember David Sylvester exclaiming, 'These minutes! Though the record of the meeting lists me as being present, I have no sense from what I read that I was actually there.'

She concluded by saying that, 'You get to the point where you just can't do another set of minutes. You feel you're almost quoting yourself.'

Annual reports

These are vital public documents, distributed each autumn to local libraries and the wastepaper bins of the nation. Titled the 'Annual Report and Accounts', they have balance sheets for the previous financial year (April to March) prefaced by 'state of the art' essays from senior staff. The original royal charter stipulated that the Council should 'as soon after the month of March as possible, prepare a General Report of its proceedings for the year preceding'.

The Arts Council of Great Britain's reports are numbered from 1 to 49. From 1994 they became the reports of the English Arts Council, numbered accordingly from the new start. It has become a tradition that the Chairman's overview comes first, followed by the Secretary-General's, and then the departmental reports, which fall under the aegis of the executive and are therefore unsigned. What the Chairman writes is usually called an Introduction, while the Secretary-General's musings are a Report, or oddly, in Luke Rittner's day, a Preface. These inspiring essentials are melded together with thrilling photos of performers, many of whom are surprised to see their pictures there, having never thought of themselves as working for the Arts Council.

The Chairman and the Secretary-General really have the same things to say, apportioned between them: The arts are precious/ give us more money. They generally end with 'a warning'. The name Oliver Twist has appeared in these discourses on eleven occasions. The dourest notes of all were penned by music director John Denison ('There were no major catastrophes this year'), while on reading Sir Kenneth Robinson's remarks you can hear the rattle of his collecting tin:

Well, we faced appalling inflation at that time, and I go on about Money, Money, Money, because the Council is a bottomless pit. It always wants to do more than it's financially able to, and that consideration rather gets to you.

Sir Roy Shaw's comments read like engaging lectures, which you suspect will be followed overleaf by an exam paper on the topics he covered.

In the early days the Council and panel members would simply be listed on the inner cover as a matter of record, and then on inside pages as the panels expanded. From 1987, a 'get to know your Council' section was introduced, together with a photo of the members trying to raise smiles. At this very time the operation was vigorously pursuing an equal-opportunities policy, so it's curious to see that a Council member's education background was supplied only if he or she went somewhere posh. While we're told, for instance, that Christopher Frayling went to Repton and Churchill College, Cambridge, and Mathew Prichard (who is 'the grandson of detective writer Agatha Christie') enjoyed Eton, poor old Clare Mulholland, among others (usually women), must have kicked balls in back alleys until she matured, for all we're told. It transpires that she went to Notre Dame High School, Glasgow and Notre Dame Primary School before that, but as there must be a clause in the royal charter that the Council can only list names of exclusive academies, they weren't mentioned.

From the eighth report (1952–1953) to the seventeenth (1961–1962), Bill Williams gave the publication doom-laden titles: 'The Public & the Arts', 'Arts in the Red' (1956–1957), 'The Struggle for Survival' (very appropriate for 1958–1959), 'A Brighter Prospect'. Abercrombie followed on – 'Policy into Practice' to 'Changes & Moves' – but Willatt desisted. Shaw took up the theme again – 'The Arts in Hard Times' to 'Critical Judgments' – but he was the last to do so.

The covers have swivelled between graphics and photos. Now that we have the Arts Council of England presenting its report, graphics have returned. What appears to be the Red Cross flag is in fact the cross of Saint George, slightly askew.

Annual accounts

The accounts are drawn up with one main aim: to give the impression that the Council is spending more on the arts than it really is.

Back in the 1940s it would quietly implant staff costs and other overheads in the artform columns of expenditure. The total sum apparently spent on visual arts, say, contained within it the salaries of the department's director and his staff, either at the headquarters or out in the regions. This had the dual effect of displaying a higher figure being spent on the artform than was the case and hiding the true cost of the Council's administration. Treasury officials challenged this neat tactic, but the accountant argued that change would create 'an inconsistency in present-ation' – and got away with it.

The staffing ledger was refashioned in the fifties at the time that Bill Williams dismantled the regional offices. That done, the cost of the office overheads looked much more acceptable, even virtuous – down from an opening high of 20 per cent to 12 per cent in 1954 and finally 8 per cent by 1959 – and only then were they allowed a column of their own. Meanwhile the government's grant had increased and that helped to camouflage the downward adjustment of artform spending in the accounts.

Bill Williams, incidentally, liked to awe readers with exuberant graphs and charts. His tuppenny-coloured fantasies were inserted in front of the balance sheet in the fifties. They purported to illustrate attendances and box-office returns, which was an odd way to tell people what you'd spent their taxes on. You were really telling them what they'd had to spend in addition to their taxes in order to see the art they'd already funded.

But Bill Williams was an amateur in contrast to the reports' compilers in the eighties at the time of Rittner and Everitt. As one former director said:

> I could make neither head nor tail of our accounts as records of business. They looked perfectly impressive as you scanned them. But if you asked a simple question like, 'How much have we spent in total on that client?' or more frankly, 'How much have the bastards in the other departments squandered away?', then it was near impossible to be comparative. In fact there was one that was a complete balls-up. Wasn't it shredded and reprinted? I think the Treasury insisted it had to be redone.

The report for 1986–1987 came to the public in two volumes, one later than the other. Only the first was widely distributed. It was not polluted by a single piece of arithmetic.

Bill Williams would have envied one tactic his successors could rely on to stupefy any reader of the accounts. As the government grant increased in the sixties and seventies, it was decided to disburse as many minor payments as possible to fatten the list of recipients for political gain. Awards to individuals, long resisted for policy reasons, were re-introduced and conspicuously headed the schedule of grants. While Bill 'few but roses' Williams tallied a grand total of 104 client grants, his successor, Hugh Willatt, could now list 281 awards solely to single artists, following those with twelve pages of artform payments (230 to drama alone). Most of these grants were impertinent and nominal, but they conveyed the impression that the Arts Council had placed its cash in every artistic nook and cranny in the country.

The first ACE report of 1994 lists no fewer than 1,700 grants. Yet the same clients keep cropping up in different columns. London's Institute of Contemporary Arts, for instance, appears on fourteen occasions: under combined arts (four times), cross-disciplinary initiatives, film and video, international initiatives, literature, and visual arts (five times). It illustrates how the carve-up of grant-giving into countless 'strategic' projects serves the Arts Council's quantitative aspirations. Further, it exposes how far organisations now have to faff around the Arts Council's capricious network of fleeting, one-off schemes. The majority of grants are tiny: 53 per cent of them are lower than £5,000; 107 are no higher than £500. Seventeen of those are for £120, less than the cost of administering them.

One of the strangest figures in the accounts is one that goes out and comes straight back in again with a different name, like this:

	£
Cash grant-in-aid voted by Parliament 1993–4	225,630,000
Supplementary grant-in-aid	200,000
Less: Debtor for grant-in-aid accrued at 1 April 1993	11,874,000
Total	213,956,000
Plus: Debtor for accrued grant-in-aid outstanding at 31 March 1994	11,874,000
Total	225,830,000

The origins of this peculiar business began in the fifties. It's a consequence of two different accounting systems and two separate calendars trying to mesh into one piece of information. In the early days of the Arts Council, the government's annual grant-in-aid would arrive as a single cheque. The finance department put it on deposit to accrue interest, which was not strictly speaking allowable as they were supposed to be passing the money on to clients. Treasury officials finally cottoned on. Subsequently, in the middle fifties, the grant was broken into quarterly amounts, but not equal ones, because the Council pointed out that its theatre clients, for instance, needed more money when they were closed in the summer months and less when the Christmas show was packing them in. The Treasury cheques came out something like this:

25%	1 April
40%	1 July
18%	1 October
17%	1 January

Tony Field also introduced double-entry book-keeping, while the Treasury maintained a cash accounting system. He did so in order that he could take in creditors and debtors, acknowledging that most of the clients didn't work on an April-to-March financial year, but through seasons, where spring sometimes carried over into July. He also needed, he believed, to build up a reserve for the Council to cover unforeseen problems – a snowstorm in Manchester erasing a Hallé concert, for instance. At the same time he divided the cash sent to clients into two different lumps: a grant and a guarantee against loss.

The latter amount, which might be 10 to 15 per cent of the full sum offered, was held back by the Council until the client could produce accounts to show it had not done better on the box office than it had anticipated when it sent in its application a year before. Critics of the guarantee system complained that it 'penalised success', and for a period after Field left in 1984 it was dropped, which Field considered an 'appalling lapse'. It was the Treasury that stampeded over and said, 'Right, now he's gone, we're going to do it *this* way,' which is another example of Whitehall's growing intrusions on the Council in the eighties.

The complications resulting from these increasingly subtle transactions didn't faze Field. In fact, he marshalled the situation brilliantly to the Council's advantage and his skill at 'playing with the last quarter's figures [January–March]' is still fondly remembered by his artform colleagues, which is a remarkable achievement seeing as how he made them squabble for the very large and useful crumbs spilling from this process, which became known as the 'cash and commitment gap'.

John Faulkner, the drama director who fought for the money each winter, explained it this way:

Cash was the grant, commitment the guarantee. Guarantees were
not always called on, and so 'fall-ins' became evident during the
last quarter. In other words, we had more money left to spend than
we thought we had. That was backed up by the percentage of grant-
in-aid winging in from the Treasury. Very often it was possible to
massage these figures together so that you could actually commit
more than you had in cash. Tony was a master at this; he understood that kind of financing to a hair. Some of us in the artform
departments were able to arrange our budgets perfectly legiti-
mately in such a way that we benefited from this bit of arbitrage
between the cash you had and what you could commit, and what
would fall in from guarantees unclaimed. It gave us leeway. When
the Treasury took it away, the removal of that buffer was like a cash
cut.

Field insisted that the money was central before it was
apportioned to departments and he would not hear of a director
talking about 'my money'. Each final quarter, 'I would beat them
into making judgments *together*. The directors had to be
corporately responsible, so that I didn't end up looking like a
dictator.' The art director Joanna Drew admired 'the way Tony
could turn 80 into 90, but I have to say that he'd imply it was to my
tactical and financial advantage to run a Renoir exhibition in the
last quarter!'
Once we take into account the seasonal variances and the fact
that the Council funded a number of festivals which ran in
sequence from May (Bath) to September (Ludlow), we can see
how Field could use the same money twice or three times over in
the same year.

If a spring festival presented its accounts in August, I could modify
what might be needed at the end of the season. This made the flow
of information, of course, between the artform departments, my
department and the clients themselves much closer and regular
than outsiders sometimes realise.

It's said that Manchester's Royal Exchange Theatre benefited year
end by year end thanks to the prompt exchange of information.
This, then, is the background relating to the debtor figure that
appears each year and it came about because the Treasury started
to hold back around 5 per cent of the grant-in-aid in line with the
Council's manipulations. The change took place dramatically in

1979, that very significant year when Callaghan lost to Thatcher. Up to then, the government grant figure was followed by an additional but small sum of money simply defined as 'provision for grants and guarantees not required', which was the amount Field persuasively saved for the Arts Council in the annual round of negotiations with the Treasury officers who might otherwise have clawed it back as unused grant. His technique was invariably persuasive, though the Council still came a cropper under the Tories in 1973 when the civil servants listened politely but still took back £250,000 (£1.5 million at today's values).

In 1979, according to the Arts Council, 'the [Labour] Government was unable to pay part of the grant-in-aid voted by Parliament for 1978–9. The Council therefore negotiated an overdraft [with Coutts] in anticipation of receiving this sum in 1979–80' (the account in fact shows an unprecedented overspend by the Council of £21,345, which is close to £80,000 today). The large sum unpaid by the Government was £1,525,000. It was finally included within the following year's grant, which was determined during Labour's last year in power and was therefore voted in but not actually fixed before Mrs Thatcher's Conservative Government took over. The incoming regime snipped £1,100,000 off the voted budget, in effect taking back the substantive sum that had caused the problem the previous year. Roy Shaw called it a 'cut', which it was, but he was not able to profit by it because that would have exposed the background to the loss.

Quite simply the Treasury had called into question the way the Arts Council was handling unfinished business from previous periods and commitments to future ones. In the huffy rhetoric of the 1980 Arts Council accounts:

> The Parliamentary grant-in-aid is issued to meet the Council's expenditure falling due for payment during the financial year including payments to meet commitments incurred in a previous year. The Council may incur commitments during a financial year in the full knowledge that they will not fall due for payment until the following year.

In other words the Council had started borrowing from future grants not confirmed or even determined. No Arts Council client would have been allowed to do that (at least, not officially) and all clients would have been curious to know to whom the Arts Council was making promises 'in the full knowledge that they will not fall due for payment until the following year'. Stand up the Big Four.

The £1,510,000 not paid out in 1978 related to the similar total of 'unmatured commitments' mentioned in the previous year's accounts. The Treasury wanted a new method to establish such sums as borrowings, really an overdraft arrangement. The debut of the new format in the 1980 accounts was lumbering but comparatively explicit:

Reconciliation of parliamentary grant-in-aid	£
Amount voted by Parliament	61,476,000
Less: Amounts earmarked at 31.3.79 to be met out	
of future amounts to be voted by Parliament	2,725,000
Underpayment of 1978–1979 cash, paid 1979–1980	1,525,000
Total	57,226,000
Plus: Amounts earmarked at 31.3.80 to be met from	
future amounts to be voted by Parliament	6,404,000
Total	63,630,000

The £11,874,000 mentioned in the 1994 accounts amounts to 5 per cent of the total grant-in-aid offered to the Council by the Government. The finance director of the time, Lew Hodges, confirmed that:

This practice has now been ceased and the note [in 1994] reflects the accumulated position. The Government agreed the current position some time ago, but required that in future the Arts Council's income should be the same as the actual amount provided by Government. Thus there will be no repeat of the practice of the 1980s, but the accounts will have the present note for the foreseeable future.

One crucial item in the accounts has never been truly calculable. This is the amount of money directly spent on the arts in England – England because the government grant to the Arts Council ('of Great Britain') used to be cut up and passed on in part to the Arts Councils of Wales and Scotland, likewise inside England to the Regional Arts Associations. In effect the money to be spent on the arts was actually passed down the line to a second tier of administration. As most arts companies had administrative costs themselves it could be argued that the government's money was drained through three levels of administration before it reached the work of art – four, if the government's own distributing department was included.

Nevertheless the accountants would play with these figures to offer as benevolent a picture of the Arts Council as they could. The grand total of 'general expenditure on the arts' would include within it the grants to the associate bureaucracies. 'General expenditure' is an impressively subtle term. For example, the final ACGB accounts of 1993–1994 display a sum for 'general expenditure on the arts in Britain' which carefully indicates that it does not include the cost of the Arts Council's 'management and services'. It sounds jolly good, too, when the Secretary-General can say to Parliament or the press, 'Our government grant last year was £225 million, and we spent £217 million of that on general expenditure on the arts in this country.' Yet the Arts Council only spent £133 million of that in grants to the arts, with another £4 million for its own promotions. In reality it handed over £80 million to associate bureaucracies who, by the time of the 1993 accounts we can be sure, would have passed some of that not to companies and artists but to 'consultants', a generous name for old colleagues who write reports about things their staff should know already.

A version of this can be found in a promotional pamphlet from 1995, unwisely titled 'The Arts Council of England: Facts About the Arts'. Over an imposing set of bar charts with elaborate costings against a range of artforms, it states, 'In 1995/6 the Arts Council and Regional Arts Boards allocated the £191 million grant as follows . . .' yet the figures underneath add up to a sum £20 million short of the balance.

Another hard Fact About the Arts lies undeclared.

Chapter 25

The unpaid

It is said that Sir William Emrys Williams – Pelican Bill – gave an off-the-cuff chat to a group of visitors from a Women's Institute. 'The Arts Council is run like a town council. It has two limbs. Indeed, it is like the human body with its two systems: the blood system and the nerve system.' A lady piped up, 'Don't you mean lymph?' Pelican Bill smiled and answered, 'Ah, lymph is our money which is distributed as grants.' Another lady asked, 'And where do we, the public, fit in?' Williams wondered aloud, 'Well now, what system's left?' Someone from the staff mumbled, 'Waste, Sir William.'

A hierarchy of around 190 staff (nerves) are paid to service nearly 300 unpaid advisers (blood). The great and the good are distributed among twenty-four or so committees; some of them sit on more than one. The nerves are divided into twenty-two departments, determined by artform (the combined arts department, say) or function (finance and resources). Decisions are made by a bloody council of twenty-one advisers, while the committees underneath make 'recommendations' which inform those decisions. But, like the collection of plasma, nerves, lymph and excrement by which Williams conjured his establishment, it's not quite that simple.

Take the 300 advisers. Their council meets almost monthly, at least ten times a year, and each agenda takes all day. Indeed the council has recently taken to assembling in the evening and working through to dinner, then reconvening in the morning to end with lunch. Back in the forties and fifties the meetings ran for a mere afternoon, and Sir Roy Shaw would have welcomed the return of that, for 'no committee does any decent work after two hours'. The expansion is blamed on more clients, more arguments. 'The early meetings were decorous,' recalled Mary Endacott, the Council's renowned minute-taker, who recorded discussions between 1950 and 1986.

> There weren't any of the verbal fisticuffs of later years. Ladies wore hats, some of them rather flamboyant, actually, though I was a secretary and wasn't called on to do so. Some time after the war the Council met every three months and there was an executive committee that conferred monthly. I really feel that arts practitioners with more eminence were willing to serve in those days, when everything seemed more manageable – I daren't say more reasonable – in contrast to recent times.

A Council member is someone who can spare twenty days a year and more, sifting through the heap of papers posted a week beforehand; officers assume, however, that Council members never really read them. They *scan*. Though food and drink is provided, Lord Palumbo still preferred to have his own cook and butler. Mary Endacott remembers that in the early years of frugal afternoons, the writer Richard Capell would hide a bar of chocolate in the back pocket of his trousers and chew on lumps when he thought no one was looking, 'like a schoolboy in class'.

The Council is composed of people invited by the Chairman, who checks first with the Arts Minister whether the appointment is acceptable to the government. The Chairman is himself appointed by the Minister. Critics argue that it's not the government's place to meddle in such matters, though it's pretty much accepted as common practice on other quangos, and anyway the Minister is answerable to Parliament for the behaviour of the Council and therefore has a right to be advised about appointments. Since the 1995 Nolan Commission on public appointments, the Council's membership is now formally regulated by Sir Len Peach, the Commissioner for Public Appointments (OCPA). His code of practice confirms that 'the ultimate responsibility for appointments is with ministers'.

Ministers prefer to say they don't select or even approve but are merely 'consulted' on Council appointments. Yet the 1946 charter specified that Council members should be 'appointed by Our Chancellor of the Exchequer after consultation with Our Minister of Education'. The 1967 charter changed this to approval by the Secretary of State for Education and Science 'in consultation' with the Welsh and Scottish Secretaries of State, and the 1994 charter states that 'members shall be appointed by our Secretary of State': the Secretary of State for what it doesn't say, but practically it means the one for the Department of Culture, Media and Sport.

It's quite possible for the Chairman to put before the Minister an argument as to why someone customarily unacceptable, that is politically so, might be a useful choice. Recently the Earl of Gowrie put up as Vice-Chairman the architect Richard Rogers. The former Tory Minister was second-guessing a 1997 general election. Gowrie chose Rogers because he was a prominent Labour supporter. Most ministers would appreciate the political wisdom of that appointment, although two previous Labour-friendly deputies were discharged during Tory regimes: Denis Hodson and Richard Hoggart.

Decisions are made by the Council, while all the panels one step below it can pass merely on 'recommendations'. Keynes set up this system when he found he hadn't time to control the original artform subcommittees by chairing them. He decided that if he couldn't be there at the table they couldn't have power. Those who chair the panels are given a place on the Council; that is an ancillary task that most members of the Council have to take on, and chairing a panel eats up a great deal more time and energy. The recommendation formula also explains why an applicant may wheedle out of a panellist or an officer the news that he or she is going to get the money applied for: this takes place off the record as all such information is considered confidential. Yet the applicant hears nothing formally until the Council has ratified the panel's recommendation at a subsequent meeting. Never call a Council member a councillor, by the way: they'd loathe to be mistaken for the newsagents and freemasons who run parish politics.

The Council

In 1998 there were twenty-three Council members: ten chairmen of the Regional Arts Boards, eleven panel chairs, one 'independent' and the Council Chairman. The original size back in the forties was sixteen, determined by the notion of five Londoners, five provincials and a further four representing Scotland (two) and

Wales (two), plus the Chairman and Vice-Chairman (who, it was assumed, would be Welsh or Scottish – a touch of the Tom Joneses there). Then it expanded, up to twenty-one, as panels grew. In 1993 the Government commissioned the consultants Price Water-house to review the Arts Council's structure, and it recommended a reduction of the Council to twelve. Peter Brooke, the Arts Minister at the time, nevertheless declared in the Commons:

> I intend to move to a Council of sixteen members, including the Chairman and Vice-Chairman. This will allow the inclusion of five regional representatives, each of the seven artform panel chair-men, and four independents.

Until Palumbo came along at the start of the nineties, the Council meetings were additionally crammed with a motley selection of staff (all the directors but also six minor officers selected by ballot) and observers from the ministry. Rees-Mogg tried to cut the thing down but faced the gall of the directors who wanted to be there to keep a hand on the throats of their panel chairs. On finding something like fifty people packed into the room, he decided to bang a gavel to bring order to bear between items. Palumbo agreed to succeed Rees-Mogg only if he could eliminate all but the decision-makers. He threw out the general staff and when the Arts Council became that of England in 1994, the Scottish and Welsh had no excuse to be there anyway.

Subsequently there was an inartistic ploy to add all the chairs of the ten Regional Arts Boards, which brought the Council back to twenty-one members in 1997. Already half of them had sat on the 1995 Council, as Brooke proposed; this is part of the Council's 'integrationist' approach in evolving a liaison with the RABs. It created an intriguing new consequence for those bodies because it meant that the Minister had to be consulted on the regional appointments if they were also to take up a place on the Council. As the RABs are never chaired by artists, but by unexciting academics or businessfolk with a suspicious amount of time on their hands, the decision to include them all made even more remote the involvement of authentic practitioners at the executive level.

Between 1945 and the summer of 1997, 202 members had sat on the Council. Of these, 170 (84 per cent) were male, thirty-two (16 per cent) female. Only forty-one (20 per cent) of the total could be called creative or re-creative artists of any kind, and only nineteen (9 per cent) of those have worked in the performing or visual arts. Representation of writers stands way above the Council's concern for literature; in principle that's no bad thing, though secretary Sheila Gold said, 'I'd see these famous authors sitting there, and I wanted to tell them they would better help the arts by writing rather than enduring one more uneventful debate.' Despite the odd distinguished presence, the list makes rather rum reading. Rather than articulating the grand sweep of British artistic endeavour through half a century, it amounts to an odd collection of artisans who might be relied on to vote Conservative or Labour as appropriate in an election and have been rewarded with a Council seat by the Minister of the time for doing so.

Theatre	*Novelists*
Peggy Ashcroft	Melvyn Bragg
Richard Attenborough	Buchi Emecheta
Lewis Casson	P.D. James
Constance Cummings	Marghanita Laski
Michael Elliott	C.P. Snow
Martin Esslin	Angus Wilson
Peter Hall	
Benn Levy	*Poets*
James Bridie/O.H. Mavor	Joseph Compton
Jonathan Miller	Roy Fuller
Trevor Nunn	C. Day Lewis
Brian Rix	Andrew Motion
Donald Sinden	
	Other writers
Visual arts	Richard Capell
William Coldstream	Antonia Fraser
Henry Moore	Richard Hoggart
	Michael Holroyd
Architecture	Frank Kermode
Richard Rogers	Bryan Magee
Colin St John Wilson	Myfanwy Piper
	C.V. Wedgwood
	Raymond Williams
Music	Angus Wilson
Philip Jones	
Denis Mathews	*Dance*
Ralph Vaughan Williams	Annette Page

It might surprise his critics to learn that the artistic capacity of the Council bothered Lord Rees-Mogg.

> I never thought – and in this my fellow members of the Council got rather irritated with me – that we actually had the proficiency to make very discriminating artistic judgments. My own view of the Council's record on this was that, roughly speaking, we could limit our judgments to three categories – excellent, good, or inadequate. We could make fairly firm judgments of that sort, but anything more sensitive became a matter of taste upon which the most expert people would not agree. Invariably, the senior people on the Council had to be generalists. They were dealing with some arts of which they had no full understanding. My discernment of ballet was so negligible that provided the people didn't actually fall off the stage I didn't know whether they were doing it properly or not. They understood some arts quite well but other arts hardly at all.

Rees-Mogg sagely intimated that he preferred to read press reviews than listen to the aesthetic opinions of the Council, but then, having edited *The Times*, he would.

Rees-Mogg's adversary Sir Roy Shaw found the entirety of debate disappointing:

> People were so chuffed to be put on the Council that they felt the only decent thing was to agree with the Chairman. The critic Jack Lambert chaired the drama panel for years in the seventies. A very nice man, and after he retired from the Council he wrote an article about his time there lamenting that members would sit through a meeting *schtumm* and afterwards gossip, 'Of course, I didn't agree with that.' I've found that courage is not a widespread public quality.

However, those who do challenge the chair are often deterred. After an introductory meeting, the author C.P. Snow turned to secretary Sheila Gold and said, 'I'm not coming here again. I wasn't allowed to open my mouth.' A member at the time of Goodman recalls that:

> At my first meeting Arnold said something and I butted in with an observation. Well! It was made very clear to me that this wasn't approved; Goodman made a rather nasty, 'good-humoured' crack. Henry Moore was there and he winked at me, which made me feel

there was at least some artistic support to usurp what I thought was a rather staged affair. Afterwards Talbot Rice actually told me that it was better to keep quiet while Goodman was pontificating, because 'After all, he's rather entertaining.'

As a Council member in the sixties, Roy Shaw was also told off by a fellow member after his third meeting: 'You know, it's not done here to disagree with the Chairman.'

Panels

Below the Council sit ten or so advisory panels (currently eleven), divided by artform – music, drama and so on – or function: education, touring. There have been fifty-five different names for panels and their subcommittees since 1945: dance panel (founded 1979), dance and mime projects and awards subcommittee (founded 1973), dance and mime education and outreach committee (founded 1987), dance development advisory team (founded 1992), and so exhaustively on.

Each panel comprises around twelve unpaid members. Today's sizes complement those of the forties, from which time the panels ballooned out to Goodmanesque girth in the late sixties (each around thirty members), then dieted back to common sense through the eighties. The Minister's involvement reaches down to this level, as it's normal practice for the panel's chair to be one of the Council members on whom the Minister has been consulted. Sir Kenneth Robinson believed that this key appointment could make or break the system:

> It is extremely dependent on the prowess of panel chairmen. An effective one should certainly have a reputation within the artform, but equally he must be technically adept and thus able to communicate corporate views to the Council. A good panel with a bad chairman doesn't really get its points across.

Each panellist serves about three years, though in practice there's no hard rule. Officers admit that it's hard to find enough compliant experts to fill the panels, and so a bit of backstage manipulating is allowed to invite useful ones to extend their stay, or to get rid of awkward sorts early. It's not only at this level that there's a play of influences between the staff and the advisers. This dual system of blood and nerves allows for a degree of secondary circulation. The most common breakdown occurs when the artform director and the panel chair don't see eye to eye, or one of them is unsatisfactory. Using their separate chains of command they can appeal upwards, the director to the Secretary-General, the panel chair to the Chairman. Equally, those at the top can use either circuit to bypass obstacles without recourse to sackings or bumbling subterfuge.

Recruitment is an incontestable problem. As one former Council member said:

> There's a mythology that a variety of opinion balances itself out when a decision has to be made. That's rubbish. Committees have difficult tasks. They have a genuine job of work which has to be done in a very short time. Practical aspects limit choices – you must have clear committee procedures, or the members should be able to assimilate the routine without wasting time, but there's no mechanism that can forecast that they will. In my day the officers would devise a panel that was supposed to be composed of individuals but which really represented at the professional level an unwieldy mixture of organisations or geography or a specialist arts area: a performer or two, an academic, someone from the Regional Arts Associations, the secretary of a society of something, a chairman of a performing company who might actually be an industrialist. But all that would produce was a nightmare combination of carpet-bagging, log-rolling, petty jealousies and points-scoring, and therefore, in the end, a machine for endless, tortuous compromises. It's the toughest job to find the right people, and don't let them kid you otherwise. Experienced artists are often the best because there is a kind of professional respect for others starving in the self-employed field.

Panel and Council members attend as individuals. They are not there to represent a company or project and they must leave the room if they have a business interest in an application. Yet representation saturates the system. A Council member who chairs an artform panel represents that panel on the executive body. Former Vice-Chairman Richard Hoggart argues that:

> You immediately had a double role. One was that I had to represent the drama department's needs to Council, and sometimes I found myself fighting my corner against other artforms, which is a daft situation to be put in. The other was that you had to have an overall view and be aware of budgetary limits. You're obliged at some point

to say to panel members, 'Much as I take your point about more money, I have to say that a stronger case has been made for ballet.' There was a fellow at the panel who ran a theatre not far from 105 Piccadilly (no, it wasn't Peter Hall) and he used to rabbit on demanding this, that and the other. And I would say, 'Look, I'll make the case as well as I can but I'm not going to put it in the form you say because you're demanding too much. You can't resolutely claim there are no other arts as good as yours.' He replied, 'Your job is to ask for more and more because you represent drama on the Council.'

Hoggart ran the panel at a time when more artists and producers sat on it than they do now. Let's look at the drama panels through the years:

Drama Panel 1951: twenty members

Wyn Griffith (chairman)	Author/ACGB vice-chairman
Peggy Ashcroft	Actress
Ivor Brown	Drama critic, *Observer*
Alec Clunes	Actor/Arts Theatre Club
John Gielgud	Actor/director
Tyrone Guthrie	Stage director (ex-Old Vic)
André van Gyseghem	Director, Nottingham Playhouse
E.A. Harding	BBC drama producer, Manchester
Patrick Henderson	Council of Repertory Theatres
Hugh Hunt	Director, Old Vic
Laurence Irving	Film art director/stage designer
Ronald Jeans	Playwright/Liverpool Playhouse
Charles Landstone	ex-ACGB/theatre manager
Benn Levy	Playwright/director
Michael MacOwan	Director, London Mask Theatre
Sir Ralph Richardson	Actor
Ronald Russell	Bristol Little Theatre (commercial)
Derek Salberg	Alexander Theatre, Birmingham
Stephen Thomas	British Council drama director
Peter Ustinov	Playwright/actor/director

Drama Panel 1971: thirty-one members

J.W. Lambert (chairman)	Literary editor, *The Sunday Times*
Professor Roy Shaw (deputy)	Adult education, Keele University
Susanna Capon	BBC

Peter Cheeseman	New Vic, Stoke-on-Trent
Professor Philip Collins	Chairman, Leicester Rep
Harriet Cruickshank	Royal Court Theatre
Constance Cummings	Actress, National Theatre
Peter Dews	Birmingham Rep
Patrick Donnell	Administrator, National Theatre
Jane Edgeworth	British Council
Ronald Eyre	Stage and TV director/writer
Richard Findlater	Arts editor, *Observer*
Bernard Goss	Playwright
Nickolas Grace	(Twenty-three-year-old) actor
Jennifer Harris	Brighton Combination Co.
Philip Hedley	Midlands Arts Centre
Hugh Jenkins	Labour MP/Equity
Peter James	Young Vic, London
Oscar Lewenstein	Producer/Royal Court board
Dr A.H. Marshall	Treasurer, Coventry Belgrade
Jonathan Miller	Stage director, National Theatre
Lee Montague	Actor
Richard Pilbrow	69 Theatre Co., Manchester
Eric Porter	Actor, RSC
Owen Reed	BBC
Derek Salberg	Alexander Theatre, Birmingham
Peter Shaffer	Playwright
Donald Sinden	Actor, RSC
Caroline Smith	Library Theatre, Scarborough
Shaun Sutton	BBC
Carl Toms	Designer, National Theatre

Drama Panel 1991: fourteen members

Brian Rix (chairman)	Producer and actor of farces
Beverly Anderson	ex-TV newsreader
Paul Allen	Presenter, Radio 4, *Kaleidoscope*
Eileen Atkins	Actress
Roger Chapman	Head of touring, National Theatre
Hugh Hudson Davies	Ex-board of Coopers & Lybrand
John Gale	Producer *No Sex Please, We're British*
Stella Hall	The Green Room, Manchester
Hilary Hammond	Head of libraries, Norfolk County Council
Vikki Heywood	Contact Theatre, Manchester

Phyllida Lloyd	Director, RSC/Royal Exchange
Penny Mayes	General manager, Trestle Company
Deborah Paige	Salisbury Playhouse
Timberlake Wertenbaker	Playwright, Royal Court Theatre

We can quickly see that while the presence of celebrities dwindles, there is a corresponding move away from preoccupations with the West End. Unless it be thought that poor old Derek Salberg sat on the panel for twenty years between 1951 and 1971, he 'retired' in 1954 and was eventually invited back. This was allowed, especially when your family owned a lynchpin touring theatre. Women gradually dominate, from the 5 per cent represented by the tireless Peggy Ashcroft in the Festival of Britain year, through 20 per cent twenty years on, to 55 per cent at the start of the nineties (Hilary Hammond, by the way, is a he).

Nonetheless, there are few mavericks to be found in the latest list and no greater range of theatre embodied than there was twenty years back. In comparison, both Ralph Richardson and Peter Ustinov fifty years ago were considered 'iconoclastic, unpredictable and indubitably sharp'. A former director believes that:

> panels have become increasingly 'sensible', which is a loathsome, inartistic word. They've become banal, to be frank. And I don't think they should be so consensual. Because of the amount of practical work a panel's compelled to undertake nowadays, officers have taken the soft option in recruitment. In fact, you could say that the lifelessness of the panels mirrors the rather dreary quality of officer you get in the building at the moment.

It was the 1971 panel that drew the fiery breath of Charles Marowitz, the counterculture playwright. In a diatribe for the *Guardian* on 19 November 1971, Marowitz made the widespread mistake of whingeing that he'd failed to get an Arts Council grant of £5,000 for his Open Space Theatre. His mantra-like opening is fondly, if vaguely, remembered by wizened old hippies:

> If, by justice, we mean the hidden use of influence in order to obtain public monies, then the Arts Council of Great Britain is a just organisation. If, by justice, we mean the making of arbitrary decisions under the guise of democratic procedure, then the Arts Council of Great Britain is a just organisation. If, by justice, we mean the establishment of a cultural hierarchy which maintains

itself by deflecting opposing viewpoints, then the Arts Council of Great Britain is a just organisation.

The scent of sour grapes otherwise overwhelmed his sturdy point that most of the panel members worked for organisations already in receipt of subsidy and that these 'high-ranking officials from recipient organisations' may well have used the system to protect their needs.

> The major defence of the Arts Council in rejecting applications is that they have a wide range of existing commitments and must honour them. But the criticism they never credit is that it is these very commitments which should be re-examined . . . A member of the panel recently told an applicant that his projected grant for September might not materialise as the National had accumulated an unusually large deficit this year, and, of course, the Arts Council had to 'get them out of trouble'.

His argument remains one from which the Council can never seem to extricate itself. 'It's self-evident that you have to have had experience of the funding system in order to help others make proper use of it,' said the drama director of the time, Dick Linklater. As it stands, the panel system can't afford to be compromised by any unworldliness or fundamental questioning from its members as to its role or its biases – it hasn't the time or the structural mechanism to cope, and members know that more time spent debating policy means less time sorting out grants to clients.

Critics of Marowitz think that he promotes a more dangerous way of spending subsidy – one based on caprice and instability. 'If it's a large project you have to go with it, stick by it, give it a fair chance to achieve its aims,' stressed Sir Hugh Willatt, the Secretary-General of the period, who 'went' with the Royal Shakespeare Company. Marowitz saw a system for the defence of favoured institutions; others say he saw nothing more than a level of investment into creative structures that are worth the effort of nurturing. Yet that doesn't satisfy his point that panels seem to engage those who already benefit from the system they are now asked themselves to sustain.

In the past, panels have included artists whose fame places them above the need for self-promotion. It was easier to attract them in the fifties because the Council was considered more or less a 'good thing'. Even so, Alec Guinness felt he 'had the vague suspicion of being manipulated', and others such as Laurence Olivier complained that their name was being attached to schemes 'of which I remembered nothing'. The feeling grew that Council officers were using celebrities to endorse in print, through the minutes of the meetings, their own whims. As esteem for the Council declined, especially through the eighties, it found it increasingly hard to recruit artists of note. One such panellist confesses:

> To be honest, I joined partly because it was flattering to be asked, but also because it meant I got to see what other people were up to. You could argue that I was exploiting the system by gaining an advantage on my rivals, seeing their accounts, their programming plans – the way they operate. My gain was education. I believe I became a better administrator, but not a richer artist, for having seen how others worked. I grew to respect a whole range of drama far more by having sat at an Arts Council table for a couple of years. Now other people sit at that table and can see how I work. There's nothing wrong in that. It's not self-perpetuating, but I admit it's (slightly) self-advancing.

With this in mind, Luke Rittner, in the early eighties, improved the representation of women and ethnic minorities, as they were first called. While the move was generally valued, new black members found themselves patronised and corralled into personifying this new agenda. As one said:

> My professional background was jazz and a bit of reggae, and whenever those words or anything 'ethnic' appeared somewhere on an application the chairman would expect me to lead the discussion, even when it was something like steel bands on which I'm not an expert. If the application was one for an orchestra, nobody looked at me, even though the applicants had filled in the same form for the budget which anyone could read as well as any other. Although I was told I was chosen as an individual, it was soon plain that I was there to cover the 'ethnic' applications. It seemed to be quite manipulative. It was tokenist, and badly prepared, because you were limited to representing black culture while the other members could generalise, and I suppose they said of me, 'Well, he only talks about jazz, he only cares for his own livelihood.'

Another panellist found her experience Kafka-esque:

I'd mentioned in passing after my first meeting that I was surprised how little we talked about policy – the meetings have a tight agenda because there are scores of applications and you want to sort them out, say something supportive, or honest. So at my next meeting, I suppose as a sop to my little moan, the panel's chairman went around the table asking us one by one what we thought the Really Big Issues were in [our artform]. An officer stood at a whiteboard and wrote Really Big Issues at the top with a sort of crayon. Well, everyone said education was a matter of concern (I think that's always the way, whatever the artform), and there were some other things, which the officer duly listed on the board. After lunch, we noticed that the board had disappeared. It turned out someone had borrowed it for another meeting and wiped it clean. The chairman said, 'Never mind. We know what the issues are.' That was that; the discussion wasn't even minuted. It was as though policy existed by some means of osmosis from on high, not through the thoughts and debates of practising artists.

The downgrading of the panels was not at first a matter of recruitment, but of internal politics. In 1978 Sir Kenneth Robinson and Roy Shaw set up the OWP, the Organisational and Procedures Working Party, under their Vice-Chairman, lawyer Lord Hutchinson. He reported that the relationship between the panels and the Council was messy. The panels were trying to push arguments upwards that the Council had no time to digest – in fact they were really asking fundamental questions about policy which the Council couldn't answer. Rather than fix this, the OWP decided that the Council's officers should have much more executive authority. The panels should be constrained to advise. From that moment the staff were rigorous in calling them 'advisory panels'.

This devaluing of the panel's leverage may have deterred experts from getting involved with them. At the same time, while the OWP gave officers more jurisdiction, it also stressed that they should be able to explain their decisions to all and sundry. This contributed to the navel-gazing 'retreats' and development of 'strategy-speak' that critics deem the start of the Council's decline. Through this the quality of staff started to slacken, while marginal committees and 'boards' dealing with matters unrelated to the artforms were introduced. These clogged the lines of communication that the artform panels had once enjoyed. While recent readjustments have simplified the system, the panels still lack the authority of earlier years, and as they're the only place in the Council system where actual practitioners sit, it's generally agreed by those outside the Council that more reform is vital.

One former panel chair believes that the 'Glory of the Garden' devolution process has damaged the work of panels.

> I found at panel a rather false view of the overall picture across the country. It only gradually occurred to me that we were being fed a lot of information about clients in our list and nothing about the ones handled since devolution by the Regional Arts Boards. We never saw the full picture. I think this explains why a degree of bad decision-making goes on now. And I'd also like to know why we have to have a financial relationship with someone before we can talk to them. That seems to me to be something that comes from Whitehall – a Whitehall view of communication – which the recent Arts Council has accepted too easily.

Below the panels stand a dozen or so committees that deal with very specific matters that would otherwise choke the work of the assemblies above them. It is here that officers look out for potential panellists. If their panellist peers find that their time is too occupied with practicalities, the committee members who sift applications are saddled with sticky, restricted decisions from the word go. They usually handle the applications for projects and bursaries, the one-off grants that emergent or even established artists rely on once a year to survive. The members will probably receive colour-coded copies of applications, already sifted by officers into what they consider to be recommended 'for approval', 'for discussion', or 'for rejection'. A committee member can question an officer's view and open out the discussion – and that's where the schedule runs askew and time vanishes.

A projects committee member recalls:

> We'd been stuck in that hell hole of a boardroom on the top floor of Great Peter Street since 11am, and by 6.30pm we had something tiny like £80,000 left and four applications that totalled £200,000, each of which was worth supporting. The building shuts down at 7pm, so you can imagine the pressure: you are going to ruin the lives of some competent artists because a caretaker's about to go off duty.

They ended up with the chairman – who was actually a Council member – desperately stabbing at a whiteboard with a line on it shouting at the committee to decide whether company A,B,C or D should go above or below a line that represented £40,000. Meanwhile an officer was barking down a wallphone to the security guard, 'Don't switch the alarm on, don't turn the lift off, we're still up here. Hello? Hello!' The committee member adds: 'If artists could see how their hours of work end up, filling in those fucking forms, they would commit suicide.'

If an applicant thinks he or she might be rejected at this humble level, even though they have lobbied the members of the committee beforehand at social functions, then they have two further opportunities – at panel, at Council – to get the 'recommendation' (that is, the rejection) challenged. By that time though, the members will see one sheet of paper with a summary of recommendations from the committee below them – not the application itself nor supporting data of any sort.

The applicants can play safe and lobby panellists or Council members, even though they don't themselves know the outcome of the committee's meeting. However, members are rarely going to stick their necks out for something that other people further down the line seem to have considered of dodgy value. The structure is such that personal credibility is at play at every turn.

'I found the committees and the panels I served on rather ill-informed,' a panellist observed.

> A lot of the time they hadn't seen an artist in action, and therefore they were reduced to picking at a detail on the application form, to show they hadn't totally fallen asleep. There was a tendency, though, for a rapid consensus simply because of the pressure of time. If you've rocked the boat once, and realised that the time spent debating a relatively small matter could be better spent on bigger issues later in the day, you tend to hold back. You're also most likely to find that, at the level where artists are starting out, they don't know how to play the system and they don't find out who the Arts Council is using on its panels and committees, so nobody useful to them gets to see their work. At committee you may find one member who's seen them and can speak out; the decision is then based on someone's sole ability to excite or discourage the others sat round the table. Otherwise the officers, who cover their backs by seeing nearly all applicants once, have it their own way.

Conversely, two mime artists found the selection system so arbitrary and shallow that they would invent intricate arguments between themselves simply to break the boredom.

At the bottom of the advisory ladder perch the forlorn advisers and assessors who spend solitary nights filling in show reports about grant-aided companies or newcomers working in their 'patch'. The information required in these personal accounts, on a single A4 sheet, have mutated through the years in line with the Council's preoccupations. They are now expected to include the following:

Background: audience size, cultural mix: length of piece, size of company: access to theatre, event programme: suitability of venue.

Assessment: competence, originality, coherence, courage, power of communication, sincerity, faithfulness.

Consensus: personal response/audience response.

The reports are signed by the advisers, but their names are clipped off before they reach the committee, where they're used to assemble a general, round-the-country view of a company. 'The trouble is,' a former panellist points out, 'they reach us as nameless reports. If you don't know who wrote it you can't trust it. I think it's very arrogant of the Arts Council to assume we can depend on all of its advisers to the point of anonymity.' Another member recalls the day a black dance company nearly lost its final chance of funding because two negative show reports were passed around. The one panellist who'd actually seen the company in action spotted that both authors had misread the printed programme and got the pieces mixed up, which is why their deliberations were so unfavourable. 'In other words,' he claimed, 'the company was being wiped out because of the carelessness of a couple of provincial PE teachers. At least one could assume that's who they were, by the way they couldn't spell – or read.'

That is the unpaid advisory system, from the Earl of Gowrie at the head to PE teachers at its feet – blood all the way down. Yet for their unpaid work, there are rewards.

No one would claim that personalities in the arts have received a royal honour merely because they were serving on committees at the Arts Council at the time. Harold Pinter or Judi Dench were not honoured solely for attending meetings of the drama panel, though they probably deserved it. Yet the list reveals how it can aid non-artists, and how often chairmen of all kinds receive honours, as Mr Keynes (Chairman number 1), Mr Goodman (32), Mr Crawshay (60), Mr Gibson (65), Mr Hutchinson (81), Mr Robinson (89), Professor Peacock (98), Mr Grierson (102), Mr Palumbo (103) and Mr Gummer (118) experienced.

Nor did it preclude Sir Ernest Pooley (5), Sir Kenneth Clark (20), Lord Cottesloe (24), Lord Goodman (59), nor Sir William Rees-Mogg (101) from further elevation while in office, or at the point of retirement from that office.

1942	1	J.M. Keynes CB	**Chairman**	Lord
1946	2	W.E. Williams	Council	CBE
1949	3	Bronson Albery	Chair, drama	Sir
1950	4	Joseph Compton	Chair, poetry	CBE
1951	5	Sir Ernest Pooley	**Chairman**	Bt
	6	Captain John McEwen	Council	Sir
1955	7	Lord Esher	Council	GBE
1956	8	William Coldstream	Chair, art	Sir
	9	Professor Anthony Blunt	Art panel	Sir*
	10	Peggy Ashcroft	Drama panel	CBE
	11	John Clements	Drama panel	CBE
1957	12	Professor Leslie Martin	Art panel	Sir
	13	Kathleen Long	Music panel	CBE
	14	George Devine	Drama panel	CBE
	15	Basil Grey	Art panel	CBE
1958	16	Thomas Armstrong	Music panel	Sir
	17	Celia Johnson	Drama panel	CBE
	18	Mrs K.L. Somerville	Art panel	OBE
	19	Louis MacNeice	Poetry panel	CBE
1959	20	Sir Kenneth Clark	**Chairman**	CH
	21	Alec Guinness	Drama panel	Sir
	22	David Baxandall	Scottish	CBE
	23	Leslie Woodgate	Music panel	OBE
1960	24	Lord Cottesloe	**Chairman**	KGBE
1961	25	Dr Wyn Griffith	Vice-chairman	OBE
	26	Trenchard Cox CBE	Art panel	Sir
	27	Roland Penrose	Art panel	CBE
	28	Professor Carel Weight	Art panel	CBE

* *Knighthood annulled in 1979 when it was made public that this visual arts panellist was a Soviet spy.*

1963	29	H.H. Donnelly	Scottish education	CB
1964	30	Hugh Marshall	Scottish	OBE
	31	William Glock	Music panel	CBE
1965	32	Arnold Goodman	**Chairman**	Lord
	33	Professor Gwyn Jones	Welsh chairman	OBE
	34	Jane Edgeworth	Drama panel	MBE
	35	Ian Finlay	Scottish	CBE
	36	John Neville	Drama panel	OBE
1966	37	Roland Penrose CBE	Art panel	Sir
	38	Leonard Clark	Literature panel	OBE
	39	F.E. McWilliam	Art panel	CBE
	40	Harold Pinter	Drama panel	CBE
	41	Reginald Salberg	Drama panel	OBE
	42	Elizabeth Sweeting	Drama panel	MBE
1967	43	John Witt	Art chair	Sir
	44	Robert Sainsbury	Art panel	Sir
	45	Alex Gorden FRIBA	Welsh	OBE
1968	46	Angus Wilson	Literature chair	CBE
	47	Dame V. Wedgwood	Literature panel	DBE
	48	V.S. Pritchett	Literature panel	CBE
	49	Dr J.A. MacLean	Scottish	CBE
	50	Professor Talbot Rice	Scottish	CBE
	51	J.B. Dalby	Scottish	OBE
1969	52	Tudur Watkins	Welsh	MBE
	53	T. Osborne Robinson	Drama panel	OBE
1970	54	Norman Reid	Art panel	Sir
	55	J.W. Lambert	Drama chair	CBE
	56	Judi Dench	Drama panel	OBE
1971	57	John Pope-Hennessy CBE	Council	Sir
	58	Peter Williams	Dance	OBE
1972	59	Lord Goodman	**Chairman**	CH
	60	William Crawshay	Welsh chair	Sir
1974	61	Constance Cummings	Drama panel	CBE
	62	Stuart Burge	Drama panel	CBE
	63	Alex Gordon OBE	Welsh vice-chair	CBE
	64	Wilfred Vaughan-Thomas	Welsh	OBE
1975	65	Patrick Gibson	**Chairman**	Lord
	66	Haydn Rees	Welsh	CBE
	67	Dr Philip Larkin	Poetry mss.	CBE
	68	Allen Percival	Music	CBE
1976	69	Ben Smith	Scottish	OBE
	70	I.M. Robertson	Scottish	CB

	71	Helen Crummy	Scottish	MBE
	72	Michael MacOwen	Training	CBE
	73	Alan Bowness	Art panel	CBE
	74	Colin Young	Art films	OBE
1977	75	Marchioness of Anglesey	Welsh chair	CBE
	76	Richard Rodney Bennett	Music panel	CBE
	77	Patrick Heron	Art panel	CBE
	78	Peter Moro	Housing the Arts	CBE
	79	Louise Brown	Dance	OBE
	80	Martyn Goff	Literature panel	OBE
1978	81	Jeremy Hutchinson	Vice-chairman	Lord
	82	Helen Watts	Music panel	OBE
	83	Mary Burkett	Art panel	OBE
1979	84	Christopher Cory	Welsh	MVO
	85	Gerald Forty	Art panel	OBE
1980	86	Charles Drury	Scottish	OBE
1981	87	Gerald McDonald	Training	OBE
1982	88	John Manduell	Music chair	CBE
1983	89	Kenneth Robinson	**Chairman**	Sir
	90	Albert Frost	Council	CBE
	91	David Sylvester	Council	CBE
1984	92	Lady Barbirolli	Music panel	OBE
	93	Joan Knight	Scottish	OBE
1985	94	William Mathias	Welsh	CBE
1986	95	Gerald Elliot	Scottish chair	Sir
	96	Brian Rix	Drama chair	Sir
	97	Philip Jones	Music chair	CBE
1987	98	Professor Alan Peacock	Scottish chair	Sir
	99	Cyril Davies	Touring	CBE
	100	Anthony Smith	Film panel	CBE
1988	101	Sir William Rees-Mogg	**Chairman**	Lord
1990	102	Ronald Grierson	South Bank chair	Sir
1991	103	Peter Palumbo	**Chairman**	Lord
1992	104	Sir Brian Rix	Council	Lord
	105	Mathew Prichard	Welsh chair	CBE
	106	Nargis Rashid	Education	OBE
1993	107	Ernest Hall OBE	Council	Sir
	108	Barbara Matthews	Touring	MBE
1994	109	Thelma Holt	Drama chair	CBE
	110	Michael Hopkins	Architecture	Sir
	111	Usha Prasha	Council	CBE
	112	David Puttnam	Lottery board	Sir

	113	Ruth Mackenzie	Lottery board	OBE
1995	114	Richard Burton	Art panel	CBE
	115	Fleur Adcock	Literature panel	OBE
	116	Paddy Masefield	Lottery board	OBE
1996	117	Sir Richard Rogers	Council	Lord
	118	Peter Gummer	Lottery chair	Lord
	119	David Harrison	Council	Sir

Chapter 26

The paid

The Arts Council has never kept a running tally of its staff numbers. The only figures available are the following, assembled here for the first time:

1946	34	+ 36 regional staff
1955	27	+ 15 regional staff
1957	20	(Secretary-General's forecast)
1969	215	
1972	174	
1973	194	
1974	252	
1975	271	
(1976 no record)		
1977	250	
1978	233	
1979	258	
1980	266	
1981	280	
1982	275	
1983	273	170 core staff, 103 direct promotions
1984	267	
1985	261	

1986	262	162 core staff, 100 direct promotions
1987	260	165 core staff, 95 direct promotions
1988	184	167 core staff, 17 direct promotions*
1989	164	
1990	175	
1991	183	
1992	208	
1993	161	
1994	132	+ 8.5 lottery unit under construction
1995	144	+ 18 lottery
1996	154	+ 55 lottery

* *Art collection to Hayward Gallery.*

'The secretaries have the most information. The officers have the most intrigues. The directors have the most experience. The Secretary-General has the most migraines.' In this way Mary Glasgow, the Council's first Secretary-General, summed up the staff structure as she knew it in the forties and fifties. Some say it's hardly altered, except that secretaries are now called assistants or assistant officers, 'because with new technology the traditional role of secretary has changed', and quality has dropped while wages have risen. Remarkably, though, the Council's junior positions still attract the same kinds of people – OK, women. Bill Williams called them 'daughters and spinsters'.

He meant first of all the rather Sloaney sorts who might otherwise work in private art galleries and would occasionally ask, according to Sheila Gold, 'Do you mind awfully if I have a day orf to go to a point-to-point with Mummy?' The personnel officer reckoned that 'they didn't need to earn very much, therefore they could afford to work for the Arts Council'. Even in 1995 a secretary could be found in the art department who was lady-in-waiting to Princess Diana. The other sort, corruptly described by Williams, were independent-minded, genuinely keen on one artform or another, unattached; in fact, a little like Mary Glasgow herself. Again, they are still there.

In 1996 an Arts Council assistant would earn between £10,000 and £13,000; an officer £17–23,000; a director £40–47,000; the Deputy Secretary-General around £52,000, and the Secretary-General £70,000. Until that year the pay was graded on the civil-service scale (grades 3 down to 7 for senior staff, F down to B for juniors). Whitehall deregulated its system in 1996 and now the

Arts Council negotiates directly with the one employees' body it recognises, the white-collar Manufacturing Science Finance Union (MSF). Only directors are appointed on fixed-term, renewable contracts of five years. There is a non-contributory pension scheme, decent holiday provision and opportunities for in-service training in disability equality and staff appraisal. 'The Arts Council is a nice employer,' acknowledged a former officer. 'Everything's rather nice about it. Nice is the right word for the whole place: but Laura Ashley Nice.'

The former music director John Denison defined the basic job of officers and their directors as 'how to tell people no – though they must not realise it until they have walked out of the building'. John Faulkner believes that most of the problems an officer faces start when the client

> doesn't appreciate the difference between *discuss* and *agree*. Even a smile at the wrong moment can mislead. At the same time you don't want them to think the Arts Council is faceless. You don't want to squash them but neither do you want them to have an excuse to say they were misled.

A former staffer blames the current malaise on the fact that 'Lawrence Mackintosh aside, the staff have forgotten how to be subtle'.

When CEMA started in 1940 its administration was run by the Board of Education. Mary Glasgow was paid at the same rate as CEMA Secretary as she had been on as a Board inspector, and the CEMA gradings were calculated downwards from that. At the time when her title was advanced to Secretary-General, Keynes tried to get her grade moved up to that of a principal secretary, but failed to improve her wages by more than one level. In any case women's pay was less than that for a man. By 1943 Glasgow earned a salary of £1,225, while the male directors under her received £1,200. Both figures are today valued in the region of £30,000.

Arts Council salaries were pegged accordingly from that moment, even though the Council was no longer a division of the Ministry of Education (as the Board had become), but quasi-independent. While artists moan about the 'high wages' Council officers receive, business people are often surprised how little they earn. Officers who moved over from the British Council, for instance, often accepted less money for more work.

There were two reasons why the staff tolerated this. When CEMA started its staff believed they were doing war work for the Board of Education. In those days you were given a job of 'government-approved employment'. The entire matter of salaries during the war seemed a fairly artificial one, given food and fuel rationing, and this comparatively relaxed approach carried over into CEMA. Secondly, they were recruited directly from a working arts background, like actor Lewis Casson of the Old Vic, or the conductor and orchestra-fixer Reginald Jacques. They were in the vanguard of arts administration, handling the first subsidies, but they also had freelance work and their salaries were not their sole source of income. They might have considered their work in front of the public a profession, but not their work behind it, which Casson called merely 'helping out'. The public would not have had a name for either.

In 1945 those in the services, like John Denison, or in 'approved employment', like Mary Endacott, were deregulated. 'I had been a secretary in the Foreign Office at Bush House,' recalls Endacott.

> The director of the department mentioned that his wife was working for CEMA. As I was arts-orientated, I wrote them an on-spec letter. Jobs weren't much advertised in those days. So I went along to this rather crummy office in Belgrave Square. I was interviewed by Mary Glasgow's PA, Barbara Sewell, who thought I might come in handy at some point – recruitment was that casual then. Six months later she wrote to say they needed a secretary and I started in November 1946, soon after the charter had been granted. It was at this time there was the feeling of a change. The old guard, who did drama tours and ran recital tours for music clubs and so on, thought that the Arts Council was moving from being 'hands-on' to becoming more administrative. There was certainly a change of focus, especially when Sir William Williams took over in 1951.

Mary Glasgow shaped a clear civil-service structure for her staff. She also established clean lines of contact for their involvement with the advisory system. Yet she declined to specify policy, at least anything written. They were told how to do things, but not what to do. Glasgow believed her officers should react to proposals from outside the organisation and so gradually she began to select candidates who were more disposed to support other people's bright ideas than to promote their own. This explains the old guard's fear of having their hands chopped off. She later said:

We did things ourselves in the war years, and we rather liked it. But that was an emergency measure, and when the promoting organisations regained their strength once the war was over, we had to be much more serious about supporting and regulating what they did. There were some touring things we continued to do because no one else would do them. I suppose the history of the Arts Council could be viewed as one where the hands of the officers move gradually away from the art itself. But not, I would hope, their minds.

A neat image, though several hands refused to budge and others strayed back again. Yet one of the greatest gripes of artists and producers who deal with the Council lies in their belief that officers have deteriorated in 'their minds' – in the breadth of knowledge in their field, in their ability to fight their artistic corner, and generally in their 'enthusiasm'. On this matter, one client explained:

> I think it's an essential quality. It's what I found in Chris Cooper when he was a drama and regional officer in the seventies. He was genuinely interested and driven. A bit maverick. You felt you could talk about the Living Theater or the new Godard film or Gilbert and George with almost anyone there. Today – God! It's *The Stepford Wives* in that place. There's little of what I'd recognise as enthusiasm but instead a lot of synthetic cordiality. You feel you're a victim of Customer Care.

Although the Council has fallen in with local government by adopting the public-service babble of corporate America ('Hello, my name is Grey. How may I help you?'), it wasn't always so banal. Veterans recall that while a work code imposed elements that were very fixed, others were entirely improvised. In the early days contracts stipulated that you arrived for work by 9.56am, which is a deeply civil-service practice. One or two staff were found turning up early, but they were stopped, as a senior member recalls:

> They were up to mischief, you see. There was one man who used to rifle through the drawers of colleagues in the music department to read their papers and see what they were cooking up. Another woman used to sneak in and look through diaries to check who was coming in, so that she could waylay visitors on the way up with her own invented business and find out what *they* were up to.

When Roy Shaw arrived in the late seventies he wanted the staff in by 9am, but settled for 9.30am, after complaints that officers spent their evenings watching the work they stuck their necks out for in the daytime. Rittner scheduled 8am breakfast meetings. 'You can tell when Catholics are in charge – up with the lark,' snarled one unmarried staffer.

By comparison the fifties seemed relaxed. Getting a job at the Council, for instance, was even more arbitrary than Mary Endacott experienced. When Catherine Porteous applied to assist the Chairman Sir Kenneth Clark, she was interviewed by 'a most peculiar character who was called the personnel officer, though I'm sure I never ever saw the man again'. She thought the encounter was going quite well until he interrupted her. 'I'm afraid I have to ask you a personal question. How old are you?' I was twenty-one. 'I'm afraid, then, in that case it won't do because the secretary to a principal in a quasi-civil-service establishment has to be at least twenty-three.' She decided that she wasn't going to be vetoed by this bureaucratic oddball, so she parried: 'But I'm a married woman and that adds two years to my age.' He paused, perhaps dreading that she'd read some small print he hadn't read. After an awkward silence he declared, 'The interview may continue.'

Val Bourne OBE will never forget her first day at work as the dance assistant. Up to the late seventies dance was handled within the music department and conducted by a single officer, the glorious Jane Nicholas who, on the day Ms Bourne joined to assist her, was on holiday.

I arrived at the entrance to find a ballet company chained to the railings. Press photographers were clicking away. It was a group rumoured to be backed by dodgy South African cash. For artistic reasons alone it neither deserved subsidy nor got any. But their campaign was very rowdy, and after crossing over them I sought refuge in the office only to receive minute after minute, hour after hour of phone calls from members of the public asking me to explain what the Arts Council had got against these supposedly wonderful ballet dancers. The company had circulated the Council's number at shows. By the end of the day I was drained and disheartened. I went to see the music director, John Cruft, and I asked him what I should do about the campaign. He looked at me sympathetically and said, 'Leave by the back door.'

Back in the fifties conspiratorial fear seemed to lurk everywhere the public intruded. Music secretary Sheila Gold recalled that 'there was an air of unease and caution, especially when the phone rang. If it was a member of the press we weren't allowed to say anything, so it was pretty much a fruitless, one-way conversation.' She would be given tickets for concerts at the Royal Festival Hall, but if she saw her colleagues or seniors there, there was a paranoid rule that they could do nothing more than nod acknowledgment. 'John Denison told me that Arts Council staff must never be seen talking to each other at performances. People might notice us and say, "Look, there's the Arts Council. What are *they* up to, talking over there?"'

Oddly enough the Royal Opera House presented them with the opposite problem. The Arts Council was given a box there as a grant condition: left-hand side of the audience, second level, almost opposite the royal box. But they had to occupy it for every performance or people could claim that the Council was wasting money. There would be a panic: 'Can someone cover at Covent Garden tonight? Otherwise it'll be empty.' If they did take up the offer, 'we had to dress up a bit so that we wouldn't embarrass our bosses, because we were in full public view, quite on parade'. The rules about tickets have changed now, and in general Council officers have to pay for their own seats and reclaim the cost on expenses.

At the same time, it was possible for gumptious officers to formulate and expand their own territory, so long as they didn't bring the Council into disrepute. The literature department used to interpret this largesse as a duty to contribute directly to the world of publishing. The first director there was Eric Walter White, who had stealthily turned his vague position as assistant Secretary-General (1946–1972) into a full-time poetry job, from where he expanded into prose. During White's arduous years at the Arts Council he managed to dash off the following books: *Stravinsky: A Critical Survey* (1947), *Benjamin Britten: A Sketch of His Life & Works* (1948), *Entertain Yourselves!* (1949), *The Watch Tower & Other Lyrics* (1949), *The Rise of English Opera* (1951), *Benjamin Britten: Revised Edition* (1954), *A Tarot Deck & Other Poems* (1962), *Stravinsky: The Composer & His Works* (1966), and *Benjamin Britten: His Life & Operas* (1970). Oh, there was also *Notes of Guidance on the Formation of a Regional Arts Association* (1968), but that, unlike the others, clearly had little to do with his Arts Council job.

White retired in 1972 so he could write full time, and was

replaced by his peppery Australian assistant. Charles Osborne was renowned for annoying applicant writers who deserved annoying, and for bringing his dog, Asta, into work – that is until Luke Rittner issued a famously I'm-not-getting-at-anyone-in-particular memo banning pets from the building. Osborne, a conservative in most senses, was only too happy to observe the tradition established by White with *Kafka* (1967), *Swansong: Poems* (1968), *The Complete Operas of Verdi* (1969), *Australia, New Zealand & the South Pacific: A Handbook* (1970), *Ned Kelly* (1970), *The Bram Stoker Bedside Companion* (1973), *Richard Wagner: Stories & Essays* (1973), *New Poems* (1973), *The Concert Song Companion: A Guide to the Classical Repertoire* (1974), *Masterpieces of Dobell, Masterpieces of Drysdale, Masterpieces of Nolan* (all 1975), *New Poetry: An Anthology* (1975), *New Stories: An Anthology* (1976), *Rigoletto: A Guide to the Opera* (1977), *Wagner & His World* (1977), *Verdi* (1978), *The Opera House Album: A Collection of Turn-of-the-Century Postcards* (1979), *The Complete Operas of Mozart: A Critical Guide* (1978), *Klemperer: Stories & Anecdotes* (1980), *W.H. Auden: The Life of a Poet* (1980), *The Complete Operas of Puccini* (1981), *The Dictionary of Composers* (1981), *The Life & Crimes of Agatha Christie* (1982), *The World Theatre of Wagner* (1982), *How To Enjoy Opera* (1983), *The Dictionary of Opera* (1983), *A Letter to W.H. Auden & Other Poems* (1984), *Schubert & His Vienna* (1985), *The Collins Book of Well-loved Verse* (1986). Thirty books in twenty-two years of service. Well done! It seems he even managed to finish his memoirs as he was tidying his desk. *Giving It Away* (1986) includes a wry account of his time at the Council, including a record of the writers he pissed off.

The most developed and famous, if not eventually notorious, officer empire started in 1971, when the music director of the time, John Cruft, encouraged his underling specialising in contemporary work and jazz to start a countrywide touring network for modern music. It was given the wildly catchy name of the Contemporary Music Network. Annette Morreau, a former cellist, was its feisty and far-sighted organiser. She would not have tolerated Laura Ashley Nice for a second. 'She tramped around the place like a Jewish Boadicea,' recalled one of her colleagues,

but Cruft let her get away with it because she was tackling this backwoods problem. I mean, there's hardly anyone out of trendy London who likes avant-garde blippy-bloppy tuneless rants like some of the stuff she toured on tax-payers' money. But she had a go at making the CMN a success and built her little dominion in a shabby corner of an office. Her fellow officers couldn't stand it, though, and didn't appreciate her efforts.

Nowadays the American composer Philip Glass is rather a star, but when Morreau gave him a British tour in 1975, he played to a paying public of ten in Birmingham. The vocal group Singcircle sang Stockhausen's epic *Stimmung* to an eager crowd of six in Carlisle. Yet Mik Flood of Cardiff's Chapter Arts Centre got the impression of

> an incredibly sophisticated touring system. Everything it issued looked exceptionally expensive ... which it was! The sort of luscious print, full-colour posters and leaflets on high-grade paper were sent to us Red Star. Unfortunately to little purpose, because the posters were too large for most shops and too heavy to stay on their walls. You could put them up, stand around for a minute or two, and watch them drop to the floor. We looked like pillocks.

Though everyone guessed that the printers had added 100 per cent to the bill on account of it being the Arts Council who was paying, nobody seemed to challenge it.

Wild rumours circulated of Morreau's deepening relationships with a couple of artists who were repeatedly invited to tour. Matters reached a climax when she was found in the foyer of the Bloomsbury Theatre, in front of a dumbfounded audience, wrestling with the Council's music education officer, Stephen Firth, who yelled at her in frustration, 'You bitch! You fucking bitch!' when one of her artists failed to show for a pre-concert talk. Though he was rightly reprimanded by Rittner, Morreau sought another department to work in and eventually the CMN moved into a reluctant touring unit, where she eventually left it to its own devices. Remarkably, the CMN survives and remains the most consistently impressive touring project the Arts Council has ever developed. In twenty-five years it has circulated nearly 200 ensembles and soloists, introducing around the country a splendid selection of vanguard work, especially modern jazz, and it has rightly highlighted the work of Britain's finest living musician, the saxophonist Evan Parker. That sort of thing could never be brought about by someone who was Laura Ashley Nice. It was achieved entirely by Morreau.

The overwhelming evidence of witnesses suggests that the calibre of staff was finest in the sixties and seventies, when crusading characters like Morreau were around. The routines Glasgow had set, honed by Williams, were married to personnel who had worked as artists, performers, directors, curators or producers in the past but had decided that others did it better and that they wished to help the cause of those still in the field and those about to try their best. Glasgow had handled this transition successfully, but when a second such period occurred thirty years later, it led to a sea of troubles.

In 1979 Secretary-General Roy Shaw awarded the second-in-command post to a youngish, openly gay civil servant 'who had no professional experience of the arts but just sort of wanted to muck in'. Richard Pulford went on to work in the same position, deputy Secretary-General, for Luke Rittner (himself a relative outsider to the arts). It's argued by some that they allowed a disproportionate number of non-arts people like themselves to clog the system. The artform departments were effectively demoted in the command structure. Some staff said they found themselves earning less than their new colleagues in marketing, resources or planning. 'It was literally a devaluation of the arts within the Arts Council,' claimed a former staffer.

Naturally, there is another way of looking at this. Richard Pulford began his job slightly in advance of that notable general election that threw out Callaghan's Labour Cabinet and enthroned Mrs Thatcher. Pulford had been, on his own admission, a high flyer of a civil servant who had spent twelve years at the Department of Education and Science then the Treasury. At the age of thirty-two he was the youngest assistant secretary in the service. That both he and Roy Shaw were conscious of acute political change suggests that his appointment was simply a symptom of what followed; it seems that the Council desired this civil servant as the new number two in order to send a message to Whitehall, which was sterilising its surgeon's tools ahead of plans to carve into the quangos, without anaesthetic. In the back of many civil servants' minds lay the thought that quangos were losing them work, and privatisation would lose them more unless they stemmed the flow. The Department of Education and Science had started with a management services unit review of the Council's operations, filed in October 1979.

The subsequent introduction of non-artform departments at the Council mirrors developments at other quangos. It intensified when Thatcherism promoted at second hand the accountability and profile-raising style of American not-for-profit businesses. It was the Arts Council's involvement with public-sector enterprise that absorbed free-market reformers. At the time it ran its own tours, a bookshop in Covent Garden, a concert hall (the Wigmore) and it was a monopoly in the sense that the Regional Arts Associations were dependent on it for cash and worthwhile clients. The Council was faced with 'devolving' challenges, as hiving off was called.

Grimmer still, it was increasingly asked to explain the work of its clients as businesses operating in the leisure sector. Luke Rittner and his Chairman William Rees-Mogg understood this from the first, and it might be said that they protected what they could of the old Arts Council while meeting as few as possible of the privatisation changes that the Adam Smith Institute, other radical think-tanks and civil servants themselves would have wished to impose on them. It ended up a bit of a dog's breakfast, but only as far as many such outfits did in the eighties as they attempted to accommodate the structures of contrasting ideologies in a system charged with inherited obligations.

Pulford, though, was one of the few around who'd studied the charter with a magnifying glass. With a Whitehall concern for letter-of-the-law assessment, he emphasised that a chartered body may delegate its duties in three ways only: through whatever was designated in the charter (in this case the Scottish and Welsh committees), through a committee composed of trustees, or executively through the staff. The panels had no formal role; the Hutchinson Review had put this point less rigorously. But, more important, Pulford asserted:

> There was a prevailing view amongst staff that their constitutional responsibility is to artists. But this is untrue – it is to the public. The Arts Council can discharge this responsibility through the support it gives to the artists, but this is not its prime responsibility.

This is entirely a matter of interpretation, of course, but Pulford bore the power and the boldness to lure the Council away from its former assumptions. Anyway, a responsibility to the public can be quantified much more easily than one to artists.

Nonetheless, Pulford was appointed when accountability was already an issue. The growing attacks from the new left and the community-arts cults against the Arts Council during the seventies had challenged the executive to justify itself against charges of elitism. It found it could do so in two ways only. First, it could try to defend notions of high culture, and Roy Shaw did his impressive best in a number of articles in the late seventies. Second, it could demonstrate through facts and figures that it was inclusive rather than exclusive in the range of work it supported. At this point the Council realised that it had to learn the language of accountability to do so effectively. It did this, then, to fend off not the right, but the new left. To a degree Pulford's appointment addressed this need.

The drama director of the time, John Faulkner, noticed the change in this way.

> Roy and Richard certainly marked a watershed in the Council because they came with a somewhat similar ideology. When Roy introduced a move towards education, for instance – with an education officer and education as part of the general agenda – it was a factor in their thinking that went, 'Giving money to artists hasn't really got us anywhere. It's just got the Council into a terrible squabble with artists. How can we invest the money better?' And that led to the beginning of the Council moving away from its accepted role and seeking alternatives, examining sponsorship (in Roy's case fighting it), looking at fundamentals, exploring issues of access, reforming its procedures with the Hutchinson Review [1978–1979] and so on. Formidable intellects like Richard Hoggart were also around, asking essential questions. We began to have these weekend retreats where we were really asking, 'What should we be doing with this vast machine we operate?' So, at this time the Council became somewhat internalised in seeking answers to important questions. What none of us had any control over was Parliament. We weren't ready with the answers it was beginning to ask.

The Arts Council had to learn the language of accountability in order to preserve *itself*. This explains the gradual arrival of technocrats and PR types at 105 Piccadilly, such as Dylan Hammond from Saatchi & Saatchi, who ran the seemingly fruitless marketing department. But this doesn't explain why the calibre of artform officers themselves diminished. It's generally agreed that there are three reasons. First, the foolish crises that have beset the subsidy system through the past twenty years have alienated those who would otherwise serve it. The music director's post had to be advertised and candidates actively solicited on three separate occasions before Ken Baird landed the job in the middle eighties.

On the other hand, it surprised almost everyone when the progressive curator Sandy Nairne joined the Arts Council as visual arts director from 1987 to 1992. He declared that he would work there strictly for five years to drive through a number of reforms and then leave. Nairne moved on to the Tate where, thanks to his politically correct leanings, he's now endearingly known as P.C. Nairne – he was the first member of staff at the Council to seek paternity leave. Nairne was already a renowned curator, having worked at Oxford's MOMA, the Whitechapel, then the ICA, and the Council rolled out the red carpet. When the theatre director Nick Jones arrived in 1994 as drama director, the fact that an actual practitioner was joining the Council was hotly publicised by the press department as though it was a fantastic stroke of luck. They were less keen to announce his hasty exit a few months later.

Second, Thatcherism pensioned off the notion of administration, that is, serving. It replaced it with management, that is, controlling. Administrators sit in rolled-up sleeves checking petty-cash chits; managers make presentations of strategies in suits, whichever their gender. Performers generally agree that the Council's preoccupations of the eighties removed it from directly artistic matters. It became fixated with exclusive policy issues, like its own relation to the Regional Arts Boards and its accountability to Whitehall. 'It's what happens when you start treating your organisation as a business,' argued a former panel member.

> You start thinking about yourself exclusively, and in commercial terms, with business plans, objectives and 'delivery'. It might be a good exercise to play with in an idle afternoon, but it's essentially irrelevant to subsidising the arts. That to me is a skilled task. An administrator is dedicated to shadowing and converting artistic decisions towards practical ends. But they took on people versed in management-speak who would vindicate the Arts Council rather than serve the arts.

Take Keynes' definition that 'the artist walks where the breath of the spirit blows him. He cannot be told his direction: he does not know it himself.' Romantically expressed maybe, but it describes why we have arts administrators, not managers. Indeed, the construction of arts management in the eighties duly contributed to a narrowing of the range and quality of performed work. It led to the promotion of readily sellable 'product' of little importance, though proficient to the balance sheet – theatrical adaptations of novels in particular. This in turn contributed to the retreat of challenging artistic work, which had made headway up to then, back from the subsidised heart to the insolvent margins.

Meanwhile, beyond the Council, managers seemed able to aggrandise their status with childish titles like chief executive, and stand above the artistic directors they would otherwise, and properly, support – Nottingham Playhouse was a significant example of this change in 1990. The endowment of admin- istration that the Council maintained for forty years perished. Now the arts world has a cadre of functionaries which has acquired an ever-renewable and specious vocabulary, one which foxes the artists it is supposed to engage with, and which fails to assist the production of resonant work to the public, which is what the job was supposed to be about.

Thirdly, critics consider that a drip-down effect can be detected in the staffing. Although there is still debate as to whether Sir Hugh Willatt or Sir Roy Shaw remains the 'last great Secretary- General', there is a consensus about decline. A former regional director cruelly quipped:

> Roy Shaw was a glorified night-school tutor, and Luke was a shiny
> modern Tory with a campaign badge stuck to his lapel stamped
> HEY! I'M ONE OF YOU GUYS. Anthony Everitt was a jumped-up
> journalist. And Mary Allen . . . it's no good declaring she's just a
> one-time chorus girl – Betty Boothroyd was a chorus girl too. None
> of them have the calibre of Hugh Willatt. Well, Roy – maybe.

Directors, too, are considered less fit for the task than their predecessors. Critics have claimed that progressively weak or pre- occupied secretary-generals appointed lacklustre directors, who in turn recruited deficient officers. All of them did so to ensure that the careerist ambitions of those below them remained a faint threat. In other words, the internal relations have remained fixed; the quality of knowledge, experience and capacity has diminished proportionally. Of course, Council officers might well say the same of clients, and it's hard to gain an overview of an organ- isation where so many people have worked and personal relations have coloured judgments of involved outsiders. Many clients themselves, and fellow officers, made an exception for Dr Alistair Niven, the recent literature director, who was hailed as a very bright man doing a very dull, but delicate, job. A writer said of him, 'He had meagre money to dispense to a conceited rabble of novelists and poets who were incapable of appreciating largesse, or even littlegesse.'

Crudely speaking, there have been four castes from which staff have been selected. The forerunners in the performing arts served the Church and its related scene, like Hugh Allen and George Dyson. The next generation – and others in the tradition – had been artists or practitioners of some kind, from Casson (actor) or Denison (musician) to Jane Nicholas (ballet dancer). Altern-atively, a similar group emerged from the Council's own regional offices or comparable servicing outfits, like Jo Hodgkinson or Dick Linklater (also an actor). They were followed by officials from local government engaged at a programming level in the arts, or something similar, during the municipal and education expansions of the sixties and seventies, such as Graham Marchant or Rod Fisher.

However, the trend in recent years has favoured those who may have worked in arts organisations, but in back-seat roles, or completely outside the arts, bringing 'a breath of fresh air'. An ill-famed example of fresh air was Margaret Hyde, who joined in 1991 as deputy Secretary-General under Anthony Everitt. This former executive of the National Council for Voluntary Organisations left within the year, offering only a passing comment that she couldn't fathom what the Council thought it was about. What all of these have in common, perhaps unwittingly, is that they have defined and cultivated a chimeric profession.

At the start of the Council's life the daughters and sons of the well-to-do assisted the arts and, like everything that sort did when they entered public life, they transformed it into a mystical calling, a vocation. In their eyes they have seen their opaque values vulgarised through the past twenty years. When seasoned arts administrators and artists grouse about the conduct of staff in the Council today, it could be that they are complaining about the relative transparency of operations, which artists should actually welcome. In the early days there was no written policy, no equal opportunities, no chance to call in Sir Len Peach.

For the arts, however, there has come a point when trans-parency and open procedures have a negative effect. While the Arts Council now tries to make it clear to artists what is expected of them, they in turn protest that they have to know everything about a production or project before they can apply, from the nature of the outreach work they must bolt on to it to the dates at venues willing to take on work which hasn't yet been made and in which they have no stake. Theatre director Peter Cheeseman argues:

> Too many policy decisions and principles about grant provision are
> now made out of practical ignorance, simply because some of the
> staff have had no experience with the putting on of work. As the
> level of expertise is lower, it might explain why much more is asked
> about things that simply can't be decided so far ahead.

Arts administration has mutated from a vocation to the profession we now call arts management. What was once considered a
labour of love is now simply labour. The offspring of the well-to-do
had imposed mystifications as a means of protecting their social
prestige. These have been replaced with written procedures and
strategies that can be processed by menials. This post-war shift
mirrors similar developments that have taken place wherever the
needs of the bourgeoisie for salaried security has been promoted.
The swelling fields of study at universities or the elevation of the
polytechnics are examples of this, which we'll come to. The
increasing division of labour into distinct specialisations brought
benefits to those in the arts who acquired a clearer definition of
their role than Casson's 'helping out'.

When the Council came into being, its operational vocabulary
was determined by the work in hand, not the other way round as it
is today. Veterans are deeply unsettled by the way their successors
have been urged to make their work comprehensible to the
discipline of commerce. In doing so these new brooms have
contorted some standard and favoured terms. For instance,
'investment' often replaces 'subsidy'. Yet 'subsidy' means a
financial contribution to the upkeep of something that would
otherwise perish, while 'investment' means the conversion of
money into some kind of property from which the original
investment plus profit will be recouped. 'Investment' is an apt
term only by an artful sleight of hand – the argument that money
goes in one end and audience applause comes out the other.
Politicians have now taken these twists a step further by saying that
cultural institutions must develop structures for 'enabling'
(investment), not 'dependency' (subsidy). There are other unwise
words, such as 'innovation' and 'cultural industry', which are
there to make businessfolk more approving of arts management as
a profession.

While the first generation of administrators protected their
rank no less strongly than their successors, they did so hand in

hand with artists. Tom Jones devised CEMA as an emergency employment measure, and created hybrid jobs composed of practical artistry mixed with the promotion of shows and some administration. In recent years the Arts Council has been seen to develop the work of almost everyone involved in the arts except the artists, which was what the public pointed out very clearly during the 1993 orchestra and theatre fiascos. The Arts Council has now acquired a sham responsibility to sustain and advance the arts-management profession. It has done so by devising a number of systems that require the comprehensive intervention of consultants and freelance 'specialists' or, as one theatre manager once pointed out to Anthony Everitt, 'You're telling us to hire some twerp as a consultant who's only on the market because I had to sack him from a previous job.'

The Council can't easily unburden itself of this problem. Yet it can influence the future by dissociating itself from a further development. It's one that has been spurred on by the Council's former associates who have moved away from administration and into higher education, thereby validating and classifying their otherwise vague status. This move was buoyed by the Conservative Government's Further and Higher Education Act of 1992, which allowed polytechnics and colleges to retitle themselves universities and free their subsistence from the grip of local authorities. We now have sixty-four courses devoted to arts and cultural management at fifty-two institutions. The Leisure and Food Management Department of Sheffield's Hallam University runs a BA (Hons) in Leisure and Food Studies, which includes specialist units in 'arts and entertainment, play management, customers – their need for recreation, and leisure organisation environments'. At the Liverpool Institute of Performing Arts, whose council chairman is the Council's former finance director Anthony Field, a BA (Hons) is offered in 'Performing Arts Enterprise Management'.

The nation's principal courses are provided by London's City University, a former engineering college which runs a Department of Arts Policy and Management, and the old Leicester Polytechnic, now called De Montfort University, whose School of Arts and Humanities offers an MA in European and Cultural Planning together with a plain old BA in Arts Management. City University spews seventy to eighty graduates annually out of its arts-management courses; each year around 200 people graduate nationally with degrees in arts or cultural policy management. At the secondary and higher education level the Arts and Entertainment Training Council in Bradford has developed National Vocational Qualifications (NVQs) in such areas as 'arts development enabling', 'delivering cultural products' and even 'delivering artform development sessions – for anyone who presents sessions to pass on arts skills'. Remarkably, it is the largest recipient of the Council's education and training budget.

This economy serves the needs on the one side of those who worked in the arts but now seek sanctuary in the world of tenured academe, and on the other the intensifying demand from young people and second-career types who consider the arts a snug option. The education institutions, fired by Thatcherism to serve new markets, are keen to advance the cause and bank the fees, never mind how superfluous the discipline may turn out to be to the world outside. The creative arts are being usurped as a calling by the uncreative arts.

Although the Arts Council cannot provide information on the recruitment of graduates to itself, there is an overwhelming suspicion from veterans that the development of these courses will further damage the quality of arts administration inside it. Their fingers are pointing to certain places that run arts-management courses as the cause of the decay, and they believe that the Arts Council shouldn't employ anyone with little more than an arts-management degree to recommend them. A former staff member said, 'What they should look for now is staff with values, not validation.' It would be useful to know how far we can move back to values and enthusiasm without straying into a greater mystical fog.

The paid: more rewards

The last three secretary-generals have not received the kind of honours bestowed on their predecessors (see 2, 10, 23, 31 below). Sir Roy Shaw was the last to be honoured – over fifteen years ago. Those last three resigned, which might have had something to do with it, though critics offer less generous explanations.

It's interesting to see how the Arts Council's hold on the honours system has diminished through the last decade. Some claim that this is the result of a choosy Conservative Government (choosy? Lord Archer?) while others believe it reflects the recent quality of staffing. The introduction of fixed-term contracts may also have played a part by reducing opportunities for long-term loyalty; the cynical civil-service line about 'gongs' is that you get one 'for hanging around long enough and declining to go'.

BEMs and MBEs are really the same, except the former is offered for working-class positions, the latter for middle class (see numbers 33 and 34).

1945	1	Lewis Casson	Drama director	Sir
1949	2	Mary Glasgow	**Secretary-General**	CBE
1950	3	Philip James	Art director	CBE
	4	Charles Landstone	Associate drama director	OBE
1952	5	Myra Owen	Welsh director	OBE
	6	Huw Wheldon	Festival of Britain	OBE
	7	Jo Hodgkinson	Regional director NW	OBE
	8	W.R. Fell	Visual arts	OBE
	9	C.W. Sibley	Art transport	BEM
1955	10	W.E. Williams CBE	**Secretary-General**	Sir
	11	George Firth	Scottish director	OBE
1956	12	Cyril Wood	SW director	OBE
1960	13	J. Denison MBE	Music director	CBE
	14	Stanley Vigar	Transport office	BEM
1961	15	Mona Tatham	Associate music director	MBE
1963	16	Gabriel White	Art director	CBE
1964	17	M.J. McRobert	Deputy secretary	CBE
1965	18	D.P. Lund	Accountant	CBE
	19	Douglas Craig	Opera for All	OBE
1966	20	Eric W. White	Literature director	CBE
1967	21	N.V. Linklater	Deputy drama director	OBE
	22	Elizabeth Davison	Assistant art director	OBE
1972	23	Hugh Willatt	**Secretary-General**	Sir
	24	Ronald Mavor	Scottish director	CBE
	25	Mary Endacott	Records officer	MBE
1974	26	N.V. Linklater OBE	Drama director	CBE
	27	Roy Bohana	Welsh music director	MBE
1976	28	Eric Thompson	Deputy music director	OBE
1978	29	Robin Campbell	Art director	CBE
	30	N.V. McManus	Exhibitions manager	BEM
1979	31	Roy Shaw	**Secretary-General**	Sir
	32	Stanley Leppard	Transport manager	BEM
1980	33	Nora Meninsky	Art librarian	MBE
	34	George Grant	Handyman	BEM
1984	35	Anthony Field	Finance director	CBE

1985	36	John Billings	Administration officer	MBE
	37	Joanna Drew	Art director	CBE
1987	38	William Lyne	Wigmore manager	MBE
1988	39	Jean Bullwinkle	Assistant drama director	OBE
1990	40	Jane Nicholas	Dance director	OBE
1992	41	Jack Phipps	Touring director	CBE
1994	42	Christopher Davies	Disability	OBE

Chapter 27

How to lead an Arts Council: the yes years

At the very top of the operation sit three people, one of whom validates the other two. That is the Government Minister, who is answerable to Parliament for the Arts Council's conduct.

The Minister appoints the Chairman of the Arts Council, who chairs the paramount Council and is therefore the head of the advisory structure – panels, committees, subcommittees, forums (sorry, *fora*). The Secretary-General is appointed by the Chairman in consultation with the Minister to govern the administrative structure of officers and other staff, acting as the accounting 'principal executive officer'. As Hugh Willatt discovered, when the Council is called before the parliamentary public accounts committee, it is the Secretary-General and not the Chairman who is grilled. The Minister appoints the Chairman but *approves* the Secretary-General, the difference being that the executive job is advertised and the Chairman recommends to the Minister the selected candidate. One of the recent secretary-generals, possibly Luke Rittner, wanted to change the job's title to 'chief executive', but as the royal charter stipulates 'secretary-general', it stayed. This United Nations-style name was copied from the British Council in the forties, when Mary Glasgow's status and salary were raised as CEMA became the Arts Council. In reply the British Council sniffily renamed its top post director-general, filched in turn from the BBC.

The Minister, the Chairman and the Secretary-General tend to get on with each other under a stable government. As the Minister chooses someone to chair who is acceptable to the government of the time, this is understandable. It's when there's a transition between the governments of different political parties that there is the most tension. The relation of the Chairman to the Secretary-General is often talked of as a partnership. In a straightforward company the Secretary-General would be the chief executive, answerable to the chairman of the board. As Secretary-General Bill Williams once said to his Chairman, Sir Kenneth Clark, 'You are the admiral. I am the captain. Get off my bridge.'

Ministers

The role of minister is a party-political appointment, vulnerable to job shifts inside the government and the ballot box, assassins or unemployed actresses on the make. So it will hardly come as a surprise that there have been twenty-nine appointments to date (arithmetically one every two years), only some of whom have been aware that the arts had anything to do with them. Of the twenty-nine, twenty-seven were men, and two not men. Actually it's twenty-six men, because we have to count David Mellor twice: once as Minister in the Privy Council Office in 1990 for all of four months, and then in 1992 as the first Secretary of State for Heritage and Unemployed Actresses for all of five.

The title of the post has changed nine times over fifty-eight years. MPs with nothing better to do than ask questions about the arts have acquired evasive answers from three presidents of the Board of Education, one Minister of Education, ten chancellors of the exchequer, one Under-Secretary of State for the Department of Education and Science (who was mercifully elevated to Minister of State in the same department), one Paymaster-General, two chancellors of the Duchy of Lancaster, four ministers of the Arts in the Privy Council Office, and five secretaries of state in the Department of National Heritage. Nevertheless, should one pass you in the street, the acceptable form of address is, '*Big Issue*, Minister?'

Two of those twenty-eight politicians have gone on to become prime ministers. Harold Macmillan and James Callaghan were both chancellors of the exchequer when they handled the Arts Council. Mind you, this doesn't mean they took an interest in its work. When Sir Kenneth Clark made an appointment to see Macmillan one evening, Macmillan asked him, 'Now, what's this about your art club?' Whatever the party in power or the position of the Minister in its pecking order, there is only one thing the politician wants to know of the council's Chairman. It's what Jennie Lee would ask of Lord Goodman in the sixties: 'How many votes are there in it?'

Once the war ended and the Arts Council acquired its royal charter, Keynes made sure that the Council was looked after by the Treasury instead of the Department of Education, from which it sprang in 1939. He wanted it to be as close to its source of money as possible. The Chancellor the Exchequer was therefore its Minister, which meant formally that the arts were represented at the highest Cabinet level. Yet neither the Council's Chairman nor the Secretary-General got anywhere near 11 Downing Street.

It was agreed in theory that the Council's Chairman, being an appointee of the Chancellor on a public body, should discuss matters with the Chancellor as colleagues. The Secretary-General, on the other hand, being a quasi-civil servant concerned with the Council's administration, should first discuss any necessary matters with a senior civil servant in the Treasury. Of course, no Chairman in his right mind would allow the Secretary-General to hold meetings with senior figures in Whitehall from which he was excluded, and so in practice it was decided that the Chairman and the Secretary-General should brief the Whitehall mandarin about Council decisions and he in turn would brief the Chancellor as he saw fit. As the Council meetings were held every three months, they met quarterly, and things went on in this decorous way until 1964.

When Labour came to power late in that year, the arts job was downgraded out of the Cabinet and driven down to a dependent position under the parliamentary secretary to the Education Minister. However, this very job was handed to Nye Bevan's spirited widow, Jennie Lee, to give her something to do. She enjoyed the patronage of Prime Minister Harold Wilson – so it was a demotion and promotion at one and the same time. Lee was also a close friend of the Council's Chairman, Lord Goodman, and in fact the three of them met frequently, both formally and informally. The whole business was a casual one, but effective.

From 1970 on the Arts Minister position moved all over the place, in and out of the Cabinet and becoming tied to other jobs. This came about because prime ministers tried to find appropriate personalities to do the work, in the same way as Wilson had invented the post to keep Lee around him. In Thatcher's

Government of 1983, the poem-writing Earl of Gowrie was placed in the Privy Council Office, and the role remained there for nearly a decade. Under Major's Government, David Mellor made the post part of his new Department of National Heritage in 1992, where it persists as a Cabinet position. It became a job for someone on the way up (Stephen Dorrell) or on the way down (Virginia Bottomley).

This Cabinet post is 'shadowed' by the Opposition, and though artists sigh that the Minister seems to change in every Cabinet reshuffle, Labour's recent record of shadow ministers was not impressive either – three in five years. One of those, however, finally emerged in the 1997 Government as Secretary of State, Chris Smith. He changed the department's title to the Department of Culture, Media and Sport. The Labour MP who has most kept his hand in official arts policy is Mark Fisher, an old Etonian and a Friar Tuck of a figure who lost his chances of full promotion but long ago found his niche behind the throne of culture. Fisher was made junior Arts Minister under Smith; his emollient tone suits the New Labour style. Yet another Labour arts specialist, the more radical and sparkling Tony Banks, became Fisher's cohort as the junior Sports Minister.

The Chairman, the Secretary-General, the Secretary of State and his Arts Minister meet formally every month, usually following a Council meeting, so that the Chairman can brief the ministers on decisions and issues that came up. These parleys follow an agenda and are held at the Minister's office, currently in Cockspur Street. Civil servants sit there and take notes, though the Minister can tell them to slope off any time he or she chooses. Tea and biscuits are served and the atmosphere is 'informal but slightly staged'.

Ministers can't simply turn up at the Arts Council offices. They must be invited, so they can be introduced to the work of a department or two. Officers need notice to make the appropriate ambient adjustments. A dance officer remembers a visit in 1995 from Ian Sproat, Virginia Bottomley's number two Minister, who was much more involved in sport than in art.

We had to take down all the Michael Clark posters – no naked flesh – and put up ballet ones, anything with tutus. We searched around for sporty connections to display, like a certificate we'd got from the Sheffield Student Games for giving a grant to the opening ceremony, and one officer hung her Lillywhite's carrier bag on the hatstand. Sproat came in and asked my colleague if dancers took anabolic steroids. We had to explain tactfully that dancers try hard to lose weight, not gain it.

Chairmen

Strictly speaking there have been twelve chairmen, though the Council counts Keynes as its first and numbers only ten. It excludes Tom Jones and Lord Macmillan of the CEMA years. At first chairmen tended to stay for seven years, but now it's five, in part to match more closely the tenure of a government. There's no question that the Chairman is consistently a political appointment. They tend to reflect the spirit of the party in power. Ernest Pooley had been involved in the nationalisation of hospitals when Labour came to power in 1945. Arnold Goodman was a legal adviser to the Labour Prime Minister Harold Wilson. Kenneth Robinson was a former Labour MP. Cottesloe was a Tory peer, Gowrie was once the Arts Minister in the Thatcher Government, and so on.

Chair-men all. Ministers generally find it difficult to find suitable candidates to head quangos, partly because they rely on intelligence picked up through social networks, which limits their choice to those they already know or have heard of, and sometimes because it needs to be someone who wants to advance his status in the honours system, which is the sole reward offered aside from free tickets to shows. Lord Rees-Mogg claimed that 'the unknown are not appointed', which prompted a question from one artist, 'Unknown to whom?' Rees-Mogg says of the chairmanship: 'It's not considered a difficult duty, but it's unpaid, and it's a job where you end up unpopular unless you happen to coincide with a period of expansion of public funding.' Palumbo seems to have managed to prove him wrong there.

Every one of the chairmen so far selected has been educated outside the state system. Half went to Eton, others to Winchester, Charterhouse and Oundle; Goodman first went to an independent Jewish school. Five went on to Oxford, four to Cambridge; Kenneth Robinson exceptionally went to work at fifteen as a Lloyd's broker. Two are hereditary peers (Fourth Baron Cottesloe, Second Earl of Gowrie), while six were ennobled either at the start, during, or at the end of their tenure; Kenneth Robinson was knighted at the end of his, while Pooley, Clark and

Rees-Mogg were already knighted when they joined. The age category shows how old they were when they started:

Chairman	Years in office	Age
(Lord) John Maynard Keynes	1942–1946	59
Sir Ernest Pooley	1946–1953	69
(Lord) Sir Kenneth Clark	1953–1960	50
Lord (John) Cottesloe	1960–1965	60
(Lord) Arnold Goodman	1965–1972	52
(Lord) Patrick Gibson	1972–1977	56
(Sir) Kenneth Robinson	1977–1982	66
(Lord) Sir William Rees-Mogg	1982–1988	54
(Lord) Peter Palumbo	1989–1994	54
Earl of (Grey) Gowrie	1994–1998	54

Secretary-Generals

Eight of these up to 1997, six men and two women. Their backgrounds are less integrated than those of their chairmen. Bill Williams and Roy Shaw came from northern working-class backgrounds and progressed through the state-school system to Manchester University, while Hugh Willatt and Anthony Everitt went to independent schools and Oxbridge. The ages at which they started, too, are varied, so much so that on two occasions the Secretary-General has been older than his Chairman: Williams and Clark in the fifties, Willatt and Goodman in the late sixties.

It might be said that three of them came to the job from 'outside': Mary Glasgow, of course, because she started it off; Nigel Abercrombie, who'd been a civil servant in the Admiralty; and Luke Rittner, who was running the Association for Business Sponsorship of the Arts. Bill Williams, Hugh Willatt and Roy Shaw had been Council members and had some knowledge of the structure when they started work. The last two Secretary-Generals were promoted; both had been the predecessor's deputies.

Secretary-General	Years in office	Age
Mary Glasgow	1940–1951	34
(Sir) William Williams	1951–1963	55
Nigel Abercrombie	1963–1968	55
(Sir) Hugh Willatt	1968–1975	57
(Sir) Professor Roy Shaw	1975–1983	56

Luke Rittner	1983–1990	36
Anthony Everitt	1990–1994	50
Mary Allen	1994–1997	43

Let us look at the way these three types of character mesh in what Rees-Mogg defined as the Yes Years.

1945–1953: Mary Glasgow/Sir Ernest Pooley

The former state-school inspector was the means by which a minor pen-pushing post (Secretary) evolved into a major one (Secretary-General). Together with her successor, Bill Williams, Mary Glasgow is the longest-serving executive of the lot, but her record has been neglected, mainly because Pelican Bill loathed her and succeeded in demeaning her memory. We tend to forget how young she was when she started. Glasgow was clever, elegant, a Francophile, with a touch of schoolteacher theatrics about her. She declined central heating and insisted on an open fire in her office, which was also a quirk of the BBC's Director-General, Lord Reith. Toilets she refused to have designated for male or female use, because that's how they did it in France.

Glasgow stood in awe of Lord Keynes. He was venerable, wasp-witted and rather full of himself, a celebrity, and a misogynist. She had to cope with both his neurotic interference and his prolonged absences in America, when they would communicate through flurries of memos and telegrams. When he died suddenly in 1946, she had to maintain the enterprise that he'd reconstructed around himself. To do this, Glasgow admitted that she cultivated a more authoritarian approach post-war than she had before. It was her loyal defence of Keynes' alliance with the commercial impresario Binkie Beaumont that gave the new Chairman an excuse to dump her.

As strongly as Keynes is remembered today, his successor Ernest Pooley lies forgotten. Yet he steered the Arts Council out of the harbour, and it's agreed that he was a capable committee chairman. Bulky, red-faced, silver-haired and moustached, on the verge of seventy, he was asked to take on the role by Labour's Chancellor Hugh Dalton for a curious reason. His only regular link with the arts was his trusteeship of the Old Vic Theatre Company, but he was singled out because Labour wanted someone who would develop the administrative functions of the Council without asking for more money than he was given. He was known to the Government because he chaired the King Edward

Hospital Fund in London and advised on the nationalisation of hospitals brought about by the National Health Service Act. They knew Pooley would do as he was told because he was gay. Mary Glasgow remembers being told at a drunken party by a senior civil servant that he was 'a safe little shit' because 'we've got something on him'. Homosexuality was then a criminal offence and it seems that he may have been caught in a compromising caper which was hushed up – it's hard to tell.

Ernest Henry Pooley was the son of a Victorian assistant secretary to the Board of Education. His background was not dissimilar to Glasgow's, therefore, but one generation behind. He was educated at Winchester and Pembroke College, Cambridge, where he studied law, then his father got him a job as a legal assistant at the Board. In 1905 he moved over to the Drapers' Company in the City of London, and from 1908 until his retirement in 1944 he became its clerk, leaving his job during the First World War to serve in France and Gallipoli. A clerk was a senior executive post in the City's Corporation.

Mary Glasgow agreed that people didn't know much about Pooley because they didn't quite understand what the Drapers' Company was all about. Pooley wrote a book about the guilds of the City of London to help explain the good work they did in the charity fields of education and welfare, and how this peculiar, parallel system of local government operated. The Drapers' Company bankrolled Queen Mary College at the University of London, and in his capacity as clerk he sat on the senate and the court of the institution between 1929 and 1948. He did not marry until 1953, when he wed his best friend's widow.

So Pooley was a 'safe little shit' about money, legal niceties, committees and the new welfare structures. He was concerned to make sure that the Council stayed 'below the parapet' by acting prudently with a comparatively insignificant amount of government grant-in-aid and keeping away from the attentions of press and Parliament. Between 1948 and 1952 the base grant stayed at £575,000 (around £7–8 million today). His successors laugh at his pronouncement: 'We don't need any more. An increase will only get us into trouble.' Yet he's been proved right.

Whether he didn't like Glasgow or she didn't think much of him, they didn't get on. She wouldn't let him have an office. She used the pretext that Keynes had never had one; America had been his office. Pooley would totter up the stairs to Mary Glasgow's room, stand at the door, and she'd say, 'No doubt you'll write a letter about this, won't you? I'll get you a secretary.' As that secretary might be Mary Endacott, we know what happened:

> The poor man used to walk up and down the corridor, huffing and puffing on his pipe, while one had to try and catch what he was saying. It was very daunting. I'm sure that's why he was determined to get her out.

When the Council received its charter in 1946, Glasgow signed a renewable five-year contract. Bill Williams had fought to become either the Chairman or Secretary-General after Keynes' death that year (he didn't mind which) and he would not have countenanced Glasgow as his executive had he got the chairmanship. He was horrified when Pooley got it instead, as was Kenneth Clark, who by now had been passed over twice. But when Williams saw that Pooley and Glasgow didn't get on, he sided with the Chairman to push her out. That she fulfilled her contract is a sign of her tenacity and flair. Yet in 1950 Pooley told her that her contract wouldn't be renewed the next year. She was more than livid, she was heartbroken, especially when she learned that her successor would be Bill Williams. After all, she had created the administrative structure of the Council from scratch. The civil-service elements still in evidence today in the operation are testimonies to her organisational skills.

When Mary Glasgow left at the age of forty-six she did so with a year's salary as recompense. She became a film censor, sitting in a preview theatre in Soho Square writing comments like, 'Delete rabbit-punch in reel 3.' Glasgow was partly responsible for the banning of *The Wild Ones*, starring Marlon Brando, which she agreed nevertheless was 'a brilliant film'. She also began to edit French-language magazines for school use, such as *Carrousel*, a line which she developed into her own text-book publishing company, the successful and widespread Mary Glasgow Publications, which has continued to exist after her death in 1983. She remained single.

For nine years she organised language-teaching programmes for ATV. This gave her the income she needed to buy part of an old castle in Entrechaux, Provence, where she was known to the locals as 'Madame Miss'. To travel between her home at 5 Justice Walk, Chelsea, and her castle, she part-owned a light plane, GAY-VV, 'Victor Victor', which she claimed to fly over to France, though the view behind her back was that she was really the co-pilot; it was a two-seater.

1953–1963: Bill Williams/Sir Kenneth Clark

Throughout this book Sir William Emrys Williams (1896–1977; knighted 1955) has been called Bill Williams, or Pelican Bill because of his abiding connection with Penguin Books, where he remained a company director. In fact, from 1935 to 1965 he was editor-in-chief of Penguin Books, and he must be the only Secretary-General to run two jobs simultaneously. He was stocky, well built but not tall, his hair routinely Brylcreemed, and he wore double-breasted suits, 'a cross between a headmaster and a bank manager – standard professional wear of the fifties'. Pelican Bill had a stammer, which appeared at moments of tension. He wore tiny specs over which he would view you like a magistrate. In the CEMA days he was known as Bill or Billy, and he cultivated that style. Williams was born into a working-class family from Carmarthenshire which moved to Manchester. His father was a journeyman joiner, his mother a farmer's daughter.

Fervently socialist in the thirties, he drifted languidly to the centre and by degrees a certain snobbery pervaded his outlook. He had married Gertrude Rosenblum, who became professor of social economics at London University, and they lived a full, elevated, society-parading life together. Whether his move rightwards was the cause, or whether he was disposed as a socialist against other left-wing views, he held a fervently anti-communist line during the McCarthy witch hunt in America, a stand which brought about one of the most disgraceful episodes in the history of the Council.

Tom Russell was a viola player and managing director of the London Philharmonic Orchestra when Beecham left it to fend for itself at the start of the war. Many regard him as the wisest orchestra administrator this country ever produced; he was certainly successful in sustaining and building the orchestra through an unstable and competitive period. Russell was a member of the Communist Party, and openly so. He was not alone. The LPO's chairman and principal horn, Charles Gregory, was too, as were other players. In 1952 Russell visited communist China on his annual leave. Labour's London County Council was intensely anti-communist and was looking for any excuse to break the left-wing clique in the orchestra it subsidised.

Bill Williams was contacted by London County Council in the hope that he could help to get rid of Russell on the pretext of his visit to an alien state. Williams had already decided that Russell must go. He took the orchestra's regular conductor, Sir Adrian

Boult, to lunch to persuade him that to intervene in the matter, or to back Russell in what Williams was about to do, would jeopardise the very existence of the LPO. Williams then went to three members of the orchestra board and, using the Arts Council's grant as a threat, struck a deal whereby if Russell was thrown out, the other communists could stay. Russell was sacked summarily and left without work. Meanwhile, Williams' action had exactly the opposite effect to that he'd supposed. It debilitated the ensemble entirely, the management fell to pieces and not long after the directors 'decided it was impossible to continue on a permanent basis'. This McCarthyite scandal was entirely engineered by the Secretary-General, fired by a private aversion to something he might himself have supported years before. It did him no harm; it got him a knighthood.

It was under Williams, too, that the Council made the most damaging decision of its life. The regional offices were shut down, in Williams' view simply to save money on administration, though he'd calculated, quite wrongly, that it would make the local authorities pay more for art. He held an obsessive attitude about the percentage spent on overheads and staffing, wanting it reduced from 10 per cent to 5 per cent. By closing the Council's practical links with towns outside London, he achieved his aim, but at the same time he opened the way for the feuding Regional Arts Associations to be devised, and for the regrettable waste of staffing and overheads they subsequently expended to no reasonable purpose whatsoever.

Williams was a resolute operator – a bit of a bruiser, someone called him – and in the view of the Council's long-serving finance director, Anthony Field, he was the best Secretary-General ever:

> He had a fantastic brain, and he'd use it to help you see the flaws in your own reasoning. Some found this intimidating, but it was always constructively offered. I'll give you an example of how he worked with the staff, perhaps my first one-to-one encounter with him. For many years we'd given money as grants or guarantees to companies that were registered as charities. That was how we worked. But we were encouraged, when there was considered to be a problem about play-writing or poetry in the fifties, to offer grants to individuals. The first was £250 to Shelagh Delaney. I was very worried about this precedent. I went to see Bill – Sir William we would have said then – and pointed out that to go with our grants was a detailed list of conditions by which the companies had to

abide. We had no conditions for individuals to send with her grant offer. He looked over his glasses at me. 'What sort of conditions would you apply? Should she, say, submit twelve sheets of typed paper every Monday morning at the place she is writing? And what is more, if she doesn't, what are you going to impose by means of retribution?' We agreed that we'd just have to give her the money, gulp, and hope she'd deliver. Well, she delivered *A Taste of Honey*.

Williams was the first Secretary-General to cultivate a court around him, an inner circle of reliables. Beneath him he consolidated the positions of two men who were opposed in method and reason. Matthew James McRobert (1905–1991), known as Mac, had been deputy Secretary-General since 1946. A 'steady pair of hands but awfully nice with it', Mac was a former accountant, responsible, economical, a red-taper, rather dull. Eric Walter White (1905–1985) was assistant secretary, wrote books about music during office hours using Arts Council equipment to help him, but got away with it because he fostered a flamboyant, mischievous tone. Later on he became, appropriately enough, the Council's first literature director. According to Sheila Gold:

> White was tallish and plump and pink with white hair. He always had a red flush to his cheeks after lunch. He talked with a very affected voice, which came from the egghead circle he socialised in. All in all a roguish teddy bear.

Goodman called White 'prissy' and noted that 'his joy and delight was to refuse a grant to someone he did not like'. Behind these two, the good cop and the bad cop, Williams ran a compact operation. His motto was 'Few, but roses.' Actually, he had another one, equally agronomic: 'Raising, not spreading.'

Kenneth Clark and Bill Williams had sat in on the first meeting of CEMA in 1939. Clark was then the absurdly young director of the National Gallery, while Williams ran the 'Art for the People' scheme of sending art exhibitions to galleryless towns. They crossed paintbrushes over visual-art provision several times, as we saw in Part I, and if anyone had truly thought about it for a second, they would not have put Williams and Clark together at the head of the Council. Clark treated Williams with kid gloves, but enjoyed the bolt hole he was given when, at the same time as chairing the Council, he was asked to be the inaugural chairman of the Independent Television Authority (ITA), which was setting up the country's commercial TV system to start in 1957. So both the Secretary-General and the Chairman had two jobs each.

It does appear that K. Clark did his Council work conscientiously and with good humour, though his heart would have been in it more if Williams hadn't been breathing down his neck, or up it, given that he was somewhat taller. He did manage to get an office and a secretary. Mrs Catherine Porteous was just twenty-one, but 'very lucky indeed to have K. as my boss. I had a lot of fun.' Many people can picture the good-looking Clark, even hear him, because of his famous TV series *Civilisation*, but Mrs Porteous describes him in this way:

> He must have been about six foot tall. He grew rather portly in middle age. His walk had become a kind of unathletic waddle. Otherwise he came across as very much a thirties gent, with the style, vocabulary and mannerisms of that period – I suppose *dapper* is the word. He liked good food and wine. He didn't have a drink problem, though, because his father had been a drunk, and K.'s wife Jane, poor Lady Clark, had a very bad drink problem which would get him into all kinds of jams at parties and receptions. He wore the most beautifully cut suits, and I remember being very surprised later to see him once in his shirt sleeves, how fat he'd become and how well his suits had been tailored to hide his girth.

Mary Glasgow considered Clark refreshingly unpredictable. Mrs Porteous agrees:

> You could never stereotype K. He would come out with the most unexpected reactions to political events or crimes or gossip. We might call him centrist now, even left of centre; I don't think he would think much of his son's views [Tory MP, diarist and archaic Romeo Alan Clark].

Although his friends included Winston Churchill and Rab Butler, he was also an acquaintance of Hugh Gaitskell and his centrist circle. Porteous adds:

> He appeared aloof to some of the staff, partly because he had a prominent nose which made him 'look down at you', and he was certainly shy, which may have come from his childhood, when he spent a lot of time alone, happily, so he claimed. K. was hopeless at the staff's annual Christmas dinner – he just stood around looking

embarrassed and hoping the floor would swallow him up. But he would come in and ask me things like, 'Poor Miss Somebody is looking a bit down in the mouth. Has that young man in Drama given her the push?' You see, he noticed more than he let on. He was bored easily, especially with Arts Council bureaucracy, and loved nothing better than showing people round the little exhibitions they had in the old headquarters at St James's Square. On his way to the Council something might have caught his eye in a gallery window on the way to the office, and he'd ask me to nip out and check if it really was interesting.

Leaving aside Gowrie's limited literary output, Clark has been the only Council chairman who we could say was himself involved in the arts, if only at the level of interpretation and patronage. It might therefore be thought a pity that Bill Williams blocked K.'s ability to make an impact on policy. Yet Clark was a little like Keynes in his artistic taste, endorsing the classical canon, relishing the distractions of the unruly and eccentric, but disengaged from creative experiment. 'When it comes to non-representational art I'm like Adam and Eve before the Fall,' Mrs Porteous recalls him saying. 'I have no knowledge of good or evil.' She added:

> He admired the cubist movement. He owned some Matisse drawings and some very abstractish Cézanne watercolours. He privately helped Henry Moore, John Piper and Graham Sutherland, but he was equally sympathetic to young artists he came across – encouraging, I mean – and he bought a terrific amount of work of theirs even though he hadn't the room for it. There was one who would come down with new work each year who we called the Huddersfield Genius. K. was very kind to him, but also to many others of that calibre. He presented some of these works to the Contemporary Art Society while he was still with the Arts Council.

In the eyes of the press and public, the Williams–Clark period was a relatively successful one. If we compare the scandals blowing around the Royal Opera House in the fifties and the nineties, we find that the Council was deeply damaged both times round, but Williams was much stronger at riding the storm than his successors. The secret lay with the low profile of 'Few, but roses' – the metropolitan exclusivity Williams favoured at the expense of regional provision. Fine for him, but that approach set problems for his successors – problems with which they're still battling.

1963–1968: Nigel Abercrombie/Lord Cottesloe

Lord Cottesloe was an hereditary Tory peer absorbed by rifles, rowing, dogs, Hampstead Heath and the taxation of works of art, especially his. He wanted to show the world that rifle-shooters were civilised chaps and so he cultivated the arts, or rather arts committees. At the time of his appointment to the Arts Council in 1960 he was chairman of both the Tate Gallery and the National Rifle Association. The Tate job had come about because in 1956 he inherited his father's estate and had suddenly become very interested in the export of works of art, including those in the family collection.

His down-to-earth name was John Fremantle, but he was proud to bear the title of Fourth Baron of the line a predecessor had begun in 1816 as a Baron of the Austrian Empire. He looked like a strapping version of Wilfred Hyde White:

> I am living proof that the theory that rowing strains the heart is an old wives' tale. I was a tall and weedy youth with a bad heart . . . but I was passionately fond of rowing and decided to keep on with it. Slowly my heart muscles grew stronger and all signs of weakness disappeared.

Well done! Mary Endacott, ever the diplomat, admits that the Council meetings under Cottesloe were 'not especially interesting', though he was competent enough in keeping order. Maybe the bulge in his jacket pocket helped.

Bill Williams worked with him for three years, even though the Secretary-General should have retired formally in October 1961. His sworn enemy in the Commons, Dame Irene Ward, had raised with the Chancellor a year earlier the question of why he had arranged for the Secretary-General 'a special pension although he is over the qualifying age?' Yet Pelican Bill left aged sixty-six, which is unique in the Council's history. His time with Cottesloe was spent wiping the babies' bottoms of the National Theatre and the Royal Shakespeare Company. Cottesloe backed the National, while the Council staff rather liked the look of Hall's RSC. The survival of both of them is a testament either to Williams' skill in keeping them alive if underfed, or to a lack of skill in failing to pick one or the other. The smallest of the National's three theatres is named after the huntin' shootin' lord.

There have been two occasions when the reaction of the

Council staff to the announcement of the next Secretary-General has been like that of the audience watching *Springtime for Hitler* in Mel Brooks' film *The Producers*: gobsmacked paralysis. Here was the first such moment. Nigel Abercrombie had been a lecturer in French at Magdalen, then French professor at Exeter before the war took him into Whitehall. Enlisted to the Admiralty, he stayed on comfortably as under-secretary until he moved into the Cabinet Office in 1962 and swiftly looked for any job going when the Profumo scandal rocked his boat. Abercrombie was described to the staff as a renowned author. Indeed, who hasn't lounged on a beach with *The Origins of Jansenism*, or *St Augustine & French Classical Thought*? The Council's staff clearly hadn't, and they clamorously opposed his appointment.

As might be gathered from the titles of his books, he was a devout Catholic, the first of three Sec-Genuflectors: Shaw and Rittner came after him. Abercrombie is the Alec Douglas Home of the arts world. Nobody except Sheila Gold seems to remember much about him, and she does only because she worked as his assistant. 'Nigel Abercrombie was thin, aquiline, refined, quiet. He was an academic, a toff, terribly cultivated, but not a man who had soiled his hands in the arts. His wife had been a singer, I think.' His son trained as a pianist; his son-in-law was the composer John Gardner, whose *The Moon and Sixpence* was the first opera Peter Hall directed. Aside from that, unsoiled.

Cottesloe had chosen him for a vital reason. The scandal surrounding Covent Garden, Sadler's Wells and Carl Rosa had induced the three main political parties to contemplate setting up an arts ministry, or something to replace the Council. Cottesloe needed a conservative, senior civil servant to impede challenges. (It was for a similar reason that Richard Pulford was appointed sixteen years later as deputy.) What Cottesloe had not banked on was a Labour victory in October 1964 in the wake of the Profumo affair. Abercrombie's five-year appointment had not meshed with his Chairman's. While Cottesloe stepped down in 1965 to be replaced by Labour's Goodman, Abercrombie was left exposed with another three years of his contract due to run.

Goodman did not like him one bit. At his first meeting

> I was ushered in with all the enthusiasm that Nigel Abercrombie could muster (I discovered before long this was a severely rationed quantity) . . . The cold waters he poured on my plans would have filled the reservoirs of the Water Board.

When Abercrombie's contract came up for renewal he'd reached sixty and as a deal to help him over his pension rights, the Council invented a job which was finally listed as regional adviser, but which Abercrombie fancifully called inspector-general of the regions. If his own version of the name has a witchfinder-general ring to it, it is not inappropriate. He was given the job of working out what the emerging and independent Regional Arts Associations were up to. Abercrombie rather relished what he saw out there. Tony Field warned that Abercrombie 'will do us out of jobs', and in a roundabout way he was right.

Chapter 28

How to lead: the yes, but years

1968–1972 Hugh Willatt/Arnold Goodman

Arnold Goodman (1913–1995) was a pudgy blob from first to last. He enjoyed a bourgeois Jewish Hampstead home life, got a double first in law at Downing, Cambridge, and honed his trade with Rubinstein, Nash & Co., which cultivated work from theatre people, Harold Rubinstein being a playwright. During the war, as a quarter-master sergeant, he met George Wigg, who was a close chum of Harold Wilson's, and it was through casual friendship with Wigg that he developed social relations with Hugh Gaitskell, Aneurin Bevan, Mrs Bevan (Jennie Lee) and finally the future Prime Minister, Wilson.

When in 1954 he set up his own business, Goodman Derrick & Co., he became Nye Bevan's executor. It was also through the firm that Goodman helped to set up the Royal Ballet and the National Theatre as legal entities, both of which gave him an understanding of royal charters, though he got thrown off the National job. He reaped the reward of his friendship with high-ranking members of the Labour Party when they came to power in 1964. In return for acting as the negotiating 'Mr X' in the ITV strike of that time, he asked for a knighthood and the job of succeeding Cottesloe as the Chairman of the Arts Council, both of which were swiftly granted – in fact he went one better and got ennobled at the start of his chairmanship, just as Keynes had done.

It was Goodman's idea to create an Arts Minister post for the outstanding MP Jennie Lee (1904–1988). Though the role was new, as we've already learned, the notion had been washing around all three parties for some time. Wilson had been indebted to Nye Bevan and wished to see his widow wired up to Downing Street, more or less for sentimental reasons. Goodman made the suggestion for which some will thank him, others fault him. As we've seen, it formally demoted the presence of the arts at the Cabinet table by making it a number three position in the Education Ministry for the first time since the war. In 1945 Keynes made a deal with Tory Chancellor Anderson – before Attlee was voted in – to harbour the Council within the Treasury, and Labour's Government of the time was happy to keep it there. It moved back to Education twenty years later purely to integrate Lee into the administrative system. Eventually the post improved a notch, still in the Education Ministry and still outside the Cabinet, to enable Lee to be called a (junior) minister. The one thing Wilson, Lee and Goodman cooked up together, a true achievement overshadowing anything they did for the Arts Council, was entirely educational – the Open University.

In any case, as Hugh Willatt says:

It wasn't Lee at all who determined policy. It was Arnold all along. Actually, he had just as much pull as she did in getting into 10 Downing Street any time of day or night, because Wilson used him as someone with whom to chat through all kinds of matters of state that happened to be on his mind. Meanwhile Jennie Lee would exasperate her civil servants by sticking official papers in her shopping bag and telling them, 'I'm just popping round to see Arnold.' They got their own back, eventually. She was excellent at going round the country and saying nice things about the arts to raise the profile in the press, and Arnold did this sort of thing, too, often accompanying her. There was nothing sexual in it, by the way, at least as far as I could see, though there was clearly an intimacy between them – slightly husband-and-wife.

I'm asked now and again if Goodman was homosexual. I don't know. All I can confirm is how much he enjoyed escorting widows to the opera. What that is a sign of, I wouldn't like to say. There was one in particular. She'd once been Lady Rothermere but became in the end Ian Fleming's widow – the *James Bond* writer – Ann Fleming.

Arnold looked after her financial affairs, and to some extent, it seems, her social life. She always looked bored stiff, but maybe she was weary of me and my wife when Arnold would invite us all to the Savoy Grill after a show – he enjoyed that kind of wining and dining. Arnold also liked to be seen with Eden's widow, who was a Churchill – I thought of Jennie Lee as a Labour version of her.

Hugh Willatt (1909–1996) was the solicitor from Nottingham who got the Playhouse built there in 1963. His wife, Evelyn, was an artist who set up the Midlands Art Group, which ran an arts centre in the city until one of Willatt's successors, Anthony Everitt, had it closed down in the eighties. The Willatts were regarded as a charming, chic, bohemian couple and they both remained active in the London arts scene after retirement. They lived in a fashionable artists' colony by the Thames at Hammersmith, where Evelyn died of Parkinson's Disease in 1992.

Willatt had joined the drama panel in the fifties and from 1960 he chaired that panel and thus sat on the Council. Goodman liked him because he was a solicitor working for another leftish firm in London, Lewis Silkin & Co.

'I had two blistering rows with Arnold when I chaired the panel,' Willatt recalls.

He wanted to merge the National and the RSC. 'Why have two?' he asked me. Well, to my mind, I felt it was wrong to have a monopoly at the top; it might allow a dead institution to come about. I thought competition (if that's the word) was healthier, and so did the entire drama panel, which was slightly exalted in those days – Jack Lambert, Harold Pinter, John Mortimer. I pointed out that we had two ballet companies and two opera companies. That was one of two rows I had with him – so, you see, everything comes in twos.

The other concerned the Nottingham Playhouse, when John Neville resigned in 1967 and Jennie Lee said she supported the salty director.

I called Arnold and asked if I could see him. He'd see me that night at his flat in Portland Place, where he did a lot of his negotiating – entertaining and business always seemed to go together. It was after 11 o'clock when I trotted round. We started arguing, and we got to shouting at each other, which was very unlike both of us. In the end, rather surprisingly at the time, he suddenly dropped it and agreed to back my point. He offered, 'Let's have a drink,' which was funny when he said it because he was teetotal and he only drank Perrier. He ventured, 'By the way, Abercrombie's had his time. Are you *wedded* to the law?' I went home and told my wife, but she said 'Don't be a bloody fool.' Well, I became a bloody fool and I was interviewed, though much as a formality. The only question I can remember was from a senior civil servant, who asked, 'Have you ever sacked anybody?' Luckily or unluckily, there had been a rare occasion when I had.

Hugh Willatt is considered by many to be the last great Secretary-General. While others merit Willatt's successor Roy Shaw, all agree that Willatt was a dandy chap. They say this in the full knowledge that he was too old to take it on. He was fifty-seven when he started, which in itself may be no bad thing, but he led an organisation that expanded rapidly in every direction – its grant-in-aid, its clients both large and small, artforms, the Council and its panels and their membership, staff and a huge new building. 'Goodman built his empire on Hugh Willatt's back,' claims a former Council member.

If I had a pound for every cigarette Hugh drew down to the stub getting his work done, I'd be a millionaire. Arnold exploited that man's goodwill and capacity for hard graft, and frankly it's a miracle he survived until his retirement. Hugh was like a knackered old pit pony when he finished, and like one of those ponies, everyone was proud of him. Justly so.

In timing, Willatt, Goodman and Lee were deeply lucky. Their main client was swinging London, an image from which this country has never truly recovered – vivid developments in the film, fashion and pop-music industries matched by an emerging post-war generation of artists in all fields, including new ones. Goodman, however, couldn't find it in him to escort his widows to a Gilbert and George danceathon or take a trip – if that's the word – to Jim Haynes' Arts Lab, which had applied for a grant: 'Our suspicions were that it was a place connected at least with marijuana if not with more dangerous and vicious forms of drug abuse,' Goodman wrote in his entertaining but manipulative autobiography of 1993, *Tell Them I'm On My Way*. Critic Kenneth Tynan claimed that if a committee was divided, with Goodman of one view and the entire committee of the opposite opinion,

Goodman would deem that a deadlock which he would then decide in his favour with his casting vote as chairman. This was certainly the case with the Arts Lab, which failed to get a penny from a man potently addicted – to food.

The development that Goodman encouraged above all else was Sadler's Wells Opera, which became English National Opera in his time. He was so preoccupied with it that, when he stepped down from the Council, he became its chairman and ended up its life president. He supported some regional reps, as we saw in Part II, but anything adventurist or experimental he discouraged, and in so doing he created an image of the Arts Council that the more progressive members of staff beneath him had to combat in order to secure credibility with developing artists.

Willatt, who'd been involved with a radical left-wing theatre group in the thirties, was more sympathetic to new work than Goodman. He was also responsible for the shift of resources to the regions. The nationals had moved down from 34 per cent of expenditure when he started to 24 per cent by the middle seventies; it wasn't his fault that the National hadn't yet opened at the resource-guzzling South Bank. More and more money poured into the Council year by year, and for that reason Goodman, not Willatt, is considered the saint. Yet how easy to be chairman at a time when your friends in high places are throwing money at you, to cast as you wish among the little people below. It was his successors who had to bend down and pick it all up again.

1972–1977 Hugh Willatt/Patrick Gibson

In June 1970 the Conservatives returned, now under Edward Heath. This made no difference whatsoever to the spending power of the Arts Council. Heath's championship of the orthodox arts – he was an organist and a novice conductor – guaranteed that the Council could go about expanding as before. Heath, like Wilson, used Goodman as a sounding post, but Whitehall had it in for Britain's Kissinger. Goodman stayed around the Council because he'd argued that chairmen customarily stayed for seven years (like K. Clark and Pooley), and though the charter stipulates five years in office, the Chairman can be re-appointed up to a further five. Jennie Lee was replaced by David Eccles, who walked in with grand designs of his own and wanted to show he would not let Goodman's girth stand in his way.

Goodman and Willatt received a letter from the Auditor-General, the 'civil servant dreaded by all other civil servants', who called them to appear before a parliamentary body known as the public accounts committee. First, they were accused of promising money they didn't have through the Housing the Arts fund. Officers would tell applicants that there was no more money left this time round but that their name could be added to a 'waiting list' for the following year. Civil servants thought it improper to commit speculative revenue, as the list might be used to blackmail the Treasury. Secondly, Goodman's pet, Sadler's Wells, had been allowed to run into debt after a year of operation at the huge Coliseum. Though the opera company was a client and therefore independent in its operations, Whitehall considered this to constitute bad housekeeping on the part of the Council. Frankly, these were trivial matters, picked on to rattle Goodman.

Hugh Willatt remembers Goodman's

absolute fury over this investigation. It took an enormous amount of time and energy to deal with the committee proceedings. Arnold took the business very hard indeed. I had to sit in the dreaded chair, but Goodman insisted on coming along to assist. He wasn't allowed to speak, however. He sat there fuming, mainly I think because he could have answered the questions better than me. After all that, we were exonerated. It was a terrible waste, just so somebody could gossip, 'Oh, well of course the Arts Council's being investigated by the public accounts committee. Most irregular.' But that's how civil servants get their own back, you see.

Goodman put Hugh Willatt up for a knighthood, which he had to go directly to Heath and over the heads of others to acquire. Mandarins tut-tutted that Willatt had been brought before the public accounts committee. Heath approved the award.

His Minister for the Arts, Viscount Eccles (born 1904), had been both Eden's and Macmillan's Minister of Education. Nominally, under Heath, he was the Paymaster-General, which is an odd job, involving acting as a sort of bank manager for government departments while doling out pensions to the armed forces and Whitehall. It meant that the arts were divorced again from education after five years. This was fortuitous because, had it stayed there, the Arts Minister would have answered to the new Secretary of State for Education, one Margaret Thatcher.

According to Richard Hoggart, who was then the number two at UNESCO and came across the Minister in that capacity:

David Eccles was an impressive man, tall, good-looking, very much the established, cultivated Milord in bearing – the sort who are trained to control the public with a curled lip. His hair had those handsome wings that grow silver. We were once together at an arts ministers' conference in Helsinki. The Soviet Minister of Culture was there, Madam Firsova, notorious and deeply flamboyant. She was trying to allow one of her block – Belorussia or somewhere – to enter as an extra member. Eccles had his instructions from the Foreign Office and opposed her bid. She turned to the other ministers and cried out, 'Ah! I have known this man for many years. Oh! How handsome he was! Golden hair, I remember! And courageous – then.' That evening Eccles sat with his wife and I heard him remark, 'This morning Madam Firsova said I was once handsome.' He looked rather crushed.

While Jennie Lee was happy to stick files in her shopping bag, Eccles demanded a department store. He acquired extra civil servants and made the first attempt to create a ministry rather like the Department of Culture, Media and Sport is now. To do this he invented new clients. The Crafts Council was his idea; a bloody pointless one it proved to be, because any other minister would have pressured the Arts Council to establish a crafts department, but Eccles, it seemed, wanted to expand his remit, not theirs. It has survived for the same reason the Arts Council persevered in its early days, by staying 'under the parapet'. But this whim of Eccles' became little more than a corn-dolly shop for the upper crust.

Eccles said that he was in the bath when he thought of Pat Gibson, reflecting on Gibson's ability to replace Goodman in 1972. Small, dapper, sharp-faced, bald and bespectacled, Gibson (born 1916) chaired the publishing subsidiary of the Cowdray Group, which owned the *Financial Times.* He was ennobled halfway through his Arts Council reign, in 1975. Gibson was not a 'character' like Goodman, and Mary Endacott places him in her category of 'not especially interesting Council minutes'. He liked architecture and music, mainly because his grandfather had been an architect in Newcastle-upon-Tyne and his father a baritone at Berne's Opera House in Switzerland before being wounded in the neck during the First World War. His father switched to stockbroking and sent Patrick to Eton. In summer holidays he treated his son to Glyndebourne, where they became friends of the Christie family. When Pat later moved to Sussex, he became a trustee of the private opera house. Adding the Historic Churches

Preservation Trust and the National Trust to his great and good committee work brought him to the attention of a bathing Paymaster-General.

About the time Gibson was appointed, the Gulbenkian Foundation had asked Lord Redcliffe-Maud, whom we've met elsewhere, to chair a report on the position of the arts in Britain. As Redcliffe-Maud had been responsible for the reshaping of local government, it was hardly surprising that his report, 'Support for the Arts in England and Wales', would come out in favour of local authorities taking a stronger role in the provision of the arts. As his six metropolitan authorities established themselves, they did just that. Gibson linked this in his mind with the development of the Regional Arts Associations, where he saw a beneficial alliance. In this way Gibson was responsible for a further weakening of the Arts Council's countrywide role. He told *The Times* in July 1976:

> I would like the RAAs to have substantially greater funds, to be rather differently structured from the way they are now and to take upon themselves over the next decade many of the functions that have been historically the Arts Council's.

This was the second time that, under a Conservative Government, devolution was promoted. There would be a third. And a fourth.

When Willatt retired in 1975, he was replaced by Roy Shaw, professor of adult education at Keele University near Stoke-on-Trent. Shaw was considered left-wing, though he later joined the Social Democrats. Had Willatt left a year earlier, however, it would have been unlikely that Shaw could have got in, despite a friendship with Eccles. What helped him was a change of government in March 1974, from Heath back to Wilson. There are four things we know from the job interview. One was that Richard Hoggart had applied, and many assumed he'd get it because of his fame as an author, but 'he didn't interview at all well'. When Hoggart walked up the stairs to his grilling, he met the TV arts producer Huw Wheldon coming down, so we know he was up for it, too. The deputy Secretary-General of the time was Angus Stirling (born 1933), now head of the National Trust and Covent Garden's luckless chairman at the time of the television series *The House.* Insiders were certain that Stirling would win. It was later rumoured that Pat Gibson couldn't bring himself to appoint Stirling because of the censure that would follow when outsiders learned they had something embarrassing in common: Eton.

1977–1983 Roy Shaw/Kenneth Robinson

Labour's first Minister on its return was Hugh Jenkins, now Lord Jenkins of Putney. Goodman claims that he put him there, and back in Education. Some, such as Lawrence Mackintosh, the Council's head of secretariat, consider that Jenkins was an exemplary minister, probably the finest of them all. He was undoubtedly the one out of the twenty-nine who was already closest to the performing arts, being a writer of radio plays and having been an Equity official in the early sixties (when he was also a key campaigner for nuclear disarmament). He later wrote an engaging book, *The Culture Gap*, on arts policy, but he wasn't in the game long enough to put his thoughts into action. When Wilson resigned in 1976 and James Callaghan took over as Prime Minister, Jenkins the grammar-school boy was superseded by the Etonian Lord Donaldson. We met Jack Donaldson in Part Two as the chicken farmer who was put on the board of Covent Garden. He became a friend of Labour's theorist and opera fan Tony Crosland, which is how he ended up as Minister.

When Labour searched for a Chairman, it didn't need to look far. Gibson's deputy was the lawyer Jeremy (Lord) Hutchinson, and it was commonly assumed he'd take over. But Goodman thought different. He wanted to chair English National Opera, but Ken Robinson sat there. Goodman apparently suggested to Shirley Williams (then Minister for Education) that Robinson move out to the Council so that he could move into the Coliseum. As Robinson was also chairman of London Transport at the time, the transfer was smooth, though he wasn't too happy about the increased workload because 'I'd tried to retire twice'. The Rt Hon. Kenneth Robinson (1911–1996) was the son of a doctor who died suddenly while his boy roomed at public school. It was because he then needed to support his mother that Robinson worked from the age of fifteen at Lloyd's, until the war. His solace was opera, and he followed Beecham's International Opera seasons at Covent Garden from balcony seats throughout the thirties. Unlike many of his colleagues, then, his love of opera was heartfelt and enduring.

As Labour MP for London's St Pancras North between 1950 and 1970, 'one looked around for subjects to take up, and the two I lighted on were mental health and the arts'. He would ask occasional questions in support of subsidy, but was more successful in getting suicide excluded as a common-law crime, and a number of mental-health improvements of that kind, when he became Minister of Health in the sixties under the heel of Richard Crossman. Many believe that Robinson chaired the Council under the heel of Shaw, though he felt that Shaw considered him 'too much of an executive chairman. Of course, I had *been* an executive chairman at London Transport. I think I did more work at the Council than my predecessor had done, but less than my successor would later do.'

Robinson got on fine with Lord Donaldson – 'I spent a weekend on his chicken farm in Bucks, and we clucked away about opera' – but he began to question the whole notion of arts ministers:

> You realise, don't you, that there's no real job for a minister of the arts? They get free tickets for Covent Garden; that's about it. I also question the Cabinet position. When Norman St John-Stevas first got it into the Cabinet, he made such a song and dance. But in the Cabinet you spend half the time dealing with matters for which you're not responsible. When I was Health Minister I could devote my entire time to the National Health Service. If I'd been in the Cabinet I'd have been worrying about foreign affairs.

His Secretary-General came from Sheffield, which was foreign enough to Robinson, who admitted, 'I am a London man first and last.' Roy Shaw (born 1918) spent the first half of his life in the north Midlands, devoting his career to adult education, at Leeds before Keele, where he became professor. He was the first Secretary-General to 'have an accent'. A staunch Catholic, he has five sons and two daughters. There was no question that the Council was not only getting a learned man, but also an inveterate lecturer: 'He tended to tell you things rather than ask you things, and we really felt he wanted to turn the Arts Council into the Academy for Further Education in the Arts,' a member of staff recalls. He once toyed with the idea of funding a school for showbusiness to be run by Tommy Steele.

Shaw admits he came in with change in mind. He'd chaired panels and sat on the Council, so he believed he knew what was needed:

> I had the impression from the press, for instance, that it had the same troubled image as British Railways. When I got in I appointed a press officer for the first time, with opposition from everybody. One of the directors said at a meeting, 'Why do we need a press

officer? Does the army have a press officer?' I said it had a whole bloody brigade of them. Sue Rose was my choice, and she's still there.

His other famous development was the creation of an education officer, which some see as the beginning of the end of the Arts Council in that it developed an activity that wasn't an artform. In fact this had started with touring just before his time.

Shaw and Robinson faced far more vexing problems than their predecessors, and it says a great deal for their skills that they were able to hand over to their successors an Arts Council more or less in shape. There were four mighty challenges: inflation, community arts, the Regional Arts Associations, and the inception of Mrs Thatcher's Government in 1979. On money Robinson believed that:

> We did well under Lord Donaldson. I was able to arm him with the arguments he needed. There was no ideological barrier between us. He fought hard with the Treasury for the Arts Council's case, pointing out our labour-intensive commitments and the effect of inflation. The Arts Council comes across to civil servants as a bottomless pit. We can't quantify creativity, of course, but it is possible to get them to see practical points. I think you will find that we got comfortably above the rate-of-inflation increases each year then.

Community arts had developed through the seventies, along with a number of disciplines dumped by the Council in a bin marked 'Alternative'. All of them questioned the Arts Council's commitments to national institutions and the priority it gave to orthodox practices, but community art was especially militant. As many projects were funded through local-government play-schemes and youth projects, it became a small but thorny issue between town halls and the Council: the 'do-good' emotional blackmail that community arts workers could pull had an especially sentimental effect on Labour authorities. At first Goodman's Council looked on this amateurist arena as 'social work', which is a more valid reaction than the community arts lobby was then willing to accept, recognising in it an excuse for the Council to keep the chequebook closed. Vaughan Williams would have identified and applauded some endeavours where professionals and amateurs undertook projects to mutually enhance creative skills, which is not called amateurism but animateurism.

But by the time Shaw arrived, a number or worthwhile ventures were overshadowed by mediocre, clamorous artists exploiting community schemes to sustain their failed careers and validate puerile self-expression as legitimate artistry. Shaw had worked for years in an education system based on notions of skill and quality, cultural traditions and training, and he scorned this unsophisticated challenge to his values. A book by Su Braden, *Artists & People* of 1978, especially annoyed him in its attacks on high art – not very clever ones – and he slapped it in the next annual report, an act which some considered imprudent and verging on paranoia; Shaw the lecturer at it once again.

As community art in its practice became confused with arts education and 'local arts', Shaw was bothered how much it fogged what he wished to develop through the Arts Council, especially when local authorities pressured the RAAs to support schemes they had naively taken on but couldn't sustain financially. Robinson's successor remembers being lobbied with similar demands, 'but whenever I went to community-arts things I found them, as far as I recall, to be amateurish and rather poorly attended'. This movement has withered since, the more unproductive of its activists pursuing subsistence wages through 'special needs' schemes, or peddling playgroup projects based around phoney rituals, which culminate in straggling parades of face-painted toddlers: old hippies pushing young kids around.

Meanwhile the regional scene was getting out of hand. As Shaw had been instrumental in setting up the West Midlands Arts Association in the late sixties, he became dismayed at the growing antagonism he faced as the associations challenged the Arts Council's metropolitan, high-art bias and the fact that they had to depend on it for their annual grants. The issue of community arts practice and regional conflict merged dismally together in Liverpool at this time, where the work of Merseyside Arts Association was blocked by a small group of community arts malcontents led by a local character called Bill Harpe, known to Council officers as Davy Crockett on account of his wild-frontier ways and comic hat. Robinson recalled 'that man trying to take it over. We put our deputy on it [Richard Pulford] and he saw off the misfits. That sort of thing was like a death wish by community arts.'

Of the regional crisis in general, Shaw considers that:

The regions felt the Arts Council had neglected them, and it went

right back to the middle fifties and the closure of the Council's own
regional offices ... But this fractiousness turned into malicious
in-fighting, almost personal power struggles and a lot of showing
off. At my farewell speech to the annual conference of the RAAs I
told them it was time to stop it, that they were in the same boat.
That didn't go down very well. There was a cabal of RAA directors
who were simply anti the Arts Council's existence; one of them
turned into a real bully. Crudely put, they resented the fact that the
Arts Council was bigger than them and held the purse strings. It
was a venomous period, but I have to say that not much seems to
have changed deep down since.

Thatcher's maiden Minister in 1979 was Norman St John-Stevas,
now Lord St John of Fawsley (born 1929). He was designated
Chancellor of the Duchy of Lancaster and leader of the House of
Commons, which put him in the Cabinet. For this reason he
claimed he first placed the arts onto the Cabinet table, which is a
bit cheeky of him. Of his character Robinson said:

> You could say he was a flamboyant figure. I'd been used to a
> completely informal relationship with Jack Donaldson. In direct
> contrast St John-Stevas was very formal indeed. He was a little
> distant with us, mandarin. Roy and I began to notice how he kept
> us waiting outside his office, routinely so, up to ten minutes. I once
> asked an aide what he did for all that time. He replied with a gleam
> in his eye, 'All I can say is that it's not work.'

He was the first Tory minister Robinson had met who was
genuinely interested in the arts.

> But that meant he wanted to dabble in things that were really the
> Arts Council's prerogative, and I had to head him off from time to
> time, which he took with a good grace. On policy he didn't give any
> impression that great changes were expected of us. He seemed
> secure with the *status quo*. But *she* hadn't shown her claws. And I
> think he thought he could get away with all these jokes about 'the
> Blessed Margaret' and that sort of foolishness, unaware that he was
> storing trouble for himself the whole time.

He survived one year and nine months before being thrown out by
the 'Bitch'.

The first stirrings of unease occurred when St John-Stevas told

Robinson and Shaw he wished to put the Treasurer of the Conservative Party, Lord McAlpine, on the Council. Shaw stressed that such a blatantly political appointment was not on. The Minister insisted. 'I pointed out that McAlpine was on record against public subsidy. Stevas replied, "I can only tell you that the request came from a very high source indeed." He meant Thatcher.' McAlpine joined, seemed to say next to nothing of interest, and soon left, bored to tears: 'I hated my time on the Arts Council . . . The meetings were tedious, the chairman, Kenneth Robinson . . . was pedestrian,' McAlpine later admitted in his memoirs. 'He was Mrs Thatcher's "spy". But there was nothing to "spy",' thought an officer. In 1981 St John-Stevas was replaced by Paul Channon, a moneyed and obliging chap, whom Robinson considered 'was much more at ease with us; he reverted to an informal relationship. A very comfortable sort of man, which wealthy people sometimes are when they've no need to be ambitious.' Channon lasted two years and four months.

Meanwhile Robinson retired with a knighthood. He and Pooley are the two chairmen not to be ennobled, the reason being that they joined under a government of one colour and left under one of another; the remainder got their royal rewards before political change crossed the paths of their careers. His replacement was a controversial choice, to say the least. Sir William Rees-Mogg (born 1928) had just retired from *The Times* as its editor of fourteen years' toil. He was ennobled as Lord Rees-Mogg of Hinton Blewitt in 1988, just before the final year of his Council tenure. He gave the impression of being a fossil. His school-swot haircut, chalk-stripe suits and town-clerk specs reminded one of Richard Wattis playing the stuck-up neighbour in *Sykes*. 'He would walk right past you in the corridor as though you didn't exist. At first we thought he was shy, then we put it down to short-sightedness. Finally we decided he must be a spectre,' shivered a member of staff.

Rees-Mogg and Shaw didn't get on at all, in spite of the fact that they were both staunch Catholics. Though Rees-Mogg was a decade younger he seemed older and his style was quite remote from anything Shaw had experienced before. The deputy of the time, Richard Pulford, remembers how Shaw's desk would be littered with literature. 'Look at this report from UNESCO, absolutely fascinating,' he'd enthuse, while Pulford stood over him and tipped most of it in the bin: 'You don't need to read this report, Roy, but you do need to check this memo.' In contrast

Rees-Mogg ran a spartan office. 'He changed the decoration and removed anything that belonged to the twentieth century. It became the timeworn inner sanctum of an antiquarian book-seller,' claimed a former director. Shaw called his new chairman Mogadon, after the drowsy drug.

Sir William was thought of as Mrs Thatcher's man. Not so:

I did three quango jobs in this period, and I don't think in any of these cases that I was appointed because the idea entered Mrs Thatcher's head, but because it had entered someone else's head and they felt she was not going to say no. I had only one advantage over other people she considered for such posts, and that was that she had known me for some time. You can only really say that she didn't object to me (she *did* object to people).

How I was actually appointed is absurd, as these things usually are. Paul Channon was having great difficulty filling the chairmanship. He was discussing this at home, and at that time his son Henry was going to Westminster Under School with my second son, Jacob. Henry said to his father over the lunch table, 'If you can't find anyone to do the job, why don't you give it to Jacob's father?' So, far from it being Mrs Thatcher who was the great patron of this idea, it was in fact Henry Channon, aged twelve.

Chapter 29

How to lead: the well, really years

1983–1990: Luke Rittner/William Rees-Mogg

Never has anyone entered the Council so feared and left so loved as Luke Rittner (born 1947). When his appointment was announced staff were as horrified as they had been over Abercrombie in the sixties. Resolutely hostile, they sent up a protesting petition to the Council. They had four overt complaints: at just turning thirty-six Rittner was too young, he'd only got three O-levels, he wore Union Jack underpants (how did they know about those?) and his background was sponsorship, not subsidy.

Their covert reason was that he was a Tory, and one who was too much of a puppy to prevent Rees-Mogg from running the show – the old admiral-and-captain issue once again. Bernard Levin in *The Times* guessed the staff's hidden agenda in a column of February 1983: 'The fear induced by Mr Rittner (I distinctly sense something of the same fear of Sir William himself) is that *he might start doing things differently.*' Rees-Mogg got into trouble for saying off the cuff that the staff were 'bureaucratically entrenched, resistant to change'.

Luke Rittner was, and remains, a model Next dresser of the yuppie eighties, chiselled and lithe, always ready with a winning grin, 'the finest people-manager I ever met', according to a colleague. After working for the Bath Festival in his home town, he founded in 1976 the Association for Business Sponsorship of the Arts (ABSA), which matched sponsors with arts events. Lord Goodman was his chairman. ABSA was very much an initiative of its time, one that has survived today to little purpose, putting about figures feigning to show that businesses help the arts to thrive, when arguably all they're doing are tax dodges and corporate entertainment. Shaw and Robinson detested this device, and Shaw's main gripe about the succession was Rittner's involvement in these dealings.

Rittner knew he had to charm the staff out of their shells.

> On my first full day there I didn't go into my office at all. I went into every single room in the building on my own and introduced myself to whoever was there. I got the impression that I was the first Secretary-General to knock on some of the doors, to judge by the reactions. But it was important to me to show that I was eager to find a team spirit. My second or third day, however, was marked by a young man throwing petrol all over the rubber-tyre submarine sculpture by David Mach at the South Bank. It was devastatingly awful because the man died of burns, and I dealt with his parents. I ended that day thinking, 'Oh, my God, is this what the job's about? Does this happen every day?' There is a side to the work that's fairly lonely.

Rittner was unlike Shaw in two dynamic ways. First, he could bound up the Council's staircase two at a time – 'Blimey, I don't think I ever saw Sir Roy do that,' exclaimed the caretaker, Will Stagg. Second, he got on with Rees-Mogg. Although Shaw, Rittner and Rees-Mogg were all Catholic and family-builders, the latter pair seemed to root their approach in their faith more blatantly. While they were surrounded by staff and advisers for whom the arts were everything, the greatest achievements of humankind, 'we both felt that the arts were merely a step on the way to something even better; a means to a greater end and not an end itself', Rittner revealed. They were also united in their achievements, frustrations and failures.

Rittner observed:

> Politicians and Whitehall were pandering to the screams to cut back on the welfare state and we could see that the Arts Council

would be damaged as a scrounger, even destroyed, if we were unable to show how we weren't wasting cash, and that the tax-payer was getting value for money. We addressed that pretty successfully. There were attacks and we countered them. The frustrating side was that civil servants saw the growing calls for accountability as a heaven-sent opportunity to secure their future. Over the seven years I was there I found civil servants getting more and more involved in checking our documents, our annual plans, our bids, everything. We went through endless debates, nth drafts and modifications in order to address their comments. They failed to beat us down, but in the process – and I take some blame for this – it drove us to go overboard in the planning process. The demands we made on client organisations became more and more complex and time-consuming. I see now how bureaucracy went berserk.

Rees-Mogg and Rittner placed their principles and aspirations in a document that was intended to provide a ten-year strategy: 'The Glory of the Garden' (1984). 'Basically I came to the conclusion that arts funding had to be for the benefit of the audience and not for the benefit of the performer,' explained Rees-Mogg, who was encouraged in this by the deputy, Richard Pulford.

Secondly, the arts are much more often let down by bad management than by bad art. If you're a not-very-good violinist, you don't get into a top orchestra. If you're a not-very-good accountant, then it's perfectly conceivable you'd be an accountant to a top orchestra, because it's not a particularly attractive job. Therefore one did pay a lot of attention to see that the managerial side of clients we supported was brought up to the level of the artistic side.

Rittner agrees:

We tried to alter the outlook of many arts organisations as far as their administrative, managerial and financial practices were concerned. Part of that was to do with the seismic change in the political nature of the country, and that in turn drew from us a strategy for survival, which was 'Glory of the Garden'. The trouble was that the very civil servants who should have been supporting our moves didn't give the full economic backing we needed. I know that William felt let down by that.

Rees-Mogg had to cope with three different ministers: Channon ('a man of considerable personal charm'), Richard Luce ('a nice man to deal with, his meetings were always entertaining') and in between them the Earl of Gowrie ('a degree tougher'). Gowrie was an ambitious Minister for two years, 1983–1985, the second of which brought him into the Cabinet in St John-Stevas's former seat. He resigned during a reshuffle in September 1985, complaining that his salary of £33,000 worked out at £1,500 net a month 'which is not what people need for living in central London', a remark mauled by the popular press. Rees-Mogg recalls that Gowrie was

> tough with us on reaching agreement on any matter where he had to plead our case higher up. He would give us a cross-examination as to why we needed further resources, how we could justify it. He would be rigorous.

One wonders how Gowrie the Minister would have tackled Gowrie the subsequent Chairman.

The Earl's view was that arts companies were receiving fair subsidy and if they needed more they should 'get out into the world of the real economy and hustle'. He kept back some of the Council's grant to fund an ABSA development called the Business Sponsorship Incentive Scheme (BSIS) to match money offered by new sponsors. One of the ABSA staff showed incentive by setting up false companies in the South-East Arts area and salting thousands of pounds of Gowrie's cash in bank accounts before getting jumpy and shopping himself.

It was during this time that Sir Peter Hall denounced Gowrie and accused the Arts Council of being his stooge. Prime Minister Thatcher countered, 'When are you going to be able to stop giving money to awful people like Peter Hall?' Rittner points out that Rees-Mogg was not swayed by this personal bickering but rather

> William came to the view that arts organisations were not profligate, that they were running a pretty tight ship. Certain politicians thought he'd turned native. He therefore faced some very tough and difficult negotiations with the Government, and he fought hard to secure the independence and the future of the Arts Council in a way that not many people have given him credit for.

Credit is due because when he started the staff totalled 275 and when he left there were 164; the grant rose consistently from £96 million to £155 million (a value increase from £126m to £160m, slightly tight but favourable). Credit is also deserved for getting clients to construct three-year plans, many for the first time.

A regular applicant recalled:

> They devised the Incentive Funding Scheme, which seemed to me a sleazy device on the one side to annexe more money from the Government and on the other to show it was being used to specific effect, to make us appear more businesslike. So I was sceptical. But, to be fair, the three-year plan we worked on turned out to be a wonderful exercise, both in projecting our needs and in team work. In the end it was all rubbish because we were working with standstill grants, but the project gave us focus.

Credit is also due for working with Birmingham in its cultural redevelopment, especially Simon Rattle's music schemes there. Credit is warranted for finally dealing with the undeniable obstacle of racism within the white bourgeoisie who run the arts. 'Ethnic minorities' the issue was called first; it became 'cultural diversity'. Rittner took it seriously, and his roving black monitoring committee was resented because some felt 'it was like the Spanish Inquisition' and enjoyed widespread powers of intervention, but it exposed and then rectified some weak thinking on the subject. This began with the notion that, as Britain's blacks totalled 4 per cent of the population, no less than 4 per cent of all budgets should be devoted exclusively to their work. Such a segregated calculation became resented by blacks and whites alike, and the monitoring committee was able to improve the context in which such work was discussed and supported.

It's not Rees-Mogg's fault that black administrators ripped off the collapsed Roundhouse black arts centre project, or that white administrators likewise squandered any chance of completing the National Jazz Centre in Covent Garden as a home for black classical music (as the great jazz composers prefer their work to be known). On a different level the Council also boosted limp stuff like Adzido, a dance company peddling fake pan-African goo for suburban tourists, a style which typified rejoicerism in its 'celebration of roots culture'. The Council would never have subsidised a pan-European folk-dance group.

Nevertheless, fine work was supported and developed as well as weak. The distinguished (black) theatre director Yvonne Brewster considered that:

> the Council was certainly opening up its credibility to us. But there seemed to be little quality-control going on, even perhaps a lack of vision about what was needed. It was too hands-off to be believable and maybe some took advantage of the access we were offered. On one occasion I was asked to join a panel and I replied that I'd like to think about it. 'Mrs Brewster,' I was firmly told, 'people who are invited to join the Arts Council are not in the habit of asking for time to consider.' It all moved far too fast and superficially in my opinion.

When a critically scorned show which was purported to demonstrate – by having black actors stand onstage in breeches and wigs – that Beethoven and Pushkin were black was nevertheless toured with Council money, a member of the monitoring unit tried to defend it on the grounds that, 'I only saw a happy and empowered audience'.

More credit, however, is due to Rees-Mogg and Rittner for tackling disability in the arts, strongly promoted by Lords Attenborough and Rix; and women in the arts, strongly supported by women already in the arts. Pity they overlooked the arts themselves. A lot of equal-opportunities legislation was developed in all fields during the general privatisation exercises of the period, of course, in order to project meritocratic thinking. The race issue was really impelled by the 1981 riots in Brixton and Toxteth. But how very liberal and seventies this supposedly Thatcherite arts regime turned out to be in such matters.

The whip employed to lash the efforts of Rees-Mogg and Rittner has seven strands: they let the Council become a tool of government; they moved policy away from practising artists towards audiences that didn't exist; they demoted the arts in the Council structure and promoted instead peripheral departments such as marketing; they diminished quality in the recruitment of officers; they went planning barmy; they introduced a debasing language of voguish management-speak; and they created the fattest white elephant in the Council's history when they took over the South Bank Centre.

Now that we have had a Council that truly was a tool of the Major Government and which tried to convert itself into a tool of the next one, we can see that something quite different happened back in the eighties. Rees-Mogg had to face the demands of civil servants rather more than those of the politicians who weakly allowed Whitehall its head. He did so not by refusing them or yielding to them, but by tackling their requirements, with the survival of the Council's independence in mind. It was the mandarin Clive Priestley who reported that Covent Garden and the RSC should be handled directly by the Treasury and Rees-Mogg saw off that idea. It was permanent secretary Richard Wilding who, in 1989, told the Arts Minister the way the Council should operate in the nineties. His report was followed by scrutiny of the Council by the National Audit Office.

Creeping Whitehall interference had first been sensed by Robinson and Shaw, which is supposedly why they employed the former civil servant Richard Pulford as deputy. The growing strength of Whitehall in the domain of culture started as soon as the Tories entered in 1979 and ended victoriously for them twelve years later with the opening of the extensive Department of National Heritage, now called the Department of Culture, Media and Sport and staffed by 960 civil servants. Lord Armstrong remarked how its boss, permanent secretary Hayden Phillips, was 'almost knocked over by the rush of people wanting to get out of other departments and join his one'.

Medium-term political directives definitely influenced a number of publications the Council commissioned, which suggests that the Council was better at marketing its policies than practising them. For instance, the parliamentary Select committee on public and private funding of the arts in October 1982 told the Council to spend more money in the regions, hence 'The Glory of the Garden', 'a major act of administrative decentralisation'. Heseltine's inner-city regeneration programme stimulated 'The Urban Renaissance'. Government keenness for tourism initiatives in the wake of the IRA bombs produced 'A Great British Success Story', while scrutiny into costs prompted 'Partnership: Making Arts Money Work Harder' (1986). But they were like catalogues for summer holidays with Club ACGB, where great art lies just a stone's throw from a baking beach. They were prospectuses, not manuals. Few of them had a practical effect.

'Garden' was designed to drive policy through to 1994, but few of the practical measures it set out for devolution, such as a national grid of thirteen cities, were ever effected. Civil servants blocked the financing of them. In Rees-Mogg's time the Council devised a ten-year plan, a three-year plan (1988–1991) and a one-year plan, all of which were abandoned at some point. He believes that Mrs Thatcher was keen to see more money go to the capital and that she didn't back the views of the select committee that sparked the devolution process. So, not Thatcher's man at all. When his five years were up in came a more intimate friend of Mrs Thatcher's, one who even invited her into the building for a formal visit.

1990–1994 Anthony Everitt/Peter Palumbo

It is heartlessly said that the difference between Rees-Mogg and Palumbo could be observed by their behaviour in the Chairman's seat. Rees-Mogg seemed not to be there but he understood what was going on. Palumbo might have been there, but . . .

Peter Garth Palumbo (born 1935) was equally the converse of Rittner – praised to the heavens when his appointment was announced, but out five years later judged the least fortunate of chairmen. In May 1990 Terry Hands of the RSC eulogised, 'Palumbo is very good news. He loves the arts for a start, which is a damn sight more than Rees-Mogg ever did.' Peter Jonas of English National Opera agreed: 'He is an advocate rather than a messenger of government policies. It is a complete contrast to the ascetic and acerbic presence of his predecessor.' The reason why they thought he'd be so superior stemmed from his patronage of modern art and architecture; Rees-Mogg reserved his enthusiasm for eighteenth-century literature, chiefly Samuel Johnson. Palumbo had sat as a trustee of the Tate and the Whitechapel Art Gallery during the eighties. There he had set up some projects that were considered questionable.

Elected by the Tate trustees in 1984 to become their next chairman, he loftily told the press of his plans to run a Tate Foundation in order to address some hard criticisms he had of the existing operation. His appointment was then annulled, despite him furnishing his Foundation with elegant offices. Similar issues were said to have affected his dealings with the Whitechapel's Foundation. Palumbo, it seemed, may have become less of a maker and shaker than a dreamer and a diva.

Sure enough, when he joined the Arts Council he dramatically set up a rival, grant-dispersing organisation called the Arts Foundation. He did so with £1.1 million bequeathed to the Council by a merchant banker, Francis Hoch. Palumbo used this bounty to create the Foundation, but no amount of cash could cushion its rocky start. Palumbo appointed five male friends as trustees and estimated that it would raise through sponsorship £20 million; at this time the Council was running its own sponsorship unit, which would be trawling the same patrons in competition (actually, neither of them flourished).

The Foundation's first director was a yuppie called Stephen Bayley who got off to an awkward start at its Docklands launch in May 1991. After apologising for dragging the guests into the 'hellish' East End, he and Palumbo declared that the Foundation would be distinct from the Council and have an 'intelligent' approach, by devoting its funds to 'innovative' work. 'Does that mean that what the Arts Council does is stupid?' asked a journalist. 'Are you saying the Arts Council is against innovation?' asked another. Ah, how Palumbo must have shuffled his feet and chuckled. The Arts Foundation had to be relaunched twice and appears today a tail-between-its-legs affair quietly run by a Council member Palumbo got to know, Pru Skene, who now chairs the lottery board.

Nor was this Palumbo's sole unwise project. He was a sovereign rejoicerist and opened his first annual report with the remark: 'Looking through my diary for this year, I am struck by the insistent theme of the celebration of the arts.' In heady response he invented the Millennium Initiative, to 'raise money to restore the fabric of museums and cathedrals'. Had Palumbo taken more notice of the civil servants who were looking into the Lottery once Major took power, he might not have announced this non-starter. Being a staunch Christian he saw the year 2000 as 'an event of profound symbolic significance ... that when the second hand ticks past midnight ... our house is in order socially, econom-ically, culturally, and in terms of world stability'.

He consequently marked each year leading from 1992 to that date with landmark Years of Arts, each a spell of another artform in a different city, ending with the Year of the Artist for 2000 itself. It started lamely with a year of music in Birmingham, which was having a year of music anyway, and swiftly sank into oblivion with the 1993 Year of Dance in the east Midlands. A radio journalist who followed the entire fracas felt that it was squalidly hushed up; perhaps the Council was lucky that the public tends not to notice when things *don't* happen.

One of Palumbo's chosen years covered architecture (1999), predictably enough. He even imposed an architecture unit on the

Council, surprised that this artform had not been represented earlier. In setting it up it was thought he was challenging English Heritage. Nobody had the nerve to ask him to justify in what way architecture was still a truly creative art, but at this very time architects' clients were progressively advised by the rival trade of building managers. The impatient campaign by architects to buttress their teetering status by invading their way into the Arts Council and the Royal Academy of Arts was driven by this threat, over which Palumbo naturally took a professional interest.

Palumbo seemed to believe that if it interested the Chairman, it must interest the Council. 'He was used to having his own way, but you felt that he had little idea how to work *with* people,' explained a former colleague of his. Palumbo didn't like the food in the Council canteen, so he summoned his own chef and butler. As he made clear, he refurbished his office (the one with the abbey view) to regal quality with £250,000 of his own cash. Staff claimed they knew when he'd called in by the scent of his piquant cigars loitering in the non-smoking lifts ('the place ponged all afternoon'). He sometimes travelled on Council business in his own helicopter ('We were ordered to lay a big white blanket in the nearest field so he'd know where to land,' recalled a rural client), though when he went by train staff gossiped that he had two first-class tickets purchased so he wouldn't have to sit next to anyone. That said, these luxuries were not paid for by the Council but by Palumbo himself.

When he first saw the headed notepaper, printed up with his name together with that of the Secretary-General and deputy, he was said to have exclaimed, 'It says Lord Palumbo. I'm not Lord Palumbo. I'm *The* Lord Palumbo.' The entire notepaper stockpile had to be scrapped and re-ordered. Soon after it arrived with the definite article added, Rittner resigned and a third order had to be made with Everitt's name in his place. The costs swiftly escalated. After the third batch arrived, his new deputy, Margaret Hyde, left and a fourth order had to be made.

In contrast to The Lord Palumbo's lofty style, his grandfather was an Italian immigrant who ran a café in Lower Thames Street. Peter's father, Rudolph, used commercial common sense to develop a £69 million property empire out of bombsites in the City, which he handed on to his Eton-educated son as the Rugarth Investment Trust. Peter became famous for something he wasn't allowed to do despite thirty-five years of lobbying – build a Mies van der Rohe tower by the City's Mansion House. Cynics claim that in return for taking on the Arts Council for Mrs Thatcher (he was fifth on her list; top of it was said to be Jeffrey Archer, and the others had said no too), he finally got the go-ahead to demolish listed buildings and erect his personal monument, now to a design by the late Sir James Stirling, the Mies van der Rohe design having failed to gain planning permission. 'We have something in common,' he teased as he examined Sam Wanamaker's model of the unbuilt Globe Theatre. 'We've both fought philistinism in pursuit of our visionary buildings.' It's said that Palumbo assumed that the Council would support Wanamaker, though it was not in his gift to promote anything. Early reports of this kind made officers increasingly unhappy with the situation.

Rittner was already anxious. He thought Palumbo had cancelled a couple of the regular ministerial meetings with Richard Luce, which would have been an unprecedented move in the Council's history. Rittner's unease grew when a senior civil servant suggested to him that the Chairman and the Minister might be convening without him. Having discovered that another meeting, understood to have been cancelled, had been scheduled, Rittner confronted Palumbo at the door of his office with the agenda. Behind closed doors, Palumbo told Rittner that the arts agenda was a bluff and that he was really meeting Luce apparently to reveal to him details relating to a chief negotiator for the Palestine Liberation Organisation. Rittner, overwhelmed, left it at that.

Rittner convened the staff on 28 March 1990 and announced his resignation. As he could not understand or pass on the PLO story, he said he was dismayed by the increased devolution proposed by the Wilding Report of October 1989. Staff wept at the news of the popular Rittner's departure. Palumbo replaced him with the deputy Secretary-General, Anthony Everitt. Few of those 'upstairs' were surprised by the choice, for they knew that Everitt had aspirations for the hot seat.

Well built but flabby, Everitt (born 1940) contrasted his white hair and pale skin with black-framed glasses and dark suits so that he 'looked like a black and white photograph until he got excited and his face turned into a red balloon'. He had grubbed in the seventies as the art and drama critic of the *Birmingham Post*. He advanced to features editor between 1976 and 1979 and accepted chairmanships of Birmingham's modernistic Ikon Gallery and Arts Lab. He took on the directorship of the troubled Midland Group Arts Centre in Nottingham, the one which Mrs Willatt had set up, but when the directorship of East Midlands Arts

Association came up just months later he took that and, from his position as chief funder of the arts centre, withdrew aid.

A leading producer recalled:

> I remember him as a likeable and quite bright journalist in Birmingham who championed contemporary things, but as he's got on in his career I've increasingly lost any sense of what interests him. He seems to enthuse about everything. When he was deputy at the Arts Council there was a general feeling that he'd become too political, and some felt you had to second-guess his voiced reactions. He came across to some as Mr Hidden Agenda. On the other hand, you could take him to meet the artists backstage and he'd engage with them sparklingly, which so few of the others did. He was a good guy who lost his way, I reckon.

Everitt was the first gay Secretary-General (if we may make assumptions about Mary Glasgow) and one who enjoyed a settled partnership. A former colleague of his puts forward an intriguing view that particular homosexuals find it difficult to enjoy a public, exposed position, and that through the 'inconsistencies, prevarications, nervousness, bluster, the wayward turning on and off of the hot and cold policy taps during his reign', Everitt was displaying his reticence and tensions. 'He'd been an efficient, adequate manager. When he took on the number one job he became Palumbo's right-hand man.' His predecessor as deputy, Richard Pulford, doesn't think even the number two job suited him. Then again, Pulford doesn't seem to think anyone did it as well as he did himself, and he may well be right.

Palumbo and Everitt wished to avoid the obstacles faced by their antecedents. There were two nagging problems: first the broadsides from the civil-service armada, and second the loss – of authority and function, of money running through the artform accounts, of national perspective – that derived from devolution. They decided that they must build a new alliance with Westminster to bolster defences against Whitehall: to 'keep things sweet'. The trouble was that two sets of characters got in the way. The National Audit Office issued a stinking cost-analysis report on the Council, but more prominently Permanent Secretary Richard Wilding had delivered in September 1989 his report on the national arts funding picture to Minister Luce, who'd commissioned it. Wilding advocated powerful structural changes, including a second and deeper wave of devolution. In September

1990 the new Minister, David Mellor, announced the results of consultations following the delivery of Wilding: there would be ten Regional Arts Boards to replace the twelve Regional Arts Associations, not the seven advocated by Wilding, and the Arts Council would lose a further ninety-two clients to these new RABs, retaining eighty-one of its own (in the end so many clients refused to be devolved to RABs that these figures were never realised).

Mellor, MP for Putney, was a centralist and had diluted Wilding's proposals, much to the good. Wilding's report was insightful, but no arts practitioner would have started from the same basic assumptions that guided the mandarin, who was looking at how to overcome structural inconsistencies on a national scale. Mellor's lucky intervention, nonetheless, was part of Palumbo's second problem. In 1990 alone he had to deal with three motley ministers – Luce, Mellor and Timothy Renton. All in all there were five ministers in five years, so no wonder the hot and cold policy taps spluttered or gushed by turns when the Council relied on politicians for a smooth supply. Palumbo's beloved Margaret had been ditched by her party in November of 1990. John Major took over and rewarded his supporter David Mellor with promotion to Chief Secretary of the Treasury, replacing him with the veteran Renton, who had broadcasting interests and a daughter who went to art college, but little else to single him out as Arts Minister, unlike Mellor's collection of CDs.

In contrast to Mellor, Tim Renton, MP for Mid-Sussex, was a devolutionist. Yet the combination of Mellor at the Treasury and Renton at the coalface proved constructive because Mellor was already sympathetic and ensured that the arts got healthy increases, 26 per cent over two years. At the same time they couldn't trust the Council and the new money was 'handed over on strict conditions'. Palumbo was now truly at the mercy of politicians. Unfortunately he even managed to make a gaffe over this largesse: when the second tranche arrived he publicly thanked Mellor, not his Minister, Renton. Tim Renton may have got his revenge out of office by calling for the abolition of the Council in a widely publicised newspaper article. Even in office he dropped a bomb of a question: 'What *is* the role of 150 people living in very expensive headquarters in London?'

Everitt was sure he had the answer. Before Luce left the Ministry he'd said, more or less in passing, that he'd like the Arts Council to determine its national strategy. Everitt turned this into a major marketing exercise. After all, here was a chance to secure the Council's future by defining and promoting through apparent consultation whatever it had left that only it could do: asserting and adjusting national policy, national advocacy, fielding the grant-in-aid that fuels national and regional activity, appraising clients, co-ordinating touring. The National Arts Strategy produced in 1992 forty-one consultancy documents of bubbly blather, distilled by a couple of subordinates called Webber and Challens into a final, pointless document in 1993. By that time the country was three ministers on, and in any case the Lottery was about to 'chuck its bucket of money over the wall' to the Council, changing the entire character of its operation. Incredibly, the strategy had nothing to say about *that*.

For Palumbo it must have been galling to be brought in under one government and work under another which had renounced his champion. But in the general election of April 1992 (so that's what those cash increases were all about), Major was voted Prime Minister for the first time and Mellor moved into his new department, which Rittner suspects was actually set up by Chris Patten for his friend. Unfortunately, his friend paid Patten back appallingly when three months later the *People* revealed that Mellor was having an affair with a 'resting' actress. He survived this surprisingly well, but the *People* went on to disclose that he'd also received gifts – a $20,000 holiday, a loan of a Mercedes – from Mona Bauwens, who happened to be the daughter of a financial adviser to the PLO. Mellor resigned in September. Palestinians *again*, apparently.

In came Peter Brooke, a senior and suave politician who'd recently resigned as Northern Ireland Secretary when he performed to a piano accompaniment 'Oh ma darlin' Clementine . . . you are lost and gone forever' on Irish TV during a night of atrocities even worse than his serenade. He is perhaps the only minister to have been sacked for singing. To make sense of what was going on in the arts, he commissioned from the accountants Price Waterhouse a cost analysis of the Council's administration. The report agreed that the Council had four core functions:

- Making artistic judgments and overseeing the state of the arts in England.
- Managing the grant-in-aid.
- Conducting appraisals of artistic bodies and artists.
- Advocacy on behalf of the arts.

To fulfil these it needed fewer staff. Soon afterwards, Camelot started up and the staff numbers the Council dropped were deftly transferred to the new lottery unit, to be paid for out of the chucked bucket. As a result of the Price Waterhouse findings the Council retreated for a weekend in May 1993 to the Bear Hotel in Woodstock near Oxford to consider its future. It was there that the Council made its disastrous decision about theatres, narrated in Part II.

By the end of 1993 the Council was known to the general public, in an unparalleled blaze of media publicity, as the barmy army that wished to kill off ten theatres, two symphony orchestras and three major touring companies (including the magnificent travelling wing of Glyndebourne Opera) but was willing to hand millions of Lottery pounds to the toffs of the Royal Opera House. Almost every national newspaper ran an editorial calling for the Arts Council to be scrapped and 'heads to roll'. Brooke announced that he was cutting the following year's grant by £5 million; in the end, thanks to astute accounting with allocations, the reduction shrank to £3.2 million. Nevertheless, it was the first announced cut in the Council's history and Palumbo had to live with the consequences of his 'keeping things sweet'. Everitt resigned, producing for a short time a weekly series of revisionist musings for the *Guardian* in which he revisited his recent history. He is now a freelance arts consultant.

1994– Mary Allen/Earl of Gowrie

When the press predicted who would replace Everitt, the common names were Colin Tweedy of ABSA (as if!), Timothy Mason of the London Arts Board, Clive Priestley, his chairman, and Mike Elliott of West Midlands Arts. Nobody named a woman, not even Mary Allen. Yet, though she'd sat in the number two seat as Everitt's deputy for a couple of years, no one at the interview board identified her with the most wrenching period in the Arts Council's history. When the orchestra fiasco was at its height, she was found weeping in her office. 'Mary can't handle the heat,' staff gossiped. She retorted that they were tears of rage.

Allen was the first female Secretary-General since 1951, the year she was born. Her appointment was considered a victory for the Council's policy on women, for which it has a monitoring committee. Having been educated at a private Church of England school for girls in Abingdon, she graduated from New Hall,

Cambridge to become a jobbing actress, perhaps most notably as a chorus member in a touring production of *Godspell*, the dramatic equivalent of washing windscreens at traffic lights. In fact her job record seems lean: agent London Management 1977–1978, assistant director ABSA 1982–1983, director Watermans Arts Centre at Brentford, 1990–1992. Indeed, she admitted that 'I've never done a job for more than three years'. Her sole substantive appointment took place at the turn of the eighties, when she worked in PR for Mobil Oil as a sponsorship manager. The only position weighed with any artistic gravitas was the one at Watermans, which was certainly the meagre stepping stone to her eventual appointment. She is married to merchant banker Nigel Pantling.

Four women in leading positions in the arts commented off the record about the conservative Allen for this book. Two of them came to a similar opinion, quoted thus: 'She's all front.' One continued, 'Very good at appearing firm and self-assured, which may be the actress in her, but if she's tripped up over a detail she seems to fall to pieces.' Another claimed:

> When she set out her stall in 1994 she was very impressive, and the staff were relieved that here was someone who was firm, who admitted that tough decisions had to be made. But instead of becoming a figure in her own right, she appeared to retreat in favour of the Chairman.

In a magazine interview in July 1994, Allen stated that, 'People would far rather hear something clear and honest than a statement which is more evasive', and, after declaring that she planned to be a 'highly visible Secretary-General', she ended by saying, 'The point at which I can't speak out, I will leave'. Yet an arts reporter commented, 'When she began she was the one we would be expected to contact for quotes. But pretty quickly Gowrie took over.'

Allen then seems to have sent out conflicting signals about her style. When she started as deputy, a principal female client recalls,

> I had to wait later than the appointed time, and when I got to see her I was surprised how power-dressed she was, and slightly taken aback when she introduced herself with, 'I'm afraid I've only got twelve minutes available for you. Talk to me.' It was a disconcerting 'welcome to the eighties' manner she had at the time. I wish I could say she's mellowed.

For a *Guardian* article on women managers in June 1996, Allen presented the view that, 'the kind of challenges posed in running an arts organisation are suited to women. Running an arts organisation is about creating partnerships.' But further on she indicated, 'The arts are a business. It's a tough job.'

Part of the disparity between these two stances derives from the public-relations problems bequeathed by Everitt, and part from the view of artists that they'd been railroaded by the Council for the previous decade. Allen sought redemption.

A client commented:

> She was trying to be resolute on the one side, for which she had to compete with La Bottomley, but she kept saying how consensual the Council had become, especially towards artists, and how integrationist – holding the RABs' hands, letting them into the Council chamber. One got the feeling the Arts Council wished to be reactive again, but didn't quite know how to go about it. It seemed to allow everyone to tread on its back. I think the fact that a dance company called the Kosh brought in the Ombudsman to question the Council's ability to handle clients and make decisions caused a number of tensions.

Allen was appointed by Alexander Patrick Greysteil Hore Ruthven Gowrie. This mouthful of a name is commonly shortened to Grey, which also happens to be the colour his notably wavy, 'golliwog' mane of hair has gone. The earldom Gowrie inherited tenders a rather misleading impression. There's no estate involved any more, which explains why he whined about his poverty and toils with several boardroom directorships. An Irish legacy which was disallowed in 1600 is the origin of the earldom, restored after the war to honour Grey's father, a governor-general of Australia who ended up a Victoria Cross hero, killed in Libya. Grey was raised by his grandfather at Windsor Castle, where the old man was deputy constable, and educated at nearby Eton for free thanks to his father's war record. He had a manservant called Mr Mustard.

After Balliol, Oxford, he tutored (though did not lecture) in English at Harvard, then got involved with art-dealing, which led to his appointment as chairman of Sotheby's Europe (1986–1993). He wrote a published volume of poems, *A Postcard from Don Giovanni,* in 1971. Above all, he used his inherited place in the House of Lords as a loyal Tory, especially on behalf of Mrs

Thatcher. He was her Arts Minister for two years in the middle eighties.

On his Chairman's desk at the Council for a period was propped in pride of place a postcard dated November 1995. It was not from Don Giovanni, but from Britain's Donna Elvira, Mrs Thatcher. She thanked him for his unidentified 'imaginative and historic birthday gift' which she would use on Sunday mornings for its 'proper purpose'. She went on to tell him that, as the Labour Party had critically rejected socialism and moved towards 'our' position, they had become more electable – 'But there is still *some* hope for us.' Twice married, secondly to Countess Adelheid von der Schulenburg, Gowrie has a touch of the Don Giovannis about him. The air he bears of a matured roué even led some observers misleadingly to rhapsodise on quite why he appointed a female Secretary-General and a female deputy, the elfin Sue Hoyle, and why Allen let him take the lead.

As might be expected of someone who has served steadily in government, he's been happiest dealing with Westminster, where he clearly knows his way around to the money. It's little coincidence that when Gowrie and Allen had their photo taken together, they chose not the routine work of art as a backdrop, but the Houses of Parliament. Palumbo left the Council entirely in the hands of politicians, but Gowrie tried to give it a degree of respite from interference and did rather well, at least until the first Tory female Arts Minister took over in 1995.

'Golden Virginia' Bottomley was known to have 'the terrifying self-assurance of the English middle-class woman being reasonable', as Andrew Brown of the *Independent* reported, and some said this was a quality to which Allen aspired. To be fair to this nannying Minister, she had two competing bureaucracies to deal with – the Council itself and the Department of National Heritage. As she was apparently a politician 'who needed a lot of briefing', it's little wonder her department found it easy to take the lead in the development of arts policy, buoyed by the success of the Lottery, and in consequence the Council was forced to run once more after Whitehall.

The contest between the DNH and the ACE to construct and announce new uses for Lottery funds in 1996 became an amusing sideshow, though one of little value to the arts profession. Under Gowrie and Allen the Council had a tough job keeping up with Whitehall on one side and the amateurist advocates of the Regional Arts Boards on the other. It certainly had little Lottery time for professional artists and instead had dreamed up new schemes to throw money at amateurs and 'youth', which is just what the Government was requiring in advance of a general election. Sure enough, in November 1996 Allen dutifully announced an 'Arts for Everyone' fund (A4E), which provided the Tory's publicity machine with more 'good news for the nation'.

At the same time Gowrie had been canny in courting New Labour, which he possibly assumed would win the 1997 shoot-out. He did so by placing the architect and Labour supporter Sir Richard Rogers (now Lord Rogers) as vice-chairman, then to some extent distancing himself from Bottomley by increasingly criticising her decrees, especially since she made him the second Conservative Chairman to suffer the humiliation of a grant cut, of £5 million in 1995–1996.

The Council's policy statements and initiatives were soon timed to coincide with politically charged events, such as Gowrie's public carping about Bottomley during the week of the Labour conference in October 1996. Bottomley retaliated by announcing her own advisory Arts Forum which would circumvent the traditional association between ministers and the Council. Labour also demonstrated that it was less seduced than Gowrie had hoped. In the election manifesto of early 1997 Labour declared that Lottery cash would be taken away from the arts to address health and education matters (the 'sixth good cause', as it became), and this promise turned out to receive the most positive public reaction of all pledges on its information helpline. Gowrie, Allen and Lottery chairman Gummer cannot have been happy to learn that their stewardship was to be rewarded with a removal of funds. These hiccups aside, Gowrie clearly wanted the remainder of his chairmanship, which would last until April 1999, to be pleasant.

Whether New Labour really wanted a Tory with an inherited peerage to guide arts policy is another question. Observers gossiped that the 1997 Government might dump Gowrie in favour of Baroness Blackstone or former party leader John Smith's widow in order to trail-blaze the first female chair, or Melvyn Bragg, who is probably no less than Labour's Jeffrey Archer. Yet nobody could have predicted the sensational development on 13 May 1997.

On that day – the day after the first A4E awards were presented – Mary Allen announced that she would leave the Council in September and move over as chief executive to her biggest client, the Royal Opera House. The House's current chief, the respected Genista (Jenny) McIntosh, had left after no more than four months in the job. The chairman of the House was Lord Chadlington, who, as Peter Gummer, had recently sat on the Arts Council and chaired the lottery board which in 1995 awarded the Royal Opera House its £78.5 million for a controversial redevelopment. Chadlington and Mary Allen had worked well together on that, it was said, and so it was hardly surprising that he should turn to her in a time of crisis.

Yet rumours had long circulated that Allen aspired to an Opera House top job. Colleagues thought it unusual that she hadn't formally applied for the post when it was advertised in 1996, unlike such hopefuls as Ruth Mackenzie of Nottingham Playhouse, Norman Rosenthal of the Royal Academy, or the victor, Jenny McIntosh. Insiders suspected that Allen had let it be known to the House that she was interested, but she sat in on the interviews of the other candidates to represent the concerns of the Council.

In the strange circumstances surrounding McIntosh's sudden departure, Allen acquired the post without having to pursue the common procedures, even though she would receive an increase on her Council job salary of £20,000 or so. Other Council clients swiftly phoned in to register to artform directors their disapproval of the episode, several on the lines of one company which complained, 'We wouldn't get treated so well if we landed in the shit.' On 21 and 22 May the Council met to discuss the swelling criticism and decided that Allen should not wait until September but leave with immediate effect 'in recognition of the importance of maintaining the integrity of relationships between the Arts Council and its clients'. Some clients considered this a cosmetic, 'stable-door' exercise by a Council 'that didn't grasp how out of touch it was with the general mood'. Allen's duties were taken up by her recently selected deputy, Graham Devlin.

During the week before the 13 May announcement, Chadlington had been to see the newly installed Labour Heritage Secretary, Chris Smith, to discuss Allen's advancement. It was here that observers felt the unprecedented transfer might have been challenged, if not suspended, as it didn't seem to align with equal-opportunities policy at the House or the procedural and ethical code of the Council. But no. For a man in a Government which claimed it was going to 'hit the ground running', Smith's approval of the move appeared somewhat lax.

We can only conjecture what may have been running through Smith's mind just a few days into his job. Chadlington, some felt, had moved quickly to take full advantage of the political context. When Smith was shadow Heritage Secretary back in 1995, the Covent Garden Lottery award was announced. Smith supported the grant despite a chiding from rowdy Labour colleagues. As his junior Arts Minister Mark Fisher said at the time, 'Chris didn't flinch. He held the line. If you want opera you can't throw away Covent Garden' – which is an opinion doubtless shared by Fisher.

Both of them kept an eye on subsequent developments at the House. In government from the start of May 1997, they surely knew that they would need to tackle full-on the myriad problems at Covent Garden and the Council. Yet removing key figures from the House would do little to inhibit the regime of those 'untouchable' private fundraisers who were in full swing over the redevelopment. Freeing Allen from her Council desk, however, would leave the hereditary peer Gowrie vulnerable. Maybe that was the reason for Smith's approval of Allen's move.

Sure enough, on 1 October Gowrie gave notice that he would resign the chairmanship a year early, in May 1998. His announcement coincided – true to form – with an Arts Council reception during the Labour Party conference in Brighton, which ensured him full press coverage including the front page of *The Times*. Gowrie said he was leaving to 'return to his business interests', though he hadn't actually left any. More likely he suspected that Smith and his department were plotting to impose long-term changes to the Council's remit, or possibly its erasure, and didn't want to hang about only to handle or bequeath the consequences. By resigning he was forcing Smith to speed up, which was probably a tactic of benefit to the demoralised arts scene, and one for which Gowrie deserves credit.

Chris Smith was the first parliamentary arts supremo – the first minister of any kind – able so soon in office to approve the Council's new chief officer and choose the next Chairman. Yet he allowed the organisation to run for nearly a year without a Secretary-General. Smith was also the first Labour minister in history to announce a cut in the Council's annual grant, applying Mrs Bottomley's plan to reduce the 1998–1999 sum by £1.5 million to £184.6 million. Eventually he announced as Chairman Gerry Robinson, head of Granada Television and a New Labour patron, but someone who had to be asked twice before he took on the quango. New Labour – New Arts Council, or Dead Arts Council?

Chapter 30

It could be it

Two centuries ago the San Carlo Opera House of Naples ran a gaming room. So did Vienna's Burgtheater, where *The Marriage of Figaro* was first performed. Under licence from Empress Maria Theresa it managed a casino, the profits from which went towards the court's maintenance of the opera house. As did Milan's La Scala, from 1715 to 1788 and 1802 to 1815. At least thirty other opera houses in Europe ran gambling dens. The most famous of such combinations still exists in Monte Carlo, where one door leads to the opera, the other to the casino. And it's more than chance that the opera house of Brussels is called La Monnaie.

Little surprise, then, that the creator of Britain's thriving new National Lottery is an opera conductor. He is not a well-known one, but Denis Vaughan worked in Naples and Munich, where he developed some rather good-natured but quirky ideas about youth and criminals, as conductors do. He wrote, in German, a book on 'how to kick the need for drugs', warning that

> people who need chemical drugs to discover the emotions within them can never become self-reliant. Active participation in the arts, whether creation or interpretation, is one of the simplest ways of helping the young to this state of emotional maturity.

Pity he didn't pen one for his colleagues on 'how to kick the need for drink'.

Vaughan crusaded the notion of a national lottery mainly as a financial motor to run his anti-crime campaign, with its strapline, 'Protecting the Lives of All in Britain':

> Currently 1 in 3 males has a criminal record by the age of 30. Half a class in a Glasgow school has tried heroin by the age of fifteen. More than a quarter of all young people will not go out alone at night for fear of mugging. This risk threatens everyone in Britain . . . Our lawyer, Aubrey Rose, a great humanist, sees the lottery as potentially one of the greatest pieces of social engineering this century.

Imagine Vaughan's dismay on viewing the fruits of his labours – not just the suicide who clutched a losing Lottery ticket, or the Muslim worth £17 million who was reportedly severed from his faith for gambling, or the hundreds of thousands who have eaten into their life savings to feed a growing gambling habit, but also the monthly wrangle when the Arts Council's latest tally of Lottery grants is ridiculed in the press.

Denis Vaughan first pushed the plan in 1987, though the notion of a lottery had been floated for some years, buoyed by schemes in Europe and the United States. He observed that £1,151 million a year was donated through charities to medicine, health, welfare and international aid. Only £15 million went to youth, the same to the arts and recreation and just £2 million to education. Vaughan's lottery would adjust the donated balance. 'The whole aim of my original lottery idea,' he declared, 'was to increase the availability of the arts and to increase awareness of the arts; to improve the quality of life.'

Once the wins and the costs were taken off, the Lottery would give the entire remainder to cultural regeneration through a single Lottery Foundation: 40 per cent to sport, 30 per cent to arts, 20 per cent to environment/heritage and 10 per cent to charities. He tried to sell the idea to the Prime Minister, Mrs Thatcher, overlooking the fact that she was brought up a Lincolnshire Wesleyan and probably 'signed the pledge' against gambling while still in nappies. She would not hear of a state lottery.

The merchant bankers N.M. Rothschild were avidly keen, however. Once Thatcher had been thrown out and replaced with John Major, they circulated their paper, 'A National Lottery, How

It Could Be Established'. The new Chancellor, Norman Lamont, happened to be an old Rothschilds man and he was attracted to its findings. It recommended that the 'government would leave management and operation to the private sector but with appropriate legislation', and Rothschilds made plans to run the Lottery themselves. The sympathetic chief secretary to the Treasury at the time was David Mellor, who, after the 1992 election, had a new ragbag Department of National Heritage (DNH) constructed around him. He sussed how well a lottery would connect the department's diverse commitments – sports centres, films, crumbling castles, the arts – and provide a welcome source of funds independent of the Treasury, for he ensured that the Lottery share to 'good causes' would be filtered through his department. At the same time, this former chief secretary made sure that the Treasury would get a compensatory cut through a tax on each ticket of 12 per cent, which was something to which Vaughan was implacably opposed: 'The more is invested in the arts, the more the exchequer gains from other taxes.'

Vaughan had set up the Lottery Promotion Company in 1990 with South Bank's Lord Birkett and English National Opera's Earl of Harewood, and got an office through the Royal Opera House. Yet his quirky altruism didn't fit with the growing avarice that forged the final scheme and he found his company sidelined. Increasingly peevish letters were circulated to anybody with a posh-looking address, and Vaughan has ended up as a sort of John Christie figure, baying in a wilderness of his own devising. Meanwhile, Rothschilds' groundwork led to the National Lottery emerging as a privatised monopoly regulated by the DNH. Lottery income would go to cover the start-up costs, then to the company's eventual profit; another portion would be siphoned by the Treasury, and finally just 28 per cent would be divided between five 'good causes' tied to the DNH. Rothschild formed a consortium to handle the Lottery, but to its dismay it came second. The winner was G-TECH and other businesses under the consortium with the name of Camelot. Even though G-TECH had the computer firm ICL in its cartel, Vaughan reported that the start-up costs, the systems to run the operation with over 30,000 terminals in shops, exceeded those of every other lottery in the world.

Being one of those five 'good causes', the arts received 5.6 per cent instead of the 30 per cent in Denis Vaughan's scheme. Camelot called this distribution 'chucking a bucket of money over the wall', though their bucket was five times smaller than Vaughan's. This 5.6 per cent was divided by the DNH into portions for the Arts Councils of England, Scotland, Wales and Northern Ireland. But in Vaughan's plans the Arts Councils would have got nothing at all, because he wanted a 'top down' system run by a Lottery Foundation chaired by Prince Charles, which brings us back again to the Keynes–Christie split over government and court. Nevertheless, between Saturday 19 November 1994, when the lottery balls were first drawn, and Saturday 18 November 1995, the arts would have received £1.56 billion from Vaughan instead of a mere £392 million under Camelot. Through the system finally approved by the DNH, the Arts Council of England itself got 83.33 per cent of 20 per cent of 28 per cent of the net proceeds, and there are an awful lot of 'roughlys' and 'abouts' to blur a clear picture of how the thing worked, because the Lottery routed the entire notion of annual cycles. The 5.6 per cent (the 20 per cent of 28 per cent) that came to the Arts Councils was further apportioned according – 'roughly' – to the civil-service Goschen formula of population volume, thus:

Arts Council of England	83.3% of 5.6%
Arts Council of Northern Ireland	2.8% of 5.6%
Scottish Arts Council	8.9% of 5.6%
Arts Council of Wales	5.0% of 5.6%

We must then take away from the ACE portion another 3.9% of the remaining sum, set aside to cover the cost of the fifty (at the time of writing) lottery unit staff and the fees earned by a pool of 200 assigned consultants. Then the final hurdle proves unsurmountable, for the Council can commit funds in advance of receiving them. Though the Camelot financial year ran from November, the Arts Council began distributing its cash four months later. In the first year – March 1995 to February 1996 – it received £271.6 million from the DNH's distribution fund but committed £292 million, on 522 projects. These figures have such a fairyland touch to them that it's only when we begin to pull them earthward that we appreciate the scale of the venture: the slim-sounding 3.9 per cent of staff and operating costs actually amounted in that year to £10.6 million. In contrast, the total management and services costs of the entire Arts Council in 1994–1995 (staff of 132, rents, rates, telephones, publicity, depreciation) came to £7.7 million.

*

The Arts Council has ended up with two wings to it. The 'old' Council gets around £190 million from the Government to spend on the yearly work of clients. The 'new' Council, called the Arts Council lottery unit, has one and a half times as much to spend, but only, so far, on buildings, films and puny schemes for amateurs. It's staggering to think that anyone could conceive of bolting on a unit sometimes twice as rich as its presumed boss, but what has transpired will either transform the Council into a revitalised mechanism or the Council will buckle and collapse from the weight of its conflicting responsibilities.

There was no reason why the Arts Council should have been handed the Lottery money in the first place, but it clearly came from Mellor's DNH, striving to keep control of the system. After all, his department had to invent two boards from scratch, one to look after charities and another contraption called the Millennium Commission which was really a relic of the rejoicerism of the eighties, whereby for some obscure reason a multi-ethnic, secular society was urged to celebrate the supposed 2,000th birthday of Jesus by spinning in a ferris wheel on the South Bank or plodding round a reconditioned rubbish tip in Greenwich. That a Labour Government then took on this project with signal enthusiasm served only to confirm to their bemused voters that parliamentarians in general are prone to an abiding dedication to kitsch. The Greenwich Millennium Experience is a fine example of why Britain needs an 'arm's-length' arrangement for its creative arts.

To give Lottery money for the arts to the Arts Council and sports cash to the Sports Council made sense to the DNH, which had no intention of handing over this bonanza to Vaughan's independent foundation. Yet both Councils saw the opportunity as a threat from the Treasury. Mandarins might turn to them, once Camelot had started chucking its buckets, and cut the existing government grant by a parallel amount. This became known as the 'additionality' issue. Equally, the DNH would not be happy to lose its financial stake in state spending. It was really for this reason that the Councils were determined to protect revenue funding and lock the Lottery into capital endeavours – bricks and mortar, toilets and vans. This in any case suited the Treasury, which welcomed a Keynesian trick to kick-start the construction trade following the recession of the late eighties. Keynes, though, would have considered the Lottery a deceptive and capricious tax on the poor and have disapproved, for they are the essential consumers of Lottery tickets who fuel the whole system.

The Council was divided into sceptics who considered that the Lottery might yield a containable £50 million a year, and others who hoped it would escalate beyond all hopes – the optimists won but the naysayers ran the planning. They first of all marked out a bottom line for the capital grants it would issue of £10,000 and a ceiling of £10 million, with significant levels – originally 35 per cent – of partnership funding to be scoured from other sources. By that means they limited the scope of applications to their preconceived preferences. Then they circumvented a Ministry directive, which denied the Council a prompting strategy or a chance to initiate buildings, by dragging in the 'old' Council's nineteen policy priorities and deploying the Regional Arts Boards as a second line to 'take account of local, regional and national strategies', presumably in order to deter any development that was inconvenient or superior to pet projects. No doubt to reinforce this approach the Council appointed as Lottery director Jeremy Newton, chief executive of the Regional Board Eastern Arts. What they hadn't counted on was the amount of paperwork generated by their tactical criteria. Newton brought in his sidekick from Norwich, a much-respected administrator and genial jazz fan called Andrew Milne, as deputy. The lack of common sense in the planning and the tactical interventions became clear. Unfortunately the resulting overwork may have been a contributing factor to the heart attack that killed Milne.

Financial restrictions were thrown out once the big players like the South Bank Centre and Covent Garden heard of the constraints. They also got the partnership requirement diluted to 25 per cent, while the needless mediation of the Regional Arts Boards was retained because, after all, they wouldn't trouble the 'nationals'. But no one could predict the amount or category of staff needed to process the applications, and that's where the operation first went wrong.

Some claim the aptitude of the officers recruited was insufficient, partly because this was new territory but mainly because the amount of paperwork implied by the overvalued processes put in place weighed down the system and they weren't trained to cope. The staff were basically novice bureaucrats: 'They probably came from somewhere musty like a backwater municipality,' sniffed an artform officer. However, the skills of these apparatchiks and the inarticulate conditions placed on notions of 'quality', business planning and 'community benefit' offered much scope for consultants to intercede and interpret at a minimum daily rate of £300 each. The system was soon running six months behind, and the Council had to advertise for yet more processing and monitoring staff. In its first year it cleared 522 applications, or ten a week. But there was a backlog of 786, which was bad news for the other 1,708 who had told the unit they aimed to bid. This state of affairs was basically structural and no doubt Jeremy Newton sought to overcome these opening snags. Yet each time the lottery unit began to catch up, new directives and schemes were developed.

While the Lottery officers ground their noses in the rule book, the artistic values and consequences of the projects were overlooked. Three contrasting bids on different scales, each successful in getting Lottery cash, show how. First, as the *Sun* put it on 16 October 1995:

IT'S TUTU MUCH!
EXCLUSIVE
By Lenny Lottery

Sadler's Wells Theatre is the latest in a
string of posh causes to get a windfall.
MPs and showbiz stars blasted the award to
the ageing London theatre, where tickets
cost up to £25.

Lenny's headline confused the building with the bygone ballet company, but he still managed to winkle out its career as a badly planned theatre:

1931 – even then its design was regarded as poor. During the war jokers said staff used to shout to Nazi bombers: 'Over here, over here!' In recent years it has struggled to fill seats with performances as varied as flamenco and *The Sound of Music*.

However, he stressed, the development of the theatre was backed by Labour's Tony and Cherie Blair, who lived in Islington (its local MP was Chris Smith, shadow Heritage Secretary at the time). The bidders didn't deny that it was a bad place and this was in fact their main argument in seeking Lottery aid of £30 million – they planned to knock it down and build a new one, a 'technological theatre of the future ... to satisfy the creative imagination of generations to come'. Lucky them, though this a theatre with nothing in it, for it doesn't produce, it only receives. But Sadler's Wells remains flawed for another reason. If the golden rules for a shop are location, location and location, Sadler's Wells fails three times over. It's simply too far from sufficient public transport to serve the capital or the nation. The nearest tube runs on a single branch of the Northern Line; a couple of Routemasters pass the theatre. While the £30 million of Lottery money might support its survival by pulling it to pieces and starting again, it won't do anything to solve the problem of the 38 bus.

After the opera company moved out to the Coliseum in 1968, Sadler's Wells was due for demolition but it persisted as a defective venue for hire: 'When we go down to hell, we shall find it is the Sadler's Wells foyer,' declared Britain's leading dance critic, Clement 'Salt & Vinegar' Crisp. Despite visits by foreign dance companies, part of the diplomatic baggage carried by embassies, and the blockbusters of Michael Clark in the middle eighties, the theatre tended to back the mediocre and those who otherwise couldn't get bookings in the West End. During its final week of opening in June 1996, the principals walked out of *Calamity Jane*, leaving Sadler's Wells to bail out the show at a loss. In the very same week, its plans to programme the Royalty Theatre in Holborn during rebuilding went awry when the company providing its Christmas show, London City Ballet, went bust. Maybe this is why Keynes couldn't stand the place: it too often promoted the second rate.

Sadler's Wells got its Lottery grant by appealing to its sentimental past and a high-tech future. Nobody thought to ask why someone couldn't build a high-tech theatre in a more accessible part of London for £40 million (around the cost of the new Glyndebourne). At the same time English National Opera was examining with Lottery cash five vacant spots in the West End to serve its own development, so the sites were there. As for Sadler's Wells' claims on dance, the lottery unit also funded a further feasibility study to choose another London theatre to house modern dance and ballet, called 'the National Dance House'.

What really carried the plan was the admirable gung-hoism of its new chief executive, Ian Albery, scioned from the theatrical family we encountered earlier. The magic combination of names – Sadler's Wells and Albery – lent power to whatever challenges he flung at the Arts Council. Albery not only got the £30 million for his ambitious plan, he objected that he could not raise any more than £1.4 million of the £10 million partnership funds needed from other sources to meet Lottery conditions, and went before Parliament's national heritage select committee in December 1995 to vent his frustration. In response to this high-profile dig, the Arts Council 'reconsidered' the status of the application and accepted the notion of 'gifts in kind' and services provided as allowable contributions, at their full value, to the partnership target. Even the most generous book-keeper might see how this could be used: if said book-keeper charged £5 an hour while a chartered accountant charged £35 an hour to do the same work, it might be claimed that the value of the underling was seven times the cost. Still, it seemed to suit the Arts Council. Where there's a Wells there's a way.

Our second case study was presented to the public by the *Daily Mirror* in this way on 27 November 1995:

LOTTO GIVES £150,000
TO RAVE NIGHTCLUB

Fury as cash goes
to improve toilets

Brighton's beachfront Zap Club is a popular discotheque which, by putting on 'just one or two events a year', according to the *Mirror*, reaped liberal licensing benefits from the local authority and gained the patronage of South East Arts, a Regional Arts Board burning to support novelty in its spiritless, commuter-belt parish. The nightclub was described by South East Arts as a 'live art venue', which occasionally it was in the early evening, though the 1996 Club Guide called it 'Brighton's best club night out, and rumoured to be expanding in the not too distant future [indeed] . . . Go it Girl on Saturdays is another formidable night for the town's eager club kittens.' The Zap's owners simple-heartedly invited Lord Palumbo to look round the place when once he visited Brighton. Though tolerant of its lurid, beer-soaked appearance in daylight, Palumbo left unimpressed: 'But it's a nightclub!' he explained helpfully. At the time Palumbo's estranged son Jamie had invested in the London club Ministry of Sound.

After Palumbo was replaced by Gowrie, the Zap put in a bid for £143,353 to do up the washrooms and refurbish one of its promenade arches as a 'chill-out' café. When a knowing member of the press asked if a chill-out area was the place you went to indulge in drug-taking, one wit replied that, no, it was the place you visited to 'chill out' from your drugs. 'It's a venue for a number of activities which we support,' a Council spokeswoman artlessly told reporters.

The Zap got its grant, not for an established arts programme that couldn't be supported by Lottery funds even if it ran one, but because it was argued that the enhancement of its commercial use would eventually benefit its potential as a host to cutting-edge performances. This contingent argument was backed to the hilt by the Regional Arts Board. South East Arts was then lowest in the national league for Lottery awards. The Council published a monthly league table in order that the Regional Arts Boards would be motivated to compete, though it was suspected that it merely led them to support submissions for political benefit above artistic value. Thus the true profit went to the Arts Board, at least until the tabloids seized the story. Once the renovations were completed and the club's marketable value enhanced, the Zap was sold off by its owners to a commercial leisure company. One supposes that the money was returned, having in the meantime constituted an interest-free loan. Capital.

For the third example we must plummet from the tabloids to the broadsheets, namely the *Financial Times*, 16 March 1996:

LOWRY AT LARGE IN SALFORD
But theme-park is not appropriate
argues William Packer

The news that the city of Salford is to receive £64 million from the National Lottery, and as much again in matching funds, in order to build a cultural complex by the turn of the millennium, arouses mixed feelings.

Not quite Lenny Lottery, but never mind. Salford gained a triple award: the bulk – £41.1 million – from the Arts Council; £15.65 million from the Millennium Commission; £7.65 million from the National Heritage Lottery Fund, all to 'celebrate' L.S. Lowry, the 'matchstick man' artist who was born in Manchester and died in Cheshire. He detested Salford: 'They laughed at me for thirty years in Pendlebury.' The 350 paintings already dis-

played by Salford Council in its municipal gallery will be
rehoused, and that accounts for the heritage element. The Arts
Council was attracted to the 'visionary' complex which will include
a 1,600-capacity concert hall, a small 400-seat theatre space and a
'state-of-the-art virtual reality centre with an interactive gallery for
children'.

As William Packer pointed out:

> If the work were simply, properly shown in a decent gallery, the
> visitor might still be free to come to his own conclusions. But to set
> Lowry's work into a National Industrial Virtual Reality Centre, with
> head-sets programmed to project the visitor into those weird and
> personal cityscapes, is something else. It is to turn from art into
> mere entertainment . . . Poor Lowry: poor us.

The director, Bob Stone, said he hoped to provide an 'edutain-
ment' experience. The entire centre is strap-lined as 'a waterfront
home for art, innovation and entertainment'.

If £40 million can buy Sadler's Wells a futuristic theatre in costly
London, or Glyndebourne an international opera house, it's odd
that a low-cost town like Salford should need £41 million to build a
middling, 1,650-seater, multi-purpose theatre. After all we have
learned about the failures of such spaces, it's astounding that the
Arts Council should support an effort that 'will be rapidly
adaptable to the changing needs of dance, opera, musical comedy
and drama'. In any case the mint Bridgewater Hall and a range of
theatres stand one mile away – though they, say the burghers of
Salford, are in Manchester. Some claim this incoherent scheme
was dreamed up at a town hall retirement bash. It has little to do
with Lowry, arts provision, public need or local employment, but
maybe an awful lot to do with Salford City Council's debt of £430
million, the problem of business confidence in its Salford Quays
commercial development within which the Lowry Centre is sited,
and the town's status in the shadow of mighty Manchester.

As a local columnist commented:

> Salford Council wanted a glorified civic centre and they got away
> with it by playing their hard luck card. North West Arts appeared
> lukewarm, and I doubt that anyone had seen a detailed business
> plan of how it was fully meant to work once it opened. I bet the
> little theatre will be running wedding receptions in no time.

A local editor observed, 'It's really an attempt to stave off the companies deserting Salford Quays. As for creating local employment, it'll best provide opportunities for kids nicking radios from the middle-class cars parked outside.' Insiders feel that Salford got the grant because the Arts Council was desperate to be seen putting Covent Garden-style money into something outside London, especially somewhere sickly. The Lowry Centre will exist because the *Sun* stood against £78 million for the Royal Opera House with the slogan 'Boycotto the Lotto'.

These three cases display how an astute personality, a Regional Arts Board and a local authority could each use the Council's Lottery distribution system to their capital advantage above artistic benefit. Not only do they expose the shortcomings of the Lottery scheme set up by a body committed to 'develop and improve the knowledge, understanding and practice of the arts', they also highlight the way that the Council had failed to prepare the ground for integrated funding structures once the buildings were up and running. For this we might well blame the moneyed consultants who scanned the applicants' business plans, for as one successful applicant said:

> Those plans are based on bollocks. It's impossible to make long-term projections in a short-term culture. But no doubt the Lottery consultants might be able to do it for you – they know the form, it's a bit of club, and there's plenty of work for them all.

Critics of the scheme back in 1994 warned the Council of two looming problems. First, that the partnership funding would soon balloon to a total figure impossible to meet. Second, that the running-cost implications of these capital developments could only be met in the end by diverting the Lottery fund from capital into revenue. That in turn would create a problem with its Treasury grant. It took two years for the Council to cotton on.

Against partnership, the Arts Council took the blasé line that the bulk of the successful applications – 450 – had applied for sums under £100,000, which only required 10 per cent of secondary funding. But, of course, the big players soon rolled up and by the start of 1996 the partnership target exceeded £400 million in London alone. The national estimate (why didn't the Council have this figure?) stood somewhere around £1 billion. The Sadler's Wells solution was applied to those already closest to the Council and it was thought that the partnership level would soon be dropped to 10 per cent for others, too – or as the Council subsequently put it, 'the partnership dimension will be individually negotiated according to the circumstances of the applicant'. Thus a safeguard imposed to ensure that only serious, firmly supported projects can proceed was to be slackened; possibly, though not constantly, to the good.

Acceptance of 'in kind' support might explain a worrying anomaly in the sponsorship claims that emerged between the Council and the Association for Business Sponsorship of the Arts. The latter discovered that business contributions towards capital projects fell from £14 million in 1995 to just £5 million in 1996. Yet the Council had allocated Lottery money in the belief that the corporate sector would provide no less than £91 million for 260 approved schemes above the £100,000 threshold. ABSA's boss, Colin Tweedy, asked sharp questions about this discrepancy but remained unconvinced by some of the answers: one third of the £91 million would be obtained from the commercial development of arts sites (shops, cafés), while varying amounts of cash were pledged over a number of years, and so on. It seemed that the Council was simply letting the partnership formula slip out of its sight.

On the transfer from capital to revenue, it seems that the Department of National Heritage took the lead. Seems, because Lord Gowrie believed that the Council had invented a little ploy called the 'youth talent fund', only to find himself gazumped at a press conference by the Heritage Secretary, Virginia Bottomley, who announced a similar idea as a government initiative. Bottomley was soon trounced herself as the next general election loomed; 'good news' Lottery changes were increasingly proclaimed by the Prime Minister. The DNH issued a 'new directions' policy on 1 April 1996, commanding the Arts Council to 'take into account the desirability of developing skills and creative abilities, particularly of young people'. This was interpreted by the Council to mean 'new work' on the one hand and the chance to 'make a real difference to the creative cultural experience of young people' on the other, though nowhere had it defined 'youth', or anything else. In addition, the Council 'shall take into account the desirability of facilitating access to and participation in the arts'. The Council understood this to mean supporting amateurs and 'an equal value and status on people's self-expression through the arts'. Had Vaughan Williams and Walford Davies been alive, how they would have cackled to see their ambitions converted, at the end of the century and during peacetime, into impetuous directives by a Conservative Government facing a general election. Keynes, of course, would have thrown the deed across Mrs Bottomley's office, roaring 'Come off it.' He'd have been incandescent with fury to learn that it was his own Covent Garden that brought it about.

No doubt the magnitude of the Lottery cash helped to change thinking. More forcefully, though, the 'new directions' policy was the Conservative reaction to the crippling hostility of the general public towards the inept handling of arts awards. In early 1995 the Lottery's public-relations pitch went haywire. Camelot had thrown its first bucket of money over the wall to the five good causes. The National Lotteries Charities Board was brand new and lacked a full-on computer system to process applications. Had the public heard first of its donations going to wheelchairs and orphans, there would have been little outcry. Instead they saw news pictures of the Royal Opera House chief, escorted by a giggling, tutued dancer, handing in his multi-million begging letter at the Arts Council's door. While the Council assumed it was being canny in March 1995, announcing the inaugural grants for grand pianos in Grimsby and B-flat cornets for brass bands, everyone was waiting for the 'fat cats', as they were soon called, who had widely and foolishly publicised the cost of their ambitious plans as part of their campaign to get the cash. Hence the *Sun* editorial on 22 July 1995, with its ghastly pun on TV's Oprah Winfrey:

THIS OPERA WINDFALL'S APPALLING
Not one penny more must go to the bunch of Toscas at the Royal Opera House.

The people's verdict in our *You The Jury* vote could not be clearer.

They don't want their lottery money squandered on the minority pastimes of the well-heeled while genuine causes like medical research charities are losing out. Those who hand out lottery cash lack two things: common sense and the common touch.

Heritage Secretary Virginia Bottomley must quickly demonstrate she possesses both by changing the laws that govern the lottery.

She did. While her department mused on schemes to win the public over, the Council's press department hired a journalist to teach them how to write releases for the tabloids. But far from returning of its own volition to CEMA's Pilgrimism, the Council came up with the Stabilisation Fund 'to support good management' through a programme 'aimed at giving the arts a chance to escape from the downward spiral ... with expert assistance', which was felt to be another 'fat cat' scheme to provide additional fees for consultants. The fund seemed to suggest that the recent generation of arts managers had been less than effective and that it would take a few buckets of Lottery money to sort out the administrative mess they had put themselves in.

DNH civil servants proposed a further option to help long-standing revenue clients of the Council: the Endowment Fund. This was an American ploy that the British Liberal Party, as was, picked up in the early eighties. A Lottery lump sum would be licensed to a client to invest. The annual interest would be used to cover their maintenance and overheads. By this resourceful means, the DNH was acknowledging the sheer pull of wartime and post-war commitments – the national this and that – that has dragged the Arts Council towards protectionism and creative inertia. Here lay a seemingly neat solution, through which the Lottery (which was monthly but not cyclic) and its grants (which were one-off) were turned into annual sums. It would give the perennial clients enough to get on with by their own skills, but not so much that they couldn't ignore the need to progress – or face their box-office figures.

Yet the Council turned it down. In an interview for this book the Earl of Gowrie's aide, John Dowling, admitted that 'you can endow some clients though not all', but argued that there would simply not be enough Lottery money available even for long-standing clients such as the Royal Opera House. The House, he indicated, currently needed £23.7 million a year of subsidy. An endowment sum of £330 million would be required to produce a £23 million annual return. To give the House that amount of Lottery cash would sharply penalise other applicants, he stressed. Yet in the end the endowment argument hangs on the level of investment return. The Council's estimate of £330 million seems to be calculated on an annual return of around 7 per cent, which is the routine short-term rate obtained by the Treasury when it stores Lottery largesse in advance of distribution to the five good causes. The House, however, would surely be able to invest as it pleased, no doubt using the more reliable of the City's experts to optimise its chances of superior rates and time spans. Nor would it necessarily need such a large one-off sum to start. The Council gave the impression that it hadn't done its endowment homework as thoroughly as it should before it discounted the idea.

Though it shunned a long-term scheme of endowments, the Council accepted short-term ones. Immense policy changes, such as the move to amateurism, seemed to be rushed through by a Council goaded by a Tory Minister who in turn was spurred on by the *Sun*. A fifty-page consultative document was issued by the Council in the middle of June 1996. It contained the 'new directions' proposals, with a little note on the inside cover warning: 'written submissions to be received no later than Monday 15 July'. Artists and producers had absolutely no time to react in a useful way. Their responses were crucial, though. Composers not bureaucrats drove the CEMA campaigns and did so from aesthetic commitment. This resurrection of superficially similar endeavours was steered this time by headstrong politicians hunting for quick-fix comebacks to popular contempt.

The Council didn't handle the 'new directions' issue at all well. The consultants it paid to compose the rapidly written papers relied too readily on the cloudy formulas of 'artsperanto'. Why, for instance, were 'access' and 'participation' glued together? Development workers who specialise in participation don't do so merely to raise consumer numbers, and perhaps the consultant really meant 'audience development'. But then it may be that supplementary interpretation stimulates more paid work for consultants. One of the phrases within that section, 'an equal value and status on people's self-expression through the arts', is profound, haunting and perilous. How far are the arts driven by 'self-expression' in comparison to psychiatric therapy? That phrase alone generates bulky dissertations and entire pro-grammes of academic lingo on Radio 3; it's not something to be covered in a thank-you note to Mary Allen. The Council couldn't absorb critical reaction because the Council had a deadline to meet, set by a Government with an election to gain. The 'new directions' agenda turned out to be one of the starkest signs of how far the Council had become driven by Westminster and Whitehall rather than the arts, and ironically it happened not because of its government grant, but as a result of the Lottery – money from the people. The arm's length had on the end of it a hired hand.

Anyhow, these feverish changes turned out ineffective in reassuring the public. The Arts for Everyone 'express' scheme (A4E) was designed for amateurs, but it simply exposed to a new class of arts-users how 'amateurish' the Arts Council had grown. Of the 4,700 initial applicants the majority were turned down and were sent the same outline Council letter listing no fewer than eleven separate reasons why they had been rejected, some of the points contradicting others. 'The letter was designed so that the relevant reason(s) would be highlighted for individual recipients – but this did not happen,' admitted Allen's deputy. At the same time an application form for assessors (to meet the 'unexpected' demand for A4E appraisals) asked the nominees to mark, on a list of 100 areas of skill, the six 'where you feel you have not the greatest expertise'. Only later did Council officers spot the erroneous word 'not' for 'got' and the forms had to be reissued.

Perhaps the lottery unit was so busy finding highlighters and Tipp-Ex that it lacked the time to check where its A4E money was really going. One lucky rock group got £5,000 from the Council to make cassettes poking fun at the popular band Oasis. Calling themselves Juan Kerr and the Nosebags (geddit? The Council didn't seem to), they set sarcastic words about cocaine to the tune of the Oasis hit 'Wonderwall' and handed out copies of their song to Oasis fans at a London show. They also sent a copy to Tony Blair in a plain brown envelope. This jolly jape was disclosed by the *Big Issue*. An Arts Council spokesman defended the award on the grounds that the group 'met the criteria of increasing arts participation, developing new audiences and working with young people'.

With well-publicised gaffes like these, it's little wonder that New Labour placed in its May 1997 manifesto a promise to divert Lottery money away from the arts into education and health, now known as the New Opportunities Fund, or the 'sixth good cause'. Opinion polls and a survey of manifesto enquiries showed that this particular policy point was the most popular with the public. In other words, it appeared that the Arts Council had handled the Lottery programme so poorly that to public acclaim it would be divested of a level of its stewardship. The Council, it seemed, couldn't even buy compassion.

Well before the Lottery, on 9 December 1993, the *Evening Standard* ran a flash across its front page:

AXE THE ARTS COUNCIL!
Former Minister Tim Renton hits out

'The Arts Council has become largely superfluous,' he wrote inside. 'It was a great and important institution but it is nearly 50 years old and it seems to have become out of touch.' Mr Renton was sixty-two at the time. He argued that the Council should be abolished. The bulk of the money ought to be handed directly to the ten Regional Arts Boards, while the Department for National Heritage would fund the 'major' clients: 'the national orchestras, the RSC, the two London Opera Houses, the South Bank, the National Theatre and some of the important theatres outside London'. This article was followed by a number of supportive letters and eventually a searing article by Brian Sewell, the paper's pooh-pooh art critic, 'Let's prune this poisoned rose'. In this he clipped images from 'The Glory of the Garden': 'Rees-Mogg wondered if resources were spread too thin with so many demands for dung and water – but more and more such suckers grew, and none was ever pruned.'

Tim Renton MP had written his article before the appointment of Lord Gowrie, the creation of the Arts Council of England, or the advent of the National Lottery. Once they were in place, we might have expected the Council to have used them to win friends in high papers. But on 11 June 1995 *The Sunday Times* ran this feature:

LET'S AXE THE ARTS COUNCIL!
Money from the National Lottery should be used to make the arts
self-sufficient and the Arts Council redundant.
By ROBERT HEWISON

'The Arts Council is gripped by institutional inertia,' this cultural historian argued.

> Every attempt to break free of established commitments – be they theatres or orchestras – is met with such an outcry that nothing results ... The fig leaf of the Arts Council [arm's-length independence] is looking increasingly threadbare. It is time it was blown away.

Hewison is progressive, Renton conservative, yet they both found the Council unfit to serve this country's future. They saw that the Regional Arts Boards seemed to work perfectly well without help from their London parent, while Hewison additionally regarded the Endowment Fund as a substitute for Renton's control of the 'major' clients via Whitehall. Defenders of the Council pointed out that Renton was a politician and Hewison an academic and they did not represent the artists. But the artists soon spoke too.

In May 1995 a dance theatre company called the Kosh convinced the Government's ombudsman to investigate the Arts Council for maladministration in its procedures. The Kosh, touring with Arts Council grants for twelve years, suddenly had its application for funding of £150,000 rejected on the grounds that its artistic standards had fallen. 'We believe what has happened is that a handful of people in positions of power have acted irresponsibly and with bias,' argued its artistic director, Michael Merwitzer, who is not a man to be meddled with. The Kosh was backed by its local MP, who just happened to be the shadow Heritage Secretary of the time, Chris Smith. He told the ombudsman, 'There appeared to be no proper guidelines about how organisations are assessed and no appeal mechanism at all.' The ombudsman ordered the Council to provide him with every document and note in its possession that referred to the Kosh – a formidable mound of papers. As this was the first such case of its kind, there was no way of guessing the outcome. 'You'll notice how the Arts Council's being extra nice to everyone at the moment,' observed an insider in 1996, 'but that's because it's shitting itself over the Kosh. Some officers didn't like the company because they thought it was a bit creepy.' The name of the company is an acronym. It stands for 'Kinaesthetics Of Social Harmony'. As this book goes to press the ombudsman has yet to make his ruling.

Ombudsmen aside, we must acknowledge the failure of the Council to cope with the Lottery, in contrast to the Sports Council, as well as the exposed and continued humiliation of Covent Garden which the Arts Council was created to safeguard, the devastating antipathy of the general public to the arts (for which the Council was chartered to develop 'a greater knowledge, understanding and practice . . . throughout Our Realm'), the generic decline asserted by critics in the quality of its staff and councillors. Together these have conspired to close the Council down.

Yet however much we can share the scepticism of Messrs Renton, Sewell and Hewison, it would be a mistake to sentence the Arts Council to death. Reformation yes, the noose no. However fervent the arguments for abolition that come from the Adam Smith Institute, it is fifty years too late to shut it down. Most of the problems that beset the Council can be solved. What the critics have recognised is how far the Council has drifted away from its central role, to support the arts. Unprecedented, the Lottery – rather like the Pilgrim bedrock – gives it the means to redeem itself, this time through the direction of practitioners instead of dilettantes. The Council needs a little less Keynes and a little more Vaughan Williams at its heart.

In order for their cull to make sense, Renton and Hewison have assumed that the RABs are doing frightfully well. Yet it seems there is hardly a single respected, major client of the regional bodies who backs them. The high-profile problems besieging the Arts Council have hidden from public view the workaday weaknesses of the Regional Arts Boards, who are merely a third layer of bureaucracy and, as such, the most expensive with the least return. They employ in total twice as many employees as the Arts Council. Their staff and overhead charges amount to £11 million a year, or 17 per cent of their public income. Yet as they sit in their provincial dugouts – Loughborough, Winchester, Tunbridge Wells – the RAB directors can delight in the bashing the Council gets from the mass media, because, as one RAB press consultant admitted in 1996,

> Nobody cares about the RABs. The Arts Council has famous and contentious clients. It's got a photogenic toff in charge. We've got nothing on our books to interest the media. Our press releases get us half a column inch in the *Mugchester Bugle.* On the other hand that gives us a kind of diplomatic immunity.

Both Renton and Hewison assumed, quite understandably, that the RABs could function better without the Arts Council as their probation officer. The truth is that they would function far worse. In fact, there's not even a reason to keep them. For them nooses, yes.

First, the Regional Arts Boards grew up piecemeal and in rivalry, trying to steal bits of each other's turf. There are now ten, but only ten because they themselves couldn't cope with twelve, and twelve because they couldn't cope with fifteen, and fifteen in reaction to a centralised six, when the Arts Council ran its regional offices in the forties. What we have by their existence is in no sense a nationally integrated system for serving the arts: they are autonomous, with exclusive policies, priorities, programmes and funding patterns. The amount of money they have to spend is determined not by the scale of arts activity within their regions, but by a pinstripe calculation based on the size of the population within their boundaries.

Each one has devised a mission statement, a set of aims and predilections, at the request of the Arts Council. These are drawn from the same reservoir of platitudes employed by art bureaucracies, with this difference: 'They don't understand them, they can never explain them properly, but they *believe* in them,' vouched one of their former directors. Bad news, then, for artists working in North West Arts' patch where, with ropey grammar, 'Our core activities are to support the arts in the region financially and to work to help develop the North West's arts infrastructure – its venues, festivals and promoters, and its opportunities for training and other resources.' No room for the artists themselves in this bustling agenda.

Artists there may have to move to London, where at least the London Arts Board's prime aim 'supports artistic excellence and innovation throughout London'. But of course that's exactly what developing artists tend to do, they move to London. It's a curious notion on which to build a national arts strategy – that there are ten distinct zones in England which artists address and no other, and that in a nation which, thanks to mass media, has never before been so homogeneous, creativity has ten disparate voices.

Second, the ten regions are political and economic constructions. Brussels would not give RABs the time of day, even at an hour ahead; they don't meet notions of subsidiarity, for they're not the organisations closest to the people they're charged to serve. Their regions aren't real ones, at least none that express any supposed cultural landscape. Milton Keynes has nothing to do with Dorchester, except that a councillor from each might sit at a table in Winchester a couple of times a year for the sake of Southern Arts. Liverpool and Manchester are civic rivals, which is why North West Arts has an office in each city – it can pretend to be one and two organisations at the same time.

These ten regions are really a disorganised patchwork of local authorities. Those town halls who join up pay £x a year subscription in order to get £x + y back in arts subsidy for events in their patch. In total the local authorities gave just £3.5 million (5 per cent) to the RABs in 1995, while the Arts Council paid into the Boards £58.8 (95 per cent). The work of a RAB is governed by the political demands of these member authorities, and the administration's main drudge is balancing these commitments between them.

Even worse, it's often the private bias or enthusiasm of a party-political councillor that the RAB has to address. That individual may have won fewer than 1,000 votes to gain a council seat, and 900 of those might have been awarded to the party, not the person. Yet that councillor is taking part in order to promote one district in preference to another. This explains why so many local authorities remain chaotic and capricious in their arts funding.

Improvement was sought in a recent drive to create a framework of 'arts development officers'. This administrative alliance of RABs and local government came about when rate-capping of local authorities by Thatcher's central Government diminished arts spending and staffing. By developing such schemes as Northern Arts' Local Arts Development Agencies (LADAs – indeed), the RABs were providing funds to revive local-government provision which usefully sidestepped the town halls' restrictive budget conventions. The 'development' therefore dealt with implied social deprivation rather than artistic provision, but this explains why the vogue term 'arts *development* officer' came about. In addition the term neatly though misguidedly suggested that the arts officer (as the role used to be called) was engaged in work that was more creative than bureaucratic. However, the benefit came in staffing rather than art. The RABs and their successors have failed utterly, in three decades, to vitalise and enlarge the arts capability of the town and city councils they were set up to engage with. It is geography, not creativity, which drives a Regional Arts Board.

Third, the Council runs sixty-six diverse 'development' or one-off project grants, and while the RABs between them offer a comparable total, they're semi-duplicated. The money's a different matter. Council awards range between three and ten times the amount offered by the RABs, and when an RAB sets a limit of, say, £300 on a training grant, you can be sure that most recipients will be expected to manage on £150. The Council by its very nature offers a wider range of opportunities, while RABs are financially constrained by the size of their population.

As for assessment, more creative artists are involved at the Council's panels and committees than the RABs accept. In fact, several RABs did away with committees and used instead a list of 'advisers' from which the officer could phone a selection offering him or her the answer they wanted to hear. Fourth, the Council runs a structure of checks and balances in its operation. There are four dance officers at the Arts Council, for instance. They have prejudices and loyalties, but those are exposed in front of colleagues – and the officer has to defend a recommendation to the panel. In contrast a RAB employs one dance officer whose bias eludes scrutiny; the only argument RAB officers are impelled to make is when their budget is under threat from other artform officers. A single officer can make or break a region, and scores of frustrated artists are keen to indicate which.

Finally, it's easier to reform one organisation than ten. In fact it's easier to contact one than ten, as any administrator of a touring company will tell you. The Department of Culture is dismayed by the thought that, if the Arts Council were scrapped, the arts Lottery cash would be distributed by ten separate RABs. That might well be the single practical consideration that could save the Council from extinction. At this point the reader might enjoy a little exercise: phone up the ten RABs and see if you can speak to ten drama or dance officers in a row, in the same hour, on the same day, in the same week. This is not to say that all RAB officers are sluggards. Some work industriously to make sense of the system they're burdened with for the benefit of their baffled clients. As an example, a number of interviewees for this book singled out for compliments John Kieffer, head of performing arts for the London Arts Board (LAB), pointing out how he has consistently supported new work and radical developments in difficult times. Kieffer attained his post by climbing diligently up the internal ladder from the rank of music assistant and departing for a period in between to sample the real world as an arts producer. However, his supporters go on to say that instability surrounds workers like him, and the LAB remains as capricious as the others in its conduct, which is a little surprising as it is the only RAB not encumbered with the financial patronage of local authorities. Nevertheless, it is possible to find the odd director, officer and assistant who attempt to make the unwieldy wheel of fortune that is regional provision roll smoothly. A former RAB officer considers, 'There are some decent officers in the sticks trying to make the thing work. I would say if you could bundle them together you'd get one bloody good RAB.' One out of ten won't do.

The Arts Council was there first. Regional Arts Boards exist because Bill Williams, in his psychotic search for savings in the fifties, uprooted the Council's regional offices and allowed a patchy substitute to cultivate its competing and bureaucratic weeds in the path of the arts. However, there is not the slightest evidence that regional organisations would have flourished had the Arts Council headquarters closed down instead.

Suppose, indeed, that the Arts Council never existed. Imagine that Tom Jones had got no further than John Christie; that Keynes died of his heart attack at Bretton Woods in 1944. We would probably still have Glyndebourne; the Edinburgh Festival; the National Theatre (it would have taken just as long to arrive), which the government would have funded directly; Shakespeare summer seasons at Stratford in the manner of Glyndebourne; Sadler's Wells opera and ballet at the Coliseum or the Metropolitan Opera House south of the river; two London symphony orchestras; and a miked Domingo starring in opera seasons at Wembley, produced for profit or loss by Raymond Gubbay.

Moreover, the London County Council would still have built the South Bank, where the LPO would reside, and the Corporation of London the Barbican for the LSO. The Tate wouldn't have been affected and would display new art much as it does now; the Whitechapel, too. The Royal Court Theatre might well have emerged – thanks to Oscar Lewenstein and the Queen's cousin – and also the ICA. They might be funded by the Pilgrim and the Carnegie Trusts, still busy, or the Gulbenkian, which would be sustaining organisations rather more than pump-priming them. Macmillan's Government might have introduced a sweepstake in the fifties which could have supported the arts entirely. The arts units of the British Council would still exist, and they may have developed means to support artists and companies domestically in the manner of Swedish subsidy structures, where no distinction is made between supporting work at home or abroad (in fact there are few logistical obstacles, aside from heart attacks in the Treasury, against the present Arts Council being absorbed within the British Council).

It's hard to say what we would have lost by the absence of the Council in terms of structure. Standards of performance and design would surely be lower, because, as stage director Peter Stein has confirmed, 'money buys you time to get it better'. Far fewer people would get along to see the work, thanks to touring limitations or higher ticket prices – though the government might have dropped VAT for cultural events (in 1979 Labour nearly did so). Above all, the local authorities would not have developed and sustained as much professional and educational arts activity as they have.

There is no doubt that the Council under Mary Glasgow made earnest and influential efforts to link up with local authorities and galvanise them in the domain of buildings – arts centres, civic theatres, concert halls – and the performing arts through festivals, resident companies and post-war concert seasons. The local councils had already sustained their commitments to municipal galleries and halls, though it's hard to say whether the civic-theatre movement might have gained better momentum if Keynes and Bill Williams had been less dismissive. The three civic orchestras of Bournemouth, Liverpool and Manchester would not have survived without the Council. Community arts movements would not have been affected, as much of their energy was buoyed by local political support through adventure playgrounds and community centres. A much-diminished dance scene would have been spread entirely through state education and the voluntary youth movements. Arts Council money helped to raise dancers' sights over quality and range, though sadly not those of their spooky teachers.

The Arts Council worked best as a national agency when it first engaged directly with the local authorities through its regional offices. That is what it should do now – let it scrap the ten RABs and re-open its six branches. They were distributed as follows:

1	North-Western	Manchester
2	North-Eastern	York
3	Midlands	Birmingham
4	Eastern	Cambridge
5	South-West	Bristol
6	South-East	London

Nothing in this modest structure works against the regionalist framework established by the European Community, on which we increasingly rely for funds to develop 'internal cultural develop-ment' and 'inter-regional co-operation'. In May 1997 New Labour announced that a network of Regional Development Agencies would be set up, though their number and disposition had not been determined at the time of writing; whether each association could harbour an Arts Council appointee is still open to conjecture. If there *has* to be another way, then the Sports Council's system, whereby each regional director is answerable to the headquarters executive, should be copied (in fact, it runs both systems: ten regional offices but half a dozen 'national centres').

The Sports Council's national staffing cost is £10 million a year, though the work is linked to education and not sufficiently comparable. The RABs employ in total over 300 full-time staff (£7.38 million) and a dozen offices (£3.4 million). On that generous basis, it would cost the Arts Council overheads of £300,000 and staff costs of £200,000 to employ eight officers in each of five offices (the south-east sixth within the ACE headquarters), amounting to £2.7 million and saving £8 million a year on the old system. Still more could be saved, of course.

In doing this we must squarely disregard fantasies about equal distribution, for if an elected local authority doesn't want anything to do with the arts it's not up to an unelected quango to tell it otherwise; the Council must impress the infidels with fine deeds elsewhere. Meanwhile the Council should slim the structure at its headquarters. The artform departments must be elevated again to their central position by upgrading their officers or downgrading the others, the lottery unit(s) beneath them. Peripheral departments should be closed down – touring and education among them.

In fact, all the current mechanisms of performance monitoring, appraisals and assessment should be scrapped. They eat up money and energy, yet are ineffective; it's obvious when a client is going down the pan. Appraisals are vital, but not in the sloppy manner they're done now. Though the education unit has proved itself useful, it's better to have an officer with specialist education experience appointed in each artform department. Together these officers can form a horizontal team to interface with the regional offices. All artform staff should be appointed for their working knowledge of arts practice. The interviewing board ought to rate individuality and vocationalist principles above mechanistic computations about representation; nobody with an arts-management degree should be given a job just because they've been accredited by a college.

A statistical unit should be established, but with a public function. The Council must sort out its archives by housing them for research use and appointing a full-time archivist; let the funds of the Heritage Lottery cover the start-up costs. Of the new Council of twelve, at least seven must be experienced, working artists or producers. They will come because the routine meetings will last no more than three hours. Council members should be called councillors; that'll bring them down a peg or two. The Arts Council should be led by characters with genuine, enduring arts experience. The Chairman must be drawn from the performing arts – not a film-producer, architect or novelist. The Council must also close down the incurable South Bank Centre, *pour encourager les autres*, as Nicholas Snowman might say. The Festival Hall should stay, *pour encourager l'Orchestre Philharmonique de Londres et sa pote, le Philharmonia.*

Now to money. The Arts Council can do little to shake the public's belief that it has a stronger stake in Lottery proceeds than it has in direct taxes. Though the Lottery is a form of levy, it has a completely different complexion from income tax, due to the sales pitch that patrons are donating 28p out of each pound to designated charities. Therefore a suitably conceived endowment fund, or something like it, seems a neat idea that will offer the prevailing major outfits a degree of independence and stability, so long as the stabilisation fund has sorted out their internal blemishes. If the public disagrees with their conduct, it's their prerogative to forge change through the box office and the outfits' trustees, though the endowment account will protect clients from out-and-out nutters who begrudge anything creative. In view of this, the Council should take the opportunity offered by the redevelopment closures to organise a TV debate on the six major companies, chaired by Anthea Turner or Mystic Meg: the Royal Opera and English National Opera, the National Theatre and the Royal Shakespeare Company, the Royal Ballet and English National Ballet. Let the people demonstrate how well they understand them, and let the clients state their defence directly; thanks to the Lottery, the people can afford to be more generous to the established arts than the Council.

What the general public tends not to comprehend is the unprecedented, the ephemeral, development, experiment. While we include here radical work which provokes and confronts audiences, we shouldn't forget that experimental traditions have also evolved in this country which are essentially conservative in intent. So let the government grant be devoted, as it is in defence research, entirely to the new, and let the Arts Council fund professional research and development as well as commissions and productions through its grant-in-aid rather than the Lottery, allowing projects to extend and spread beyond the annual or the one-off.

To do this it will need to scrap all of the proactive schemes and programmes it has devised, for they are disguised mechanisms through which the Council instils and polices policy of little gain to artists or their public. The Council will once again embrace a conduct of reaction. This category, by the way, can include totally new productions of existing work, even a bunch of *Toscas*.

The Lottery can handle what the public already knows – the present infrastructure – while the Arts Council's grant will support the uncertain, the future of the arts. As this work will advance the experience of the British public, a measure of the government grant must benefit audience development and public awareness – routed through artists, companies, producers and presenters, but not through the marketing agencies which have already spent money indulging themselves to little effect. This bilateral budget – for undertakings and their reception – will use less of the government's annual grant, say 50 per cent less (£100 million; the Council's own costs will rise to 10 per cent of that), allowing the Council to 'slip below the parapet' that protected it until the late sixties. Let the Department of Culture, Media and Sport face the blame for any future PR blunders.

While the Council may continue, through its endowment policy and capital unit, as a Lottery counting house for the Department of Culture, Media and Sport, the measures described here will allow the Council to assert its independence from that ministry. Not a fuck-you licence, however; the Council is a quasi, not wholly, autonomous body – a quango not a wango. It is only proper that it should account for its behaviour to Parliament so long as Parliament squirts money at it.

These steps will settle two key criticisms the Council faces from artists, producers and the public, that 'it just does what the government tells it' and that 'it keeps bringing out plans to hide the fact it doesn't know what it's doing'.

By engaging with frontier work, it will be its saving grace to say, 'We don't know what we're doing.'

Appendices

Ministers and Arts Council chiefs:
chronology
Arts Council grant-in-aid and spending
Arts Council administration structure
Arts Council advisory structure

Sources
Index

MINISTERS AND ARTS COUNCIL CHIEFS: CHRONOLOGY

Year	Organisation	Government	Minister (Arts)	Chairman	Secretary-General
Dec 1938	CEMA	Coalition Chamberlain	Lord De La Warr President: Board of Education	Thomas Jones (4 months)	Mary Glasgow ($11\frac{1}{2}$ years)
1939					
1940			Herwald Ramsbotham President: Board of Education (1 year 3 months)	Lord Macmillan (2 years)	i. Secretary (4 years)
1941		May: Churchill I	R.A. Butler i. President: Board of Education (3 years)		
1942				John Maynard Keynes (4 years)	
1943					
1944			ii. Minister of Education (1 year)		ii. Secretary-General ($7\frac{1}{2}$ years)
1945	ACGB	July: Labour: Attlee	Hugh Dalton Chancellor (2 years)	Acting Chairman: Sir John Maud Acting Chairman: Ifor Evans	
1946				Sir Ernest Pooley (7 years)	
1947			Sir Stafford Cripps Chancellor (2 years)		
1948					
1949					

Year	Organis-ation	Government	Minister (Arts)	Chairman	Secretary-General
1950	(ACGB)	(L: Attlee)	Hugh Gaitskell Chancellor (1 year)	(Pooley)	(Glasgow)
1951		October: Conservative: Churchill II	R.A. Butler Chancellor (4 years)		(Sir) William Emrys Williams (12 years)
1952					
1953				Sir Kenneth Clark (7 years)	
1954		Conservative: Eden			
1955			Harold Macmillan Chancellor (1 year)		
1956					
1957		January: Conservative: Macmillan	Peter Thorneycroft Chancellor (1 year)		
1958			Heathcote Amory Chancellor (1 year 10 months)		
1959			Selwyn Lloyd Chancellor (2 years)		
1960				Lord Cottesloe (5 years)	
1961			Reginald Maudling Chancellor (2 years)		
1962					

Year	Organis-ation	Government	Minister (Arts)	Chairman	Secretary-General
1963	(ACGB)	October Conservative: Douglas-Home	(Maudling)	(Cottesloe)	Nigel Aber-crombie (5 years)
1964	ACGB	October: Labour: Wilson I	James Callaghan Chancellor (1 year)		
1965			Jennie Lee i. Under-Secretary of State, Department of Education and Science ($2\frac{1}{2}$ years)	Lord Goodman (7 years)	
1966					
1967			ii. Minister of State, Department of Education and Science (3 years)		
1968					(Sir) Hugh Willatt (7 years)
1969					
1970		June: Conservative: Heath	Lord Eccles Paymaster-General (3 years 9 months)		
1971					
1972				Lord Gibson (5 years)	

Year	Organisation	Government	Minister (Arts)	Chairman	Secretary-General
1973	(ACGB)	(C: Heath)	Norman St John-Stevas Minister for the Arts, Department of Education and Science (4 months)	(Gibson)	(Willatt)
1974		March: Labour: Wilson II	Hugh Jenkins Minister for the Arts, Department of Education and Science (2 years)		
1975					(Sir) Roy Shaw (7 years)
1976		April: Labour: Callaghan	Lord Donaldson Minister for the Arts, Department of Education and Science (3 years)		
1977				Sir Kenneth Robinson (5 years)	
1978					
1979		April: Conservative: Thatcher	Norman St John-Stevas Chancellor: Duchy of Lancaster, Leader of the House (1 year 9 months)		
1980					
1981			Paul Channon, Minister for the Arts, Department of Education and Science (2 years 4 months)		

Year	Organis-ation	Government	Minister (Arts)	Chairman	Secretary-General
1982	(ACGB)	(C: Thatcher)	(Channon)	Sir William Rees-Mogg (6 years)	(Shaw)
1983			Lord Gowrie i. Minister for the Arts, Privy Council Office (1 year)		Luke Rittner (7 years)
1984			ii. Chancellor of the Duchy of Lancaster (1 year)		
1985			Richard Luce Minister for the Arts, Privy Council Office (4 years 10 months)		
1986					
1987					
1988					
1989				Lord Palumbo (5 years)	
1990		November: Conservative: Major	David Mellor Minister for the Arts, Privy Council Office (4 months)		Anthony Everitt (4 years)
			Tim Renton Minister for the Arts, Privy Council Office (1 year 5 months)		
1991					
1992			David Mellor Secretary of State, Department of National Heritage (5 months)		

540

Year	Organis- ation	Government	Minister (Arts)	Chairman	Secretary- General
(1992)	(ACGB)	(C: Major)	Peter Brooke Secretary of State, Department of National Heritage (2 years)	(Palumbo)	(Everitt)
1993					
1994	April: ACE		Stephen Dorrell Secretary of State, Department of National Heritage (1 year)	Lord Gowrie (4 years)	Mary Allen (3 years)
1995			Virginia Bottomley Secretary of State, Department of National Heritage (1 year 10 months)		
1996					
1997		May: Labour: Blair	Chris Smith Secretary of State, Department of Culture, Media and Sport		
1998				Gerry Robinson	

		Arts Council			Covent Garden
Financial year	Government	£ Government grant	£ ACGB * Distributed in England	£ Value †	£ Core
1939–1940	Coalition	–	25,000‡		–
1940–1941		50,000	–	2.45m	–
1941–1942		45,000	12,500‡	1.9m	–
1942–1943		100,000	12,500‡	3.7m	–
1943–1944		175,000	–	5.7m	–
1944–1945		185,000	124,196[A]	4.06m	–
1945–1946	Labour	235,000	172,579[A]	5.6m	25,000
1946–1947		350,000	278,526[A]	5.5m	25,000
1947–1948		428,000	283,006[B]	5.2m	30,000
1948–1949		575,000	432,919[B]	7.4m	145,000
1949–1950		600,000	491,806[B]	8.1m	145,000
1950–1951		575,000[C]	422,508[B]	7m	145,000
1951–1952		575,000[C]	403,842[B]	5.9m	150,000
1952–1953	Conservative	585,000[D]	538,958[B]	7.5m	200,000
1953–1954		785,000	569,451	7.8m	240,000
1954–1955		785,000	591,337	8m	250,000
1955–1956		820,000	614,670	8m	250,000
1956–1957		885,000	686,172	8.5m	270,000
1957–1958		985,000	761,962	9.2m	302,000
1958–1959		1,100,000	867,244	10.1m	362,000
1959–1960		1,218,000	985,771	11.4m	473,000
1960–1961		1,500,000	1,225,434	14m	500,737
1961–1962		1,745,000	1,438,945	16m	505,991
1962–1963		2,190,000	1,793,513	19.2m	
1963–1964		2,730,000	2,270,021	23.9m	815,000
1964–1965		3,205,000	2,689,700	27.4m	1,055,000
1965–1966	Labour	3,910,000	3,276,230	31.9m	1,026,500
1966–1967		5,700,000	4,711,597	44.1m	1,225,000
1967–1968		7,200,000	5,759,514	52.5m	1,280,000
1968–1969		7,750,000	6,099,521	53.2m	1,280,000
1969–1970		8,200,000	6,456,048	53.4m	1,400,000
1970–1971		9,300,000	7,268,124	56.5m	1,420,000

‡ Pilgrim Trust grant

	Covent Garden			Sadler's Wells – English National Opera		
Supplementary	*Total value †*	*% Core of ACGB spend*	*Core*	*Supplementary*	*Total value †*	*%*
–	–		–		–	
–	–		–		–	
–	–		–		–	
–	–		–		–	
–	–		–		–	
–	–		–		–	
–	0.82m	12%	10,000		326,700	4.5%
30,000	1.01m	17.5%	15,000	(15,000)	588,100	5%(10%)
68,000	1.8m	27%	23,000		421,800	8%
–	2.5m	34%	40,000		682,900	9%
25,000 i 10,000	2.8m	34%	52,500		867,600	11%
ii 150,000[C]	4.9m	35%	47,500		770,000	11%
-c-	2.2m[C]	37%	60,000	19,250	1,164,000	19%
65,000[D]	3.7m	37% (49%)	68,000		955,000	13%
	3.3m	42%	100,000		1.3m	17%
	3.4m	42%	100,000		1.3m	17%
	3.3m	41%	100,000		1.3m	16%
15,000	3.5m	41.5%	125,000		1.5m	18%
15,000	3.8m	41.5%	142,000		1.7m	19%
35,000	4.4m	43.5%	155,000[E]		1.8m	18% (18)
35,000	5.6m	49.5%	200,000		2.3m	20%
35,000	5.9m	42%	275,000		3.1m	19%
35,000	5.8m	36%	365,000		4m	25%
15,260	8.9m	36.5%	400,000		4.2m	17%
	10.7m	37.5%	425,000		4.3m	16%
	10m	36%	521,500		5m	17%
100	11.5m	26%	638,000		6m	13%
100	11.7m	22%	757,500		6.9m	13%
250	11.1m	22%	787,000		6.9m	13%
15,000	11.7m	22%	762,000		6.3m	12%
15,100	11.2m	20%	815,000		6.3m	11%

	Arts Council				**Covent Garden**
Financial year	_Government_	_£ Government grant_	_£ ACGB * Distributed in England_	_£ Value †_	_£ Core_
1971–1972	Conservative	11,900,000	9,101,335	64.7m	1,640,000
1972–1973		13,725,000	10,371,035	68.8m	1,750,000
1973–1974		17,138,000	13,076,682	79.5m	2,195,000
1974–1975		21,850,000	16,635,572	87.2m	2,650,000
1975–1976	Labour	28,850,000	22,337,892	94.2m	3,410,000
1976–1977		37,150,000	28,485,192	103m	4,300,000
1977–1978		41,725,000	32,201,618	100.6m	4,850,000
1978–1979		51,800,000	39,970,910	115.3m	5,475,000
1979–1980		63,125,000	48,613,763	123.6m	7,000,000
1980–1981	Conservative	70,970,000	54,679,613	117.9m	7,805,000
1981–1982		80,450,000	62,072,793	119.6m	9,020,000
1982–1983		91,300,000	70,307,100	124.7m	10,379,682
1983–1984		96,080,000	74,754,448	126.8m	11,584,776
1984–1985		101,900,000	78,738,937	127.2m	12,386,891
1985–1986		106,050,000	81,948,366	124.8m	13,474,491
1986–1987		135,600,000	110,076,600	162.1m	12,371,000
1987–1988		139,300,000	112,879,000	159.7m	13,226,960
1988–1989		152,411,000	118,875,000	160.3m	13,991,270
1989–1990		155,500,000	122,883,000	153.7m	14,722,040
1990–1991		175,792,000	136,888,000	156.4m	15,832,000
1991–1992		205,000,000	165,853,000	179m	17,815,200
1992–1993		221,200,000	176,433,000	183.6m	18,951,710
1993–1994		225,830,000	178,038,000	182.3m	19,521,000
1994–1995		185,990,000*	179,921,000	179.9m	19,521,000
1995–1996		191,100,000	–	–	
1996–1997		186,100,000	–	–	
			3,606,260,000		

* From this point, England only

544

| Covent Garden | | | Sadler's Wells – English National Opera | | | |
Supple-mentary	Total value †	% Core of ACGB spend	Core	Supple-mentary	Total value †	%
15,674	11.8m	20%	1,118,153		7.9m	12%
15,000	11.7m	18%	935,000		6.2m	9%
	13.3m	17%	1,130,000		6.9m	9%
3,150,058	30.4m	16% (35%)	1,411,000		7.4m	9%
	14.4m	15%	1,848,000		7.8m	8%
	15.6m	15%	2,225,000		8m	9%
	15.1m	15%	2,640,000		8.2m	9%
	15.8m	13.5%	3,665,000		10.6m	9%
505,000	19.1m	15%	4,800,000		12.2m	10%
350,000	17.6m	15%	4,205,000	435,000	10m	8%
750,000	18.8m	15%	4,550,000	30,000	8.8m	7%
150,000	18.7m	15%	5,440,000	35,000	9.7m	8%
	19.6m	15%	5,988,401		10.1m	8%
	20m	15.5%	5,918,250		9.6m	8%
	20.5m	16.5%	6,034,500		9.2m	7%
	18.2m	11%	6,626,000		9.8m	6%
	18.7m	12%	6,748,000		9.5m	6%
2,411,000	22.1m	11% (14%)	6,917,000		9.3m	5%
	18.4m	12%	7,056,000		8.8m	6%
16,000	18.1m	11%	7,832,000	1,291,000	8.9m [10.4m]	6%
25,000	19.2m	11%	10,432,300	i 10,800,000 ii 46,000	11.3m [23m]	7%
25,000	19.7m	11%	11,371,207	69,000	11.9m	7%
25,000	20m	11%	11,655,000	11,950	11.7m	6.5%
	19.5m	11%	11,655,000	10,000	11.7m	6.5%

NOTES

†   Value at 1994–1995 retail prices (RPI).
      Source: Central Statistical Office.

A   Grant distribution England, Wales and Scotland. Scotland published
      separate accounts from 1947–1948.

B   Grant distribution England and Wales.
      Wales published separate accounts from 1953–1954.

C   Additional sums were voted by Parliament for the 1951 Festival of Britain.
      Some of this covered the disastrous opera competitions.

D   Additional sums were voted by Parliament for the 1953 coronation of
      Elizabeth II.

E   From 1958–1959 onwards London County Council/GLC gave Sadler's
      Wells/ENO an annual grant not added here.

*   This column, composed in order to show the net amount actually spent
      on the arts in England by the Arts Council, includes grants to Regional
      Arts Associations/Boards. The devolution of certain ACGB clients to
      RAAs, especially between 1983 and 1986, clouds the consistency of the
      overall picture if they are otherwise excluded. However, some of the
      money given to RAA/RABs covers an additional layer of administration.

ARTS COUNCIL ADMINISTRATION STRUCTURE 1996

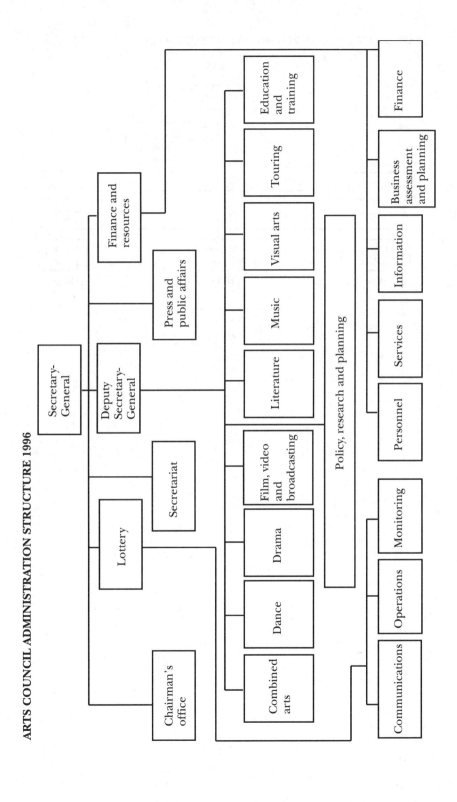

ARTS COUNCIL ADVISORY STRUCTURE 1945–1995

1945

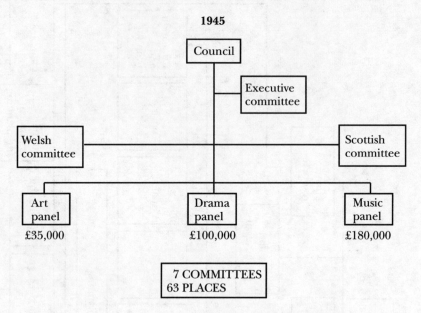

Council

Executive committee

Welsh committee

Scottish committee

Art panel
£35,000

Drama panel
£100,000

Music panel
£180,000

7 COMMITTEES
63 PLACES

1955

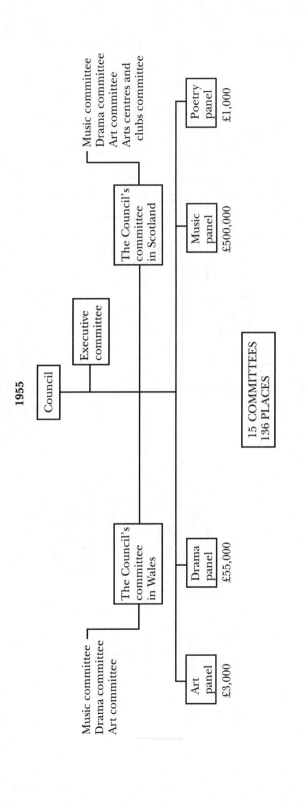

Council

Executive committee

The Council's committee in Scotland

Music committee
Drama committee
Art committee
Arts centres and clubs committee

Poetry panel
£1,000

Music panel
£500,000

15 COMMITTEES
136 PLACES

The Council's committee in Wales

Music committee
Drama committee
Art committee

Drama panel
£55,000

Art panel
£3,000

1965

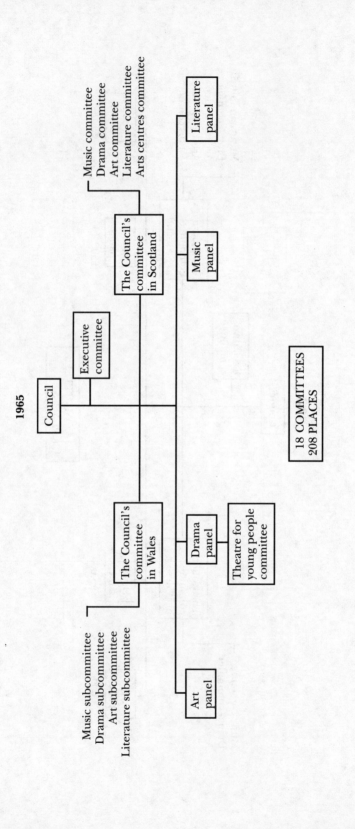

Council

Executive committee

Music committee
Drama committee
Art committee
Literature committee
Arts centres committee

The Council's committee in Scotland

Music panel

Literature panel

The Council's committee in Wales

Music subcommittee
Drama subcommittee
Art subcommittee
Literature subcommittee

Art panel

Drama panel

Theatre for young people committee

18 COMMITTEES
208 PLACES

1975

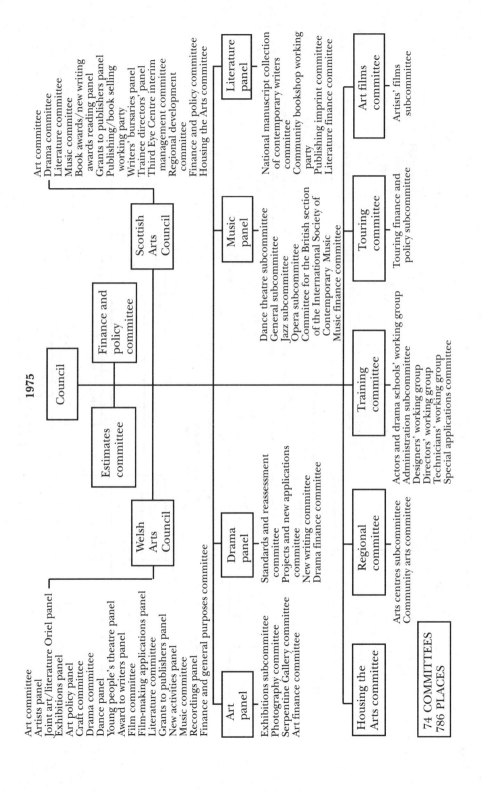

Council

Art committee
Artists panel
Joint art/literature Oriel panel
Exhibitions panel
Art policy panel
Craft committee
Drama committee
Dance panel
Young people's theatre panel
Award to writers panel
Film committee
Film-making applications panel
Literature committee
Grants to publishers panel
New activities panel
Music committee
Recordings panel
Finance and general purposes committee

Welsh Arts Council

Estimates committee

Finance and policy committee

Scottish Arts Council

Art committee
Drama committee
Literature committee
Music committee
Book awards/new writing
awards reading panel
Grants to publishers panel
Publishing/book selling
working party
Writers' bursaries panel
Trainee directors' panel
Third Eye Centre interim
management committee
Regional development
committee
Finance and policy committee
Housing the Arts committee

Art panel

Exhibitions subcommittee
Photography committee
Serpentine Gallery committee
Art finance committee

Drama panel

Standards and reassessment
committee
Projects and new applications
committee
New writing committee
Drama finance committee

Music panel

Dance theatre subcommittee
General subcommittee
Jazz subcommittee
Opera subcommittee
Committee for the British section
of the International Society of
Contemporary Music
Music finance committee

Literature panel

National manuscript collection
of contemporary writers
committee
Community bookshop working
party
Publishing imprint committee
Literature finance committee

Housing the Arts committee

Regional committee

Arts centres subcommittee
Community arts committee

Training committee

Actors and drama schools' working group
Administration subcommittee
Designers' working group
Directors' working group
Technicians' working group
Special applications committee

Touring committee

Touring finance and
policy subcommittee

Art films committee

Artists' films
subcommittee

74 COMMITTEES
786 PLACES

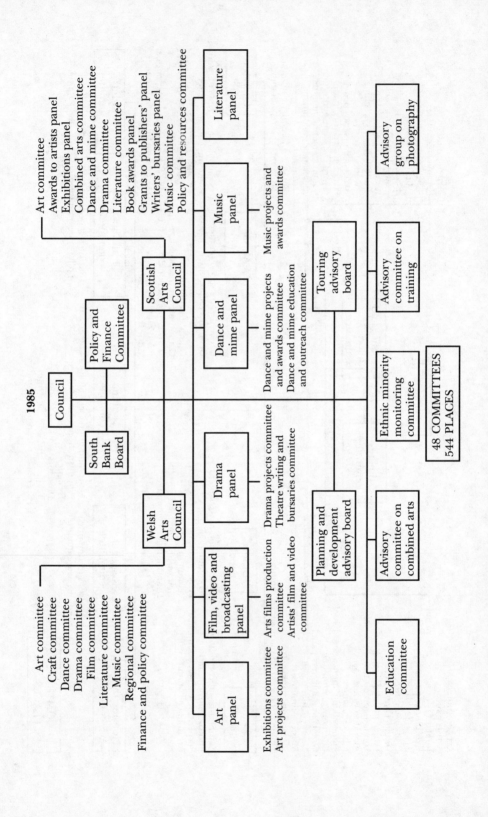

1985

Council

Policy and Finance Committee

South Bank Board

Welsh Arts Council

Scottish Arts Council

Art committee
Craft committee
Dance committee
Drama committee
Film committee
Literature committee
Music committee
Regional committee
Finance and policy committee

Art committee
Awards to artists panel
Exhibitions panel
Combined arts committee
Dance and mime committee
Drama committee
Literature committee
Book awards panel
Grants to publishers' panel
Writers' bursaries panel
Music committee
Policy and resources committee

Literature panel

Music panel

Music projects and awards committee

Dance and mime panel

Dance and mime projects and awards committee
Dance and mime education and outreach committee

Drama panel

Drama projects committee
Theatre writing and bursaries committee

Film, video and broadcasting panel

Arts films production committee
Artists' film and video committee

Art panel

Exhibitions committee
Art projects committee

Touring advisory board

Planning and development advisory board

Ethnic minority monitoring committee

Advisory group on photography

Advisory committee on training

Advisory committee on combined arts

Education committee

**48 COMMITTEES
544 PLACES**

1995

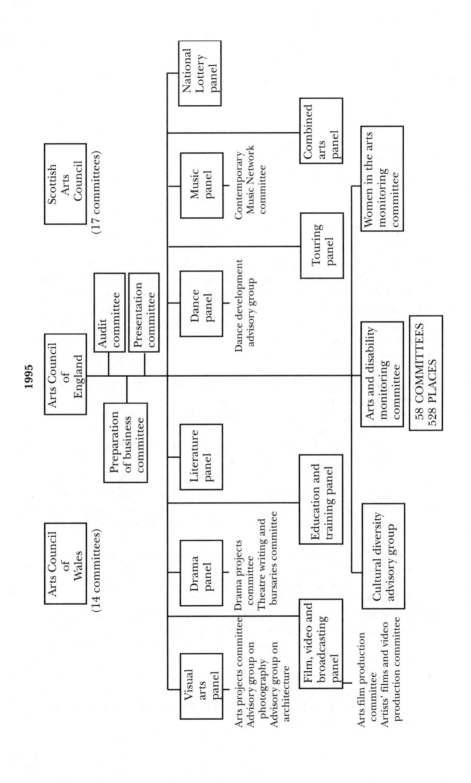

Arts Council of Wales (14 committees)

Arts Council of England

Scottish Arts Council (17 committees)

National Lottery panel

Audit committee

Presentation committee

Preparation of business committee

Music panel

Contemporary Music Network committee

Combined arts panel

Dance panel

Dance development advisory group

Touring panel

Women in the arts monitoring committee

Literature panel

Education and training panel

Arts and disability monitoring committee

58 COMMITTEES
528 PLACES

Visual arts panel

Arts projects committee
Advisory group on photography
Advisory group on architecture

Drama panel

Drama projects committee
Theatre writing and bursaries committee

Cultural diversity advisory group

Film, video and broadcasting panel

Arts film production committee
Artists' films and video production committee

Sources

Newspaper news items and articles are normally identified within the main text. Several books are cited there too, but their details are repeated here more fully. Books on general historical matters which are catalogued below were consulted to check details indicated in archives and interviews (see Acknowledgements). The British Library, the Public Record Office, the insanely undersized Arts Council Library, the City of Westminster Reference Library and the Library of the University of Sussex were the principal resources used.

Arts Council of England, 1st Annual Report (1994–1995), London, ACE, 1995; 2nd Annual Report (1995–1996).

Arts Council of England, 'Development Funds 1996–1997', leaflet, London, ACE, 1995.

Arts Council of England, 'Paying Attention – A Guide to Customer Care in the Arts', pamphlet, London, ACE, 1994.

Arts Council of England, 'Strategy for the Support and Development of Orchestras and their Audiences', report, London, ACE, July 1995.

Arts Council of Great Britain, 'A Great British Success Story – An Invitation to the Nation to Invest in the Arts', pamphlet, London, ACGB, 1985.

Arts Council of Great Britain, 'An Urban Renaissance – The Role of the Arts in Inner City Regeneration', report, London, ACGB, 1987.

Arts Council of Great Britain, Annual Reports nos. 1 (1945–1946) to 49 (1993–1994), London, ACGB.

Arts Council of Great Britain, Arts Council Collection – a concise, illustrated catalogue of paintings, drawings, photographs and sculpture purchased for the Arts Council of Great Britain between 1942 and 1978, London, ACGB, 1979.

Arts Council of Great Britain, Arts Council Collection – Acquisitions 1979–1983, London, ACGB, 1984.

Arts Council of Great Britain, Arts Council Collection – Acquisitions 1984–1988, London, South Bank Board, 1990.

Sources

Arts Council of Great Britain, 'Committee on the London Orchestras' (the Goodman Report), ACGB, 1965.

Arts Council of Great Britain, 'Housing the Arts in Great Britain', vols I and II, report, London, ACGB, 1959, 1960.

Arts Council of Great Britain, 'Incentive Funding – The First Year' (ed. Allen, M. and Webber, H.), London, ACGB, 1989.

Arts Council of Great Britain, minutes of Council meetings 30 April 1945 and subsequent meetings, London, Arts Council Archives.

Arts Council of Great Britain, monthly bulletins (following on from CEMA bulletins) no. 64 August 1945–.

Arts Council of Great Britain, 'National Arts & Media Strategy, London – Discussion Papers 1991; Towards a NA&M Strategy' (ed. Webber, H.), London, ACGB, 1992; 'A Creative Future, The Way Forward for the Arts, Crafts and Media in England', report, London, ACGB, 1993.

Arts Council of Great Britain, 'Opera and Dance, Report of the Study Group', London, ACGB, 1983.

Arts Council of Great Britain, Orchestral concerts research, qualitative findings report, Harris Research Centre, London, ACGB, 1993.

Arts Council of Great Britain, 'Organisational Review, Report of the Working Party on Assessment of Revenue Clients', London, ACGB, 1985.

Arts Council of Great Britain, 'Partnership – Making Arts Money Work Harder', report, London, ACGB, 1986.

Arts Council of Great Britain, 'Plans for an Arts Centre', booklet, London, Lund Humphries, 1945.

Arts Council of Great Britain, 'Promoting Regional Orchestral Music (PROM), a Discussion Paper' (ed. Duncan, N.), London, ACGB, 1985.

Arts Council of Great Britain, 'Report of the Advisory Committee on the London Orchestras' (the Hoffman Report), London, ACGB, 1993.

Arts Council of Great Britain, 'Report on Opera & Ballet in the United Kingdom 1966–1969', London, ACGB, 1969.

Arts Council of Great Britain, 'Report on Orchestral Resources in Great Britain' (the Peacock Report), London, ACGB, 1970.

Arts Council of Great Britain, Response to the Wilding Report, papers, London, ACGB, 1990.

Arts Council of Great Britain, 'The Glory of the Garden – The Development of the Arts in England', booklet, London, ACGB, 1984.

Arts Council of Great Britain, 'The Obscenity Laws: Report of the Working Party', London, André Deutsch, 1969.

Arts Council of Great Britain, 'Theatre Is For All – Report of the Enquiry into Professional Theatre in England' (the Cork Report), London, ACGB, 1986.

'Arts Council & What it Does', booklet, London, ACGB, 1950.

Arts Training Network, Directory of Arts Management Courses and programmes in higher and further education (ed. Dr Janet

555

Summerton), Brighton, University of Sussex, April 1996.

Arundell, D., *The Story of Sadler's Wells 1683–1977*, Newton Abbot, David & Charles, 1978.

Association of Metropolitan Authorities, 'Arts & Cultural Policy – A Discussion Document', London, AMA, 1990.

Barron, S., *Degenerate Art – The Fate of the Avant Garde in Nazi Germany*, New York, Abrams, 1991.

Bate, J. and Jackson, R. (eds), *Shakespeare, An Illustrated Stage History*, Oxford University Press, 1996.

BBC/Arts Council of England, 'National Review of Orchestral Provision' (the Ritterman Report), London, ACE, April 1995; consultation document October 1994.

Bell, C., *Civilisation*, London, Chatto, 1928.

Blair, S. (ed.), *The Original British Theatre Directory 1994*, London, Richmond House Publishing Company, 1994.

Blunt, W., *John Christie of Glyndebourne*, London, Geoffrey Bles, 1968.

Bookseller, 'Government subsidy of literature: the Arts Council's policy outlined, 16 April 1966. State Patronage Under Fire', magazine, 12 November 1966.

Bull, J., *Stage Right – Crisis and Recovery in British Contemporary Mainstream Drama*, London, Macmillan, 1994.

Callaghan, J., *Times & Chance* (Prime Minister's memoirs), London, William Collins, 1987.

Castillejo, D., *A Counter Report on Art Patronage*, London, Castillejo, 1968.

Cazalet Keir, T., *From the Wings*, London, Bodley Head, 1967.

City University, Department of Arts Policy & Management – introductory pamphlet for 1996–1997 entry, London, CU.

Clark, K., *Civilization*, London, BBC/John Murray, 1969.

Clark, K., *The Other Half – A Self Portrait*, (autobiography vol. II), London, Murray, 1977.

Committee for the Encouragement of Music and the Arts, minutes of meetings 1–12, January–April 1940, London, Arts Council Archives; miscellaneous correspondence, Public Record Office.

Conservative Political Centre, 'The Arts – The Way Forward', pamphlet, London, Conservative Political Centre, 1978.

Cook, J., *The National Theatre*, London, Harrap, 1976.

Council for the Encouragement of Music and the Arts, minutes of meeting 1 (23 April 1940) and subsequent meetings, London, Arts Council Archives.

Council for the Encouragement of Music and the Arts, CEMA bulletins: Nos 1 (May 1940) to 63 (July 1945), London, CEMA.

Covent Garden Community Association, Annual Report 1995–1996, London, CGCA, 1996.

Covent Garden Community Association: 'Il Rigmarole della Casa d'Opera Regale', leaflet (parody of Royal Opera programme), London, CGCA, 1995.

Sources

Dalton, H., *High Tide & After – Memoirs 1945–60*, London, Muller, 1962.

Davies, A., *Other Theatres – The Development of Alternative and Experimental Theatre in Britain*, London, Macmillan Education, 1987.

De Grazia, *The Culture of Consent – Mass Organisation of Leisure in Fascist Italy*, Cambridge University Press, 1981.

Dent, E.J., *Selected Essays* (ed. Taylor, H.), Cambridge University Press, 1979.

Donaldson, F., *The Royal Opera House in the Twentieth Century*, London, Weidenfeld & Nicolson, 1988.

Dorrell, L.J., Notes and transcript of meetings with Miss M.C. Glasgow (property of Ms Dorrell), 1983.

Double Exposure Ltd, TV series of six programmes, *The House*, on Royal Opera House, Covent Garden, videotape, London, 1996.

Drogheda, Earl of, *Double Harness*, London, Weidenfeld & Nicolson, 1978.

Duff, C., *The Lost Summer – The Heyday of West End Theatre*, London, Nick Hern Books, 1995.

Duncan, R., 'The Tories & the Arts', *Spectator*, 29 May 1964.

Dyson G., *Fiddling While Rome Burns – A Musician's Apology*, Oxford University Press, 1954.

Economist, 'Ministry for the Arts?', magazine, vol. 211, 11 April 1964.

Ehrlich, C., *The Music Profession in Britain since the Eighteenth Century – A Social History*, Oxford, Clarendon Press, 1985.

Elcock, H., *Local government – policy and management in local authorities*, London, Routledge, 1994.

Elsom, J. and Tomalin, N., *The History of the National Theatre*, London, Cape, 1978.

Encounter, 'Does the Arts Council know what it is doing?' Karen King and Mark Blaug, magazine, September 1973.

Endacott, M., retirement speech, April 1986 (property of Miss Endacott).

Evans, B. Ifor, *The Arts in England*, London, Falcon Press, 1949.

Evershed-Martin, L., *The Impossible Theatre – the Chichester Festival Theatre Adventure*, London, Phillimore, 1971.

Evershed-Martin, L., *The Miracle Theatre – the Chichester Festival Theatre's Coming of Age*, David & Charles, 1987.

Fay, S., *Power Play – The Life and Times of Peter Hall*, London, Hodder & Stoughton, 1995.

Foss H. and Goodwin N., *London Symphony – Portrait of An Orchestra*, London, Naldrett Press, 1954.

Fuscher, L.W., *Neville Chamberlain and Appeasement – A Study in the Politics of History*, Norton, 1982.

Gallo, M., *Mussolini's Italy – 20 Years of the Fascist Era*, Paris, Perrin, 1964.

Gielgud, J. (with Miller, J.), *Shakespeare – Hit or Miss?* London, Sidgwick & Jackson, 1991.

Gilbert M. and Gott R., *The Appeasers*, London, Weidenfeld & Nicolson, 1967.

Glasgow, M.C., 'The Concept of the Arts Council', in *Essays on John Maynard Keynes* (ed. Milo Keynes), Cambridge University Press, 1975.

Glasgow, M.C., *The Nineteen Hundreds – A Diary in Retrospect*, Oxford University Press (privately published), 1986.

Golomstock, I., *Totalitarian Art in the Soviet Union, Third Reich, Fascist Italy and the People's Republic of China*, London, 1990.

Goodman, Lord, *Tell them I'm On My Way* (memoirs), London, Chapmans, 1993.

Gourlay, J., *Olivier*, London, Weidenfeld & Nicolson, 1973.

Granville-Barker, Harley, *A National Theatre – Schemes & Estimates*, London, 1907 (revised Sidgwick & Jackson, 1930).

Greater London Council, 'The state of the art or the art of the state: strategies for the cultural industries in London', report, GLC Department for Recreation and the arts, 1985.

Green, M. and Wilding, M. 'Cultural Policy in Great Britain, Paris', *UNESCO Studies & Documents on Cultural Studies*, 1970.

Hall, P., *Making An Exhibition Of Myself* (memoirs), London, Sinclair-Stevenson, 1993.

Hampton, W. *Local Government & Urban Politics*, London, Longman, 1987.

Harcourt, G.C., (ed.), *Keynes and his Contemporaries*, London, Macmillan, 1985.

Harewood, Earl of, *The Tongs & the Bones – The Memoirs of Lord Harewood*, London, Weidenfeld & Nicolson, 1981.

Harkin, D. *Inside the Royal Court Theatre 1956–81*, USA, Louisiana State University Press, 1990.

Harris, J.S., *Government Patronage of the Arts in Great Britain*, London, University of Chicago Press, 1970.

Harrod, R.F., *John Maynard Keynes*, London, Macmillan, 1951.

Harwood, R., *Sir Donald Wolfit – His Life and Work in the Unfashionable Theatre*, London, Secker & Warburg, 1971.

Haydon, G., *John Tavener – Glimpses of Paradise*, London, Gollancz, 1995.

Hayes, N., *Municipal Subsidy & Tory Minimalism (1942–63)*, Birmingham, Midland History, vol 19, 1994.

Hayward Gallery: Art & Power – Europe under the dictators 1930–45 (the XXIII Council of Europe exhibition), catalogue, London, 1995.

Hennessy, P., *Never Again – Britain 1945–51*, London, Cape, 1992.

Hoggart, R., *An Imagined Life – Life & Times 1959–91*, London, Chatto & Windus, 1992.

Holden, A., *Olivier*, London, Weidenfeld & Nicolson, 1988.

Horne, A., *Macmillan Vol. II – 1957–86*, London, Macmillan, 1989.

Huggett, R., *Binkie Beaumont – Eminence Grise of the West End Theatre 1933–73*, London, Hodder & Stoughton, 1989.

Hughes, S., *Glyndebourne – A History of the Festival Opera*, London, Methuen, 1965.

Hughes, S., *Great Opera Houses – A Traveller's Guide to Their History and*

Traditions, London, Weidenfeld & Nicolson, 1956.

Hutchinson, G., *The Last Edwardian at Number Ten – An Impression of Harold Macmillan*, London, Quartet, 1980.

Hutchinson, R., *A Hard Fact To Swallow – the division of Arts Council expenditure between London and the English regions*, London, Policy Studies Institute, 1982.

Hutchinson, R., *The politics of the Arts Council*, London, Sinclair Browne, 1982.

Ibberson, M., *For The Joy That We Are Here – Rural Music Schools 1929–50*, Hitchin, RMSA, 1977.

Jenkins, H., *The Culture Gap – An Experience of Government and the Arts*, London, Marion Boyars, 1979.

Jenkins, R., *Baldwin*, London, Wm Collins, 1987.

Johnson, E., *The Shadow of Keynes*, London, Blackwell, 1978.

Jones, T., *A Diary with Letters 1931–50*, Oxford University Press, 1954.

Jones, T., *Lloyd George*, Oxford University Press, 1951.

Jones, T., *Whitehall Diary, Vol. II (1926–30)*, Oxford University Press, 1969.

Kallaway, W., *London Philharmonic – Music Makers Since 1933*, Havant, Kenneth Mason, 1972.

Keller, S.I., *Beyond the Ruling Class – strategic elites in modern society*, New York, Random House, 1963.

Kenyon, N., *The BBC Symphony Orchestra 1930–80*, London, BBC, 1981.

Keynes, J.M., *Collected Writings, Vol. XXVI (1943–6), Vol. XXVIII*, Royal Economic Society, Macmillan/Cambridge University Press, 1989.

Keynes, J.M., 'The Arts Council – its policy and hopes', radio transcript, *Listener*, vol. XXXIV, 12 July 1945.

Kiernan, T., *Olivier – The Life of Laurence Olivier*, London, Sidgwick & Jackson, 1981.

King-Smith, B., *Crescendo! 75 Years of the City of Birmingham Symphony Orchestra*, London, Methuen, 1995.

Koestenbaum, W., *The Queen's Throat*, London, Penguin, 1994.

Labour Party, 'The Arts & The People – Labour's policy towards the arts', London, 1977; 'Arts & media – our cultural future', London, Labour Party, 1991.

Lambert, J.W., *Drama in Britain 1964–73*, London, British Council, 1974.

Landstone, C. and Williamson, A., *The Bristol Old Vic*, London, 1951.

Landstone, C. *Off-Stage – A Personal Record of the First Twelve Years of State-Sponsored Drama in Great Britain*, London, Elek, 1953.

Langhorne, E., *Nancy Astor & her Friends*, London, Arthur Baker Ltd, 1974.

Lebrecht, N., *Music in London – A History and Handbook*, London, Aurum Press, 1992.

Levi, E., *Music in the Third Reich*, London, Macmillan, 1994.

Lewenstein, O., *Kicking Against The Pricks – A Theatre Producer Looks Back*, London, Nick Hern Books, 1994.

Lewis, N., *Naples '44*, London, Collins, 1978.

Lindsay, J., *British Achievement in Art & Music*, London, Pilot Press, n.d. (1940s).

Littlewood, J., *Joan's Book – Peculiar History as She Tells It*, London, Methuen, 1994.

London County Council, 'Report of the independent Committee of Inquiry on Sadler's Wells', London, LCC, 1959.

London Orchestral Concert Board, 'The Four London Orchestras – A Report to the LOCB' (the Figgures Report), London, LOCB, 1978.

Lynford, A., 'The new arts patrons – I Lord Goodman', *Illustrated London News*, 8 July 1967.

Mackerness, E.D., *A Social History of English Music*, London, Routledge & Kegan Paul, 1964.

Macmillan, H.P., *A Man of Law's Tale – Reminiscences*, London, Macmillan, 1952.

Marquard, D.I., *Politics and the Arts – An Historical Perspective*, Council of Regional Arts Associations, 1980.

McAlpine, A., *A Jolly Bagman* (memoirs), London, Weidenfeld & Nicolson, 1997.

McIntyre, Ian, *The Expense of Glory*, London, HarperCollins, 1993.

Miller, J., *Ralph Richardson – The Authorised Biography*, London, Sidgwick & Jackson, 1995.

Mirskii, D.P., *The Intellectuals of Great Britain*, London, Gollancz, 1935.

Moggridge, D.E., *Maynard Keynes – An Economist's Biography*, London, Routledge, 1992.

Money, E., *The Conservatives and the Arts*, London, Conservative Central Office, 1974.

Moran, Lord, *Winston Churchill – The Struggle for Survival 1940–65*, London, Constable, 1966.

Morgan, A., *Harold Wilson – a life*, London, Pluto Press, 1992.

Morley, I., *Soviet Ballet*, London, Collins, 1945.

Morpurgo, J.E., *Allen Lane – King Penguin*, London, Hutchinson, 1979.

Mosse, G.L., *Nazi Culture – Intellectual, Cultural & Social Life in the Third Reich*, London, Allen Lane, 1966.

National Audit Office, Review of the Arts Council of Great Britain, report, HMSO, 1990.

Netzer, D., *The Subsidized Muse*, Cambridge University Press, 1978.

Norman, J.O. (ed.), *New perspectives in Russian and Soviet artistic culture – selected papers from the World Congress for Soviet and East European studies*, London, Macmillan, 1994.

O'Connor, G., *Ralph Richardson – An Actor's Life*, London, Hodder & Stoughton, 1982.

OCPA, The Commissioner for Public Appointments' Guidance on Appointments to Executive Non-Departmental Public Bodies, London, Office of the Commissioner for Public Appointments, 1996.

Osborne, C., *Giving it Away – Memoirs of an Uncivil Servant*, London, Secker & Warburg, 1986.

Sources

Parkinson, M. (ed.), *Reshaping Local Government*, Hermitage, Policy Journals, 1987.

Parliament, 8th Report of the Estimates Committee: sessions 1967–1968; 1969.

Parterre Box, New York, USA: website: http://www.anaserve.com/~parterre/lacieca.htm

Peacock, A., 'Welfare Economics & Public Subsidies to the Arts', Manchester School of Economic & Social Studies, vol. 37, December 1969.

Pearton, M., *The London Symphony Orchestra at 70 – A History of the Orchestra*, London, Gollancz, 1974.

Pettitt, S.J., *Philharmonia Orchestra – A Record of Achievement 1945–1985*, London, Robert Hale, 1985.

Pick, J., *The Theatre Industry – subsidy, profit and the search for new audiences*, London, Comedia Publishing Group, 1985.

Pick, J., *Vile Jelly – the birth, life and lingering death of the Arts Council of Great Britain*, Doncaster, Brynmill Press, 1991.

Pimlott, B., *Hugh Dalton*, London, Jonathan Cape, 1985.

Ponting, C., *1940 – Myth and Reality*, London, Hamish Hamilton, 1990.

Pound, R., *Sir Henry Wood*, London, Cassell, 1969.

Priestley, J.B., *The arts under socialism*, London, Turnstile Press, 1947.

Quayle, A., *A Time to Speak*, London, Barrie & Jenkins, 1990.

Redcliffe-Maud, Lord, *Support for the Arts in England & Wales*, London, Calouste Gulbenkian Foundation, 1976.

Redgrave, M., *In My Mind's Eye – An Autobiography*, London, Weidenfeld & Nicholson, 1983.

Rix, B., *Farce About Face*, London, Hodder & Stoughton, 1989.

Robbins, B., *Secular Vocations – intellectuals, professionalism, culture*, London, Verso, 1993.

Roberts, P., *The Old Vic Story – A Nation's Theatre 1818–1976*, London, W.H. Allen, 1976.

Robertson, William, *Welfare in Trust 1930–63* (account of the Carnegie UK Trust), London, Constable, 1964.

Rock, W.R., *British Appeasement in the 1930s*, London, Arnold, 1977.

Rosenthal, H., *My Mad World of Opera*, London, Weidenfeld & Nicolson, 1982.

Rosenthal, H., *Opera at Covent Garden, A Short History*, London, Gollancz, 1967.

Rowell, G., *Old Vic Theatre*, London.

Royal Opera House, annual reports, Royal Opera House Covent Garden Limited, London, ROH.

Russell, G., *The Old Vic Theatre, A History*, Cambridge University Press, 1993.

Russell, Thomas, *Philharmonic Decade*, London, Hutchinson, 1945.

Sadie, S. (ed.), *The New Grove Dictionary of Opera* (vols 1–4), London, Macmillan, 1992.

Artist Unknown

Scheslinger, A.M., *The Age of Roosevelt, Vol II – The Coming of the New Deal*, London, Heinemann, 1959.

Shaw, R., *The Arts & the People*, London, Cape, 1987.

Shepherd, R., *A Class Divided – Appeasement and the Road to Munich 1938*, London, Macmillan, 1988.

Sinclair, A., *Arts & Cultures – The History of the 50 Years of the Arts Council of Great Britain*, London, Sinclair-Stevenson, 1995.

Skidelsky, R., *John Maynard Keynes, Vol. I – Hopes Betrayed; Vol. II – The Economist as Saviour*, London, Macmillan, 1983, 1992.

Sorley Walker, K., *Ninette De Valois – Idealist Without Illusions*, London, Hamish Hamilton, 1987.

South Bank Centre, 1st annual review 1986–1987 ('Now We Are One'), and subsequent annual reviews to 1994–1995, London, SBC.

South Bank Centre, 'Transforming the South Bank' (briefing pack), May 1996.

Sports Council, 'What Is The Sports Council?' (introductory pamphlet); accounts 1994–1995; also factsheet on the National Sports Centres, London, 1994 (the Sports Council was undergoing restructuring at the time of writing this book, and the policy unit provided information on these developments as far as they were known at the time).

Sunday Times, 'Why everyone sends for Lord X', 26 February 1967.

Tanitch, R., *Olivier – The Complete Career*, London, Thames & Hudson, 1985.

Tannenbaum, E.R., *The Fascist Experience – Italian Society and Culture 1922–45*, London, Allen Lane, 1973.

Telegraph, Daily, report on Robert Forbes' address to the ISM, 29 December 1937.

Thirwall, A.P., *Keynes as a Policy Adviser*, London, Macmillan, 1982.

Tippett, M., *Those Twentieth Century Blues – An Autobiography*, London, Hutchinson, 1991.

Trussler, S.R., *The Cambridge Illustrated History of British Theatre*, Cambridge University Press, 1994.

Walton, S., *William Walton – Behind the Facade*, Oxford University Press, 1988.

White, E.W., 'Architect of the Arts Council', in *Keynes – Aspects of the Man & his Work*, from the first Keynes Seminar held at the University of Kent, London, Macmillan, 1974.

White, E.W., *The Arts Council of Great Britain*, London, Davis-Poynter, 1975.

White, J.F., *Art in Action – American arts centers and the New Deal*, Metuchen, Scarecrow Press, 1987.

Whitaker's Almanac: 1929–1951 for names, titles and salaries of civil servants; royal institutions; dates and repertoire of Vic-Wells, Sadler's Wells Ballet, Opera and Old Vic seasons in London; Beecham's grand opera seasons at Royal Opera House, subsequently first productions of Covent Garden Opera; also date references to Tennent productions in West End.

Who Was Who – A Cumulated Index 1897–1980, London, A&C Black, 1981.

Wilding, R., *Supporting the Arts – A Review of the Structure of Arts Funding*, London, Office of Arts & Libraries, 1989.

Willatt, H., 'The Economic Situation and the Arts Council of Great Britain', in *The Arts, Economics & Politics – Four National Perspectives*. USA, Aspen Institute for Humanistic Studies, 1975.

Williams, H., *The Old Vic Saga*, London, Winchester Publications, 1940s.

Williams, R., *Resources of Hope – Culture, Democracy, Socialism*, London, 1989.

Williams, R., 'The Arts Council', in *Political Quarterly*, Spring 1979.

Williams, W.E., 'Public Patronage of the Arts', in *New Society*, 16 May 1963.

Williams, W.E., 'The pre-history of the Arts Council' in *Aim & Action in Adult Education, 1921–1971*, London, 1971.

Williams-Ellis, C., *Britain & The Beast – Visionary Essays by J.M. Keynes & Others*, London, Dent, 1937.

Williamson, B., *The Temper of the Times – British Society since World War II*, London, Basil Blackwell, 1990.

Wood, ELF (Earl of Halifax), *Fullness of Days*, London, Collins, 1957.

Woolf, V. (ed. Bell, A.), *Diaries, Vol. I (1915–1919); Vol. IV (1931–1935)*, London, Hogarth Press, 1982.

Young, K., *Stanley Baldwin*, London, Weidenfeld & Nicolson, 1976.

Ziegler, P., *Wilson – The Authorised Life of Lord Wilson of Rievaulx*, London, HarperCollins, 1993.

INDEX

21, 23–4, 105, 106–7; in the Soviet
Union 29; *see also* animateurism
American Ballet 128
Amory, Derick Heathcoat, 1st
Viscount Amory 237, 284, 298, 379
Anderson, John *see* Waverley, John
Anderson, 1st Viscount
André, Carl: *Equivalent VIII* 366
Andry, Peter 200
Angerstein, J.J. 368–9
Anglo-American Concerts Ltd 172
animateurism 23, 88, 89, 146, 150,
270, 480–1; music 62, 67, 105
Annual Register 107
Anouilh, Jean 279, 297
anti-communism 36, 462–3
anti-Semitism 193, 227
anti-Victorianism 162–3, 166, 319, 389
Apollo Leisure 119
'Appeasers' set 13, 51, 53, 59
Araeen, Rasheed 387
Archer Shee, Martin 367–8
architecture 116–17, 493–4
Arden, John 293, 327
Arlen, Stephen 234, 235
Armitage, Kenneth 387
Armstrong, Robert, Baron Armstrong
of Ilminster 402, 491
Army Bureau of Current Affairs
(ABCA) 71
Arnolfini gallery, Bristol 383
art department 365–90, 445; art
collection 370, 371, 372–7, 387; at
CEMA 97, 98, 109–14; fakes
109–11; funding 381, 389;
National Touring Exhibitions 377;
'Percent for Art' scheme 390;
spending 311; touring programme
377–8, 383, 384; *see also* 'Art and
the People' touring exhibitions
'Art and the People' touring
exhibitions 63, 64, 71–2, 79, 89,
96–7, 109, 112–14, 149, 372
Art Monthly 387, 388
Arts Club Theatre, London 297
Arts Council: accounts 404–11;
administration versus management
445–6, 448–9; advisers 412–13,
428; annual reports 403–4;
bookshop 397, 443; *see* Arts

Council of England (1994–); Arts
Council of Great Britain (1945–
94); Arts Council of Northern
Ireland; Arts Council of Wales;
committees; Committee for the
Encouragement of Music and the
Arts (1939–40); Council; Council
for the Encouragement of Music
and the Arts (1940–45);
departments; lottery unit; panel
system; policy; premises; Regional
Arts Associations; Regional Arts
Boards; royal charters; Scottish
Arts Council; staff
Arts Council of England (ACE):
annual accounts 406; investigated
524; and Lottery money 509; name
changed to 195, 415; royal charter
for 401; *see also* Arts Council of
Great Britain (ACGB); Council for
the Encouragement of Music and
the Arts
Arts Council Gallery, Cambridge 380
Arts Council Gallery, London 379,
380, 395
Arts Council of Great Britain (ACGB)
148–53, 155–533; annual accounts
410, 411; name 144–5; owns Royal
Opera House 259; policy 157–8,
166; premises 385; royal charter
150, 151–2, 400–1; *see also* Arts
Council of England (ACE);
Council for the Encouragement of
Music and the Arts
Arts Council Lottery Board 261
Arts Council of Northern Ireland
(ACNI) 145, 509
Arts Council of Scotland *see* Scottish
Arts Council
Arts Council of Wales (ACW) 167,
410, 509
arts development officers 527
Arts and Entertainment Training
Council, Bradford 450
Arts for Everyone (A4E) 503, 521–2
Arts Forum 503
Arts Foundation 492–3
Arts Lab, London 309, 473, 474
Arts League of Service 38
arts management 445–6, 448–9, 487,